October 29–31, 2014
Tsukuba, Japan

 **Association for
Computing Machinery**

Advancing Computing as a Science & Profession

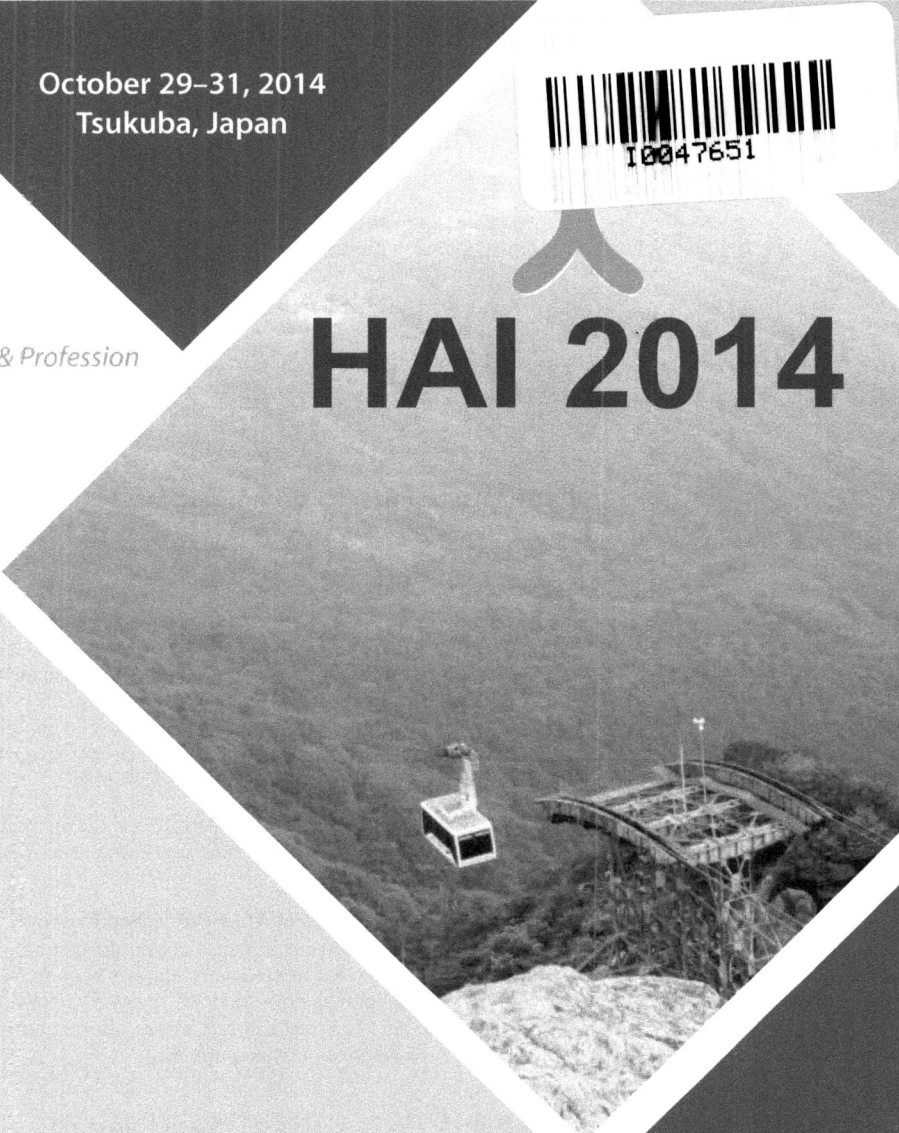

HAI 2014

HAI 2014

Proceedings of the Second International Conference on
Human-Agent Interaction

In cooperation with:
ACM SIGCHI

**Association for
Computing Machinery**

Advancing Computing as a Science & Profession

The Association for Computing Machinery
2 Penn Plaza, Suite 701
New York, New York 10121-0701

Notice to Past Authors of ACM-Published Articles
ACM intends to create a complete electronic archive of all articles and/or other material previously published by ACM. If you have written a work that has been previously published by ACM in any journal or conference proceedings prior to 1978, or any SIG Newsletter at any time, and you do NOT want this work to appear in the ACM Digital Library, please inform permissions@acm.org, stating the title of the work, the author(s), and where and when published.

ISBN: 978-1-4503-3035-0 (Digital)

ISBN: 978-1-4503-3383-2 (Print)

Additional copies may be ordered prepaid from:

ACM Order Department
PO Box 30777
New York, NY 10087-0777, USA

Phone: 1-800-342-6626 (USA and Canada)
+1-212-626-0500 (Global)
Fax: +1-212-944-1318
E-mail: acmhelp@acm.org
Hours of Operation: 8:30 am – 4:30 pm ET

Printed in the USA

HAI 2014 Chairs' Welcome

Welcome to Tsukuba! *The Second International Conference on Human-Agent Interaction (HAI 2014)* is a premier interdisciplinary and multidisciplinary conference that showcases state-of-the-art research in human-agent interaction. Work presented here has implications that cross conventional research boundaries including robots, software agents and digitally-mediated human-human communication. HAI gathers researchers from fields spanning engineering, computer science, psychology and sociology, and covers diverse topics, including human-robot interaction, affective computing, computer-supported cooperative work, social computing, gaming and serious games, artificial intelligence, and more.

HAI this year has grown well beyond our expectations. Submissions more than doubled from last year, and the call for papers attracted submissions from 16 different countries around the world. Papers, posters, and presentations cover a range of areas, including new ways that people and agents can interact with each other, ways agents can be integrated into other technologies, and novel insights into how people will interact with agents and what their expectations are. We hope that this program will continue to help fuel cross pollination of ideas across fields wherever interactive agents are used.

We are honored this year to have three exciting keynote talks by world leaders in areas related to human-agent interaction:

Ellen Do, Georgia Tech, NUS: Creative Design Computing for Happy Healthy Living

Jane Hsu, National Taiwan University: Crowdsourcing Agents for Smart IoT

Takeo Igarashi, The University of Tokyo: Design Everything by Yourself

HAI 2014 in Tsukuba could not have happened without the team effort of many people, including the organizing committee, program committee, reviewers, and authors. We would also like to thank the keynote speakers for their participation. Finally, we thank the Faculty of Engineering, Information and Systems, University of Tsukuba as the host institution, and our sponsor, the Tsukuba EXPO'85 Memorial Foundation.

We hope you can enjoy the Tsukuba countryside and forget the hustle and bustle of city life for a while, and enjoy a valuable opportunity to exchange diverse ideas on human-agent interaction with other researchers from around the world.

Hideaki Kuzuoka
HAI'14 General Co-Chair
University of Tsukuba, Japan

Tetsuo Ono
HAI'14 General Co-Chair
Hokkaido University, Japan

Michita Imai
HAI'14 Program Co-Chair
Keio University, Japan

James E. Young
HAI'14 Program Co-Chair
University of Manitoba, Canada

Table of Contents

HAI 2014 Organization..x

Workshops

- **AS 2014: Workshop on Augmented Sociality and Interactive Technology**............................1
  Michita Imai *(Keio University)*, Tetsuo Ono *(Hokkaido University)*, Kazushi Nishioto *(JAIST)*

- **CID 2014: Workshop on Cognitive Interaction Design**..3
  Michita Imai *(Keio University)*

- **IWME 2014: First International Workshop on Mood Engineering: Creating Effective Moods with Robots/Agents. What Makes a Good Mood?**..5
  Masahide Yuasa *(Shonan Institute of Technology)*, Kazuki Kobayashi *(Shinshu University)*,
  Takahiro Tanaka *(Nagoya University)*, Daisuke Katagami *(Tokyo Polytechnic University)*

Keynote Talk I

- **Creative Design Computing for Happy Healthy Living**...7
  Ellen Yi-Luen Do *(National University of Singapore & Georgia Institute of Technology)*

Session: Agents for Support and Learning

- **PEKOPPA: A Minimalistic Toy Robot to Analyse a Listener-Speaker Situation in Neurotypical and Autistic Children Aged 6 Years**..9
  Irini Giannopulu *(Pierre & Marie Curie University)*, Valérie Montreynaud *(Center of Medical Psychiatry)*,
  Tomio Watanabe *(Okayama Prefectural University)*

- **User-Friendly Autonomous Wheelchair for Elderly Care Using Ubiquitous Network Robot Platform**..17
  Masahiro Shiomi, Takamasa Iio, Koji Kamei, Chandraprakash Sharma, Norihiro Hagita
  (ATR Intelligent Robotics and Communications Laboratories)

- **Tangible Earth: Tangible Learning Environment for Astronomy Education**..........................23
  Hideaki Kuzuoka *(University of Tsukuba)*, Naomi Yamashita *(NTT Communication Science Laboratories)*,
  Hiroshi Kato *(The Open University of Japan)*, Hideyuki Suzuki *(Ibaraki University)*,
  Yoshihiko Kubota *(Utsunomiya University)*

- **Daily Support Robots that Move on the Body**..29
  Tamami Saga, Nagisa Munekata, Tetsuo Ono *(Hokkaido University)*

- **Simplification of Wearable Message Robot with Physical Contact for Elderly's Outing Support**..35
  Hirotake Yamazoe *(Osaka University)*, Tomoko Yonezawa *(Kansai University)*

Session: Novel Interaction Techniques

- **Ningyo of the CAVE: Robots as Social Puppets of Static Infrastructure**..............................39
  Nico Li, Stephen Cartwright, Ehud Sharlin, Maric Costa Sousa *(University of Calgary)*

- **Personal and Interactive Newscaster Agent Based on Estimation of User's Understanding**..45
  Naoto Yoshida, Miyuki Yano, Tomoko Yonezawa *(Kansai University)*

- **Emotional Cyborg: Complementing Emotional Labor with Human-agent Interaction Technology**..51
  Hirotaka Osawa *(University of Tsukuba)*

- **Calamaro: Perceiving Robotic Motion in the Wild**..59
  John Harris *(University of Waterloo)*, Stephanie Law *(University of Calgary)*,
  Kazuki Takashima *(Tohoku University)*, Ehud Sharlin *(University of Calgary)*,
  Yoshifumi Kitamura *(Tohoku University)*

Session: Telepresence and Teleoperation

- **Volume Adaptation and Visualization by Modeling the Volume Level in Noisy Environments for Telepresence System** 67
  Akira Hayamizu, Michita Imai *(Keio University)*,
  Keisuke Nakamura, Kazuhiro Nakadai *(Honda Research Institute Japan)*

- **An Affective Telepresence System Using Smartphone High Level Sensing and Intelligent Behavior Generation** 75
  Elham Saadatian *(Keio-NUS CUTE Center)*, Thoriq Salafi *(National University of Singapore)*,
  Hooman Samani *(National Taipei University Taiwan)*, Yu De Lim *(National University of Singapore)*,
  Ryohei Nakatsu *(Keio-NUS CUTE Center)*

- **Can a Social Robot Help Children's Understanding of Science in Classrooms?** 83
  Tsuyoshi Komatsubara, Masahiro Shiomi, Takayuki Kanda, Hiroshi Ishiguro, Norihiro Hagita
  (ATR Intelligent Robotics and Communication Laboratories)

- **Robotic Tele-Presence with DARYL in the Wild** 91
  Christian Becker-Asano, Kai O. Arras, Bernhard Nebel *(Albert-Ludwigs-Universität Freiburg)*

- **Nodding Responses by Collective Proxy Robots for Enhancing Social Telepresence** 97
  Tsunehiro Arimoto, Yuichiro Yoshikawa, Hiroshi Ishiguro *(Osaka University)*

Keynote Talk II

- **Crowdsourcing Agents for Smart IoT** 103
  Jane Yung-jen Hsu *(National Taiwan University)*

Session: Interactive Session

- **A Fixed Pattern Deviation Robot That Triggers Intention Attribution** 105
  Kazunori Terada, Yuto Imamura *(Gifu University)*, Hideyuki Takahashi *(Osaka University)*,
  Akira Ito *(Gifu University)*

- **The Sharing of Meta-Signals and Protocols Is the First Step for the Emergence of Cooperative Communication** 109
  Takakazu Mizuki, Akira Ito, Kazunori Terada *(Faculty of Engineering Gifu University)*

- **FIONA: A Platform for Embodied Cognitive Agents** 113
  Celestino Alvarez, Lucía Fernández Cossío *(Adele Robots)*

- **A Cooking Assistant Robot Using Intuitive Onomatopoetic Expressions and Joint Attention** 117
  Mutsuo Sano Sano, Yuka Kanemoto, Syogo Noda, Kenzaburo Miyawaki *(Osaka Institute of Technology)*,
  Nami Fukutome *(Ochanomizu University)*

- **Synchrony Based Side by Side Walking: An Application in Human-Robot Interactions** 121
  Syed Khursheed Hasnain, Ghiles Mostafaoui, Caroline Grand, Philippe Gaussier *(ETIS Laboratory)*

- **Image Recognition Method Which Measures Angular Velocity from a Back of Hand for Developing a Valve UI** 125
  Hirotsugu Minowa *(Okayama University)*

- **Development of a Dialogue Scenario Editor on a Web Browser for a Spoken Dialogue System** 129
  Ryota Nishimura, Daisuke Yamamoto, Takahiro Uchiya, Ichi Takumi *(Nagoya Institute of Technology)*

- **Notification Design Using Mother-like Expressions** 133
  Marie Uemura, Keiko Yamamoto, Itaru Kuramoto, Yoshihiro Tsujino *(Kyoto Institute of Technology)*

- **Will You Follow the Robot'S Advice? The Impact of Robot Types and Task Types on People's Perception of a Robot** 137
  Hyewon Lee, Jung Ju Choi, Sonya S. Kwak *(Ewha Womans University)*

- **Multimodal Bodily Feeling Analysis to Design Air Conditioning Services for Elderly People** 141
  Shinya Kiriyama, Kenichi Shibata, Shogo Ishikawa *(Shizuoka University)*, Kei Ogawa, Harunobu Nukushina *(Toshiba Carrier Corporation)*, Yoichi Takebayashi *(Shizuoka University)*

- **Portable Robot Inspiring Walking in Elderly People** 145
  Yuri Kumahara, Yoshikazu Mori *(Ibaraki University)*

- **Can You Touch Me? The Impact of Physical Contact on Emotional Engagement with a Robot** 149
  Chaehyun Baek, Jung Ju Choi, Sonya S. Kwak *(Ewha Womans University)*

- **Social Acceptance by Elderly People of a Fall-detection System with Range Sensors in a Nursing Home** 153
  Takamasa Iio, Masahiro Shiomi, Koji Kamei, Chandraprakash Sharma, Norihiro Hagita *(ATR IRC.)*

- **Preliminary Investigation of Supporting Child-Care at an Intelligent Playroom** 157
  Masahiro Shiomi, Norihiro Hagita *(ATR IRC.)*

- **Recovery of Virtual Object Contact Surface Features for Replaying Haptic Feeling** 161
  Yongyao Yan, Greg S. Ruthenbeck, Karen J. Reynolds *(Flinders University)*

- **Toward Playmate Robots That Can Play with Children Considering Personality** 165
  Kasumi Abe, Chie Hieida, Muhammad Attamimi, Takayuki Nagai *(The University of Electro-Communications)*, Takayuki Shimotomai, Takashi Omori *(Tamagawa University)*, Natsuki Oka *(Kyoto Institute of Technology)*

- **Affective Agents for Enhancing Emotional Experience** 169
  Takahiro Matsumoto, Shunichi Seko, Ryousuke Aoki, Akihiro Miyata, Tomoki Watanabe, Tomohiro Yamada *(NTT Corporation)*

- **The Hybrid Agent MARCO: A Multimodal Autonomous Robotic Chess Opponent** 173
  Christian Becker-Asano *(Albert-Ludwigs-Universität Freiburg)*, Eduardo Meneses *(National Polytechnic Institute)*, Nicolas Riesterer, Julien Hué, Christian Dornhege, Bernhard Nebel *(Albert-Ludwigs-Universität Freiburg)*

- **Artificial Endocrine System for Language Translation Robot** 177
  Wu Jhong Ren, Hooman Samani *(National Taipei University)*

- **Pointing Gesture Prediction Using Minimum-Jerk Model in Human-Robot Interaction** 181
  Ren Ohmura *(Toyohashi University of Technology)*, Yuki Kusano *(ShinMaywa Soft Technologies, Ltd.)*, Yuta Suzuki *(Tokai Rika Co., Ltd.)*

- **Digital Play Therapy for Children with Learning Disabilities** 185
  Yukako Watanabe, Yoshiko Okada *(Shibaura Institute of Technology)*, Hirotaka Osawa *(University of Tsukuba)*, Midori Sugaya *(Shibaura Institute of Technology)*

- **Amae and Agency Appraisal as Japanese Emotional Behavior: Influences on Agent's Believability** 189
  Koushi Mitarai, Hiroyuki Umemuro *(Tokyo Institute of Technology)*

- **Weight-Aware Robot Motion Planning for Lift-to-Pass Action** 193
  Oskar Palinko, Alessandra Sciutti, Francesco Rea, Giulio Sandini *(Istituto Italiano di Tecnologia)*

- **Emotion Recognition and Expression in Therapeutic Social Robot Design** 197
  Jie Sun *(National University of Singapore)*

- **Luminous Device for the Deaf and Hard of Hearing People** 201
  Akira Matsuda, Midori Sugaya, Hiroyuki Nakamura *(Shibaura Institute of Technology)*

- **Development of Werewolf Match System for Human Players Mediated with Lifelike Agents** 205
  Yu Kobayashi *(Tokyo Polytechnic University Graduate School of Engineering)*, Hirotaka Osawa *(University of Tsukuba)*, Michimasa Inaba *(Hiroshima City University)*, Kosuke Shinoda *(University of Electro-Communications)*, Fujio Toriumi *(University of Tokyo)*, Daisuke Katagami *(Tokyo Polytechnic University)*

- **Development of Smart Infant-Parents Affective Telepresence System** 209
  Elham Saadatian *(Keio-NUS CUTE Center)*, Rehaneh Hosseinzade Hariri *(University Putera Malaysia)*, Adrian David Cheok *(City University, London)*, Ryohei Nakatsu *(National University of Singapore)*

- **COLUMN: Persuasion as a Social Mediator to Establish the Interpersonal Coordination** 213
  Yasutaka Takeda, Kohei Yoshida, Shotaro Baba, P. Ravindra S. De Silva, Michio Okada
  (Toyohashi University of Technology)

- **Towards Better Eye Tracking in Human Robot Interaction Using an Affordable Active Vision System** 217
  Oskar Palinko, Alessandra Sciutti, Francesco Rea, Giulio Sandini *(Istituto Italiano di Tecnologia)*

- **Evaluation of a Video Communication System with Speech-Driven Embodied Entrainment Audience Characters with Partner's Face** 221
  Yutaka Ishii, Tomio Watanabe *(Okayama Prefectural University)*

- **Dynamic Dialog System for Human Robot Collaboration - Playing a Game of Pairs** 225
  Andreas Kipp, Franz Kummert *(Bielefeld University)*

- **Unification of Demonstrative Pronouns in a Small Group Guided by a Robot** 229
  Takashi Ichijo, Nagisa Munekata, Tetsuo Ono *(Hokkaido University)*

- **Evaluating an Intuitive Teleoperation Platform Explored in a Long-Distance Interview** ...233
  Ritta Baddoura *(Université Lyon 1)*, Gentiane Venture *(Tokyo University of Agriculture and Technology)*,
  Guillaume Gibert *(Université Lyon 1)*

- **Analysis of Personality Traits for Intervention Scene Detection in Multi-User Conversation** 237
  Shochi Otogi, Hung-Hsuan Huang, Ryo Hotta, Kyoji Kawagoe *(Ritsumeikan University)*

- **A Design Method Using Cooperative Principle for Conversational Agent** 241
  Masahide Yuasa *(Shonan Institute of Technology)*

- **Experimental Study of Empathy and Its Behavioral Indices in Human-Robot Interaction** 245
  Yuichiro Tsuji, Ami Tsukamoto, Takashi Uchida, Yusuke Hattori, Ryosuke Nishida, Chie Fukada,
  Motoyuki Ozeki *(Kyoto Institute of Technology)*, Takashi Omori *(Tamagawa University)*,
  Takayuki Nagai *(The University of Electro-Communications)*, Natsuki Oka *(Kyoto Institute of Technology)*

- **Huggable Communication Medium Encourages Listening to Others** 249
  Junya Nakanishi *(ATR & Osaka University)*, Hidenobu Sumioka, Masahiro Shiomi *(ATR)*,
  Daisuke Nakamichi, Kurima Sakai *(ATR & Osaka University)*, Hiroshi Ishiguro *(ATR)*

- **Tap Model to Improve Input Accuracy of Touch Panels** 253
  Takahisa Tani *(The Graduate University for Advanced Studies)*, Seiji Yamada *(National Institute of Informatics)*

- **Modeling of Cooperative Behavior Agent Based on Collision Avoidance Decision Process** 257
  Kensuke Miyamoto, Hiroaki Yoshioka *(Keio University)*, Norifumi Watanabe *(Tokyo University of Technology)*,
  Yoshiyasu Takefuji *(Keio University)*

- **Representation of Gaze, Mood, and Emotion: Movie-watching with Telepresence Robots** 261
  Ken Yonezawa, Hirotada Ueda *(Kyoto Sangyo University)*

- **A Hierarchical Structure for Gesture Recognition Using RGB-D Sensor** 265
  Hyunsoek Choi, Hyeyoung Park *(Kyungpook National University)*

- **Communicating Emotions: A Model for Natural Emotions in HRI** 269
  Oliver Damm, Britta Wrede *(Bielefeld University)*

- **How Does Emphatic Emotion Emerge via Human-Robot Rhythmic Interaction?** 273
  Hideyuki Takahashi, Nobutsuna Endo, Hiroki Yokoyama, Takato Horii, Tomoyo Morita,
  Minoru Asada *(Osaka University)*

- **Determining Robot Gaze According to Participation Roles in Multiparty Conversations** 277
  Takashi Yoshino *(Seikei University)*, Yuki Hayashi *(Osaka Prefecture University)*,
  Yukiko I. Nakano *(Seikei University)*

- **Interactions on Eyeballs of Humanoid-Robots** 281
  Takayuki Todo, Takanari Miisho *(Institute of Advanced Media Arts and Science (IAMAS))*

- **Video-Based Emotion Identification Using Face Alignment and Support Vector Machines** 285

  Gil-Jin Jang *(Kyungpook National University)*, Ahra Jo *(Ulsan National Institute of Science and Technology (UNIST))*, Jeong-Sik Park *(Yeungnam University)*

- **Social Networking Sites Photos and Robots: A Pilot Research on Facebook Photo Albums and Robotics Interfaces for Older Adults** 287

  Angie Lorena Marin *(Self-Scholar)*

- **Telepresence Robot That Exaggerates Non-Verbal Cues for Taking Turns in Multi-Party Teleconferences** 293

  Komei Hasegawa, Yasushi Nakauchi *(University of Tsukuba)*

- **Emotional Scene Understanding Based on Acoustic Signals Using Adaptive Neuro-Fuzzy Inference System** 297

  Taewoong Kim, Minho Lee *(Kyungpook National University)*

Session: Techniques and Strategies for Developing Agents

- **SB Simulator: A Method to Estimate How Relation Develops** 301

  Taichi Sono, Toshihiro Oosumi, Michita Imai *(Keio University)*

- **Modeling Perception-Action Loops: Comparing Sequential Models with Frame-Based Classifiers** 309

  Alaeddine Mihoub *(GIPSA-Lab & LIRIS)*, Gérard Bailly *(GIPSA-Lab)*, Christian Wolf *(Université de Lyon)*

- **PaintBoard – Prototyping Interactive Character Behaviors by Digitally Painting Storyboards** 315

  Daniel J. Rea *(University of Manitoba)*, Takeo Igarashi *(The University of Tokyo)*, James E. Young *(University of Manitoba)*

- **Voice Interaction System with 3D-CG Virtual Agent for Stand-alone Smartphones** 323

  Daisuke Yamamoto, Keiichiro Oura, Ryota Nishimura, Takahiro Uchiya, Akinobu Lee, Ichi Takumi, Keiichi Tokuda *(Nagoya Institute of Technology)*

Session: Social Interaction Strategies for Agents

- **Assigning a Personality to a Spoken Dialogue Agent through Self-disclosure of Behavior** 331

  Yoshito Ogawa *(Waseda University)*, Kouki Miyazawa *(RIKEN Brain Science Institute)*, Hideaki Kikuchi *(Waseda University)*

- **Potential of Imprecision: Exploring Vague Language in Agent Instructors** 339

  Leigh Michael Harry Clark, Khaled Bachour, Abdulmalik Ofemile, Svenja Adolphs, Tom Rodden *(University of Nottingham)*

- **Sharedo: To-Do List Interface for Human-Agent Task Sharing** 345

  Jun Kato *(National Institute of Advanced Industrial Science and Technology)*, Daisuke Sakamoto, Takeo Igarashi *(The University of Tokyo)*, Masataka Goto *(National Institute of Advanced Industrial Science and Technology)*

- **A Design Model of Emotional Body Expressions in Non-Humanoid Robots** 353

  Jekaterina Novikova, Leon Watts *(University of Bath)*

- **Signaling Trouble in Robot-To-Group Interaction. Emerging Visitor Dynamics with a Museum Guide Robot** 361

  Raphaela Gehle, Karola Pitsch, Sebastian Wrede *(Bielefeld University)*

Keynote Talk III

- **Design Everything by Yourself** 369

  Takeo Igarashi *(The University of Tokyo)*

Session: Understanding Users

- **Methodology for Study of Human-Robot Social Interaction in Dangerous Situations** 371

  David J. Atkinson, Micah H. Clark *(Institute for Human and Machine Cognition)*

- **More Human than Human? A Visual Processing Approach to Exploring Believability of Android Faces** 377
  Masayuki Nakane, James E. Young, Neil D. B. Bruce *(University of Manitoba)*

- **Differences of Expectation of Rapport with Robots Dependent on Situations** 383
  Tatsuya Nomura *(Ryukoku University)*, Takayuki Kanda *(ATR Intelligent Robotics and Communication Laboratories)*

- **Stage of Subconscious Interaction in Embodied Interaction** 391
  Takafumi Sakamoto, Yugo Takeuchi, Yugo Takeuchi *(Shizuoka University)*

Author Index 397

HAI 2014 Organization

General Chairs:	Hideaki Kuzuoka *(University of Tsukuba)*
	Tetsuo Ono *(Hokkaido University)*
Program Chairs:	Michita Imai *(Keio University)*
	James E. Young *(University of Manitoba)*
Finance Chair:	Yugo Takeuchi *(Shizuoka University)*
Poster Chair:	Kazunori Terada *(Gifu University)*
Publication Chair:	Kazuki Kobayashi *(Shinshu University)*
Local Chairs:	Hirotaka Osawa *(University of Tsukuba)*
	Yugo Hayashi *(Ritsumeikan University)*
Sponsorship Chairs:	Yoshihiko Murakawa *(Fujitsu Lab)*
	Natsuki Oka *(Kyoto Institute of Technology)*
Publicity Chair:	Daisuke Katagami *(Tokyo Polytechnic University)*
Web Chair:	Daniel J. Rea *(University of Manitoba)*
Design Chair:	Nagisa Munekata *(Hokkaido University)*
Program Committee:	Fereshteh Amini *(University of Manitoba)*
	Sean Andrist *(University of Wisconsin)*
	Christian Becker-Asano *(Albert-Ludwigs-Universitat Freiburg)*
	Christoph Bartneck *(Canterbury University)*
	Jeffrey Boyd *(University of Calgary)*
	Andrea Bunt *(University of Manitoba)*
	Mauro Dragone *(University College Dublin)*
	Hironori Egi *(Kobe University)*
	Barret Ens *(University of Manitoba)*
	Dylan Glas *(ATR)*
	Guy Hoffman *(IDC Herzliya)*
	Chien-Ming Huang *(University of Wisconsin-Madison)*
	Julien Hue *(Albert-Ludwigs-Universitat Freiburg)*
	Michimasa Inaba *(Hiroshima City University)*
	Pourang Irani *(University of Manitoba)*
	Kentaro Ishii *(University of Tokyo)*
	Gil-Jin Jang *(School of Electronics Engineering, KNU)*
	Koh Kakusho *(Kwansei Gakuin University)*

Program Committee (continued):

Yusuke Kanai *(Keio University)*
Masayoshi Kanoh *(Chukyo University)*
Jun Kato *(AIST)*
Kheng Koay *(University of Hertfordshire)*
Tomoko Koda *(Osaka Institute of Technology)*
Takanori Komatsu *(Meiji University)*
Sonya S. Kwak *(Ewha Womans University)*
Shaun Lawson *(University of Lincoln UK)*
Karon MacLean *(University of British Columbia)*
Setareh Manesh *(University of Calgary)*
Fulvio Mastrogiovanni *(University of Genoa)*
Amir Meghdadi *(University of Manitoba)*
ChunYan Miao *(Nanyang Technological University)*
Kouta Minamizawa *(University of Tokyo)*
Hideyuki Nakanishi *(Osaka University)*
Yasushi Nakauchi *(Carnegie Mellon University)*
Victor Ng-Thow-Hing *(Honda Research Institute USA)*
Haruno Noma *(Ritsumeikan University)*
Tatsuya Nomura *(Ryukoku University)*
Mohammad Obaid *(Chalmers University of Technology)*
Kohei Ogawa *(Osaka University)*
Mai Otsuki *(Ritsumeikan University)*
Hyeyoung Park *(School of Computer Engineering, KNU)*
Rui Prada *(INESC-ID)*
Ferdian Pratama *(JAIST)*
Irene Rae *(University of Wisconsin-Madison)*
Juan David Hincapie Ramos *(University of Manitoba)*
Matthias Rehm *(Aalborg University)*
Daisuke Sakamoto *(University of Tokyo)*
Satoru Satake *(ATR)*
Ehud Sharlin *(University of Calgary)*
Solace Shen *(University of Washington)*
Masahiro Shiomi *(ATR)*
Sowmya Somanath *(University of Calgary)*
Yuta Sugiura *(Keio University)*
Osamu Sugiyama *(ATR)*
Yasuyuki Sumi *(Future University)*
JaYoung Sung *(Google)*
Hideyuki Takahashi *(Tohoku University)*
Kazuki Takashima *(Tohoku University)*
Bob Wang *(National Taiwan University)*
Tomoko Yonezawa *(Kansai University)*
Huang Zhiyong *(I2R)*
Jakub Zlotowski *(University of Cantebury)*

In-cooperation with: **acm** *In-Cooperation*

SIGCHI

Supported by:

公益財団法人
つくば科学万博記念財団
TSUKUBA EXPO'85 MEMORIAL FOUNDATION

Faculty of Engineering, Information and Systems
Univ. of Tsukuba

AS 2014: Workshop on Augmented Sociality and Interactive Technology

Michita Imai
Keio University
3-14-1 Hiyoshi Kohokuku,
Yokoama, Japan
michita@ailab.ics.keio.ac.jp

Tetsuo Ono
Hokkaido University
9Chome Nishi, 14 JoKita, Kita
Ward, Sapporo, Japan
tono@ist.hokudai.ac.jp

Kazushi Nishimoto
JAIST
1-1 Asahidai, Nomi, Ishikawa,
Japan
knishi@jaist.ac.jp

ABSTRACT

Researchers have developed computer systems which interact with people by recognizing situations around people. On the other hand, people behave socially based on perceived relations with others, being aware of a gaze from others, public pressure from others, and so on. If the computer systems can recognize the social relation and manage/control it, a new interactive service will emerge by enhancing the social skill of people. Designing, visualizing, and simulating relations also prepare a new socially interactive environment for people. The workshop named "Augmented Sociality and Interactive Technology" discuss the technologies which can deal with social relations and augment the social behaviors of people. Moreover, the workshop discuss interactive services using the technologies of the augmented sociality.

Author Keywords

Augmented Sociality; Social Behavior; Social Interaction; Communicate Technology

ACM Classification Keywords

H.5.m. Information interfaces and presentation (e.g., HCI): Miscellaneous.

HAI '14 , Oct 28-31 2014, Tsukuba, Japan
ACM 978-1-4503-3035-0/14/10.
http://dx.doi.org/10.1145/2658861.2662950

CID 2014: Workshop on Cognitive Interaction Design

Michita Imai
Keio University
3-14-1 Hiyoshi Kohokuku,
Yokoama, Japan
michita@ailab.ics.keio.ac.jp

ABSTRACT
Mutual adaptation plays an important role when people build a relation with the others and communicate with them. We can observe the adaptations not only in human-human communication but also in human-animal communication. For example, a service dog learns proper behaviors while reading the verbal and nonverbal expressions of a human. Also, the human behaves in response to what the dog learns. The workshop named "Cognitive Interaction Design" discusses the nature of the mutual adaptation between people or between a person and an animal. Moreover, it discusses the area of a field where the design of using the mutual adaptation for an interactive system shows exceptional performances.

Author Keywords
Cognitive Design; Interaction Design; Mutual Adaptation; Human-Agent Interaction; Human-Animal Interaction; Human-Human Interaction;

ACM Classification Keywords
H.5.m. Information interfaces and presentation (e.g., HCI): Miscellaneous.

IWME 2014: First International Workshop on Mood Engineering
Creating effective moods with robots/agents. What makes a good mood?

Masahide Yuasa
Shonan Institute of Technolog
1-1-25 Tsujido Nishi-Kaigan,
Fujisawa, Kanagawa 251-8511
Japan
yuasa@sc.shonan-it.ac.jp

Kazuki Kobayashi
Shinshu University
4-17-1 Wakasato, Nagano
380-8553 Japan
kby@shinshu-u.ac.jp

Takahiro Tanaka
Nagoya University
Furo-cho, Chikusa-ku, Nagoya
464-8601 Japan
tanaka@coi.nagoya-u.ac.jp

Daisuke Katagami
Tokyo Polytechnic University
1583 Iiyama, Atsugi,
Kanagawa 243-0297 Japan
katagami@cs.t-kougei.ac.jp

ABSTRACT
The first international workshop on mood engineering (IWME) is held in Tsukuba, Japan on October 28, 2014 and co-located with the second international conference on human-agent interaction (HAI). The main objective of the workshop is to create artificial moods by robot and agents and to clarify the mechanism of a mood created by a group including humans, robots, and agents. We have constructed an exciting program of demonstrations, posters, and video materials as interactive sessions that will provide participants creative a mood for collaborative research.

Author Keywords
Mood modeling; artificial mood; human-agent interaction; human-robot interaction; human-computer interaction;

ACM Classification Keywords
H.5.m. Information Interfaces and Presentation (e.g. HCI): Miscellaneous

INTRODUCTION
The purpose of the workshop is to bring together researchers from multiple disciplines associated with the study of robots or agents' mood, such as multiparty or multimodal interactions, human-agent interaction, robotics, verbal and nonverbal behaviors, social robots or agents and social psychology.

Humans have the capacity to read the emotions of other people and understand their moods, such as friendliness, excitement, and boredom, by observing verbal and nonverbal expressions. Thus it will be useful to develop conversational robots or agents that can recognize our moods, and create effective moods in each situation. However, unified principles of conversational agents or robots have not been found until now. What makes a good mood? Which verbal and nonverbal cues facilitate conversational moods? How can robots or agents create a good mood with us?

The workshop will discuss interaction models, principles, and techniques for developing robots or agent to comprehend mood. We will invite researchers from relevant field to deliberate on a good mood with robots or agents.

SCOPE
The theme of the IWME 2014 is to create artificial moods by robot and agents and to clarify the mechanism of a mood created by a group including humans, robots, and agents. This workshop welcomes posters, demonstrations, and video materials that address fundamental research issues in the mood engineering research area, with an emphasis on mood creation and mood control. Topics of interest include, but not limited to:

- Mood modeling
- Mood creation by robots and software agents
- Mood extraction from Twitter and SNS time lines
- Mood detection in multipaty interactions
- Mood analysis on cross cultural interactions
- Mood control by ambient computing
- Development of mood monitoring devices
- Interpretation of moods by artifacts
- Emergence control of moods in a group
- Mood interaction between groups

Acknowledgements
We would like to thank all authors who submitted contributions for IWME 2014 and the program committee members of HAI 2014 for their excellent work to support workshops.

Creative Design Computing for Happy Healthy Living

Ellen Yi-Luen Do
Keio-NUS CUTE Center, National University of Singapore
& Georgia Institute of Technology
ellendo@acm.org

ABSTRACT

The age of ubiquitous/pervasive/ambient computing is upon us. We see more and more connected objects and devices embedded in everyday life. Design and Human-Computer Interaction are crucial components of information technologies that color our experience. As designers and technologists, we have the unique opportunity to imagine, design and create interesting, intelligent and interactive technologies for a smart living environment.

A smart living environment is responsive, reconfigurable and transformable, embedded with sensors and actuators, to support everyday happy, healthy living with things that think, spaces that sense and places that play. Specifically, we see opportunity for investigating creative design computing to consider the built environment as an interface. We aim to engage people in playful, creative ways in which computing technologies embedded in the built environment (e.g., objects, furniture, building, and space) can support everyday happy healthy living.

We build wellness technologies in different scales (e.g., in human-centered view: hand, body and environment), for various applications (e.g., to support emotional, physical, and intellectual wellness) to unlock human potential and augmenting human capabilities through digital design innovations. Opportunities exist for integrating multidisciplinary perspectives together to create innovation with impacts.

For example, the Mobile Music Touch, a light-weight fingerless instrumented glove provides passive haptic learning of piano playing but also works as an effective rehabilitation tool. The ClockMe system, not only converts traditional pencil-and-paper Clock Drawing Test on a digital tablet for automatic scoring and analysis for detection of Alzheimer's disease and related disorders but also provides more information of the drawing behavior such as drawing sequence and pressure. The Digital Box and Block Test employs image processing to automatically detect and record a clinically validated post-stroke rehabilitation assessment for in-home use and a tangible gaming system to increase patient motivation.

The Dodo game provides pictures of cute animals for color matching, and serves as a clinical screening test to detect color deficiency in young children. The Taste + bottle and spoon provide stimulation to alter the sense of taste without any chemical flavoring using electric pluses and color LED lights. It could encourage water drinking or enhance taste for people with restrictive diets or diminished taste sensations. The Sensorendipity is a real-time smartphone-based web-enabled sensor platform for designers to create sensor-based applications such as monitoring activities, in exergaming or safe driving.

Now is an exciting time to engage in creative design computing, to implement physically and computationally enhanced environment, to explore experience media, to build prototypes, towards a smart living environment. Advancing technology offers new ways to solve problems, discover opportunities, and create new objects and experience that delight our senses and improve the way we live and work. Let's begin with the spark of creativity and enthusiasm and follow up with design and computational thinking towards the goal of creating unique technology for everyone.

Author Keywords

Creative Design Computing; Human Computer Interaction; Happy Healthy Living

ACM Classification Keywords

H.5 INFORMATION INTERFACES AND PRESENTATION (e.g., HCI); H.5.2 [Information Interfaces and Presentation]: User Interfaces; Interaction styles; Prototyping;

BIOGRAPHY

Ellen is a professor in the School of Industrial Design and the School of Interactive Computing, in the College of Architecture, and the College of Computing, at Georgia Institute of Technology. Before joining Georgia Tech in January 2006, Ellen was on the faculty in the computational design program at Carnegie Mellon University, where she co-directed the Computational Design Laboratory – CoDe Lab (Sep 04-Dec 05), and was an affiliate faculty at the Human Computer Interaction Institute - HCII and the

HAI'14, October 29–31, 2014, Tsukuba, Japan.
ACM 978-1-4503-3035-0/14/10.
http://dx.doi.org/10.1145/2658861.2658947

Institute for Complex Engineered Systems - ICES at Carnegie Mellon University. Before CMU, she was a faculty at University of Washington (99-04) where she co-directed the Design Machine Group - DMG, served as faculty director for the MS program in Design Computing and taught for the Honors Program. Prior to UW, Ellen worked at University of Colorado at Boulder (94-99) as a researcher and instructor for the Sundance Lab for Computing in Design and Planning. Since April 2013, Ellen has been serving as the Co-Director (NUS side) for the Keio-NUS CUTE (Connective Ubiquitous Technology for Embodiments) Center, at Interactive and Digital Media Institute, National University of Singapore.

Ellen received a Bachelor degree of architecture (Honors) from National Cheng-Kung University - NCKU in Taiwan, with a minor in Urban Planning, a Master of Design Studies from the Harvard Graduate School of Design - GSD, and a Ph.D. in design computing from Georgia Tech, with a minor in cognitive science & computer science.

Ellen has built creative computing tools, from understanding the human intelligence and creativity involved in the design process to improving our interaction with computers beyond the desktop into the physical world. Ellen's research interests are in: (1) computer aided architectural design, especially sketch computing, (2) creativity and design cognition, including creativity support tools and design studies, (3) tangible and embedded interaction, including architectural robotics and augmented learning, and most recently (4) computing for health, including experience media for wellness technologies.

ACKNOWLEDGEMENT

This material is based upon research work supported by the US National Science Foundation under Grant No 1117665 (SHB) and the National Research Foundation, Prime Minister's Office, Singapore under its International Research Centre @ Singapore Funding Initiative and administered by the Interactive & Digital Media Programme Office.

Any opinions, findings, and conclusions or recommendations expressed in this material are those of the author and do not necessarily reflect the views of the funding agencies

REFERENCES

1. Do, EY-L, Designing Interactive Computing for Happy Healthy Life, Intelligent Interactive Technologies and Multimedia Communications in Computer and Information Science Volume 276, (2013), pp 1-13 pdf
2. Do, EY-L and Gross, MD, Environments for Creativity: a lab for making things, in ACM SIGCHI conference on Creativity & Cognition, 27-36 (2007)
3. Weller, MP and Do EY-L. Architectural Robotics: A new paradigm for the built environment. in EuropIA.11: 11th International Conference on Design Sciences & Technology, Montreal (2007); 353-362
4. Huang, K, T Starner, E Do, G Weinberg, D Kohlsdorf, C Ahlrichs, R Leibrandt, Mobile music touch: mobile tactile stimulation for passive learning, in CHI '10 Proceedings of the 28th international conference on Human factors in computing systems pp 791-800 (2010)
5. Kim, H, C-P Hsiao and EY-L Do, Home-based computerized cognitive assessment tool for dementia screening, in Journal of Ambient Intelligence and Smart Environments 4 (2012) 429–442
6. Zhao, C, C-P Hsiao, NM. Davis, EY-L Do: Tangible games for stroke rehabilitation with digital box and blocks test, CHI Extended Abstracts 2013: 523-528 (2013)
7. Nguyen, LC, W Lu, EY-L Do, A Chia, Y Wang: Using digital game as clinical screening test to detect color deficiency in young children. IDC 2014: 337-340 (2014)
8. Ranasinghe, N, G Suthokumar, KY Lee, EY-L Do, The sensation of taste in the future of immersive media, in 2014 ACM international workshop on Immersive media experiences (MM '14), ACM (2014)
9. Lu, W, C Sun, T Bleeker, Y You, S Kitazawa, EY-L Do, Sensorendipity: a real-time web-enabled smartphone sensor platform for idea generation and prototyping, in Chinese CHI '14, Second International Symposium of Chinese CHI, Pages 11-18 ACM, NY (2014)
10. Camarata, K, MD Gross, EY-L Do, A Physical Computing Studio: Exploring Computational Artifacts and Environments, in International Journal of Architectural Computing, (2003) Volume 1, Issue #2. Multi-Science Publisher, UK, Pp 169-190

PEKOPPA: A Minimalistic Toy Robot to Analyse A Listener-Speaker Situation in Neurotypical and Autistic Children Aged 6 Years

Irini Giannopulu
Pierre & Marie Curie University
Cognitive Neuroscience
75005 Paris, France
igiannopulu@psycho-prat.fr

Valérie Montreynaud
Center of Medical Psychiatry
75017 Paris, France
v.montreynaud@gpspv.fr

Tomio Watanabe
Okayama Prefectural University
Department of Systems Engineering
719-1197 Okayama, Japan
watanabe@cse.oka-pu.ac.jp

ABSTRACT

Using a "speaker-listener" situation, we have compared the verbal and the emotional expressions of neurotypical and autistic children aged 6 years. The speaker was always a child (neurotypical or autistic); the listener was a human or an InterActor robot named Pekoppa, i.e., a small toy robot which reacts to speech expression by nodding only. The results suggest that an InterActor robot characterized by small variance nonverbal behavior better facilitate verbal and nonverbal emotional expressions of autistic children than a human. This might be related to autistic children preferences: autistic children are rather interested in minimalist objects to which they can assign mental states of their own or of others. Everything happens as if the InterActor robot could allow autistic children to elaborate a multivariate equation encoding and conceptualizing within his/her brain, and externalizing into unconscious emotion (heart rate) and conscious verbal speech (words).

Author Keywords

brain development; autistic children; minimalistic InterActor robot; language; emotion; listener-speaker

INTRODUCTION

Imagine two people, one speaking the other listening. The speaker is elaborating a multivariable equation. S/he is trying to conceptualize within his/her brain and encode according to rules of semantics and syntax, and then externalize into spoken form. Speech engenders an avalanche of neuronal responses in the listener. Such neural reaction seems to mirror a multitude of computations associated with multiple processing information incorporated in the received signal.

The received information needs to be decoded and encoded according to linguistics rules and finally encrypted into representation in the neurons of the listener [1]. The listener is computing and trying to solve the proposed equation displaying various verbal and nonverbal (emotional or not) reactions in response to the utterances of the speaker. Verbal reaction necessitates the elaboration of coherent (grammatical and syntactically) sentence. Nonverbal reaction takes the form of head nods and/or various kinds of facial expressions. Intimately connected with the utterances of the speaker, these responses signify that the utterance is being accepted, understood, integrated [2, 3]. Successful communication requires that both speaker and listener accurately interpret (via verbal, nonverbal and emotional processes) the meaning of each other referential statement.

Neurotypically developing listeners and speakers are able to consider verbal, nonverbal (i.e, head nods), emotional (i.e., facial expressions) conventions and rules as well as each other referential statement. This is potentially due to the formation of a neural multimodal network, which naturally follows the evolution of the brain [4]. Using a modeling approach, recent neuroimaging studies have reported that both speech comprehension and speech expression activate a bilateral fronto-temporo-parietal network in the brain, fully characterized by the dynamic interaction among all the components [5]. Different studies emphasize the importance of multiple cortical (e.g., prefrontal cortex, temporal and parietal cortices) and subcortical areas (e.g., basal ganglia, hippocampus and cerebellum) not only for production and reception of speech but also for cognitive nonverbal emotional processes [6, 7, 8, 9].

Failure of the exterior superior temporal sulcus [8], of the interior temporal lobe, amygdala included [9], of the connectivity between temporal regions [10] as well as of the inferior prefrontal cortex [11] i.e., the mirror neurone system, is accepted as an explanation for atypical neurodevelopment, such as autism [12, 13]. The atypical neural architecture causes impairment in social interaction, in communications skills and interests [14, 15, 16, 17] and reduces the ability of mentalizing, i.e., represent the referential statement of other people [18].

Imagine now that in the aforementioned situation of "speaker and listener", the speaker is an autistic child trying to elaborate a multivariable equation. Complex in nature, the elaboration of this equation becomes more complex notably when the listener is a human, who is characterized by a high degree of variability on verbal and nonverbal reactions, (i.e., unpredictable reactions) [19]. Adding the fact that the child is impaired in interpreting the referential statement of other people [13], listener's verbal and nonverbal contributions are not always scrutinized. Based on the atypical neural architecture, there are at least two main reasons for this. The first reason is associated with the fact that autistic children have continual comprehension and language expression problems. Even if autistic children acquire language, it is often lacking any depth and is characterized by a paucity of imagination [20]. The second reason is that autistic children experience difficulties in perception and emotion, functions which are linked to language [21, 22] and also to social interaction and mentalizing [10].

Advances in recent years have enabled robots to fulfill a variety of human-like functions with autistic children. Different approaches have shown that animate robots using different stimulation encourage interaction in autistic children [23, 24]. Quantitative metrics for autism diagnosis and treatment including robots have been developed [25]. Despite these studies, only marginal attention has been paid to the comparison of neurotypical and autistic children in human-human and human-robot interaction. Using a "speaker-listener" situation, we have compared the verbal and nonverbal emotional expressions of neurotypical and autistic children aged 6 to 7 years. The speaker was always a child (neurotypical or autistic); the listener was a human or an InterActor robot, i.e., a robot which reacts to speech expression by nodding only. Given the fact that the InterActor robot is characterized by a low degree of variability in reactions (i.e., predictable reactions) and the human by a high degree of variability in reactions (i.e., unpredictable reactions), our general hypothesis is that verbal and emotional expressions of autistic children could better be facilitated by the InterActor Robot than by the human.

METHOD

A. Participants

Two groups of children, one "neurotypical" and one "autistic" participated in the study. Twenty neurotypical children (10 boys and 10 girls) composed the "neurotypical group"; twenty children (14 boys and 6 girls) composed the "autistic group". The developmental age of typical children ranged from 6 to 7 years old (mean 6.1 years; sd 7 months). The developmental age of autistic children ranged from 6 to 7 years old (mean 6 years; sd 8 months). Their mean age when first words appeared was 28 months (sd 7 months). The autistic children were diagnosed according to the DSM IV-TR criteria of autism [26]. The Childhood Autism Rating Scale-CARS [27] has been administrated by an experienced psychiatrist. The scores varied from 31 to 35 points signifying that the autistic population was composed of middle autistic children. They were all verbal. All autistic children were attending typical school classes with typical educational arrangements. The study was approved by the local ethics committee and was in accordance with the Helsinki convention. Anonymity was guaranteed.

B. Robot

An InterActor robot, i.e., a small toy robot, called "Pekoppa", was used as a listener [28]. Pekoppa is shaped like a bilobed plant and its leaves and stem make a nodding response based on speech input and supports the sharing of mutual embodiment in communication (Figure 1). It uses a material called BioMetal made of a shape-memory alloy as its driving force. The timing of nodding is predicted using a hierarchy model consisting of two stages: macro and micro (Figure 2). The macro stage estimates whether a nodding response exists or not in a duration unit, which consists of a talkspurt episode $T(i)$ and the following silence episode $S(i)$ with a hangover value of 4/30 s. The estimator $Mu(i)$ is a moving-average (MA) model, expressed as the weighted sum of unit speech activity $R(i)$ in (1) and (2). When $Mu(i)$ exceeds a threshold value, nodding $M(i)$ also becomes an MA model, estimated as the weighted sum of the binary speech signal $V(i)$ in (3). Pekoppa demonstrates three degrees of movements: big and small nods and a slight twitch of the leaves by controlling the threshold values of the nodding prediction. The threshold of the leaf movement is set lower than that of the nodding prediction.

Figure 1. Pekoppa

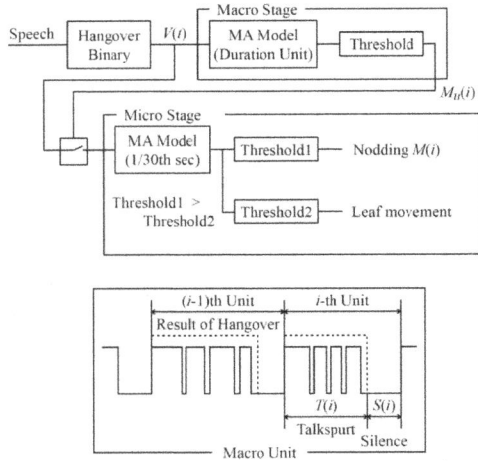

Figure 2. Listener's interaction model

$$M_u(i) = \sum_{j=1}^{J} a(j)R(i-j) + u(i) \qquad (1)$$

$$R(i) = \frac{T(i)}{T(i) + S(i)} \qquad (2)$$

$a(j)$: linear prediction coefficient
$T(i)$: talkspurt duration in the i-ht duration unit
$S(i)$: silence duration in the i-th duration unit
$u(i)$: noise

$$M(i) = \sum_{k=1}^{K} b(j)V(i-j) + w(i) \qquad (3)$$

b(j) : linear prediction coefficient
V(i) : voice
w(i) : noise

C. Procedure

For both groups, the study took place in a room which was familiar to the children. We defined three conditions: the first one was called "rest condition", the second was named "with human" (child-adult) and the third one was called "with robot" (child-Robot, i.e., child-Pekoppa). The second and third conditions were counterbalanced across the children. The duration of the "rest condition" was 1 minute; the second and third conditions each lasted approximately 7 minutes. The inter-condition interval was approximately about 30 seconds. For each child, the whole experimental session lasted 15 minutes (figure 3).

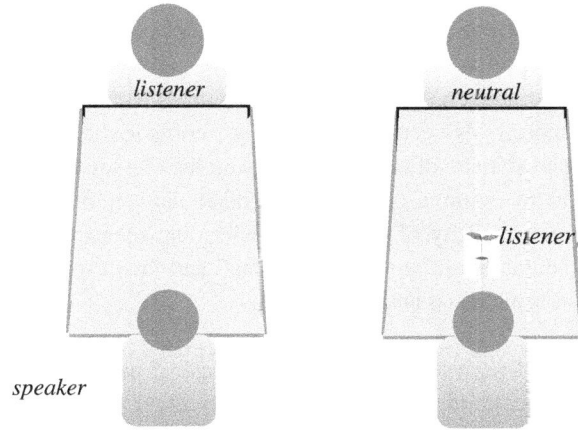

a) Human InterActor   *b) Robot InterActor*

Figure 3. Listener-Speaker Situation

At the beginning of each session, the experimenter presented the robot to the child explaining that the robot nods whenever the child speaks. Then, the experimenter hid the robot. The session was run as follows: during the "rest condition", the heart rate of each child was measured in silence. At the end of that condition, the child was also asked to estimate the intensity of her/his own emotion on a scale ranging from 1 (the lowest intensity) to 5 (the highest intensity) [29]. During the "with human" condition, the child was invited to discuss with the experimenter. The experimenter initiated discussion and after listened to the child acting as the speaker. The heart rate, as well as the frequency of words and verbs expressed by each child was measured. During the "with robot" condition, Pekoppa was set to nod movements; the experimenter gave the robot to the child inviting the child to use it. The robot was the listener, the child was the speaker and the experimenter remained silent and discreet. The heart rate and the frequency of words and verbs expressed by the child was recorded once again. At the end of the session, the child was invited to estimate the intensity of its own emotion on the same aforementioned scale. At the end of the experiment, each child was invited to respond to two questions: 1) *how did you find Pekoppa? 2) did you enjoy yourself with Pekoppa?* [22].

D. Analysis

The analysis was based on the following dependent variables a) the heart rate b) the number of nouns and verbs expressed by each child and c) the intensity of emotional feeling (auto-estimation of emotion). The data analysis was performed with SPSS Statistics 17.0. [30]

RESULTS

The distributions of heart rate, words and emotional feeling reported in both age groups approximate a parametric shape. With such distributions, the mean was been chosen as central index for comparisons. We performed statistic of comparisons using the chi-square test ($\chi 2$ Test) to examine differences in heart rate[1], number of words and intensity of emotional feeling between the two experimental conditions ("with human" and "with robot"), for neurotypical and autistic children.

Figure 4 represents the mean heart rate of neurotypical and autistic children both at inter-individual and intra-individual levels.

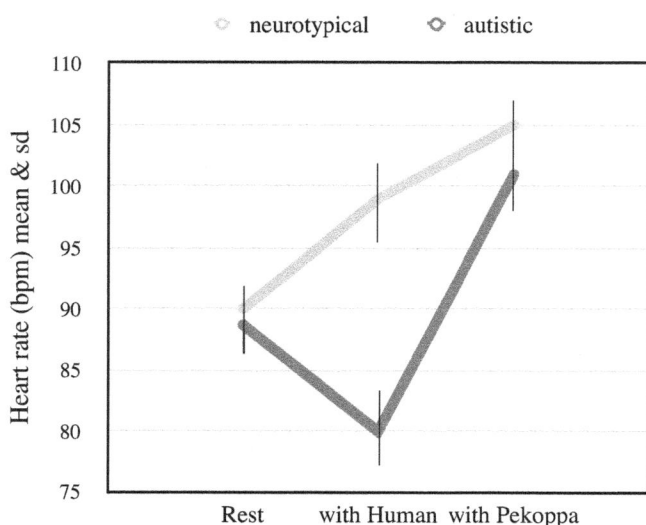

Figure 4. Mean Heart Rate

At the intra-individual level, the statistical analysis showed that relative to the "rest condition", the mean heart rate of neurotypical children was higher when the children were in contact with the InterActor robot ($\chi 2=6.68$, $p<0.01$) than when they were in contact with the human ($\chi 2=4.09$, $p<0.05$). However, the mean heart rate of neurotypical children didn't differ when they interacted with the human or with the InterActor robot ($\chi 2=2.83$, $p>0.05$). Similarly, relative to the "rest condition", the mean heart rate of autistic children was higher when they interacted with the InterActor robot ($\chi 2=7.01$, $p<0.01$) than when they interacted with the human ($\chi 2=5.01$, $p<0.05$). Finally, the mean heart rate of autistic children was higher when they were with the InterActor robot than when they were with the human ($\chi 2=7.84$, $p<0.01$).

At the inter-individual level, the mean heart rate of neurotypical and autistic children was similar ($\chi 2=2.06$, $p>0.10$) in the "rest condition". However, compared to the heart rate of neurotypical children, the mean heart rate of autistic children was lower when they interact with the human ($\chi 2=8.68$, $p<0.005$). The mean heart rate of autistic children didn't differ from that of neurotypical children when the InterActor was the robot ($\chi 2=2.85$, $p>0.05$).

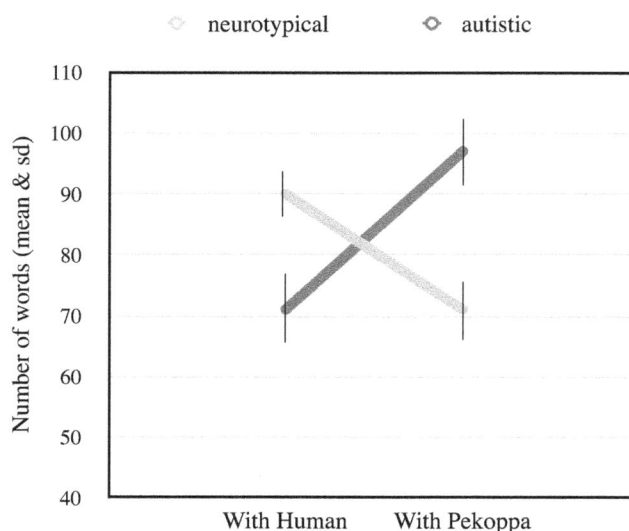

Figure 5. Number of words (nouns & verbs)

At the inter-individual level, as shown in figure 5, the mean number of words (nouns and verbs) was low in the "with human" condition for autistic children ($\chi^2=4.86$ $p<0.05$) and in the "with robot" condition for neurotypical children ($\chi^2=5.98$, $p<0.025$). The mean number of words expressed by autistic children in the "with robot" condition didn't differ from the mean number of words expressed by neurotypical children in the "with human" condition ($\chi^2=1.34$, $p>0.10$). At intra-individual level, the mean number of words was higher when the autistic children had the robot as interlocutor than when the interlocutor was a human ($\chi^2=5.97$, $p<0.025$). The quasi opposite configuration was observed for the neurotypical children ($\chi^2=4.78$, $p<0.05$).

---

[1] Heart rate is measured in beat per minute (bpm) using a frequency counter ring placed on the index finger of each child. The physiological heart rate limits correspond to 95 bpm (±30) at the age of 6 to 7 years.

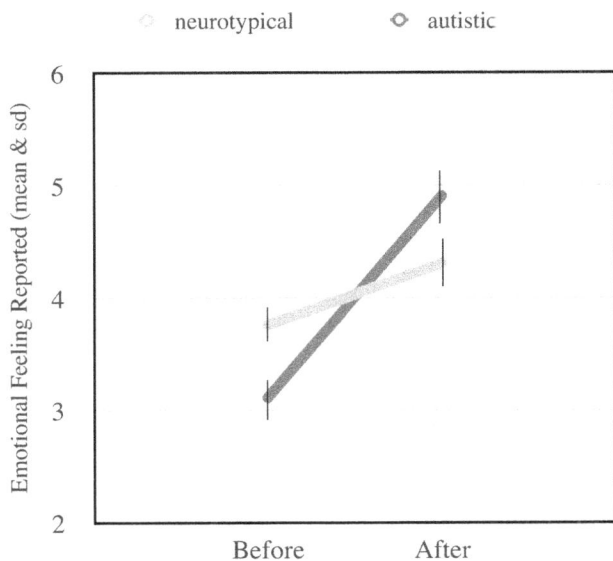

Figure 6. Intensity of Emotional Feeling Reported

Figure 6 illustrates that at inter-individual level, the intensity of emotional feeling reported didn't differ between neurotypical and autistic children within both conditions: "before robot" and "after robot" ($\chi^2=3.38$, $p>0.05$; $\chi^2=3.90$, $p>0.05$ respectively). However intra-individually, the intensity of emotional feeling is higher "after" than "before" the interaction with the InterActor robot for autistic children ($\chi^2=6.43$, $p<0.025$) but it didn't vary for the neurotypical children ($\chi^2=2.98$, $p>0.05$).

DISCUSSION

The present study aims at analyzing the embrainment of verbal and emotional expressions in neurotypical and autistic children aged 6 to 7 years. Our approach centered investigating the effects of a human or an InterActor robot in the context of a "speaker-listener" situation: the speaker was always the child; the listener was a human or an InterActor robot. To this end physiological data (i.e., heart rate), as well as behavioral data (i.e., number of nouns and verbs in addition to the emotional feeling reported) were considered. The results showed that 1) the heart rate of autistic children is low when the listener was a human and increased nearer to levels of neurotypical children when the listener was the InterActor robot; 2) the number of words expressed by the autistic children was higher when the interlocutor was the robot; 3) the emotional feeling reported increased after the interaction with the InterActor robot.

Fundamentally, the results are consistent with our hypothesis according to which the predictability of the InterActor robot would facilitate the emotional and verbal

expressions of autistic children. Our results showed significant differences of heart rate depending on whether the listener was a human or a robot. When the listener was a human, the children showed a low heart rate; when the listener was an InterActor robot, their heart rate increased. Such a result cannot be attributed to an order effect as the order of "human-human" and "human-robot" conditions have been counterbalanced. On the contrary, it can be understood as an effect of the InterActor robot on autistic children's mental state. This interpretation is also supported by the fact that when the autistic children had the InterActor robot as listener, their heart rate didn't differ from the heart rate of neurotypical children in the same condition. It is also interesting to note that the heart rate of the neurotypical children didn't differ when the listener was a human or a InterActor robot. Such difference reveals that an InterActor robot might improve autistic children behavior. This inference is reinforced by the fact that the physiological data we recorded reflects the modifications of orthosympathetic and parasympathetic autonomous nervous system which is dynamically (and bidirectionally) connected to the central nervous system [34, 35]. Physiologically, the lower regulation of heart rate (in "with human" condition) reflects poorer action of the myelinated vagus nerve [36] which in turn would signify poor neural activity in temporal cortex (amygdala included), in cingulate cortex and in prefrontal cortex [37, 38]. This neural architecture is hypo-activated in children with autism [12, 13], causing impairment in cognitive verbal, nonverbal and emotional behavior [14, 15, 16, 17, 18]. Such hypo-activation might explain autistic children's behavior when the listener is the human. Contrary to research suggesting that autistic children show disruptions in autonomic responses to environmental (human) stressors [39, 40, 41], our findings indicate that not only are there no disruptions in autonomic responses but that these responses don't exceed the physiological limits. Apparently, when the listener is the InterActor robot, the heart rate of children with autism increases indicating a "mobilisation" of a given mental state. Such "mobilisation" provides support for the social engagement of autistic children. Namely, by making the autistic children available to engage emotionally (and verbally), the InterActor robot seems to modify their neural activity: the children enjoyed participating. It is noteworthy that they also verbalized such pleasurable sentiments at the end of the experiment. Essentially, the present results are consistant with our previous assumptions following which toy robots would improve autistic children brain functioning [23, 32].

The above considerations could account for the number of words (nouns and verbs) expressed by the children. Even if the autistic children were verbal, the present finding indicated that when the listener was an InterActor robot, the number of words expressed by the autistic children was higher than the number of words they express when the listener was a human. Interestingly, such verbal behavior doesn't differ from that of neurotypical children when these latter had a human as listener. Once again, the use of the InterActor robot seems afford autistic children to express themselves as neurotypical children do with humans. This data is consistent with previous studies which have demonstrated that verbal expression can be facilitated by the active (but discreet) presence of a robot [21].

Although neurotypical children didn't report emotional feeling changes after their interaction with the robot, autistic children felt better after interaction with the robot. This is coherent not only with the physiological data we observed but also with parent accounts. At the end of the experiment, many parents announced: "s/he is happy", "s/he likes your robot". Autistic children also conceded that the robot was "cute", "cool" "genius", some of them even said: "if I had the robot, I would talk to it all the time". Some of them imitated the robot verbally (and emotionally).

It could be argued that the "autistic group" was made up verbal children and that the results we observed might be due to the actual verbal capabilities of the children. However, we must underline that these children expressed themselves (both emotionally and verbally) only when the listener was the InterActor Robot. Although our results are statistically significant, we recognize that the size of our group is limited to twenty children only. We aim to study the behavior of other age groups as well. Finally, it is obvious that what we need to develop is a follow up study to prove that the InterActor robot is the robot which can sustainably improve the emotional and verbal behavior of autistic children.

CONCLUSION

Given the present findings, it can concluded that an InterActor robot characterized by small variance nonverbal behavior, (i.e., nodding when children speak), better facilitates verbal and emotional expressions of autistic children than a human. This might be related to autistic children preferences. Autistic children are rather interested in minimalist objects to which they can assign mental states of their own or of others [22]. Such a behavior might be interpreted as reflecting the children's willingness to communicate with humans using the robot: the InterActor toy robot is a miniature of a human listener, i.e., the autistic autistic children can handle the head nods (as neurotypical children do with humans). These results (consistent with previous studies) appear to indicate that minimalistic artificial environments could be considered as the root of neuronal organization and reorganization with the potential to improve brain activity in order to support the embrainment of cognitive verbal and emotional information processing.

ACKNOWLEDGMENTS
To all the participants and their parents, the Major, the Pedagogical Inspector, the Educational Advisor, the Director and the team of principal elementary school of the first district of Paris, and the National Department of Education and Research.

REFERENCES
1. Dick, A.S., A. Solodkin, A., and Small, S.L. Neural development of networks for audiovisual speech comprehension. *Brain and Language*, 114 (2010), 101–114.

2. Bavelas, J.B., Coates, L. and Johnson, T. Listener responses as a collaborative process: the role of gaze. *Journal of Communication,* 52, (2002), 566–580.

3. Clark, H.H. *Using language*. Cambridge University Press, Cambridge, 1996.

4. Giannopulu, I. Multimodal interactions in typically and atypically developing children: natural vs. artificial environments. *Cognitive Processing*, 14, (2013), 323-331.

5. Davis, M.H. Johnsrude, I.S. Hearing speech sounds: Top-down influence on the interface between audition and speech perception. Hearing Research, 229, (2007), 132-147.

6. Cangelosi, A. Grounding language in action and perception: from cognitive agents to humanoid robots. *Physics of Life Reviews,* 7, (2010), 139-151.

7. Fedorenko, E., Hsieh, P.J., Nieto-Castañón, A., Whitfield-Gabrieli, S. and Kanwisher, N. New Method for fMRI Investigations of Language: Defining ROIs Functionally in Individual Subjects. *Journal of Neurophysiology,* 104, (2010), 1177–1194.

8. Pelphrey, K.A. and Caster, E.J. Charting the typical and atypical development of the social brain.

Developmental Psychopathology, 20, (2008), 1081–1102.

9. Corbett, B.A., Carmean, V., Ravizza, S., C. Wendelken, C., Henry, M.L., Carter, C. and Rivera, S.M. A functional and structural study of emotion and face processing in children with autism. *Psychiatry Research*, 30, (2009), 196-205.

10. Frith, U. and Frith, C.D. Development and neurophysiology of mentalizing. *Philosophical Transaction of the Royal Society B Biological Science*, 358, (2003), 459-473.

11. Brothers, L. The social brain: A project for integrating primate behaviour and neurophysiology in a new domain. *Concepts Neuroscience*, 1, (1990), 27–51.

12. Iacoboni, M. and Mazziotta, J.C. Mirror neuron system: basic findings and clinical applications. *Annals of Neurology*, 3, (2007), 213–218.

13. Baron-Cohen, S. Mindblindness. MIT Press, Cambridge 1995.

14. Adolphs, R., A. Jansari, A. and Tranel, D. Hemispheric perception of emotional valence from facial expressions. *Neuropsychology*, 15, (2001), 516–524.

15. Aggleton, J.P. The Amygdala: A Functional Analysis. Oxford University Press, Oxford, 2000.

16. Nacewicz, B.M., Dalton, K.M., Johnstone, T. Long, M., McAuliff, E. M., Oakes, T.R., Alexander, A.L. and Davidson, R.J. Amygdala Volume and Nonverbal Social Impairment in Adolescent and Adult Males with Autism. *Archives of Genetic Psychiatry*, 63, (2006), 1417-1428.

17. Kana, R.K., Murdaugh, D.L., Libero, L.E., Pennick, M.R., Wadsworth, H.M., Deshpande, R. et al. Probing the brain in autism using 807 fMRI and diffusion tensor imaging. *Journal of Visualized Experiments*, 55, (2011), e3178.

18. Baron-Cohen, S., Leslie, A.M. and Frith, U. Does the autistic child have a theory of mind? *Cognition* 21, (1985), 37–46.

19. Pierno, A.C., Mari, M., Lusher, D. and Castiello, U. Robotic movement elicits visuomotor priming in children with autism. *Neuropsychologia*, 46, (2008), 448–454.

20. Pelphrey, K.A., and Caster, E.J. Charting the typical and atypical development of the social brain. *Developmental Psychopathology*, 20, (2008), 1081-1102.

21. Puyon, M. and Giannopulu, I. Emergent emotional and verbal strategies in autism are based on multimodal interactions with toy robot in spontaneous game play. In Proc. IEEE International Symposium on Robot and Human Interactive Communication, (2013), 593–597. [*22nd Annu. Conf. RO-MAN, Korea*].

22. Giannopulu, I., Montreynaud, V. and Watanabe, T. Neurotypical and Autistic Children aged 6 to 7 years in a Speaker-Listener Situation with a Human or a Minimalist InterActor Robot. In Proc IEEE RO-MAN, (2014), 942-947.

23. Giannopulu, I. Multimodal cognitive nonverbal and verbal interactions: the neurorehabilitation of autistic children via mobile toy robots. *IARIA International Journal of Advances in Life Sciences*, 5. (2013) 214–222.

24. Giannopulu, I. Embedded multimodal nonverbal and verbal interactions between a mobile toy robot and autistic children. In Proc. ACM/IEEE International Conference on Human-Robot Interaction, (2013), 127-128. [*8th Annu. Conf. RHI Japan*].

25. Diehl, J.J., Schmitt, L.M., Villano, M. and Crowell, C.R. The clinical use of robots for individual with autism spectrum disorders: a clinical review. *Research in Autism Spectrum Disorders*, 61, (2012), 249–262.

26. DSM-IV-TR *Manuel diagnostique et statistique des troubles mentaux*. Paris, Editions Masson, 2003.

27. Schopler, E., Reichler, R.J., De Vellis, R.F. and Daly, K. Toward objective classification of childhood autism: Childhood Autism Rating Scale (CARS). *JADD10*, (1980), 91-103.

28. Watanabe, T. Human-entrained Embodied Interaction and Communication Technology. *Emotional Engineering*, (2011), 161-177.

29. Giannopulu, I. and Sagot, I. Ressenti émotionnel positif dans une tâche expérimentale chez l'enfant (Positive emotion in the course of an experimental task in children). *Annales Médico-Psychologiques*, 168(10), (2010), 740-745.

30. SPSS STATISTICS 17.0. Python Software Foundation, (2008).

31. Giannopulu I. and Watanabe, T. Give Children Toy Robots to Educate and/or to Neuroreeducate. MESROB, (2014), EPFL-Lausanne.

32. Giannopulu, I. and Pradel, G. From child-robot interaction to child-robot-therapist interaction: a case

study in autism. *Applied Bionics and Biomechanics*, 9, (2012), 173–179.

33. Barres, B.A. and Barde, Y. Neuronal and glial cell biology. *Current Opinion in Neurobiology*, 10, (2000), 642–-648.

34. Servant, D., Logier, R., Mouster, Y. and Goudemand, M. Heart rate variability. Applications in psychiatry. *Encéphale*, 35, (2009), 423-428.

35. Porges, S. The polyvagal perspective. *Biological Psychology*, 74, (2007), 116-143.

36. Porges, S.W. and Furman, S.A. The Early Development of the Autonomic Nervous System Provides a Neural Platform for Social Behavior: A Polyvagal Perspective. *Infant Child Development*. 20(1), (2011), 106–118.

37. Manta, S. Effets Neurophysiologiques de la stimulation du nerf vague : Implication dans le traitement de la dépression résistante et optimisation des paramètres de stimulation. Thèse de Doctorat, Université de Montréal, Canada, 2012.

38. Schmitt, J.E., Neale, M.C., Fassassi, B., Perez, J., Lenroot, R.K., Wells, E.M. and Giedd, J.N. The dynamic role of genetics on cortical patterning during childhood and adolescence. *PNAS*, (2014), Early Edition.

39. Kylliäinen, A. and Hietane, J.K. Skin conductance responses to another person's gaze in children with autism. *Journal of Autism and Developmental Disorders*, 36, (2006), 517–525.

40. Toichi, M. and Kamio, Y. Paradoxal autonomic response to mental tasks in autism. *Journal of Autism and Developmental Disorders,* 33, (2003), 417-426.

41. van Hecke, V.A., Lebow, J. Bal, E. et al. Electrocephalogram and heart rate regulation to familiar and unfamiliar people in children with autism spectraum disorders. *Child Development,* 80, (2009), 1118–1133.

User-friendly Autonomous Wheelchair for Elderly Care Using Ubiquitous Network Robot Platform

Masahiro Shiomi, Takamasa Iio, Koji Kamei, Chandraprakash Sharma, and Norihiro Hagita
ATR Intelligent Robotics and Communication Laboratories
2-2-2 Hikaridai, Keihanna Science City, Kyoto, Japan
m-shiomi@atr.jp, iio@atr.jp, kamei@atr.jp, chandraprakash@atr.jp, hagita@atr.jp

ABSTRACT

The importance of assistive robots for elderly people is increasing to match the needs of rapidly aging world societies. This paper develops a wheelchair robot to support the movement of the elderly to decrease caregiver workloads from the perspective of physical load and time consumption. We observed the behaviors of caregivers at a private residential care home when they are wheeling elderly people in wheelchairs. The behavior includes appropriate utterances for reducing the anxieties of senior citizens based on properties of place, e.g., "Here the path is a little narrow" while passing a narrow space or "Now let's go into elevator." They also adjusted to the wheeling speed preference of each individual because their preferred speeds were different. We implemented these two functions for elderly care using the Ubiquitous Network Robot Platform that allows the management of users and environment properties. Experimental results with elderly participants at a pseudo resident home show that the seniors prefer a wheelchair robot on which the above functions have been implemented.

Author Keywords

Autonomous Wheelchair; Human-Robot interaction; Ubiquitous Network Robot Platform

ACM Classification Keywords

I.2.9. Artificial Intelligence: Robotics

INTRODUCTION

As the number of senior citizens continues to increase in many countries including Japan, Italy, and Germany, assisting them is one of the major purposes of robotics research field. Such physical assistance as walking aid [1, 2] and carrying baggage [3] are especially promising applications for assistive robots.

Recent research has also focused on the social acceptance of assistive robots due to the advances in their development. Even if stable and safe wheelchair robots are realized, integrating them in the world is difficult without acceptance

by the actual users: elderly people. Such a gap between researchers (or engineers) and users is always experienced when new technologies are introduced to the world.

User-friendliness is one key for acceptance from elderly people. Assistive robots must consider both their individual properties and their preferred interaction style. For example, the walking speeds of seniors vary widely and tend to be slower than younger people. Therefore, assistive robots that accompany users need a function to adjust their moving speed based on each elderly person's preference. Moreover, a past research work reported that elderly people prefer a conversational robot more than a non-conversational one [4]. Such behavioral considerations are useful to design assistive robots for the elderly.

We are developing a moving support system using a wheelchair robot for the benefit of the elderly. We analyzed the typical behaviors of caregivers in a private residential care home. Such behaviors include appropriate utterances to reduce the anxieties of the elderly that reflect the places and changing wheeling speeds based on individual preferences. To implement typical behavior in a wheelchair robot that adapts to such personal properties as a preferred walking speed, we employed a Ubiquitous Network Robot Platform (UNR-PF) service, which manages interaction between users and wheelchair using UNR-PF. It also manages environment information such as the spatial attributes of a corridor; the robot used this information to make appropriate comments to reduce stress, as caregivers do (Fig. 1). We experimentally evaluated the effectiveness of these functions with elderly participants at an experimental private residential care home facility.

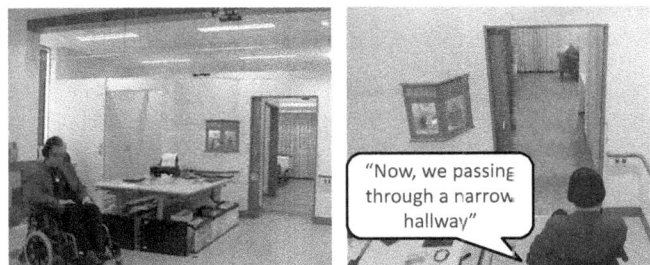

Fig. 1 Wheelchair robot with an elderly person

RELATED WORK

Assistive robots for elderly people are seeing greater development in the world. For example, researchers have developed them as walking aids [1, 2]. Mutlu et al.

developed a conveyance robot to assist hospital staffs, which indirectly assists elderly people [6]. Developing a wheelchair robot is one straightforward approach to physically support elderly people [7]; such basic navigation methods as path planning [8], obstacle avoidance [9], and simultaneous localization and mapping [10, 11] are stabilizing due to the hardware and software advances of wheelchair robots. Therefore, researchers are focusing on various stages of research, e.g., such as a user interface as a voice interface [12] and a brain machine interface [13] for easily controlling wheelchair robots, comfortable driving by considering human perceptions [14], and safe autonomous navigation for multiple wheelchairs [15].

Related to the development of such physical assistant robots, social robots, which focus on effective communication with the elderly, are also becoming a major topic in this research field. For example, social robots have been developed for healthcare assistance that give verbal instruction to provide reminders about medicine schedules [16, 17]. Paro, a seal robot, is used for therapy purposes in elderly care homes [18]. Iwamura et al. investigated the effectiveness of the conversation and the appearances of a physical assistant robot for elderly people [4] and concluded that seniors prefer a conversational robot as a shopping assistant partner.

Similar to these related works, in this research we investigate the effectiveness of a wheelchair robot that provides moving support to elderly people instead of caregivers through an experiment with actual elderly people. One of the unique points of our research work is its investigation of the perception of elderly people about two implemented functions that were designed by observing the behavior of actual caregivers for such moving support as speaking behavior for wheelchair robots. Past related works developed several wheelchair robots to provide moving support [7], but they did not focus on such perceptions.

SYSTEM DESIGN AND OVERVIEW

Design Policy for a Wheelchair Robot
We investigated how actual caregivers interact with the elderly at a private resident home (Good Time Living Kōrigaoka, Osaka) to design the functions for our wheelchair robot. About 100 elderly live in the home, among whom 20 only use wheelchairs every day.

The minimum number of daily wheelchair trips for a person in the home was 10: six times between the bedroom and the dining area (three round trips for meals), twice between the bedroom and the bathroom, and twice between the bedroom and the recreation room. Therefore, at least 20*(10-times) wheelchair uses for the moving support of elderly people occur in this home.

We observed how the caregivers wheeled the elderly people around the home. From ten observations of a 11-m hallway between an elevator and a dining hall/cafeteria, the average wheeling speed was around 600 mm/second, which resembles the slow walking speed of an adult. Caregivers often made comments based on the locations or about arriving at or waiting for the elevator or entering the cafeteria/recreation room, even if the elderly people did not respond.

After observing the caregiver behaviors during the moving support, we discussed them with the home's administrator. Even though the caregivers carefully maintained a slow wheeling speed, we learned that some of the elderly people desire an even slower wheeling speed because they want to move at their own walking speed. The administrator also emphasized that caregivers must engage in small talk to help reduce the anxiety of the seniors, even if they failed to respond.

Based on these observations, we implemented two functions to realize a friendly wheelchair robot for moving support: 1) adaption of moving speed based on individual preference and 2) small talk about position-related events.

System Overview
We used an UNR-PF to manage the preferred speed of the individuals as a personal characteristic and environmental information to support position-related events to implement the observed functions. Fig. 2 shows an overview of the system, which consists of three components: user interface (UI), UNR-PF, and a wheelchair robot. The details are described as follows.

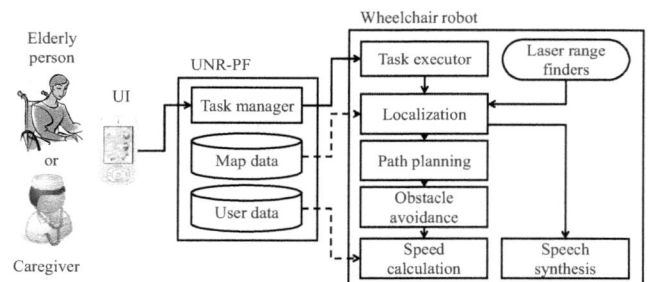

Fig. 2 System overview

User Interface
We used an Android tablet (Nexus 7) to control the wheelchair robot. The user interface consists of three panels: settings, user selection, and navigation (Fig. 3). By using a "login" system, the system automatically retrieves and changes the moving speed of the wheelchair robot to the preferred speed of the user who is riding on the robot wheelchair. Destination options are displayed by simple icons that the elderly or the caregivers can touch to select a target location.

Fig. 3 UI to determine wheelchair location

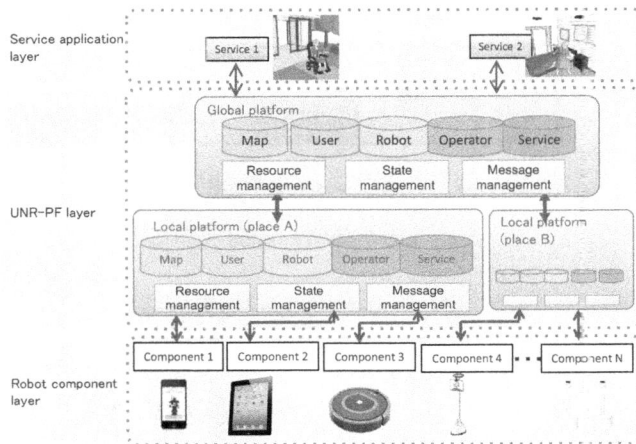

Fig. 4. UNR-PF overview

UNR-PF

The UNR platform is an open standard infrastructure for networked robot services [5]. Its salient point is that it focuses on abstraction over the underlying low level robotic hardware layer to develop robotics services, unlike other common libraries and middleware such as ROS and RTM. Even if such systems enable robotics researchers to develop functions for robot control, it remains difficult to manage robot service applications with different kinds of robots/sensors. To bridge the gap between robot development and service applications, our UNR platform design has three layers: service application, platform, and robot component (Fig. 4).

To achieve interoperability with different robots and sensors by sharing information among the robots and the service applications, the specifications of the data structures and the interfaces must be standardized. Even though part of the UNR platform has already been proposed to several organizations as international standards, the standardization details are beyond the scope of our research focus (see [5]

for details). We used the UNR Platform to connect the wheelchair robot and a client user interface system and to manage both the elderly and environment information.

Wheelchair Robot

In this work, we used a differential drive robotic wheelchair from Nissin Medical Industries (NEO-PR45, Fig. 1), which is equipped with three laser range finders (Hokuyo UTM-30LX). It is 59-cm wide, 85-cm-tall, and 104-cm-long and we set it to move forward at a maximum velocity of 900 mm/sec and at 30 degree/sec. The forward acceleration and the rotation are 600 mm/sec^2 and 30 degree/sec^2, respectively. The laser range finders are used for localization and obstacle detection. For safe navigation, we implemented a time varying dynamic window (TVDW) [9] and used speech synthesis software, XIMERA [19], for the robot's speech.

For speed adaption and speaking behavior, the wheelchair robot changes its moving speed using the preferred speed information from UNR-PF to realize the first function. For the second function, the robot makes pre-defined small talk based on its position and registered map information in UNR-PF around narrow spaces and slopes. The robot also uses the elderly person's name who is riding in the wheelchair and informs her of departures and arrivals.

EXPERIMENT

Hypotheses and Prediction

We implemented two functions on our wheelchair robot by referring to the actual caregiver behaviors. If these functions are prepared well, we believe that the elderly will more positively evaluate the robot than a robot without them.

As an alternative method, we used a wheelchair robot without our implemented functions that was designed based on the observations of caregivers. The safety functions are the same as the developed system. The moving speed is 600 mm/sec, which is the average speed of the caregivers measured at the private residential care home. We also prepared a caregiver condition to compare the evaluations with the robots as an additional alternative method. Based on the above idea, we made the following predictions:

Prediction 1: The wheelchair robot with the implemented functions will be rated higher in terms of comfortable moving speed than the wheelchair robot with an alternative method.

Prediction 2: The wheelchair robot with the implemented functions will provide more enjoyment during movement than the wheelchair robot with an alternative method.

Participants

Twenty eight elderly people (14 women and 14 men, who averaged 74.0 years old, S.D 6.85) participated in the experiment. 10 people, who require daily care, are living in private residential care homes; five usually use wheelchairs. One or two senior staff members from the care home also participated in the experiment to support the elderly people who are living in the home.

Environment
We conducted the experiment in an experimental residential care home facility that consists of a bedroom, a bathroom and a lobby. The room sizes and designs are the same as the actual care home where some of the participants are actually living. Fig. 5 shows a map of the environment.

Conditions
We used a within-participant experiment design to evaluate and compare the effects of the implemented functions.

Simple navigation condition
In this condition, the wheelchair robot automatically moved with the participants who are riding on it after selecting the target location by UI. As written above, the wheelchair's usual speed was 600 mm/sec. The robot did not use its speech synthesis function. Fig. 6 shows a wheelchair robot moving around in the experimental environment.

Proposed condition
In this condition, the wheelchair robot also automatically moved after selecting the target location by UI. It speaks based on the robot's location. We adjusted the usual speed to each participant's preferred speed that was measured at the beginning of the experiment (details are described below).

We set two kinds of place information in this environment: a narrow place at the bedroom's door and a slope in front of the bathroom. This information was sent to the robot from the UNR-PF using the robot's position, and then the robot says pre-defined dialogues before passing these places. For example, the robot said, "here is relatively narrow" before passing the bedroom's door, and "now we are going slightly uphill" at the beginning of the slope. Fig. 1 shows a scene where a wheelchair robot speaks before passing the door.

Caregiver condition
In this condition, a caregiver wheeled the participants as the caregivers usually do. Therefore, this condition reproduces a daily situation of the elderly who are using wheelchairs and need help to move around.

If the participants were living in the care home, a staff member of the home wheeled them in the experiment in the usual fashion; we did not specify moving speed or conversation behavior. For the rest of the participants, the experimenter wheeled them at around 600 mm/sec, which is the average speed at which the caregivers wheeled the elderly people, as measured by the private resident home. The experimenters talked to the participants using similar contents to the *proposed* condition that was described above.

In Fig. 7, a caregiver is pushing a participant in a wheelchair.

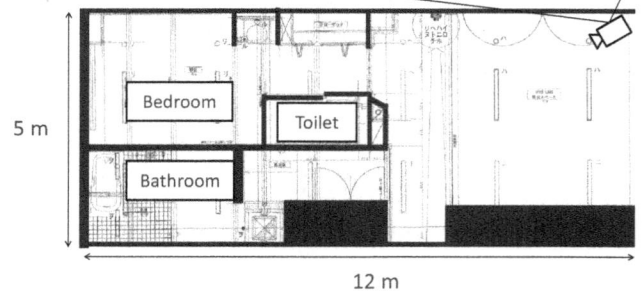

Fig. 5 Environment

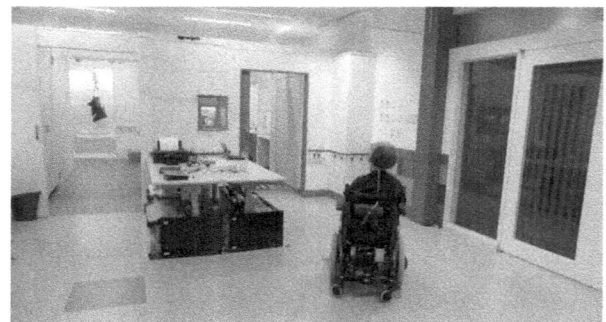

Fig. 6 Wheelchair in simple navigation condition

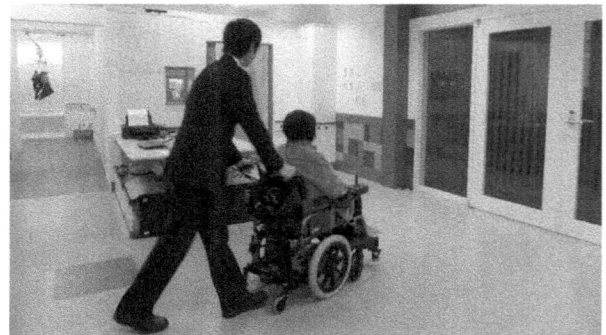

Fig. 7 Caregiver condition

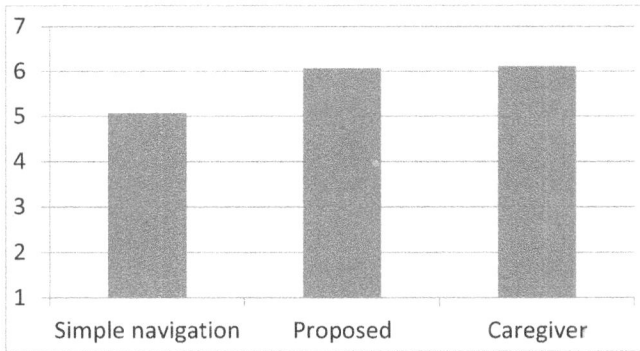

Fig. 8 Comfort of moving speed

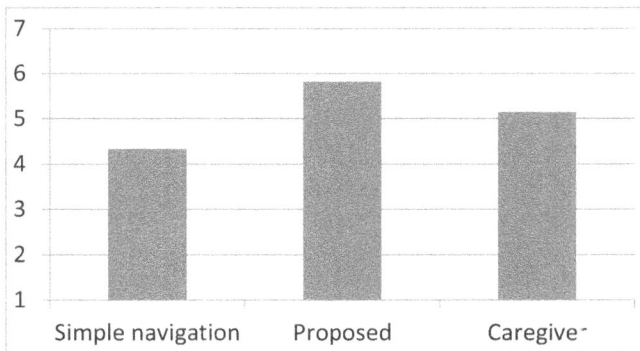

Fig. 9 Enjoyment during movement

Procedure

Before the first session, the participants were given a brief description of our experiment's purpose and procedure. We also determined their preferred speed; the participants rode in the wheelchair robot at three different speeds: 300, 600, and 900 mm/sec. Most of the preferred speeds reported by the participants are used for controlling the wheelchair robot under the *proposed* condition. Seven participants preferred 300 mm/sec, 19 preferred 600 mm/sec, and two preferred 900 mm/sec.

Since the experiment had a within-participant design, each participant participated in three sessions of different conditions. The order of the conditions was counterbalanced. Staff members remained in the environment for safety and to record videos. The participants filled out a questionnaire after each session.

The experiment's route was designed based on the daily situation of a representative elderly person who is using a wheelchair at the private resident home in the evening. She leaves her bedroom to go to the bathroom to take a bath and returns to her bedroom. Since this is an experiment, the wheelchair robot makes a round trip between the bedroom and the bathroom.

Measurements

We measured two items in this experiment: comfort at the preferred moving speeds and enjoyment during the

movement. All questionnaire items were evaluated on a 1-to-7 point scale.

RESULTS

Verification of Prediction 1

Figure 8 shows the result of the comfort of the moving speed. We conducted a one-factor within subject ANOVA and found a significant difference among the conditions (F $(2, 52) = 10.419$, $p<.001$, partial $\eta^2=.286$). Multiple comparisons with the Bonferroni method revealed significant differences: *caregiver > simple navigation* ($p = .001$) and *proposed > simple navigation* ($p = .001$). No significance was found between *caregiver* and *proposed* ($p = 1.0$). Therefore, prediction 1 was supported.

Verification of Prediction 2

Figure 9 shows the result of enjoyment during the movement. We conducted a one-factor within subject ANOVA and found a significant difference among the conditions (F $(2, 52) = 12.026$, $p<.001$, partial $\eta^2=.316$). Multiple comparisons with the Bonferroni method revealed significant differences: *caregiver > simple navigation* ($p = .029$) and *proposed > simple navigation* ($p <.001$). A significant trend was found between *proposed* and *caregiver* ($p = .096$). Therefore, prediction 2 was supported.

DISCUSSION

Limitations

Since this study was conducted for moving support at an experimental residential care home in Japan, we cannot generalize about our predictions from it. Even though this experiment was held in a realistic situation with participants who used the wheelchair robot, it was conducted within the framework of an academic study. The elderly participants only used the wheelchair robot a few times. Thus, the effect shown in the experiment would probably be moderated if they got accustomed to the wheelchair robot: the diminishment of any novelty effect. For example, the robot needs to change its words to avoid negative impressions caused by repeating the same speeches. The preferred speed of individuals might also change based on experiences with the wheelchair robots. These limitations of our study will be tested in the future, perhaps with the realistic deployment of wheelchair robots in society.

CONCLUSION

This paper investigated whether elderly people prefer a wheelchair robot that makes comments based on place while providing moving support and changes its moving speed according to individual preferences. To implement these functions, we used a wheelchair robot and UNR-PF, which can manage individual properties and environment information for robot services. We conducted an experiment with elderly people at an experimental residential care home that consists of a bedroom and a bathroom. The elderly people more highly evaluated a wheelchair robot with the implemented functions than a wheelchair robot without them; we found no significant differences from the questionnaire results between caregiver support and the wheelchair robot with our implemented functions.

ACKNOWLEDGMENTS

This research was supported by the Ministry of Internal Affairs and Communications of Japan and JSPS KAKENHI Grant Number 25730165. We thank the staff at the ORIX Living Innovation Center and the Good Time Living Kōrigaoka for their helpful participation. We also thank Shinobu Masaki, Naoki Kusakawa, and Eiko Fukumori for their help.

REFERENCES

1. Dubowsky, S. Genot, F., Godding, S., Kozono, H., Skwersky, A., Yu, H., and Yu, L.S. PAMM: A Robotic Aid to the Elderly for Mobility Assistance and Monitoring: A "Helping-Hand" for the Elderly. *IEEE Intl. Conf. On Robotics and Automation, (2000),* 570-576.

2. Graf, B. An Adaptive Guidance System for Robotic Walking Aids. *Journal of Computing and Information Technology*, 17, 1, (2009), 109-120.

3. Kulyukin, V., Gharpure, C., and Nicholson. J. RoboCart: Toward Robot-Assisted Navigation of Grocery Stores by the Visually Impaired, *IEEE/RSJ Int. Conf. on Intelligent Robots and Systems,* (2005), 2845-2850.

4. Iwamura, Y., Shiomi, M., Kanda, T., Ishiguro, H., and Hagita, N. Do Elderly People Prefer a Conversational Humanoid as a Shopping Assistant Partner in Supermarkets? In *Proc. HRI2011*, (2011), 449-456.

5. Shiomi, M., Kamei, K., Kondo, T., Miyashita, T., and Hagita, N. Robotic Service Coordination for Elderly People and Caregivers with Ubiquitous Network Robot Platform, In *Proc. ARSO2013*, (2013), 57-62.

6. Mutlu, B. and Forlizzi, J. Robots in organizations: the role of workflow, social, and environmental factors in human-robot interaction, *ACM/IEEE Int. Conf. on Human Robot Interaction,* (2008), 287-294.

7. Faria, BrígidaMónica, Reis, LuísPaulo, and Lau, Nuno. A Survey on Intelligent Wheelchair Prototypes and Simulators, New Perspectives in Information Systems and Technologies, Volume 1, (2014), Rocha, Á., Correia, A.M., Tan, F. B., Stroetmann, K. A. (Eds.)

8. Henry, P., Vollmer, C., Ferris, B., and Fox, D. Learning to navigate through crowded environments, In *Proc. of IEEE Int. Conf. on Robotics and Automation.* (2010), 981-986.

9. M. Seder and I. Petrovic, "Dynamic window based approach to mobile robot motion control in the presence of moving obstacles," In Proc. of IEEE Int. Conf. on Robotics and Automation, pp. 1986-1992, 2007.

10. Durrant-Whyte, H. and Bailey, T. Simultaneous localization and mapping (slam): Part I the essential algorithms, *IEEE ROBOTICS AND AUTOMATION MAGAZINE*, 13, 2, (2006), 99-110.

11. T. Bailey and H. Durrant-Whyte, "Simultaneous localization and mapping (SLAM): part II," *IEEE ROBOTICS AND AUTOMATION MAGAZINE,* 13, 3, (2006), 108–117.

12. Boucher. P., et al., Design and Validation of an Intelligent Wheelchair Towards a Clinically-Functional Outcome, Journal of Neuroengineering and Rehabilitation, 10, 1, (2013), 58-73.

13. Kanemura, A., Morales, Y., Kawanabe, M., Morioka, H, Kallakuri, N., Ikeda, T., Miyashita, T., Hagita, N., and Ishii, S., A waypoint-based framework in brain-controlled smart home environments: Brain interfaces, domotics, and robotics integration," *IEEE/RSJ International Conference on Intelligent Robots and Systems (IROS)* (2013), 865-870.

14. Morales, Y., Kallakuri, N., Shinozawa, K., Miyashita, T., and Hagita N., Human-Comfortable Navigation for an Autonomous Robotic Wheelchair, In *Proc. IROS2013*, (2013), 2737-2743.

15. Kobayashi, Y., Kinpara, Y., Shibusawa, T., and Kuno, Y. Robotic wheelchair based on observations of people using integrated sensors, *IEEE/RSJ International Conference on Intelligent Robots and Systems (IROS)*, (2009), 2013-2018.

16. Montemerlo, M. Pineau, J. Roy, N. Thrun, S., and Varma, V. Experiences with a Mobile Robotic Guide for the Elderly. *Int. Conf. on Artificial Intelligence. Edmonton,* (2002), 587-592.

17. Pollack M., E. Intelligent technology for an aging population: The use of AI to assist elders with cognitive impairment. *The AI magazine*, 26, 2, (2005), 9-24.

18. Shibata, T. An overview of human interactive robots for psychological enrichment. *The Proceedings of IEEE*, 92, 11, (2004), 1749-1758.

19. Kawai, H. Toda, T. Ni, J. Tsuzaki, M., and Tokuda, K. XIMERA: a new TTS from ATR based on corpus-based technologies. *5th ISCA Speech Synthesis Workshop*, (2004), 179-184.

Tangible Earth: Tangible Learning Environment for Astronomy Education

Hideaki Kuzuoka
University of Tsukuba
Tsukuba, Ibaraki, Japan
kuzuoka@iit.tsukuba.ac.jp

Naomi Yamashita
NTT Communication Science Labs
Seika-cho, Kyoto, Japan
naomiy@acm.org

Hiroshi Kato
The Open University of Japan
Mihama-ku, Chiba, Japan
Hiroshi@Kato.com

Hideyuki Suzuki
Ibaraki University
Mito, Ibaraki, Japan
hideyuki@mx.ibaraki.ac.jp

Yoshihiko Kubota
Utsunomiya University
Utsunomiya, Tochigi, Japan
kubota@kubota-lab.net

ABSTRACT
To support astronomy education, we developed a tangible learning environment called the tangible earth system. To clarify its problems, we defined an assessment framework from the aspects of curriculum guidelines, design guidelines of tangible learning environments, and epistemology of agency. Based on the analysis of our small-scale user study, we identified problems of the system in terms of location, dynamics, and correspondence parameters.

Author Keywords
Astronomy education; educational technology; tangible bits.

ACM Classification Keywords
H.5.2. Information interfaces and presentation (e.g., HCI): User Interfaces.

INTRODUCTION
Among astronomy curricula, concepts related to earth-sun relationships are difficult since students need to understand how the spatial and temporal relationships between the sun and earth cause daily and seasonal variations in various phenomena [5, 8], including the sun's diurnal motion. Even some preservice elementary school teachers fail to fully understand these relationships [1].

One promising approach that helps students effectively grasp basic astronomy concepts is using a globe [1, 5] and a doll-like figure on it [9]. Indeed, many studies have applied a tangible user interface (TUI) for educational purposes [4, 10] and astronomy is one major target for educational technology. TUI's physicality and intuitive user interface seem to be effective in learning scientific phenomena.

By taking these approaches, we developed a tangible learning environment (TLE) called *tangible earth system* to support the learning of earth-sun relationships (Figure 1) and have been applying it in experimental classes for junior high students. Although most of the students and teachers were enthusiastic about the system, we also saw instances where it was not effectively embraced. Therefore, we conducted a small-scale observational study to understand the pros and cons of our approach.

In the rest of this paper we first explain our assessment framework. Next we introduce our tangible learning environment and use it to describe an observational study and its results. Finally, we discuss design implications of TLE for astronomy education.

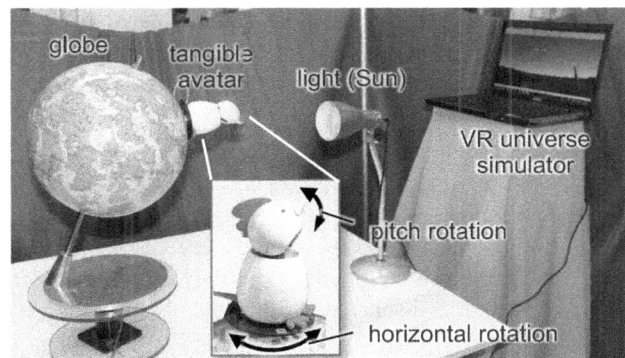

Figure 1. Tangible earth system.

ASSESSMENT FRAMEWORK

Curriculum Guidelines
The earth-sun relationship is part of the science curriculum for junior high schools in Japan. According to a report on curriculum guidelines for science education from the Ministry of Education [3], the purpose of astronomy education is to teach students how to understand the earth's movement through observations of celestial bodies and the characteristics of the sun and the planets with figures and physical models. Through such activities, the curriculum enables students to form spatial and temporal concepts so that they can develop skill in perceiving the positions and motions of astronomical bodies as relative concepts. Based

on the government report, we derived the following specific curriculum goals to enable students to form temporal and spatial concepts:

- Temporal concept: teaches students to relate the earth's rotation to the recorded observations made by students of the sun's diurnal motion.

- Spatial concept: teaches students to relate the sun's celestial positions to the positions and orientations of an observer on earth.

Our analysis focuses on our system's influence on learning temporal and spatial concepts.

Design Guidelines for Tangible Learning Environments

TLEs are one of the trends in educational technology research, and many systems have been proposed [4, 5, 10]. Researchers have also started to discuss design frameworks [2, 6]. Particularly Price's framework highlights the effect of the external representations of the TLE on learning. As the aim of the curriculum for astronomy is to enable students to form temporal and spatial concepts through *observation* of various phenomena, appropriateness of our system's external representations to be observed is our main concern. Thus, in this study, we employ Price's framework for the analysis of the tangible earth system.

Price proposed a "conceptual framework for systematically investigating how different ways of linking digital information with physical artefacts influence interaction and cognition, to gain a clearer understanding of their role for learning [6]." Framework parameters included location, dynamics, correspondence, and modality. We will briefly explain all of them.

Location parameters refer to how physical artifacts and digital representations are located to each other. They are *discrete* if the tangible input device and the digital output device are located separately; they are *co-located* if the input and output are contiguous; and they are *embedded* if the digital output is displayed within a tangible object.

Dynamics parameters refer to the information association between artifact and representation. More specifically, they discuss whether "digital effects can occur contiguously with intentional action, generating an expected effect, or they can be inadvertently triggered according to pre-determined configurations, causing an unexpected effect [6]."

Correspondence parameters "refer to the degree to which the physical properties of the objects are closely mapped to the learning concepts." They are *symbolic* if the objects act as common signifiers. For example, blocks are symbolic because they can be used to represent various entities. They are *literal* if the objects' "physical properties are closely mapped to the metaphor of the domain it is representing [6]."

Modality parameters refers to how audio and tactile modes affect learning. Since our tangible earth system does not utilize these modalities, we do not consider this parameter in this study.

Based on the parameters, we analyzed the influence of our system on learning temporal and spatial concepts from the aspects of *location*, *dynamics*, and *correspondence* parameters.

Epistemology of Agency

As an effective way to assist learners to understand scientific phenomena, Saeki proposed the conceptual theory of "epistemology of agency." He discussed the effectiveness of a learner's agents in understanding various scientific phenomena [7]. According to his theory, it becomes much easier for a learner to understand scientific phenomena if he/she imagines placing his/her agents (or surrogates) in various places of a scientific model and posits what they would observe from their perspectives. Based on this theory, we assumed that the doll-like figure on the globe would play a role of the learner's agent and it should be effective in learning earth-sun relationships.

In our analysis, we are interested in if learners actually perceive the doll-like figure as their surrogate.

SYSTEM OVERVIEW

Our TLE, called the tangible earth system, was designed to support the learning of the relation of the sun's diurnal motion and the earth's rotation. It consists of a doll-like figure (tangible avatar or avatar), a globe, a rotating table, an electrical light, and a laptop PC (Figure 1). The electrical light represents the sun. The laptop runs a publicly available VR universe simulator, Mitaka[1] to show the diurnal motion of the sun in the celestial sphere (ground-level view).

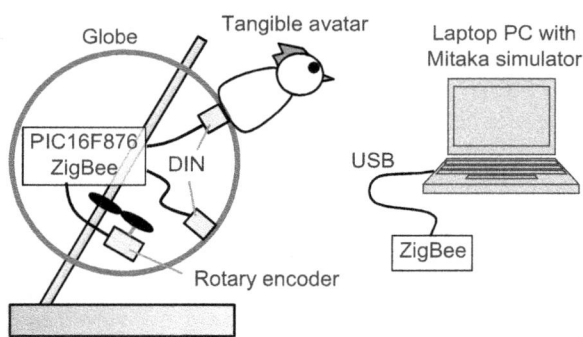

Figure 2. Mechanism of tangible earth system.

Figure 2 shows mechanism of the system. The globe is rotated around the earth's axis either forward or reverse during the simulation to change the sun's position in the celestial sphere. Rotation of the globe is detected by a rotary encoder inside the globe. DIN type connectors are embedded at the locations of Japan, Australia, and

---

[1] http://4d2u.nao.ac.jp/html/program/mitaka/index_E.html

Honduras to plug the avatar into those places and to change the location of the ground-level view. The avatar's body rotation angle and pitch rotation angle are detected by potentiometers embedded in the avatar. The information of the globe rotation, the avatar's position, and the avatar's posture is captured by a PIC16F876 microcontroller and wirelessly sent to a note PC using ZigBee protocol.

With this mechanism, the simulator's line of sight can be changed by the horizontal rotation of the avatar's body and its head's pitch rotation. The clock time in the simulator, the compass point names, and the azimuth altitude of the line of sight are displayed on the PC screen.

To see the sun in the simulator, a learner simply rotates the globe and reorients the avatar's body and its head toward the light. With this configuration, learners are expected to naturally relate the earth's rotation, the avatar's posture, the relative position of the earth and the sun, and the sun's diurnal motion.

OBSERVATIONAL STUDY

We conducted an observational study with junior high students who interacted with the tangible earth. During the activity, they completed a worksheet that had questions. The activity was videotaped for subsequent analysis.

Participants and Apparatus

Seven Japanese 8th graders were participated in our study. They were divided into three groups: two males, three females, and two females. Each group was given a tangible earth system and allowed to freely interact with it during the activity. Note that to breed a congenial atmosphere, we accepted all the students who wished to participate in the activity and did not strictly control the gender balance and the number of students in a group.

Before the subjects started to work on their worksheets, they were given a short lecture to recall such basic knowledge about astronomy as the earth's rotation direction, compass directions, revolutions, and axial tilt. They also learned how to manipulate the system.

For simplicity, we did not use the rotating table, and the simulator's date was fixed around June 22nd, which is the summer solstice.

Procedure and Data Analysis

The worksheet consisted of seven questions. For instance, participants were asked 1) to illustrate the earth's rotational direction, 2) to answer four azimuth on the globe, 3) 4) to find the compass directions of the sunset and the sunrise, 5) to find the sun's culmination altitude for Japan, 6) to draw diurnal motion on a celestial chart, and 7) to do answer the same questions for Australia.. During the exercise, the experimenters occasionally asked the students to explain their answers, e.g., concerning why the compass directions of the sun's culmination of Japan and Australia are opposite.

We videotaped the student activities and drew on the conversation analysis and recent studies of multi-modal interaction. In this respect, participant learning interactions were classified into temporal and spatial concepts. Then the interactions for each concept were further classified into location, dynamics, and correspondence.

RESULTS

Since all three groups took about an hour to finish their worksheets and answer our questions, we gathered about three hours of videotaped data.

Temporal Concept

Learning temporal concepts is mostly related to the globe's rotational manipulation, particularly when the participants changed the points in time to sunrise, noon, and sunset. In general, these interactions seemed quite intuitive for all of them.

When the participants sought the three points in time, they instantly confidently started to rotate the globe. In many cases, they did not even look at the globe while they were controlling the time, causing other problems described later. This shows that they had no problem with the *location* parameter. Furthermore, the interface is clearly appropriate in terms of *dynamics* and *correspondence* parameters because the participants easily related the sun's diurnal motion to the earth's rotation.

Spatial Concept

However, we observed various problems for supporting spatial concept learning.

```
P2: The Sun is going down.
P1:                         Okay.
                      *a

P2: I can't see the compass point. Let it look down.

P2: Something is written.                West-northwest.
P1:                         West-northwest.
                      *b

P1: (Sunset) Direction is the same (as Japan).
P2:

P2: I wonder why. I wonder why. It is intriguing.
```

Figure 3. Participants observing sunset. "*" indicates the time when corresponding image is captured.

Location

In this experiment, since most of the worksheet answers (compass point names and the sun's azimuth altitude) could be found on the PC screen, the participants tended to concentrate on their PC screen.

In Figure 3, participants are trying to determine the compass point for the sunset in Australia. P1 is manipulating the avatar attached to Australia. Then, they find that the Sun goes down to west-northwest. P1 then is aware that compass points of sunset are the same for Japan and Australia. Although P2 wonders why they are the same, he cannot find the reason.

To understand why the compass points of the sunset is the same for Japan and Australia, participants must look at the avatar's orientation on the globe. However, during this activity, they rarely looked at the avatar and instead mostly focused on their PC.

Dynamics
In Figure 4, P1 is trying to find the sunrise by manipulating the avatar and the globe. To do so, she first tries to capture the sun in the field of view of the PC screen. While P1 is rotating the globe, both P1 and P2 keep looking at the PC screen. When the avatar is located around the noon position, P1 orients the avatar to the north and makes it look up almost straight up. Then the sun enters the PC screen's field of view and she says "Oh, I found the sun" (Figure 4a). She orients the avatar's body to the west, horizontally tilts its head down, and rotates the globe clockwise again (Figure 4b). Since the avatar's head is now orienting toward a quite different direction from the light, the sun in the PC screen disappears. Failing to understand the reasons for the disappearance, P1 says, "The sun sun sun . . it's gone!"

Figure 4. Participants trying to keep the sun in the PC screen while rotating the globe.

For the sun to be seen in the PC screen, P1 had to keep the avatar's head orientation toward the light. However, her intentional manipulation of the avatar failed to cause the effect that she intended. We have seen other examples where participants manipulated the interface without being conscious of its meaning.

Considering the fact that the participants manipulated the avatars back and forth like manipulating a game controller, facile manipulation of the tangible interface may be one factor that prevented the participants from conceptually understanding the intentional action of manipulation.

Correspondence
One of the experimenters asked a group of two boys why the compass directions of the sun's culmination were different between Japan and Australia. One of the participants gave the following answer:

Because the sun is at the height of the equator (Figure 5a-i), if the avatar is above the equator, the sun is seen in the south (Figure 5a-ii). If the avatar is below the equator, it is seen in the north (Figure 5a-iii).

Although this answer is correct within the given physical properties of the TLE, it is wrong in the real world. The problem which led them to a misunderstanding was that the light was too small, and the distance to the globe was too close compared to the actual relationship between the sun and the earth. In reality, since the sun is quite far from the earth, its rays come almost in parallel (Figure 5b).

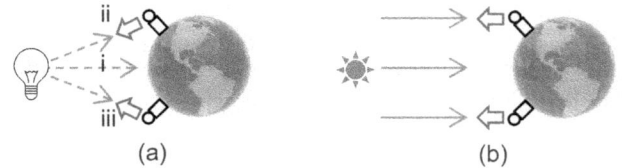

Figure 5. Misunderstanding caused by misleading representation

DISCUSSION
The analysis in this paper revealed that our system has problems in its learning spatial concept. This section proposes design some design implications of TELs for astronomy education.

The *location* parameter of astronomy education tends to be discrete because it must show multiple images of different points of views, typically a ground-level view of the celestial sphere and a birds-eye-view of the solar system. Therefore, the auxiliary information's location must be carefully considered so that it draws student's attention to appropriate objects. Careless choices may lead to disregarding important views, as seen in Figure 2. In our case, the compass point names and the azimuth altitudes of the sun should have been co-located/embedded with avatars.

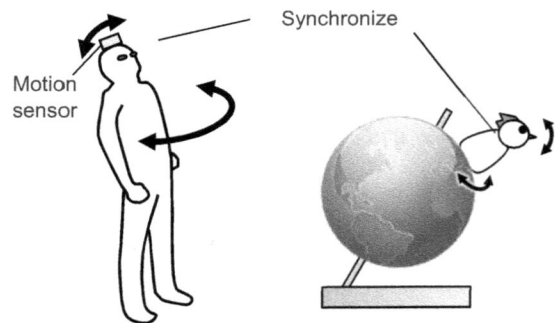

Figure 6. Synchronizing motions of a learner and the tangible avatar

As for the *dynamics* parameter, our example (Figure 4) indicates that students tend to manipulate a TUI like an unfamiliar game controller, without being conscious of the properties it represents. One way to alleviate this problem is to make a learner deem that the avatar is their surrogate. For example, we are planning to synchronize the avatar's motion with the learner's head motion. As shown in Figure 6, the learner's motion can be detected by attaching a motion sensor to his/her head. We also need to embed motors into the avatar to control head and body movement. We will not synchronize the motion of the avatar and the learner all the time while he/she is learning. Instead, we will temporarily synchronize them at the beginning of a learning session and let the learner observe the synchronized motion. With this experience, we are expecting that the learner can have a sense that the avatar is his/her surrogate.

The *correspondence* parameter can be a problem not only for astronomy contents but also for various scientific contents because many physical models that represent scientific phenomena are inevitably symbolic to some extent. We also need to keep in mind that there is a trade-off between *being literal* and other factors. In our case, for example, we could have placed the light further away from the globe than the current setup, i.e., behind the PC. This setup might have been better for students to deliberate the issues of sun's culmination. Conversely, the setup might have diminished the participants' awareness to the earth-sun relationship which might not be preferable for other activities.

One solution is to make the system flexible in terms of reconfigurability and changeability of tangible objects. Then, during an activity, a teacher chooses the suitable configuration/objects corresponding to the perspectives students need to learn. In that case, appropriate explanation for the change should be provided to the students as well.

CONCLUSION
We developed a tangible earth system to support astronomy education. Based on curriculum and general design guidelines for tangible learning environments, we discussed a framework to assess a tangible learning system for astronomy education. The observational study with junior high school children revealed problems of the system in terms of location, dynamics and correspondence parameters. Our next step is to apply our ideas to improve our tangible earth system and conduct a large-scale user study.

ACKNOWLEDGEMENT
This work was supported by JSPS KAKENHI Grant Number 26282030. We thank Mr. Takeshi Ichimura and Mr. Tatsuya Saito of Namiki Secondary School for supporting our experiments.

REFERENCES
1. Atwood, R. K. and Atwood V. A. Effects of Instruction on Preservice Elementary Teachers' Conceptions of the Causes of Night and Day and the Seasons. *Journal of Science Teacher Education* 8, 1 (1997), 1-13.

2. Marshall, P. Do tangible interfaces enhance learning?, In *Proc. TEI 2007*, ACM Press (2007), 163-170.

3. Ministry of Education, Culture, Sports, Science and Technology-Japan. http://www.mext.go.jp/component/a_menu/education/micro_detail/__icsFiles/afieldfile/2011/04/11/1298356_5.pdf

4. Moher, T., Hussain, S., Halter, T., and Kilb, D. RoomQuake: Embedding dynamic phenomena within the physical space of an elementary school classroom. In *Proc. CHI 2005,* ACM Press (2005), 1655-1668.

5. Morita, Y. and Setozaki, N. Practical Evaluation of Tangible Learning System: Lunar Phase Class Case Study. In *Proc. of SITE 2012*, (2012), 3718-3722.

6. Price, S. A representation approach to conceptualizing tangible learning environments. In *Proc. of TEI 2008*, ACM Press (2008), 151-157.

7. Saeki, Y. Cognition and Learning by Imaging (Ime-jika niyoru chisiki to gakushu) (in Japanese), Toyokan Publishing, Tokyo (1978).

8. Shelton, B. and Hedley, N. Using Augmented Reality for Teaching Earth-Sun Relationships to Undergraduate Geography Students, In *Proc. ART02*, IEEE (2002), 8 pages.

9. Vosniadou, S., Skopeliti, I., and Ikospentaki, K. Modes of knowing and ways of reasoning in elementary astronomy. *Cognitive Development* 19, 2 (2004), 203-222.

10. Zuckerman, O., Arida, S. and Resnick, M. Extending tangible interfaces for education: digital Montessori inspired manipulatives. In *Proc. of CHI 2005*, ACM Press (2005), 859-868.

Daily Support Robots that Move on the Body

Tamami Saga   **Nagisa Munekata**   **Tetsuo Ono**
Hokkaido Univ., Japan
Kita 14 Nishi 9, Kita-ku, Sapporo Hokkaido 060-0814, Japan
{saga, munekata, tono}@complex.ist.hokudai.ac.jp

ABSTRACT

Today, wearable devices such as Google Glass[1] and Smart-Watch[2] are gathering attention. These devices can constantly support us by being worn on a daily basis. In contrast, although we can also find an increase of personal robots in daily life, "wearable robots" are not so prevalent.

We focus on wearable robots and the "fixed" points on which they are worn. We believe that they can provide more continuous and suitable support in a variety of ways by moving automatically on our bodies. Therefore, we propose a daily support system with a wearable robot that moves on the body, and we developed a small prototype robot that can move on a rail fixed on a belt worn on the human body.

Author Keywords

robot; wearable; daily support; communication;

ACM Classification Keywords

H.5.2. Information Interfaces and Presentation (e.g. HCI): User Interfaces

INTRODUCTION

Wearable robots have bodies with which they can express their personality and support us effectively, e.g., telexistence robots, but the bodies are so obstructive that it is difficult to wear them when performing other tasks, such as running and working. Accordingly, the functions of these robots tend to be limited to individual purposes. We speculate that a robot that automatically moves on the human body on the basis of the person's current state can make using the robot more practical. Furthermore, the ability to move may lead to new uses and functions. Moving about all portions of the human body could enable them to collect physical information on the user that they can use to point out health problems.

In addition, we also focus on a robot whose touch we can feel constantly so that users can be aware of the robot's behavior without paying attention to, and especially watching, it. We believe that this could cause users to grow fond of the robot and enable natural, not stressful, daily use.

There are other possible uses for such a robot. For example, the robot could check and study users' life styles, health, and habits. Such information could be used for not only taking corrective actions but also communication support. By interacting with these robots, we may be able to get more chances to communicate with others because we can show our mental state, what we are trying to do, or problem we are facing, and they could be aware them. They may even be able to speak to us in consideration of our current emotion, mental state, what we are doing at the time, and the context.

On the basis of this idea, we propose a daily support system that involves a wearable robot that can move on the body. Figure 1 shows this system.

Figure 1. Future goal

To achieve this concept, we developed a prototype robot that can be worn by equipping users with a belt, in which a system for estimating a user's state is implemented, and we performed a user study to see how users felt using this robot. We also investigated the difference between users' and bystanders' recognition of the purpose of the robot, the type of support, and the relationship between user and robot so that we could speculate whether the robot can change its presence or role for users and bystanders to be less intrusive and to present information efficiently.

RELATED WORKS

Wearable Robots

Wearable robots have a variety of forms[3][4]. One example of wearable robots that have been studied is the "telexistence robot." Kashiwabara et al. presented a wearable telexistence robot called "TEROOS"[5] that is remotely operated and that enables affective communication between the wearer and others in remote locations. From their field work, they explained that a person talking with the wearer naturally treated TEROOS, who was operated remotely by a human, as a person; in other words, the person could recognize the personality of TEROOS's operator from the remote location because TEROOS has a body that bystanders see.

Yonezawa et al. proposed a robot that clings to the arm[6] and that gives information and expresses emotion and love by changing its temperature and pressing the arm softly. They suggested the possibility that a robot that uses these methods to communicate can give users a higher rate of awareness toward given information and more affection toward the robot than one that does not use them.

Social Effects on Human-Robot Interaction

Focusing more on the effects of touch, Fukuda et al. indicated the possibility that robots can have a social effect on humans by touching them[7]. According to the results of their study, it tended to be more acceptable for humans for a robot to make a profit when the robot touches us than when the robot it does not. Hieida et al. investigated the effects of holding hands on building a relationship between children and robots[8]. They obtained the result that a hand connection lead to an improvement in the relationship between a child and robot by watching the distance between them and by collecting the children's answers to a questionnaire. They consider that this improvement resulted from not only a high sense of security given by the social act of "holding hands" but also from physical contact itself and restraint. They anticipated that a sense of unity brought about by sharing the direction and speed of movement and the high predictability of the robot's behavior increased their affinity for the robot.

The distance between a robot and user is also important for us when considering the social relationship between them. According to the "proxemics" proposed by T. Hall (1966)[9], the distance between people is closely related to their social relationship. He classified this distance into four types and proposed that physical distance corresponds to psychological distance.

Small Robots Moving along Surfaces

The surface of the human body is very complex, possibly moves during wear, and the orientation varies depending on posture. As a result, a mounted robot is likely to be lateral or upside down. For these reasons, small robots have already been developed with the expectation that gravity acts downward or that wall-climbing robots[10][11][12] cannot move freely enough on the surface of the human body.

CLASH[13], developed by Birkmeyer et al., is able to climb cloth by hooking its toes into the cloth like an insect, but it

needs to be very light (15 g), so it is hard to mount sensors, cameras, or other motors on it. Clothbot[14], developed by Liu et al., also climbs on cloth such as shirts and pants by gripping wrinkles, but it is hard for the robot to climb cloth with no wrinkles.

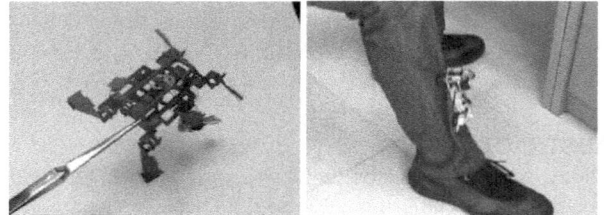

(a) CLASH   (b) Clothbot

Figure 2. Cloth climbing robot

SYSTEM PROTOTYPING

Figure 3 shows a prototype robot developed for our concept. It can move up or down on a user's body by moving along a rail fixed on a belt that the user wears. Figure 4 shows a user wearing this prototype. The motored ears and LED eyes indicate its state, emotion, or other information. The robot is equipped with a nine-axis sensor for getting information on its position and motion, from which it can estimate the pose of the part of the body it is on. A microcomputer, IOIO-OTG, which is connected to an Android phone via Bluetooth, controls all motors, sensors, and LEDs.

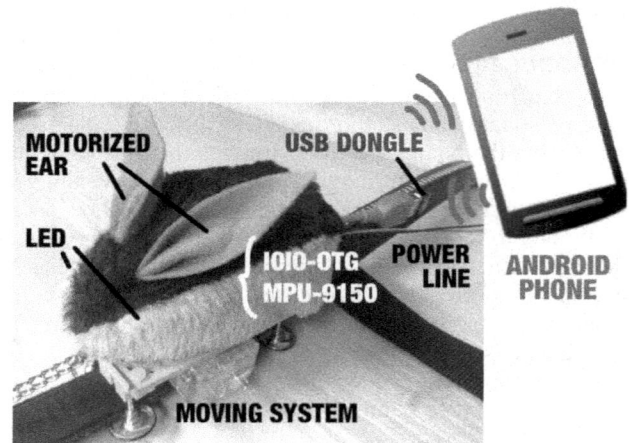

Figure 3. Prototype robot

Hardware

At this time, our main subject was not creating the moving system but the support provided by the system. Therefore, we implemented a simple prototype system as an initial step, accepting some level of constraint. To be more specific, by fabricating the prototype such that it was able climb over rails laid on the body, we created a robot that moves on the body artificially. As shown in Figure 5, we sandwiched a driving sprocket between two driven sprockets so that the chain could be captured regardless of the direction of gravity.

Table 1. Classifying User States

Shoulder/back		Arm	
Posture	Movement	Posture	Movement
standing	no motion	standard position	no motion
inclining forward	walking	falling	swinging
lying on face	running	rising	irregular movement
inclining backward	irregular movement		
lying on back			

Figure 4. Wearing the prototype robot

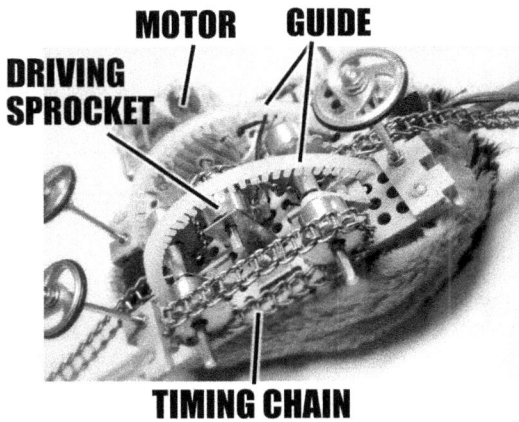

MOTOR   GUIDE

DRIVING SPROCKET

TIMING CHAIN

Figure 5. Moving system

To indicate its emotion and information, the robot can use its eyes and ears. The eyes are full-color LEDs, which can change color or flicker. The ears are motored so that the robot expresses itself such as by swinging, lowering, and raising its ears.

The robot has a photo interrupter to count the number of revolutions of the motor and a sensor module (MPU-9150), which contains a 3-axis gyroscope, 3-axis compass, and 3-axis accelerometer. The sensor module is controlled through a microcomputer board, the Arduino Mini.

These parts are connected to a microcomputer board (IOIO-OTG). The board controls all sensors and motors by i²c com-munication while communicating wirelessly with an Android phone through a Bluetooth dongle connected to the tail.

Software

Scanning the Surface

At any point in time, the direction of the robot's nose roughly equals the direction of the next point to which it will advance. Therefore, the robot can estimate the track it will take from information on its direction and moving speed. In other words, the robot can recognize the surface it moves on.

We implemented sensors for the acceleration, geomagnetic field, gyro, and the sprocket revolutions so that the robot is able to calculate the nose's direction and moving speed. Once moving along the belt (scanning), the robot partly recognizes the user's body line partly. Figure 6 shows an example of an estimation result. The sampling width was 2.5 cm.

Figure 6. Estimating path

Estimating Relationship with User's Body

After the scanning phase, the robot knows the surface and its own relative position. Next, the robot has to estimate where this position corresponds to on the user's body. With this mapping, the robot can know its own position on the body regardless of whether the user's pose changes, unless the user shifts the belt.

Furthermore, the robot can get information on the user's pose and motion depending on its position with this mapping. For example, a robot located on the shoulder may know the direction of the trunk of the body, and one located on the arm may know how the arm swings.

As a prototype, we implemented a simple function for the robot to estimate its position on a body under the assumption that users wear the belt from the back to either arm. The robot scans the user's body line from the back, through the shoulder, and to the arm. After that, from this information, it recognizes a range of 10 cm around the highest point as the "shoulder," the side behind as the "back," and the side before as the "arm." Figure 7 shows an example of mapping.

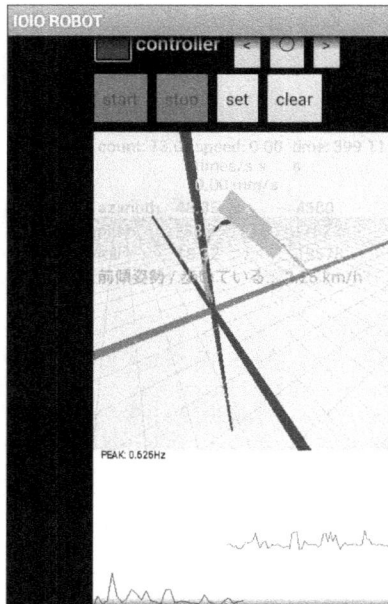

Figure 7. Estimating relationship with user's body

Classifying User State
Furthermore, the robot estimates the user's state and classifies it from the change in acceleration frequency analyzed (FFT treated). Table 1 shows the class we implemented.

USER STUDY
We held a user study to research how users feel about the prototype robot, which provided information while moving on them.

Cases
We asked three subjects to perform a task in each of the following cases.

1. The robot is located on the table.

2. The robot is worn on the left arm.

3. The robot is worn on the left arm and moves while providing information.

The task was a simple game, the "high-low game," in which a player forecasts either a higher or lower number for a hidden card, which is then revealed. We explained to them that the robot had known the answers and it would tell them the answers by using the color of its eyes (red: high, blue: low) but that it would possibly make mistakes. Figure 8 shows the study being performed. We took videos and asked them to write comments on how they felt.

Results and Discussion
The subjects tended not to seek direction from the robot when it was easy to expect the answer, e.g., the number of the revealed card was the smallest number, "2," but in Case 3, they

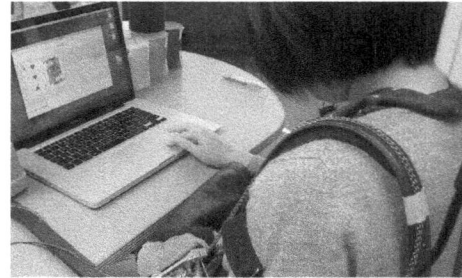

Figure 8. Study being performed

were apt to look at the robot in these situations, too. Subject B and C did not touch the robot in the interval between Cases 1 and 2, but they did several gestures such as stroking the back of the robot after Case 2. Subject A never touched the robot.

The following comments were received on the subjects' impressions of the robot giving information while moving on the body.

┌─ Positive Comments ──────────────────────

- The robot is like a guinea pig being playful and cute.

- I didn't feel disappointed when the robot made a mistake.

- I excused the robot if it made a mistake because the robot was cute.

- I felt a bond with the robot when the answer was correct.

┌─ Negative Comments ──────────────────────

- I felt a little itch.

- If the robot moved when I was thinking, it attracted my attention. At the time, if the robot gave me wrong information clearly, e.g., when it changed the color of its eyes to blue when the revealed card was "2," I was confused.

We also received the comment, "When the robot stayed at a distance from me, there was a sense that it was not involved in my affair. I grew fond of it as the robot approached me."

From the result of the observation and comments, it may be able to be said that the wearers' affinity, love, sense of unity, and tolerance to failure of the robot tended to increase if the robot was worn on the arm. In addition, the robot being worn and moving on the body might increased the strength of inspiring or convincing the subjects, too.

PAPER EXPERIMENTATION
We investigated the difference between users' and bystanders' recognition of the purpose of the robot, the type of support, and the relationship between the user and the robot in a paper experimentation.

| (a) arm | (b) shoulder | (c) back |

Figure 9. Illustrations shown in question

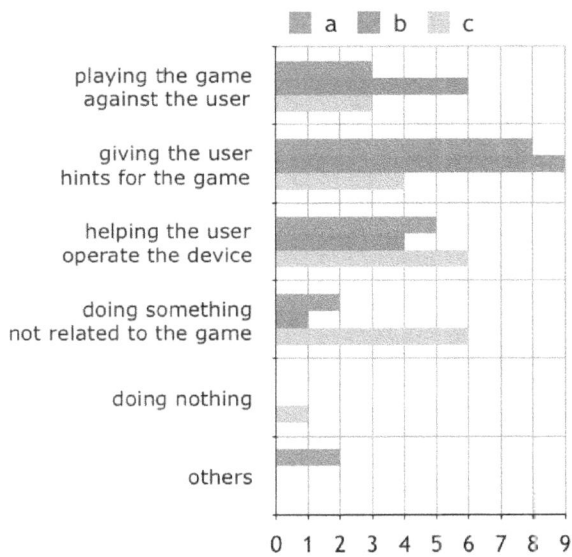

Figure 10. Selections and number of answers

Questions

We showed test subjects the three illustrations shown in Figure 9 and asked them to guess what the robot is doing and to choose one from a selection. At the same time, we also asked them to freely write comments about what they feel from the illustrations. The test subjects were 11 men and 9 women, which comprised college students (Faculty of Letters, Human Life, Engineering and Science) and working people. They didn't know anything about the prototype and the system we suggested.

Results and Discussion

Figure 10 shows the result and provided selections.

We can see that (a) and (b) showed similar results in terms of the number of each answer. In contrast, (c) performed different from these cases. In particular, the number of people who answered "doing something not related to the game" demonstrates this clearly when comparing (a) and (b). We consider that the behavior of the robot to turn away from the device and user led to this result as the robot was regarded as paying no attention to them.

Between (a) and (b), we found a difference in the tendency of the answers through the comments. For (a), we received these comments:

- like a pet.
- cheering up the man.

and for (b):

- like a buddy.
- cheeky.
- doing something together with the man.

From the difference between "pet" and "buddy," it can be said that there is a possibility that the robot in position (b) was recognized as a more close and more social presence to the wearer than it was for position (a). Also, it can be seen from the expression "cheeky" that the robot in (b) tended to be regarded as an equal presence to the wearer than it was for (a). It is also interesting that comments such as "doing something together" were made for (b) in contrast to comments such as "cheering up," which were made for (a). We can see the robot in (b) was more regarded as an existence that shares the same goal.

From these results, we can hypothesize that a robot changes its familiarity or role by changing its position. In particular, by focusing on the distance from the center of the wearer's body or face, we may be able to recognize this distance as an extension of the proxemics of Hall.

CONCLUSION

We proposed a daily support robot that moves on the human body to achieve more complex and suitable support for users. Additionally, for this concept, we developed a prototype robot that can be worn by equipping a belt. The robot is equipped with a system for estimating the user's state. We performed a user study to see how users felt when using this robot. We also investigated the difference between users' and bystanders' recognition of the purpose of the robot, the type of support, and the relationship between the user and the robot.

The results of an experiment suggested that the wearers' affinity, love, and tolerance to the failure of the robot and the strength of inspiring or convincing the wearer were increased by the robot moving about the body. Furthermore, it was suggested that factors such as the mounting position, direction, posture, and line of sight made a difference in bystanders' interpretation of the robot, the kind of support the robot was providing, and what they thought about the wearer.

FUTURE WORK

We plan to develop a prototype robot that is smaller and lighter and to improve the moving system so that it can move more smoothly, quickly, and freely, not in a one-dimensional way but in a multidimensional one. Additionally, we need to implement functions for interacting with users and bystanders such as voice, touch sensors, and so on. When it comes to software, we need to generalize the estimation of the position on the body and of the user state so that the robot makes autonomous decisions depending on the context.

We are also planning more experiments to investigate the effects on users wearing the moving robot.

REFERENCES

1. "Google Glass." http://www.google.com/glass/start/, (2014).

2. "SmartWatch - Sony Smartphones" http://www.sonymobile.com/smartwatch, (2014).

3. Masa Ogata, Yuta Sugiura, Hirotaka Osawa, Michita Imai. "Pygmy: A Ring-shaped Robotic Device for Storytelling." *IJICIC*, (2013).

4. Y. Tsumaki, F. Ono, T. Tsukuda. "The 20-DOF Miniature Humanoid MH-2 for a Wearable Communication System." *Proc. of the IEEE Int. Conf. on Robotics and Automation*, pp. 3930–3935 (2012).

5. Tadakazu Kashiwabara, Hirotaka Osawa, Kazuhiko Shinozawa, Michita Imai. "TEROOS: A Wearable Avatar to Enhance Joint Activities." *CHI 2012, Proceedings of the SIGCHI Conference on Human Factors in 524 Computing Systems*, pp. 2001–2004 (2012).

6. Tomoko Yonezawa, Hirotake Yamazoe, Shinji Abe. "Investigation of a haptic communicative robot with anthropomorphic expressions." *Human-Agent Interaction Symposium 2011*, II-1B-3 (2011).

7. Haruali Fukuda, Masahiro Shiomi, Kayako Nakagawa, Kazuhiro Ueda. "Social Touch in Human-Robot Interaction." *Human-Agent Interaction Symposium 2012*, 3-C-1 (2012).

8. Chie Hieida, Kasumi Abe, Takayuki Nagai, Takayuki Shimotomai, Takashi Omori. "How Important Is Holding Hands on Building Relationship Between Children and Robots." *Human-Agent Interaction Symposium 2013*, S-3 (2013).

9. Edward T.Hall. "The Hidden Dimension Doubleday & Company." NY, (1966).

10. Stacey Kuznetsov, Eric Paulos, Mark D. Gross. "WallBots: interactive wall-crawling robots in the hands of public artists and political activists." *Conference on Designing Interactive Systems 2010*, pp 208–217 (2010).

11. Murphy, M. P., Tso, W., Tanzini, M. and Sitti, M. "Waalbot: An agile small-scale wall climbing robot utilizing pressure sensitive adhesives." *Proc. of the 2006 IEEE/RSJ Int. Conf. on Intel. Robots and Systems*, pp. 3411–3416 (2006).

12. Krahn, J., Liu, Y., Sadeghi, A., and Menon, C. "A tailless timing belt climbing platform utilizing dry adhesives with mushroom caps." *Smart Materials and Structures*, 20:1–11 (2011).

13. P. Birkmeyer, A. G. Gillies, and R. S. Fearing. "CLASH: Climbing vertical loose cloth." *IEEE/RSJ Int. Conf. on Intelligent Robots and Systems 2011*, pp. 5087–5093, (2011).

14. Yuanyuan Liu, Xinyu Wu, Huihuan Qian, Duan Zheng. "System and design of Clothbot: A robot for flexible clothes climbing." *IEEE Int. Conf. on Robotics and Automation 2012*, pp. 1200–1205 (2012).

Simplification of Wearable Message Robot with Physical Contact for Elderly's Outing Support

Hirotake Yamazoe
Osaka University
1-31 Machikaneyama, Toyonaka,
Osaka 560-0043, Japan
yamazoe@osipp.osaka-u.ac.jp

Tomoko Yonezawa
Kansai University
2-1-1 Ryozenji, Takatsuki,
Osaka 569-1095, Japan
yone@kansai-u.ac.jp

ABSTRACT
In this paper, we introduce a wearable message robot that transmits messages to the user and alerts him/her immediately and affectionately through physical contact. This robot is aimed at supporting elderly people who would like to participate in outings but suffer from anxiety. The system creates haptic stimuli corresponding to the user's clothing and posture. We implemented two versions of the system: the first combines haptic stimuli and anthropomorphic motion to express physical contact, while the second is a simplified system for application on smartphones to provide ubiquitous services.

Author Keywords
simplified wearable robot; physical contact; outing support;

ACM Classification Keywords
H.5.2. Information Interfaces and Presentation (e.g. HCI): User Interfaces

INTRODUCTION
Recent aging societies are faced with a variety of serious problems related to changes in their lifestyles such as an increase in nuclear families. In these societies, elderly and disabled people living alone sometimes need the support of caregivers to overcome their anxiety when participating in social outings. A shortage of volunteers and the burden of asking for help often make these people withdraw from society. However, large scale withdrawal from society causes even greater problems such as advanced dementia.

When participating in outings, individuals are faced with both physical and cognitive problems. Physical problems, especially for elderly people, stem from impaired body functions. Such problems can result in serious accidents. The use of power suits [11] can solve some of these physical problems by compensating for partial power loss. On the other hand, cognitive problems can cause memory loss and attention deficit issues. Instructions may be forgotten and especially those with dementia are at risk [9] during outings.

To mitigate these problems, outing support services such as toilet maps and navigation systems for transportation or walks have been created. Information for these services is provided through applications on mobile devices. Network systems give the user appropriate real-time information based on his/her information including the GPS location. Although these applications compensate for the user's cognitive problems, almost all of the services are limited to push-based information, or are reliant on the user continually checking the mobile device to obtain the latest information. In order to cuddle up to, watch over, and notify the user, the system should behave like an attentive caregiver during the outing. Previously, we proposed a wearable stuffed toy with physical contact [13]. Considering a minimum design for portability, we developed a system with appropriate simplifications of the functionality and structure.

RELATED RESEARCH
Various studies have been carried out on haptic stimuli as displays for mobile devices, such as vibration stimuli as feedback [5] directional indicators [4], skin stretch feedback [2], and traction force feedback [1]. All these studies aimed to present information in a physical manner to the user.

Furthermore, considerable research has been conducted on anthropomorphic behavior, such as affection and the attention of robots and agents [7], and wearable haptic interfaces [3, 12]. Physical interaction between the user and pet robots has also been investigated. As a first step toward reaching our goal, we have combined haptic stimuli and anthropomorphic behavior of a robot to implement a feeling of physical contact by the robot.

Communication robots or agents as media have also been developed based on the premise of ongoing communication between people [10]. In addition, there are wearable avatar robots that sit on the user's shoulder [6]. A mobile phone type robot has also been proposed [8]. In this paper, we propose a wearable robot that is able to make physical contact by placing its hand on the wearer's arm like a caregiver, and a system designed for supporting the elderly during outings.

SYSTEM CONFIGURATION
Our proposed system has two specific characteristics: the first is the anthropomorphic presence, and the second is its physical contact. To indicate appropriate physical interaction corresponding to the user's situation and the content of the robot's expression, we implemented two types of physical

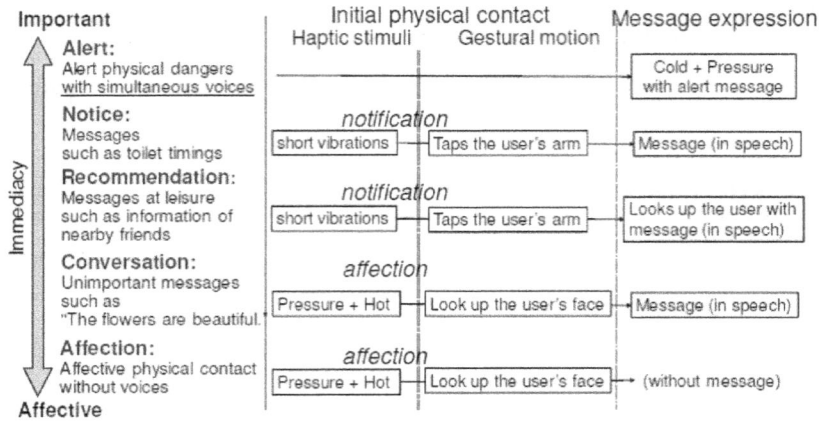

Figure 1. Gradual communication model for physical contact.

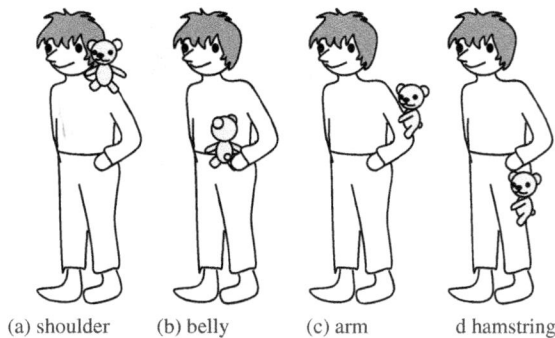

Figure 2. Considered locations for fixing the robot.

Table 1. Preferred ranking scores by six people.

region	shoulder	belly	arm	hamstring
score	13	16	23	8

Minimum and maximum scores are, respectively, 6 and 24 for each.

interaction: *notification* and *affection* based on the gradual communication model of physical contact [14].

Figure 1 shows our gradual communication model of physical contact corresponding to the importance of the message. The robot system provides physical contact at five importance levels (*Alert, Notice, Recommendation, Conversation, and Affection*) corresponding to the immediate/affective aspect of the information in two communication steps, *initial physical contact* and *message expression*.

To realize such gradual communication by physical contact, we designed and implemented a detailed prototype [13]. In this paper, we introduce a new simplified prototype.

As push-type notification schemes for mobile devices, "sound notification" and "vibration" are generally used. But when the user is notified in these ways, s/he needs to operate the device to ascertain the content of the notification. On the other hand, visual notifications are easy to understand, but cannot easily attract the user's attention. When caregivers communicate with elderly people, they transfer care and communicate after first attracting the aged person's attention by touching his/her shoulder. Our system employs such preliminary communication.

Preliminary Experiment on Appropriate Positions

Before explaining the details of the prototypes, we present preliminary experimental results on appropriate locations for the robot [13].

To determine the ideal placement of the wearable robot, various parts of the body were considered by comparing preliminary data. The quality and performance of the wearable partner robot, including its ability to behold and cuddle up to the user, and provide intuitive and comfortable communication, need to be altered according to the part of the body to which it is attached.

To investigate the appropriate position of a wearable robot, we considered the following four fixation locations: a) shoulder, b) belly, c) upper arm, and d) hamstring (upper leg), as shown in Figure 2.

It was previously assumed that placement on the user's torso such as the shoulder and belly was better than on the limbs. As a result, the precedent research proposed that placement on the user's shoulder [6] would provide the optimal performance. However, we focused on the following important aspects:

- a robot as communication medium for the user,
- the anthropomorphic presence as an emotional medium, and
- performance and comfort as a wearable robot.

Table 1 gives some of the preliminary experiment's results (detailed results are given in [13]). From these results, we determined that the arm is the best position for the message robot.

Detailed Prototype of Message Robot

Next, we introduce the detailed prototype of the message robot [13].

People communicate to relay messages (notifications). However, additional, unproductive communication, such as emotional expressions (affection) can enrich their personal relationships. A mixture of both expressions and a change in their intensity is expected to lead to human-like behavior. For

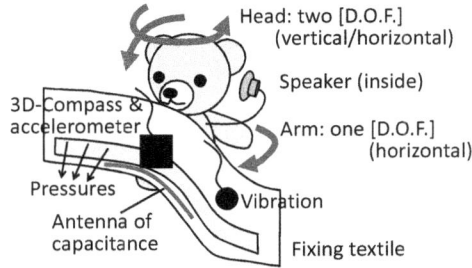

Figure 3. System configuration.

Figure 4. System view.

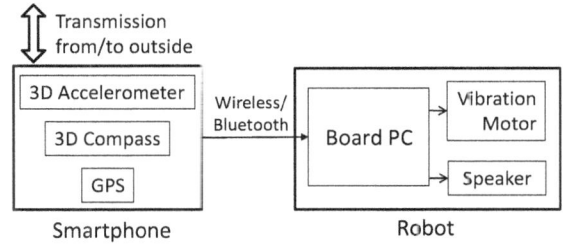

Figure 5. Configuration of simplified system.

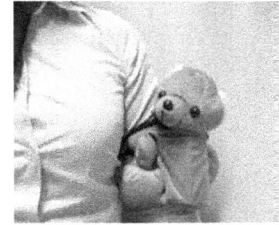

Figure 6. Appearance of simplified system.

example, a human expresses affective emotions or alerts in different ways based on their importance. Accordingly, we adopted two different types of physical contact using a two-step method: initial physical contact and message transmission. This approach ensures that messages are received without apprehension compared with unexpected sudden messages.

Combining motion of the robot and haptic stimuli simultaneously, our proposed system aims to provide the user with a feeling of physical contact from the robot. In the expression of notification, the robot repeatedly strokes the user's arm, while a short-term vibration creates haptic stimuli at the same time to express the physical contact of the robot's touch. This behavior is seen when a caregiver makes initial contact with a patient. In the expression of affection, the robot turns its face toward the user, and a simultaneous pressure stimulus relays the physical contact of the robot's enfolding behavior.

Figure 3 shows the wearable stuffed-toy message robot with the appropriate haptic actuators and sensors. An antenna of capacitance (as used in theremins) is placed on the lower part of the fixing strap to measure the thickness of the user's clothes, so that the strength of the haptic actuations can be adjusted accordingly. To detect the activity of both the user and robot, a 3D-accelerometer with a 3D-compass is attached to the system.

Figure 4 illustrates the use of the system. The fixed part of the system weighs about 350 g, including the stuffed-toy robot, actuators, and battery. However, since a small PC (400 g) is required in this prototype, the user needs to carry a bag for the PC.

We need to consider the user's clothing to provide appropriate physical contact from the robot and adjust the strength and timing of the physical contact depending on the user's clothes. As used in touch-panels or theremins, capacitances between the human body and a device change depending on the distance between the body and the device. Using this mechanism, we estimate the thickness of the user's clothes.

In our system, an antenna is placed inside the fixing strap, and we measure the thickness of the user's clothes from the capacitances between the antenna and user's body. Here we have composed an oscillator from an inductance and certain capacitances including the capacitance between the antenna and the body. Changes in the thickness of the clothes, d, (i.e., changes in capacitance) can be observed as changes in the oscillating frequency, f, as follows:

$$f = \epsilon/\sqrt{(\alpha + d)/(\beta + \gamma d)}, \qquad (1)$$

where α, β, γ, and ϵ are parameters calculated from the inductance and capacitances used in the oscillator. Based on the estimated thickness, the strength and duration of the physical contact can be controlled appropriately.

The wearable message robot also changes its behavior depending on the user's current activity. For example, if the user moves his/her arm to make it easy to see the wearable robot, the robot looks at the user's face. If the user is walking or running, the robot does nothing else than hold onto the user's arm tightly. To realize such behaviors, we estimate the user's situation using a 3D digital compass and accelerometer as follows. First, we perform a short-time Fourier transform on the accelerometer data. Based on the results, the robot is able to perform the appropriate behavior corresponding to the user's activity.

Simplified Design for Elderly Outing Support

Next, we introduce the simplified message robot. The detailed version introduced in the previous section includes several sensors and actuators and can realize various behaviors and tactile notification. On the other hand, considering actual use cases for elderly people or patients with dementia, the robustness of the detailed system is not sufficient. Thus, we designed a simplified construction of the message robot to achieve greater robustness. In this case, to create a simplified system, we attached high importance to the use of commodity devices like smartphones, while realizing a robust and easy-to-use message robot system.

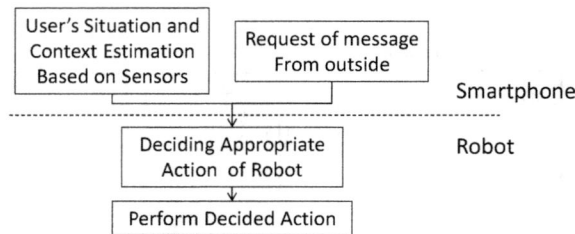

Figure 7. Process flow of simplified system.

Figures 5 and 6 show the configuration and appearance of the simplified system. In the simplified system, we employ smartphones proactively. Since most recent smartphones are equipped with a triaxial accelerometer and a compass, these sensors are used to estimate the user's situation and activities. In addition, since smartphones are also equipped with a global positioning system (GPS), we are investigating using the location and velocity information obtained from the GPS to estimate the user's context. The robot includes a vibration motor for tactile presentation and a speaker for auditory presentation. These actuators are controlled by a small board PC (Raspberry PI). The board PC and smartphone are connected through Wifi or Bluetooth. A pocket is included on the fixation strap for storing the smartphone. The weight of the robot including a battery is about 250 g and the size of the robot is about 18 cm. Thus, the total weight of the entire system including the robot and the smartphone is about 350-400 g (most smartphones weigh less than 150 g).

Next, Figure 7 shows the process flow of the simplified system. First, the user's situation and activity are estimated periodically based on sensor information from the smartphone and are transmitted to the board PC through Wifi or Bluetooth. If there is a request to send a message from outside users such as the user's family, the request is also transmitted to the robot. In the robot, behaviors of the robot are determined based on the estimated user's context and any requests to send messages, and then the robot performs the determined behavior.

We are planning an actual experiment on elderly people and patients with dementia using this simplified system. In addition, we are investigating an interface to transmit the user's situation to their family as well as a watching and monitoring scheme for the elderly using the message robot.

CONCLUSION

In this paper, we proposed a portable message robot, which cuddles up to the user's arm in order to transmit messages to the user after making physical contact. The robot is expected to enable the elderly to participate in outings without anxiety. We have implemented two versions of the robot system: the first implementation combines haptic stimuli and anthropomorphic motion using a pocket PC to realize physical contact, while the second is an simplified system for application on smartphones for ubiquitous services. The original sensors in smartphones could be used as alternative components of the basic structure of the message robot. As future work, the experiment with target users, especially elderly folk, will be conducted to evaluate the effectiveness of the simplified system.

Acknowledgments
This research was supported in part by JSPS KAKENHI 24300047, 25730114, and 25700021. The authors would like to thank those who participated in the experiment.

REFERENCES
1. Amemiya, T., and Sugiyama, H. Haptic handheld wayfinder with pseudo-attraction force for pedestrians with visual impairments. In *Proc. ASSETS09* (2009), 107–114.
2. Bark, K., Wheeler, J., Premakumar, S., and Cutkosky, M. Comparison of skin stretch and vibrotactile stimulation for feedback of proprioceptive information. In *Symposium on Haptic Interfaces for Virtual Environment and Teleoperator Systems* (2008), 71–78.
3. Bonanni, L., Vaucelle, C., Lieberman, J., and Zuckerman, O. Taptap: a haptic wearable for asynchronous distributed touch therapy. In *CHI'06 extended abstracts* (2006), 580–585.
4. Cassinelli, A., Reynolds, C., and Ishikawa, M. Augmenting spatial awareness with haptic radar. In *ISWC'06* (2006), 61–64.
5. Fukumoto, M., and Sugimura, T. Active click: tactile feedback for touch panels. In *CHI'01 extended abstracts* (2001), 121–122.
6. Kashiwabara, T., Osawa, H., Shinozawa, K., and Imai, M. Teroos: a wearable avatar to enhance joint activities. In *CHI'12* (2012), 2001–2004.
7. Kozima, H. Infanoid: A babybot that explores the social environment. In *Socially Intelligent Agents: Creating Relationships with Computers and Robots* (2002), 157–164.
8. Minato, T., Sumioka, H., Nishio, S., and Ishiguro, H. Studying the influence of handheld robotic media on social communications. In *Social Robotic Telepresence in ROMAN'12 Workshop* (2012), 15–16.
9. Rowe, M. A., Feinglass, N. G., and Wiss, M. E. Persons with dementia who become lost in the community: a case study, current research, and recommendations. *Mayo Clinic Proceedings 79*, 11 (2004), 1417–1422.
10. Sekiguchi, D., Inami, M., and Tachi, S. Robotphone: Rui for interpersonal communication. In *CHI'01 extended abstracts* (2001), 277–278.
11. Tanaka, T., Satoh, Y., Kaneko, S., Suzuki, Y., Sakamoto, N., and Seki, S. Smart suit: Soft power suit with semi-active assist mechanism-prototype for supporting waist and knee joint. In *ICCAS 2008* (2008), 2002–2005.
12. Wang, R., Quek, F., Tatar, D., Teh, J., and Cheok, A. Keep in touch: Channel, expectation and experience. In *CHI'12* (2012), 139–148.
13. Yonezawa, T., and Yamazoe, H. Wearable partner agent with anthropomorphic physical contact with awareness of clothing and posture. In *The 18th International Symposium on Wearable Computers (ISWC2013)* (2013), 77–80.
14. Yonezawa, T., Yamazoe, H., and Abe, S. Physical contact using haptic and gestural expressions for ubiquitous partner robot. In *IEEE/RSJ International Conference on Intelligent Robots and Systems (IROS2013)* (2013), 5680–5685.

Ningyo of the CAVE:

Robots as Social Puppets of Static Infrastructure

Nico Li
University of Calgary
2500 University Dr. NW
Calgary, AB, Canada
Nico.HaoLi@gmail.com

Stephen Cartwright
University of Calgary
2500 University Dr. NW
Calgary, AB, Canada
sgcartwr@ucalgary.ca

Ehud Sharlin
University of Calgary
2500 University Dr. NW
Calgary, AB, Canada
ehud@cpsc.ucalgary.ca

Mario Costa Sousa
University of Calgary
2500 University Dr. NW
Calgary, AB, Canada
smcosta@ucalgary.ca

ABSTRACT

In this paper, we present a view of robots as physical agents submitting to a static infrastructure, allowing a computerized static system to use the robot as a dynamic puppet, which is a social agent that can communicate on physical and social terms with its human users and visitors. We demonstrate our approach with *Ningyō of the CAVE*, a prototype designed to allow a virtual reality CAVE facility to introduce its capabilities to human users and visitors. Through the robot, the CAVE is able to highlight capabilities and uses of the facility through performance, showmanship and physical actions to create an engaging interaction that conveys an overview of the facility and demonstrates its key functionalities. We examine the quality of the resulting engagement with preliminary reflection by several human visitors to our CAVE system. We believe that viewing robots as components of a greater and more capable computerized ecosystem is a less explored research path in social human-robot interaction, and hope that our *Ningyō of the CAVE* prototype could set the stage and inform some of the future research on this topic.

Author Keywords

Social Physical Agents; Robot Theater Play; Human-Robot Interaction; Human Factors; CAVE Automatic Virtual Environment

ACM Classification Keywords

I.2.9. Robotics: Commercial robots and applications; J.5. Arts and Humanities: Performing arts; K.3.2. Computer and Information Science Education: Information systems education; H.1.2. User/Machine Systems: Human factors

INTRODUCTION

Many static infrastructures have sufficient computational power to allow them to mimic logical thinking and employ synthetic emotions in order to act as intelligent agents. However, due to the lack of mechanical physicality, it can be difficult or impossible for such static facilities to interact with their human users and visitors in a dynamic and social way. For example, a modern high-performance computer has tremendous computational capability and potential to leverage this capability to interact with the world in interesting ways, but this potential may be hindered without some physical medium to facilitate it.

With this in mind, the challenge is to find a way to give a static infrastructure the opportunity to interact and communicate with people, not only scientifically and logically but also socially and artistically. Inspired by the Japanese Bunraku play, in this paper we explore the use of humanoid robots as a physical representation of a computerized static infrastructure to provide a socially engaging means of interaction with people. Ningyō (人形) is the Japanese term for the puppet that commonly used in Bunraku or Ningyō Jōruri, which is a form of a traditional Japanese puppet play (Figure 1). During the performance, puppeteers control mechanically sophisticated human-like figures, providing the illusion that the puppets perform under their own agency and will. In our *Ningyō of the CAVE* prototype, the humanoid, like a Ningyō puppet, is indeed teleoperated by the static CAVE infrastructure, which plays the role as a puppeteer.

Figure 1: Bunraku puppeteers manipulate Ningyō [20]

The CAVE [1] system is a highly capable computerized static infrastructure, used to puppeteer *Ningyō of the CAVE* in order to demonstrate its capabilities to visitors, and to physically engage its users. We believe that our approach can scale to other highly computerized static infrastructures, and explores a variation on the common social human-robot interaction design approach, which usually views robots as egocentric autonomous intelligent agents rather than as agents of a larger computerized entity, which fully controls them.

RELATED WORK

Use of robots has been explored in a wide range of public interactive settings, including lobby interaction [2], museum guidance and navigation assistance [3][4], as well as museum interaction [5]. Interaction patterns and strategies among robots and humans in public spaces have also been explored and discussed [3][6][7]. Human-like motions, such as head movements, eye contact, hand gestures, etc. were shown to significantly improve the experience of visitors during their interactions [8][9]. These works show not only the possibility to use human-like robots as a means of meaningful and dynamic social interaction, but also the potential to enhance and enliven static infrastructures.

There have been several novel attempts at robotic theatrical performances. These efforts evolve from the early study of Bunraku puppet [10], science shows [11], to recent professional theater plays such as *I, work*, *In the heart of the forest*, and *Sayonara*, where robots perform physical feats along with real actors [12][13][14]. In the play *Sayonara*, the android actor, Geminoid F, has been said to be almost indistinguishable from a human actresses. The Bunraku master Kanjūrō III was also involved in the play, demonstrating the existence of commonality between the traditional puppet show and modern robot theater [12]. In other recent approaches, both humanoid robots and androids with a less human appearance are being used in performances where the robot is acting as itself, playing the role of a robot interacting with the human players [15][16].

Virtual agents have also been explored as cost effective solution for education and training purposes, requiring advanced graphical technologies and a large amount of technical work to provide a believable experience [17][18][19]. However, virtual agents inherently cannot support the physicality that interaction with a robotic agent provides.

The design of *Ningyō of the CAVE* was informed by both artistic intent and research objectives. The core focus of the design may be summarized with two primary goals: building on the important role robots can play when guiding or introducing people to static infrastructure, and on their inherent ability to act as perfect puppets in a carefully orchestrated play.

A unique design angle of *Ningyō of the CAVE* is that the static infrastructure itself, in our case a highly computerized one, is the director which fully controls the robot as its

interactive puppet, serving its need to communicate and engage visitors and users in a physical and socially meaningful manner.

DESIGN

In this project we are using the CAVE system, located in the Foundation CMG / Frank and Sarah Meyer Collaboration Centre at University of Calgary, as the static infrastructure, which puppeteers our *Ningyō of the CAVE* prototype. Our CAVE has four projected surfaces: three walls and floor, and a high quality Vicon tracking system with 8 high-resolution infrared motion capture cameras mounted above (Figure 2).

Figure 2: CAVE area, surrounded by display screens

Both the CAVE and Vicon systems are connected to and driven by a powerful server. The visual appeal of a visualization facility such as a CAVE, along with the high-performance computational capability attached, represent an excellent computerized static infrastructure. This CAVE system is used extensively to showcase and explore oil-and-gas processes and data, particularly for reservoir engineering applications. This often necessitates the introduction of the facilities technological capabilities, tools and applications to oil-and-gas domain experts with little knowledge of technology and facilities such as a CAVE. The use of an environment such as a CAVE by users, which often lack the skills and knowledge to effectively interact with it, creates an interesting interaction space for a robotic agent that will physically represent the CAVE facility. Motivated by the overall vision of robots as puppets of static computerized environments, and by the instance of our CAVE, we designed the *Ningyō of the CAVE* to help demonstrate the validity of our concept.

The goal of our prototype is to give an interactive introduction of the CAVE infrastructure to visitors. These visitors range from students and researchers on campus, to members of other institutions and industrial partner organizations, to members of the public. The introduction, or the self-introduction from the perspective of the CAVE, is delivered in the form of an interactive theater play. This is accomplished by using multiple autonomous agents on the server synchronized to control the humanoid robot and provide the illusion that the robot controls the CAVE, while in practice it is being controlled by it. This impression is

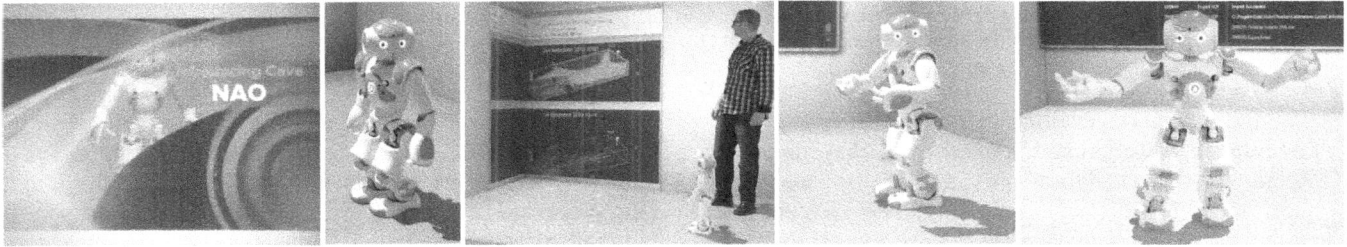

Figure 4: snapshots during the performance

From left to right: the virtual robot; the physical robot "steps out" of the screen; robot manipulates an application window; robot shows its Vicon makers; robot has personality traits and makes jokes

accomplished through manipulation of content and demonstrations on the CAVE screens while interacting with an audience in a human-like fashion. We endeavored to further enrich the performance by assigning the humanoid a certain personality, and then examined the consequent social impact.

IMPLEMENTATION

In our system, an Aldebaran Robotics NAO robot is used as the physical humanoid agent that is puppeteered by the CAVE. The NAO is a humanoid with 25 degrees of freedom that allows it to perform basic human-like gestures and legged locomotion (Figure 3). Our *Ningyō of the CAVE* prototype is designed as an interactive theatre play, which is controlled by the CAVE and delivered to the human audience by the humanoid within the CAVE area, on the floor projection screen.

Figure 3: NAO with Vicon markers attached on it

The Vicon cameras are used to track the motion of the robot. Reflective markers, arranged in an asymmetrical pattern, are attached to the torso of the robot (Figure 3), in order to allow the system to monitor the precise location and orientation of the robot in real time. By tracking the robot in this manner, the necessary orientation and positioning is maintained so that the impression that the robot is interacting with the audience is preserved. For instance, the robot's head orientation is adjusted in real time based on the robot's body position; hence the robot is always looking in the direction where the audience is located. This seems to greatly enhance the experience by

creating a sense of direct communication between the robot and the CAVE visitors and users.

At the beginning of the act the CAVE attempts to introduce its capabilities using a virtual robot, which appears on its screens. However, shortly after the introduction starts, it is interrupted by an error message, creating an interesting twist (Figure 4).

Following the error message, the virtual robot on the screen appears to be surprised by the technical issue and tries to comfort audiences by saying: *"...What the... Please don't panic, this happened before"*.

Next, the virtual robot walks toward the edge of screen. When the virtual image reaches the middle of the side screen, the physical robot is brought to life and stands up from a slightly hidden compartment placed at a corner of the stage, and starts marching toward the center of the CAVE area. The transition gives audiences the illusion that the robot breaks the fourth wall, walks out of the screen, and turns into a real one, which is a metaphor often used in cinema, for example in Woody Allen's *the Purple Rose of Cairo*.

The physical robot expresses itself in a slightly grumpy and dramatic manner. For example, because the robot is less than a meter tall, right after coming out, it faces the audience and exclaims, *"Yes, I'm short, stop staring at me"*.

Then robot starts walking around the CAVE area, introducing various functionalities of the facility according to the arrangement of the lab environment, including the screens of the CAVE system and other attached equipment such as the Vicon cameras above the interactive area. The robot also describes applications that are used to visualize and explore different domains in this environment. Since the robot is tracked using the Vicon cameras (Figure 2), the content on the CAVE screens is completely synchronized with the robot motion and actions. The impression is that the robot indeed controls the entire facility through the use of motion, gaze, and hand gestures. For example:

One simple scenario unfolds when the robot points at a screen and says, *"Let me open a program."*

The application window appears at exactly the location where the robot is pointing. Next, the robot says, *"And let me move the window to a different screen."*

As the robot waves its hand across and eventually pointing at a different CAVE screen, the application window floats across the CAVE to the new corresponding location smoothly, as if controlled directly by the robot gestures.

The robot is able to not only give system level instructions, such as moving or resizing an application window, but is also able to manipulate the application contents, for example rotating the reservoir model inside an oil-and-gas visualization, or a molecule structure inside a biochemistry simulation.

From the software perspective, our prototype implementation includes four software modules: the "tracking agent", the "window control agent", the "robot control agent", and the physical robot (Figure 5).

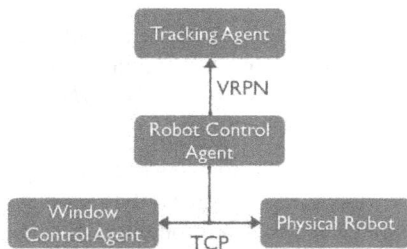

Figure 5: block diagram of the software implementation

The "tracking agent" reads data from the Vicon system via Virtual Reality Peripheral Network (VRPN). VRPN is a standard protocol dedicated to support communication of devices within virtual reality systems. The Vicon system uses the VRPN channel to communicate the spatial location and orientation of objects that are being tracked by it, in *Ningyō of the CAVE* the robot's torso is one such object (Figure 3).

The "window control agent" determines when and where an application window should be displayed in the CAVE screens directly. It is also able to initialize a new program at a given screen coordinate, or move an existing window to a new location in the screen. We calculate the direction at which the robot points, and make the window move corresponding to the motion of the robot arm. The combination of the robot's movements and the window animation provides the illusion that the robot is directly manipulating the selected application window on the corresponding CAVE screen with its hands.

The "robot control agent" module is the core of the system: it fetches the robot's spatial information from the "tracking agent" in real time, and gives synchronized instructions to both the "window control agent" and to the physical robot. In our system we use Aldebaran Robotics Choregraphe to interpret and apply the robot's physical actions. We either

use standard postures and movements provided by the graphical programming interface of the software, or program custom ones if the there is nothing in the standard library that is sufficient.

Ningyō of the CAVE is designed with loose coupling as a goal, so any of its components may be changed without impacting other parts of the system. We implemented a several minute interactive sequence that first introduces visitors to our CAVE facility, describing its main components and features, and then walks them through some of our CAVE's interactive visualizations such as those used to explore reservoir engineering and biochemistry simulations. However, since *Ningyō of the CAVE* is an generic entity, which can interactively engage with any content the system displays on its screens, the CAVE can deploy it to serve as needed to execute any interactive task or show any application it needs to engage users with.

CRITIQUE

Since the goal of our current *Ningyō of the CAVE* prototype is to introduce the CAVE system to visitors and users we held preliminary critique sessions and collected feedback from five stakeholders and visitors to the CAVE. Our evaluation is very preliminary and based on a limited number of participants who visited the facility and interacted with *Ningyō of the CAVE*.

According to observations from these sessions, all viewers enjoyed watching the introduction given by *Ningyō of the CAVE* to the CAVE facility. Most of the viewers were focused on following the humanoid's movements, gestures, and interaction with the content on the CAVE's screens. One observation brought forward by the CAVE stakeholders was the difficulty of both retaining and ensuring availability of high quality human guides to demonstrate the facility to visitors, which is a common need that occurs sometimes on short notice. Using *Ningyō of the CAVE* as a key tool for introducing the facility and its various applications to visitors on an ongoing basis was proposed as a result of the critique sessions. Based on the reaction of the viewers and feedback received, we believe that *Ningyō of the CAVE* has the potential to become an effective method of introducing environments such as ours to visitors and users.

In addition, all audiences noticed and appreciated the personality of the robot and reported being entertained by its jokes and actions. Several reported that the human-like appearance and behavior caught their attention effectively and in a positive manner as evidenced by smiles and laughter. We observed that people treated the robot as a living creature rather than a machine or equipment, and attached emotive state to it. We believe this treatment to be due to the appearance and behavior of the robot.

Both visitors to the facility and stakeholders were excited by *Ningyō of the CAVE*, and a lot of suggestions were collected to further improve both the structure and content of the humanoid performance.

FUTURE WORK
We consider *Ningyō of CAVE* to be at the proof of concept stage, and believe there are many possible extensions of this work.

In particular, we would like to execute a user study to quantify and qualify the difference between our robot theater play and traditional in-person active or passive touring. Two major questions that we would like to answer are:

1. What changes to user response and feedback does *Ningyō of the CAVE* evoke? We assume our performance of the robot is able to create a strong positive impression of the facility and will motivate users to request more information and participate in future events or projects at the facility. To find supporting evidence for this assumption would show clear benefit to the use of an agent in this manner and for this purpose.

2. Does *Ningyō of the CAVE* help the audience understand the facility in a better way? Using this performance as an engaging learning tool that can be continuously improved over time could provide a consistent and effective means of introduction and information dissemination. Assuming this is the case, how much benefit could this technique provide over traditional tutoring methods and what factors contribute to the effectiveness of the performance as a communication technique?

The humanoid, NAO, which we are using as the physical agent in *Ningyō of the CAVE*, has limitations due to its physicality. For instance, the humanoid's lack of an expressive face may be reducing the effectiveness and users' engagement during interaction. We are hoping to integrate different robotic platforms in our project, allowing us to explore whether different robotic physical capabilities, such as facial expression, could create stronger social engagement with visitors.

In the longer term, we would like to apply the *Ningyō of the CAVE* approach to other computerized static infrastructure. Of particular interest is infrastructure comprised of "smart" technology. Smart buildings and smart homes are currently gaining popularity and there is an ever-increasing selection of sensing and tracking devices as well as a greatly increased capability to communicate both among these devices and other machines. Further to this, many things now have the label "smart" on them, from light bulbs to washing machines to thermostats. Such devices are improving our daily lives in an intelligent way, yet their lack of dynamic physicality limits any possible physical interaction with human users. It is an exciting and potentially very impactful research objective to experiment and examine the possibility to embody and reflect the "smartness", embedded in this new world of static infrastructure to create an engaging and interactive experience that may provide information and entertainment to humans. For example, would it be a more impressive and positive experience to be handed fresh clothing from a personable robot, rather than receiving a text message, "job done", from your washing machine?

CONCLUSION
In this paper we presented a view of robots as physical agents submitting to static infrastructure, where a computerized system uses the robot as a dynamic social agent, which can communicate physical and social needs to human users and visitors. We demonstrate our approach with *Ningyō of the CAVE*, a prototype designed to allow our virtual reality CAVE facility to introduce its technical capabilities and uses to human visitors through interaction with a physical agent. We provided a detailed description of the current *Ningyō of the CAVE* prototype, and presented a preliminary evaluation of our concept and its validity.

We believe that viewing robots as mere physical components of a much larger and more capable computerized ecosystem is a less explored research path in social human-robot interaction, and we hope that our *Ningyō of the CAVE* prototype could set the stage and inform future research on this topic, potentially bringing this design concept to other advanced and highly computerized static infrastructures.

ACKNOWLEDGMENTS
We are very grateful to the Foundation CMG / Frank and Sarah Meyer Collaboration Centre for enabling our research. This research was supported by the NSERC / AITF / Foundation CMG Industry Research Chair program in Scalable Reservoir Visualization at the University of Calgary.

REFERENCES
1. Cruz-Neira, Carolina, et al. "The CAVE: audio visual experience automatic virtual environment." *Communications of the ACM* 35.6 (1992): 64-72.

2. Gockley, Rachel, et al. "Designing robots for long-term social interaction." *Intelligent Robots and Systems, 2005. (IROS 2005). 2005 IEEE/RSJ International Conference on.* IEEE, 2005.

3. Burgard, Wolfram, et al. "The interactive museum tour-guide robot." *AAAI/IAAI.* 1998.

4. Siegwart, Roland, et al. "Robox at Expo. 02: A large-scale installation of personal robots." *Robotics and Autonomous Systems* 42.3 (2003): 203-222.

5. Shiomi, Masahiro, et al. "Interactive humanoid robots for a science museum." *Proceedings of the 1st ACM SIGCHI/SIGART conference on Human-robot interaction.* ACM, 2006.

6. Satake, Satoru, et al. "How to approach humans? Strategies for social robots to initiate interaction."

Human-Robot Interaction (HRI), 2009 4th ACM/IEEE International Conference on. IEEE, 2009.

7. Hayashi, Kotaro, et al. "Humanoid robots as a passive-social medium-a field experiment at a train station." *Human-Robot Interaction (HRI), 2007 2nd ACM/IEEE International Conference on.* IEEE, 2007.

8. Kuno, Yoshinori, et al. "Museum guide robot based on sociological interaction analysis." *Proceedings of the SIGCHI conference on Human factors in computing systems.* ACM, 2007.

9. Faber, Felix, et al. "The humanoid museum tour guide Robotinho." *Robot and Human Interactive Communication, 2009. RO-MAN 2009. The 18th IEEE International Symposium on.* IEEE, 2009.

10. Hattori, Motofumi, et al. "An analysis of the Bunraku puppet's motions based on the phase correspondence of the puppet's motions axis-for the generation of humanoid robots motions with fertile emotions." *Systems, Man, and Cybernetics, 1999. IEEE SMC'99 Conference Proceedings. 1999 IEEE International Conference on.* Vol. 2. IEEE, 1999.

11. Lin, Chyi-Yeu, et al. "The realization of robot theater: Humanoid robots and theatric performance." *Advanced Robotics, 2009. ICAR 2009. International Conference on.* IEEE, 2009.

12. Paré, Zaven. "Robot drama research: from identification to synchronization." *Social Robotics.* Springer Berlin Heidelberg, 2012. 308-316.

13. Lu, David V. "Ontology of robot theatre." *Proceedings of the workshop Robotics and Performing Arts: Reciprocal Influences, ICRA.* 2012.

14. Ogawa, Kohei, Koichi Taura, and Hiroshi Ishiguro. "Possibilities of Androids as poetry-reciting agent." *RO-MAN, 2012 IEEE.* IEEE, 2012.

15. Złotowski, Jakub, et al. "I sing the body electric: an experimental theatre play with robots." *Proceedings of the 8th ACM/IEEE international conference on Human-robot interaction.* IEEE Press, 2013.

16. Lemaignan, Séverin, et al. "Roboscopie: a theatre performance for a human and a robot." *Proceedings of the seventh annual ACM/IEEE international conference on Human-Robot Interaction.* ACM, 2012.

17. Kopp, Stefan, et al. "Max - A Multimodal Assistant in Virtual Reality Construction." *KI* 17.4 (2003): 11.

18. Kenny, Patrick, et al. "Building interactive virtual humans for training environments." *The interservice/industry training, simulation & education conference (I/ITSEC).* Vol. 2007. No. 1. National Training Systems Association, 2007.

19. Swartout, William, et al. "Ada and Grace: Toward realistic and engaging virtual museum guides." *Intelligent Virtual Agents.* Springer Berlin Heidelberg, 2010.

20. "Noh and Kyogen." Yokohama Noh Theater. N.p., n.d. Web. 25 May 2014.

Personal and Interactive Newscaster Agent based on Estimation of User's Understanding

Naoto Yoshida
Kansai University
2-1-1 Ryozenji, Takatsuki
Osaka 5691095, Japan
k463362@kansai-u.ac.jp

Miyuki Yano
Kansai University†
2-1-1 Ryozenji, Takatsuki
Osaka 5691095, Japan
† presently with
The Senshu Ikeda Bank, Ltd.

Tomoko Yonezawa
Kansai University
2-1-1 Ryozenji, Takatsuki
Osaka 5691095, Japan
yone@kansai-u.ac.jp

ABSTRACT

In this paper, we propose a virtual agent system that introduces the current news on the Webs depending on the user's reactions to the understanding. We focused on the gesture of the user to estimate the user's state of understanding based on the head motion. The goal of the research is the user's understanding of the news regardless of the knowledge level. The system controls 1) the level of the news content corresponding to the user's gesture of inclining her/his head and 2) the audibility of the agent's speech (the volume and the speed) by the user's head motion to turn her/his ear to the agent. The results of the evaluations showed the effectiveness of the interactive change of the reading behaviors to be understandable and audible.

Author Keywords

User's understanding; virtual agent; personal newscaster; gesture of audience; head movement.

INTRODUCTION

Recent advances of communication networks such as the Internet and ubiquitous service devices have developed various types of information representations. One of the important features of these communications is the independence of time and place. The other feature is the variance of the communication media, such as texts, sounds, images, and movies. Thus, the Internet communications include conventional media and the multiple uses of it for comprehensive and intuitive understanding. From the view point of multiple communication media, it is important for the information devices to appropriately integrate these representations.

One of the ideas for intuitive integration of the information media is anthropomorphic interactions, as can be seen in various research on robotics [14, 12] and virtual agents [1, 9, 13].

Text-to-speech services have been proposed in the application research field of speech synthesis [2, 7] while the infor-

mation on the Web is updated in time, and we can access the information anytime without limitation. Recent portal sites provide us images and movies of the news, not just text information. Broadcasting media has an important advantage of the shared information among a large number of passive audiences. On the other hand, these media present unidirectional information, and the acceptability of the information is different according to each person. A news channel on the Web is a passive information acquisition such as TV news and radio news. Some recent young people who have experience with Internet use can overcome the weakness by searching the unclear or unknown keywords in the news in unidirectional media. However, most of users are not interested in news with many unknown keywords. Consequently, the audience gets biased knowledge of the news fields. Nevertheless, reading many sentences and looking up collected meanings needed for positive learning will takes labor. Consequently, users cannot sufficiently look up news on the Web.

In this paper, we propose a virtual agent system, *Personal Newscaster*, that introduces the current news on the Web depending on the user's reactions of the understanding.

The role of newscaster is to read the news of incidents, accidents, disasters, politics, economy, international situations, and local events widely and accurately. A newscaster should announce the truth objectively and impartially. In addition, the manuscript is standardized to observe many rules so that as much audience as possible understands it in mass media. Nevertheless, the user must have had an interest in news content and needs simple explanation and concrete accounts of events. In most cases, these users cannot be given support.

Announcements from *Personal Newscaster* are optimized for the user. The agent explains the news topic to the user using simple and easy words. Understanding of the user is recognized from the gestures of introspective consciousness of his/her understanding. The aim of this system is to provide the user with as much news as possible regardless of quantity of the knowledge.

In this research, we focused on the gesture of an audience and estimated what the audience did not understand. We developed the virtual newscaster agent system, which changed the reading manner depending on the understanding of the audience.

HAI 2014, October 29–31, 2014, Tsukuba, Japan.
Copyright © 2014 ACM 978-1-4503-3035-0/14/10 ...$15.00.
http://dx.doi.org/10.1145/2658861.2658877

Figure 1. Appeararance of Personal Newscaster Agent.

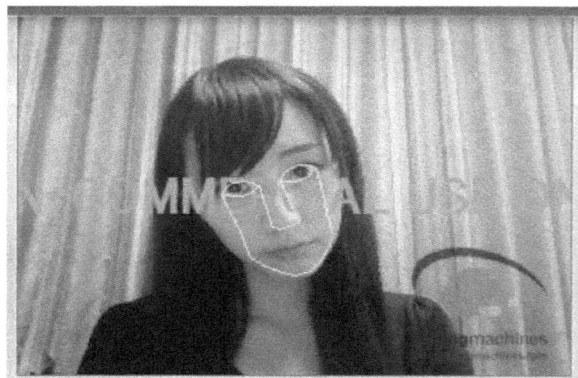

a) gesture without understanding

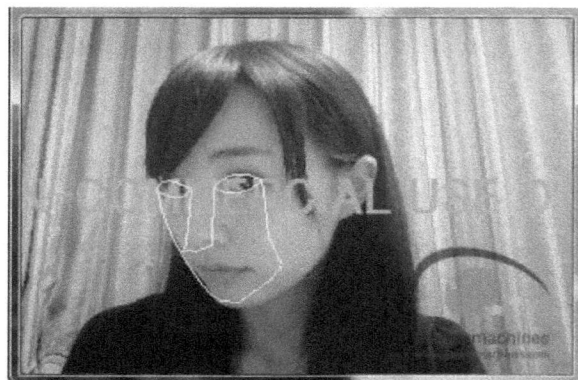

b) inaudible gesture

Figure 2. Gesture without understanding.

RELATED RESEARCH

There have been many studies of news navigation systems for individuals. Some researchers have proposed the systems with personalized news lists from a large number of news clips from TV and Web [5, 15]. The news is selected by the user's interest, estimated by the user's search words. However, video media is not able to be edited during the playback in real time. In addition, explanation of words in the movie in real time are difficult. There are other researches about news recommendation. Based on the text news, the relevance of the keywords in the news are used for the selection and filtering of various news articles [3, 6]. In these approaches, the user could become satisfied while the user's knowledge becomes biased to her/his original tendency. In order to kindly provide the chance of discovery, the system should prepare an appropriate environment to intelligibly give news of the unselected keywords.

Daniel [4] et al. proposed the system that widens the interest of the user for various articles by classifying the following options of the feedbacks: interesting, not interesting, already known, tell me more, and explain. The recommendation model of the system selects the news based on the feedback.

Contrary to this, we still assume that the user cannot train herself/himself to read the articles in new fields with difficult keywords. In such situations, the user might lose the learning motivation if the system never gives the user supportive information immediately. The user should want to know the meaning of the words immediately. The user might lose the learning motivation if the user cannot receive the support of the system immediately.

Consequently, our proposed system estimates the understanding level of the user from her/his head motion of the introspective gestures and the under-conscious behaviors. It is expected that the repeat function of the news reading in different manners not only helps the users understanding but also stimulates the interest of the user. Reading again using easy words helps the user to have an interest in the news.

PERSONAL NEWSCASTER

Agent Drawing and Voice Control

The system consists of a Windows 7 PC, a 13-inch liquid crystal monitor and a three-mega-pixel camera attached to the upper part of the monitor. The system was implemented by Processing[11]. The drawing screen is layered with background image, agent, and table. The agent's expression is animated changing with plural images (Figure 3): default/worried face expression, opening/closing agent's mouth and opening/closing agent's eyes.

The voice of the agent's speech is generated by a text-to-speech software, CeVIO Creative Studio FREE [1], and recorded into multi-audio files. The speech voice was generated with a female voice, frequency from 200 [Hz] to 420 [Hz]. We prepared two speeds of speech: normal speed is set at 9.5 phonemes per second and slow speed is set at 7.6 phonemes per second. We also prepared two volumes for speech voice; normal volume is set at 70 [db] and loud volume is set at about 79 [db] assuming one-meter distance between the speaker and the user.

---

[1]Japanese speech synthesizer, http://cevio.jp/

		Expression	
		Default	Worried
Eyes Open	Mouth Open		
	Mouth Close		
Eyes Close	Mouth Open		
	Mouth Close		
Nod			

Figure 3. Agent's face images.

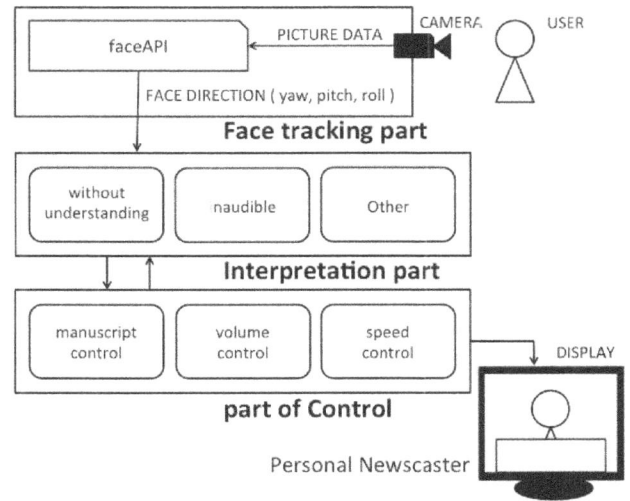

Figure 4. The structure of the Personal Newscaster system.

Gestures Related to User's Understanding

Our proposed *Personal Newscaster* (Figure 1) is the news-reader agent system that changes its reading manners and the content level of the news according to each user's state of understanding. Basically, the agent makes a one-directional announcement with minimum conversations such as the notification of a change in the reading manner or the content level. We focused on the user's involuntary gestures during the news announcement, while the target users are passive audiences who do not show their own questions or unclear points. Attention must be directed toward gestures of the audience while they are listening closely. Nakamura et al. had estimated the difficulty in learning by the user's voice analyses [10]. However, the intentions of speech are varied in the utterances of the news compared to the learning system. We then focused on the understanding states that may generate various types of the gestures. We hypothesized that the users without reactions are understanding the information of the announcement and that the users who do not understand the news or who consider the news difficult to understand lean their heads to the side.

On the other hand, there is another problem with the one-directional news announcements. The audiences cannot sometimes hear the words in the news, even in TV broadcasting programs. Moreover, in this system, the agent makes speech using text-to-speech synthesis. It is assumed that the agent's voice is more difficult to hear than the human announcer's one. The main factors of inaudible situations are 1) the volume and 2) the speed of the speech. These factors cause not only the inaudible sentence but also the low understanding of the total contents. In order to appropriately control these factors, we hypothesized that the users turn ears to the agent in the inaudible situations.

Attitudes and Contents Corresponding to Estimated Understanding Level

In order to implement the reactive agent system for the user's understanding state, we prepared a mapping between the estimated understanding level and the change of the agent's behavior.

Automatic Estimation of the User's Understanding

Figure 4 shows the structure of the Personal Newscaster system. In the face-tracking part, the user's head direction is acquired by face API [8]. In the interpretation part, the user's states of understanding, "could not listen" or "could not understand," are recognized by the analyses of the head-directional data when the user inclines her/his head to the side or turns an ear to the agent. In the part of control, the level of the news manuscript is changed by the understanding level of the user, and the volume of the voice and the reading speed of the agent are changed by the audibility. In addition, the control part makes the agent's reactive behaviors, such as nod and eye blinking, to the user's delicate gestures.

The face directions acquired by face tracking are the pitch, yaw and roll angles. The lower limit threshold of the gesture without understanding is defined as ten degrees of the roll. The lower limit threshold of the inaudible gesture is defined as ten degrees in absolute value of the yaw (Figure 2-a). The continuous durations for the detection are set to be over two seconds (Figure 2-b).

Parameter of the Agent's Behaviors

There are two types of agent behaviors depending on the user's gestures: a) reading speed and voice volume and b)

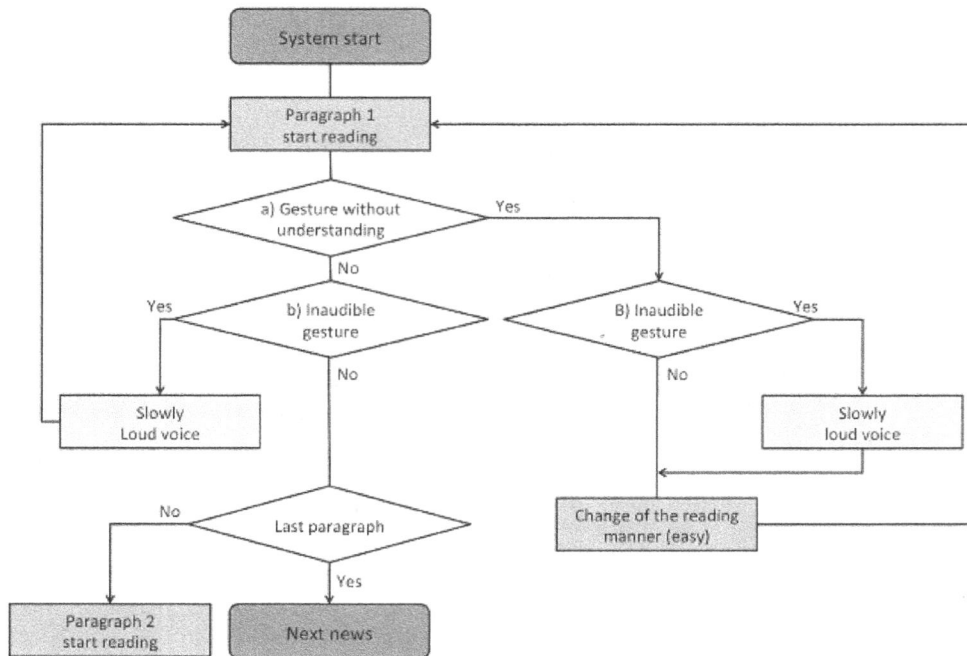

Figure 5. Flowchart of the agent's scripts.

difficulty of words in sentences. Figure 5 shows the agent's script flow. The user's understanding level estimated in the timing of every paragraph decides both a) and b) behaviors. When the system detects the user's gesture without understanding during the sentence, the agent repeats the same sentence with appropriate change of the reading manner corresponding to the detected gesture.

The mappings of the reading manners are shown as follows. The reading manner a) is conducted when users incline their head. And the reading manner b) is conducted when users turn their ears to either the right or the left. There are three types of the change of the reading manners.

1. Reading with easy words.

2. Reading slowly in a loud voice.

3. Reading slowly in a loud voice with easy words (with both manners).

In the case of the agent reading the paragraph again, the agent will speak the words below.

1. "I'll reread clearly that phrase one more time."

2. "I'll reread slowly and loudly that phrase one more time."

3. "I'll reread clearly and slowly that phrase one more time in a loud voice."

EVALUATION OF UNDERSTANDING AND VERIFYING CHANGE OF IMPRESSION OF PERSONAL NEWSCASTER

The objective is to verify the proposal method to improve user's understanding. Furthermore, in order to clarify differences in impressions for the speaker, another objective is to make a comparison between Personal Newscaster and conventional media (TV news).

Hypotheses: User's involuntary gesture of inclining their head and turning their ear toward the screen show users without the understanding state. The agent's response manner for giving understanding to users is appropriate. The user feels consideration for the agent's support.

Subject: Twenty-four people ages nineteen through twenty-three (five males and nineteen females) participated in the experiment. They were university students in faculty of informatics.

Conditions: There are four conditions with two factors. The first factor is the patting motion of the robot's left hand, as if the experimenter instructed a participant to incline and turning his/her head or turn his/her head when he/she cannot understand (DT) or the experimenter did not give such instructions (dt). The second factor of the condition is changing the agent's reading manner (RM) or not changing the agent's reading manner (rm). The DT/dt factor was prepared in order to confirm whether the user can naturally interact with the system without consciousness of the control.

	dt – DT		rm – RM		intr.	
	F	p	F	p		
Q1	5.552	$=0.27$	17.209	$<.01$	3.45	$=0.07$
Q2	15.374	$<.01$	22.136	$<.01$	9.51	$<.01$
Q3	30.803	$<.01$	16.043	$<.01$	2.69	$=0.11$
Q4	15.620	$<.01$	22.702	$<.01$	5.24	$=.03$
Q5	7.494	$=.012$	11.521	$<.01$	4.92	$=.03$
Q6	11.088	$<.01$	11.384	$<.01$	8.90	$<.01$
Q7	12.663	$<.01$	11.175	$<.01$	2.09	$=0.16$
Q8	11.717	$<.01$	17.286	$<.01$	0.89	$=0.35$
Q9	2.917	$=.101$	22.139	$<.01$	3.76	$=0.06$
Q10	3.431	$=.077$	23.923	$<.01$	2.23	$=0.15$
Q11	11.088	$<.01$	21.600	$<.01$	1.30	$=0.27$

Table 1. ANOVA for subjective evaluations.

Procedures and Instructions: The participants were instructed to sit at the indicated chair (1.2 meters from the display screen,) and wait for the reading of the news in each experiment. The participants were not instructed to react to the agent. The news manuscript is constructed in two paragraphs. The length of one news article was about 20 seconds if paragraphs were not repeated. While news was read, the agent changed the manner and reread the paragraph if the user behaved the gesture of not understanding. After the reading ended, the subject evaluated their impression of agent and their own understanding of the news. Participants used this system four times. Four types of news stories were prepared, and participants listened to different news every test. News used in the experiments was fictional and these were randomly selected.

Evaluation Items: Participants performed five phases of impression rating for each item against four conditions. The participants made an evaluation using a five-point rating scale of the relevance (5: very relevant, 4: somewhat relevant, 3: even, 2: somewhat irrelevant, 1: irrelevant) of the following statements. Q1 to Q8 are evaluations about the user's impression for the newscaster agent.

Q1 I felt the agent was friendly.

Q2 I felt the agent was kind.

Q3 The agent understood my hearing attitude.

Q4 The agent showed an interest in me.

Q5 I felt the agent was close to me.

Q6 I felt affection for the agent.

Q7 I could trust the agent.

Q8 The agent was intelligent.

Q9 to Q11 are evaluations about understanding of participants.

Q9 I could understand the news.

Q10 I could capture the meaning of the news.

Q11 I could listen to the agent's voice.

Result: Table 1 and Figure 6 show the results of means opinion score (MOS) for each statement, and Table I shows the results of two-factor repeated measures ANOVA. In the analyses, α, the level of significance was .05 and ϕ, the degree of freedom (DOF) was $(1, 25)$. There were significances of both factors from the results of statement 2, 3, 4, 5, 6, 7, 8, 10, 11. There were significances only by the factor of agent's reading manner from the results of the statements 1 and 9.

DISCUSSIONS

In this section, we first discuss the positive impressions for intuitive and communicative system of "Personal Newscaster." As our expectation, the reactive repeat of the news generally improved the impressions for the agent while the behaviors of the agents correspond to the user's gestures of low understanding or inaudible situation. The results related to the agent's kindness showed that the agent was regarded as a presence that is attentive to the user's situation. From these results, it is conjectured that the personality of the news agent was differently interpreted by the correspondence of the repeating manners to the user's situation.

Next, we discuss the appropriateness of the gestural mappings. Regardless of with or without the instruction of the gesture, the subjective results for understanding were significantly high when the gesture of head inclining changed the level of the news. From the result, we could confirm the appropriate mapping of the understanding gesture. In addition, the inaudible gesture could also provide the audible speech with slow and loud voices so that the user could understand the news.

Consequently, the system provided the user with understandable and audible speech of the agent according to the user's under-conscious or introspective gestures of her/his head. The subjective impression for understanding could also be elevated by the appropriate manner of the news. From the viewpoint of the understanding level in the unknown or uninterested field, it is suggested that the user can acquire the chance to know and get interest in the news field that she/he is going to learn.

CONCLUSIONS

In this paper, we proposed a virtual agent system, *Personal Newscaster*, that speaks the current news on the Web depending on the user's under-conscious or introspective reactions of understanding. We employed a face-tracking method to capture pitch, yaw and roll angles of the user's head in order to detect the gestures of 1) head inclining to the side and 2) ear turning toward the agent. From the results of the experiment, it is suggested that the appropriate change of the agent's reading manner that corresponds to the user's gestures of the understanding level could not only improve the subsequent understanding level but also be familiar to the user. This system can be adapted to universal information services, especially for educating and cultivating the user's interest on the Internet regardless of the current interest and ability of the user. As future work, we should discuss the balance between the familiar personalization and the fairness of the information in the agent, which simulates a member of mass media.

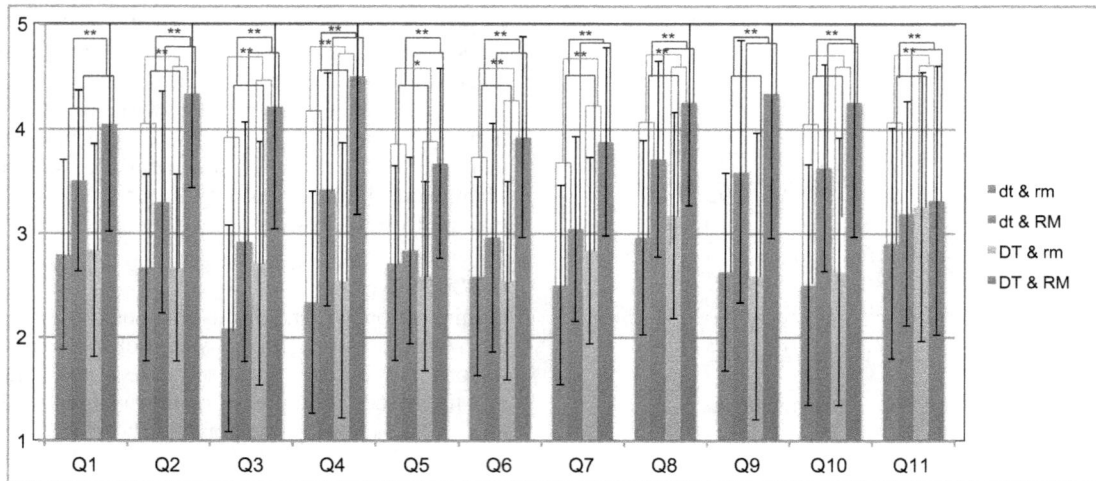

Figure 6. Results of subjective evaluation.

ACKNOWLEDGMENTS

This research was supported in part by KAKENHI 24300047 and KAKENHI 25700021. The authors would like to thank the participants in the experiment.

REFERENCES

1. Abbattista, F., Paradiso, A., Semeraro, G., and Zambetta, F. An agent that learns to support users of a web site. *Applied Soft Computing 4*, 1 (2004), 1–12.

2. Asakawa, C., and Itoh, T. User interface of a home page reader. In *Proceedings of the third international ACM conference on Assistive technologies*, ACM (1998), 149–156.

3. Banos, E., Katakis, I., Bassiliades, N., Tsoumakas, G., and Vlahavas, I. Personews: a personalized news reader enhanced by machine learning and semantic filtering. In *On the Move to Meaningful Internet Systems 2006: CoopIS, DOA, GADA, and ODBASE*. Springer, 2006, 975–982.

4. Billsus, D., and Pazzani, M. J. A personal news agent that talks, learns and explains. In *Proceedings of the third annual conference on Autonomous Agents*, ACM (1999), 268–275.

5. Hopfgartner, F., and Jose, J. M. Semantic user modelling for personal news video retrieval. In *Advances in Multimedia Modeling*. Springer, 2010, 336–346.

6. Jennings, A., and Higuchi, H. A personal news service based on a user model neural network. *IEICE Transactions on Information and Systems 75*, 2 (1992), 198–209.

7. Kuhn, T., Jameel, A., Stumpfle, M., and Haddadi, A. Hybrid in-car speech recognition for mobile multimedia applications. In *Vehicular Technology Conference, 1999 IEEE 49th*, vol. 3, IEEE (1999), 2009–2013.

8. Machines, S. Faceapi. *URL: http://www. seeingmachines. com/product/faceapi* (2009).

9. Müller, W., Spierling, U., Alexa, M., and Rieger, T. Face-to-face with your assistant. realization issues of animated user interface agents for home appliances. *Computers & Graphics 25*, 4 (2001), 593–600.

10. Nakamura, K., Kakusho, K., Murakami, M., and Minoh, M. Estimating learnersf subjective impressions of the difficulty of course materials in e-learning environments. In *APRU 9th Distance Learning and the Internet Conference* (2008), 199–206.

11. Reas, C., and Fry, B. Processing: programming for the media arts. *AI & SOCIETY 20*, 4 (2006), 526–538.

12. Shiomi, M., Kanda, T., Ishiguro, H., and Hagita, N. Interactive humanoid robots for a science museum. In *Proceedings of the 1st ACM SIGCHI/SIGART conference on Human-robot interaction*, ACM (2006), 305–312.

13. Theune, M., Hofs, D., and Kessel, M. The virtual guide: A direction giving embodied conversational agent. *International Speech Communication Association (ISCA)* (2007).

14. Thrun, S., Bennewitz, M., Burgard, W., Cremers, A. B., Dellaert, F., Fox, D., Hahnel, D., Rosenberg, C., Roy, N., Schulte, J., et al. Minerva: A second-generation museum tour-guide robot. In *Robotics and automation, 1999. Proceedings. 1999 IEEE international conference on*, vol. 3, IEEE (1999).

15. Zimmerman, J., Dimitrova, N., Agnihotri, L., Janevski, A., and Nikolovska, L. Myinfo: a personal news interface. In *CHI'03 Extended Abstracts on Human Factors in Computing Systems*, ACM (2003), 898–899.

Emotional Cyborg: Complementing Emotional Labor with Human-agent Interaction Technology

Hirotaka Osawa

Faculty of Engineering, Information and Systems, University of Tsukuba

1-1-1 Tenno-dai, Tsukuba, Ibaraki, 305-8573, Japan

osawa@iit.tsukuba.ac.jp

ABSTRACT

The author proposes the notion of an emotional cyborg as a new application proposal in the human-agent interaction (HAI) field. This paper is a summary of what kind of human processes maintain emotional labor and how such kind of social labor is supported by HAI technologies. The author implemented AgencyGlass, a prototype application, as a tool for realizing an emotional cyborg. The device is attached on a user's face and displays the user's eye gestures. The author created a prototype application for supplementing emotional labor with AgencyGlass and presented this as a video. Reactions from media and online feedback on the prototype are analyzed, and the future of HAI applications is illustrated.

Author Keywords

emotional labor, human-agent interaction, human robot interaction, human interface, augmented human

ACM Classification Keywords

H.5.m Information interfaces and presentation (e.g., HCI): Miscellaneous.

INTRODUCTION

Our society is supported by many workers. Some types of labor includ sophisticated social services for other people like caring, welcoming, and greeting. These services are named "emotional labor" in contrast with physical labor and mental labor. Emotional labor is the sort of work that requires workers to control their emotion. Flight attendants, nurses, and teachers are examples of handling this kind of labor. Hochschild suggested the relationship that the role of emotional labor is increased as technology develops. She suggested that commoditization of physical labor and mental labor by technology accelerates the arms race of emotional labor for human workers [16].

Emotional labor causes a mismatch between workers'

required emotions and workers' real emotions. For example, similarity of emotion between patients and nurses makes a good impression on patients [29]. However, this forced synchronization causes a cognitive load on the workers because they cannot laugh or appear sad without caring for patient's emotions.

Virtual agents and social robots are used as technological solutions for emotional labor [25]. Several human-agent interaction (HAI) technologies like affective computing, persuasive technology, intelligent virtual agent, and social robotics contribute to substituting for emotional labor by replacing human labor with computers. However, emotional labor is a highly social and context oriented task, and it requires an intelligent and multimodal computing process (social brain hypothesis suggests that this ability is categorized as a higher-order ability in the brain [3]). Because of technological difficulty both in robotics and artificial intelligence, these autonomous agents support our emotional labor incompletely.

Figure 1. Emotional cyborg using AgencyGlass. Although the staff member (person on right) is not concentrated on the customer (person in middle), the glasses show gaze gestures in accordance with the customer's movement. As a result, the customer accepts enough "emotional labor" from the staff member. This reduces the amount of labor required from the staff member.

In this study, the author proposes another use of HAI technology called the "emotional cyborg" – not to substitute for emotional labor but to complement it. The emotional cyborg has the technology to generate the autonomous emotional behavior of workers. Complementary

HAI 2014, October 29–31, 2014, Tsukuba, Japan..

Copyright is held by the owner/author(s). Publication rights licensed to ACM.

ACM 978-1-4503-3035-0/14/10…$15.00.

http://dx.doi.org/10.1145/2658861.2658880

technologies are more applicable for commercial use because they produce solutions that combine human ability and technology. For example, HAL cybernetic suits are a good solution for physical labor and are commercialized well [34]. Wearable computing and augmented human technologies are also solutions for mental labor [33]. The author proposes the notion of the emotional cyborg as a complement to emotional labor through HAI technologies.

First, the author models the relationship between emotional labor and HAI technologies by reviewing several studies about our brain functions. Next, the author discusses what is achievable with an emotional cyborg. The author produced a prototype application for the emotional cyborg named "AgencyGlass," which is is an attachable fake-eye display that imitates human eye-gestures, as shown in Fig. 1. Last, the author examines feedback on our prototype by checking reactions in media and online comments and discusses the future vision for the emotional cyborg.

This paper is organized as follows. In section 2, the author describes details on how social brain theory grows our emotional ability and generates emotional labor by referring to several studies, including science, engineering, and humanity studies. Section 3 illustrates an emotional cyborg that is realizible with today's HAI technology and illustrates the functions of our prototype, AgencyGlass. In section 4, the author examines feedback from media articles and comments on AgencyGlass and discusses what kind of reactions on the emotional cyborg from society may be generated. Section 5 concludes the author's work.

BACKGROUND

Routes for Emotional Labor: Social Intelligence requires Arms Race of Caring

Emotional labor is brain activity first defined by Hochschild [17]. Before Hochschield, mental labor and emotional labor were both categorized as brain activity. She defined two kinds of brain activity for work. The first activity is the process of producing some solution regardless of the reaction from other people, for example, computation, logstics, searching, etc. This activity is categorized as mental labor. The other is the process of producing an appropriate behavior for other people, for example, caring, welcoming, greeting, etc. This activity is categorized as emotional labor (Note that emotional labor is not limited to just "emotions," but it is every social behavior that requires workers to control their own emotions). Hochschield proposed that emotional labor is more required in developed countries because physical labor and mental labor are already replaced by technologies. For example, if two companies both have enough technological solutions for customers for physical and mental tasks, customers select the service for social reasons. As a result each company requires its workers to make more emotional labor toward customers.

At a glance, emotional labor seems to be relatively light because smiling at customers is mannerful and not a big issue. However, emotional labor becomes a heavy social task because it requires estimating the customer's intention and making the appropriate reactions in accordance with them. Each company or employee requires workers to internalize their emotions. As a result, emotional labor causes depression and several mental disorders in workers [23]. This is because it causes a difference between a worker's real emotion and required emotion.

Why does our society view emotional labor as having significant value even though it sometime causes suffering in workers? In other words, why do we accept flattery as a reward even though it does not give us a visible reward? Biological and cognitive science studies suggest that this social reward is programmed as our innate ability. Cognitive science suggests that we have a module called the "theory of mind" (ToM), which is the brain function for understanding other's intentions from the environment [31]. The social brain hypothesis in biology states that humans must handle communication with each other for the benefit of trading in a society by using ToM [3][28]. A friendly attitude is rewarding to other people, and intentional behavior is appreciated [40]. Our brain accepts social attitude as value, and this process requires emotional labor, indispensable in our society. It is also suggested that this emotional labor is an evolutional factor that encourages appreciation in people such as customers because social intelligence is a higher-order ability in the brain [4]. Emotional labor is the message that "You are special. We care more about you than others." It is an inseparatable factor of our society.

HAI as Substitute to Emotional Labor

Our society has replaced human labor with technology [27]. For example, several types of human physical labor were replaced by machines and robots after the industrial revolution. Mental labor is still human labor but has also been gradually replaced by computers. With abduction, the replacement of emotional labor is not an untouched sanctruary forever. Therefore, what kind of technology replaces emotional labor? HAI technology does.

The HAI method is an engineering process that uses intentional social agents as an interface between humans and systems. If an agent's behaviors are cognitively intentional (meaning that an agent is accepted by the human intentional stance noted on Dennett's work [8]), they are accepted as agents – social actors. The process of finding social agents is triggered even by very subtle levels. For example, studies on media equations suggest that media devices like displays are sometimes handled as social actors by users even though they are not noticed [32]. These agents substitute some of emotional labor and even force their authority on users [6]. Even though a user recognizes that the interfaces are fake and there is no real intelligence, they accept emotional behavior as emotional if such kind of cognition causes less cognitive load [9]. HAI technologies use several social manners and stereotypes. Gender stereotypes are also the central theme in the study of emotional labor. Hochschield's research comes from female flight attendants and nurses. Eyssel et al. suggested that users confronted with agents accept several gender and racial stereotypes [10][11].

Emotional Cyborg: HAI as Complement to Emotional Labor

Findings and technologies for HAI have been used mainly for creating social agents. However, these agents have not been successful in our society. This is because emotional labor is a highly context-dependent brain process and not manualized well. Remember that companies requires workers to do emotional labor for customers because "it is not easily replacable by technology." The author estimates that creating autonomous agents for handling emotional labor is the ultimate goal for HAI, but it is not achieved easily. There is also opposition toward replacing human work with robots [21].

If we attach technology in a complementary fashion such as a prosthesis, it becomes more useful because it is a collaboration between human ability and technology. For example, Glas et al. proposed using a partial autonomous agent controller operated by a human [13].

There has been a lot of success with enhancing human ability for solving mental labor with computational technologies like the Parasitic Humanoid [18] proposed by Iizuka et al. and the PossessedHand proposed by Rekimoto et al. [39]. With the Parasitic Humanoid, a user's motion is partially controlled by galvanic vestibular stimulation, and the system guides the user without being noticed by him/her. The PossessedHand forces human fingers to move by electric stimulus.

On the basis of previous challenges, the author proposes the notion that emotional labor is a prosthesis for human emotional labor. The author estimates that enhancing human ability is a more acceptable notion in our society. Few studies have beed tried to substitute emotion with technologies. However, they are incomplete in the aspect of autonomy. In Maeda and Rekimoto's studies, users inevitably realize that their behaviors are forced by the system. With the emotional cyborg, a user's cognitive load is needed to be decreased more. Some kinds of emotional support are more explicit, like the HappinessCounter proposed by Tsujita et al. [41]. The author focuses on providing more implicit help through technology.

The emotional cyborg is inspired by Hallaway's controversial proposal in "A Cyborg Manifesto" [14]. In this article, she proposed overcoming gender stereotypes by attaching gender roles technologically. This challenge is also an engineering method for realizing Hallaway's vision.

AGENCYGLASS: PROTOTYPE FOR EMOTIONAL CYBORG

First Step for Emotional Cyborg: Complementing Gaze

Emotional gesures such as face gestures contribute mainly to producing emotional labor [7]. Picard proposed applications with emotions [30]. The most functional gestures for representing emotions use the eyes and mouth. Gestures especially have many roles for regulating other's behaviors. For example, several studies suggested that eyes evoke behavioral reponses in others [1][2]. Appropriate eye gazes generate fruitful discussion by signaling for appropriate turn-taking [35]. People in eastern cultures accept eyes as the main trigger for understanding intention, more so than the mouth [42].

On the basis of the above studies, the author created a device for showing eye gestures as a first prototype to demonstrate the possibility of the emotional cyborg. This device is named "AgencyGlass," which has agency inside the glasses. Utilizing HAI technologies and previous findings, the author implemented two functions. One is to extend and to calculate a user's emotional states by monitoring the user's behavior with sensors. The other is to show intention to other people through sharing gazes, called "joint attention" [26].

Hardware Implementation

The assembly of the prototype is shown in Fig. 2. This prototype was constructed with OLED displays the same size as the eyes and with a sunglasses-like interior.

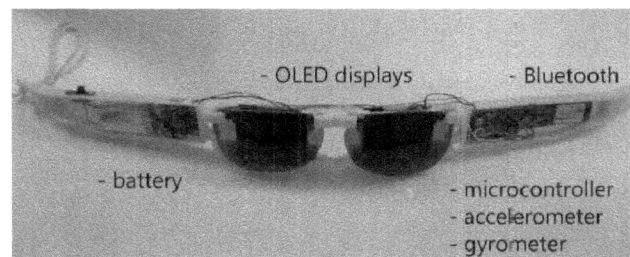

Figure 2.   Prototype of AgencyGlass. The eye area includes thin displays. The frames have a battery and electrical circuits.

A user's emotions are pre-recorded and played by using a program. The glasses have a 3-axis gyrometer and 3-axis accelerometer for monitoring a user's behaviors, and it connects to a PC or a smartphone via Bluetooth. A connected computer detects and monitors the user's environmental conditions. Support for emotional labor is achieved by both the glasses and a computer. Dark lenses (made by black acryl) around the OLED displays hide your real eyes and sustain the user's field of vision (Fig. 3). A user can perform daily tasks as usual while wearing the glasses. This sunglasses-like setup also provides more natural eye representation. Showing the eyes insides glasses is more natural than just showing the displays. The author implemented several prototypes to make represntations natural.

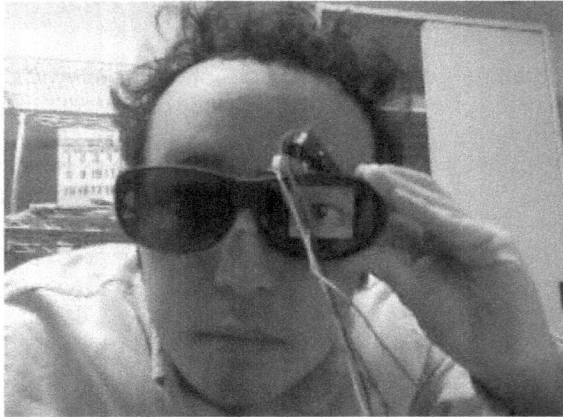

Figure 3. Real eyes hidden with black acryl (in prototype version of AgencyGlass, these glasses have only one display and are connected by wire)

The glasses extends user's emotional labor in several situations. For example, if the user nods to someone, the glasses show a blink. If the user shakes their head, the glasses show more blinks. If the user tilts his/her head, the glasses show an upward glance. In group discussion with facial recognition, if another member gazes at the user, the glasses display the motion of gazing toward the user. Although these expressions are simple, a person or group members could feel that they are cared for by the user. This emotional support reduces a user's cognitive load for social manners.

Prototype Video

The author created a prototype video to demonstrate AgencyGlass. The video shows several functions of AgencyGlass, shown in sections 3.1 and 3.2. For example, the glasses show several eye gestures made by monitoring the user's motion. The video also shows several cases of wearing AgencyGlass, such as reading books, walking, meeting people in a corridor, and having discussions. Figures 4, 5, 6, and 7 show examples of how AgencyGlass works. Figure 4 shows that these eye gestures are controllable depending on the user's behavior by using wearable sensors in the glass. Figure 5 shows that daily tasks are achievable with this prosthesis device. Figure 6 and 7 show working examples that combine face detection and eye gestures to accomplish social tasks.

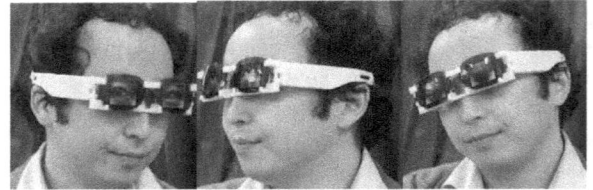

Figure 4. Extention of eye behavior with accelerometer and sensor. Head shaking is detected with the sensor and translated as left and right gazes. Head direction is detected with the accelerometer and translated as thinking and sleeping eye gestures.

Figure 5. Daily work (reading and walking) are achieved because field of vision is sustained.

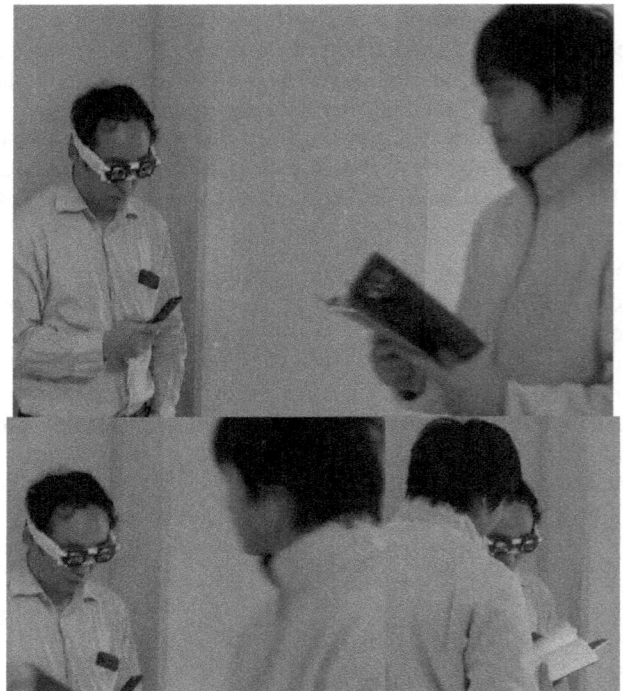

Figure 6. Automatic gaze-drawing helps avoid being talked to by others (upper figure is first frame, bottom left figure is second frame, and bottom right figure is third frame). Human motion is detected by external camera on his chest, and it shows gaze motion.

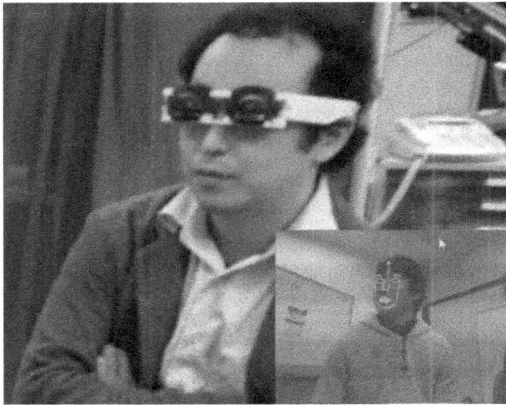

Figure 7. Image of proposal video for using AgencyGlass in group discussion. Face detection algorithm detects opponents motion and produces gaze reactions.

ANALYZING FEEDBACK

Feedback from Articles

The prototype video was presented at an international conference on human-robot interaction. After the presentation, several media outlets reported on the prototype. This author analyzed articles in which the author was directly interviewed and on feedback on the articles.

The earliest article was published in New Scientist [24]. This article focused more on the aspect of the technological advantage of AgencyGlass than on the purpose for solving emotional labor. The IEEE Spectrum was next to write about the prototype [22]. It exemplified the purpose of the study on emotional labor. This aspect is discussed in a BBC report [20]. An article by the Asia Press Front provided the specifications of the device [15]. These three news articles were translated and released in the USA, Autralia, New Zealand, the United Kingdom, France, Germany, Switzerland, Spain, Russia, Sweden, the Peoples Republic of China, Chile, Brazil, Taiwan, Israel, Vietnam, Idonesia, India, and Japan. Due to resource limitations, the author cannot analyze reactions other than those in English and Japanese reports.

Feedback from Comments: Positive and Negative

The above articles enhanced discussion. The IEEE Spectrum also accepted comments on the idea of emotional cyborg. The prototype video was also uploaded onto Youtube and played more than 100,000 times. also generating discussion. On Youtube, 81% of viewers rated the video positive (245 thumbs up) and 19% negative (58 thumbs down) [43]. There were 14 positive comments, 10 negative comments, and 36 uncategorized comments in the comment section of the video. Found in the positive comments was praise for complementing emotional labor, the hope of being able to use the technology because of suffering from emotional labor, and advice on attaching the

device to people who are not good at expressing emotions. Amongst the negative comments were people who claimed that the proposal and appearance are scary and horrible. There was a hypothesis that Japanese society requires such a social solution in the uncategorized comments. In the IEEE Spectrum article, there were three positive comments, four negative comments, and seven uncategorized comments. In the article, there was the comment that if people know that someone is wearing AgencyGlass, the solution becomes useless. There was also the comment that emotional labor is also found on Facebook and that this is an offline version of the solution.

Several people also discussed AgencyGlass beyond weblogs and websites. On BBC News, Dr. Berthouze proposed the possibility of an emotional cyborg as a translated cultural representation by referring to Jack et al.'s work that shows different cultures have different emotions [19]. Garcia noted that this kind of emotional translation is a hard task [12]. A Huffington Post article contained much fruitful discussion in the comments, with people saying that those with Asperger's and myopia would be more naturally able to express emotion by using this prosthesis technology [5]. Sanova proposed the ethical issue that this kind of automation of emotional labor decreases our ability to drive emotion [36].

Discussion

The demonstrated proposal caused fruitful discussion online. There were both positive and negative comments about the notion of emotional cyborgs. Negative comments included those that claimed that the prototype is scary. There were two kinds of reactions here. The first found fault in the current implementation. The author estimates that these claims are solvable because we can precisely modify the lighting conditions and size of the eyes in the future. We may get more positive comments if other implementations are proposed. The second kind of reaction found fault in the idea itself. Some people felt that complementing emotional labor is not ethical. It is important that this aspect is discussed well. Sanova's article is important. From the author's viewpoint, these ethical questions are also the same as those surrounding physical and mental labor. As shown in section 2, emotional labor is fundamentally implemented in our brain, so the question needs to be generalized to what kind of labor is needed to be replaced and what is not. In the future, to use an emotional cyborg as well as AgencyGlass, we need to focus on what kind of area is socially accepted.

It is important that although the current implementation has several defects, a rather large group of people require such a kind of prosthesis technology for emotion. Some comments noted the cultural difference in the background of the author. There is a study that states that Japanese society invests a lot of energy in social interactions both offline and online [38]. However, emotional labor is found in several countries [37], and the feedback on the prototype suggests that solutions are needed by people all over the world. This result suggests that although the expressions of emotion is different according to the culture, the need for an emotional cyborg is universal.

Limitation
In this paper, emotional labor as new application of HAI technologies is proposed. The author demonstrated the proposal with an organized demonstration video and evaluated the result with feedback from media and comments. This paper should contribute to evaluating what kind of reactions will be gained from society. However, this feedback is given just by video and not given through direct user interaction. Making a working prototype for emotional labor in the real world is a more difficult technological task. In the next phase, The author will implement a working application of AgencyGlass by attaching several sensors and evaluate how the technology compensates for emotional labor in a user study.

CONCLUSION
The author proposed a novel kind of HAI application called the "emotional cyborg." The author summarized the route of emotional labor and how such a kind of social labor is supported by HAI technologies. The author implemented AgencyGlass, which is attached on the user's face and produces the user's eye gestures. The author proposed a prototype application for supporting emotional labor with AgencyGlass as a video presentation. The author analyzed the reactions from media and online feedback on the prototype and illustrated the future of HAI applications. Reactions revealed that although there are critical comments on the unease of using the implementation, the proposed emotional cyborg is accepted by many people.

ACKNOWLEDGMENTS
This work was supported by the JST PRESTO program.

REFERENCES
1. Bateson, M., Nettle, D., and Roberts, G. Cues of being watched enhance cooperation in a real-world setting. *Biology Letters 2*, 3 (2006), 412–414.

2. Bourrat, P., Baumard, N., and Mckay, R. Surveillance cues enhance moral condemnation. *Evolutionary Psychology 9*, 2 (2011), 193–199.

3. Byrne, R.W. and Whiten, A. *Machiavellian Intelligence: Social Expertise and the Evolution of Intellect in Monkeys, Apes, and Humans*. Oxford University Press, USA, 1989.

4. Colman, A.M. and Browning, L. Evolution of cooperative turn-taking. *Evolutionary Ecology Research 11*, (2009), 949–963.

5. Cooper-White, M. These 'Wearable Eyes' Make Your Face Look More Friendly Than You Feel. *The Huffington Post*, 2014.

6. Cormier, D., Young, J., Nakane, M., Newman, G., and Durocher, S. Would You Do as a Robot Commands? An Obedience Study for Human-Robot Interaction. *International Conference on Human-Agent Interaction*, (2013), I–3–1.

7. Darwin, C. *The expression of emotions in man and animals*. John Murray, 1872.

8. Dennett, D.C. *The Intentional Stance*. A Bradford Book, 1989.

9. Duffy, B.R. and Zawieska, K. Suspension of Disbelief in Social Robotics. *International Conference on Social Robotics*, (2012), 484–489.

10. Eyssel, F. and Hegel, F. (S)he's Got the Look: Gender Stereotyping of Robots. *Journal of Applied Social Psychology 42*, 9 (2012), 2213–2230.

11. Eyssel, F. and Loughnan, S. "It Don't Matter If You're Black or White"? *Social Robotics 8239*, October (2013), 422–431.

12. Garcia, M.I. Avatar eyes: Can cyborg glasses mimic all the complex emotions expressed by real eyes? *Rappler*, 2014. http://www.rappler.com/science-nature/ideas/science-solitaire/56286-science-solitaire-avatar-eyes.

13. Glas, D.F., Kanda, T., Ishiguro, H., and Hagita, N. Simultaneous teleoperation of multiple social robots. *Proceedings of the 3rd international conference on Human robot interaction*, ACM Press (2008), 311.

14. Haraway, D. A Cyborg Manifest: Science, technology, and socialist-feminism in the late twentieth century. In *The cybercultures reader*. Psychology Press, 2000, 291–324.

15. Hiyama, H. Skipping Emotoinal Cotnrol by Glass-type Device Developed by Japanese Scientist. *Asia Press Front*, 2014. http://www.afpbb.com/articles/-/3013259.

16. Hochschild, A.R. *The Managed Heart: Commercialization of Human Feeling*. 1983.

17. Hochschild, A.R. *The Managed Heart: Commercialization of Human Feeling*. University of California Press, 1983.

18. Iizuka, H., Ando, H., and Maeda, T. The Anticipation of Human Behavior Using "Parasitic Humanoid."In *Human-Computer Interaction. Ambient, Ubiquitous and Intelligent Interaction*. 2009, 284–293.

19. Jack, R.E., Garrod, O.G.B., Yu, H., Caldara, R., and Schyns, P.G. Facial expressions of emotion are not culturally universal. *Proceedings of the National Academy of Sciences of the United States of America 109*, 19 (2012), 7241–4.

20. Kelion, L. Cyborg glasses save users the need to control emotions. *British Broadcasting Corporation*, 2014. http://www.bbc.com/news/technology-27052773.

21. Kirman, B., Linehan, C., Lawson, S., and O'Hara, D. CHI and the future robot enslavement of humankind. *CHI '13 Extended Abstracts on Human Factors in Computing Systems on - CHI EA '13*, ACM Press (2013), 2199.

22. Lim, A. 'Wearable Eyes' Make You Appear Friendly, Social Even When You're Not. *IEEE Spectrum*, 2014. http://spectrum.ieee.org/automaton/robotics/artificial-intelligence/wearable-eyes-agencyglass-emotional-cyborgs.

23. Mann, S. and Cowburn, J. Emotional labour and stress within mental health nursing. *Journal of psychiatric and mental health nursing 12*, 2 (2005), 154–62.

24. Marks, P. Goggle-eyed glasses swap your lying eyes for fake ones. *NewScientist*, 2014. http://www.newscientist.com/article/dn25234-goggleeyed-glasses-swap-your-lying-eyes-for-fake-ones.html.

25. Matsukuma, K., Handa, H., and Yokoyama, K. Subjective Evaluation of Seal Robot: Paro - Tabulation and Analysis of Questionnaire Results -. *Journal of Robotics and Mechatronics 14*, 1 (2002), 13–19.

26. Ono, T. and Imai, M. A model of embodied communications with gestures between humans and robots. *23rd meeting of the Cognitive Science Society*, (2001), 760–765.

27. Osawa, H. Agentphobia and Emotional Labor : How Human-Agent Interaction Contributes to the Preservation of our Humanity. *The 1st International Conference on Human-Agent Interaction*, (2013), II-p1.

28. Osawa, H. Intelligence Arms Race: Delayed Reward Increases Complexity of Agent Strategies. *International Conference on Autonomous Agents and Multiagent Systems*, (2014), 789–796.

29. Phillips, S. Labouring the emotions: expanding the remit of nursing work? *Journal of Advanced Nursing 24*, 1 (1996), 139–143.

30. Picard, R.W. *Affective Computing*. MIT Press, 1997.

31. Premack, D. and Woodruff, G. Does the chimpanzee have a theory of mind? *Behavioral and Brain Sciences 1*, 04 (1978), 515–526.

32. Reeves, B. and Nass, C. *The Media Equation: How people treat computers, television, and new media like real people and places*. Stanford, 1996.

33. Rekimoto, J. and Saitoh, M. Augmented surfaces: a spatially continuous work space for hybrid computing environments. *ACM annual conference on Human Factors in Computing Systems*, ACM Press (1999), 378–385.

34. Sankai, Y. Leading Edge of Cybernics: Robot Suit HAL. *2006 SICE-ICASE International Joint Conference*, IEEE (2006), P–1–P–2.

35. Sato, R. and Takeuchi, Y. Coordinating Turn-Taking and Talking in Multi-Party Conversations by Controlling a Robot's Eye-Gaze. *International Conference on Human-Agent Interaction*, (2013), I–1–1.

36. Savona, S. AgencyGlass – the digital eyes that show emotion so YOU don't have to. *Think Inc.*, 2014. http://thinkinc.org.au/agencyglass-the-digital-eyes-that-show-emotion-so-you-dont-have-to/.

37. Smith, P. and Gray, B. Emotional labour of nursing revisited: Caring and Learning 2000. *Nurse Education in Practice 1*, 1 (2001), 42–49.

38. Takahashi, T. Youth, Social Media and Connectivity in Japan. In P. Seargeant and C. Tagg, eds., *The Language of Social Media: Community and Identity on the Internet*. 2014, 1–48.

39. Tamaki, E., Miyaki, T., and Rekimoto, J. PossessedHand: a hand gesture manipulation system using electrical stimuli. *Proceedings of the 1st International Conference on Augmented Human*, ACM Press (2010), 1–5.

40. Terada, K., Shamoto, T., Ito, A., and Mei, H. Reactive movements of non-humanoid robots cause intention attribution in humans. *International Conference on Intelligent Robots and Systems*, IEEE/RSJ (2007), 3715–3720.

41. Tsujita, H. and Rekimoto, J. HappinessCounter: smile-encouraging appliance to increase positive mood. *ACM annual conference on Human Factors in Computing Systems*, (2011), 117–126.

42. Yuki, M., Maddux, W.W., and Masuda, T. Are the windows to the soul the same in the East and West? Cultural differences in using the eyes and mouth as cues to recognize emotions in Japan and the United States. *Journal of Experimental Social Psychology 43*, 2 (2007), 303–311.

43. Video: Wearable Eyes Turn You Into Emotional Cyborg. *IEEE Spectrum*, 2014. https://www.youtube.com/watch?v=GhvHxz1NePQ.

Calamaro: Perceiving Robotic Motion in the Wild

John Harris[1] **Stephanie Law**[2] **Kazuki Takashima**[3] **Ehud Sharlin**[2] **Yoshifumi Kitamura**[3]

[1]University of Waterloo
Waterloo, Ontario, Canada
john.harris@uwaterloo.ca

[2]University of Calgary
Calgary, Alberta, Canada
{sjlaw;ehud}@ucalgary.ca

[3]Tohoku University
Sendai, Japan
{Takashima;kitamura}@riec.tohoku.ac.jp

ABSTRACT

We present our study of *Calamaro*: a robotic platform designed to investigate the impact of emotive motion on people, and its deployment in an extensive field study in a busy public space at the University of Calgary campus. Our paper details the design of the *Calamaro* robot, the field study conducted with it, including hundreds of observers and 88 participants, and our quantitative and qualitative findings. The paper provides a thorough discussion of the implications of our results on the design of robotic emotive motions, and reflections on the deployment of robotic interfaces in field studies.

Author Keywords

emotive motion; robot interaction in-the-wild; HRI

ACM Classification Keywords

H.5.m. Information Interfaces and Presentation (e. g. HCI): Miscellaneous

INTRODUCTION

Motion is a powerful channel of expression and as robots begin to take on increasingly personal roles in our daily lives it is expected that their inherent motion capabilities will become an important method for people to be able to communicate and interact with them in socially intuitive and easily understandable ways. In this paper we explore the concept of *emotive motion* as a design tool for social human-robot interaction research (HRI) by exploring how low-level style and characteristics of robotic movement (e.g. slowly, smoothly, sporadically, etc.) affect people's social and emotional interpretations of them when deployed in the public space.

The essence of life and liveliness is intimately linked to the concept of motion. From an etymological perspective, the Latin word *anima* refers to the concepts of "soul", "life",

"spirit", and "vital principal" and from this root we encounter the words *animal* ("living creature") and *animate* ("to impart life"). Intuitively, we gain that same impression from the world around us: things that are moving, changing, and reacting are seen as somehow "alive" whether they are biological creatures or not.

Besides simple liveliness, motion is also a powerful channel for emotional expression. For thousands of years, humans have been expressing emotions through theatre, dance, and gesture; conveying frustration, sorrow, jubilation, and an entire spectrum of powerful emotions using only the movement of our bodies. In contrast, a person who is entirely motionless (e.g. their chest not even breathing) are quickly presumed to be in distress, injured or deceased. In the world of film, master animators have demonstrated for decades that there is emotional power to be expressed in *how* characters move, above and beyond the specific gestures of *what* those characters are doing [1].

Arguably, motion is also one of the primary differentiating features between robots and other computerized agents. Unlike virtual agents, robots are capable of moving through their environment: gesturing, reacting, exploring, communicating, and affecting their surroundings in very dynamic, physical ways. Whether a robot's purpose is to serve, create, explore, or destroy, it is this ability to move, interact, and affect the same physical world that we, as humans, live in which distinguishes them from almost all other forms of modern technology.

This paper presents the evaluation of *Calamaro* (Figure 1) a robotic platform designed specifically for the study of *emotive motion*, which we deployed in a field study in a busy public space gathering finding on the impact of emotive motion as well as on the challenges of running HRI studies in-the-wild.

RELATED WORK

The importance of pursuing HRI research challenges in-the-wild, and of understanding how social HRI experiences change when they move from the laboratory into the "real world" has been highlighted by several HRI researchers. A few examples include in-the-wild observations of a robotic conference attendee, and a robotic receptionist [2], in the field observations of robot guides in a train-station [3], and in a building [4], and observations of androids deployed in public spaces [5,6].

Figure 1 - The *Calamaro* prototype with its eight arms

Emotive motion is arguably inherent to all robotic interfaces, with seminal work on the affective capabilities of moving, non-living, abstract objects dating to the 1944 experiment by Heider and Simmel [7]. Emotive motion was explicitly explored in several recent HRI efforts: for example, Hoffman and Breazeal's robotic desk lamp assisted its human partners with what was perceived as intelligent and often emotive actions through simple physical gestures and movements [8]. Mutlu et al. projected a collection of abstract moving geometric shapes onto a display with the intent of eliciting specific emotional responses such as happiness, nervousness, or fear by animating the displayed shapes according to designated patterns [9]. In [10] the authors demonstrated how motion paths could be used to express different robot personalities and intents. A study by Saerbeck and Bartneck [11] investigated emotive motion by asking participants to rate their emotional responses to robotic motions with different acceleration and curvature. Nomura and Nakao studied how age and cultural differences affect the interpretation of robotic emotive motion [12], and the Stem project [13] used movements by an abstract robotic-stick for emotive expression. Takayama et. al. proposed to employ animation principles in HRI motion design [14], and recent efforts mapped emotive motion to future, actuated, semi-robotic mobile phones [15,16]. The *Calamaro* effort presented in this paper can inform these HRI research threads through its focus on exploration of robotic *emotive motion* via an extensive field study.

CALAMARO

Our goal was to design a robot with semi-zoomorphic attributes which is capable of a range of engaging *emotive motion*s and can be deployed in the field. Rather than seclude our participants in a serene and reflective but practically unnatural lab environment we wanted to take an in-the-wild approach. Our motivation was to pursue a greater sense of how our findings might generalize to robotic *emotive motion* in daily life.

The prototype we designed, *Calamaro* (Figure 1) is named after the singular of the Italian word "calamari" (a food recipe involving squid). In line with our original design goal, this articulated robot has visual appearance which is vaguely animalistic (e.g. an octopus) while still being heavily robotic. *Calamaro* has multiple distinct appendages, including wheeled legs, a 3-axis "head", and eight individual arms with three degrees of freedom each. *Calamaro*'s movements were designed to allow us to explore a spectrum of *emotive motion* themes relating to the speed, repetition and coordination of its appendages.

Calamaro was programmed to perform a set of 5 motion sequences using a combination of 3 different motion styles. In between each motion, the robot returns to a neutral position where its head is facing forward and all of its arms are evenly spaced around it, leveled, and pointing outwards like the spokes of a wheel. We attempt to describe each of the five *Calamaro* motions as clearly as is possible in text as follows:

1. *Simple Breathing* – *Calamaro*'s arms would begin laid out flat in an evenly spaced circle around its body. They would then rise to +25°, fall to -25°, and then return to level. At the same time, the robot's head would rise and fall slightly. The desired impression was that *Calamaro* was taking a deep breath and then exhaling slowly.

2. *Defensive Cage* – The robot would look once from side to side, roll backwards, and then raise its arms around itself; turning them about their axis so as to form a defensive wall around the perimeter of its head and body. Once "caged", *Calamaro* would look around again before lowering its defensive wall and returning to its neutral position. The desired impression was that *Calamaro* was guarding itself against some threat in front of it; as a boxer raises their hands to block incoming punches.

3. *Table Tap* – First, the robot would align all of its arms so that the four arms on its left side pointed directly left, all parallel, and the four arms on its right pointed directly to its right, also all parallel. It would then look over and down to its right and tap the table with its right arms and then return the arms to level. It would then repeat this tapping motion on its left side and then return to the neutral position. The desired impression was that *Calamaro* was "checking" the feel/sound of the table next to it.

4. *Ebb and Flow* – Similar to "Table Tap", but more closely resembling a smooth dancing manoeuvre. Without aligning its arms, *Calamaro* would roll sideways to the right while lowering its right arms and raising its left arms. Its head would roll into the slide and briefly dip down. It would then repeat this move to the left; lowering its left arms, raising its right, and dipping its head down and to the left before returning to its neutral position. The desired impression was

that *Calamaro* was suavely sliding from side to side, as if dancing.

5. *Prairie Chicken* – *Calamaro* arranges its four rear arms like the tail feathers of a turkey or peacock; sticking straight up into the air behind the robot's head. The remaining four front arms (two pairs of two) are arranged like "wings" to the front and sides of its body. The robot then rolls forward while rocking all of its arms side to side repeatedly before retreating. The desired impression was that *Calamaro* was presenting an aggressive display and challenging the observers in front of it; much as a real bird might try to intimidate an opponent and scare it away.

The content of *Calamaro*'s five motion patterns was not the primary focus of our research of *emotive motion*. Instead, we designed our experiment to study three simple "styles" under which these five motions would be performed. Each "style" had two attributes which were systematically combined in a 2 x 2 x 2 schema of conditions. Each motion sequence was scripted in such a way that there was only one sequence of steps for each and it was the combination of the different style conditions that would dictate how those steps were interpreted. *Calamaro*'s three styles of movements are described below:

A. *Fast or Slow* – A given sequence of motion steps would be interpreted and performed either quickly or more slowly. Each condition was just as smooth as the other, with only the time taken for each step being elongated or shortened.

B. *Sequential (Mechanical) or Simultaneous (Organic)* – *Calamaro*'s motion sequences consisted of discreet gestures. In the Sequential condition, these individual gestures would be performed separately, one after the other. (E.g. Raise arms, then turn head, and then roll forward.) In the Simultaneous condition, all of the distinct gestures would be performed at the same time. (E.g. Raise arms while turning head and rolling forward.) This style distinction also extended to individual gestures involving multiple motor axes working in unison and was especially evident with arm gestures. (E.g. either each of the eight arm motors would move one after the other until all of the arms were "raised", or the arms would all rise at the same time.)

C. *Repeating or Non-Repeating* – In the Repeating condition, once a complete motion sequence was finished, *Calamaro* would perform the same motion again and again. (E.g. Breathing, breathing, breathing...) In the Non-Repeating condition, *Calamaro* would randomly select a new motion each time. (E.g. Breathing, Defensive Cage, Prairie Chicken...).

During interactive sessions *Calamaro* cycles between motion styles approximately every half hour, ensuring that during a study participants interacting with *Calamaro* viewed only one type of motion style.

STUDY

The study was conducted in a crowded public space at the food court area of the University of Calgary campus, in three different sessions with over 12 hours of *Calamaro* interaction, and hundreds of observers and participants. The *Calamaro* robot was placed in the center of a large, round, 150cm diameter wooden table (Figure 2). Attached to the front and mounted on stands to either side of the table were three large information posters describing that a research study was being conducted and that the study area was being recorded via both video and audio.

Two experimenters were present with handheld audio recorders to interview passing visitors who expressed interest in the robot. In order to maintain some element of serendipity, these interviewers specifically avoided soliciting interest in the study and did not actively approach any passersby. If however someone chose to stop and examine the robot or speak with the interviewers, these people were then approached and questioned about their thoughts and impression of *Calamaro*. These people were classified as Category 1 participants.

Generally the participants would immediately begin a dialog with the interviewer. Otherwise, the interviewers would eventually prompt Category 1 participants with open-ended questions such as "*What do you think of the robot?*", "*What do you think it's doing?*", or "*Why do you think it is doing that?*" The interviewers would then ask more focused questions such as "*What can you say about the way the robot is moving?*" or "*Do the robot's motions remind you of anything?*"

Figure 2 - *Calamaro* deployed at the University of Calgary's food court

When answering questions posed by the participants, interviewers would attempt to avoid biasing the participants; often by deflecting the participant's inquiries back at them. For example, if a participant asked *"What is the robot for?"* the interviewer would respond with *"What do you think it's for?"* Depending on how persistent a participant would be with their inquiries, interviewers would eventually defer to email addresses displayed on the information posters and assure the participant that their detailed questions would be answered at a later time. The purpose of this was to avoid revealing the purpose of the study to the general population. We wanted to avoid having new participants arrive, having been briefed by their friends, with a pre-conceived focus on the robot's motions.

After being interviewed, the Category 1 participants were invited to fill out an additional questionnaire that asked more specific questions about their emotional interpretation of the robot and its motions. These survey sheets also included a section asking the participants for consent to a) analyze their survey results and/or b) use their un-blurred recorded video footage for academic publications. If these people chose to fill out a questionnaire sheet, they were then classified as Category 2 participants and were led to one of the nearby cafeteria seats where one of the experimenters would explain and administer the survey.

Having had an opportunity to observe and interact with *Calamaro*, Category 2 participants were presented with the Bartneck, et al. "Godspeed Questionnaire Series" Likert-scale style questionnaire [17]. The participants were asked to rate how applicable they felt different pairs of emotionally descriptive adjectives were to the robot and its motions. The Godspeed Questionnaires allow participants to reflect on concepts such as anthropomorphism, animacy, likeability, perceived intelligence, and perceived safety of robots; all of which relate to *emotive motion* and its impact on social HRI. For each participant, the order of each individual adjective pair was randomized, as was the ordering of all adjective pairs within the list (e.g. the order of the first, second, third, word pairs would differ randomly between participants.) Having completed the questionnaire, Category 2 participants were thanked and then allowed to depart.

RESULTS

The *Calamaro* study was conducted over the course of three sessions on separate days. Each session lasted from 11AM in the morning until 3PM in the afternoon; covering the high-traffic lunch hours of each day for a net total of 12 hours. Over the course of these three study sessions, hundreds of people observed *Calamaro* from afar; either watching it while walking through the food court or while sitting and eating. Of these, many dozens of people stopped to closely inspect the robot and talk with the experimenters about the study (Category 1). Of these, a total of 88 participants (70 male, 18 female) completed our written survey (Category 2). The average age of our Category 2

participants was 24.59 (standard deviation of 7.42). Part of the written survey was demographic and asked participants to describe their professional or academic background. We grouped their responses into four major categories: robotics oriented (e.g. mechanical/electrical engineering, computer science), technical but non-robotics oriented (e.g. chemistry, astronomy), non-technical but creative (e.g. artists, musicians, teachers), and non-technical non-creative (e.g. secretary, plumber). (Figure 3)

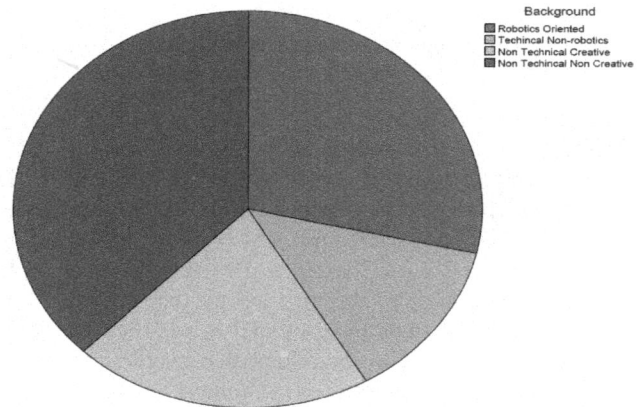

Figure 3: participants' demography

Quantitative Results

We performed an analysis of variance (ANOVA) on our collected survey data and found multiple main effects and 2-way interactions between our movements style conditions. We chose to run a factorial analysis of variance (ANOVA) because we were interested in comparing the different conditions of movement, speed and repetition. A covariance analysis was not conducted as there were no significant correlations found between the data and the demographic data we collected.

Main Effects

1) Comparing the simultaneous (organic) condition to the sequential (mechanical) condition, the following main effects were observed:

a) Participants rated the robot as significantly more natural under the organic movement type condition (M = 3.26) than under the mechanical movement type condition (M = 2.59) averaged over speed and repetition. $F(88) = 4.95, p = .029$.

b) Participants rated the robot as significantly more organic under the organic movement type condition (M = 2.50) than under the mechanical movement type condition (M = 1.83) averaged over speed and repetition. $F(88) = 5.41, p = .023$

c) Participants rated the robot as significantly more interactive under the organic movement type condition (M = 3.16) than under the mechanical movement type condition (M = 2.95) averaged over speed and repetition. $F(88) = 5.25, p = .025$

d) Participants rated the robot as significantly more kind under the organic movement type condition (M = 3.82) than under the mechanical movement type condition (M = 3.33) averaged over speed and repetition. F(88) = 4.43, p = .039

2) Comparing the repeating condition to the non-repeating condition, the following main effects were observed:

a) Participants rated the robot as significantly more relaxed with repetition (M = 3.80) than without repetition (M = 3.08) averaged over speed and movement type. F(88) = 4.46, p = .038

b) Participants rated the robot as significantly more calm with repetition (M = 4.12) than without repetition (M = 2.82) averaged over speed and movement type. F(88) = 22.52, p = .000

Two-way Interactions
1) There were two-way interactions between movement style and repetition:

a) For the fake/natural pair, participants rated the robot as more fake under the mechanical movement condition (M = 2.50) than the organic movement type condition (M = 3.79) when there was no repetition, t = 4.47, p = .026. There was no significant difference in ratings found when there was repetition between the mechanical movement type (M = 2.67) and organic movement type (M = 2.72) conditions.

b) For the mechanical/organic word pair, participants rated the robot as more mechanical under the mechanical movement type condition (M = 1.53) than the organic movement type condition (M = 2.67) when there was no repetition, t = 4.10, p = .002. There was no significant difference in ratings found when there was repetition between the mechanical movement type (M = 2.13) and the organic movement type (M = 2.33).

c) For the unfriendly/friendly word pair, participants rated the robot as less friendly under the mechanical movement type condition (M = 3.63) than the organic movement type condition (M = 4.22) when there was no repetition, t = 2.15. The effect of movement type was not the same for all levels of repetition as with repetition, the participants rated the robot as more friendly under the mechanical movement type condition (M = 4.19) than the organic movement type condition (M = 3.61).

d) For the anxious/relaxed word pair, participants rated the robot as more relaxed when repeating under the mechanical condition (M = 4.27) than when not repeating under the mechanical condition (M =2.75), t = 4.40, p = .001. There was no significant difference found in ratings under the organic movement type condition with repetition (M = 3.33) or without repetition (M = 3.41).

2) There were two-way interactions between speed and movement style:

a) For the mechanical/organic word pair, participants rated the robot as more mechanical under the mechanical movement type condition (M = 1.56) than under the organic movement type condition (M = 2.83) when the speed was slow, t = 3.90, p = .001. There was no significant difference in ratings found between the mechanical movement type (M = 2.10) and organic movement type (M = 2.17) when the speed was fast.

b) For the foolish/sensible word pair, participants rated the robot as more foolish under the mechanical movement type condition (M = 3.08) than under the organic movement type condition (M = 4.39) when the speed was slow, t = 4.35, p = .002. There was no significant difference in ratings found between the mechanical movement type (M = 3.42) and organic movement type (M = 3.03) when the speed was fast.

3) There were two-way interactions between speed and repetition:

a) For the ignorant/knowledgeable word pair, participants rated the robot as more ignorant with repetition (M = 2.78) than without repetition (M = 3.62) when the speed was slow, t = 2.76, p = .042. There was no significant difference in ratings found between the with repetition condition (M= 3.67) and the no repetition condition (M = 2.82) when the speed was fast.

b) For the agitated/calm word pair, participants rated the robot as more agitated with repetition (M = 4.50) than with no repetition (M = 2.11) when the speed was fast, t = 7.52, p = .000. There was no significant difference in ratings found between the repetition condition (M = 3.75) and no repetition condition (M = 3.53) when the speed was slow.

Qualitative Results
Over the course of the three separate sessions of the *Calamaro* study, a number of interesting interaction themes emerged. These are summarized as follows:

A Sense of Entitlement
An unforeseen consequence of this new study environment was a distinct "sense of entitlement" from many of the passersby. Often the very first question the experimenters received from many people was *"Ok, so what's this about?", "What's the story here?",* or *"Ok, give me the spiel. What's going on?"* followed by the participant crossing their arms and waiting for an explanation. Unlike a more classical ethnographic field study (where the experimenters are almost completely hidden and attempt to never interfere with the population they are studying), our study was designed (and our ethics clearance necessitated) that the experimenters be present and visible at all times during each session. Together with the large, highly visible information posters, this turned the experiment into more of a "kiosk" or "information booth at a convention" experience than a "natural encounter with a robot in-the-wild"-style experience as we initially intended.

Hands-on Interaction

While we felt a true "robot in-the-wild" experiment would be even more interesting, we learned over the course of preparing and mounting our *Calamaro* study that it would also take a tremendous amount of preparation and safety precautions (for both the participants and the robot) that we do not think would have been feasible given the resources available to us, in retrospect. *Calamaro* is a relatively fragile robot and, even with the experimenters present, the robot often came close to being man-handled and physically abused by the public participants to the point of being broken and needing to be repaired. It appeared that these hands-on participants were generally interested in testing *Calamaro*'s strength out of a natural sense of curiosity.

On one hand, it is highly likely that the current *Calamaro* prototype would not have survived for very long if participants were allowed free-reign of their physical interaction with it. This is primarily because the available motors and control programming did not account for extreme motor loads. *Calamaro* simply interpreted its motion scripts and performed its movements unthinkingly. If one of *Calamaro*'s motors were to become obstructed, it would continue to push against the obstacle until either the blockage was removed or the motor overloaded and shut down. While rare, the nearby experimenters worked to avoid this scenario by asking particularly hands-on participants to treat the robot more gently and discouraged aggressive handling.

On the other hand, we find it interesting that so many participants at least asked if they could touch and interact with *Calamaro*. Despite its unfamiliar appearance, unknown purpose, and often rapidly moving appendages, relatively few people appeared to be afraid of the robot. Instead, most participants seemed more to be intrigued, curious, or entertained by *Calamaro* and hence their desire to see just how closely they could interact with it.

We feel that this level of comfort arose out of two possible factors: 1) The "information booth" appearance of the study area; complete with waiting "information attendants" (e.g. the nearby experimenters with microphones). 2) The small, pet-like size of the robot, its lack of physically intimidating presence, and its relatively slow locomotion speed. One could easily "escape" from the robot, if necessary, so people may have felt bolder when approaching it.

The Effect of Background Training, and Self Selection

As could be expected the academic or professional background of a participant often greatly affected the tone of their interview responses. Technically oriented individuals, particularly those with engineering backgrounds or work involving robotics, approached *Calamaro* by comparing it to their own work or analysing its construction. E.g. "*So what did you use for the controller?*", "*How powerful are the motors?*", "*If it doesn't have any sensors, then it's just a toy.*"

Alternatively, there were numerous non-technically oriented participants for whom *Calamaro* was an entertaining curiosity. These participants were more likely to ask about the robot's name, refer to it as "*Calamaro*" or "he" as opposed to "it", and generally treated is as something with character rather than just as a machine. These participant's inquiries were more often directed towards the nature of the study and the experimenters' motivations.

Regardless of their technical background, all of the *Calamaro* study participants were self-selected. That is, participants decided to stop by the *Calamaro* food court table and join our study due to their interest in the robot. By negation, we assume that our study may be missing a subset of the population that had little interest in the robot and thus decided not to stop-by and participate. This self-selection bias is an interesting challenge for the design of future in-the-wild HRI studies, which may look for ways to "force" interaction with the robot, or seek mechanisms that will enable input also from people that decided against interaction with the robot.

Public vs. Private Reflection

Unlike usability lab settings *Calamaro*'s in-the-wild settings generated a unique atmosphere and challenges. First and foremost, we felt that the internally reflective comments from *Calamaro* participants was of low quality. When asked about their impressions of the robot participants were generally quick to respond, as if being quizzed for a known answer, rather than pausing to reflect and present their own well-formed thoughts. Part of this might be attributable to the high-pace nature of the public food court: people are either there to study, eat or are passing through on their way to different destinations. Some of the most popular comments from all of our participants were variations on "*That's cool!*" or "*That's impressive!*"; commenting on the robot and the study itself rather than their thoughts on the specific qualities of the robot's motions or visual characteristics. That any robot at all was moving and gesturing in the middle of the food court was more noteworthy and more unexpected than details about the robot itself or its motions.

Group Reflection

Unique to the *Calamaro* study was the possibility for participants to reflect as a group. A number of groups (e.g. sports teams, groups of colleagues out for lunch, student club members, conference attendees, etc.) stopped to observe the robot and were subsequently interviewed as a whole. Individual comments would be proposed, reiterated, added-to, or countered by other members of the collective. Often this would lead to the formation of consensus (E.g. "*Yeah, you're right... it does kind of look like an octopus.*"). We question whether this apparent group-think also had the effect of suppressing some of the less popular or more esoteric responses.

In other cases, in particular a group of robotic engineers and their non-engineer friend, the deliberation led to subtle conflict: a set of engineering graduate students that were working on a search-and-rescue robot for the University were particularly critical of *Calamaro*. They immediately regarded the robot as a machine with no intelligence or emotive impact and, once they recognized the relative simplicity of the robot's mechanics and control technology, were visibly unimpressed with *Calamaro*'s technical aspects as well.

However, a single non-engineering-oriented member of the group who claimed to have no understanding of how either *Calamaro* or the search-and-rescue robot worked clearly expressed a dissenting opinion and drew laughs and mild indignation from his friends. This participant then went on to explain that, because *Calamaro* actually "worked" (e.g. continued to move and perform without outside intervention for dozens of minutes at a time, despite his not having been told what the robot's "purpose" was), he was far more impressed with *Calamaro* than with his companions' more advanced, more capable, and more expensive platform that constantly suffered from technical problems which prevented it from consistently "working". "Reliability" was a characteristic that we had so far not considered in our experimental designs. Similar statements were also made by other participants with technically-oriented backgrounds. They complimented us on how well *Calamaro* appeared to be functioning and expressed exasperation over how difficult it often was to keep robot prototypes in good working order; especially when operating "in the field".

DISCUSSION

Running *Calamaro* as a field study was an attempt to bring some "real world legitimacy", or external validity, to our exploration of *emotive motion*. Although we encountered unexpected challenges in terms of how we were able to mount our study and publicly portray our robot, we gained important insights into both different *emotive motion* characteristics, the differences between conducting controlled laboratory studies and experiments in-the wild, and how that difference in setting affects emotional interpretations of social robots.

Impact on the Design of *Emotive motion*

The statistical analysis of our *Calamaro* survey results reveal that the more repetitive segments of the motion were perceived as being calmer and more relaxed. We believe that regardless of the complexity or duration of a robot's motion pattern, once an observer has perceived it to have fallen into a predictable pattern, a sense of expectedness and calm arises.

Robot motion that is smoother and more complex (e.g. simultaneous coordination of multiple appendages) was generally interpreted as more natural, more organic, more interactive, more friendly, more intelligent, more calm, and

more kind; all of which can be viewed as beneficial traits when attempting to design pleasant social interactions between humans and social robotic agents. In contrast, "typical" robotic motion (e.g. jerky, linear, rigid, sequential, and repetitious) may be failing to take advantage of the expressive power of *emotive motion*.

We view these themes as our most important experimental results: The quality and style of a robot's motions, regardless of that robot's purpose or visual form, carried with it an important emotional weight and should be a deliberate focus when designing social human-robot interaction scenarios.

Impact on Social HRI Study Design

Our study proved an eye opener for us on the realities of deploying a robot into a busy public space, with little ability to gain personal and reflective interaction between the robot and participants. Social HRI researchers should be prepared for the practical challenges of bringing their robot prototypes out of the safety of the lab and into the unpredictable chaos of public spaces.

Most current robots are often relatively fragile and largely helpless devices which require constant supervision and regular maintenance. However, if social robots are to become the ubiquitous, daily experience that many envision they will become, then they must be capable of dealing with overzealous humans (and potentially overt vandalism), mechanical failure, complex and dynamic public environments, and many other challenges.

Even in the semi-controlled scenario of an academic field study, researchers must be aware of the unique social interactions (e.g. group consensus, time pressures, public expectations) that are simply not possible to emulate in a laboratory setting.

CONCLUSION AND FUTURE WORK

In this paper we discussed the development of our *Calamaro* robot prototype and its deployment in a field study. The study's results revealed some of the unique influences and challenges that rise when running HRI studies in-the-wild, and that can affect the design of robotic *emotive motion*. Our initial investigations into the expressive capabilities of *emotive motion* remain far from exhaustive, and much future work is called for.

In the short term a thorough, grounded-theory analysis of the *Calamaro* study video data could perhaps uncover some more interesting, if subtle, trends. We would also like to redesign *Calamaro* in a more locomotive fashion: although our current prototype has wheels, due to safety concerns about it accidentally rolling off the table *Calamaro*'s locomotion was extremely limited during our field study. This is a major limitation since locomotion is another entire aspect of motion that we did not really address in our current set of studies. We would also like to evaluate an interactive *Calamaro*: although some participants still thought the robot was able to react to their presence and actions, *Calamaro* never exhibited true interactivity. Adding an interactive layer could allow us to explore the role of interactivity in emotive motion with the *Calamaro* platform.

Through movement, humans and robots can express both powerful and subtle emotions. As robots continue to advance in complexity and capability, it is predicted that they will play increasingly larger roles in our daily lives, and that it will becoming increasingly important that robots will be able to communicate and interact naturally with their human counterparts. Robotic *emotive motion* will play an important role in the design of such future robotic agents and we hope that our *Calamaro* effort will help with additional insight on this research direction, and will add to the accumulated experience of running HRI studies in-the-wild.

ACKNOWLEDGMENTS
We thank the HAI'14 reviewers for their helpful comments, and NSERC Discovery Grant for enabling our research.

REFERENCES
1. Johnston, O. and Thomas, F. *The Illusions of Life: Disney Animation*. Disney Editions (1995)

2. Sabanovic, S., Michalowski, M. P., and Simmons, R. Robots in the Wild: Observing Human-Robot Social Interaction Outside the Lab. The 18th IEEE International Symposium on Robot and Human Interactive Communication, (pp. 816-821). Standbul, Turkey. (2009).

3. Shiomi, M., Sakamoto, D., Kanda, T., Ishi, C. T., Ishiguro, H., & Hagita, N. A semi-autonomous communication robot: a field trial at a train station. Proceedings of the 3rd ACM/IEEE international conference on human robot interaction. Amsterdam, Netherlands. (2008).

4. Bohus, D., Saw, C., and Horvitz E., Directions Robot: In-the-Wild Experiences and Lessons Learned, AAMAS'14. Proceedings of the 2014 international conference on Autonomous Agents and Multi-Agent Systems. Pages 637-644. (2014).

5. Becker-Asano, C., Ogawa, K., Nishio, S. and Ishiguro, H., Exploring the Uncanny Valley with Geminoid HI-1 in a Real-World Application, IADIS International Conference Interfaces and Human Computer Interaction (2010)

6. Pütten, M. A., Krämer, N., Becker-Asano, C., and Ishiguro, H., An Android in the Field, HRI'11, Proceedings of the 6th international conference on Human-robot interaction, March 6–9, 2011, Lausanne, Switzerland. (2011)

7. Heider, F., and Simmel, M. An Experimental Study of Apparent Behavior. *The American Journal of Psychology*, 57 (2), 243-259. (1944)

8. Hoffman, G., and Breazeal, C. Anticipatory Perceptual Simulation for Human-Robot Joint Practice: Theory and Application Study. Proceedings of the Twenty-Third AAAI Conference on Artificial Intelligence. (2008)

9. Mutlu, B., Forlizzi, J., Nourbakhsh, I., and Hodgins, J. The Use of Abstraction and Motion in the Design of Social Interfaces. DIS 2006. University Park, Pennsylvania, USA. (2006)

10. Young, J., Sharlin, E., and Igarashi, T. Teaching Robots Style: Designing and Evaluating Style-by-Demonstration for Interactive Robotic Locomotion. *Human-Computer Interaction*, 28(5), 2013. Taylor. (2013)

11. Saerbeck, M., and Bartneck, C. Perception of affect elicited by robot motion. Proceedings of the 5th ACM/IEEE international conference on Human-robot interaction (pp. 53-60). Osaka, Japan. (2010)

12. Nomura, T., and Nakao, A. Comparison on Identification of Affective Body Motions by Robots Between Elder People and University Students: A Case Study in Japan, *International Journal of Social Robotics*, 2(2). (2010)

13. Harris, J., and Sharlin, E. Exploring the Affect of Abstract Motion in Social Human-Robot Interaction, RO-MAN'11, the 20th IEEE International Symposium on Robot and Human Interactive Communication, July 31 - August 3, 2011, Atlanta, GA, USA. (2011).

14. Takayama, L., Dooley, D., and Ju, W., Expressing Thought: Improving Robot Readability with Animation Principles, HRI'11, Proceedings of the 6th international conference on Human-robot interaction, March 6–9, 2011, Lausanne, Switzerland. (2011)

15. Dawson, J. et al., It's Alive! Exploring the Design Space of a Gesturing Phone, Proceedings of Graphics Interface Conference GI'13, Regina, Saskatchewan, Canada (2013)

16. Hemmert, F., Löwe, M., Wohlauf, A., and Joost, G., Animate Mobiles: Proxemically Reactive Posture Actuation as a Means of Relational Interaction with Mobile Phones, TEI'13, Proceedings of the International Conference on Tangible, Embedded, and Embodied Interaction, Feb. 2013, Barcelona, Spain. (2013)

17. Bartneck, C., Kulic, D., Croft, E., and Zoghbi, S. Measurement Instruments for the Anthropomorphism, Animacy, Likeability, Perceived Intelligence, and Perceived Safety of Robots. January 2009, *International Journal of Social Robotics*, 1 (71-81). (2009)

Volume Adaptation and Visualization by Modeling the Volume Level in Noisy Environments for Telepresence System

Akira Hayamizu, Michita Imai,
Keio University
3-14-1, Hiyoshi, Kohokuku,
Yokohama, Japan
michita@ailab.ics.keio.ac.jp

Keisuke Nakamura, Kazuhiro Nakadai
Honda Research Institute Japan
8-1, Honmachi, Wakoshi, Japan
{keisuke, nakadai}@jp.honda-ri.com

ABSTRACT

The Lombard effect is the involuntary tendency of speakers to increase their vocal effort when speaking in a loud noise to enhance the audibility of their voice. There is a problem in telecommunication due to the Lombard effect. A speaker talks at a louder volume than necessary for the conversation partner at a remote location. This paper proposes a volume model that is required in order to automatically adjust the volume of an operator's voice at a remote communication via a telepresence robot, and develops an optimal volume control system LombaBot equipped on a telepresence robot with the model. The volume model measures the level of noise around the robot and the distance between a conversation partner and the robot to adjust the volume of the operator's voice. It has two types of volume adjustments. Those are called comfortable volume and secret talk volume. LombaBot enables people at a remote site to listen comfortably to the voice of a robot operator. Moreover, the operator is able to talk in low voices when s/he wants to talk in secret with nearby people. We confirmed that LombaBot adjusted the volume of an operator's voice properly in the noisy remote location.

Author Keywords

Tele-presence robot; Tele-communication; Volume Model; Adjusting Volume;

ACM Classification Keywords

H.5.m. Information interfaces and presentation (e.g., HCI): Miscellaneous.

HAI '14, October 29 - 31 2014, Tsukuba, Japan
Copyright 2014 ACM 978-1-4503-3035-0/14/10···$15.00.
http://dx.doi.org/10.1145/2658861.2658875

INTRODUCTION

Telepresence robot is based on the physical presence of the robot. Commercialized telepresence robots already exist such as Texai of Suitable Techmology's and QB of the Anybots Inc 1 & 2. Some studies examined the benefit of using a telepresence robot in daily situations 3 & 4. On the other hand, a sound environment around the telepresence robot is severer than that of a video conference system because the sound environment around the robot varies dynamically depending on the movement of the robot. The telepresence robot needs to take into account the sound environment around the robot in order to assist a verbal communication between the operator and people around the robot.

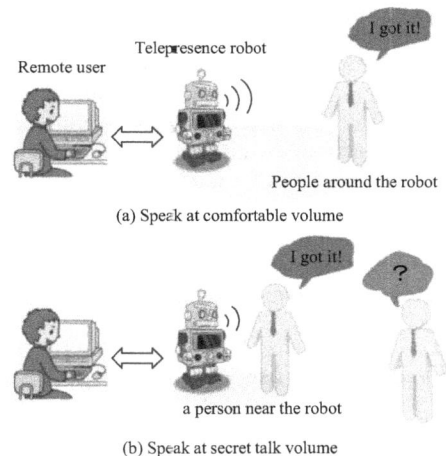

Figure1: an optimal volume control system

The main problem in telecommunication is the difference in the sound environment between a local site and a remote site. The operator of a telepresence robot is in the remote site, and controls the robot in the local site. It is hard for the operator to recognize the sound environment of the local site via the robot and to adjust her/his voice volume to the local site. In addition, there is a phenomenon called the Lombard effect which has an effect on a human's voice volume 5. The volume of the speaker's voice becomes larger, if noise increases around the speaker. The Lombard effect also makes the operator of the telepresence robot talk at a louder volume than necessary for the others at a remote location. The operator cannot speak at an optimal volume under a noisy environment even though the noise comes via the speaker or the headset of the telepresence system.

There are studies to deal with the sound environment in a telecommunication. For instance, the studies 6 & 7 developed systems which assist a user to listen to the voice of a remote conversation partner by localizing the sound source of the voice and separating it from other sounds. Also, Takeda, et al. 8 developed a system which cancels the effect of a robot's utterance when recognizing a user's utterance. The 3-D audio system named wave field synthesis 9 can duplicate the whole sound field of a remote room with many speakers. Ambisonic 10 and Amplitude panning 11 employed a panning technique which produces virtual sound sources at various locations by controlling the output amplitude of the loudspeakers. Myung-Suk Song et al. 12 made listeners localize the sound source by using geometric model.

Although these studies can assist a user to understand the sound environment of a remote place, these do not guarantee that the user speaks at an optimal volume through a telepresence robot. The telepresence robot requires a function to adjust the voice volume of the remote user based on the auditory characteristics of people around the robot.

This paper proposes an optimal volume control system LombaBot which adjusts the voice volume of a telepresence robot depending on the noise level around the robot and the distance between a conversation partner and the robot. We have measured the auditory characteristics of humans and developed a volume model for LombaBot (Fig. 1). In particular, LombaBot prepares two types of volume control: the comfortable volume control that produces the comfortable sound of voices for a user around the robot, and the secret talk volume control that produces a minimum sound level for a particular person near the robot. LombaBot can not only communicate with people at a comfortable volume, but also perform personal conversations with nearby people.

RELATED WORK AND APPROACH OF THE PAPER

Studies of Lombart Effect

Many studies of the Lombard effect have been done 13, 14, & 15. W. Van Summers et al. 16 measured word accuracy rates under three different noise levels. The results indicated that a bigger masking noise toward a human utterance causes a lower word accuracy rate. Also, voices under a noisy environment showed higher word accuracy rates than voices under a quiet environment. The Lombard effect decreases the performance of a speech recognition system because it changes the fundamental frequency and the formant frequency of an utterance. Therefore, researchers of speech recognition have tackled the Lombard effect to improve the speech recognition accuracy. On the other hand, the Lombard effect also induces a problem in a telecommunication system if the system reproduces the sound environment of the other remote site. A user speaks at a louder volume than necessary. However, there are few telepresence systems which deal with the problems of the Lombard effect.

Studies of assisting volume adaptation

There are two studies of assisting the voice volume of a remote user for a telepresence robot. Andreas et al. 17 employed a side tone to assist the remote user to adjust the volume of her/his utterance. The side tone is the method to make the remote user hear a part of her/his utterance for feedback. Although the authors reported that the side tone whose delay is less than10 msec works properly without disturbing a user's talk, the work of Andreas et al. employs a constant sound environment to use the system and did not consider a dynamic noisy environment. In addition, Kimura, et al. 18 employs visual feedback to assist volume adaptation. The study makes the remote user adjust the volume of her/his voice by showing a graphical icon which represents the current volume of the user's utterance. However, it is impossible for the user to check whether s/he talks at a proper volume by the system.

Automatic Gain Control

There are several studies of Automatic gain control (AGC) 19 & 20. The studies observe the level of the received signal, and calculate a gain from the ratio of an appropriate level to the observed level. However, the studies did not discuss a dynamic environment such as the use of a robot. In this paper, we consider applying AGC to a telepresence robot.

Our approach to adjusting volume

The previous studies give a kind of feedback to a user to make her/him adjust the volume of her/his voice. The other way to adjust the voice volume is that a system reproduces a whole field and makes a user imitate the voice volume of a remote partner. However, there is a possibility that the voice volume of the partner is bigger than necessary one if the partner is in a noisy environment. Moreover, the system needs to estimate the voice volume of the partner if the system assists the volume adaptation automatically based on the volume of the remote partner. However, estimating the volume requires the direction of the head of the remote partner and the echo model of a remote room 21. It is impossible to prepare the echo model for a telepresence robot which moves inside a room because the echo model depends on a certain location in the room. Thus, we decided to measure an auditory characteristic of humans under a noisy environment and to develop a volume model based on the measurement. We can develop a system which can adjust an appropriate volume based on the model.

Our Approach to make a volume model

The volume model includes two types of volume. One is the volume where people around a telepresence robot can hear the voice of the robot operator comfortably. The other is the volume where the operator selects a person near the robot and talks with her/him in secret. This paper calls them comfortable volume and secret talk volume respectively. Strictly speaking, the secret talk volume is a minimum volume where the only person who is in a small distance from the telepresence robot can hear an utterance coming from the robot. This paper develops a system which enables the operator to select the comfortable volume and the secret talk volume depending on the contents of their conversation.

The volume model employs two parameters: the distance between a person and the telepresence robot, and the level of noise around the robot. W. Van Summers 16 found out that it becomes harder that a voice carries according to the level of noise. Also, Hall, et al. 22 reported that a person adjusts a distance or a space against others depending on the contents of a conversation or the relationship between them. M.L Walters, et al. 23 measured the comfortable distance between a person and a robot. The result indicates that the distance is smaller than 2m. The volume model takes account of the findings of the distance and the noise when considering the decay of a speech power against the distance

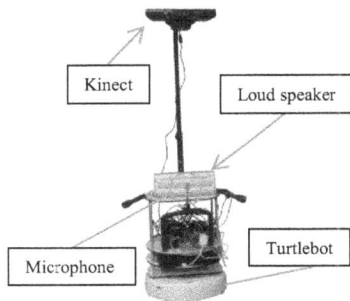

Figure2: Turtlebot with Kinect sensor

between the person and the robot.

We investigated the volume model with a higher resolution for the distance within 2m because we expect that people frequently stand at this distance to communicate with the robot. We also investigated a lower resolution outside 2m. We expect that the volume model outside 2m is used for the operator to call people around the robot. We employ 50-70 dB(A) of noise when investigating the volume model.

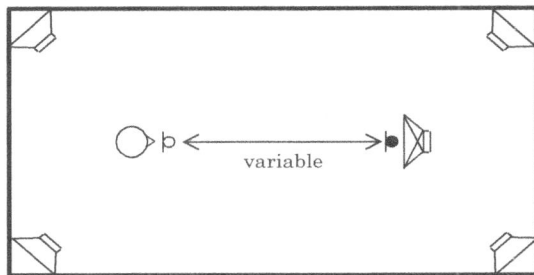

Figure 3: The arrangement of a speaker and recording device

The levels of noise correspond to a real situation such as a shopping mall.

We used a mobile robot named Turtlebot as a basis of a telepresence robot (Fig.2). Kinect is used to measure the distance between a person and the robot.

MEASUREMENT EXPERIMENT AND MODELING

Experimental Environment and Condition

We recruited 24 participants to develop the volume model. The range of their age was from 20's to 50's. Their genders were male.

Figure 3 shows an experimental arrangement. There are four loudspeakers at the four corners of the room to emit noise. The loudspeakers face the walls of the room to make the level of noise constant at any place in the room. We employed a sound file recorded at a shopping mall as the sound of noise to develop the volume model which can be used in a real environment 24.

We played recorded sound files randomly from the loudspeaker at the center of the room. The sound files included the voice of a man. We employed the names of Japanese prefectures as the contents of the sound files because Japanese adult males have knowledge of the places and it is difficult for them to answer the name based on an inference. We measured the volume of the sound file by a microphone placed at 10cm from the center loudspeaker. We calibrated the microphone by using a noise level meter.

The participants wrote down what the man said, and answered 7 scale questionnaires to measure the degree of comfort. The center value of the 7 scale is 0 which denotes a comfortable volume. Participants select a positive value (max. 3) if they consider the sound to be loud, and select a negative value (min. -3) if they consider the sound to be low.

We prepared 4 noise conditions: 50 dB(A), 60 dB(A), 70 dB(A), and no noise. There are 7 distance conditions: 40 cm,

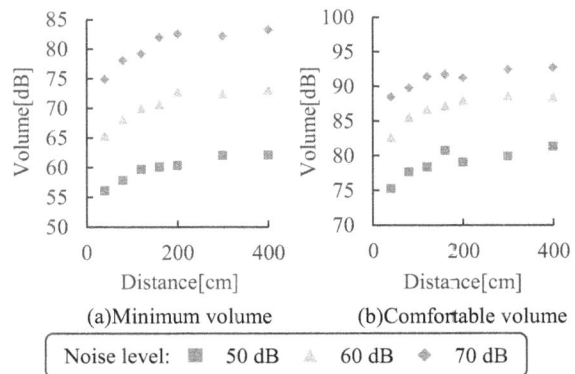

(a)Minimum volume   (b)Comfortable volume

Noise level: ■ 50 dB   ▲ 60 dB   ◆ 70 dB

Figure 4: The result of measuring the volume model

80 cm, 120 cm, 160 cm, 200 cm, 300 cm, 400 cm. We

played 10 kinds of prefectures names for 10 sec at each condition. We calculated the signal-to-noise ratio between the volume in playing the sound file and the volume without playing the file. We estimated the volume model by adding the volume of noise to the signal-to-noise ratio.

Result and the Volume Model

We confirmed that all participants could give the correct answers of Japanese prefectures names at any distances in the condition without noise. The result indicates that participants can hear the voice if the volume of the sound is appropriate.

The right graph of Fig.4 shows the plots of the comfortable volume. The plots are an average volume when participants selected 0 on the questionnaire which means that they considered that the sound volume is comfortable. The level of the comfortable volume increases according to the increase of the noise level. Moreover, the comfortable volume increases depending on the distance from the loudspeaker.

The left graph of Fig.4 shows the result of the secret talk volume. The plots are the average of a minimum volume when participants could give a correct answer at each condition. The secret talk volume also has the same tendency as the comfortable volume. The volume level increases according to the level of noise and the distance from the loudspeaker.

We employ a log approximation for the distance and a linear approximation for the level of noise to make the volume model from the result. Equations (1) and (2) represent the volume model. Here, V_{sec} denotes the secret talk volume and V_{opt} denotes the comfortable volume. x denotes the level of noise and d does the distance from a person.

$$x \geq 60 \begin{cases} V_{sec} = 3.46\ln(d) + 69.0 + \dfrac{(x-60)(0.246\ln(d)+9.90)}{10} \\ V_{opt} = 2.59\ln(d) + 85.7 + \dfrac{(x-60)(-0.704\ln(d)+4.73)}{10} \end{cases} \quad (1)$$

$$x \leq 60 \begin{cases} V_{sec} = 2.71\ln(d) + 58.7 + \dfrac{(x-50)(0.753\ln(d)+10.3)}{10} \\ V_{opt} = 2.43\ln(d) + 77.9 + \dfrac{(x-50)(0.167\ln(d)+7.74)}{10} \end{cases} \quad (2)$$

LOMBABOT

An optimal volume control system LombaBot measures the level of noise around the robot and the distance from a conversation partner. Then, it modifies the volume of an operator's voice with an appropriate gain based on the volume model.

We employed robot audition software HARK 25 & 26 to process sound signals and ROS (Robot Operating System) 27 & 28 to control Turtlebot.

There are five remarkable functions in LombaBot.

i) LombaBot adjusts the volume of an operator's voice if the conversation partner changes. Since LombaBot prepares a user interface to select a conversation partner, the operator can talk with the partner at a comfortable volume by selecting her/him.

ii) The operator can talk at a minimum volume which is appropriate for a situation. For example, the operator can reduce the voice volume when talking in a public space or in the middle of the night.

iii) The operator can talk with people under a noisy environment such as a party. The volume model can calculate an appropriate gain based on the level of noise. Moreover, LombaBot observes the noise level just before the beginning of an operator's utterance. The fresh information of the noise level improves the adaptation of the voice volume. LombaBot can adjust the volume under a dynamic noisy envi-ronment.

iv) The operator talks with someone in secret. People who are outside the range of the secret talk volume cannot hear what the robot says. The feature guarantees a personal communication via the terepresence robot.

v) LombaBot keeps the comfortable volume even if the robot moves around. LombaBot tracks a selected person by kinect sensor and measures the distance from her/him. Since LombaBot calculates a gain continuously, changes in the distance results in the change in the gain to adjust the volume properly.

User Interface

Figure 5 shows a captured image of the user interface (UI) of LombaBot. UI generates a black square on a human face when a Kinect sensor detects the human's location. The color of the square turns to yellow by pushing the left button of a mouse on the human's face. LombaBot uses the comfortable volume toward the selected person. LombaBot uses the secret talk volume when the operator pushes the right button on the selected face. The person's face who is the target of the secret talks has a red square on it. The operation is cancelled if the operator does the same operation to the same user again. The visualization of the selected person assists the operator to understand how people around the robot hear the voice of the operator via LombaBot.

Volume Adaptation

LombaBot records the voice of the operator at a sampling frequency of 16kHz, 16bit. After short-term Fourier transformation, LombaBot finds the region of an utterance by Voice Activity Detection (VAD). If it finds the utterance region, it normalizes the sound in the utterance region by calculating the power of the sound within 0.032 sec. The normalization plays a role of cancelling the difference in the input level of voices. LombaBot produces the same

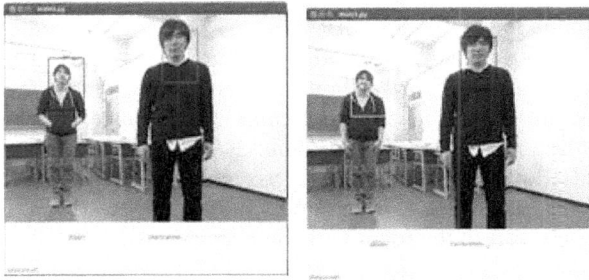

Figure 5: User Interface of LombaBot

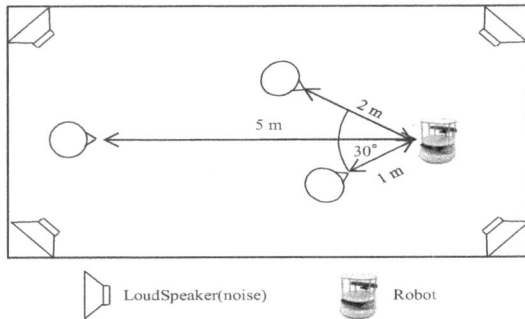

Figure 6: Room setting for the first evaluation

volume of a voice even if the operator speaks loudly or quietly. Finally, LombaBot modifies the normalized sound of the voice with a calculated gain and plays the sound via a loudspeaker. In addition, LombaBot turns the gain to 0 if the input does not include a voice.

PERFORMANCE EVALUATION

Evaluation of the concept of the comfortable volume

Goal: We evaluated how the comfortable volume works depending on the level of noise and the distance from the target person.

Experiment environment: A robot said the name of Japanese prefectures. We asked the participants to listen and repeat it to check his understandings of the robot's utterance. We recorded the voice sounds of the robot prior to the evaluation.

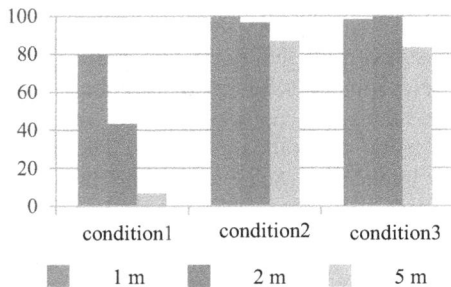

Figure 7: Ratio of correct names under 70dB

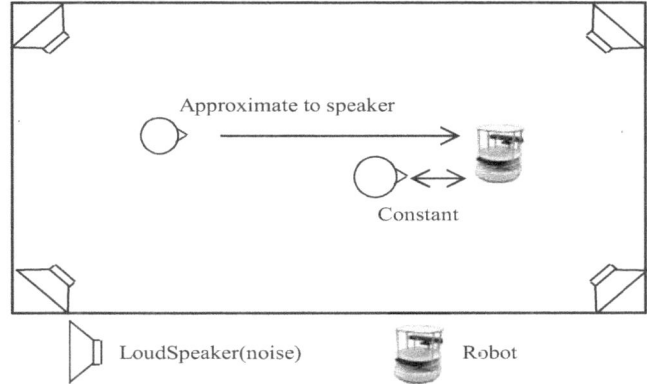

Figure 8: Room setting for the second evaluation

The volume of the robot's speaker was statically set to a certain level and there are three types of volume levels as conditions for the evaluation. We compared the volume levels in terms of the difference of noise level and the difference of the distance between the participants and the robot.

The first condition employed a volume level configured to be comfortable for a person who was within 2m from the loudspeaker under a 50dB noise sound. The second condition also employed a volume level set to be comfortable for a person within 5m under a 70dB of noise sound. The comfortable volume was decided manually based on Equation (1) and (2). The third condition employed a volume level set to a level which LombaBot calculated for a person within 5m distance under a 70dB noise sound. The difference between the first condition and the others is to confirm the effect of the level of noise. Also, the difference between the third condition and the others is to confirm how properly LombaBot works.

Participants: We recruited three adult males for the evaluation.

Experimental procedure: The robot told the participants the names of twenty Japanese prefectures at each evaluation. The timing of the utterance was once every 5 second.

At first, we set the level of noise in the room to 50 dB(A). Then, the participants sat at 2m from the robot and the robot gave the names of Japanese prefectures at the volume of the first condition. The participants repeated the utterance of the robot if he could hear it.

Next, we set the level of noise in the room to 70 dB(A). The participants sat at 1m, 2m, and 5m from the robot respectively as Fig.6 indicates. The position of the participants intended to prevent the power of sound from decaying by the body of the participants near the robot. We tested all volume conditions (from 1st to 3rd) under 70 dB(A) of noise. All participants experienced all positions at each condition.

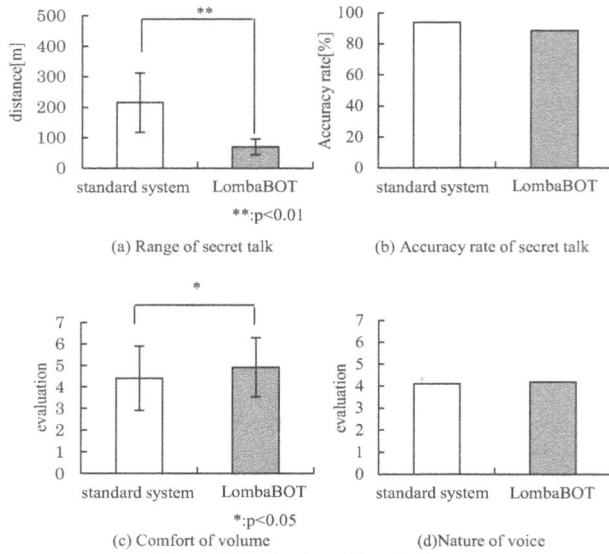

(a) Range of secret talk   (b) Accuracy rate of secret talk

**:p<0.01

*:p<0.05

(c) Comfort of volume   (d)Nature of voice

Figure 9: Evaluation of LombaBot

Result: All participants could say the correct prefecture names when the volume was set to the first condition and the noise level was 50 dB(A).

The graph of Fig.7 shows the ratio where the participants could say the correct prefecture names under 70 dB(A). In the first condition, the correct ratio of the participants sitting at 2m from the robot decreased by almost half according to the change in the noise level from 50 dB(A) to 70 dB(A). The reason is that the volume level of the first condition was proper for 50 dB(A) of noise. The volume level was too weak under 70 dB(A) of noise. The result indicates that the telepresence robot system needs to adjust the volume depending on the noise level even if a conversation partner is at the same distance.

The participants sitting at 5m from the robot could not give the correct names under the volume of the first condition in contrast to the same place of the second and the third conditions. The result also indicates that the system of the telepresence robot has to adjust the volume of the operator's voice.

The correct ratios are almost the same between the second condition and the third condition. The result indicates that LombaBot can produce the voice sound based on the comfortable volume.

Evaluation of the secret talk volume and the comfortable volume

Goal: We evaluated the functions of the secret talk volume and the comfortable volume of LombaBot. We expect that only selected participants can understand the robot's utterance at the secret talk volume. Also, we expect that the selected participants feel comfortable in hearing the robot's voice at the comfortable volume.

Experimental environment: We prepared two levels of noise: 58 dB(A) which we did not use to develop the volume model, and 37 dB(A) which was a natural noise in the experimental room without adding a noisy sound from loudspeakers. Figure 8 shows the room arrangement for the evaluation. The noise sound came from four loudspeakers at the four corners of the room. There was a robot which had a loudspeaker and a Kinect sensor in the center of the room. LombaBot measured the distance from the participants to the robot with the Kinect sensor.

The experiment needed a pair of participants. One of the pairs stood at 50cm from the robot. The other stood at 400 cm. We prepared the place of 50 cm to evaluate the secret talk volume.

Participants: We recruited 10 adult males. They were in their 20's.

Experimental procedure: we conducted the evaluation of the secret talk volume at the beginning. Then, we did the evaluation of the comfortable volume.

The operator of the telepresence robot gave the participants a simple addition question via the robot in the evaluation of the secret talk volume. We asked the participants to raise their hand if they could hear the question. If only the participant at 50cm raises his hand, we asked the participant far from the robot to move 50cm toward the robot and repeated the same question. If both participants raised their hands, we asked the participants further away the answer. If he could not give a correct answer, we asked him to move 50cm again. If both participants could give a correct answer, we finished the evaluation and recorded the distance between the participants further away and the robot.

We asked the participant further away to go back to his original position (400cm) after the evaluation of the secret talk volume. The operator selected the furthest participant as the target of the comfortable volume then. The participants were asked to answer a 7 Likert scale questionnaires such as "Can you hear the voice appropriately?" and "Can you hear the voice naturally?"

We prepared a standard system to compare LombaBot for both evaluations of the secret talk volume and the comfortable volume. We asked a participant to set the volume of the standard system to make a person who was within 4m from the robot hear the voice of the robot regardless of the level of the noise. In particular, the operator of the telepresence robot tried to reduce his own voice to give an additional question to only the nearest participant when using the standard system. The effort of the operator was intended to achieve a secret talk via the standard system.

Result: Figure 9 indicates the result of the evaluations. The distance between the pair of the participants was 20 cm on average when both of them could answer the question.

On the other hand, the distance between the pair was 165cm if they used the standard system. The result indicates a large difference in the distance to hear the robot's utterance. The result indicates that the operator of the telepresence robot achieve secret communication if there is a distance between a conversation partner and the others. LombaBot succeeded in making the target participtans of the secret talk volume answer 88 percent of the additional question. Moreover, LombaBot succeeded in preventing participants who were in more than 100cm from hearing the secret conversation, while the standard system could not.

Also, the participants gave LombaBot a positive evaluation related to comfort and there is a significance in contrast to the standard system. LombaBot has the same quality as the standard system in terms of naturalness.

CASE STUDY

We conducted a case study by using LombaBot. We set a game task where a telepresence robot chaired the game at a comfortable volume to make all participants understand the scenario of the game. The telepresence robot also asked a participant to give the others a question. The request was done at the secret talk volume to prevent the others from knowing the answer of the question.

The scenario of the game was as follows. The asked participant performed gestures to express the given question and the others inferred what the gestures meant. The telepresence robot gave the same kind of question to one of the others after someone could answer the meaning of the gesture. The case study repeated this several times.

Figure 10 shows a scenario of the case study. The above three photographs are the scenes of the room. Three photographs below them are captured images of UI each of which corresponds to each of the above scenes. At first, the operator selected one of the participants who was not near the robot as a target of the comfortable volume (two photos at the left of Fig.10). Then, the operator explained the scenario of the game to all participates. After that, the operator moved the robot toward a participant and selected him as the target of the secret talk volume (two photos at the center). The operator succeeded in giving him a question without the others noticing. The operator turned the robot to the direction of the participants who were not near the robot and selected one of them as the target of the comfortable volume (two photos at the right of Fig.10). Then, he chaired the game such as prompting the participant to start gestures, giving the answer, and so on.

The case study indicates that the operator managed the game by using the functions of LombaBot. After the game, we asked participants whether they could hear the secret talk. All participants could not hear the talk at the secret talk volume. Moreover, all participants answered that they could talk with the robot comfortably even in a noisy environment.

The operator answered that the color visualization of LombaBot UI was useful to identify the current volume setting. However, the function of tracking a person sometimes failed during the case study. We have to improve the robustness of LombaBot.

CONCLUSION

This paper developed an optimal volume control system LombaBot for telecommunication via a robot. LombaBot tackled a problem where the operator of a robot cannot talk at a proper volume via the telepresence robot. We developed a volume model by investigating a person's auditory characteristics depending on the level of noise in an environment and the distance from a sound source. And we equipped LombaBot with the model. LombaBot has two types of volume: the comfortable volume and the secret talk volume. The comfortable volume produces a voice sound at the level of voice volume comfortable for a selected person. The secret talk volume produces it at the minimum level of voice volume for the selected person and prevents the others from hearing the talk. The remarkable point of LombaBot is that a user can talk with people in secret if s/he gives a private information to them

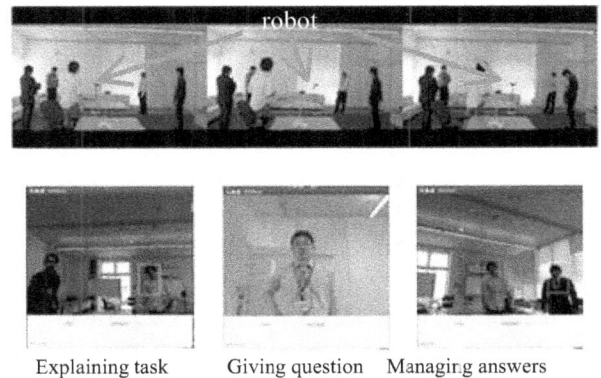

Figure 10: Chairing and giving game task via the robot

by change the level of volume dynamically according to the current noise in a room and the position of people. We evaluated LombaBot by comparing it with the telepresence robot which cannot adjust the voice volume. LombaBot can generate a comfortable sound of voice under a noisy environment based on the distance from a person. Moreover, LombaBot achieved a secret talk perfectly. We confirmed the function of LombaBot in a casual game task. The result indicated that LombaBot could be used in realistic situations.

REFERENCES

1. Texai:
   http://www.willowgarage.com/pages/texai/principles
2. QB: https://www.anybots.com/
3. Min Kyung Lee et al. ""Now, I Have a Body": Uses and Social Norms for Mobile Remote Presence in the Workplace", in Proc. of CHI2011, pp.33-42, 2011.

4. F. Tanaka et al., "Child-operated telepresence robot: A field trial connecting classrooms between Australia and Japan," in Proc. of IEEE/RAS IROS2013, pp. 5896 - 5901, 2013.

5. Lombard, E. "Le signe de le elevation de la voix," Ann. Malad. l'Orielle. Larynx. Nez. Pharynx 37, 101-119, 1911.

6. Barbara Hilsenbeck et al., "Listening for people: Exploiting the spectral stracture of speech to robustly perceive the presence of people" in Proc. of IEEE/RAS IROS 2011, pp. 2903–2909, 2011.

7. A, Deleforge et al., "The Cocktail Party Robot: Sound Source Separation and Localisation with an Active Binaural Head," in Proc. of HRI2012,pp.431-438,2012.

8. R.Takeda et al., "ICA-Based efficient dereverberation and echo cancellation method for barge-in-able robot audition" in Proc. of IEEE ICASSP2009, pp. 3367–3680, 2009.

9. A.Berkhout et al., "Acoustic control by wave field synthesis," J. acoust. Soc. Amer., vol.93, pp. 2764-2778, 1993.

10. D.Malhan et al., "3-D sound spatialization using ambisonic techniques," J. Conput. Music, vol. 19, no. 4, pp. 58-70, 1995

11. V. Pullki, "Virtual sound source positioning using vector base amplitude panning" J. Audio Eng. Soc., vol. 45, pp. 456-466, 1997.

12. Myung-Suk Song et al.,"An Interactive 3-D Audio System With Loudspeakes"IEEE TRANSACTION ON MULTIMEDIA, vol.13, no.5,pp. 844-855, 2011.

13. Goldenberg et.al, "R.,The Lombard Effect's Influence on Automatic Speaker Verification Systems and Methods for its Compensation, Information Technology: Research and Education,pp.233-237, 2006.

14. Ogawa,T et.al.,"Adequacy Analysis of Simulation-based Assessment of Speech Recognition System", " in Proc. of IEEE ICASSP'98, pp. 1153–1156, 1998.

15. John H.L.Hansen et.al., "Analysis and Compensation of Lombard Speech Across Noise Type and Levels With Application to In-Set/Out-of-Set Speaker Recognition",IEEE TRANSACTIONS ON AUDIO, SPEECH, AND LAUNGUAGE PROCESSING, Vol.17, No.2, pp.366-378, 2009.

16. W. Van Summers, D. B. Pisoni, R. Bernacki, R. Pedlow, and M. Stokes, "Effects of noise on speech production:Acoustical and perceptualanalyses," J. Acous. Soc. Amer., pp. 917–928, Sep. 1988.

17. Andreas Paepcke et al., "Yelling In the Hall: Using Sidetone to Address a Problem with Mobile Remoto Presence Systems," in Proc. of ACM UIST2011, pp 107-116, 2011.

18. A.Kimura et al, "Visual Feedback: Its effect on teleconferencing," in proceeding of HCI international, pp.591-600, 2007

19. P.L.Chu, "Voice-Activated AGC for Teleconferencing," in Proc. of IEEE ICASSP'96, pp. 929–932, 1996.

20. G.R.Steber, "Digital Signal Processing In Automatic Gain Control Systems,"Industrial Electonics Society(IECON), pp. 381–384,1988.

21. J. J. Lopez et al, "Measurement of cross-talk cancelation and equalization zones in 3-D sound reproduction under real listening conditions," in Proc. of Audio Engineering Society 16th Int. Conf.,1999.

22. E. T. Hall, The Hidden Dimension. Doubleday, NY, 1966.

23. M. L. Waltes, "Human Approach Distance to a Mechanical-Looking Robot with Different Robot Voice Styles,", in Proc. of IEEE RO-MAN2008, pp 707-712, 2008.

24. http://www.sunrisemusic.co.jp/database/database00.html

25. Kazuhiro Nakadai, Toru Takahashi, Hiroshi G.Okuno, Hirofumi Nakajima, Yuji Hasegawa, Huroshi Tsujino: Design and Implementation of Robot Audition System "HARK," Advanced Robotics, vol.24 pp.739-761, 2010.

26. HARK Main Page: http://winnie.kuis.kyoto-u.ac.jp/HARK/ .

27. Morgan Quigley, Brian Gerkey, Ken Conley, Josh, Faust, Tully Foote, Jeremy Leibs, Eric Berger, RobWheeler, Andrew Ng: ROS: an open-source Robot Operating System in IEEE-RAS International Conference on Robotics and Automation (ICRA) Work shop on Open Source Software in Robotics, 2009.

28. ROS: http://www.ros.org

An Affective Telepresence System Using Smartphone High Level Sensing and Intelligent Behavior Generation

Elham Saadatian
Keio-NUS CUTE Center
Singapore
elham@nus.edu.sg

Thoriq Salafi
National University of
Singapore
thoriqsalafi@nus.edu.sg

Hooman Samani
National Taipei University
Taiwan
hooman@mail.ntpu.edu.tw

Yu De Lim
National University of
Singapore
lim.yudee@hotmail.com

Ryohei Nakatsu
Keio-NUS CUTE Center
Singapore
idmnr@nus.edu.sg

ABSTRACT

A new approach in telepresence robots via automatic behavior generation is proposed in this paper. The robot behavior is generated using the Smartphone high level sensing, and personality based mood transition. The current telepresence systems require the simultaneous presence of both communication parties. Therefore, due to the time and context differences in distant communication, the opportunity of connectedness is reduced. This is especially important for more intimate telecommunications, that ongoing connectedness is more required. To solve these problems, we developed an automatic behavior generation system, that produces behaviors on behalf of the remote person. In order to be able to infer the state of the remote person more frequently and dynamically, Smartphone sensors are used for automatic high level sensing. Furthermore, to produce more believable affective expressions by the robot, the expressions correspond to the remote user's personality stereotype. Fuzzy Kohonen Clustering Network (FKCN), is utilized to linearly fuse the inferred mood states and regenerate them on the agent. To evaluate the results 120 samples of the user's Smartphone usage and the mood in different times of the day were logged. The state estimated by the model were compared against the users self report data. The results showed that there was no significant difference between the user's self-perceived feelings, and the feelings recognized by the model.

Author Keywords

Affective Telepresence, Smart Sensing, Artificial Intelligence

HAI 2014, October 29–31, 2014, Tsukuba, Japan.
Copyright © 2014 ACM 978-1-4503-3035-0/14/10 ...$15.00.
http://dx.doi.org/10.1145/2658861.2658878

INTRODUCTION

Lately, there has been a growing interest in developing technologies for affective telepresence ranging from abstract media [1] to holistic telepresence robots [2, 3]. These technologies are named "phatic technologies". It refers to the technologies that are not aiming to exchange any particular thought or facts about the world; they however focus on establishing and sustainability of communication [4].

One important issue during communicating through current affective telepresence technologies is the need for availability of both interacting parties. This opposes to the need for ongoing connectedness in intimate communications [5]. To address this issue we propose an intelligent affective telepresence system that can automatically detect the remote user's stochastic affective status through the smartphone sensors' data, and emulate it in another location. This study mainly focuses on affective behavior generation module of the intimate telepresence system.

Theoretical and design considerations

In order to maintain the intimate bonds, our goal is to have an agent which could be perceived as a natural extension of the remote person, and not merely an artificial agent that acts as a mediator. In intimate telepresence technologies, one of the design approaches to achieve this goal is attribution to the remote partner. For this purpose researchers have mainly focused on the appearance of the media and the form factor. For instance, a study on telepresence through the transition of heartbeats suggested that heartbeat can be perceived as an intimate signal provided that it is associated to the remote partner [6]. In another study on intimate telepresence through mediated hand holding, artificial hand prototypes had personalized appearance for each couple instead of a standard form factor. The hand prints of couples and sleeve pattern were used in the design of the hands to promote intimate telepresence through attribution to their owners [7]. magic sock drawer" [8] which supports serendipitous sharing of hand-written notes in a drawer. In our previous studies about intimate telepresence through humanoid robot, affectivity was increased via attribution of the robot in terms of attire, hair, and accessories [9] and kiss force and pressure to a remote intimate partner [10]. However, to the best of our knowledge, there is no attempt in intimate telepresence technologies through attribution of the remote user's personality stereotype to the media. Giving personality to the robot could also enhance the naturalness and believability of the robot [11]. Therefore, in this study we have considered remote user's personality in mood transitions of the agent.

Besides, establishing and maintaining the possibility of communication is another requirement of phatic technology. Therefore, we suggest the user of the smartphone as a platform for perception system. Considering the wide and the constant use of the Smartphones and their potentials in detecting users' state, it could be a suitable platform for emotion and behavior detection. However, since the smartphone environment is uncertain, noisy, and changes rapidly the perception system should be able to handle uncertainties [12]. In this paper, we propose a solution that performs high, level mood sensing through the Smartphones and handles the uncertainties.

In this respect, an artificial intelligence module for a pair of affective telepresence robots aimed to support phatic communication for Long Distance Relationships (LDRs) is presented. The module dynamically generates emotionally expressive behaviors on behalf of the remote partners, considering their estimated mood state. It is capable of expressing mood transitions based on the personality stereotypes. The artificial intelligence model has the potential to be applied in a broad range of applications such as telepresence through virtual agents, emotional robots and many other social robotic systems.

Section II introduces the overall architecture of the proposed affective telepresence system. Section III describes the affective behavior generation system and its components. Section IV presents an experiment with robot simulator and the result, and finally, the conclusion is described in section V

OVERALL ARCHITECTURE OF THE AFFECTIVE TELEPRESENCE SYSTEM

The system is composed of a pair of telepresence robots and two Smartphones. As illustrated in Figure 1, sensing is done using the smartphone sensors, then the acquired data is analyzed in the server and as a result corresponding actions are generated and visualized through the agents in the remote location. The main difference between this architecture and conventional cognitive robotic systems is that the action happens in the remote location (in relation to the sensors) for telepresence.

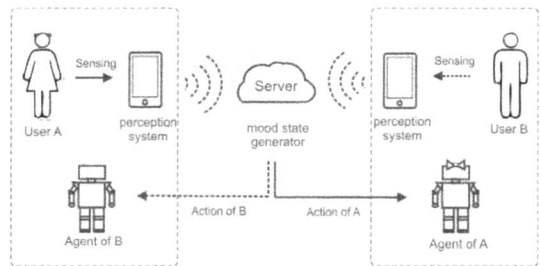

Figure 1. Overall Architecture of the proposed affective telepresence system

AFFECTIVE BEHAVIOR GENERATION SYSTEM

Affective behaviors are an embodied reaction of pleasure and displeasure, which are influenced by personality, mood, emotion and many other internal and external factors. Whereas moods are slowly changing affective expressions, and emotions are very short term affective state [13]. In this study, we have chosen to focus on mood generation on behalf of a remote user, considering his/her personality type. Inclusion of the personality increases the accuracy as well as the association of the affective expressions to the remote user and perception of the co-presence.

To identify the personality stereotype the big five personality model is applied [14]. Big five personality model is a framework to determine the personality stereotype of a person at the broadest level of abstraction. This model has received substantial support in psychology [15].The five models of personality consist of extraversion (E), agreeableness (A), conscientiousness (C), neuroticism (N) and openness (O).

As shown in Figure 2, the valence–arousal two-dimensional space model [16] is used to generate the mood state of the users. The horizontal axis is valence, which ranges from displeasure to pleasure and the vertical axis is arousal, which infers the user state from calm to arouse. Linear regression is utilized to reveal the mood state and its transitions between sad, bored, sleepy, relax, happy, delighted, aroused, alarmed, and distressed.

Figure 3, shows the architecture of the affective behavior generation module of the telepresence system. The inputs of the system are the Smartphone hard and soft sensory data and manual entries of users. The low-level data from the Smartphone sensors will be processed in the perception system and high level data describing the state of the user will be recognized. The high level data which describe the mood state of the user are sent to the mood and gesture generation system to produce the facial expressions and body languages of the agent. The user facial expressions and body movements, then could be transmitted to a remote user in the form of a robotic agent or a virtual character.

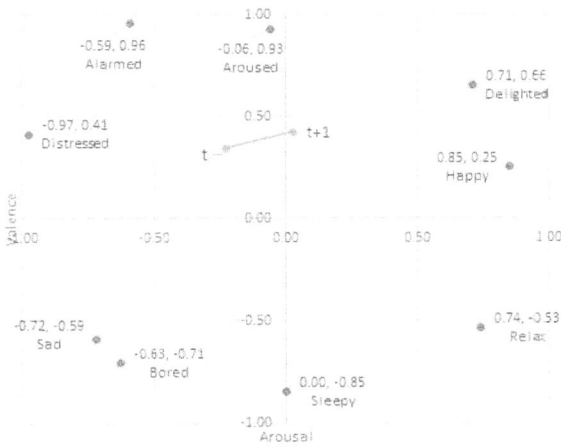

Figure 2. Nine mood coordinates in two dimensional valence–arousal plane

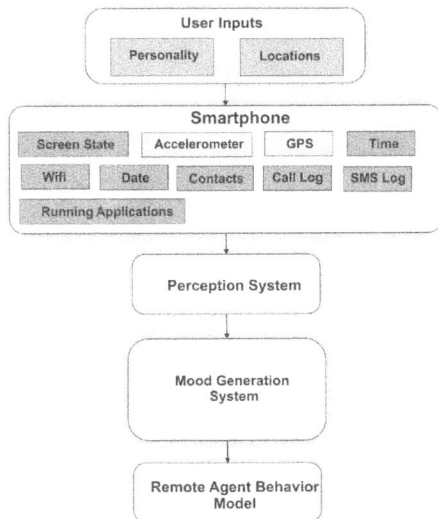

Figure 3. Architecture of affective behavior generation.

Smartphone sensing and perception

Smartphone contains useful data about its active users, that can be obtained through its built-in hard and soft sensors. The relevant data can be extracted and processed to infer the user's state. For instance, the user call log can identify the number of calls, duration and the most contacted person by the user. The running applications can identify what types of applications are used; Where GPS and accelerometer can describe the activity state of the user. Such data are useful to determine the user state such as idle or busy.

In our proposed method, in the Smartphone data extraction phase, some data will be requested to be manually logged by the user. The required manual entry by the users are their home and office location and answers to the questions regarding their personality stereotype. Location labeling is done by tagging the longitude and latitude value of their home and offices, which is detected by Global Positioning System (GPS). The personality stereotype is detectable by answering a questionnaire at the beginning of the Smartphone app usage.

Table 1 describes the used sensors and their components. The automatically sensed low level data from the soft and hard sensors combined with the manual entry of the user is gathered in the perception system.

Table 1. Soft and hard sensors

Type	Class	Components
Hard Sensors	GPS	Latitude, Longitude, Speed
	Accelerometer	X,Y,Z
Soft Sensors	Time	Clock/Date
	Screen	State: On/Off
	Aplicatios	Type, Number
	Call and SMS log	Number , Name, Duration

In this, study we have focused on mood sensing. Therefore, those sensors that could be associated to the mood are chosen. These data are retrieved in real-time using "Funf" open sensing framework [17] and processed in the server.

Mood estimation system

The mood estimation system is a combination of Support Vector Machines (SVM) and Dynamic Bayesian network (DBN). SVM will be used to classify the user state to idle and moving, based on the trained accelerometer data. Idle refers to stationary positions, whereas moving refers to the dynamic behaviors such as walking and running. GPS data are processed with regards to the user inputs to detect the user's home and office locations. Finally, these data combined with other sensor data is analyzed using DBN to estimate the stochastic mood state of the user. Due to the high level of uncertainty, dynamic change of Smartphone data and insufficient data about the user DBN is used. Bayesian Network is an established formalism for inference under uncertainty [18, 19]. In BN on the top of the network, there are observed nodes, which values are changed based on the Smartphone sensor data. After that the conditional probability is implemented from the top of the nodes to the valence and arousal nodes using the chain rule. DBN will estimate the probability of nodes using the conditional probability distribution in time-series data [20]. In our model the output of BN at time $t - 1$ affects the mood estimation in time t. It defines $P(X_t|X_{t-1})$ with a directed acyclic graph as 1

$$P(X_t|X_{t-1}) = \prod_{i=1}^{n} P(X_t^i|Pt(X_t^i)) \qquad (1)$$

where X_t^i is the *ith* node, at time t, and $Pt(X_t^i)$ are the parents of X_t^i in the graph. The nodes in the first slice of a two segment temporal Bayesian network has an associated conditional probability distribution, which defines $P(X_t|X_{t-1})$ for all $t > 1$.

Figure 4 shows the Probabilistic Mood Estimation (PME) module of the system, which is developed based on DBN. It infers the probabilistic position of the mood (α_k, β_k) and its changes $\Delta\alpha_k, \Delta\beta_k$ on valence–Arousal space model in each time interval. Coordinates are generated using expected utility node to convert these probabilities to the utility value from -1 to 1 as equation 2:

$$\Delta\alpha_k = \sum_{i=1}^{n} P(x_i)x_i \quad and \quad \Delta\beta_k = \sum_{j=1}^{n} P(x_j)x_j \qquad (2)$$

where $P(x_i)$ is the probability of valence for state i, and $P(x_j)$ is the probability of arousal for state j and x_i and x_j are the value for its respective state.

The conditional probability value of App usage is generated from self-Assessment Manikin (SAM). The SAM is a 9-rating pictorial scale that is a nonverbal self-report measure of affective state using simple manikins pictures [21]. This method is known to be used for psychology study of affection. To get valence score, a set of manikins was employed for the experiment. In this set, ratings for valence were scored from one (displeasure) to nine (pleasure). Participants were asked to perceive a virtual situation whereby they use a specific application in the Smartphone and rate the situation based on the SAM valence rating system. This online survey was participated by 38 participants, and the raw result will be processed such that the probability of each situation can be obtained and employed for the proposed DBN. The summary of the result is tabulated in table 2.

To consider the influence of the personality in mood transition, a reliable mapping method developed in [22] is applied to relate the big five personality model and the valence–arousal plane which results in the personality parameters (St_α, St_β) as eq. :

Table 2. Application types and their respective valance probability

App Type	Valence		
	P(low)	P(Medium)	P(High)
Social	0,16	0,39	0,45
Productivity	0,16	0,63	0,21
Entertainment	0,08	0,39	0,53

$$St_\alpha = 0.21E + 0.59A + 0.19N, St_\beta = 0.15O + 0.3A + 0.57N \qquad (3)$$

This equation translates the result of the personality questionnaire into the personality parameter. This personality parameter will be employed later to weight the mood variables on the valence (α axis) and arousal (β axis) plane.

Adopting the methodology in [23] to consider the personality influence, the personality parameters obtained from are incorporated to the mood variable and resulted in user mood (UM_t) at $t = 0$ as in eq. 4.

$$UM_0 : (\alpha_0, \beta_0) = (St_\alpha\Delta\alpha_0, St_\beta\Delta\beta_0) \qquad (4)$$

To show the mood transition in the agent behavior, this valence and arousal coordinates value will be passed to the next time slice $(t + 1)$ in the DBN as in eq. 5

$$UM_k : (\alpha_k, \beta_k) = UM_{k-1} + (St_\alpha\Delta\alpha_k, St_\beta\Delta\beta_k) \qquad (5)$$

where (α_k, β_k), refers to valence-arousal coordinates. This equation generates the mood transition of a remote user, considering his/her big five personality parameters.

Remote user mood expression model of the agent
The acquired mood state values from eq. 5, will be utilized to classify the affective states to sad, bored, sleepy, relax, happy, delighted, aroused, alarmed, and distressed. Fuzzy Kohonen Clustering Network (FKCN), can be utilized to linearly fuse the inferred mood states and regenerate them through the agent [24]. The obtained valence–arousal coordinate from 5 is passed to the input layer of the FKCN as shown in Figure 5. Distance layer calculates the Euclidean error distance between the input and the center of each mood (L_{ij}) using 6.

$$L_{ij} : \|X_i - M_j\|^2 = (X_i - M_j)^T(X_i - M_j) \qquad (6)$$

where $X_i : (\alpha_k, \beta_k)$ refers to the network input and M_j points to the center of *jth* emotion. The distance between these two points reflects the dissimilarity between the input and that particular mood state. This Euclidean

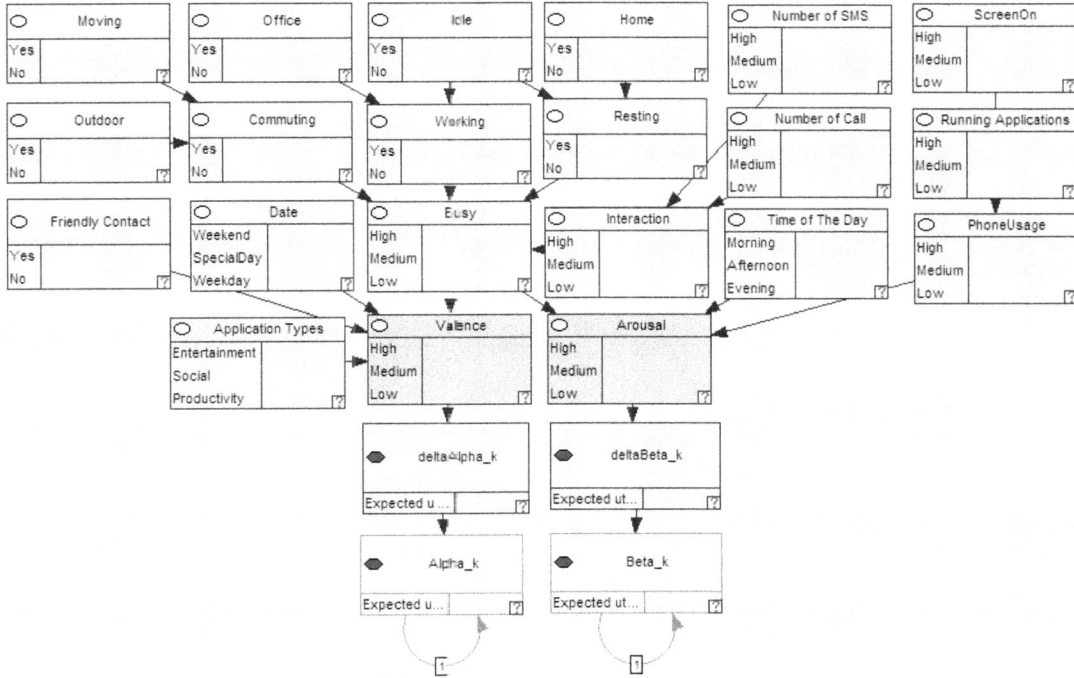

Figure 4. Probabilistic Mood Estimation (PME) for inferring mood through Smartphone data.

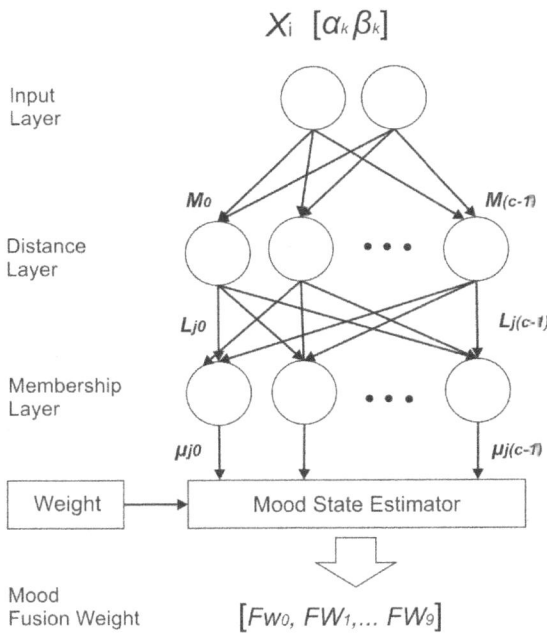

Figure 5. Fuzzy Kohonen Clustering Network for mood expression

distance error is adopted to calculate the membership value as:

$$\mu_{ij} = \begin{cases} 1 & if \quad d_{ij} = 0 \\ 0 & if \quad d_{ik} = 0 (k > 0, j \leq c - 1) \end{cases} \quad (7)$$

where c represents the number of mood patterns; otherwise:

$$\mu_{ij} = \sum_{l=0}^{c-1} [\frac{L_{ij}}{Ld_{il}}]$$

The sum of the membership layer is always equal to 1. The membership value for distance of zero with jth mood pattern is 1, and the membership value for another mood pattern is automatically 0, otherwise the membership value is the probability of the input to be classified as a member of each mood pattern. Each mood pattern has its respective weight such as sad has weight (w) of (1, 0, 0, 0, 0, 0, 0,0,0). Finally the remote agent behavior can show its mood as a linearly combined mood as in eq.8

$$FW_i = \sum_{l=0}^{c-1} \mu_{ij} w_{ji} \quad (8)$$

where μ_{ij} is the membership value and w_{ji} is the weight of each mood pattern. Table 3 shows the emotion pattern with respect to its weight.

Action generation module

Table 3. Mood pattern coordinates

Mood pattern			Weight								
j	alphak	betak	Sad	Relax	Distressed	Sleepy	Happy	Aroused	Bored	Alarmed	Delighted
1	-0.72	-0.59	1	0	0	0	0	0	0	0	0
2	0.74	-0.53	0	1	0	0	0	0	0	0	0
3	-0.97	0.41	0	0	1	0	0	0	0	0	0
4	0	-0.85	0	0	0	1	0	0	0	0	0
5	0.85	0.25	0	0	0	0	1	0	0	0	0
6	-0.06	0.93	0	0	0	0	0	1	0	0	0
7	-0.063	-0.71	0	0	0	0	0	0	1	0	0
8	-0.59	0.96	0	0	0	0	0	0	0	1	0
9	0.71	0.66	0	0	0	0	0	0	0	0	1

This module enables to regenerate the mood state of a remote user in another location, through embodied robot or animated virtual agent. To evaluate the effectiveness of the developed model in generation of appropriate affective behaviors, an animated virtual character is simulated by adopting the Grimace model [1]. The results are also visualized through a minimal robotic concept prototype by augmenting the Smartphone screen on top of a humanoid robot. The simulator can express the remote user's mood using the weight values and fusion of mood expressions.

The agent will also express the mood state through hand moves. Corresponding hand movement for each state is generated using eq.9

$$RH_k = 0.5\beta_k + 0.5 \qquad (9)$$

where $RH_k \in [0, 1]$ represents the agent's hand position. β_k is the user arousal–value obtained from the mood state generator. The hand position varies from down to up with 0 value represent the maximum hand down, and 1 represent the maximum hand up.

WORKING PROCESS OF THE SYSTEM

In order to demonstrate the working process of the system, changes of a user's mood state over a course of a day is shown based on the following scenario. The user was a 21-year-old intern student who actively uses Smartphone for managing personal information, communication, as well as entertainment. The experiment was done on a weekday, and the user was asked to manually input the Smartphone data and the SAM valence–arousal ratings on each hour. Before the experiment, the user was asked to perform the big five personality test, and the user's result was 0.40 for A, 0.78 for C, 0.68 for N, 0.15 for E and 0.40 for O. From the equation , the user personality parameter (St_α, St_β) of the user is (0.57, 0.32). Table 4 illustrates the result of the experiment made throughout a course of the day.

The data obtained from the user is processed as an input in the proposed method, and the result of the mood transition in a whole day for the user is shown in Figure 6.

---

[1] http://www.grimace-project.net/

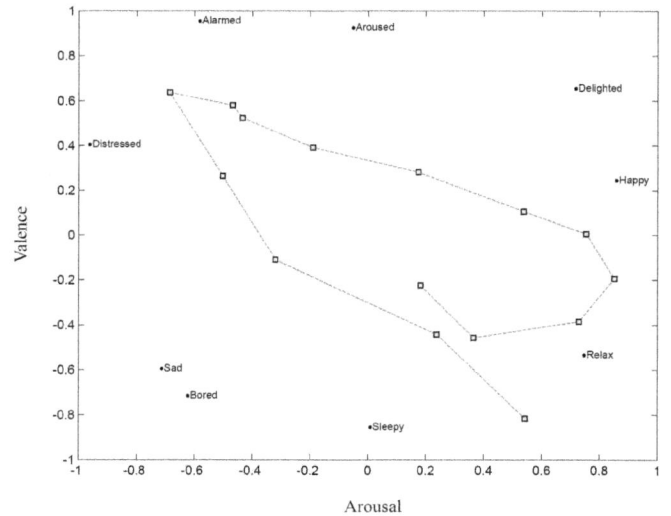

Figure 6. Estimated valence arousal coordinate transition throughout the whole day. The transition made from morning to evening is anticlockwise

Figure represents simulator and concept prototype facial and body expression for 5th, 11th and 15th mood data points from the estimated user mood state. The 5th mood is representing agent with 62% happy, and the hand's position is 50 %. The 11th mood represents the agent with 30% distressed and 40% of alarmed with hands position of 83%. The 15th mood represents the agent with 22% of sleepy and 50% of relaxed with hand's position of 10% down.

System Evaluation

To evaluate the model, $(n = 10)$ active Smartphone users (5 *Females* and 5 *Males*), Age, between 21 to 33, $(Mean = 25.8, SD = 3.82)$, were randomly selected from National University of Singapore's staff and students. The Results of 120 samples of the user's Smartphone usage and the mood in different times of the day were logged. The processed SAM user manual input was compared against the result of the proposed model. The Mann-Whitney U test is performed to test whether there is a significance difference in the proposed model estimated affective state the and user manual input in the

Table 4. User valence-arousal probe

Clock Time	Time	Location	Movement	Screen	Running apps	SMS Number	Friendly Contact	Call Number	V	A
07:00-08:00	Morning	Home	Idle	Low	Social	Low	No	Low	5	2
08:00-09:00	Morning	Home	Idle	Medium	Social	Low	No	Low	6	3
09:00-10:00	Morning	Outdoor	Moving	High	Entertainment	Low	Yes	Low	5	5
10:00-11:00	Morning	Office	Idle	Medium	Productivity	Low	Yes	Low	4	6
11:00-12:00	Morning	Office	Idle	Low	Social	Medium	No	Low	7	7
12:00-13:00	Afternoon	Outdoor	Moving	Medium	Entertainment	Low	Yes	Low	8	8
13:00-14:00	Afternoon	Office	Idle	Medium	Productivity	Medium	No	Low	5	7
14:00-15:00	Afternoon	Office	Idle	Low	Social	Medium	Yes	Low	2	7
15:00-16:00	Afternoon	Office	Idle	Low	Entertainment	Low	No	Low	3	7
16:00-17:00	Afternoon	Outdoor	Moving	High	Social	Low	No	Low	3	4
17:00-18:00	Afternoon	Outdoor	Moving	High	Entertainment	Medium	Yes	Low	3	4
18:00-19:00	Evening	Home	Idle	Medium	Social	Low	No	Low	6	3
19:00-20:00	Evening	Home	Idle	Low	Social	Low	No	Low	7	2
20:00-21:00	Evening	Home	Idle	Medium	Entertainment	Low	Yes	Low	7	1
21:00-22:00	Evening	Office	Idle	Low	None	Low	No	Low	7	1

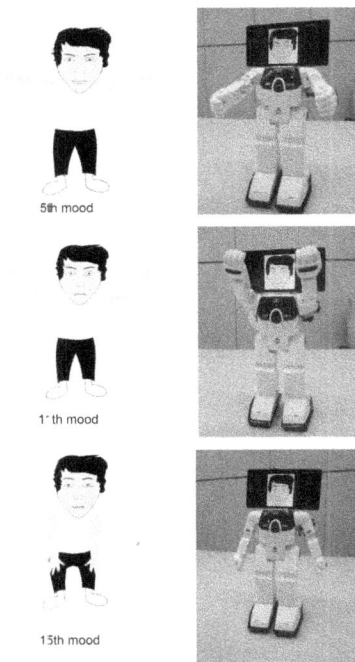

Figure 7. Visualization of the agent behavior through simulator

valence arousal space. The p value for two tailed are 0.64 for the valence space, and 0.73 for the arousal space. These two p values are higher than 5%. This suggests that there is no significance difference in the proposed model and user self perceived affective state. Therefore, the model can be applied to the proposed telepresence agent to convey the users affective state to the remote partner

CONCLUSION

In this study, an artificial intelligence model for automated affective telepresence is proposed. The system is designed for active Smartphone users to maintain the possibility of connectedness with a remote partner. The PME system supports mood inference through the Smartphone, considering the uncertain, insufficient, and dynamically changing available data. To generate natural mood transition on the agent, as well as the association of the robot expressive behaviors to the remote partner, personality stereotype of the remote user's affects the generated mood. The system evaluation results supported the success of the proposed mathematical model in emulation of the affective state. The model could also contribute towards lots of other applications such as personalized digital assistant services on Smartphones, mood sharing on social networks, empathetic agents and many more.

ACKNOWLEDGMENTS

This research is supported by the Singapore National Research Foundation under its International Research Center Keio-NUS CUTE Center @ Singapore Funding Initiative and administered by the IDM Program Office.

REFERENCES

1. J. Kaye, "I just clicked to say i love you: rich evaluations of minimal communication," in *CHI'06 Extended Abstracts on Human Factors in Computing Systems*. ACM, 2006, pp. 363–368.

2. S. O. Adalgeirsson and C. Breazeal, "Mebot: a robotic platform for socially embodied presence," in *Proceedings of the 5th ACM/IEEE international*

conference on Human-robot interaction. IEEE Press, 2010, pp. 15–22.

3. J.-D. Yim and C. D. Shaw, "Design considerations of expressive bidirectional telepresence robots," in *CHI'11 Extended Abstracts on Human Factors in Computing Systems.* ACM, 2011, pp. 781–790.

4. F. Vetere, J. Smith, and M. Gibbs, "Phatic interactions: Being aware and feeling connected," in *Awareness systems.* Springer, 2009, pp. 173–186.

5. F. Vetere, S. Howard, and M. Gibbs, "Phatic technologies: Sustaining sociability through ubiquitous computing," in *First International Workshop on Social Implications of Ubiquitous Technology. ACM Conference on Human Factors in Computing Systems, CHI,* 2005.

6. J. H. Janssen, J. N. Bailenson, W. A. IJsselsteijn, and J. H. Westerink, "Intimate heartbeats: Opportunities for affective communication technology," *Affective Computing, IEEE Transactions on,* vol. 1, no. 2, pp. 72–80, 2010.

7. D. Gooch and L. Watts, "It's neat to feel the heat: how can we hold hands at a distance?" in *CHI'12 Extended Abstracts on Human Factors in Computing Systems.* ACM, 2012, pp. 1535–1540.

8. D. Gooh and L. Watts, "The magic sock drawer project," in *CHI'11 Extended Abstracts on Human Factors in Computing Systems.* ACM, 2011, pp. 243–252.

9. E. Saadatian, H. Samani, A. Vikram, R. Parsani, L. Tejada Rodriguez, and R. Nakatsu, "Personalizable embodied telepresence system for remote interpersonal communication," in *RO-MAN, 2013 IEEE.* IEEE, 2013, pp. 226–231.

10. E. Saadatian, H. Samani, R. Parsani, A. Vikram Pandey, J. Li, L. Tejada Rodriguez, A. David Cheok, and R. Nakatsu, "Mediating intimacy in long-distance relationships using kiss messaging," *International Journal of Human-Computer Studies,* 2014.

11. K. M. Lee, W. Peng, S.-A. Jin, and C. Yan, "Can robots manifest personality?: An empirical test of personality recognition, social responses, and social presence in human–robot interaction," *Journal of communication,* vol. 56, no. 4, pp. 754–772, 2006.

12. E.-J. Malm, M. Jani, J. Kela *et al.,* "Managing context information in mobile devices," *IEEE pervasive computing,* vol. 2, no. 3, pp. 42–51, 2003.

13. L. Moshkina, S. Park, R. C. Arkin, J. K. Lee, and H. Jung, "Tame: Time-varying affective response for humanoid robots," *International Journal of Social Robotics,* vol. 3, no. 3, pp. 207–221, 2011.

14. R. R. McCrae and O. P. John, "An introduction to the five-factor model and its applications," *Journal of personality,* vol. 60, no. 2, pp. 175–215, 1992.

15. F. Hegel, S. Krach, T. Kircher, B. Wrede, and G. Sagerer, "Understanding social robots: A user study on anthropomorphism," in *Robot and Human Interactive Communication, 2008. RO-MAN 2008. The 17th IEEE International Symposium on.* IEEE, 2008, pp. 574–579.

16. M. Ouwerkerk, "Unobtrusive emotions sensing in daily life," in *Sensing Emotions.* Springer, 2011, pp. 21–39.

17. N. Aharony, A. Gardner, C. Sumter, and A. Pentland, "Funf: Open sensing framework," 2011.

18. T. Gu, H. K. Pung, and D. Q. Zhang, "A bayesian approach for dealing with uncertain contexts," *Advances in Pervasive Computing,* p. 136, 2004.

19. J.-W. Yoon and S.-B. Cho, "An intelligent synthetic character for smartphone with bayesian networks and behavior selection networks," *Expert Systems with Applications,* vol. 39, no. 12, pp. 11 284–11 292, 2012.

20. K. P. Murphy, "Dynamic bayesian networks: representation, inference and learning," Ph.D. dissertation, University of California, 2002.

21. M. M. Bradley and P. J. Lang, "Measuring emotion: the self-assessment manikin and the semantic differential," *Journal of behavior therapy and experimental psychiatry,* vol. 25, no. 1, pp. 49–59, 1994.

22. A. Mehrabian, "Analysis of the big-five personality factors in terms of the pad temperament model," *Australian Journal of Psychology,* vol. 48, no. 2, pp. 86–92, 1996.

23. M.-J. Han, C.-H. Lin, and K.-T. Song, "Robotic emotional expression generation based on mood transition and personality model," *Cybernetics, IEEE Transactions on,* vol. 43, no. 4, pp. 1290–1303, 2013.

24. C.-C. Tsai, C.-C. Chen, C.-K. Chan, and Y. Y. Li, "Behavior-based navigation using heuristic fuzzy kohonen clustering network for mobile service robots." *International Journal of Fuzzy Systems,* vol. 12, no. 1, 2010.

Can a Social Robot Help Children's Understanding of Science in Classrooms?

Tsuyoshi Komatsubara, Masahiro Shiomi, Takayuki Kanda, Hiroshi Ishiguro, Norihiro Hagita
ATR Intelligent Robotics and Communication Laboratory
2-2-2 Hikaridai, Keihanna Science City, Kyoto, Japan
{komatsubara.tsuyoshi, m-shiomi, kanda, hagita}@atr.jp, ishiguro@sys.es.osaka-u.ac.jp

ABSTRACT

This study investigates whether a social robot which interacts with children via quiz-style conversations increases their understanding of science classes. We installed a social robot in an elementary school science classroom where children could freely interact with it during their breaks. The robot asks children questions related to their latest science classes to support their understanding of the classes. During interaction, the robot says children's name and distribute its gaze among the group of children by using a face recognition system and a human tracking system. Still, speech recognition is difficult in the noisy elementary school environment; therefore the operator takes over this function during interactions. In this study our result did not show significant effects of the robot for helping children's understanding, but we found several interesting interaction scenes which shows that the robot had a certain effect on specific children.

Author Keywords

Robots for children; social robot; field study.

ACM Classification Keywords

I.2.9. Artificial Intelligence: Robotics

INTRODUCTION

Robotics researchers are investigating possibilities of robots as learning support systems under the context of the Science Technology Engineering and Math (STEM) education. For example, small robot-kits like Lego mindstorms have been used for teaching materials as a tool [1, 2]. Visual programming language is particularly useful for children [1], and such trials contributed to children's math scores [2].

Robots are also used as an agent, which interacts with children in STEM education. Other studies have reported

the effectiveness of interactive robots for vocabulary and language learning [3, 4]. The presence of a social robot would contribute to realize an enjoyable learner-centered class and encourage children to participate more [5].

We are setting up a social robot into a real elementary school to increase the science curiosity of children. Following this context, in this paper, we try to support children's understanding towards contents related to science classes through interaction with a social robot at the school. In previous studies, the fact was found that a design of group interaction is essential for a social robot which interacts with children.

For realizing an interaction with a group of children that would help their understanding, we employed a quiz-style conversation which elicits interaction from the children. We designed quizzes to include important topics related to the latest science classes therefore the children can review the topics again through interactions with the robot. We implemented a face recognition function and a human tracking system for the robot to say children's name with gaze behaviors to accomplish more natural interactions with the groups of children.

In this paper, we try to make a robot which helps children's understanding towards science classes through quiz-style conversations. For this purpose, we implemented a gaze model for a robot to distribute the gaze among the group of children. We installed the robot into the science room of an elementary school where science classes are conducted. The robot interacted with children during the free time before/after science classes (Figure 1).

Figure 1. Children raised their hands to answer a question from the robot.

RELATED WORK

Gaze model

Gaze behaviors in human-robot interaction have been broadly evaluated: turn-taking [6], joint attention [7], influences towards infants' perceptions [8], and eye contacts [8, 9]. For example, Yamazaki et al. constructed a gaze model that enables a robot to provide information with precise timing [6]. Nagai et al. investigated how a robot's gaze behavior is essential to show the intention of the robot to others [7].

Several research works focused on gaze behaviors in an interaction between a robot and a group of people. Mutlu et al have reported that people appropriately distribute their gaze to interacting people and environments during conversation with three people and investigated the effectiveness of such gaze behaviors in the case of human-robot interaction [10]. Kircher et al designed an imitated gaze cue for nonverbal robot-group interaction [11]. In their study, a gaze cue is used to show the robot's intention to interact with a specific person among group of people. However, the past works did not focus on distributing robot's gaze under interactions with more than four people; our study focused on a model to appropriately distribute the robot's gaze in such situations.

Interactive robots for learning and motivating

Researchers have investigated effectiveness of several interaction styles of interactive robots in the context of promoting children's learning. For example, Saerbeck et al have employed game-like interaction for vocabulary and language learning [12]. Han et al also focused on vocabulary and language learning at home environments [3]. Tanaka et al focused on "learning by teaching" style to promote children's learning [13]. Kanda et al installed a social robot which only speaks English into an elementary school in order to encourage interaction in English for children [4].

Researchers are tackling a couple of long-term motivation issues by using agents and robots. For example, Bickmore et al. developed a screen agent to motivate people to exercise [14]. Kidd et al. used a robot to motivate users to continue their weight-loss activities [15]. In both studies, agents and robots are designed to engage human-like daily conversations to explicitly motivate users for exercise activities. Yet these studies did not focus on group interaction with children at a real environment, unlike our study.

SYSTEM OVERVIEW

Figure 2 shows an overview of the system we implemented, which involves an operator. The system estimates positions of both children and robot by using depth sensors which are installed in the environment. Children's faces are recognized by using camera images from the robot's camera. Unlike these automatic functions, an operator takes over speech recognition because with current technology it

is difficult to realize robust speech recognition in noisy environments, such as real classes in an elementary school. The system integrates the results of face recognition, estimated positions and speech to decide its actions by using our gaze model and rules for utterance.

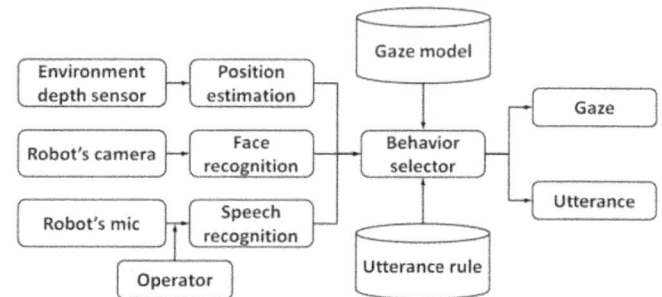

Figure 2. System overview

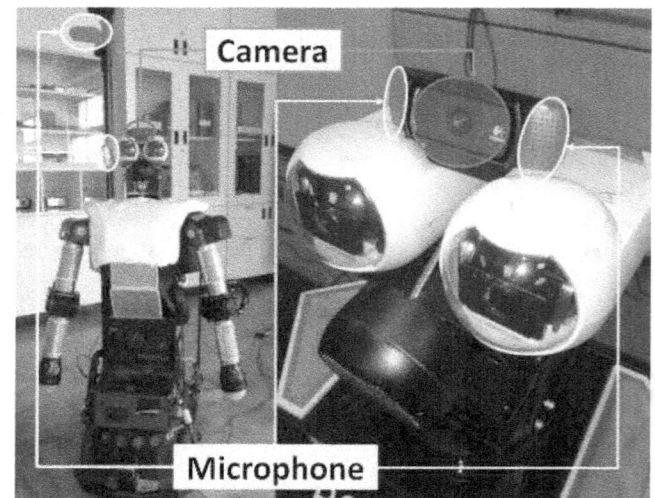

Figure 3. Robovie with an external camera

Robot

We used a communication robot, Robovie, which is 120-cm tall with two arms (4*2 DOF) and a head (3 DOF) (Figure 3). Robovie has two cameras as eyes, microphones, and a speaker. We used speech synthesis software for utterances [16].

We attached external camera for face recognition to the head of Robovie. For face recognition, we used a OKAO Vision-based face-recognition software [17]. Before field trial, the robot interacted with each child around 1~2 minutes to introduce itself; during interaction, face images were collected through the camera to build a database for face recognition.

For this study, an operator takes over the speech recognition function by using a tele-operation system (Wizard of Oz [18]). This system enables the operator to select the results of speech recognition based on pre-determined candidates. The robot decides its actions by using the speech recognition results.

The fact has been revealed that robot's best approach to human depends on situations of human and robot [19][20]. Therefore it is important to change robot's position depending on interlocutors. However, in this study, robot did not move for safety because many children irregularly move in classroom.

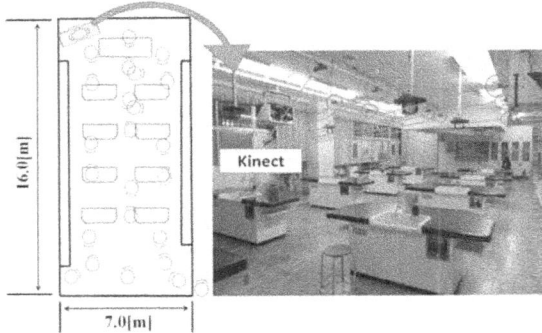

Figure 4. Environments and sensors

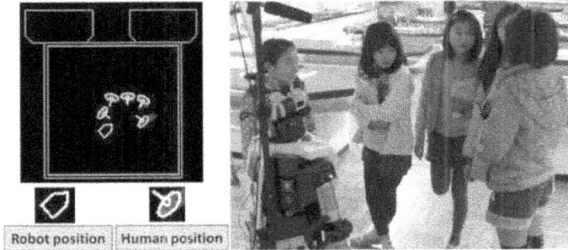

Figure 5. Human tracking system. A pentagon and ellipses represent positions of the robot and children.

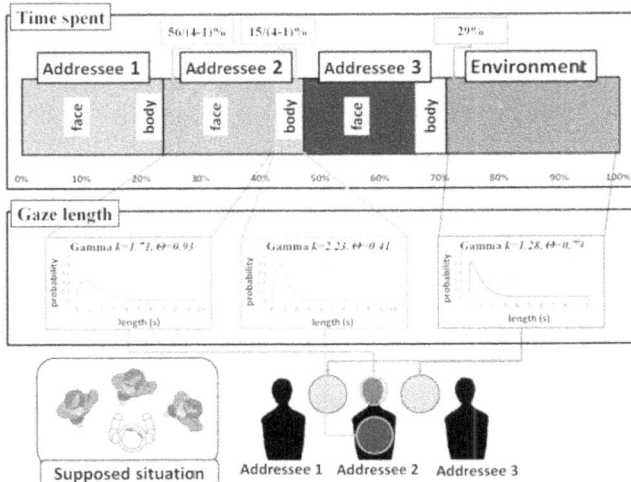

Figure 6. Gaze model for 4-party conversation.

Human tracking system

Figure 4 shows a science room at an elementary school that has eight desks in front of a blackboard, where children attend science classes. We installed 24 depth sensors (Kinect) on the ceiling of the room for position estimation. We employed a human tracking system proposed in [21]; the system allows us to track the positions of all the persons

in the area at 30 Hz with accuracy of around 30 cm. More details of the tracking technique are reported in [21]. Figure 5 shows a tracking result (left) of a situation where Robovie is interacting with five children (right).

We also implemented a function to integrate the estimated position information and the results of face recognition. Face positions from the human tracking system are converted to the X-Y coordinate on robot's external camera images. Then, the system associated face ID to a nearest person within a certain distance on the X-Y coordinates on robot's external camera images.

Environment and setup

Robovie was installed in an elementary school science room (Fig. 4). The science room remained open before and after science lessons. During science classes, Robovie did not initiate conversation; if children talked to it, it suggested, "I'm sorry. I'm prohibited talking during class." This feature was designed to avoid disturbing class activities. During breaks, children were allowed to freely interact with Robovie in the free space.

Gaze model

To implement a gaze model for n-party conversation in this study, we extended Mutlu's gaze model which considered three-party conversation [10]. In this model, they followed Clark's classification model [22], i.e., they classified interlocutors into addressees, bystanders and overhearers to build the gaze model (the details of definitions of the categories are reported in [22]). The authors focused on three situations for modeling gaze behaviors: (1) two-party conversation with a speaker, an addressee and an overhearer, (2) two-party-with-bystander conversation with a speaker, an addressee and a bystander, and (3) three-party conversation with a speaker and two addressees.

We focused on the third situation. They modeled speaker's gaze behaviors in three-party conversation by defining the ratios of gazing targets, i.e., addressee 1's face, addressee 2's face, addressee 1's body, addressee 2's body, and environment. The values were 21%, 35%, 7%, 8%, and 29%, respectively. These values were calculated by observing three-party conversation in laboratory. We added up probabilities and divided by the number of addressees toward the ratios for faces and bodies to extend the model for n-party conversations ($n > 3$).

Figure 6 shows the proposed gaze model. In this model, the speaker's gaze will be distributed into three kinds of areas: addressee's face, addressee's body, and environments. In n-party conversation with a speaker and n-1 addressees, we defined the probability of gazing at an addressee k's face is $56/(n-1)\%$, the probability of gazing at an addressee k's body is $15/(n-1)\%$. The rest of percentages are equally distributed among candidates in the environment. The number of candidates is n-2; the areas are defined between faces of two addressees.

We also used gamma distributions, defined by parameters θ for shape and k for scale, to calculate gaze duration toward each target similar to [10]. Figure 6 shows the distribution parameters values for each target; horizontal axis and vertical axis represent gaze duration and probability which is used in the calculation process to decide the gaze duration. For our model, we used the same parameter values as in [10]. In [10], calculated parameters of addressee 1's face, addressee 2's face, addressee 1's body, addressee 2's body, and environment were (θ, k)=(1.25, 1.26), (1.71, 0.93), (1.61, 0.62), (2.23, 0.41), and (1.28, 0.70) in three-party conversation. We selected their addressee 2's parameters as addressee k's parameters simply in our model because gazing ratios of addressee 2 were more than those of addressee 1. We equalized parameters of all addressees so that robot can gaze equally.

We defined three rules to decide the target person. The first rule is to express acknowledgement to the new addressee. The robot looks at a person who approached the robot within 2.0 m. The second rule is to distribute robot's gaze to person when it calls his/her name. Gaze duration in these two rules follows the gamma distribution there the robot looks at the face. The third rule is to distribute robot's gaze to interacting people. The robot looks at people who are within 3.5 m of the robot and within angle of 160 degrees in front of the robot. If there are people within a range of 2.0 m from the robot, it does not look at people who are within 2.0~3.5 m from the robot. These distance thresholds were experimentally decided by considering with the size of space where the robot is interacting with children, and knowledge of social distance reported by Hall [23]. Figure 7 shows scenes where the robot looks at children's faces based on our gaze model.

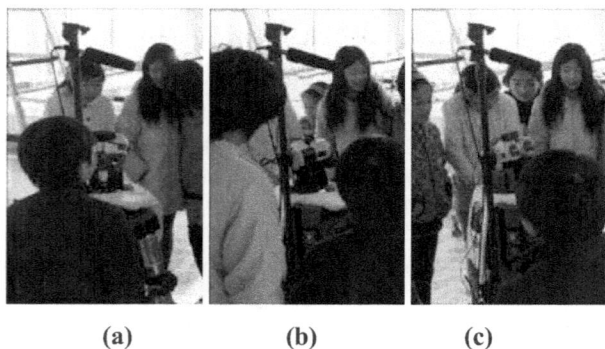

(a)   (b)   (c)

Figure 7. Example of gaze motion.

Details of implemented behaviors

An overview of the dialogue flow is summarized in Fig. 8. When children lingered around Robovie during breaks, it started to gaze at them and initiated conversation. Robovie autonomously interacts with children, except for speech recognition and behavior selections towards unexpected conversation flow.

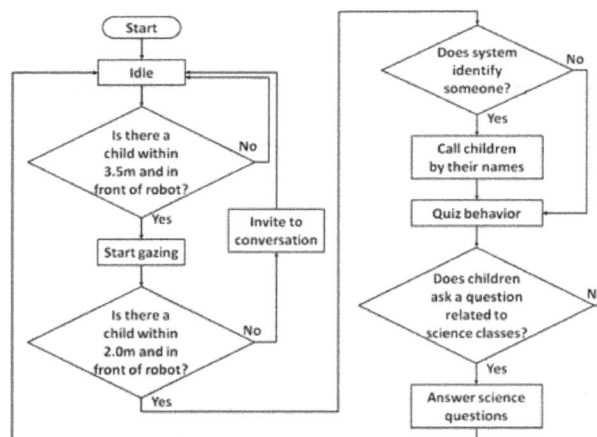

Figure 8. Flow of Robovie's dialogue

Calling children by their names Since the fact was found that people appreciated their name being called by robots[4], we considered this strategy and prepared behaviors to greet the children by names, such as "Hello, Tanaka-san (pseudo name)." If the system did not identify children, the robot only greets them in a generic way.

Quiz behavior After greeting, the robot starts a quiz related to science classes. Before the quiz the robot says a topic related to the latest class: "I think that you already learned about a spawn of medaka (Japanese rice fish). It is very small, but I'm wondering what size the human ovum is". In this study, almost of all quizzes consist of two or three choices.

We designed the robot to repeat important parts of quiz in conversations, such as "I'll give you a question about the size of the human ovum. What is the size of the human ovum? No.1 1.4 mm, No.2 0.14 mm, or No.3 0.014 mm. Pick an answer." After explaining choices, the robot tells the correct answer of the quiz and gives a simple explanation about it.

Answering science questions When a question was asked, the operator judged its relevance to science classes. To answer it, the operator employed two strategies. When typical questions were asked, he selected from pre-implemented behaviors; otherwise, he directly typed utterances to implement new behaviors after the session.

FIELD TRIAL

Participants

In this field trial, we targeted four classes of 114 5th grade students at a public elementary school. They usually used the science room for science classes.

Procedure

Each class had ten lectures during experiment term. Pendulums and human birth were taught during the lectures.

We separated the installation term of Robovie due to the lecture unit; two of four classes learned pendulums with Robovie, and rest of four classes learned human birth with Robovie. Science classes have 45 minutes, followed by a five to twenty minute break. During breaks, children could freely interact with Robovie.

We administered questionnaires to the children. Pre-tests were conducted before the first science class, and post-tests were conducted after the final science class of each unit.

Measurements

In both the pre- and post-tests, we measured their understanding about each learning unit through quizzes, which are developed based on examinations of the elementary school and entrance examinations for junior high schools in Japan. We evaluated and modified the difficulties of the quizzes with 6th grade students of the elementary school. An example of the quizzes is as follows:

- Which of the following changes would speed up a metronome's tempo?

A: Increase the amplitude of the pendulum rod

B: Decrease the amplitude of the pendulum rod

C: Lower the position of the weight

D: Heighten the position of the weight

RESULTS

General trend

The children's interaction with Robovie gradually changed during our two weeks trial which was conducted twice. In the first week many children seemed interested and gathered around Robovie to answer the quizzes. Figure 9 shows a situation where children raised their hands during answering. Moreover, the robot's greeting-by-name behavior attracted their attention (Figure 10). For example, they often asked, "Do you know my name?".

Figure 9. Children raised their hands when they regarded choice robot told as answer.

Figure 10. A child raised her hand when robot called her name.

On the other hand, in the second week, the size of groups became small. Maybe because some of them lost interest towards Robovie. Still almost all of the children continued to greet and to request to hear their name from Robovie during breaks, only about half continued to join quizzes. Typically, a group of active children interacted with Robovie after classes; after they left, children who were waiting of Robovie took turns interacting with it.

Evaluation

Scores of quizzes under the situation where Robovie was installed and not installed were 7.65 and 7.52 relatively on average. Each standard deviation were 1.92 and 2.01 relatively. There is no significant difference between them from paired t-test results ($t(96)=0.50$, $p=0.62$).

Observation

In the whole experiment, 68 children listened to Robovie's quizzes 183 times in total (2.7 times on average). The maximum number of times for a single child was 11 times. This child made conversations with Robovie in every break, and spent about 30minutes interacting with it. 46 children never listened to Robovie's quizzes (40.4% of all children).

Even if the questionnaires results did not show significant differences, we found several interesting scenes and descriptions in the questionnaires during the field trial. For example, at the post-test, three children who interacted with Robovie and participated to quizzes explicitly indicated that they learned specific knowledge about the roles of amniotic fluid in the answers to the questionnaires. Actually they only learned that amniotic fluid has a role of protecting unborn child through their science classes; therefore interaction with Robovie provided new knowledge to them and they could remember them at the post-test. Figure 11 shows situation where one of these children talked with Robovie about this knowledge. (Child B in Figure 11)

Figure 11. A child told the teacher about the knowledge the robot gave him. (Child A: Left in (a), Child B: Right in (a), Teacher: Right in (b))

Robot: Do you know what a role amniotic fluid has? (Figure 11a)

Child B: It protects unborn child against danger from outside.

Robot: You are familiar with that. But actually, it has two other roles. Do you know about them?

Child B: What's? I don't know.

Child A: (Child A was considering the question with Child B)

Robot: Actually, the amniotic fluid has a role of rehydration and ... (At this time, teacher entered the classroom and the conversation ended.)

Child B: Wow! Amazing! (He talked to the teacher) He is awesome (Figure 11b).

Teacher: What happened?

Child B: He told that unborn child can rehydrate because of amniotic fluid.

Teacher: Wow!

He had never listened to Robovie's quiz until this time. However in the next break, he talked with Robovie for about ten minutes and listened to four quizzes.

Figure 12 shows a situation where the child made a mistake in the quiz and then he asked the robot to explain the correct answer. The children had learned the principle that the period of the pendulum has nothing to do with its weight in the previous class.

Figure 12. A child directed a question at the robot when the robot gave the quiz answer. (Child A: Center, Child B: Second from the right, Child C: Right)

Robot: What happens to the period of a pendulum if its weight becomes heavier? If its weight becomes heavier, the period gets shorter, longer, or doesn't change. Pick an answer.

Child B, C: The period gets longer.

Robot: Who thinks the period gets shorter if the weight becomes heavier?

Children: ...

Robot: Who thinks the period gets longer?

Child B, C: (They raised their hands.)

Robot: I see. Finally, who thinks the period doesn't change if the weight becomes heavier?

Child A: (She raised her hand)

Robot: I'll tell you answer. If the weight become heavier, the period doesn't change.

Child: Why?

Robot: You may already know, but actually both heavy matter and light matter fall at the same speed.

Figure 13 shows an example of conversations between Robovie and the child who listened to Robovie's quizzes the most times in this experiment.

In this case, an interesting observation is that she took some actions other children did not take. On the last day of experiment, she came to Robovie immediately after finishing class (Figure 13a) and talked with it for about fifteen minutes. In that conversation, she seemed to be curious to hear Robovie's quiz on her own initiative: she said "Please give me another quiz." She also showed her textbook to ask a question about a topic on it (Figure 13b). In addition, when Robovie's farewell party was held for the whole school after experiment, she came to greet it after the party.

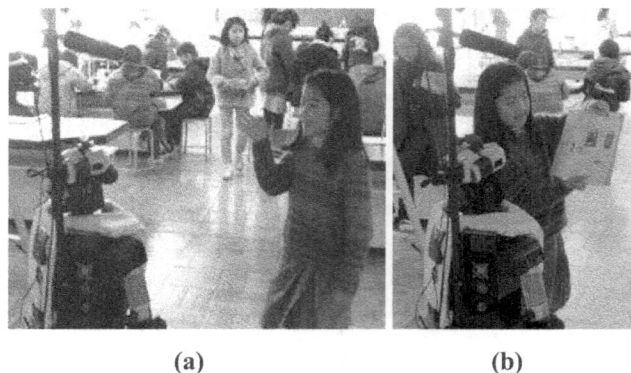

Figure 13. A child seemed to build a close relationship with the robot.

Child: What is this? (Pointing at a topic on the textbook which has no relevance to the class)

Robot: Well, I don't know about it because that topic is not related to today's class.

Child: (Child nodded.) Hey Robovie, what principle does this toy apply? (Pointing at a pendulum-based toy on the textbook)

Robot: Well, that toy applies the principle that the period of a pendulum changes depending on its length. We can play with the toy to change the length to swing the claws of the crab.

No other children got into similar actions. It seems that she had an interest in science or Robovie from the fact that she listened to Robovie alone in the beginning of the experiment. We conjecture that her interest in science or Robovie graded into relationship such as friendship between them through having conversation several times. These facts show that robots have a potential to make a strong impact on specific children.

DISCUSSION

Why robot could not increase children's score?

In our study, in the cases of figures shown in **Observation,** children replied reaction to robot well. There were only one to six children around Robovie. And there was no child who was not interested in Robovie's quiz or interfered with its utterance. In addition, the classroom was relatively quiet because there were few children in classroom. It was thus a suitable situation for children to concentrate on listening to Robovie's utterance. In almost of all such situations in this experiment, conversations between children and Robovie through the quizzes were successful. We conjecture that children replied reaction well due to this suitable situation.

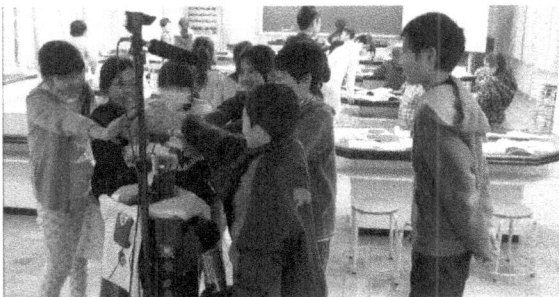

Figure 14. Children covered the robot's eyes with their hands.

However, in our study, Robovie could not increase the understanding of science classes for children significantly. We conjecture that the effect on understanding was not significant because situations where children cannot be absorbed in listening to Robovie happened most of the time. Figure 14 is an example of such situations. Figure 14 shows that children had an interest not in conversation with Robovie but covering its eyes with their hands. A similar observation was reported in Hato et al. [24]. They suggested that this behavior is due to human's understanding of robot's communicative and informative

intention. In terms of this suggestion, at least, Robovie could have a role of a communication partner.

We conjecture that there are two reasons why children could not be absorbed in listening to Robovie: no significant flexibility and answering design. Firstly, Robovie could not deal flexibly with children's behaviors. For example, Robovie continued explanation for a quiz though children answered it immediately. In addition, since we designed the Robovie to repeat important parts of quiz, children sometimes seemed to find it boring. As a result, situations were often observed where children had their attention caught by something other than conversation (Figure 15).

Secondly, it seemed that Robovie bored children because of its design that it answers only questions related to the science class. For its design, Robovie could not sometimes answer a very easy question which is not related to science class. Once, a child said "You can answer that question, can't you?" after it could not answer his question: "How much is $1 + 1$?" Avoiding such simple questions would hinder the children's interest in conversation with Robovie.

Figure 15. Children directed their attentions on Robovie's microphone.

CONCLUSION

Our field study investigated whether a social robot which interacts with children via quiz-style conversations can increase the understanding of science classes for them. Robovie was installed in a science room for five weeks, where children were allowed to freely interact with it during breaks. Although Robovie could not increase the children's score, some interesting scenes were observed, which shows that Robovie has a potential to make a strong impact on children in specific situations: it gives them knowledge they do not know, or it builds a close relationship with them so that they could ask a question freely. We conclude that Robovie can have an effect on children in suitable situations, in which children can listen to Robovie sufficiently. However, in situations where children tend to take actions besides conversation, it is difficult for Robovie to have an effect on them.

ACKNOWLEDGMENTS

We thank the staff at the Higashi-Hikari elementary school, its students, and their parents for their cooperation. We also thank Prof. Naomi Miyake (Univ. of Tokyo) for her helpful advice, Kanako Tomita who helped conduct the experiment, and Thomas Kaczmarek who helped system development. This work was supported by JSPS KAKENHI Grant Numbers 21118001, 21118003, 21110008, and 25240042.

REFERENCES

1. Chioccariello, A., Manca, S., and Sarti, L., 2001, Children's playful learning with a robotic construction kit, in Developing New Technologies for Young Children, S.-B. J. and J. Siraj-Blatchford eds., pp. 93-174.

2. Hussain, S., Lindh, J., and Shukur, G., 2006, The effect of LEGO Training on Pupils' School Performance in Mathematics, Problem Solving Ability and Attitude: Swedish Data, Educational Technology & Society, vol. 9, pp. 182-194.

3. Han, J., Jo, M., Jones, V. and Jo, J. H., 2008. Comparative Study on the Educational Use of Home Robots for Children. Journal of Information Processing Systems. 4, 4, 159--0.

4. Kanda, T., Hirano, T., Eaton, D., and Ishiguro, H., 2004, Interactive Robots as Social Partners and Peer Tutors for Children: A Field Trial, Human-Computer Interaction, vol. 19, pp. 61-84.

5. Kanda, T., Shimada, M., and Koizumi, S., 2012, Children learning with a social robot, ACM/IEEE Int. Conf. on Human-Robot Interaction (HRI 2012),

6. Yamazaki, A., Yamazaki, K., Kuno, Y., Burdelski, M., Kawahima, M., and Kuzuoka, H. 2008. Precision timing in human-robot interaction: coordination of head movement and utterance. In Proceeding of the 26th SIGCHI Conference on Human Factors in Computing Systems. ACM, pp.131–140.

7. Nagai, Y., K. Hosoda, A. Morita, and M. Asada 2003, A constructive model for the development of joint attention, Connection Science, vol. 15, no. 4, pp. 211–229.

8. Arita A., Hiraki K., Kanda T., and Ishiguro H., 2005, Can we talk to robots? Ten-month-old infants expected interactive humanoid robots to be talked to by persons. Ccog nition, vol. 95, pp. B49-B57.

9. Shimada M. and, Yoshikawa Y., 2011, Effects of Observing Eye Contact between a Robot and Another Person, International Journal of Social Robotics, Vol. 3, No. 2, pp. 143-154.

10. B, Mutlu., T, Kanda., J, Forlizzi., J, HodGins., H, Ishiguro., Conversational Gaze Mechanisms for Humanlike Robots. ACM Transactions on Interactive Intelligent Systems, 2012.

11. Kirchner, N., Alempijevic, A., "A Robot Centric Perspective on HRI", Journal of Human-Robot Interaction, vol. 1, no. 2, pp.135–157, DOI 10.5898/JHRI1.2.Kirchner, 2012

12. Saerbeck, M., Schut, T., Bartneck, C., and Janse, M. D., 2010, Expressive Robots in Education: Varying the Degree of Social Supportive Behavior of a Robotic Tutor, ACM Conference on Human Factors in Computing Systems (CHI2010), pp. 1613-1622.

13. Tanaka, F. and Matsuzoe, S., 2012, Children Teach a Care-Receiving Robot to Promote Their Learning: Field Experiments in a Classroom for Vocabulary Learning, Journal of Human-Robot Interaction, vol. 1, pp. 78-95.

14. Bickmore, T. W. and Picard, R. W., 2005, Establishing and Maintaining Long-Term Human-Computer Relationships, ACM Transactions on Computer-Human Interaction (TOCHI), vol. 12, pp. 293-327.

15. Kidd, C. D., 2008, Designing for Long-Term Human-Robot Interaction and Application to Weight Loss, ed: Massachusetts Institute of Technology

16. Kawai, H., Toda, T., Ni, J., Tsuzaki, M., and Tokuda, K., 2004, XIMERA: A new TTS from ATR based on corpus-based technologies, ISCA Speech Synthesis Workshop, pp. 179-184.

17. OKAO Vision, OMRON Corporation. http://www.omron.com/r_d/coretech/vision/okao.html

18. N, Dahlbäck., A, Jönsson., L, Ahrenberg., Wizard of Oz studies: why and how, Proceedings of the 1st international conference on Intelligent user interfaces, pp.193-200

19. K, Dautenhahn., M, Walters., S, Woods., K, L, Koay., C, L, Nehaniv., A, Sisbot., R, Alami., T, Siméon., How may I serve you?: a robot companion approaching a seated person in a helping context., Proceedings of the 1st ACM SIGCHI/SIGART conference on Human-robot interaction, pp.172-179

20. M,L, Walters., K, Dautenhahn., R, Te Boekhorst., K, L, Koay., D, S, Syrdal., C, L, Nehaniv., An Empirical Framework for Human-Robot Proxemics., Procs of New Frontiers in Human-Robot Interaction symposium at the AISB09 convention, pp.144-149

21. Brscic, DT. Kanda, T. Ikeda, and T. Miyashita, Person tracking in large public spaces using range sensors, IEEE Transaction on Human-Machine Systems, vol.43, pp.522–534, 2013.

22. H. H. Clark, , "Using Language," Cambridge University Press, 1996

23. E, T, Hall., The Hidden Dimension: Man's Use of Space in Public and Private. The Bodley Head Ltd, 1966

24. Y, Hato., T, Kanold., K, Ishii., M, Imai., Showing Awareness of Humans' Context to Involve Humans in Interaction, IEEE RO-MAN 2009, pp.663-668

Robotic tele-presence with DARYL in the wild

Christian Becker-Asano
Albert-Ludwigs-Universität
Freiburg, Department of
Computer Science
Georges-Köhler-Allee 052
basano@informatik.uni-
freiburg.de

Kai O. Arras
Albert-Ludwigs-Universität
Freiburg, Department of
Computer Science
Georges-Köhler-Allee 074
arras@informatik.uni-
freiburg.de

Bernhard Nebel
Albert-Ludwigs-Universität
Freiburg, Department of
Computer Science
Georges-Köhler-Allee 052
nebel@informatik.uni-
freiburg.de

ABSTRACT

This paper describes the results of a qualitative analysis of questionnaire data collected during a public exhibition of our robotic tele-presence system. In Summer 2013 the mildly humanized robot DARYL could be tried out by the general public during our University's science fair in the city center. People were given the chance to communicate through the robot with their peers and to perceive the world through the "eyes" and "ears" of the robot by means of a head-mounted display with attached headphones. An operator's voice was instantaneously transmitted to the robot's location and his or her head movements were tracked to enable direct, intuitive control of the robot's head movements. Twenty-seven people were interviewed in a structured way about their impressions and opinions after having either operated or interacted with the tele-operated robot. A careful analysis of the acquired data reveals a rather positive evaluation of the tele-presence system and interesting opinions about suitable application areas. These findings may guide designers of robotic tele-presence systems, a research area of increasing popularity.

Author Keywords

robotics; tele-operation; survey; head-mounted display

ACM Classification Keywords

I.2.9 Robotics: Operator interfaces; J.4 Social and behavioral sciences: Sociology

INTRODUCTION

Recently, many new robotic telepresence systems have been advertised to be released to the global market. They are supposed to be used by the general public affording only a short initial training phase. By "replicating a person in a distant location" they are advertised as helpful tools in domestic and professional domains including remote working, assisted living or telemedicine. A key promise of such systems is that they allow to cut down travel costs because users can remotely meet face-to-face embodied as a robotic avatar.

As with many other technological advancements these claims remain to be tested. Are the different operator interfaces really so well designed that they can be used intuitively and efficiently by non-professionals? Are these systems indeed appropriate substitutes for face-to-face meetings under all possible conditions? What does the general public think about a future with remote controlled robotic avatars?

The remainder of the paper is structured as follows. In the next section related work is going to be introduced and discussed, before the system setup is presented. This is followed by a description of the general scenario that the visitors of the science fair were invited to take part in. Subsequently, the data collection methodology will be detailed and results of a qualitative analysis of the interviews are presented. Finally, conclusions are drawn and possible implications for the applicability of robotic tele-presence systems are discussed.

RELATED WORK

Apart from prominent product announcements (as discussed in [6], e.g., Ava by iRobot, Beam by Suitable Technologies (former Texai by Willow Garage), VGO by Vgo Communications, Giraff by HeadThere, RP-VITA by InTouch Health, TiLR by RoboDynamics, Double by Double Robotics) telepresence robotics is also a hot topic in academic research. In the following an overview of recent work is given.

Indications for the usefulness of HMD-based teleoperation of humanoid robots have been found even for rather passive remote social interaction. A participant embodied as a robot significantly increases a presenter's feeling of being listened to as compared to a video conferencing setup [8].

The 'Giraff' mobile telepresence robot together with a console interface [7] was utilized in a study of a task featuring social and mainly physical interaction (monitoring elderly people). Both spatial and social presence felt by the operator were assessed using questionnaires and, because the Giraff robotic platform is mobile, the study focused on six types of formations realized by the robot operator together with the interlocutors. A number of correlations between the operator's spatial/social presence and these formations are reported, which are interesting even though they were detected post-hoc. They also employed an actor to act in the role of the remote partner making it unfeasible to collect and analyze impressions from remote interaction partners.

The mobile robot "Robonaut" [5] has been tele-operated by means of sophisticated tracking and wireless video transmission of stereo video feeds. The subjective experiences, described only on an informal level, indicate that an HMD-based interface is easy to manage and intuitively operated.

Thirty-two participants used the "double telepresence robot" to collaboratively construct either small or big versions of a geometrical object in a two-by-two empirical study [9]. The impact of operator mobility on task performance and presence was investigated. Although an operator's feeling of presence is higher in the two mobile conditions (as compared to the two stationary conditions), task completion times were on average significantly lower for the two high-mobility tasks as compared to the low-mobility tasks. Again, no measures regarding overall ease of use or user satisfaction were taken in this study.

During a public demonstration of the highly anthropomorphic android robot "Geminoid HI-1" at Ars Electronica a survey of visitors, who had interacted with the tele-operated android, revealed mostly positive attitudes towards this type of interaction device [4]. In addition, results of an empirical study [10] indicate that Geminoid HI-1 can remain unnoticed in a public space suggesting the possibility that the illusion of social presence can be achieved by sophisticated design alone.

Results of a previous empirical study in a laboratory environment [2, 3] suggest that using a head-mounted display (HMD) to tele-operate the mildly humanized robot DARYL in many respects outperforms the use of a standard console interface. Especially, subjective evaluations of an operator's spatial and social presence were significantly higher when an HMD was used as compared to a console.

All these works carry out laboratory studies which are commonly known to be prone of a selection bias regarding the participants' backgrounds and motivations. In this work, however, we take our tele-presence system into the wild collecting data from ordinary people in a public space in the aim to complement the insights gathered from a previous laboratory study [2].

Figure 2. The head unit of the mildly-humanized robot DARYL with annotated degrees of freedom.

SYSTEM SETUP

Fig. 1 shows two views of the setup realized at the exhibition of the tele-operation system during the public science fair in Summer 2013 in the city center of Freiburg, Germany. The

operator (see bottom of Fig. 1(a) and left side of Fig. 1(b)) wears Sony's head-mounted display "HMZ-T1" with a "Colibri" inertial measurement unit mounted on top of it.

The robot DARYL features several degrees of freedom in wheels, torso and head, three of which are used by our telepresence setup (cf. Fig. 2). Two cameras in the robot's eyes and two binaural microphones in the robot's ear-like modalities provide stereoscopic vision and hearing.

Thereby, the operator can see herself from the back through DARYL's two cameras. She can also intuitively change the robot's viewing direction by turning hear head accordingly in all three dimensions. A small wireless microphone allows the transmission of the operators voice and DARYL's stereo microphones let her hear the surroundings of the robot. A more detailed technical description of this setup is provided elsewhere [2].

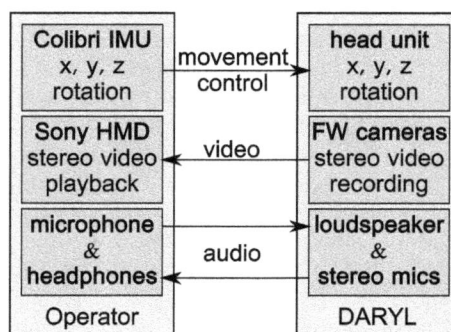

Figure 3. System schematics

A schematic of the connections between the operator and the robot DARYL in presented is Fig. 3. Only audio transmission is bi-directional with the limitation that the operator's voice is transmitted to the robot's location monophonic, whereas a stereophonic transmission is realized for the direction from the robot to the operator. Together with stereo video transmission in the same direction highest levels of social presence can be achieved [2].

SCENARIO DESCRIPTION

The science fair took place in the center of Freiburg city mainly inside show tents. We were provided with an area measuring two meters by four meters in total. Only one side of this area was closed by a partition panel leaving enough opportunity for visitors to see our robotic tele-presence setup from a distance.

Accordingly, visitors of the science fair could always engage the staff during the opening hours from 10am until 6pm on both exhibition days, July 12 and 13, 2013. Under such circumstances, a controlled study is hard to carry out soundly. Thus, we decided to target groups of at least two people and let them freely try out the system. In most cases only one of them operated the robot (N=23) and all others interacted with him or her through the robot. Sometimes, however, people took turns with operating the robot so that these people reported on their impressions from both perspectives (N=4).

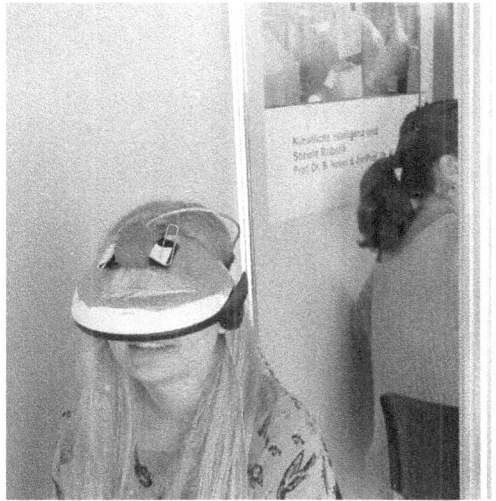

(a) Overhead camera view   (b) Side view with the operator to the left and the operated robot to the right

Figure 1. The robot DARYL installed at the science fair operated by a visitor

DATA COLLECTION

After their experience with the tele-operation system every group was asked, if they were willing to report on their feelings and impressions by taking part in a short interview. The scientific background of this interview was explained to them and, if they agreed (which was the case for all visitors that we asked), the interview was recorded using digital audio equipment.

A total of twenty-seven visitors (17 male, 10 female) agreed to be interviewed. Fifteen (11 male) had only operated the robot DARYL, eight (three male) only interacted with it, and four (three male) had done both before the interview began. On average the participants were 30 years old (standard deviation (STD) 15 years) and the majority of them (N=18) described their friendship relationship with the person they had just interacted with as "very good" (as opposed to "good", N=3, and "none", N=6). For all 27 visitors except one this was the first time to see the robot DARYL face-to-face and, again, the majority of them (N=23) had never heard of or read about this robot before.

After this background data was collected, the subsequent open-response part of the interview consisted of the following four sections:

1. Please describe the robot "DARYL".

2. Did you hesitate to participate in the experiment? Please elaborate.

3. How did you feel, when you had the conversation with another person through DARYL?

4. Do you believe that robots such as "DARYL" could be used in the future to participate in meetings/conferences in another country? Which other applications could you possibly imagine for this technology?

With this we followed a very similar interview structure used in previous research on the "uncanny valley" employing the android robot "Geminoid HI-1" in a public exhibition [4]. The resulting audio files were transcribed and a qualitative analysis of these interviews is presented next.

QUALITATIVE ANALYSIS

1. Descriptions of DARYL

At first, visitors described the robot DARYL in their own words. Their descriptions are summarized here distinguishing positive and negative adjectives.

As can be seen in Table 1, the descriptions of many visitors included technical descriptions (N=11), which are rated as neutral adjective in this list (N=16). In summary, the descriptions contained far more positive (N=28) than negative adjectives (N=4).

Interestingly, some visitors chose to describe the robot positively but in a way that could imply a negative attitude, because they negated a negative adjective such as "scary" or reported their "surprise". It also seemed difficult for some to focus on describing the robot and not their experience with it, as in case of those who reported, for example, a "strange feeling" or "jerking".

2. Hesitation to participate

Of all 27 visitors only two reported having hesitate for a moment before trying out the system. The remaining 25 visitors stated not having hesitated at all.

3. Feelings during conversation

The most frequently reported feeling "strange" is not necessarily a negative one, because it can be described as both being curious, which is a slightly positive feeling, and embarrassed, a slightly negative feeling [11]. Even when "strange" is being counted as negative, the number of positive feelings

adjective	positive	negative	neutral
technical			11
funny	7		
human-like			5
interesting	4		
fascinating	3		
friendly	2		
good looking	2		
very good	2		
frightening		2	
jerking		1	
strange feeling		1	
beautiful	1		
clever	1		
cool	1		
innovative	1		
not scary	1		
reacts very fast	1		
impressive	1		
surprising	1		
$\sum$	28	4	16

Table 1. List of adjectives derived from descriptions of the robot DARYL sorted by total count and split up into positive, negative, and neutral connotations respectively. Visitors, who provided longer descriptions, contributed more than one adjective to this list.

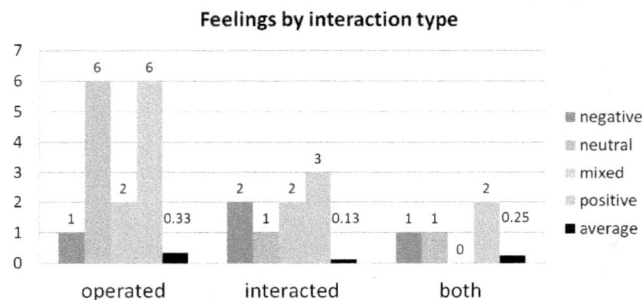

Figure 4. Bar plot showing the interaction between self-reported overall feeling and interaction type group

feeling	positive	negative	neutral
strange		7	
fascinating	4		
like Skype or better	4		
funny	4		
normal			3
jerky		2	
unusual		2	
alien		1	
insecure		1	
amusing	1		
exceptional	1		
impressive	1		
works very well	1		
interesting	1		
comfortable	1		
close to partner	1		
curiosity	1		
positive	1		
nice	1		
great	1		
changing perspective			1
direct			1
present			1
$\sum$	23	13	6

Table 2. List of feelings reported by the visitors when being asked about how they felt during their remote conversation sorted by total count and split up into positive, negative, and neutral connotations. Visitors, who provided long answers, contributed more than one token to this list.

(55%) outweighs the sum of the negative (31%) and the neutral feelings (14%) listed in Table 2.

The bar plot presented in Fig. 4 presents a summary of the acquired data cross-correlated with the "interaction type" of each participant. First, for each participant's answer it was determined whether it contained only *negative* adjectives, both positive and negative adjectives (labeled *mixed* in Fig. 4), only *positive* adjectives, or purely *neutral* ones. This was then cross-correlated with the participant either only having *operated* the robot, or *interacted* with it, or *both*. In addition, the normalized *average* is calculated per interaction type (int_type) according to the formula:

$$N_{avg}(int\_type) = \frac{-1 \times N_{neg}(int\_type) + N_{pos}(int\_type)}{N_{total}(int\_type)}$$

In effect, the data suggests that the system was evaluated most positively by those participants who had solely operated the

robot DARYL ($N_{avg}(operated) = 0.33 > N_{avg}(both) = 0.25 > N_{avg}(interacted) = 0.13$). However, the rather low number of participants per interaction type needs to be taken into account when critically assessing the general value of this result.

4. Future applications

A summary of all applications discussed and/or proposed by the visitors is presented in Table 3. It is not surprising that *conference* was mentioned and discussed very often, because the questionnaire item mentioned this application as an example of a particular application. Therefore, the fact that on average two out of nine participants responded negatively to this proposition seems most informative.

Interestingly, six individuals independently came up with the idea of using this system for *emergency management* and another four even considered an application *at home* possible. Both of these application scenarios were not even once judged as inappropriate, whereas health care-related applications, such as working in the *hospital* or taking care of *disabled persons*, were much more controversial.

CONCLUSIONS AND DISCUSSION

We set out to test our HMD-based robotic tele-presence system with regard to the general population's degree of acceptance, their subjective feelings, and their opinion of its usefulness in real-world applications. On average more positive

application type	yes	no
conference	14	4
emergency management	6	0
at home	4	0
skype++ / video conference	3	1
site inspection	2	0
hospital	2	1
disabled person	2	1
assisting disabled person	1	0
space	1	0
mining	1	0
computer games	1	0
entertainment	1	0
shopping	1	0
in the movies	1	0
$\sum$	42	7

Table 3. List of applications that were deemed appropriate (yes column) or inappropriate (no column) for the tele-presence system sorted by total count. Again, visitors giving long answers potentially contributed more than once to this list.

than negative responses were given regarding, both, the general likability of the robot DARYL itself as well as the feelings whilst tele-operating it. Also, nobody seemed to have hesitated to try out the system, which might indicate that the robot is not perceived as threatening and the whole system is expected to be intuitive to use.

When asked about possible applications of such a system, it is surprising that health-care applications (e.g. in a hospital as proposed by [7] or in a day care center for the elderly [12]) are seen very critical by the public. Of course, this might only be the case for this particular robotic setup. However, other applications such as "emergency management" might be better accepted and, thus, should be investigated and developed further.

In the light of previous results on social and spatial presence [2], we have to admit that DARYL's appearance might be too far away from human-likeness to expect similarly strong body ownership transfer as found for HMD-based tele-operation of Geminoid HI-1 [1]. Nonetheless, this expectation is one more piece of the puzzle, which is going to be investigated in future studies on the effects of cross-combining operator modalities with robotic embodiments [3].

ACKNOWLEDGMENTS

The authors would like to thank Severin Gustorff for his help with developing and implementing the tele-presence system.

REFERENCES

1. Alimardani, M., Nishio, S., and Ishiguro, H. Humanlike robot hands controlled by brain activity arouse illusion of ownership in operators. *Scientific reports 3* (2013).

2. Becker-Asano, C., Gustorff, S., Arras, K. O., and Nebel, B. On the effect of operator modality on social and spatial presence during teleoperation of a human-like robot. In *Third Intl. Symposium on New Frontiers in Human-Robot Interaction at AISB50* (2014).

3. Becker-Asano, C., Gustorff, S., Arras, K. O., Ogawa, K., Nishio, S., Ishiguro, H., and Nebel, B. Robot embodiment, operator modality, and social interaction in tele-existence: A project outline. In *Proc. of Intl. Conf. on Human-Robot Interaction (HRI2013)*, IEEE (2013), 79–80.

4. Becker-Asano, C., Nishio, S., Ogawa, K., and Ishiguro, H. Exploring the Uncanny Valley with Geminoid HI-1 in a real-world application. In *IADIS Intl. Conf. on Interfaces and Human Computer Interaction* (Freiburg, 2010), 121–128.

5. Goza, S. M., Ambrose, R. O., Diftler, M. A., and Spain, I. M. Telepresence control of the NASA/DARPA robonaut on a mobility platform. In *Proceedings of the SIGCHI Conference on Human Factors in Computing Systems*, CHI '04, ACM (New York, NY, USA, 2004), 623–629.

6. Kristoffersson, A., Coradeschi, S., and Loutfi, A. A review of mobile robotic telepresence. *Advances in Human-Computer Interaction 2013* (2013).

7. Kristoffersson, A., Severinson Eklundh, K., and Loutfi, A. Measuring the quality of interaction in mobile robotic telepresence: A pilot's perspective. *Intl. Journal of Social Robotics 5*, 1 (2013), 89–101.

8. Morita, T., Mase, K., Hirano, Y., and Kajita, S. Reciprocal attentive communication in remote meeting with a humanoid robot. In *Procs. of the 9th Intl. Conf. on Multimodal Interfaces*, ACM (2007), 228–235.

9. Rae, I., Mutlu, B., and Takayama, L. Bodies in motion: Mobility, presence, and task awareness in telepresence. In *Procs. of CHI2014* (2014).

10. Rosenthal-von der Pütten, A. M., Krämer, N. C., Becker-Asano, C., Ogawa, K., Nishio, S., and Ishiguro, H. The uncanny in the wild. Analysis of unscripted human-android interaction in the field. *Intl. Journal of Social Robotics* (2013), 1–17.

11. Russell, J., and Mehrabian, A. Evidence for a three-factor theory of emotions. *Journal of Research in Personality 11*, 11 (1977), 273–294.

12. Yamazaki, R., Nishio, S., Ishiguro, H., Nørskov, M., Ishiguro, N., and Balistreri, G. Acceptability of a teleoperated android by senior citizens in danish society. *Intl. Journal of Social Robotics* (2014), 1–14.

Nodding Responses by Collective Proxy Robots for Enhancing Social Telepresence

Tsunehiro Arimoto, Yuichiro Yoshikawa, and Hiroshi Ishiguro
Graduate School of Engineering Science, Osaka University
1-3 Machikaneyama Toyonaka Osaka 560-8531 Japan
{arimoto.tsunehiro, yoshikawa}@irl.sys.es.osaka-u.ac.jp, ishiguro@sys.es.osaka-u.ac.jp

ABSTRACT

It is expected that the social presence of a distant person can be well conveyed in telecommunication using a robot as a proxy of that person. This paper proposes a novel form of robotic telecommunication, which consists not only of a proxy robot but also an additional bystander robot that autonomously responds to the interlocutor in front of them. The second robot is expected to complement the responses of the proxy robot so that the interlocutor feels stronger social telepresence of the distant person. A psychological experiment using two small humanoid robots as proxy and bystander reveals a positive effect on conveying a stronger feeling of social telepresence of the distant person.

Author Keywords

Telepresence; robot mediated-communication; bystander robot.

ACM Classification Keywords

H.5.1. Information Interfaces and Presentation: Multimedia Information Systems - Artificial, augmented, and virtual realities

INTRODUCTION

With the conventional method of telecommunication (ex. telephone), we are able to communicate with persons in remote places. However, due to the lack of presence of the interlocutor, telecommunication sometimes is more difficult than face-to-face communication where nonverbal channels are available to express acknowledgment for smooth communication. Several studies have been carried out about enabling social telepresence in telecommunications[6]. In particular, humanoid robots are expected to assume the role of proxy for a person in a remote place [8][2][9] [7][5] and convey nonverbal information for enhancing his or her social telepresence.

One straightforward way of utilizing the nonverbal behavior of a proxy robot is the direct control over a network by the

Figure 1. Experiment conditions: (a) shows condition 1, (b) shows condition 2

person in the remote place (i.e., teleoperation). However, due to limitations in the channel capacity of the network, as well as in the interface, which should enable the teleoperator to manipulate the many degrees of freedom of the proxy robot, controlling the proxy robot so that it keeps producing adequate responses for smoother communication is a formidable task. Since the nonverbal responses toward the interlocutors are too prompt or complex for the teleoperator to directly manipulate, an autonomous mechanism should be developed to manage them. In order to introduce such autonomy into the teleoperated robot, it is necessary to design the entire system so that the control signals from the teleoperator and the autonomous mechanisms do not conflict with each other.

In this study, we propose a novel form of telecommunication media using multiple robots. Unlike the conventional telecommunication system that uses only a single proxy robot teleoperated from a remote place (see Figure 1(a)), we make another bystander robot participate in the communication and autonomously exhibit nonverbal responses, instead of requiring the teleoperator to produce them via the proxy robot (see Figure 1(b)). This extension is expected to provide the interlocutor in front of the proxy robot with the opportunity to obtain rapid responses, while releasing the teleoperator of the burden to precisely and rapidly control his or her proxy robot to express acknowledgment when necessary to maintain communication. The first basic question in this approach is whether the responses of the bystander robot work to complement the proxy robot so that the interlocutor facing the proxy robot feels sufficient social presence of the teleoperator.

In this paper, we develop a telecommunication system using both a teleoperated proxy robot and an autonomous bystander robot and use it to conduct a psychological experi-

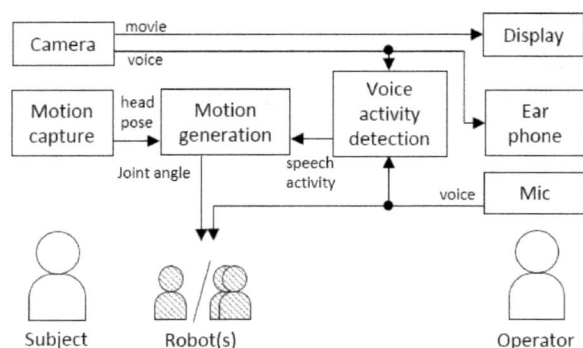

Figure 2. System overview

Figure 3. Appearance of Synchy2

ment. We report the experimental result using the Wilcoxon signed ranks test, a non-parametric, within-subject test that shows the psychological effect of the bystander robot on the feeling of the telepresence, namely the feeling that the subject is in the same room with the teleoperator who is actually in a distant room and talks to them through the proxy robot. Finally, we discuss the implications and limitations of the experimental result.

METHOD

The nodding response of a listener robot is an important listening behavior, which is regarded as a nonverbal acknowledgment to the speaker [10]. A recent study of HRI has shown that the nodding behavior of a robot can be easily misinterpreted by the speaker as the acknowledgment of another robot or person accompanying the nodding robot, even though they did not actually nod [11]. This phenomenon can be exploited in telecommunication to enhance the speaker's feeling of acknowledgment from a person who attends the conversation from a remote place through a proxy robot, which would consequently influence the speaker's feeling of sharing time and space in the conversation, i.e., the social telepresence of the remote person. In this paper, the authors propose to introduce an autonomous robot as a bystander in the telecommunication using a proxy robot. A telecommunication system with two small humanoid robots is deployed in two laboratory rooms which are separated by sound proof walls. One robot is used as a proxy for a teleoperator in one room, while the other is used as a bystander robot displaced beside the proxy robot. Aiming to promote the subjects' confusion of nodding between the two robots, the same type of robot is used for both the proxy and the bystander. A Within-subject test is adopted to compare the subject's feelings of social telepresence of the remote person. More practically, questionnaire scores on the social telepresence are compared in Condition 1, where only a proxy robot is used, and in Condition 2, where both a proxy and a bystander are used.

Subjects

Fourteen Japanese adults (eight males and six females) are hired through a temporary employment agency. Written informed consent is obtained from the subjects. All of them participate in the two styles of telecommunication. They talk to a teleoperator using a telecommunication system with only a single proxy robot in Condition 1. In Condition 2, they use an extended version of the same telecommunication system with both a proxy and a bystander robot. Seven subjects participate in a conversation under Condition 1 first, and then in another, under Condition 2. The remaining seven subjects participate in the reversed order. Note that a male experimenter takes part in the experiment as instructor, as well as the teleoperator of the proxy robot. All subjects are not personally acquainted with the experimenter. Some data are removed from the analysis due to failures in the experiment, namely the occurrence of much vibration or a halt in the robot's functions during conversation. Data from five subjects who participate under Condition 1 first, and seven who participate under Condition 2 first are used in the analysis in this paper.

Apparatus

The telecommunication system using one or two robots (see Figure 2) is setup in two laboratory rooms named "the visitor room" and "the teleoperator room", which are separated by soundproof walls. In the visitor room, one (or two) robot(s) as well as sensors, namely a microphone and an image and depth sensor (i.e., Microsoft Kinect[4]) are placed on a conventional table. The microphone is used for capturing the subject's voice, and the Kinect is used to detect the position of the subject's head. Note that the subject is asked to attach the microphone to his or her body during the conversation. A conventional chair is prepared for the subjects in front of the robot(s). Two video cameras are used to allow the experimenter to monitor and record the behavior of the subject and the robot(s) during the experiment. One is placed close to the proxy robot to capture the subject's behavior, while the other is placed beside the subject to capture the robot(s)'s behavior. In the teleoperator room, a TV interface for the telecommunication is installed on a table. The TV is used to show the images of the subject and the robot(s), captured by the cameras in the visitor room. The teleoperator wears a head-set consisting of a microphone to capture his voice and a headphone speaker to listen to the voice of the subject.

The operator's voice is conveyed to a speaker embedded in the proxy robot's body. Mouth movement is produced in the robot according to the volume of the teleoperator's voice. Although there is almost no delay in the system since the two rooms are directly connected via an analog line, we adjusted the parameters of the system so that 500 milliseconds of delay is introduced to both sound streams between the visitor and teleoperator rooms in order to test the proposed system under realistic conditions.

Communication robot

Two small humanoid robots named named M^3-Synchy2 are used in this experiment (see Figure 3). One of them assumes the role of a proxy agent for the teleoperator in both Conditions and is therefore called "proxy robot". In Condition 2, another M^3-Synchy2 is used as a "bystander robot" in the conversation between the subject and the proxy robot driven by the teleoperator. M^3-Synchy2 is an extended version of M^3-Synchy[1], with decreased motor noise. Its height is about 35 centimeters and it has a head with seven degrees of freedom, an upper body with 10 DOF, and a movable base with two wheels. In this experiment, we use only the DOFs in the head, namely the 3 DOF neck, two eye balls with independent pan axes and a common tilt one, and an open-close mouth. By sending a sequence of commands representing the desired joint angles to the microcontroller of the robot motors, the robots can produce nonverbal actions such as nodding and watching, and so on. The mouth of the robot is automatically opened and closed in such a way that it is synchronized with the sound played through the speaker embedded in the robot's chest, so that the sound appears to be produced from the robot's mouth.

Behavior of the robots

The neck movement of the proxy robot is automatically produced depending on which agent, the subject or the teleoperator is talking in the visitor room, as well as on the position of the subject's head. Sounds captured by the microphones in both rooms are used to detect who is talking. In both Conditions, we used a function of voice activity detection (VAD) included in Julius [3], which is one of the most popular voice recognition systems and provides API libraries. The VAD of the subject's voice is used by the proxy robot to produce nodding actions to make it appear to be listening to the subject. Practically, when it detects the end of an utterance in the subject's voice, it is controlled to produce a nodding action by moving its head up and down. The VAD of the operator's voice is used to produce the mouth movement of the proxy robot as if it is speaking. The face tracking function of the Kinect is used in order to measure subject's head position. The proxy robot of the operator basically moves his head position as if it is looking at the head part of the subject during conversation. In Condition 2, a bystander robot is automatically controlled so that it produces the appropriate behavior of a by-standing listener agent. When the teleoperator does not speak, the bystander robot looks at the face of the subject, which is detected by the face tracking system using a Kinect sensor (see Figure 4(a)). On the other hand, when the teleoperator talks, the bystander robot is controlled to look at the head of the proxy robot (see Figure 4(b)). Furthermore, when a short stop in the subject's utterance is observed, the bystander robot produces a nodding action (see Figure 4(c)

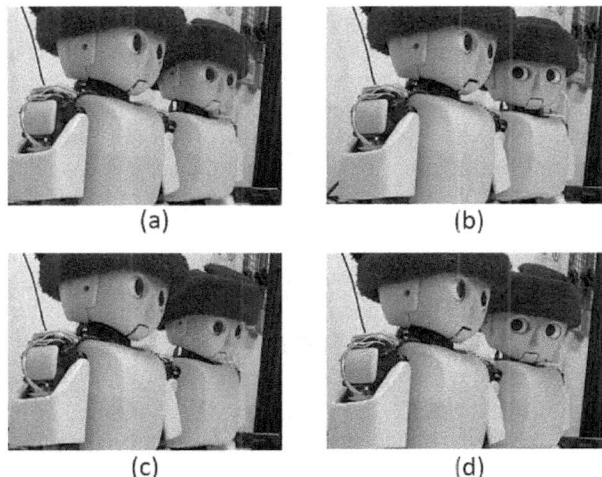

Figure 4. Motion of bystander robot:Bystander robot. In each figure: bystander robot (right), proxy robot (left). (a) shows the normal bystander robot position, (b) shows the bystander robot as it is looking to the proxy robot during operator's utterance, (c) shows it nodding to the subject and (d) shows another nod motion toward the proxy robot.

Robot type	Motion	Timing
Proxy	Mouth movement	During operator's utterance
	Nod	End of subject's utterance
Bystander	Look proxy	During operator's utterance
	Nod & Speak	End of subject's utterance

Table 1. Motion of robots during conversation

and (d)), as if expressing acknowledgment to the subject's utterances, which is considered to be a behavior enhancing the social presence of the teleoperator. The nodding action of the bystander robot is produced along with a sound that is randomly chosen from predetermined voice patterns like "*hai*", "*hai, hai*" and "*hun, hun*" in Japanese, which work as backchannel feedback such as "oh" or "uh" in English. Table 1 summarizes the motion types of both robots. Note that both the proxy and the bystander robot nod with a probability of 0.8 when they detect a chance, to avoid the impression of nodding too frequently.

Procedure

The subjects enter a room located beside the visitor and teleoperator rooms. All instructions regarding the experiment, including the informed consent, are given to the subjects by way of written documents. The experimenter reads the explanation aloud while the subjects listen and read their own copies. Each subject is instructed that he or she will participate in two sessions of about five minutes of telecommunication with the experimenter in order to evaluate the robot system. The subjects are asked to read some graphs describing many kinds of statistics before the experimental conversation. The data are about daily life such as survey results on the habit of Japanese citizens to eat breakfast everyday. Such documents are prepared in order to avoid breaks in conversation in the experiment due to the lack of common topics between the subjects and the experimenter. After each subject finishes reading, the documents are collected so that the subject can focus on the conversation itself. If the subject understands the instructions, the subject and the experimenter have a face-to-face conversation practice session. The experimenter then guides the subject to the visitor room and adjusts the volume of the robot's voice so that the subject can hear it without any problems. Finally, the experimenter shows some of the robot's movements like head movement for nodding, and lip movement for speaking, in order to help the subject get accustomed to the robot. The subject is also told that the robot might shake due to a system problem and he or she should touch the robot to stop it if the vibration becomes large.

In Condition 1, the subject is told that the experimenter will "enter" the body of the proxy robot from the teleoperator room to talk to him or her. In Condition 2, he or she is told that the experimenter will "enter" the body of the proxy robot while a bystander robot, placed to the left side of the proxy robot, will automatically take part in the conversation. The subject is also asked to evaluate his or her impressions about the conversation by answering a questionnaire immediately after each conversation session. The order of the sessions under Condition 1 and 2 are randomized for counterbalance. After both sessions are over, the subject is interviewed by the experimenter to provide further comments on the experiment in a more casual way.

Measurement

The subjects are required to fill in a questionnaire about their impressions formed through the conversation. The questionnaire consists of items for evaluating basic success of conversation, and social telepresence. To evaluate the basic success of conversation, two items are prepared to check the overall impression of the conversation as follows:

- I could talk with the partner.

- I could hear the partner's voice.

To evaluate the effect of our proposed method on social telepresence, we adopt the same item that was used in previous work on social telepresence [6]:

- I felt as if I were talking with the partner in the same room.

Since the improvement of social telepresence might bring about other by-product effects in other aspects of social cognition in communication, we prepared some items as follows:

- The partner tried to listen to my comments very proactively.

- The conversation with the partner was lively.

- It was easy for me to talk with the communication partner.

- The behavior of the proxy robot was natural.

- I felt that the responses of the partner were slow.

- I felt as if the proxy robot behaved against the operator's intention.

- I sometimes felt that I established eye contact with the proxy robot.

Because the style of telecommunication using two robots is currently rather experimental and looks complex, it might violate the subject's ease to use it as it is. Therefore, we prepared another item to evaluate it as following:

- It was difficult to talk with the distant person in the current way using X robot(s).(X is 1 or 2)

The total number of questionnaire items was thirteen in Condition 1, and seventeen in Condition 2 (some items for the evaluation of the bystander robot were added in Condition 2). Subjects were provided with a Likert scale, with expressions such as "1 = strongly disagree", "4 = neutral", "7 = strongly agree", from one to seven for each item in the questionnaire.

RESULT

In all sessions, the subjects and the experimenter could keep talking for five minutes without long breaks (see example sequences of conversation under Condition 1 and 2 in Table 2 and 3, respectively). Figure 5 shows box plots of the scores for questionnaire items in both conditions. We can see that median scores for the item "I could talk with the partner" are positive both in Condition 1 (median = 6, average = 5.4, SD = 1.2) and in Condition 2 (median = 6, average = 5.6, SD = 1.0). The same is true for the item "I could hear the partner's voice." both in Condition 1 (median = 7, average = 6.5, SD = 0.67) and in Condition 2 (median = 6, average = 6.3, SD = 0.65). These results seem to show that the conversation itself was successful in both Conditions.

The Wilcoxon signed ranks test, a non-parametric, within-subject test is adopted to compare scores for the questionnaire items obtained from the same subject in the two conditions. For the item "I felt as if I were talking with the partner in the same room", we found that the subjects feel stronger social telepresence in Condition 2 than in Condition 1 because the scores are higher (Z = 1.96, p < .05) in Condition 2 (median = 5.5, mean = 4.7, SD = 1.8) than in Condition 1 (median =

Time	ID	Subject	Behavior
1:54	1	P	"Hai, hai."
1:55	2	S	"I would like to see the Aurora Borealis. Aurora!"
1:59	3	P	"I see. The Aurora Borealis..."
2:02	4	S	"But ..."
	5	P	"Can you see it from there?(Overlapping) "
2:03	6	S	"I heard that we can see it in a Russia."
	7	P	Nod
2:04	8	S	"I don't know whether it is true."
2:06	9	S	"How about in Alaska?"
2:09	10	P	Nod

Table 2. Example conversation under Condition 1: The column "Time" shows the elapsed time since the start of the conversation. In the "Subject" column, "P" refers to the proxy robot and "S" refers to the subject in conversation with the robot.

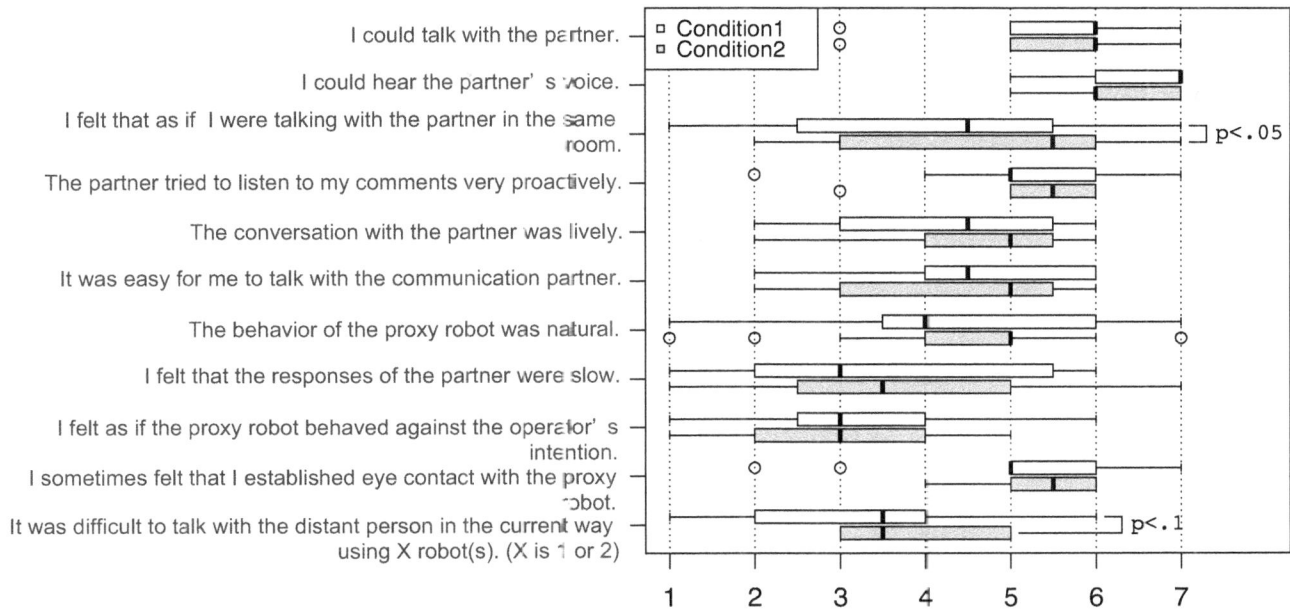

Figure 5. This figure shows scores from the questionnaire. The circles indicate outliers. The dark vertical line in each box shows the median.

4.5, mean = 4.1, SD = 1.9). However, we did not find any other significant difference between the two Conditions for the items related to by-product feelings that are considered to be potentially induced by an improvement of social telepres-

Time	ID	Subject	Behavior
1:37	1	P	"Yeah, I sometimes lose my way in Tokyo. "
	2	B	Look at proxy robot.
1:40	3	S	"Me too."
1:42	4	B	Look at subject, then nod. "Yes"
	5	P	Nod
1:43	6	S	"We sometimes get confused about which train to take."
1:46	7	P	*"Hai, hai "*
	8	B	Look at proxy robot.
1:48	9	S	"It looks very complicated."
1:50	10	B	Look at subject, then nod. "Yes"
1:54	11	S	"The train, umm..."
	12	P	"I think so too.(Overlapping)"
	13	B	Look at proxy robot.
1:56	14	S	"It should be simple, but..."
1:58	15	P	*"Hai, hai "*
2:00	16	S	"I think even taking a train is difficult. "
2:02	17	P	Nod
	18	B	*"Hun, hun"*

Table 3. Example conversation under Condition 2: The column "Time" shows the elapsed time since the start of the conversation. In the "Subject" column, "P"refers to the proxy robot , "S" refers to the subject in conversation with the robot and "B" refers to the bystander robot.

ence. There is a marginal difference between the scores about ease of use of the system between Conditions (Z = 1.72, p < .1). Scores for the item "it was difficult for you to talk with the distant person in the current way using X robot(s) (X is 1 or 2)" were larger in Condition 2 (median = 3.5, mean = 3.8, SD = 0.9) than in Condition 1 (median = 3.5, mean = 3.2, SD = 1.6).

DISCUSSION

Since the scores for the item "I felt as if I were talking with the partner in the same room" are higher in Condition 2 than in Condition 1 (Z = 1.96, p < .05), it is possible likely that introducing an autonomous bystander robot alongside the proxy robot can enhance the social telepresence of the teleoperator represented by the proxy robot. In this experiment, we introduce a large delay (500 milliseconds) for transmitting voice to the opposite room, assuming that non-zero delay must be involved in a real system. This makes it difficult for the teleoperator (as well as the subject) to respond to the interlocutor promptly and frequently. However, as in the response of ID-10 in the example dialog (Table 3), the bystander robot sometimes responds to the subject even though the teleoperator does not produce such acknowledgments. In other words, the bystander robot could produce socially correct responses in lieu of the proxy robot. Previous study [11] has found a psychological phenomenon called nodding confusion where the nodding action of one agent can be regarded as that of another agent sitting close by the nodding agent. It is considered that a similar phenomenon is likely to have occurred in this experiment. Since the two robots have the same appearance and one of them is the proxy of the teleoperator, a nodding action by the bystander robot is accepted as one by the proxy robot, and this nodding is attributed to the teleoperator. Therefore, the social telepresence of the distant person represented by the proxy robot can be enhanced by introducing such a bystander robot.

Furthermore, as in the response of ID-17-18 in the example dialog (Table 3), the proxy and bystander robots sometimes produce nodding actions at the same time. Such collaborative responses might also contribute to the subject's stronger impression of being there. In other words, the social telepresence conveyed through the proxy robot might be enhanced by the actions of the bystander robot made in imitation of, or in response to the proxy robot. Further experiments, including more specific control of the bystander robot's behavior, are necessary to correctly evaluate the influence of these two potential effects of introducing a bystander robot.

Other kinds of impressions about the teleoperator are expected to improve according to the improvement of social telepresence; however, we could not find significant improvement between Conditions (see Figure 5) regarding the seven questions of possible by-product effects. This might be due to the fact that the conversation is allowed to progress naturally through the interaction of the subject and the experimenter rather than being controlled to provide results involving less variance. Therefore, we could confirm improvement regarding only the basic aspect of telecommunication. To examine the influence on the by-product aspects, further experiments should be carefully designed according to the aspects to be focused on.

By contrast, there is a marginally significant difference observed for the item regarding the ease of the telecommunication. This might be caused by the subject being insufficiently accustomed to the new style of communication. Another reason might be the insufficient explanation about the necessity of introducing a second robot. These issues are expected to be solved by improving the behavior of the bystander robot as a natural listener since it is rather simply implemented in this experiment. However, it does not seem to be such a serious problem partially because the median score for this item of the easiness is still positive in both conditions and also because there is no other significant difference in the negative direction.

CONCLUSION

A new telecommunication system with multiple robot was developed: one of them assumed the role of a proxy for the remote person as in previous work, while another assumed the role of a bystander listener in the conversation between the proxy robot and a human. Experimental results confirm the basic, beneficial effect of introducing a bystander robot into the telecommunication, on the enhancement of the social telepresence of the teleoperator. Clarifying the influential factors in this improvement in further experiments is an important future study. Improvement of the robot's behavior to enhance or utilize the effects on social telepresence should also be considered in the future.

ACKNOWLEDGMENTS

This work was supported by JSPS KAKENHI Grant Numbers A246800220, A252200040.

REFERENCES

1. Ishiguro, H., Minato, T., Yoshikawa, Y., and Asada, M. Humanoid platforms for cognitive developmental robotics. *International Journal of Humanoid Robotics 8*, 03 (2011), 391–418.

2. Kashiwabara, T., Osawa, H., Shinozawa, K., and Imai, M. Teroos: A wearable avatar to enhance joint activities. In *Proc. the SIGCHI Conference on Human Factors in Computing Systems*, CHI '12, ACM (New York, NY, USA, 2012), 2001–2004.

3. Lee, A., and Kawahara, T. Recent development of open-source speech recognition engine julius. In *Proc. APSIPA ASC 2009: Asia-Pacific Signal and Information Processing Association, 2009 Annual Summit and Conference* (2009), 131–137.

4. Microsoft Kinect. `http://www.xbox.com/en-US/kinect/`(accessed on 20 May 2014).

5. Minato, T., Nishio, S., Ogawa, K., and Ishiguro, H. Development of cellphone-type tele-operated android. In *Proc. the 10th Asia Pacific Conference on Computer Human Interaction* (2012).

6. Nakanishi, H., Murakami, Y., and Kato, K. Movable cameras enhance social telepresence in media spaces. In *Proc. the SIGCHI Conference on Human Factors in Computing Systems*, ACM (2009), 433–442.

7. Nishio, S., Watanabe, T., Ogawa, K., and Ishiguro, H. Body ownership transfer to teleoperated android robot. In *Social Robotics*. Springer, 2012, 398–407.

8. Sakamoto, D., Kanda, T., Ono, T., Ishiguro, H., and Hagita, N. Android as a telecommunication medium with a human-like presence. In *Human-Robot Interaction (HRI), 2007 2nd ACM/IEEE International Conference on*, IEEE (2007), 193–200.

9. Sekiguchi, D., Inami, M., and Tachi, S. Robotphone: Rui for interpersonal communication. In *CHI '01 Extended Abstracts on Human Factors in Computing Systems*, CHI EA '01, ACM (New York, NY, USA, 2001), 277–278.

10. Watanabe, T., Danbara, R., and Okubo, M. Effects of a speech-driven embodied interactive actor" interactor" on talker's speech characteristics. In *Robot and Human Interactive Communication, 2003. Proc. ROMAN 2003. The 12th IEEE International Workshop on*, IEEE (2003), 211–216.

11. Yoshikawa, Y. Cognitive Neuroscience Robotics A: Synthetic Approaches to Human Understanding. (in printing). ch. Attention and Preference of Humans and Robots.

Crowdsourcing Agents for Smart IoT

Jane Yung-jen Hsu
Intelligent Agents Lab
Computer Science and Information Engineering
National Taiwan University
yjhsu@csie.ntu.edu.tw

ABSTRACT

Activity recognition is a key capability for a smart environment to offer timely services and intelligent interactions with people, especially with the growing number of connected devices. While logging data from connected sensors is no longer beyond reach, it is still quite difficult to collect the labels required by machine learning approaches to activity recognition. In this research, crowdsourcing agents are designed to acquire status labels from people situated in the environment.

Experiments on crowdsourcing in a typical building on campus have been conducted to improve air conditioning and space utilization. In particular, we will discuss how crowdsourcing agents in the form of simple physical objects can significantly improve user engagement as well as data quality. Collaboration among cyber-physical agents can lead to better user experience and overall performance.

Author Keywords

Activity Recognition; Internet of Things; Crowdsourcing; Intelligent Agents; Cyber-Physical Systems

ACM Classification Keywords

I.2.11 Distributed Artificial Intelligence (Intelligent Agents)

BIO

Jane Hsu is a Professor of Computer Science and Information Engineering at National Taiwan University. Her research interests include multi-agent systems, knowledge mining, commonsense computing, and context-aware services. Prof. Hsu is the director of Intel-NTU Connected Context Computing Center, featuring global research collaboration among NTU, Intel, and the Ministry of Science and Technology of Taiwan. She serves on the editorial board of Journal of Information Science and Engineering (2010-), International Journal of Service Oriented Computing and Applications (Springer, 2007-2009) and Intelligent Data Analysis (Elsevier/IOS Press, 1997-2002). She is actively involved in key international conferences as organizers and members of the program committee. In addition to serving as the President of Taiwanese Association for Artificial Intelligence (2013-2014), Prof. Hsu has been a member of AAAI, IEEE, ACM, Phi Tau Phi, and an executive committee member of the IEEE Technical Committee on E-Commerce (2000) and TAAI (2004-current).

HAI'14, October 29–31, 2014, Tsukuba, Japan.
ACM 978-1-4503-3035-0/14/10.
http://dx.doi.org/10.1145/2658861.2658948

A Fixed Pattern Deviation Robot that Triggers Intention Attribution

Kazunori Terada
Gifu University
Yanagido 1-1
Gifu, 501-1193, Japan
terada@info.gifu-u.ac.jp

Yuto Imamura
Gifu University
Yanagido 1-1
Gifu, 501-1193, Japan
yuto@elf.info.gifu-u.ac.jp

Hideyuki Takahashi
Osaka University
2-1 Yamadaoka
Suita, Osaka, 565-0871, Japan
hideyuki@ams.eng.osaka-u.ac.jp

Akira Ito
Gifu University
Yanagido 1-1
Gifu, 501-1193, Japan
ai@gifu-u.ac.jp

Abstract

Attributing intention to others is a difficult task for
individuals with autism spectrum disorders (ASD). We
hypothesize that individuals with ASD ascribe a lower
level of abstraction to observed behavior than typically
developing individuals. In this study, we discuss the
development of a robot that gradually increases the level
of abstraction to observed behavior, inducing
individuals to ascribe a greater level of abstraction to
observed behavior.

ACM Classification Keywords

J.4 [Social and Behavioral Sciences]: Psychology.

Introduction

Autism spectrum disorders (ASD) are developmental
disorders that are characterized by impaired social and
communication abilities and repetitive behaviors. The
repetitive behaviors associated with ASD are explained by
hypersensitivity to errors, and we hypothesize that the
impaired social and communication abilities are caused by
the same cognitive impairment.

Abstracting the world in terms of intention involves an
assumption that a wide variety of behaviors are the same
by attributing an intention to these behaviors. In
pragmatic language understanding, which is known to be

a deficit of ASD [5], one intention should be attributed to utterances with different superficial similarities. For instance, the two sentences "can you pass me the salt?" and "there is a salt bottle in front of you" are superficially different. The former is an interrogative sentence, so the hearer should answer yes or no. The latter is a declarative sentence, so the hearer has no obligation to respond. However, both sentences carry the intention "I want you to pass me the salt." To place these two sentences into one category, the hearer must allow for a large categorization error. In other words, to understand pragmatic expression, a high level of cognitive granularity must be allowed [4].

We assume that intentions are abstracted states that are expediently and arbitrarily created by humans to represent a wide variety of behaviors. Researchers suggest that the intention of an action is recognized after the action is initiated, indicating that a higher order abstracted intention is not the cause of the action [3]. Ayaya, an individual with ASD, reported that she does not recognize the state of hunger; instead, she recognizes various types of internal body states, such as anemia and hollowness in the stomach [1]. The level of abstraction for these states is lower than that for the concept of hunger. A concept of hunger is not required for animals to induce foraging behavior. We believe that intention is an illusion. The concept of intention might have evolved as a protocol of communication [2].

People use a different strategy to understand the behavior of artificial entities: the design stance [2]. The behavior of designed entities is described in terms of fixed rules of a one-to-one relationship between an input and an output. These rules ensure that the input-output relations involved in behavior remain constant. A deviation from

the fixed rule of an artificial entity thus indicates that the entity is broken. However, a person who deviates from fixed behavior, for example, when assembling a product in a factory, will not be assumed to be broken but instead will be assumed to be bored or tired. The understanding of fixed rule deviation is the critical difference between the intentional stance and the design stance. The intentional stance permits a deviation from the fixed pattern of an observed entity's behavior because the entity's intention may generate a wide variety of behaviors (i.e., a one-to-many relationship exists between the input and the output of an intentional entity). The difficulty of intention attribution is that the problem to be solved is an ill-posed inverse problem.

Our study aims to support individuals who have difficulty attributing intention to others because of their inability to eliminate higher order representations from a wide variety of observed behaviors. To accomplish this aim, we gradually increase the mapping complexity among the sensor input, the internal state, and the behavioral output of a robot. Therefore, the robot gradually increases the level of deviation from a fixed pattern of behavior. In this study, we report the basic implementation of this fixed pattern deviation robot.

A fixed pattern deviation robot

Figure 1 shows the fixed pattern deviation robot. We modified a commercially available, omnidirectional mobile robot (Revast Co., Ltd., Omni 3WD 13). The robot's shape is cylindrical. The diameter is 310 mm, and the height is 230 mm. Three ultrasonic sensors are mounted around the circumference of the body for obstacle avoidance and human detection. Further, three button switches are mounted on the upper surface of the robot for user input, and a full-color LED covered by a translucent white plastic half dome is mounted on the top of the robot to indicate internal representations of its behavior. We also prepared a remote control switch box, which has the same three button switches mounted on its upper surface.

The flow of information for our robot is modeled as follows: sensor input, internal representation, and motor output. At the beginning of the interaction, the relationship among the input, the internal state, and the output is fixed. After the user becomes habituated to the relationship, the robot deviates from this fixed relationship. The mapping complexity increases based on the user's cognitive development and abstract thinking ability.

Figure 1: A fixed pattern deviation robot

Acknowledgments

This study was supported by MEXT KAKENHI "Constructive Developmental Science" (25119502).

References

[1] Ayaya, S., and Kumagaya, S. *Hattatsu Syougai Toujisha Kenkyu (in Japanese)*. Igaku Shoin, 2008.

[2] Dennett, D. C. *The Intentional Stance.* Cambridge, Mass, Bradford Books/MIT Press, 1987.

[3] Eagleman, D. *Incognito: The Secret Lives of the Brain.* Vintage Books, 2012.

[4] Kozima, H. Cognitive granularity: A new perspective over autistic and non-autistic styles of development. *Japanese Psychological Research 55*, 2 (2013), 168–174.

[5] Lam, Y. G., and Yeung, S. S. S. Towards a convergent account of pragmatic language deficits in children with high functioning autism. Depicting the phenotype using the pragmatic rating scale. *Research in Autism Spectrum Disorders 6*, 2 (2012), 792 – 797.

The Sharing of Meta-signals and Protocols is the First Step for the Emergence of Cooperative Communication

Takakazu MIZUKI
Faculty of Engineering
Gifu University
1-1,Yanagido,Gifu,
501-1193,Japan
mts@elf.info.gifu-u.ac.jp

Akira ITO
Faculty of Engineering
Gifu University
1-1,Yanagido,Gifu,
501-1193,Japan
ai@gifu-u.ac.jp

Kazunori TERADA
Faculty of Engineering
Gifu University
1-1,Yanagido,Gifu,
501-1193,Japan
terada@gifu-u.ac.jp

Abstract

We investigated how people communicate in a situation where there is no shared languages among them. We designed "image sharing game", in which players must cooperate to solve it. The only communication media available for the players is the exchange of gestures represented by skeleton diagrams. In this game, some of the player-pairs developed not only signals for objects, but also meta-signals that controlled communication. Those with meta-signals were oberved to perform better than those without meta-signals.

Author Keywords

non-verbal communication; kinect; gesture;

ACM Classification Keywords

I.2.7. [Artifical Intelligence]: Natural Language Processing

Introduction

Let us consider communication between a human and an agent where there is no common language between them. When a target task is simple, communication goal may be achieved by the above simple signal exchange method.

However, with the increase of complexity of a target task, signals becomes more complex, and understanding of signal meanings by the partner becomes more difficult. To cope with this difficulty, a human can develop signals which controls communication process — i.e., meta-signals.

The signals representing objects could be limited in number, and could be prepared in advance, for they must correspond to the objects necessary in achieving the target task. On the other hand, the possible meta-signals are unbounded, for how we represent the target task may be quite different from human.

Therefore, it is more difficult for an agent to understand meta-signals than to understand object signals. Our goal is to make an agent understand meta-signals a human uses. For that purpose, we investigated the sharing process of meta-signals between humans.

Experimental Setup

We designed "image sharing game," in which players must cooperate to solve it. The game is played by two players. To each player in a separate room, four images are shown through PC window — i.e., one image is missing. The task is to find out which image is missing in the partner's window. The missing image is different from that of the partner. We selected a set of five images from Japanese popular folklores, i.e., Kintaro, Turu no ongaeshi, Momotaro, Issunbousi, Ant and Grasshopper(Fig.1).

During the game, players can communicate by body gestures which is displayed to the partner as a skeleton diagram consisting of head, body, arms, and feet as shown in Fig.2, Game window.

When the game starts, players try to find out which image in his window is missing in the partner's window. Since there is no regularity on the location of images, players can not solve the game by communicating the position of images.

Figure 1: Five images used in the game

Figure 2: Game window

When both the players select the answer, the result is returned to the players. The game is regarded as success if both of the players are able to select the correct image which is missing in the images of the partner. Otherwise the game is regarded as failure. Only the success/failure is informed to the players.

Since there is no limitation on the time for selecting an image, the players are able to communicate with the partner until they are satisfied with their communication.

Experimental Procedure

22 men and women of age 19-23 were recruited for the experiment. Before the experiment, subjects were instructed how to play the game, and were shown five images used in the experiment. Moreover, they were instructed that they should think beforehand how to

Pair	Meta signals	FAS
1	-	-
2	Make a circle above the head to convey the answer is found	2
3	Make a circle above the head when the gestured image is in his window, otherwise make an x-mark	1
4	-	-
5	Both hands down to a breast to tell his own turn. Raise a hand to tell the start of a gesture	1
6	Make a circle above the head when the gestured image is in his window, otherwise make an x-mark	3
7	Make a circle above the head in front of the chest when the gestured image is missing in his window	3
8	Make an x-mark when the gestured image is not in his window	3
9	Imitate the partner's gesture when it is in his window, otherwise make an x-mark	3
10	Make a circle above the head when gestured image is in his window, otherwise make an x-mark	3
11	Make a circle above the head when gestured image is in his window, otherwise make the x-mark	1

Table 1: Meta-signals at each pair

express the given five images as gestures, and wrote down the strategies in the questionnaire before the experiment. The subjects were also instructed that the reward is determined by the number of successes of the game.

Each subject pair performed the game in six consecutive stages. At each stage, four images to be displayed to the players are newly selected, and subjects are asked to solve the problem, i.e., to find out the image missing in the partner's windows.

Experimental Result

Fig.3 shows the action sequences of subject pair 2 in stage 6. In the figure, gestures are tagged with labels of a format Sn. First character S represents "a gesture meaning", and the number n distinguishes a different gesture pattern of the same meaning.

We classified gestures into two types: image signals representing images, and meta-signals used to control the communication.

Table1 shows meta-signals each pair used. In this table, the column of FAS means the stage number in which meta-signals were first used. " - " means meta-signals were not used.

The standard meta-signals are gesture of a circle or a x-mark with arms, representing some kinds of positive or negative attitudes. In the experiment, other types of meta-signals were also observed. For example, raising and lowering both hands, raising one hand, were observed in some pairs. The meaning of these gestures could not been negotiated beforehand, but later came to be shared by some of the player pairs.

As to the meta-signals, Y and N each represent (some kind of) positive or negative attitudes. The exact meanings of Y and N depend on the situation, and may differ among subject pairs. In the example of Fig.3, Y1 is a meta-signal. With these tools, we analyzed action sequences of the subjects.

In Fig.3, firstly player P2 gestured Issunbousi, Turu no ongaesi, Momotaro, Ant and Grasshopper consecutively. Then player P1 gestured Kintaro, Ant and Grasshopper, Turu no ongaeshi, Issunbousi. The same number in the label means that P1 and P2 used the same gesture for the same images. Lastly each exchanged a confirmation signal Y1, meaning that the both were satisfied, and could solve the stage.

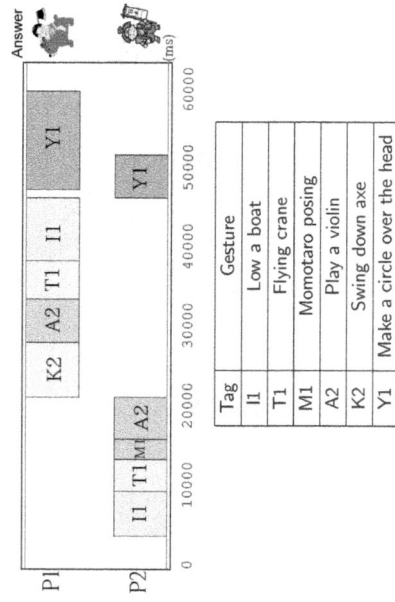

Figure 3: The action sequence of the pair 2 in stage 6.

Tag	Gesture
I1	Low a boat
T1	Flying crane
M1	Momotaro posing
A2	Play a violin
K2	Swing down axe
Y1	Make a circle over the head

Discussions

Occurrence of Gestures Imitation

At an early stages of experiments, imitation of the partner's gestures were often observed. For the gesture of the partner, the player must respond somehow. Otherwise, the partner would stop gesturing, and communication broke down from the start. Taking into account the fact that there are no shared signals, mimicking of the partner's gesture may be a good strategy for communicating an intention to communicate.

Necessity of Meta-signal

After confirming mutual intention to communicate, the players want to communicate something substantial. Even if the information content could be communicated by the gesture representing the information content, the sender could not be sure if it is understood by the receiver. As mimicking may already have been used as communicating "an intention to communicate", it cannot be used for communicating "understanding of the partner's gestures".

Here comes the necessity for communicating confirmation/negation, or meta-signals. In the experiment, most frequently used meta-signals are circle mark for confirmation, and x-mark for negation. For those pairs who failed to establish meta-signals, the communication necessarily tended to be on-sided, and average correct-answer rates were low.

Conclusion

In this study, we investigated how humans establish communication where there were no shared protocols or symbols for communication. The communication media available is the exchange of gestures, which are represented as skeleton graph. Through the experiments, subjects developed not only the sharing of signals for objects, but also meta-signals controlling the communication. Those who succeeded in developing meta-signals performed better in the average correct-answer rate.

Acknowledgements

This study was supported by JSPS KAKENHI 23500327 and MEXT KAKENHI 25119502 and 2611800S.

References

[1] Bruno Galantucci; An Experimental Study of the Emergence of Human Communication Systems: Cognitive Science 29, 737-767, 2005

[2] Garrod S1, Fay N, Lee J, Oberlander J, Macleod T; Foundations of Representation: Where Might Graphical Symbol Systems Come From?: Cognitive Science 31, 961-987, 2007

[3] Ayumu Arakawa, Naoto Suzuki; Is gesture a part of conversational style?: The relationships between paralinguistic features of speech and rates of hand gestures and its sex differences (in Japanese): Interpersonal social psychology research (Taizin syakai sinrigaku kenkyuu) 6, 57-64, 2006

[4] Soutaro Kita; Why do people gesture? (in Japanese): Cognitive Studies 7, 9-21, 2000

FIONA: A Platform for Embodied Cognitive Agents

Celestino Alvarez

Adele Robots

PT Asturias, Llanera, 33428

Asturias, Spain

celestino.alvarez@adelerobots.com

Lucía Fernández Cossío

Adele Robots

PT Asturias, Llanera, 33428

Asturias, Spain

lucia.cossio@adelerobots.com

HAI '14 , Oct 29-31 2014, Tsukuba, Japan

ACM 978-1-4503-3035-0/14/10.

http://dx.doi.org/10.1145/2658861.2658900

Abstract

For sixty years a great effort has been done to create different kinds of artificial intelligence, although achieving human-like performance is still far away. In this poster, authors propose a collaborative approach to achieve better results and transferring them to citizenship. The FIONA platform is described and a call to contribute and participate is done.

Author Keywords

FIONA, artificial intelligence, virtual robots, virtual agents, artificial vision, cognitive architectures, dialog systems, speech recognition system, deep learning, neural networks

ACM Classification Keywords

D.1.7 Programming Techniques: Visual Programming

D2.2 Software Engineering: Design Tools and Techniques

H5.2 Information Interfaces and Presentation (e.g., HCI): User Interfaces

I.2. Artificial Intelligence

I.4. Image Processing and Computer Vision

Introduction

The term Artificial Intelligence was coined on the fifties and, what at that time seemed to be easy to achieve, it has been demonstrated over the years that in fact it is an enormous challenge, maybe of a similar magnitude as putting a man on the moon, which required the collaboration of more than 400,000 people. Nowadays, the Artificial Intelligent systems still show several problems, mainly related to spontaneous dialogue, as well as inadequate communicative, affective, and cognitive capabilities, which are hindering their wider deployment. In addition, as it is also widely recognized, Robotics is a very broad field, not only in terms of the technologies and disciplines it involves, but also with regard to markets and stakeholders. Indeed, virtual robotics has to face similar challenges as Robotics in general: those related to advances in robots' capabilities, and the same challenge that so many new technologies have, to bridge the "death valley" between academia and the market.

Objectives

FIONA platform [1] aims to achieve the following objectives:

- To define a set of interfaces that enable to encapsulate, in modules, current research and development in Human-Machine Interaction (HMI), Perception and Cognition technologies, independently of the technology and programming languages used, to maximize reusability of the research already done.

- To research and develop an architecture which is able to instantiate and run the code for already existing implementations of algorithms and technologies, encapsulated as modules,

independent of the application domain and suitable for supporting distributed system components.

- To provide visual tools for model-driven software development at the design and implementation phases of new virtual robots.

- To improve and implement this architecture as a cloud platform (FIONA), as a mechanism to share resources related to Virtual robotics development.

- To define and develop a common software system to integrate and share the HMI technologies which will be shared and used within the platform.

- To outfit FIONA with appropriate software materials, sources and their improvements relevant to the most advanced state of the art in social and virtual robotics.

- To advance the definition of standards with respect to the HMI implementations, and the Robotics' components and development protocols.

The problem

The growth of the Internet as a communication and market tool requires the development of valuable solutions that enable people to easily and effectively access digital services. These solutions can be realized through the development and use of technologies known as embodied cognitive agents, intelligent avatars, virtual assistances, virtual agents, social virtual robots, etc. (which will be referred here only as "Virtual Robots"). Methodologies developed in this field address human-like social agents that can handle conversational speech; learn from interaction and react proactively to new communicative situations; recognize and generate social cues. With respect to this and the rest of social robotics, the final frontier of Virtual Robotics in terms of R&D perfectly matches with the goals that need to be achieved in order to obtain its market and social success: to develop more natural virtual robots, more intelligent and emphatic avatars, able to cope with spontaneous dialogue and with ample communicative, affective and cognitive capabilities.

In achieving such a frontier, the field itself and the current practical application of social and virtual robotics face two important challenges:

- Dispersion of Human-Machine Interaction technologies. It may have been proved the difficulties of providing human-level results on related technologies (natural language processing, speech recognition and generation, gesture recognition and gestural communication, emotion recognition and expression,). This has conducted to the existence of large number of research group working to solve each of these problems with an isolated approach.

- Consumer expectations are not met. This is due to lack of utility (capabilities) and reliability of current available robots and specially understanding of human orders and desires when natural communication is used.

Our proposal

The FIONA Platform has been conceived to overcome the existing innovation gap between markets and stakeholders, as well as to close the currently broad fragmentation in terms of technologies and disciplines Robotics involves. The OP's logic of working is inspired in Open Innovation, and Open-Source and Cooperative R&D processes, because these kinds of multidisciplinary and participatory approaches involve and consider direct experiences and resources from all the main

technology value chain's actors to feed diverse steps of the innovation cycle. To this respect, important methodical steps will be followed to analyze and search for the actors' own terms in order to reach better and more effective results with respect to the market transference and public appropriation of technologies and innovations.

Therefore, the FIONA platform will close the traditional gap between Robotics R&D and potential Markets for Robotics, becoming a real incubator and accelerator of Robotic services and applications more useful and efficient for market and society.

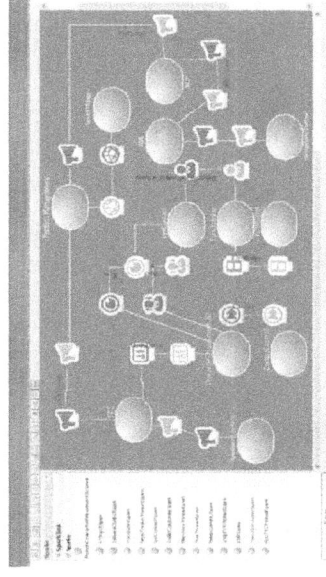

Figure 1. Screenshot from FIONA platform.

The main expected result is that in a medium-term future, developers, researchers, companies, geeks and designers from around the world will be able to contribute to the resulting online platform uploading their killer application, a detector of a new feature, a specific behavior, an amazing character or the best of their knowledge in a topic. At the same time, this enriched platform will be available to allow the end-users (who will be also professional or amateur developers of ICT products and/or services) to create or improve their own intelligent virtual robots and/or to do them more interactive, more striking and smarter.

The pursued concept is reaching a platform, aligned with current cloud-centered systems and approaches, to create, improve and use virtual robots. This cloud infrastructure will run the whole intelligence of the agent, and will also be the platform to share the experience gained by the individual agents (transfer learning).

The FIONA Platform allows users to create and co-create their own intelligent virtual robots and/or to do them more interactive, more striking and smarter. In this way, developers, researchers, companies, geeks and designers from around the world will contribute to the platform uploading their killer feature, a specific behavior, an amazing character or the best of their knowledge in a topic.

Those contributions are encapsulated as "Sparks" and can be combined to create different behaviors and personalities for the characters, enabling different skills and capabilities. While, as a simple approach, the end-user of the platform will be able to run on his/her PC, telephone, tablet, home automation controller or domestic robot, basically like doing a videoconference against an application that renders the video at the server.

This approach represents a new way of interacting with technology which will imply access to information, webservices and actions over intelligent environments. The FIONA platform ultimately facilitates the widely use of technology by general public, since it will support an easy creation of more friendly and comfortable interfaces (the social robots as avatars) to take

advantage in ordinary usage of the existing and future intelligent technologies.

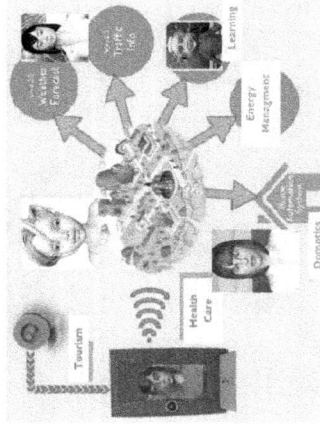

Figure 2. Screenshot from FIONA platform.

But, while the FIONA idea aims being able to run the whole intelligence of a virtual agent, and also its modeling, to easily transfer this technology into market and society, the previous platform provisioning of new agents for different end-users (each one requiring different computing power depending on the sparks being used) is not elastic and tighten enough to cluster capacity.

Conclusion

In the poster the problem of researching on Artificial Intelligence with a mass market target has been addressed. We propose FIONA as a collaborative platform that accelerates the research and transfer the results to the market.

Reference

[1] FIONA. http://www.sparkingtogether.com/.

A Cooking Assistant Robot using Intuitive Onomatopoetic Expressions and Joint Attention

Mutsuo Sano

Osaka Institute of Technology

1-79-1 Kitayama Hirakata-City

Osaka 573-0196 Japan

sano@is.oit.ac.jp

Yuka Kanemoto

Osaka Institute of Technology

1-79-1 Kitayama Hirakata-City

Osaka 573-0196 Japan

e1c0924@info.oit.ac.jp

Syogo Noda

Osaka Institute of Technology

1-79-1 Kitayama Hirakata-City

Osaka 573-0196 Japan

e1c09063@info.oit.ac.jp

Kenzaburo Miyawaki

Osaka Institute of Technology

1-79-1 Kitayama Hirakata-City

Osaka 573-0196 Japan

miyawaki@is.oit.ac.jp

Nami Fukutome

Ochanomizu University

2-1-1 Otsuka Bunkyo-ku

Tokyo 112-8610 Japan

namif@oregano.ocn.ne.jp

Abstract

A novel cooking assistance interface is proposed that guides users in the precise timing of cooking actions by means of intuitive onomatopoetic expressions associated with different cooking states and nonverbal movements on the part of a cooking assistant robot such as focusing attention through eye-gazing and gestures. The effectiveness of the scheme is demonstrated using the system to assist subjects in preparing a familiar recipe (pancakes).

Author Keywords

Cooking assistant agent; onomatopoetic expression; cooking state recognition; joint attention

ACM Classification Keywords

H.5 Information interface and presentation: User Interfaces

Introduction

In this study, we propose a cooking assistant agent-based scheme that not only promotes interest in cooking among children and young adults but also serves as a cooking rehabilitation system for people with cognitive disabilities. Specifically, we describe an intuitive user-friendly system that builds a relationship of mutual trust between user and cooking assistant agent (robot) by adopting a multimodal scheme that includes onomatopoetic terms and expressions to represent different cooking states, speech, music, gestures, and so on. This navigation approach not only heightens the user's enjoyment and interest in cooking[1], it also provides detailed timing suggestions that have proven so difficult to implement in the past.

Concept of the Proposed Cooking Assistant Agent

As illustrated in Figure 1, the system automatically recognizes the cooking state of the food being prepared then makes users aware of the tricky timing involved in cooking through sensory interaction (hearing, vision, smell, taste, etc.) based multimodal information: for example, written descriptions are converted and emphasized using intuitive easy-to-understand onomatopoetic expressions such as *putsu-putsu* (indicating the time to flip something over in Japanese) and *kun-kun* (indicating that the food is almost finished cooking), bolstered by auditory stimulus, gestures, and other techniques.

Kojima et al.[2] demonstrated the effectiveness of joint attention in achieving empathetic communication with autistic children, but our objective is to promote interest in cooking and empathetic understanding of the cooking state between user and agent through the communication environment made possible by sensory interaction in the cooking environment.

Cooking Assistant Dog-Mediated Joint Attention based on Intuitive Stimulus

We focused on preparation of a very familiar item, pancakes, and determined the proper timing to flip the pancake based on a binarization process of counting the air bubbles that form on the surface.

Japanese language is particularly rich in onomatopoetic expressions that are associated with physical and/or chemical reactions of cooking; for example, *koto-koto*, *gutsu-gutsu*, *gura-gura* for boiling, *puchi-puchi* or *pachi-pachi for frying*, and so on. We employ the term *putsu-putsu* to express formation of air bubbles, and indicate progress or change in cooking state—*i.e.*, the formation of air bubbles on the surface of the pancake—with rhythmic repetition of the expression: *putsu-putsu, putsu-putsu-putsu…, etc*.

We designed the cooking assistant agent as a realistic robotic dog with a cute and loyal appearance that interacts with people and has eye-gazing capabilities. The agent is controlled by an Arduino Uno microcontroller board and uses servomotors to emulate typical canine actions such as neck and head movement, ear-cocking, and tail-wagging.

The agent exchanges emotion with the user through eye-gazing and other expressive behavior (showing enthusiasm through tail-wagging and attentive listening though ear-cocking), draws attention to the cooking state with sensory information (appearance, cooking

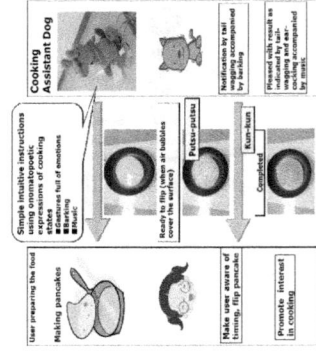

Figure 1. Sensory interaction by intuitive presentation of cooking timing

sounds, smells, etc.), and provides empathetic understanding while exploiting the joint attention function to make the user aware of the cooking state.

Demonstration Experiment

We conducted as series of trials with the cooperation of ten university student subjects to assess the effectiveness and value of the proposed cooking assistant agent. Figure 2 shows a schematic of the experimental environment.

Trial pattern	Content	Gesture when flipping is complete	Alcohol when flipping is complete	Eye gazing indication	Ear cooking indication	Joint attention through empathetic expression
A	System for guiding users to just the timing	○	○	×	×	×
B	Add eye gazing indication in Pattern A	○	○	○	○	×
C	Add joint attention indication in Pattern B	○	○	○	○	○

Table 1. Trial methodology

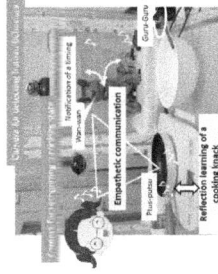

Figure 2. A schematic of the experimental environment

Question number	Content
1	Did you feel at ease in cooking together with a robotic agent?
2	Did you feel a sense of familiarity with in a robotic agent?
3	Did you find the cooking enjoyable?
4	Would you like to try using this system again?

Table 2. Survey questions

A comparison of the survey items is shown in Table 1, and the survey questions themselves are presented in Table 2. Three experimental patterns were presented in random order, and a brief survey (seven-point scale) was administered after each experimental round was completed. The timing at which to flip a pancake is tricky, so not surprisingly we found that without the system, the pancakes tended to be scorched or burned. The system, however, provided guidance on exactly when to flip the pancakes, so they came out perfectly for all three experimental patterns (A, B, and C). Figure 3 shows multiple comparison results using the Bonferroni method.

(Question 1): The significance probability of both Patterns B and C is 0.0059 for a significance level of 1% with respect to Pattern A, so Patterns B and C have no significant difference (. In other words, C = B > A. (Question 2): The significance probability of Pattern B is 0.0395 for a significance level of 5% with respect to Pattern A, while Pattern C has a significance probability of 0.0004 for a significance level of 1% with respect to Pattern A (Figure 6) . We are thus able to confirm using the t distribution to test the average difference in the two populations (correspondence) of Patterns C and B a significant difference of 5%. Thus, C > B > A. (Question 3): The significance probability of Pattern B with respect to Pattern A is 0.0182 for a significance of 5%, while the significance probability of Pattern C with respect to Pattern A is 0.0008 for a significance of 1%. In other words, B > A, and C > A; and the average value of Pattern C exceeds that of Pattern B.

(Question 4): The significance probability of Pattern C with respect to Pattern A is 0.0426 for a significance level of 5%. Thus, C > A.

It will be apparent, based on the results of survey questions 1-4, that when we compare the joint attention mechanism based on eye-gazing and onomatopoetic expressions with the case where cooking time is only shown at the time, that the affinity factor among questions 1-3 was significantly improved. This indicates that the environmental factor for continued interest in cooking is enhanced. Turning to the forth question, we were able to verify the effectiveness of focusing joint attention based on onomatopoetic phrases, which suggests likely continued use of the system.

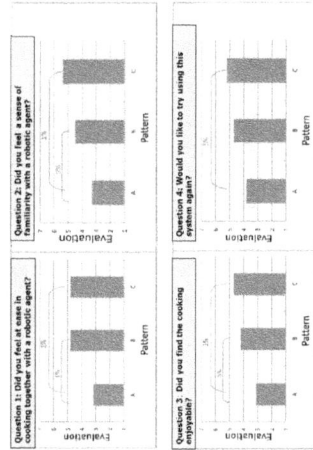

Figure 3. Multiple comparison (A, B, and C) by Bonferroni: Top left; Question1, Top right: Question 2, Bottom left; Question 3, Bottom right; Question 4.

Next, we examined the validity of the survey results by assessing the actions of subjects through video analysis. Specifically, we compared Patterns A, B, and C by measuring the ratio (%) of eye-gazing time and the number of joint attention episodes during the course of

the trials (Table 3). One can see that Pattern C revealed considerably more eye-gazing and joint attention(number of times attention was focused on the cooking object by eye-gazing) episodes than Patterns A and B, and naturally this stirred greater emotional exchange and empathetic understanding on the part of users, which again supports the survey findings.

Pattern	Ration of eye-gazing (%)	Number of joint attention episodes
A	7.3	8
B	40.4	12.3
C	49.8	17

Table 3. Video analysis results

Summary and Issues to be addressed

In this study, we proposed an intuitive and enjoyable cooking navigation system that employs user-friendly onomatopoetic phrases for a cooking assistant agent to interact with human subjects and clearly identify different cooking states and provide tricky timing guidance. We also assessed the usefulness and efficiency of the system through trials in which subjects were asked to prepare a familiar recipe, pancakes. This work was supported by the KAKENHI Grant-in-Aid for Scientific Research (C) 24500245.

References

[1] Kenzaburo Miyawaki, Mutsuo Sano: A virtual Agent for a Cooking Navigation System using Augmented Reality, *IVA*, volume 5208 of Lecture Notes in Computer Science, pp.97-103, (2008)
[2] Hideki Kozima, Marek P. Michalowski, Cocoro Nakagawa: Keepon: A playful robot for research, therapy, and entertainment, *International Journal of Social Robotics*, Vol.1, No.1, pp.3-18,(2009).

Synchrony based Side by Side Walking: An Application in Human-Robot Interactions

Syed Khursheed Hasnain
ETIS Laboratory
Site de St Martin I
2, avenue Adolphe Chauvin
95302 CERGY PONTOISE
syed-
khursheed.hasnain@ensea.fr

Ghiles Mostafaoui
ETIS Laboratory
Site de St Martin I
2, avenue Adolphe Chauvin
95302 CERGY PONTOISE
ghiles.mostafaoui@ensea.fr

Caroline Grand
ETIS Laboratory
Site de St Martin I
2, avenue Adolphe Chauvin
95302 CERGY PONTOISE
caroline.grand@ensea.fr

Philippe Gaussier
ETIS Laboratory
Site de St Martin I
2, avenue Adolphe Chauvin
95302 CERGY PONTOISE
gaussier@ensea.fr

Abstract

Previously, we proposed a model that allows a robot to
select an interacting partner and locate its focus of
attention on the basis of synchrony between its own
internal dynamics and the perceived visual stimuli. Here,
we extend our approach for human-robot interactions in a
"synchronous walking" scenario. Our inspirations come
from the notion of unintentional synchrony indicated by
psychology and motor coordination studies as a
fundamental parameter in social interactions. When two
persons walk together, unconsciously, their steps are
synchronized by constantly adjusting the length and the
frequency of their steps. Here, we are interested in
replicating this human-human behavior in a human-robot
interaction. we propose a neural network architecture that
allows a robot to follow and walk synchronously with a
human by adapting the robot's dynamics according to the
human gait using low level motor and visual primitives.

Author Keywords
Synchrony, human-robot interaction and neural networks

ACM Classification Keywords
I.2.9 [ARTIFICIAL INTELLIGENCE]: Robotics.

Introduction

In early communication among humans, synchrony was found to be a fundamental mechanism relying on very low-level sensory-motor networks, inducing the synchronization of inter- individual neural populations from sensory flows (vision, audition, or touch). Yet, to become a partner in a working together scenario, a robot also needs a minimal level of autonomy and adaptation. Predicting the rhythmic structure of the interaction could be used to build reinforcement signals for adapting the machine behavior. For more long-term interactions, the challenge is to maintain the user's interest in the interaction.

Here, we will discuss these questions in the specific case of a *walking side by side* HRI scenario. We propose a neural model allowing a mobile robot to adapt its locomotion and rhythm of interaction relative to the human partner's gait. In fact, when two people walk together, their movements appear to be interdependent and coupled to a degree [6]. Interestingly, unintentional gait synchronizations are observed as each person unconsciously adapt his speed, step size and rhythm [8].

Experimental setup

We use a mobile Robosoft Robulab 10 equipped with four wheels, two for directions and two for stabilization, proximity sensors for obstacle avoidance, an embedded computer, and for the visual perception, an Unibrain's Fire-i camera. The experiments were performed in a real indoor environment. Here, to analyze the synchronizations we use the Phase Locking Value (PLV) (see [4] for more details).

Learning and predicting the ego-motion

When a mobile platform moves, two independent motions are induced in the visual field: the ego-motion generated by the robot's own motion and the one created by moving objects in the visual field. As these two optical flows are blended together and difficult to differentiate, in order to analyze and segment human (or objects) movements while moving, the robot must first learn to predict and compensate the ego-motion generated by its own actions. To solve this question, we adopt a Perception-Action approach permitting the mobile robot to learn the cross-modal link between its motor controller (locomotion velocities of the Robulab) and the induced visual stimuli (optical flow) while moving. A classical optical flow algorithm [3] is used to extract the velocity vectors from the images acquired by the embedded camera. The computed velocity vectors are modulated by the image gradient intensities to give more importance to the contrasted regions where more accurate optical flow can be found. An architecture based on least mean square neural networks (LMS [7]) is then used to associate the motor controller orders (motor velocities) to the mean visual extracted motion intensity. Consequently, after this learning step, when the robot starts moving with a given velocity, the LMS will be able to trigger (for each velocity) the correct visual motion intensity mean value which can be subtracted from the current optical flow in order to compensate the induced ego-motion.

Synchronizing the robot's arm with the human gait

The objective is to adapt the robot's "walking"' rhythm to the human gait. Unfortunately, our robot is not endowed by legs and moves using wheels. Consequently, we added a small and "rough" arm to the Robulab Robot. The underlying reason is to make that arm oscillating relative to the robot's locomotion speed illustrating the locomotion dynamic. Moreover, this added arm's oscillations represent's external visual stimuli permitting possibly to "entrain" unintentionally the human walking dynamic leading to a more intuitive and bi-directional interaction.

To extract the human legs and arms motion, the computed visual optical flow is coded by 8 neurons sensitive to different motion directions; 0^0, 180^0, 45^0, -45^0, 90^0, -90^0, 135^0 and -135^0. In the case of forward walking, by summing the responses of the neurons sensitive to the directions 45^0 and -45^0 we obtain an approximate periodic signal. This signal, noted f thereafter, will be used to synchronize the robot's behavior with the human gait.

The robot's arm movements are controlled by an oscillator. It consists of two neurons $N1$ and $N2$ inhibiting and exciting each other proportionally to a variable β as proposed in [5]. Using the neural model we proposed in [2], this motor controller is then synchronized with the human motion signal (f) modulated by a coupling factor C_f.

Experimental Results

Let's consider the experimental scenario. First, the robot is immobile. When a human enter's in its visual field, the robot will automatically imitate and start following him. While following the human, the robot compensates the ego-motion and extracts the oscillating optical flow (f signal) due the human arms and legs movements. This signal feeds the oscillator controlling the robot's arm and adapts it to the human gait leading to a synchronized behavior while walking side by side.

To validate our results, a series of experiments were carried out. We present the results for two scenarios.

- **1)** The Human was instructed to walk with the robot with his preferred frequency regardless to the robot behavior

- **2)** The human was asked to walk by varying his moving speed as he wants to regardless to the robot behavior

To measure the synchrony between the agents, three parameters are recorded : the human gait signal f, the robot's modifiable arm oscillator controller ($N1$) and the robot's speed. The PLV is then calculated between f and $N1$. In order to see the effects of varying the coupling factor C_f, two coupling values are examined: 0.05 and 0.1.

For a coupling factor of 0.05, f and $N1$ are episodically synchronized with high PLV values. It is due to the fact that this low coupling factor is not sufficient to correctly modify the robot's arm controller relative to the optical flow induced by the human walking. Obviously, the results are even worst in the case of interaction with a human modifying his walking rhythm. Episodic synchronizations can also be seen if the human stabilizes his walking frequency during a long period.

Using a coupling factor $C_f = 0.1$, we obtained good synchronizations with high PLV values for the two different scenarios. Some difficulties in gait synchronizations can be noticed beacause the possible linear speeds of the robot's wheels (locomotion) are discretized (7 possible velocities) making it sometimes difficult to follow correctly, synchronize and match with certain human speeds.

Conclusion

We proposed a neural model for obtaining a robot able to automatically follow a human partner and to synchronize its movements relative to the human gait using very low level primitives (proprioception and visual optical flow). In our bio-inspired method, the robot learns the cross-modal link between the motor controller (possible velocities of the mobile robot) and the induced visual stimuli (optical flow) to be able to predict and compensate its visual ego-motion. After this learning, when a walking human is perceived, the robot starts imitating and following him due to visual ambiguities as proposed in our previous works [1]. After compensating the ego-motion while moving, our architecture extracts a periodic signal from the optical flow induced by the human arms and legs oscillatory movements. Using the approach we proposed in [2], the neural model adapts the oscillator controlling the robot's dynamics relative to the previously extracted signal. We experimentally tested the model in a real indoor environment and proved that our mobile robot is able to "walk" synchronously side by side with a human partner.

Acknowledgements

This work was supported by the DIRAC French ANR project.

References

[1] Gaussier, P., Moga, S., Quoy, M., and Banquet, J.-P. From perception-action loops to imitation processes: A bottom-up approach of learning by imitation. *Applied Artificial Intelligence 12*, 7-8 (1998), 701–727.

[2] Hasnain, S. K., Mostafaoui, G., and Gaussier, P. A synchrony-based perspective for partner selection and attentional mechanism in human-robot interaction. *Paladyn 3*, 3 (2012), 156–171.

[3] Horn, B. K., and Schunck, B. G. Determining optical flow. *Artificial intelligence 17*, 1 (1981), 185–203.

[4] Lachaux, J.-P., Rodriguez, E., Martinerie, J., Varela, F. J., et al. Measuring phase synchrony in brain signals. *Human brain mapping 8*, 4 (1999), 194–208.

[5] Revel, A., and Andry, P. Emergence of structured interactions: From a theoretical model to pragmatic robotics. *Neural networks 22*, 2 (2009), 116–125.

[6] van Ulzen, N. R., Lamoth, C. J., Daffertshofer, A., Semin, G. R., and Beek, P. J. Characteristics of instructed and uninstructed interpersonal coordination while walking side-by-side. *Neuroscience Letters 432*, 2 (2008), 88–93.

[7] Widrow, B., Hoff, M. E., et al. Adaptive switching circuits.

[8] Zivotofsky, A. Z., Gruendlinger, L., and Hausdorff, J. M. Modality-specific communication enabling gait synchronization during over-ground side-by-side walking. *Human movement science 31*, 5 (2012), 1268–1285.

Image Recognition Method which Measures Angular Velocity from a Back of Hand for Developing a Valve UI

Hirotsugu Minowa
Okayama University
Kita-ku, Tsushimanaka 3-1-1
Okayama, Okayama, Japan
minowa@sys.okayama-u.ac.jp

Abstract

The training that uses virtual reality technology is expected to be useful for preventing the accidents caused by human factor. However, there is a problem that a trainee cannot train due to lack of the UI such as realizing the real valve operations in industrial plant.

We propose an image recognition method to measure the valve opening manipulation velocity for developing UI to realize the training of valve manipulation in virtual environment. The method to measure the

HAI '14, Oct 29-31 2014, Tsukuba, Japan
ACM 978-1-4503-3035-0/14/10.
http://dx.doi.org/10.1145/2658861.2658903

angular velocity of the circular handle uses the optical natural feature points on the handle turning the valve. The advantages of our valve manipulation UI are that one is low cost and another it can be applied to various valves with circular handle.

The evaluation experiment revealed that our method could measure the angular velocity of 22.5-90 degree/s.

Author Keywords

Image recognition; Virtual reality; Training & Learning; Machine learning; Natural language processing

ACM Classification Keywords

H.5.2. INFORMATION INTERFACES AND PRESENTATION (I.7): User Interfaces (D.2.2, H.1.2, I.3.6).

Introduction

There are some accidents caused by rapid opening a valve in accidents of human factor [1-3]. The heat generation [4] occurs from the friction and collision between the pipe and fine particles by the compression heat which is caused from the valve rapid open. As an example of measurement of the ignition characteristics of the valve open, the paper [4] introduces the result of evaluation of the firing rate due to the compression heat of Nylon66, PCTFE used in the organic material

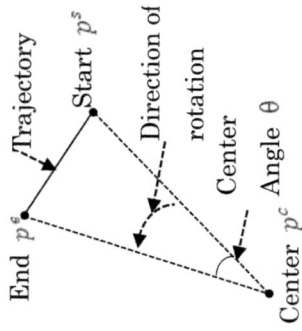

Fig. 1. Symbols to measure the rolling

$$\theta = atan\left(\frac{|y^e - y^c|}{|x^e - x^c|}\right) - atan\left(\frac{|y^s - y^c|}{|x^s - x^c|}\right)...\text{Eq (1)}$$

Eq. 1. Angular between before and after of feature points.

$$\omega = \theta / t ...\text{Eq (2)}$$

Eq. 2. Calculation of angular velocity

gasket. It reported that the firing rate of Nylon66 was about 45% when opening the valve over the period of 10 seconds, and was about 90% when opening in 0.3 seconds. The risk that causes accident is increases in proportion with the firing rate increasing according to the difference of the valve opening speed.

Therefore, we propose an image recognition method that measures angular velocity of rotation of a circular handle of the valve for constructing a VR environment to train the valve manipulation. The advantage of our method is that it can measure angular velocity by a cheap web camera, and it has general-purpose that can be applied to any valve with circular handle even if there are differences on size of the its handle or its types. Our study will give to trainees an opportunity to get the safe operation themselves through it reminds trainees whether their own manner opening the valve is safe or not by the trainees can know the angular velocity opening valve of their own.

Method to measure angular velocity

Methodology

The natural feature points are obtained from the intersection of the edges on the back of the hand or the change of brightness, and are used for detecting the object moving or image recognition. The locus of the natural feature point on the hand which rotates the handle of valve is an arc. The angular velocity can be measured if our method can know the moving distance (=length of chord of the arc) of the feature point per unit time and the central coordinates of this arc.

The relationship of the each variable to explain the logic measuring the angular velocity shows in Fig.1. The center angle θ is computed by the tangent function

from 3 points that the start point $p^s = (x^s, y^s)$ and the end $p^e = (x^e, y^e)$ as the coordinate of both ends of the locus and the central coordinate of handle $p^c = (x^c, y^c)$. The central angle θ is calculated as in Eq (1). The time that the feature point moves to the end point p^e from the start point p^s is defined as t. An angular velocity ω is calculated as in Eq (2). Therefore, the angular velocity ω can be calculated if the central coordinate P_c of the back of the hand is determined. The center of coordinate of the handle assumes to coincide with the center of coordinate of back of hand. Next paragraph explains the reason that the two coordinates were corresponded.

People put your fingers evenly on a handle so that it can turn the handle with a light force. Then, the center coordinate of the back of a hand comes near spontaneously to the rotation axis of the valve. The author searches the distance between the rotating axis of the valve and the back of empty-hand and the vertical and horizontal length in gripping the valve of which the diameters are 50, 60, and 70 mm in preliminary studies. The result shows in **Table 1**. The distance between the two coordinates became 20mm by forming that grip with the thumb, index finger, middle finger in the natural posture because the diameter of handle was small 50mm. However, the distance of the coordinates of the both axis was found to be close to 5-20mm when gripped the handle of 50-70mm. Therefore, the angular velocity turning the handle of the valve can be measured from the movement of the hand because the coordinates of the both axes are almost coincide due to the rotation amount of the valve and the handle are coincide. The valve can be rotated by manners other than those previously described. However, the other manners are excluded from application target because workers are taught from work manual the manner which rotates the valve which put the finger with hand-force evenly.

Circle handle diameter (mm)	50	60	70
Longitudinal length of the back of the hand (mm)	105	105	110
Landscape length of the back of the hand (mm)	90	90	100
Distance of centers between the hand and the handle (mm)	20	10	5

Table 1. Distance of both centers on Valve and Back of Hand

Algorithm

The camera image is defined as g^{Base}.

Step. 1 Noise reduction

A media filter applies to g^{Base} for noise reduction.

Step. 2 Conversion to HSV color space

g^{Base} is converted to a image with HSV color space g^{HSV}.

Step. 3 Binarization

A binarized image g^{Bin} is retrieved from g^{HSV}.

Step. 4 Calculation of distance image

A distance image g^{Dist} is retrieved from g^{Bin}.

Step. 5 Extraction of contour group

The group of contour lines $Cont$ is retrieved from g^{Bin} by 8-neighborhood method.

Step. 6 Determination of the contour of the hand

One of $Cont$ which includes max intensity in g^{Dist} is defined as the region of hand $Cont^{H}$.

Step. 7 Calculation of the central of the back of hand

The center coordinate $p^{c}(x^{c}, y^{c})$ is calculated from $Cont^{H}$.

Step. 8 Calculation of angular velocity

This step calculates the average angular velocity ω^{Ave} from each velocity $\omega_l(1 \leq l \leq N_l)$ which were calculate from many set of 3 points p^{s}, p^{e}, p^{c} as in Eq. (1), (2). The average angular velocity ω^{F} every time t is calculated from average of ω'_1 which is fitted within $\omega^{Ave} - \sigma \sim \omega^{Ave} + 2\sigma$ for removing error of Kanade method by using the property which ω^{Ave} follows a normal distribution.

Estimation experiment

Implementation

This software was implemented in C language using DirectShow, Open CV 1.1, not to support multi-threading. The CPU was i7-2640M 2.80GHz.

Experiment Environment

Evaluation was performed in front of white wall for measuring without effect of noise to measure nature performance. The diameters of valves used in this evaluation were ϕ 50mm, ϕ 60mm and ϕ 70mm. The location of camera and valve shows in Fig.2&3.

Experimental procedure

An image g^{Base} obtained from the camera, which is shown in Fig. 4. The median filter applied to the image g^{Base} according to Step. 1. The image g^{Base} was converted to an image g^{HSV} according to Step. 2. The image g^{HSV} was binarized to an image g^{Bin}, is shown in Fig. 5, according to Step. 3. The distance image g^{Dist}, is shown in Fig. 6, was obtained according to Step. 4. The contour lines $Cont$ obtained according to Step. 5. The hand region $Cont^{H}$ was determined as in Step. 6 is shown in Fig.7. Fig 8 shows our program recognized the hand gripping the valve. The angular velocity ω^{F} was

Fig. 2. Layout of camera and valve (distance: 250mm)

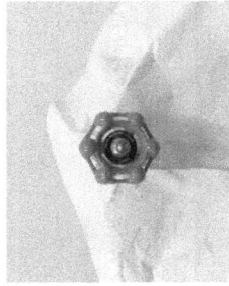

Fig. 3. View of valve from camera

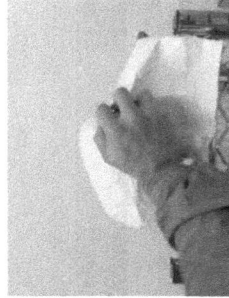

Fig. 4. Raw camera image

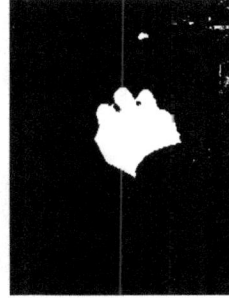

Fig. 5. Binarization image

128

computed based on average points ($N = 100$) that are left points after excluded errors in $Cont^H$ where 500 features points are obtained from g^{Base}. The optical flow image obtained from these natural feature point is shown in Fig. 9. The acquisition speed of the image came to 30 fps which is the camera limitation.

Result & Discussion

A boxplot, is shown in Fig.10, shows the velocity of each measuring item calculated from 5 measurements which was excluded the 60% both ends (30% one-side) which coincides with data of a start and end of the handle operation. Each unit of the item label is that ω is degree/s, ϕ is mm. The standard deviation was confirmed to have increased in proportion to angular velocity in 25-75% range of the waveform. The reasons of that there is a part where the velocity was dropped rapidly in measurement or there is a problem where the image acquisition rate was not keeping up with the movement of the hand because the web camera cannot get only up to 30fps.

Conclusion

Our image recognition method was confirmed to be able to be applied to the valve opening manipulation UI for constructing VR training system which allows trainees to train the risk of the opening manipulation of valve which causes the accident with the 45-90% high ignition rate when opening the valve of the tank filled with Nylon 66 in 10.0 to 0.3 seconds.

References

[1] Service Studies Committee Kinki Air-Conditioning and Refrigeration Institute, Service engineers valuable – Gas Welding and Cutting Edition (In Japanese), http://www.kinreiko-marutoku.com/safety/images/04.pdf, viewed at 2014.5.2.

[2] High Pressure Gas Safety Institute of Japan, High Pressure Gas Safety Law list accident that occurred in 2010 (1) Accident of manufacturing sites: Disaster Accident (In Japanese), http://www.khk.or.jp/activities/incident_investigation/hpg_incident/pdf/H22jikoitiranr1.pdf, viewed at 2014.5.2.

[3] Kanagawa Prefectural Government, High-pressure gas accident case information sheet - Gas injection of liquefied carbon dioxide disposal (In Japanese), http://www.pref.kanagawa.jp/uploaded/attachment/422110.pdf, viewed at 2014.5.2.

[4] Tsuchiya Shigeru, Experimental Studies on the Flammability of Materials in the Pressurized Oxygen Atmospheres (In Japanese), *TAIYO NIPPON SANSO Technical Report*, vol. 26, pp. 12–17, 2007.

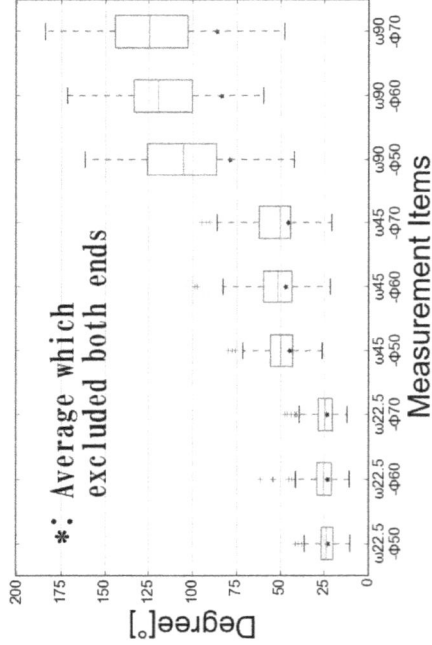

*: Average which excluded both ends

Fig. 10. The measured valve opening velocity

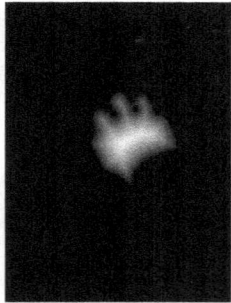

Fig. 6. Distance image

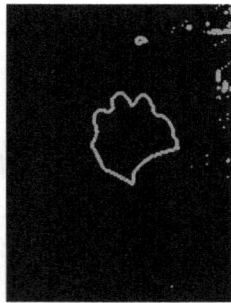

Fig. 7. Contour plots of hand

Fig. 8. Rectangle region

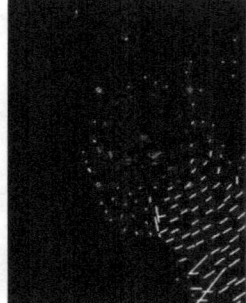

Fig. 9. Locus of optical flow

Development of a Dialogue Scenario Editor on a Web Browser for a Spoken Dialogue System

Ryota Nishimura
CREST, JST
Nagoya Institute of Technology
Gokiso, Showa, Nagoya, Japan.
nishimura.ryota@nitech.ac.jp

Takahiro Uchiya
CREST, JST
Nagoya Institute of Technology
Gokiso, Showa, Nagoya, Japan.
t uchiya@nitech.ac.jp

Daisuke Yamamoto
CREST, JST
Nagoya Institute of Technology
Gokiso, Showa, Nagoya, Japan.
daisuke@nitech.ac.jp

Ichi Takumi
CREST, JST
Nagoya Institute of Technology
Gokiso, Showa, Nagoya, Japan.
takumi@nitech.ac.jp

HAI 2014, October 29–31, 2014, Tsukuba, Japan.
ACM 978-1-4503-3035-0/14/10.
http://dx.doi.org/10.1145/2658861.2658904

Abstract

We developed a scenario editor to improve the environment of scenario editing for a spoken dialogue system. The purpose of this study is to improve the editing environment of the spoken dialogue system. We have developed MMDAgent (a fully open-source toolkit for voice interaction systems), which runs on a variety of platforms such as personal computers (running Windows, Mac OS, or Linux) and smartphones (running Android). So that MMDAgent can be used in a similar environment, the scenario editor is also implemented on a Web browser. Experiments were conducted for subjects using the scenario editor of our system. It was found that our system provides better readability of a scenario and allows easier editing.

Author Keywords

spoken dialogue system; scenario editor; web browser;

ACM Classification Keywords

H.5.2. [Information Interfaces and Presentation (e.g. HCI)]: User Interface

introduction

Various techniques of speech processing have recently been developed. Among these, techniques of speech recognition and speech synthesis are widely used. Spoken dialogue systems (SDSs) integrating these technologies have also been developed.

Therefore, for anyone to be able to use an SDS easily, we constructed a fully open-source toolkit for voice interaction systems (MMDAgent [1]) using speech processing technology. SDS software has been developed for the personal computer (PC; running Windows, Mac OS, or Linux), and it has also been ported to Android so as to work on any smartphone [2].

The MMDAgent toolkit includes software for speech recognition, speech synthesis, character drawing as part of 3D computer graphics and dialogue management to meet the requirements of an SDS. An environment to build an SDS can easily be created using this toolkit. However, even to create the environment, expert knowledge of the spoken dialogue is necessary in constructing an SDS. Novice users find it difficult to build a dialogue system without such knowledge. In the construction of the SDS, it is necessary to edit the dialogue scenario of the contents of the conversation. However, in the current editing environment, it is difficult to read in a complex dialogue scenario, and editing is thus difficult even for the expert user. Therefore, in this paper, we develop a dialogue scenario editor to improve the editing environment.

Dialogue scenario

In the scenario file, such as that in Figure 1, the indenting of each item is performed manually using a space or tab. In some cases, indentations are not aligned and readability is thus poor. Additionally, the user must remember the commands to describe the scenario. Scenario editing in a text editor is therefore difficult even for the expert user.

```
1 10 RECOG_STOP|Hello <eps>
1 10 RECOG_STOP|Good morning <eps>
10 11 <eps> MOTION_ADD|mei|greet|greet.vmd
11 12 <eps> SYNTH_START|mei|normal|Good morning.
12 13 SYNTH_STOP|mei MOTION_ADD|mei|happy.vmd
13 14 <eps> SYNTH_START|mei|happy|It is a nice morn-
ing.
14 1 SYNTH_STOP|mei <eps>
```

Figure 1: Example of a dialogue scenario FST (Some notation is simplified)

Dialogue Scenario Editor (MMDAE)

To improve the created environment of speech dialogue scenarios and thus solve the problems described above, we developed a scenario editor. The scenario editor is named MMDAE (MMDAgent scenario Editor). Three features of MMDAE are discussed in the following .

1: Completion of the input

To create a scenario, the input of four items is required, as shown in Figure 1. It is difficult to type all the dialogue scenarios (conditions and commands). An input complement function was thus implemented in the system. Furthermore, after the command is entered, the text area in which to enter arguments is displayed.

2: Execution on various platforms

The developed MMDAgent can be run on a variety of platforms such as PCs (running Windows, Mac OS, or Linux) and smartphones (running Android). So that MMDAgent can be used in a similar environment, the scenario editor can also be implemented on a Web browser. Furthermore, MMDAgent has the ability to share the dialogue scenario on the Internet, and in this respect, the use of a Web browser is effective.

3: Changing the edit mode

Notepad (the standard text editor in Windows) and MMDAE were compared in the evaluation of the editing environment of the dialogue scenario. In the experiment, subjects appended the contents of the dialogue in the scenario file. The order of use of editing tools may affect the experimental results, because the subject may become used to editing. Therefore, subjects were divided into two groups, and the order of the use of editing tools was different for each group. The duration of editing by each subject was recorded. Experiments were performed using a PC that is usually used by the subjects in the laboratory.

A questionnaire was conducted after the experiment. For the following items, the subjects gave a score on a five-point Likert scale. In the case of Q1, for example, a response that the subject found it difficult to edit is awarded 1 point, and a response that it was easy to edit is awarded 5 points.

- Easy to edit (Q1: Notepad, Q2: MMDAE)
- Readability (Q3: Notepad, Q4: MMDAE)
- Easy to understand the usage (Q5: Notepad, Q6: MMDAE)
- Convenience of function
  - Q7: input complement function
  - Q8: focus switched by TAB key
  - Q9: text area division in accordance with the number of arguments
- About MMDAgent
  - Q10: Were you aware of MMDAgent previously?
  - Q11: Have you used MMDAgent previously?
- For the following items, subjects wrote freely
  - Q12: What functions does the system require?
  - Q13: Other comments (good and bad points about the system)

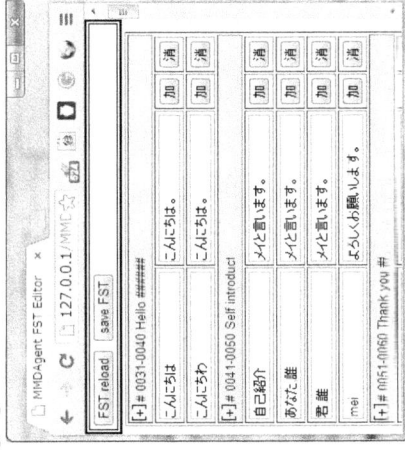

Figure 2: Simple edit mode

To change the ease of editing the dialogue scenario according to the userfs knowledge and experience of using an SDS, it is possible to change the edit mode. Only a few items are displayed to the novice user. In this way, the user can edit the dialogue scenario without knowledge of the scenario description method.

Expert users are presented many items and are provided an environment in which to create a scenario using the full functionality of MMDAgent. Furthermore, according to the hardware used to edit a scenario (e.g., a PC or smartphone), it is possible to select an appropriate display method. For example, a compact display is presented for the small screen of a smartphone, as shown in Figure 2.

evaluation

An experiment was performed to evaluate the performance of MMDAE. Subjects were 13 male bachelorfs and masterfs students in their twenties.

132

Table 1: edit time

	Notepad	MMDAE
average	4:50	3:58

results

The results of subjective evaluation based on the five-point Likert scale and objective evaluation based on the editing duration are presented below.

Subjective evaluation

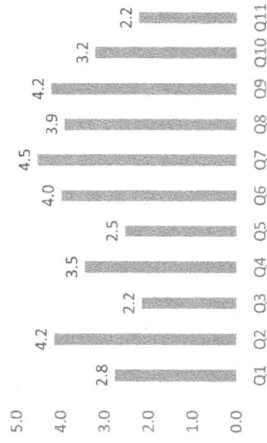

Figure 3: Results of subjective evaluation (five-point scales)

Experimental results are shown in Figure 3. The questions Q1–11 are as listed in the previous section. Figure 3 shows that, in comparing the two editing systems (i.e., Q1 vs. Q2, Q3 vs. Q4, and Q5 vs. Q6), MMDAE obtained higher marks for all items, and the difference between scores was more than 1 point. In particular, in terms of easy editing and easy understanding of use, MMDAE scored 4 points or more on average. Additionally, the functionality of MMDAE (Q7, Q8, and Q9) scored highly. According to these results, MMDAE is more suitable than Notepad for dialogue editing.

Objective evaluation

The editing duration and efficiency were compared between editing systems. The results are given in Table 1. Whereas the editing duration using Notepad was 4 min 50 s on average, that using MMDAE was 3 min 58 s on average; i.e., the editing time was reduced on average by 52 s (or about 18% of the average duration using Notepad) when using MMDAE.

conclusion

To improve the environment for editing the scenario of an SDS, we developed a scenario editor (MMDAE). In an experiment, subjects preferred to edit a scenario in MMDAE than in Notepad, and the editing duration was about 18% less when using MMDAE. In terms of usability, MMDAE rated higher than Notepad in a survey of users.

acknowledgments

This research was partly funded by the Japan Science and Technology Agency (JST) through Core Research for Evolutionary Science and Technology (CREST).

References

[1] Lee, A., Oura, K., and Tokuda, K. MMDAgent - A fully open-source toolkit for voice interaction systems. *In Proc. of ICASSP 2013* (2013), 8382–8385.

[2] Yamamoto, D., Oura, K., Nishimura, R., Uchiya, T., Lee, A., Takumi, I., and Tokuda, K. Voice Interaction System with 3D-CG Modeling for Stand-alone Smartphones. *In Proc. of international Conference on Human-Agent Interaction (iHAI) 2014* (2014), xxx–xxx (to appear).

Notification Design Using Mother-like Expressions

Marie Uemura
Kyoto Institute of Technology
Matsugasaki, Sakyo-ku, Kyoto,
Japan
marie@hit.is.kit.ac.jp

Itaru Kuramoto
Kyoto Institute of Technology
Matsugasaki, Sakyo-ku, Kyoto,
Japan
kuramoto@hit.is.kit.ac.jp

Keiko Yamamoto
Kyoto Institute of Technology
Matsugasaki, Sakyo-ku, Kyoto,
Japan
kei@kit.ac.jp

Yoshihiro Tsujino
Kyoto Institute of Technology
Matsugasaki, Sakyo-ku, Kyoto,
Japan
tsujino@kit.ac.jp

Abstract

People often ignore their reminders or schedulers, which
notify them about their requisite tasks using monotonous
message expressions, usually because they do not pay
sufficient attention to their notifications and they feel that
they are under no pressure to respond. In this study, we
propose a notification design method that uses
mother-like expressions to enhance user acceptability of
notifications. Mother-like expressions are highly variable,
such as euphemistic expressions and imperative forms, and
notifications that use them may apply different levels of
pressure on users. To implement a reminder system that
provides notifications regarding various tasks using
mother-like expressions, we classified tasks collected from
actual reminders, schedulers, and diaries. As a result, we
found that the tasks could be classified into six verb-based
categories, which could be adapted using mother-like
expressions.

Author Keywords

notification, message design, character, mother-like
expression, agent

ACM Classification Keywords

H.5.m [Information interfaces and presentation (e.g.,
HCI)]: Miscellaneous;

Introduction

A reminder or scheduler is a system used to provide notification about tasks or events at designated times. They are useful for managing tasks in our daily life as well as in business contexts. However, we might ignore notifications on occasions, which means that we will not respond to notifications in a timely manner. We consider that this situation is caused by two problems, as follows.

A) Users do not pay sufficient attention to notifications.

For example, let us assume that a person must leave his house to attend a meeting at work at 8 AM on the following Tuesday. He has already registered this event (for example, "Meeting at work") on his scheduler, thus the scheduler sends him a message such as "It's time to go to work" via an e-mail or a pop-up window as a notification. In this case, the message is usually quite simple and it is similar to many other messages from the scheduler. If he reads dull and monotonous notifications every time, his attention decreases gradually and the next time he might think: "I have the same notification again. I can remember it, so I do not need to read the next one." Finally, he begins to ignore the notifications.

B) Users do not experience any pressure to respond to notifications.

For example, let us assume that a person must do her homework. In this case, her scheduler sends a monotonous and polite message about the task repeatedly, such as: "It's time to start your homework." These repeated messages do not apply sufficient pressure, thus she might think: "I don't have to do the homework now," and she begins to ignore the notifications from the system.

Figure 1: Scenario using notifications with mother-like expressions, compared with conventional one.

Keeping to a schedule is one of the principal rules of social life, thus ignoring notifications may cause serious problems. In order to address this problem, we propose a method for designing notification messages based on mother-like expressions (Fig. 1).

Effects of Mother-like Expression

Honda[1] showed that university students have the following two types of impressions regarding their mothers.

- Tenderness:

  Mother always feels concern for her children.

- Dependence:

  A mother always wants to do something for her children, or wants them to do something for her.

We can represent many stereotypical mother-like expressions based on these two impressions. We introduce these impressions into notification messages by using the mother-like expressions to address problems A and B, as follows.

- Notification messages that contain mother-like expressions are sufficiently diverse to keep our attention. In addition, the expression gives the impression of tenderness, thus we can feel our mother's consideration for us. This can increase the level of attention paid to notifications, thereby solving problem A.

- Notifications that contain mother-like expression increase the impression of dependency. This allow various levels of pressure to be applied, because mothers use various expressions to represent their dependency such as instructions and orders. This addresses problem B.

With respect to addressing problem B, we might not accept a notification because we may feel discontent that successive messages might contain severe expressions. However, this is not problematic because although we feel severity, we also experience sufficient tenderness to make us calm, which is prompted by the mother-like impression.

To clarify the actual and practical expressions used by mothers, we held two brainstorming sessions. Based on these sessions, we obtained the following types of expressions.

- Mothers use indirect expressions when the deadline for their child's work is not close:

  – In a roundabout manner: "When is the deadline for your homework?"
  – In a rhetorical manner: "You will do your homework shortly, won't you?"

- Mothers use direct expressions when the deadline is close:

  – In a simple manner: "Why don't you do your homework now?"
  – In an imperative manner: "Do your homework right now!"

Thus, we propose a method for designing notification messages based on these two types of mother-like expressions. We created a set of examples of mother-like expressions using the design method. Table 1 shows the set of examples where the user has the task of: "Handing in my homework by 3 PM."

Table 1: Examples of notifications using the proposed expressions and the times of the messages

# of notification	time	message
1st	12 : 00PM	When is the deadline for your homework?
2nd	01 : 00 PM	You will do your homework shortly, won't you?
3rd	02 : 00 PM	Why don't you handed in your homework?
4th	03 : 00 PM	Do your homework or it will be too late!
5th	03 : 05 PM	Do your homework! It's already late!!!

Notification Design

We want to support as many notification types as possible on reminders/schedulers, thus we explored the notification types that were actually used by reminders, schedulers, and diaries during a period of approximately two years. There were 495 tasks, most of which could be categorized into six verb-based categories (Fig. 2), as follows.

- Based on a certain person's movement
  - Come
  - Exist
  - Go

- Based on a certain item's movement
  - Need
  - Have
  - Hand in

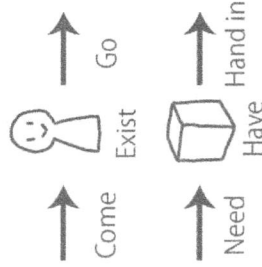

Come   Exist   Go

Need   Have   Hand in

Figure 2: Six verb-based categories of tasks on schedulers.

We plan to create six sets of templates for notification messages using mother-like expressions that correspond to these categories, thereby ensuring that notifications with mother-like expressions can cover a wide range of tasks that are actually registered by schedulers.

Conclusion and Future Work

In this study, we proposed a method for designing notifications that contain mother-like expressions to improve the user acceptability of notifications from reminders or schedulers. We utilized two impressions of mothers, i.e., "tenderness" and "dependency," to overcome the problems that messages are too monotonous to maintain the attention and users feel that they are under no pressure to respond to a notification. In addition, we classified the tasks that are actually used by schedulers into six categories.

In future research, we plan to implement a reminder system using the proposed mother-like expressions and we will evaluate the effectiveness of these expressions in daily life.

References

[1] Honda, T. On chronological changes of how children are viewed and the images of images of father and mother in adolescents and their parents. *Bulletin of Human Science 26, pp.87–93(in Japanese)* (2004).

Will You Follow the Robot's Advice?

The Impact of Robot Types and Task Types on People's Perception of a Robot

Hyewon Lee

Ewha Womans University, Seoul, Republic of Korea
sabrina.hyewon.lee@gmail.com

Jung Ju Choi

Ewha Womans University, Seoul, Republic of Korea
meloncreamm@naver.com

Sonya S. Kwak*

*Corresponding Author
Ewha Womans University, Seoul, Republic of Korea
sonakwak@ewha.ac.kr

HAI 2014, October 29–31, 2014, Tsukuba, Japan.
ACM 978-1-4503-3035-0/14/10.
10.1145/2658861.2658906

Author Keywords

Art appraiser; Autonomous robot; Human-robot interaction; Quantitative task; Qualitative task; Tele-operated robot

ACM Classification Keywords

H.5.2 [**Information Interfaces and Presentation**]: User Interfaces – *User-centered design*

Abstract

Robots could be classified into an autonomous robot and a tele-operated robot according to the levels of autonomy. As a match between robot types and task types is important, we explored the impact of robot types and task types on social presence, trustworthiness, and willingness to follow the robot's advice in art appraising situation. We executed a 2(robot types: autonomous robot vs. tele-operated robot) X 2(task types: quantitative task vs. qualitative task) mixed-participants experiment *(N=30)*. Participants perceived more social presence toward the tele-operated robot than the autonomous robot while the autonomous robot was perceived more trustworthy than the tele-operated robot. The robot types and the task types had an interaction effect on the perceived trustworthiness and the willingness to follow the advice. Implications for the appropriate design by the robot types and the task types regarding human-robot interaction are discussed.

I.INTRODUCTION

Robots are classified into an autonomous robot and a tele-operated robot according to the degrees of autonomy. Autonomous robots carry out their tasks by their own while tele-operated robots are controlled by a remote operator [11]. Several studies have been done on comparing autonomous robots and tele-operated robots. For example, social presence of the robot was perceived differently by the level of autonomy in embarrassing situation [3]. Moreover, participants felt more secure and were more motivated when interacting with a tele-operated robot than an autonomous robot [4, 5]. These studies showed that a tele-operated robot is effective in emotional communication between a person and a robot. On the other hand, Choi et al. [2] demonstrated that an autonomous robot was perceived as having more intelligence than a tele-operated robot. As an autonomous robot and a tele-operated robot have different attributes, it is expected that appropriate tasks would be different by robot types. Thus, the objective of the study is to explore the impact of robot types and task types on people's perception of a robot.

II.RELATED WORKS

Robots are classified into an autonomous robot and a tele-operated robot according to the degrees of autonomy and the amount of human intervention. An autonomous robot has higher degrees of autonomy and less amount of human intervention compared to a tele-operated robot [11]. Several studies have been done on comparing autonomous robots and tele-operated robots. Dole et al. [4] showed that in rescue situation, a tele-operated robot was evaluated more positively than an autonomous robot. According to Weiss et al.'s study [10], participants displayed more positive attitudes toward a tele-operated robot than an autonomous robot in a collaboration situation. In a situation of exercising, people were better motivated when interacting with a tele-operated robot than with an autonomous robot. According to Kwak et al., [8] a tele-operated robot was more effective than an autonomous robot in emotional communication. In embarrassing situation, such as when having an interview, people felt more embarrassment to tele-operated robots than autonomous robots as they perceived more social presence to them [3]. On the other hand, the perceived intelligence of autonomous robots was evaluated higher than that of tele-operated robots [2]. These studies showed that a tele-operated

robot could be more effective in emotional communication whereas an autonomous robot could be more effective in situations related to intelligence. Therefore, it is needed to explore how the different attributes by the levels of autonomy affect people's perception of a robot. These analyses led to the following hypotheses:

H1-1. There would be a main effect of robot types on the social presence of the robot.

H1-2. There would be a main effect of robot types on the trustworthiness of the robot.

H1-3. There would be a main effect of robot types on the willingness to follow the robot's advice.

We expect that there would be appropriate task types depending on the attributes of a robot. Kiesler et al. [5] reported that people's compliance would differ whether the given task is playful or serious. In addition, people's preference of the tasks given to the robots was different by robot appearances. Given these studies above, we proposed the following hypotheses:

H2-1. There would be a main effect of task types on the social presence of the robot.

H2-2. There would be a main effect of task types on the trustworthiness of the robot.

H2-3. There would be a main effect of task types on the willingness to follow the robot's advice.

Although there have been several studies about the match between task types and a robot's attributes, such as appearance [9], status [7], etc., limited work has been done on the impact of robot types and task types on people's perception of a robot. Since a tele-operated robot has higher human intervention level than an autonomous robot, we anticipated that it would be more effective in situations where emotional engagement is needed. On the other hand, an autonomous robot has higher autonomy level than a tele-operated robot, hence we expected that it would be more effective in situations related to the intelligence. According to the analyses above, we proposed the following hypotheses:

H3-1. There would be an interaction effect between robot types and task types on the social presence of the robot.

H3-2. There would be an interaction effect between robot types and task types on the trustworthiness of the robot.

H3-3. There would be an interaction effect between robot types and task types on the willingness to follow the robot's advice.

III. STUDY DESIGN

We executed a 2(robot types: autonomous robot vs. tele-operated robot) X 2(task types: quantitative task vs. qualitative task) mixed-participants experiment.

Participants Thirty people aged from 19 to 35 participated in this study.

Materials The robot we used in the experiment was an art appraising robot, Ra-i. It recognizes images and facial features with a camera and generates speech interfaces. We developed two robots by different human intervention levels. The autonomous robot appraises art pieces autonomously while the tele-operated robot transfers the appraisal of the remote user. The robots were controlled via Wizard-of-Oz technique.

Procedure Participants were introduced the explanation about the experiment. The robot appearance and the expertise of the robot as an art appraiser were the same across the conditions. After the three same pictures were shown to the robot and the participant, the moderator asked a quantitative ("Which one does consist of more than 1136 dots?") and a qualitative question ("Which one is the most effective in psychotherapy session?") to the robot in random order. Then, the robot chose one of the

pictures in each question. After the participants experienced each condition, a questionnaire regarding each stimulus was administered, and an interview was proceeded.

Measure Participants answered 9 Likert-type items which were combined into three scales. The three scales were social presence (5 items, Cronbach's $\alpha=$ .85), which were drawn from Heerink et al.'s research [6] and trustworthiness (3 items, Cronbach's $\alpha=$ .95), which were drawn from Andrist et al.'s research [1]. Willingness to follow the robot's advice was measured by a single item. The item was "I'm going to follow the advice."

IV. RESULTS

Social Presence H1-1 was supported by the data $(F(1,28)=5.413, p<.05)$. Regardless of the task types, participants felt more social presence to the tele-operated robot $(M=4.09)$ than the autonomous robot $(M=3.09)$. H2-1 was not supported by the data $(F(1,28)=1.593, p=.22)$, and H3-1 was not supported by the data $(F(1,28)=000, p=1.00)$. Consistent with Choi et al.'s study [2], social presence was perceived differently by the robot types.

Trustworthiness As predicted by H1-2, the main effect of the robot types on trustworthiness was significant $(F(1,28)=5.301, p<.05)$. Regardless of the task types, the autonomous robot was evaluated as more trustworthy $(M=4.98)$ than the tele-operated robot $(M=4.13)$.

H2-2 was not supported by the data $(F(1,28)=5.582, p=.052)$. H3-2 was supported by the data $(F(1,28)=7.734, P=.01)$. Participants evaluated the autonomous robot as more trustworthy when it answered to the quantitative task $(M=5.70, SD= 0.95)$ than to the qualitative task $(M=4.25, SD=1.68)$. On the other hand, participants thought that the tele-operated robot was more trustworthy when they answered to the qualitative task $(M=4.25, SD=0.98)$ than to the quantitative task $(M=4.02, SD=1.43)$. It is inferred that an autonomous robot is more trustworthy than a tele-operated as the perceived intelligence of the autonomous robot was evaluated higher than that of the tele-operated robot [2].

Willingness to follow the robot's advice H1-3 was not supported by the data ($F(1,28)=1.593$, $p=.22$), and H2-3 was not supported by the data ($F(1,28)=3.689$, $p=.07$). As predicted by H3-3, the interaction effect between the robot types and the task types on the willingness to follow the robot's advice was significant ($F(1,28)=5.406$, $p < .05$). Participants were more willing to follow the autonomous robot's advice than that of the tele-operated robot when the task was quantitative, and vice versa. This shows that there would be an appropriate match between the robot types and the task types.

V. CONCLUSION

This study investigated the impact of the robot types and the task types on social presence, trustworthiness and willingness to follow the robot's advice in art appraising situation. Perceived social presence of the tele-operated robot was evaluated higher than that of the autonomous robot, while trustworthiness of the autonomous robot was evaluated higher than that of the tele-operated robot. When the autonomous robot made a quantitative decision or the tele-operated robot made a qualitative decision, participants evaluated the robot as more trustworthy and were more willing to take the robot's advice. This implies that robot developers or designers should consider the match between the robot types and the task types.

VI. REFERENCES

[1] Andrist, S., Spannan, E., and Mutlu, B. Rhetorical robots: Making robots more effective speakers using linguistic cues of expertise. *In Proc. HRI'13* (2013), 341–348.

[2] Choi, J. J., Kim, Y., and Kwak, S. S. The autonomy levels and the human intervention levels of robots. *To be presented in Proc. RO-MAN 2014* (2014).

[3] Choi, J. J., Kim, Y., and Kwak, S. S. Are you embarrassed?: The impact of robot types on emotional engagement with a robot. *In Proc. HRI'14* (2014), 138-139.

[4] Dole, L. D., Sirkin, D. M., Currano, R. M., Murphy, R. R., and Nass, C. I. Where to look and who to be: Designing attention and identity for search-and-rescue robots. *In Proc. HRI'13* (2013), 119-120.

[5] Goetz, J., Kiesler, S., and Powers, A. Matching robot appearance and behavior to tasks to improve human-robot cooperation. *In Proc. RO-MAN'03* (2003), 55-60.

[6] Heerink, M., Kröse, B., Evers, V., and Wielinga, B. The influence of social presence on acceptance of a companion robot by older people. *Journal of Physical Agents 2*, 2 (2008), 33-40.

[7] Hinds, P., Roberts, T., and Jones, H. Whose job is it anyway? A study of human-robot interaction in a collaborative task. *Human-Computer Interaction 19*, (2004), 151–181.

[8] Kwak, S. S., Kim, Y., Kim, E., Shin, C., and Cho, K. What makes people empathize with an emotional robot?: The impact of agency and physical embodiment on human empathy for a robot. *In Proc. RO-MAN'13* (2013), 180-185.

[9] Powers, A., and Kiesler, S. The advisor robot: Tracing people's mental model from a robot's physical attributes. *In Proc. HRI'06* (2006), 218-225.

[10] Weiss, A., Wurhofer, D., Lankes, M., and Tscheligi, M. Autonomous vs. tele-operated: How people perceive human-robot collaboration with HRP-2. *In Proc. HRI'09* (2009), 257-258.

[11] Yanco, H. A. and Drury, J. L. A taxonomy for human-robot interaction. *In Proc. AAAI Fall Symposium on Human-Robot Interaction* (2002), 111-119.

Multimodal Bodily Feeling Analysis to Design Air Conditioning Services for Elderly People

Shinya Kiriyama
Shizuoka University,
3-5-1, Johoku, Naka-Ku,
Hamamatsu,
Shizuoka, 432-8011, JAPAN
kiriyama@inf.shizuoka.ac.jp

Shogo Ishikawa
Shizuoka University,
3-5-1, Johoku, Naka-Ku,
Hamamatsu,
Shizuoka, 432-8011, JAPAN
ishikawa-s@inf.shizuoka.ac.jp

Harunobu Nukushina
Toshiba Carrier Corporation,
336, Tadewara, Fuji,
Shizuoka, 416-8521, JAPAN
harunobu.nukushina
@toshiba.co.jp

Kenichi Shibata
Shizuoka University,
3-5-1, Johoku, Naka-Ku,
Hamamatsu,
Shizuoka, 432-8011, JAPAN
shibata@kirilab.net

Kei Ogawa
Toshiba Carrier Corporation,
336, Tadewara, Fuji,
Shizuoka, 416-8521, JAPAN
kei1.ogawa@glb.toshiba.co.jp

Yoichi Takebayashi
Shizuoka University,
3-5-1, Johoku, Naka-Ku,
Hamamatsu,
Shizuoka, 432-8011, JAPAN
takebay@inf.shizuoka.ac.jp

Abstract

In order to create air conditioning service scenarios adaptive to elderly people, we have conducted detailed situational analyses focusing on bodily feeling information. The practical experimental environment has introduced our constructed indoor interaction system to understand situations based on bodily feeling and to control air conditioners properly. The experiments consists of 7 sessions participated by 6 elderly people have accumulated 228 times of bodily feeling inputs. The detailed analyses have done utilizing our developed multimodal behavior observation tool equipped with the functions of behavior description from multiple viewpoints and flexible retrieval. The analysis results indicate the possibility of correspondence of the scenes of situational changes in conversation like topic transitions and turn-taking events or those of reading to the changes of bodily feeling. The multimodal bodily feeling analysis has produced valuable findings to enhance situation understanding.

Introduction

In recent years, the population of elderly people in Japan has increased rapidly, which has brought a super aging society experienced by no other country. Much research about universal design intended for elderly people to use [1] is ongoing and many home appliances for them have been produced [2].

Sensory organs and cognitive abilities for each elderly person become diverse due to aging. In order to provide suitable services to elderly people in their living spaces, it is necessary to design customized functions for each person and environment by understanding the different ways of feeling in each person. For realizing such progressive personalized services, situation understanding technologies utilizing subjective feeling information for each elderly person as well as objective information obtained from multiple sensors are required.

We had already developed a prototype of intelligent interaction system to provide adaptive air conditioning services for each user's environment [3]. The system equipped with the framework of situation understanding based on bodily feeling information and utilizing commonsense knowledge about living spaces.

This paper describes situational analysis results of experiments conducted by using the interaction system when bodily feeling information is conveyed for studying practical air conditioning service scenarios.

Intelligent interaction system for living spaces based on multimodal sensing

Multimodal sensing is a sensing method of integrated signal processing through combining multiple sensors. The progress of miniaturization of sensors has promoted research works on wearable sensing or situational estimation using mobile devices equipped with multiple sensors like smart phones [4]. The mainstream of multimodal sensing research is situation understanding based on objective sensory information, therefore, user's subjective information has not been used actively. From this viewpoint, we put a focus on how to utilize the subjective information for situation understanding in multimodal sensing environments. As an effective clue for estimating user's internal mental states, bodily feeling has been adopted to study. Bodily feeling is one of the subject information and expresses the state of oneself and its circumstances, which include the person's problem, request, and intention at the instant.

We designed and developed an interaction system to acquire user's bodily feeling information and to utilize it for understanding situation and providing suitable air conditioning services. The outline of the system is shown in Figure 1, which consists of the following subsystems; situation understanding and service providing system utilizing bodily feeling (**Indoor Interaction System**), schedule management system for interaction events (**Task Manager**), knowledge structuring system about living spaces (**Frame System**), commonsense knowledge database about living spaces (**Indoor Commonsense**) [6], and interaction interface system for bodily feeling acquisition (**Room Touch**).

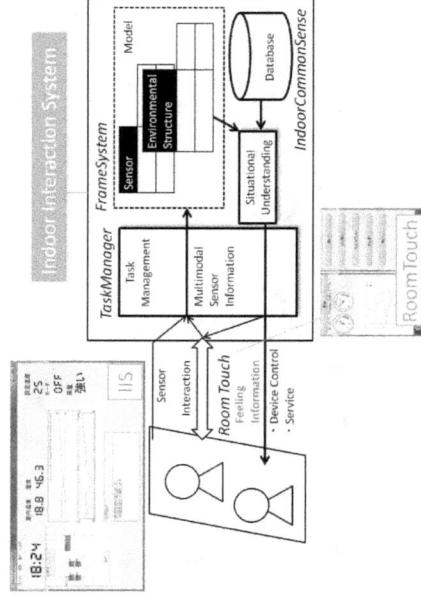

Figure 1: A framework of situation understanding and service providing by multimodal sensing.

Multimodal situation analysis when conveying bodily feeling

6 elderly people participated in the experiments. They were asked to stay the prepared experimental room for around an hour from the state where the temperature was about 13 degrees centigrades to the state where it was moderate warmed by air conditioning. Total 7 sessions were conducted where 2 to 6 elderly people got together for each session. The subjects were a circle of friends through volunteering. They were allowed to spend freely on the experiments. The only restriction was not to get out of the room. All subjects could convey their own bodily feeling at any time via personal tablet using "Room Touch" described in the previous section. The target kinds of bodily feeling were 5 items for temperature (hot, warm, moderate, chill, and cold), 2 items for noise (annoying, and don't care), and 2 items for air volume (disturbing, and don't care).

The subjects conveyed their bodily feeling total 228 times, and 8.1 times per person per session. Table 1 shows the input counts of bodily feeling for each subject in the experiments. Except subjects A and E, the variance of input counts among three items of bodily feeling was little.

In order to analyze in detail from the viewpoint of situational differences for each event of bodily feeling inputs, A multimodal behavior observation tool [5] shown in Figure 2 was introduced, equipped with the functions to describe behavioral features in the target video from multiple viewpoints in multilayered form, and to retrieve required scenes flexibly by the proper combination of behavioral features.

The tool helped us investigate the situations of every bodily feeling input event. The results revealed that some particular situations caused the subjects to convey bodily feeling; "conversation" and "reading." Table 2 indicates the counts of feeling input under these situations. About a half of feeling input events concerned conversational situations like starting or stopping conversation and listening to others. Reading was also one of characteristic situations to perceive changes in bodily feeling.

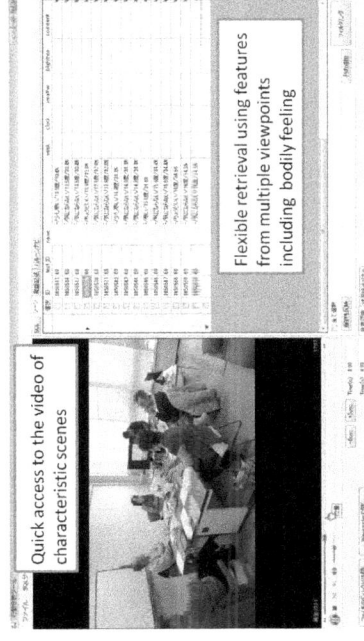

Quick access to the video of characteristic scenes

Flexible retrieval using features from multiple viewpoints including bodily feeling

Figure 2: A multimodal behavior observation tool.

Table 1: Bodily feeling input counts for each subject.

Subject	A	B	C	D	E	F	Total
Temperature	13	7	21	11	19	12	83
Sound	6	6	21	10	26	14	83
Wind	6	6	21	9	7	13	62
Total	25	19	63	30	52	39	228

Table 2: Bodily feeling input counts under some particular situations.

Situation	A	B	C	D	E	F	Total
Conversation	8	8	44	11	21	10	102
Reading	1	0	0	0	16	9	26
Others	16	11	19	19	15	20	100

Session ID	Feeling temperature	Time	°C	Position	Situation
1	Moderate	16:05:34	16.5	At door	Listening to conversation
	cool	16:27:54	18.0		Listening to conversation
2	Moderate	14:06:12	12.3		Conversation stopped
	cool	14:39:00	15.6		
3	cool	15:17:21	14.7		
	Moderate	15:36:58	16.2		Conversation stopped
	cool	16:00:22	17.2		Conversation stopped
4	Moderate	14:01:32	14.1	Near window	
	cool	14:41:56	17.2		Reading book
5	cool	15:13:55	15.0	Near window	
	Moderate	15:24:19	15.2		Listening to conversation
	cool	15:46:55	17.0		Listening to conversation

Figure 3: An example of analysis results: feeling of temperature of a 65-year-old female subject.

A typically unique trend was also observed by using the tool; the scenes were included where felt temperature was decreasing, nevertheless actual temperature was increasing. An example-based analysis was conducted to investigate the gaps between felt and actual temperature.

As a part of analysis results, Figure 3 shows the scenes of conveying bodily feeling for temperature. The cases of gaps between felt and actual features were extracted and the scenes preceding each of them were observed using the tool. The observation results indicated that the scenes of the gaps corresponded to the changes of communicative activity levels from high to low, such as when the conversation stopped, when the interest to the conversation was lost, and when reading a book started.

The experimental results suggested that to understand situations by a clue of bodily feeling was useful to design smart air conditioning services considering personal activity levels.

Conclusion

In order to create air conditioning service scenarios adaptive to elderly people, the situations when bodily feeling was conveyed were analyzed in detail from multiple viewpoints. An interaction system for living spaces to understand situations based on bodily feeling and to provide air conditioning services was introduced into the experimental environment. The experiments consisted of 7 sessions participated by 6 elderly people accumulated 228 times of bodily feeling inputs. The detailed analyses were conducted utilizing our developed multimodal behavior observation tool equipped with the functions of behavior description from multiple viewpoints and flexible retrieval. The analysis results indicated the possibility of correspondence of the scenes of situational changes in conversation such as topic transitions and turn-taking events or those of reading to the changes of bodily feeling. The analysis on the scenes of the gaps between felt and actual temperature suggested that the changes of degree to participate in communicative activities correlated with the variations of bodily feeling. The multimodal bodily feeling analysis produced valuable findings to enhance situation understanding.

References

[1] Oya Demirbilek and Halime Demirkan, Applied Ergonomics, 35, 361-370, 2004.

[2] Association for Electric Home Appliances, 2012, http://ud.aeha.jp/ (in Japanese).

[3] K. Shibata, et. al., Multimodal Feeling Information Understanding for the Elderly in Living Space, INTER-ACADEMIA 2013.

[4] Y. Suzuki; et. al., 2012-GN-83, 1-5, 2012 (in Japanese).

[5] S. Kiriyama, et. al., ICMI2007, 186-192.

[6] Open Mind Indoor Common Sense, http://www.crowdsourcing.org/site/open-mind-indoor-common-sense/openmindhri-uscomloginjsp/7438, 2012.

Portable Robot Inspiring Walking in Elderly People

Yuri Kumahara
Ibaraki University
4-12-1 Nakanarusawa,
Hitachi-shi, Ibaraki, 316-8511,
Japan
13nm911a@hcs.ibaraki.ac.jp

Yoshikazu Mori
Ibaraki University
4-12-1 Nakanarusawa,
Hitachi-shi, Ibaraki, 316-8511,
Japan
mori-zen@mx.ibaraki.ac.jp

HAI 2014, October 29–31, 2014, Tsukuba, Japan.
ACM 978-1-4503-3035-0/14/10.
http://dx.doi.org/10.1145/2658861.2658908

Abstract

In Japan, which has already become a super aging
society, it is important that elderly people maintain
their healthy condition both physically and mentally.
We have developed a portable robot, "TechTech," which
encourages them to take a walk. We infer that the
human–robot interaction is crucially important for
increasing their motivation to exercise by walking.
TechTech talks to elderly people based on information
obtained from various sensors: TechTech can judge
weather and indoor–outdoor environments. It can also
detect sounds and to count steps. It can vary the words
and the intervals in conversations. Results obtained
from experiments demonstrate that the impressions of
dialogues with the robot differ according to a person's
age. Elderly people prefer long intervals in
conversations.

Author Keywords

the elderly; communication robot; walk

Introduction

In recent Japan, the population over the age of 65 has
increased, even as the total population has decreased.
Elderly people now number about 24% of the total
population [1]. Of those elderly people, 23% live alone.
Therefore, demand has been increasing for
communication robots to be conversation partners [2].

The average time for elderly people to stay at home is about 20 hr. Social withdrawal of elderly people, which might lead to dementia, has become increasingly common [3]. In recent years, various companies have developed communication robots for elderly people. Some robots are actually used today in nursing homes. However, such robots are not intended for use outdoors. These robots do not give elderly people sufficient motivation to go outdoors, even if they become good conversation partners. Their size and weight are important factors to be considered when going out.

As described herein, we have developed a mobile robot that can walk together with elderly people and help them to maintain their healthy condition.

Description of robot

Walking supports healthy lifestyles of elderly people. Many people take walks with dogs, but the care of a pet becomes a burden for elderly people. At this point, we presume that the demand for robots will be high.

We considered the functions used to go out and to invite a user to walk. From the functions of the robot, the following flow occurs when using the robot.

1. Judgment of the weather to determine sunny, cloudy, and rain conditions.
2. With different probabilities by the weather, the robot selects actions to encourage going out.
3. It judges indoor–outdoor environments, and ascertains whether a user has gone outside.
4. At the timing of the user, it starts counting the steps.
5. It recognizes an image and utters a word.

Through initial judgment of the weather, it becomes possible to encourage walking with high probability on a suitable day to go out. We thought that it is important to set a goal so that people who do not usually go out to walk can make it a personal habit. We use the number of steps because it accounts for daily results as a numerical value.

Experiment

Basic experiment

We developed the robot actually. "TechTech" is depicted in Figure 1. We conducted the following basic experiments. A microcomputer (Coron; STM32, 72 MHz, Techno Road Co., Ltd.) and sensors are installed in a stuffed-toy-shaped pen case.

- Judging the weather by rain sensor (Asahi Electric Chemical Co., Ltd.) and CdS, and sending the results to PC using another microcomputer (SH7125, 50MHz, Renesas Technology Corp.) and XBee (see Figure 2)
- Recognizing indoor–outdoor environments using an ultraviolet sensor (G6262, Hamamatsu Photonics K. K.)
- Counting steps using an acceleration sensor (KXM52-1050, 2G, Akizuki Denshi Tsusho Co., Ltd.)

By these experiments, we confirmed these operations.

Choice method of action to encourage going out

This robot was developed to encourage users to go out and to give opportunities to take a walk using robot speech and movement. We use probability so that the robot can choose an action that increases a user's probability of going out.

1. As a learning period, the robot performed 12 actions in all from four patterns, selected three

(a) Appearance (b) Electronic circuit inside of the robot

Figure 1. Appearance of "TechTech".

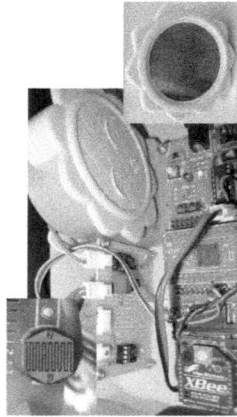

Figure 2. Device for weather judgment.

times randomly. The patterns are (1) utter a sound from a speaker, (2) move a tail with a motor, (3) utter a sound and move, and (4) do nothing.

2. After the robot acted, examinees begin walking down a corridor if they feel that want to go out. That action is regarded as going out. Furthermore, the PC calculates the probability of going out for every action. The calculation of the probability (1) is done using Bayes theorem: $P(A \mid B)$ is the probability that the robot acts as α when examinees go out; $P(A \cap B)$ is the probability that examinees go out when the robot acts as α; and $P(B)$ is the probability of robot action α.

$$P(A \mid B) = \frac{P(A \cap B)}{P(B)} \qquad -(1)$$

3. Results showed for 2 that the robot acts by two programs five times. One program often chooses an action having high probability. It chooses low probability actions less frequently. The other program selects an action randomly.

4. Examinees write a feeling they have for going out, which tells the robot how to act. We count the times to go out. Then we investigate the impression by the SD method.

The examinees were three elderly people and five students. In 3, we used a program using probability and random to test earlier and grouped it. In the SD method, we scored 1–5 points so that positive words became higher.

The result of the impression investigation is presented in Figure 3. Both programs showed wide dispersion for the item "not boring", which is based on the personal traits of the examinees for the repeated actions. We infer a method to invite a user to walk by combining

learning and random selection. Using the probability yielded high total points of the impression investigation in elderly people and students. We regard the choice method as effective.

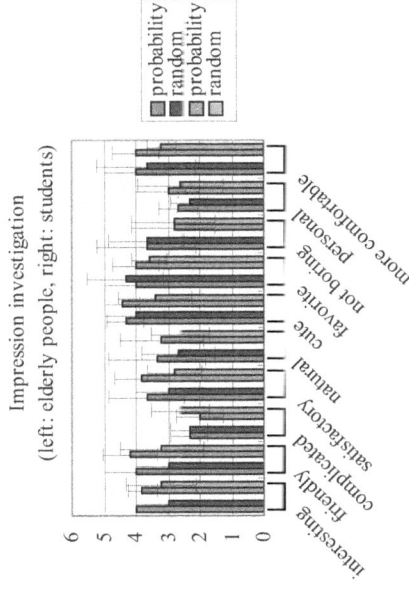

Impression investigation
(left: elderly people, right: students)

Figure 3. Result of the action choice experiment.

Production and experiments of the robot that matches the sensitivity of elderly people

Currently, we proposed " utterance of a sound" and "motion of swinging the tail" as actions that promote a decision to take a walk. Because the target of this paper is elderly people, we decided to match the robot actions with sensitivity of the elderly people. When elderly people get an opportunity, the robot reaction time has a good impression that is slower [4]. It exhibits kindness for elderly people when it pauses slightly. An immediate reply when elderly people talk might appear as anger by the robot. Back-channeling and using many questions about feelings and the contents of the story are important in conversations with elderly people [5]. The robot might be regarded as showing a manner or style of accepting a partner and building a relationship of trust.

From the above, to create the robot that matches the sensitivity of elderly people, we devised a reaction time experiment and a question-form experiment. These experimentally obtained results are used to ascertain the actions used for inviting a user to go for a walk and as a method to communicate during a walk.

In the reaction time experiment, when the robot recognizes the voice of a person, it utters random words. At that time, a time is changed before uttering words because a voice breaks off. Then we determine an optimal reply time for elderly people. The reaction time sets early and late responses mainly according to a time that students judge as moderate. Examinees talk about self-introduction to the robot with different reaction times. According to the results, we can ascertain which reaction time is good. The examinees were four elderly people and five students. Elderly people were easy to feel that the reaction of the robot was rapid. Elderly people tended to have a better impression about later reactions. Students preferred rapid reactions. In the question-form experiment, after the robot recognizes a voice, we investigated whether a user's impression changes if the robot utters the words in question form. Examinees talked about a theme with the robot uttering random words in "question form" or "non-question form" in random order. Examinees can suggest some topics when they talk with the robot. The examinees were five elderly people and five students. The differences show no trends among elderly people or students.

From results of two experiments, we regard that the time range of 0.8s to 1.3s is appropriate as the pausing time before the next utterance and it is necessary to use an appropriate combination positive and question.

Conclusion

As described in this paper, we examined a mobile robot that walks with elderly people. In addition, we devised its functions. Furthermore, we confirmed the flow obtained when using the robot, and experimented with the action choice using probability. The robot was designed and tested experimentally to match the sensitivity of elderly people. Challenges to be undertaken in future studies are explained below.

- Reexamination of the robot, which matches elderly peoples' actions

- Addition of image processing and a voice recognition function

References

[1] Statistics Bureau, Population Estimates by Age (5-Year Age Group) and Sex, January 1, 2014.
http://www.stat.go.jp/english/data/jinsui/tsuki/index.htm.

[2] Ministry of Health, Labour and Welfare, Trends in the number of households and average number of household members, by structure and type of household, 2011.

http://www.mhlw.go.jp/english/database/db-hss/dl/report_gaikyo_2011.pdf.

[3] Statistics Bureau, Survey on Time Use and Leisure Activities, 2011.

http://www.stat.go.jp/data/shakai/2011/pdf/gaiyou3.pdf.

[4] Michio Okada, Weak robot, IGAKU-SHOIN.

[5] Yuya Otake, Masafumi Hagiwara, A Dialogue System for the Elderly Considering Utterance Intention, proceeding of the Japan Society of Kansei Engineering, Vol.13, 2011.

Can You Touch Me?

The Impact of Physical Contact on Emotional Engagement with a Robot

Chaehyun Baek

Ewha Womans University,
Seoul, Republic of Korea
baek.chaehyun@gmail.com

Jung Ju Choi

Ewha Womans University,
Seoul, Republic of Korea
meloncreamm@naver.com

Sonya S. Kwak*

*Corresponding Author
Ewha Womans University,
Seoul, Republic of Korea
sonakwak@ewha.ac.kr

Author Keywords

Communicator types;
Humanness;
Productness; Robot
characteristics;
Shyness; Social
presence

ACM Classification Keywords

I.2.9 [**Artificial Intelligence**]:
Robotics –
*Commercial robots
and applications*

HAI 2014, October 29–31, 2014, Tsukuba, Japan.
ACM 978-1-4503-3035-0/14/10.
http://dx.doi.org/10.1145/2658861.2658909

Abstract

As a robot has both characteristics of humanness and
productness, we explored which characteristic is more
dominant between them. In order to explore the impact of
communicator types on social presence and shyness in
physical contact, we executed a 3 (communicator types: a
human vs. a robot vs. a product) with-in participants
experiment (N=30). Participants felt more social presence
to a person than a robot, and a product. On the other hand,
participants felt more shyness to a person than a product,
and a robot.

1. INTRODUCTION

As social robots became social companions building
relationship with humans, the importance of emotional
communication between humans and robots has been
increased in the field of Human-Robot Interaction (HRI).
Many studies have been done on developing robotic
interface, which recognizes people's emotions and
generates emotional responses [2,5]. However, it
needs to be investigated whether such developed
algorithm could make people to substantively engage in
emotional communication with robots.

According to Kashibuchi et al.'s study, participants
categorized the ten stimuli (human, animal, machine,
inanimate object (e.g., rock), and the three humanoids

and animalike robots including AIBO, PaPeRo, and ASIMO) into the three different groups: human-animal group, robot group, and machine-inanimate object group. They demonstrated that people perceived robots as having both characteristics of living creatures and artificial objects [8]. Moreover, Disalvo et al. suggested that robots have the characteristics of humanness, productness, and robotness [4].

As robots have both characteristics of humanness and productness, it needs to be investigated which characteristic is more dominant between them. Social emotions are emotions that require the representation of other social being [1]. Since a robot is a physically embodied agent [15], we focus on shyness which is one of the social emotions evoked by physical contact with others. If a robot has characteristics of humanness dominantly, a robot could yield people to feel shy toward the robot in physical contact with a robot. On the other hand, if a robot has characteristics of productness dominantly, there would be limitation on evoking people to feel shy. Thus, in this study, we compared communicator types, a human, a robot, and a product and examined its impact on substantive emotional engagement.

2. RELATED WORKS

2.1. Characteristics of Robots

As the importance of emotional interaction between a person and a robot increased, many studies have been done on developing robotic interface which recognizes people's emotions and generates emotional responses [2,5]. However, these robotic emotional expressions do not guarantee substantive emotional engagement between a person and a robot. Thus, the way of enhancing emotional engagement should be investigated. Several studies have been done on the impact of robot types on substantive emotional engagement between a person and a robot. Choi et al. explored the effect of robot types on perceived social presence of a robot and people's embarrassment toward robots [3]. Kwak and her colleagues [9] examined the effect of robot types on people's emotional empathy toward a robot. Even though several studies have been done on the impact of robot types on substantive emotional engagement between a person and a robot, limited work has been done on the impact of communicator types including a person and a product.

According to Kashibuchi et al. [8], robots are categorized in between people and products. Moreover, a robot has both characteristics of living creatures and artificial objects. Disalvo et al. [4] demonstrated that characteristics of robots are humanness, productness, and robotness. Thus, in this study, we compared a person, a robot, and a product, and examined the effect of communicator types on substantive emotional engagement between a person and a robot.

2.2. Emotional Engagement

Social presence is the concept of being with another social being, and leads people to engage in emotional communication [7]. As social presence plays a significant role in users' social responses toward the machine [10], various studies have explored the ways of increasing social presence of robots in the field of HRI. For example, Heerink et al. [6] examined the effect of sociability of robots on social presence for increasing elders' acceptance of robots. Moreover, Schermerhorn et al. [14] explored the effect of participants' gender on perceived social presence of robots. Even though several studies explored the ways of increasing social presence of robots, it needs to be investigated the impact of communicator types considering the robot's characteristics.

According to Choi et al.'s study [3], the degrees of human intervention contribute to the sense of social presence when interacting with robots. Thus, we anticipated that social presence of a person, a robot, and a product would be different since they had different levels of human intervention.

This analysis led to the following hypothesis:

H1. Participants will feel social presence differently by communicator types.

Social emotions, such as embarrassment, guilt, shame, shyness, and pride are emotions that require the representation of other social being and the connection to others unlike basic emotions, such as happiness and sadness [1,12]. As a robot is a physically embodied agent [15], it could make physical contact with a person. Since physical contact with others yield shyness, we focused on feeling of shyness among social emotions. How much people estimate others' presence affects how much people feel shyness and vice versa [12]. As we anticipated that participants would feel different social presence by communicator types, it is also expectable that people would feel shy differently when interacting with a person, a robot, and a product.

This analysis led to the following hypothesis:

H2. When there is physical contact, participants will feel shy differently by communicator types.

3. STUDY DESIGN

We used three (communicator types: human vs. robot vs. product) with-in participants experiment design.

Participants Thirty female university students participated in the experiment. We recruited the same sex group of the participants with the communicators

since sex difference could yield negative emotion in accidental interpersonal touch [16].

Stimuli In the human condition, participants made physical contact with a woman. In the robot and the product condition, participants made physical contact with the MyKeepon [13]. It has an array of invisible sensors underneath its skin and makes motion feedback depending on the types of external touch. We turned on the MyKeepon in the robot condition, and turned off it in the product condition.

Procedure Participants were welcomed to the lab and introduced the explanation about the experiment. They were then had physical contact with three communicators in random order. In each condition, participants were asked to put their hands on each communicator's cheeks. After the participants experienced each condition, a questionnaire regarding each stimulus was administered.

Measure The post-experimental survey was composed of 3 Likert-type items, which were combined into one scale. The one scale was social presence (5 items, Cronbach's α=.93), which were drawn from Heerink et al.'s research [10]. The duration of physical contact with the communicator was recorded.

4. RESULTS

We investigated the impact of communicator types on social presence and shyness. Statistical analyses were conducted using the one-way ANOVA test.

4.1. Social Presence

H1 was supported by the data. Social presence was significantly different depending on the communicator types ($F (2,58) = 63.292$, $p < 0.0005$). Participants perceived more social presence to a human communicator ($M=6.41$, $SD=0.89$) compared to a robot communicator ($M=4.31$, $SD=1.20$) and a product communicator ($M=2.83$, $SD=1.44$). Consistent with Kashibuchi et al.'s study [8], robot was positioned in between a person and a product.

4.2. Shyness

H2 was supported by the data. The duration of physical contact was significantly different depending on the communicator types ($F (2,58) = 13.185$, $p < 0.005$).
The duration of physical contact with a human communicator ($M=11.16$sec., $SD=13.55$) was shorter compared to a robot communicator ($M=45.24$ sec., $SD=49.55$) and a product communicator ($M=33.87$sec., $SD=39.88$). Even though social presence of a robot was evaluated higher than a product, participants had longer physical contact with a robot than a product. This implies that people felt less shy to a robot than a product. It is inferred that the longer physical contact was resulted from the interactivity of a robot.

5. CONCLUSION

We explored the impact of communicator types on social presence and shyness. People felt more social presence to a person than a robot, and a product. On the other hand, people felt more shyness to a person than a product, and a robot. This result implies that even though a robot is categorized in between a person and a product, a robot has difficulty to evoke social emotion.

REFERENCES

[1] Burnett, S., Bird, G., Moll, J., Frith, C., and Blakemore, S.J. Development during adolescence of the neural processing of social emotion. Journal of Cognitive Neuroscience 21, 9 (2012), 1736-1750.

[2] Breazeal, C. Emotion and sociable humanoid robots. International Journal of Human-Computer Studies 59, 1 (2003), 119-155.

[3] Choi, J.J., Kim, Y., and Kwak, S.S. Are you embarrassed?: The impact of robot types on emotional engagement with a robot, In Proc. HRI'14 (2014), 138-139.

[4] DiSalvo, C.F., Gemperle, F., Forlizzi, J., and Kiesler, S. All robots are not created equal: The design and perception of humanoid robot heads, In Proc. DIS'02 (2002), 321-326.

[5] Fong, T., Nourbakhsh, I., and Dautenhahn K. A survey of socially interactive robots. Robotics and Autonomous Systems 42, 3 (2003), 143-166.

[6] Heerink, M., Kröse, B.B., Evers, V., and Wielinga, B. The influence of social presence on acceptance of a companion robot by older people. Journal of Physical Agents 2, 2 (2008), 33-40.

[7] Heeter, C. Being there: The subjective experience of presence. Presence: Teleoperators and Virtual Environments 1, 2 (1992), 262-271.

[8] Kashibuchi, M., Suzuki, K., Sakamoto, A., and Osada, J. How should we perceive robots?: The research at RoboFesta Kanagawa 2001 Yokohama Competition. Faji Shisutemu Shinpojiumu Koen Ronbunshu (2003), 579-580.

[9] Kwak, S.S., Kim, Y., Kim,E., Shin,C., and Cho, K. What makes people empathize with an emotional robot? The impact of agency and physical embodiment on human empathy for a robot. In Proc. RO-MAN'13 (2013), 180-185.

[10] Lee, K. M., and Nass, C. The multiple source effect and synthesized speech: Doubly disembodied language as a conceptual framework. Human Communication Research 30 (2004), 182-207.

[11] Libin, A. V., and Libin, E. V. Person-robot interactions from the robopsychologists' point of view: The robotic psychology and robotherapy approach. In Proc. IEEE 92, 11 (2004), 1789-1803.

[12] Miller, R.S. On the nature of embarrassability: Shyness, social evaluation, and social skill. Journal of Personality 63, 2 (1995), 315-339.

[13] MyKeepon. http://beatbots.net/

[14] Schermerhorn, P., Scheutz, M., and Crowell, C.R. Robot social presence and gender: Do females view robots differently than males?, In Proc. HRI'08 (2008), 263-270.

[15] Shibata, T., and K. Tanie. Physical and affective interaction between human and mental commit robot. In Proc. Robotics and Automation (2001), 2572-2577.

[16] Stier, D.S., and Hall, J.A. Gender differences in touch: An empirical and theoretical review. Journal of Personality and Social Psychology 47, 2 (1984), 440-459.

Social Acceptance by Elderly People of a Fall-detection System with Range Sensors in a Nursing Home

Takamasa Iio
ATR IRC.
2-2-2 Hikaridai, Keihanna
Science City, Kyoto, Japan
iio@atr.jp

Masahiro Shiomi
ATR IRC.
2-2-2 Hikaridai, Keihanna
Science City, Kyoto, Japan
m-shiomi@atr.jp

Koji Kamei
ATR IRC.
2-2-2 Hikaridai, Keihanna
Science City, Kyoto, Japan
kamei@atr.jp

HAI 2014,
October 29–31, 2014, Tsukuba, Japan.
ACM 978-1-4503-3035-0/14/10.
http://dx.doi.org/10.1145/2658861.2658910

Chandraprakash Sharma
ATR IRC.
2-2-2 Hikaridai, Keihanna
Science City, Kyoto, Japan
chandraprakash@atr.jp

Norihiro Hagita
ATR IRC.
2-2-2 Hikaridai, Keihanna
Science City, Kyoto, Japan
hagita@atr.jp

Abstract

This study developed a fall detection system for elderly people in a nursing home and investigated their acceptance of it. The system obtained their positions and heights from range sensors and used that information to correctly detect 89.5% of the falls based on data where the elderly crouched in a mockup room of a nursing home. We investigated the social acceptance with elderly people by comparing three conditions: (1) only detecting out-of-bed, (2) detecting falls in a room and always showing the human position, and (3) detecting falls in a room and only showing the human position when a fall happened. The results showed that intention to use were significantly higher in the second and third conditions than the first condition.

Author Keywords

Smart care home; fall detection; safety system for elderly persons

ACM Classification Keywords

H.1.2 Human factors;

Introduction

In Japan, according to an official government survey in 2006, about ten percent of seniors over sixty had fallen down in a room that year [1]. Experiences of falling

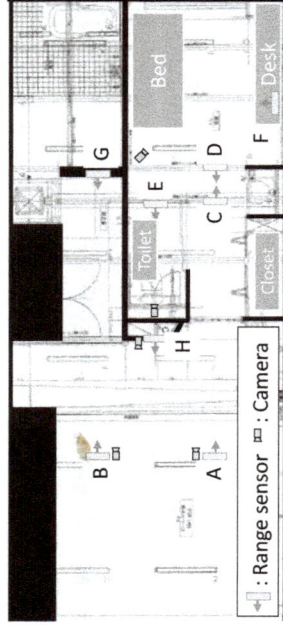

Figure 1. Environmental settings

down reduce elderly people's activity levels and then it would make a wide range of health problems including isolation from society and depression [2]. Even if it is difficult to prevent a falling of elderly people, caregivers need to help elderly people immediately if they fallen down.

In this context, a monitoring falling event for elderly people would be one of promising applications for smart home environment. Already various fall detection systems are proposed to support fall identification [3-7]. These systems enabled us to detect falling down of elderly people rapidly.

However, these studies failed to adequately look into the user impressions of fall detection systems. In this study, we develop a fall detection system with range sensors in the mockup room of a real nursing home and show video scenes of the system to the elderly people to evaluate their impressions toward the system.

System Design

Our fall detection system has three components: sensing, human tracking, and fall detection modules. The sensing module receives range images from a sensor (Asus, Xtion Pro) and sends them to a 3D human tracking module, which detects and tracks humans by processing the received range images from the sensing modules [8], and then the data of the tracked humans (ID, position, height) are sent to the fall detection module to judge whether the person fell.

The eight sensors were located in the environment shown in Fig. 1. We used a mockup room of a nursing home as an experimental environment.

Based on position and height, the fall detection module determines whether a tracked person's state can be defined as a fall. If she is in a low position or in places where people don't normally lie, the possibility of a fall is high. The module judges that a person has fallen under the following two conditions: (1) when the person's height is lower than a threshold and (2) when the person is in places where people cannot normally lie. In this study, the threshold was 110 cm, and the places were defined as other than on the bed.

User evaluation

We experimentally evaluated the user impressions of our fall detection system. In the experiment, participants watched videos that explained the fall detection systems.

Participants

Twenty eight seniors (14 females and 14 males), who averaged 74.0 years of age (SD=6.85), participated in the experiment.

Conditions

To compare our fall detection system with the conventional fall detection system that uses out-of-bed sensors, the experiment had three conditions.

Out-of-bed detection condition: This video showed a fall detection system using a dummy out-of-bed sensor. Instead of using an actual out-of-bed sensor, we developed the same function using a 3D human tracking module; if people exist in a specific area, the system changed the area from green to red.

Fall detection condition: This video showed the fall detection system using the fall detection module with a range sensor. Human positions are shown in green, but if the system detects a fall then the color becomes red.

Fall detection and privacy protection condition: This video showed the fall detection system using a fall detection module with a range sensor. The difference from the second condition is that the information only showed when people fallen down.

Procedure

Before the experiment, we explained the overview of the fall detection systems. We counter-balanced the order of showing the videos of the experimental conditions. After each condition, we gave questionnaires.

Measurements

We measured intention to use by questionnaires; the index of this measurement is composed of multiple questionnaire items, but it was difficult for elderly persons to answer many questionnaire items because of the mental and physical strain. So we only posed one questionnaire item:

Intention to use: You would like to use this fall detection system.

The questionnaire item was evaluated on a 1-to-7 point scale.

Results

Figure 2 shows the results of intention to use. The repeated-ANOVA results indicated a significant difference among these conditions ($F(2,54)=17.223$, $p<.001$, $\eta2=0.389$). In addition, multiple comparisons with the Bonferroni method showed that the evaluation value of fall detection condition was significantly higher than the out-of-bed condition ($p<.001$) and that the evaluation value of fall detection and privacy protection condition, respectively, was significantly higher than that of the out-of-bed condition ($p<.001$). We found no significant difference between the last two conditions.

Conclusion

In this paper, we developed a fall detection system for elderly persons using range sensors and described our system performance and user evaluation results. We investigated the user impressions of our fall detection system under three conditions. The elderly participants had greater intention to use with our fall detection system than the conventional system that uses out-of-bed sensors.

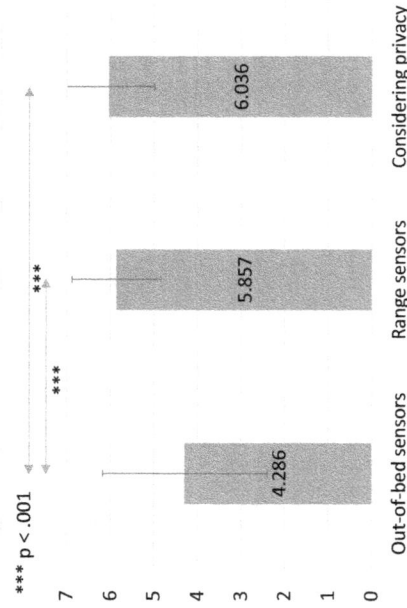

Figure 2. Results of intention to use

Acknowledgements

This research was supported by the Ministry of Internal Affairs and Communications of Japan and MEXT KAKENHI Grant Number 25730165. We wish to thank the staffs at ORIX Living Innovation Center and Good Time Living Kōrigaoka for their helpful participation. We also thank Shionobu Masaki, Naoki Kusakawa, and Eiko Fukumori for their help.

References

[1] http://www8.cao.go.jp/kourei/ishiki/h17_sougou/19html/2syou-2 (in Japanese)

[2] Steele, R., Lo, A., Secombe, C., & Wong, Y. K. Elderly persons' perception and acceptance of using wireless sensor networks to assist healthcare. *International journal of medical informatics, 78*, 12, (2009), 788-801.

[3] Yu, X. Approaches and principles of fall detection for elderly and patient. In *e-health Networking, Applications and Services, 2008. HealthCom 2008*, (2008), 42-47.

[4] Doukas, C., Maglogiannis, I., Tragas, P., Liapis, D., & Yovanof, G. Patient fall detection using support vector machines. In *Artificial Intelligence and Innovations 2007: from Theory to Applications*, (2007), 147-156.

[5] Töreyin, B. U., Dedeoğlu, Y., & Çetin, A. E. HMM based falling person detection using both audio and video. In *Computer Vision in Human-Computer Interaction*, (2005), 211-220.

[6] Alwan, M., Rajendran, P. J., Kell, S., Mack, D., Dalal, S., Wolfe, M., & Felder, R. A smart and passive floor-vibration based fall detector for elderly. In *Information and Communication Technologies, 2006*. (2006), 1003-1007.

[7] Mastorakis, G. & Makris, D. Fall detection system using Kinect's infrared sensor. *Journal of Real-Time Image Processing*, (2012), 1-12.

[8] Brscic, DT. Kanda, T. Ikeda, and T. Miyashita, Person tracking in large public spaces using range sensors, IEEE Transaction on Human-Machine Systems, 43, (2013), 522-534.

Preliminary Investigation of Supporting Child-Care at an Intelligent Playroom

Masahiro Shiomi
ATR IRC.
2-2-2 Hikaridai, Keihanna
Science City, Kyoto, Japan
m-shiomi@atr.jp

Norihiro Hagita
ATR IRC.
2-2-2 Hikaridai, Keihanna
Science City, Kyoto, Japan
hagita@atr.jp

HAI 2014,
October 29–31, 2014, Tsukuba, Japan.
ACM 978-1-4503-3035-0/14/10.
http://dx.doi.org/10.1145/2658861.2658911

Abstract

This study reports a preliminary investigation of a trial to support child-care at an intelligent playroom. We installed a human tracking system and a toy-like robot into the playroom to record children/parents activities. Moreover, we interviewed nurses at nursery schools to study their attitude towards use of robotics technologies for child-care to investigate the social acceptance of robots for supporting child-care.

Author Keywords

Child-care; Intelligent playroom; Ambient intelligence

ACM Classification Keywords

I.2.9 Artificial Intelligence: Robotics

Introduction

Declining birthrate is one of the common problems faced by developed countries. Most of the countries, which are facing this problem, are also on the verge of becoming super-aging societies. A recent trend in robotics research seems to be focusing on supporting elderly people to solve the approaching aging society problem; however there hasn't been any heed towards childcare support using robots. Childcare support should also be considered an equally important task as elderly care in order to realize sustainable development of oncoming social structures in developed countries.

Bartneck argued the importance of having a more child friendly environment to encourage young researchers in the HRI community [1]. This paper is mainly focused on HRI researchers. But, we think that necessity of creating such environment is important not only for the researchers, but also for the societies.

Traditional top down approach used by authorities would be the best way to encourage research in some particular field. But in our case, to initiate use of robotics in supporting childcare, we would like to use a bottom up approach to draw attention towards possibilities in this field by realizing a friendlier child-care environment and sharing the outcomes. In our first trial, we constructed an intelligent playroom, which consists of a human tracking system and a toy-type robot. The tracking system is used for analyzing children's activities, and the robot is used for controlling their attention. This trial is still halfway; therefore this paper reports the current system settings and preliminary investigation results of the system and interviews.

Interview with nurses at nurse schools

To investigate attitude and needs of real nurses, we surveyed 26 nurses from three nursery schools. Firstly, we explained the purpose of this research and showed videos about human tracking system and scenes where children are playing with their parent in our playroom. Then, we asked them to describe their attitude towards such systems, purposes and their opinions.

The use of human tracking system and camera recording is basically accepted positively as some of the nursery schools are already using cameras to record daily activity in the school for security purpose. Moreover, nurses have to note children's daily activities; recording data through the system would be helpful for their purpose, in case if they are too busy to monitor the activities, the system can show how children spent their time. Some of the negative responses are related to dependence on the system; they expressed their concerns about long-term ramifications. A few nurses were afraid that reliance on robots might cause laxity in parents or nurses about such an important issue as childcare. They also said that robots might not be able to notice subtle expressions of a child indicating some sort of need or emotion. Such anxiety might be common for tasks those need monitoring of people like care for elderly people.

The use of robot is also positively accepted as an addition to intelligent toys. Nowadays, there are many intelligent toys such as smartphone; therefore the use of robot is not so different for nurses. From the perspective of child-care, nurses preferred a robot, which can tell good manners to children; this might be an interesting aspect to consider for the design of robots that are used in kindergartens or nursery schools.

System overview

Figure 1 shows an intelligent playroom. Several toys and books are installed for children and parents, and 11 depth sensors are also installed into celling to track people in the environment [2]. The size of the room was big enough to accommodate more than 10 people.

We also installed a ball-type toy robot, Sphero, to investigate how children interact with it. The robot was tele-operated by the operator in some pre-defined behaviors, i.e., Wizard of Oz style [3]. We defined the behaviors to try to tempt children to chase the robot, e.g. the robot runs away from children if approached.

In the preliminary trial, 36 participants (16 children under five, 18 parents and two nurses) participated in total. Total time for the trial was 10 hours (two hours, five times). We asked participants to freely play in the environment. We played with children during the first hour because they needed some time to acclimatize to this environment.

In last one hour, we showed the robot and started tele-operation of it to investigate interactions between children and it. All children were attracted to the robot; children who could already walk tried to capture the robot by chasing the robot, children who could not walk tried to hold the robot by crawling or reaching with their hand.

Human tracking system mostly tracked children and parents, but under some conditions the system failed to track children when they are hugging their parents or their parents are changing their diapers; we will use gathered depth data through this trial to increase the performance of the system to deal with such situations.

Conclusion

In this research we constructed an intelligent playroom consists of a human tracking system and a toy-type robot to realize childcare-support with robotics technologies. Firstly we interviewed nurses who are working in nursery schools to investigate their attitude towards our approach and needs from such a system. Secondly, we conducted a preliminary trial to study the performance of our system in child-care situations and observe interactions between children and the robot. Gathered data and observations showed the possibility of acceptance of our system by children, and we could understand the issues related to such a system through feedback from parents and nurses.

Acknowledgements

This research was supported by the Strategic Information and Communications R&D Promotion Programme (SCOPE), Ministry of Internal Affairs and Communications (132107010). We wish to thank the children, parents and nurses for their helpful participation.

References

[1] Christoph Bartneck, Create children, not robots! Proceeding of the 5th ACM/IEEE international conference on Human-robot interaction (2010), pp. 75–76.

[2] Brscic, D. T., Kanda, T. Ikeda, and T. Miyashita, Person tracking in large public spaces using range sensors, IEEE Transaction on Human-Machine Systems, 43, (2013), 522–534.

[3] D. Dahlback, A. Jonsson, and L. Ahrenberg. Wizard of oz studies-why and how. Knowledge based systems, 6(4):258–266, 1993.

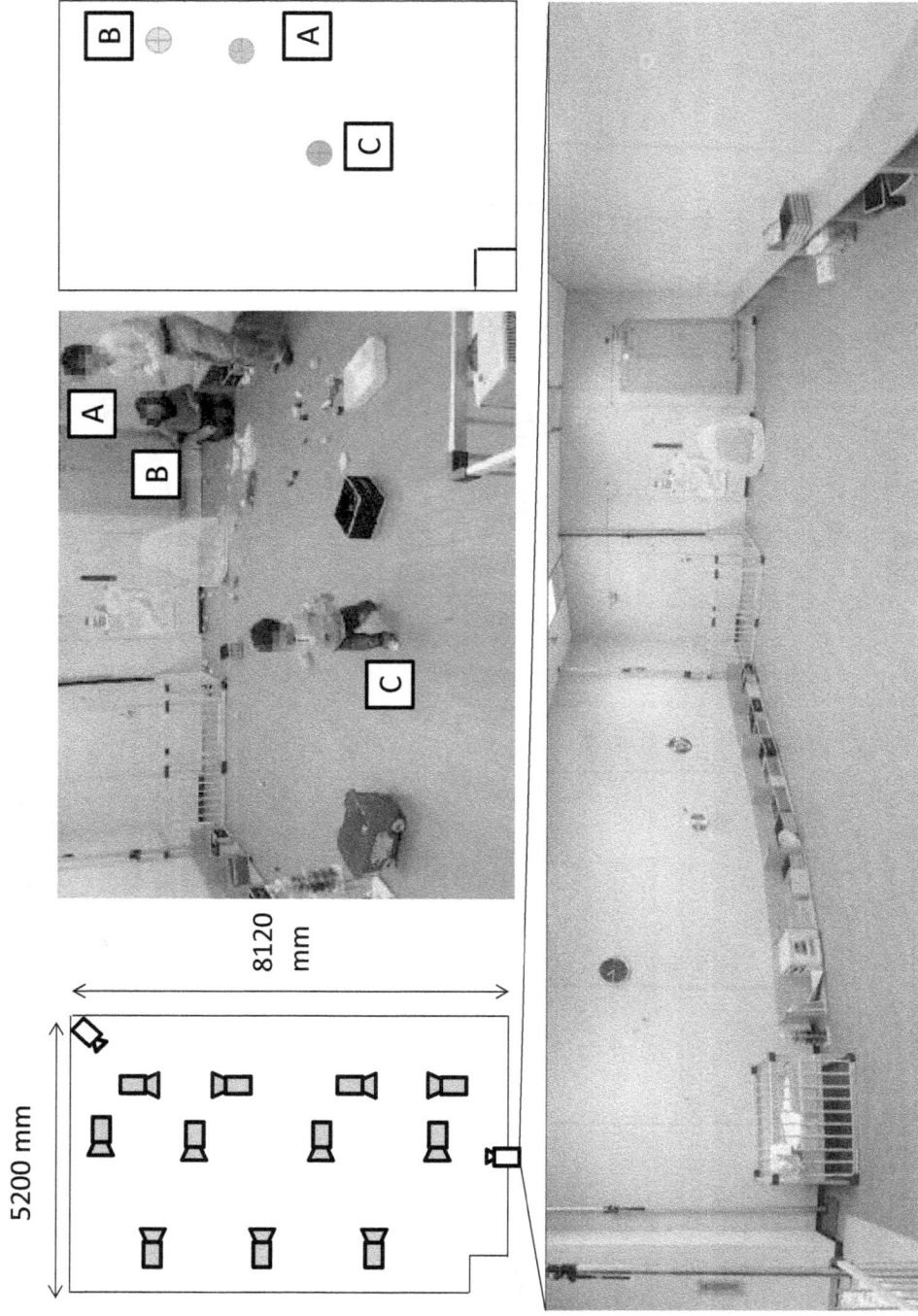

Figure 1. An intelligent playroom. Orange camera icons represent positions and directions of depth sensors.

Recovery of Virtual Object Contact Surface Features for Replaying Haptic Feeling

Yongyao Yan
The Medical Device Research Institute, Flinders University
Adelaide, Australia
yongyao.yan@flinders.edu.au

Greg S. Ruthenbeck
The Medical Device Research Institute, Flinders University
Adelaide, Australia
greg.ruthenbeck@flinders.edu.au

Karen J. Reynolds
The Medical Device Research Institute, Flinders University
Adelaide, Australia
karen.reynolds@flinders.edu.au

Abstract

In this paper, we improve our previous work to recover the user interacting virtual object's contact surface features based on the recorded visual-haptic data for replaying haptic feeling. First the haptic stylus motion is tracked from the recorded screenshot images of the haptic virtual environment (HVE). The virtual object's contact surface can then be modeled after the coordinate transformation process which transforms the haptic stylus position from screenshot image coordinate space into the haptic coordinate space. Finally, the genetic algorithm (GA) is used to identify the contact surface physical properties.

Author Keywords

Haptic virtual environment; replaying haptic feeling; visual-haptic data; genetic algorithm.

ACM Classification Keywords

H.5.2 [User Interfaces]: Haptic I/O.

Introduction

Haptics has provided people with new computer interaction styles across a range of applications. However it is difficult to share haptic experiences from HVEs. In our previous research work [4], we introduced a new system called Hapteo which enables users to capture the visual-haptic information from HVEs. By using the modeling approach, the system identifies the frictionless virtual object's stiffness and models the contact surface based on the recorded haptic data so that users are able to replay the haptic feeling without requiring the HVE software to be deployed. For frictional virtual objects, it is a challenge to estimate the physical and geometric features of the virtual object's contact surface based on the recorded data, because, at each recording step, the surface normal is unknown and, as shown in Figure 2, the recorded haptic data is actually from the position of the haptic interface point (HIP), which penetrates under the contact surface. Assuming the virtual object geometric shape is known, we introduced the GA approach [3] to identify a virtual circle physical and geometric properties at the same time. For general cases, it is hard to estimate the physical and geometric properties all together for a virtual arbitrary contact surface due to the big search space for the GA. This paper estimates the geometric and physical properties of the virtual object's contact surface in separated processes based on the recorded visual-haptic data from a HVE.

Methods

As shown in Figure 1, taking the user manipulating a 2D virtual frictional quadratic shape with a point based haptic stylus as an example, the recorded HIP trajectory presented in Figure 2 shows that the user moves the haptic stylus towards the virtual object (i.e. the section AB), slips on the surface (i.e. the section BC), and finally moves away (the section CD). Assuming the recorded visual-haptic data is synchronized at each recording step i, we get the recorded HVE screenshot images S_i, the HIP positions P_i and the haptic forces F_i, where $i = 1 \dots N$, N is the total number of samplings. A quadratic function is used to model the contact surface by tracking the haptic stylus motion in recorded screenshot

images. The physical properties such as stiffness and friction coefficient are then identified by the GA.

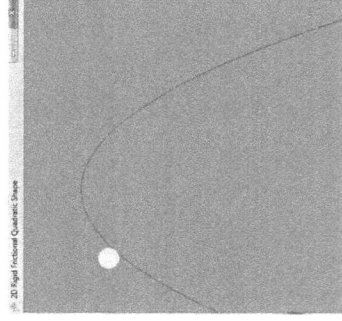

Figure 1: The quadratic shape (red) and the point based haptic stylus (yellow) in the 2D HVE.

Figure 2: The recorded HIP trajectory (green) and the virtual object surface (red).

Contact Surface Modeling

The hue-saturation-luminance (HSL) image thresholding is used to detect the haptic stylus positions Q_i from S_i. It is also easy to detect the radius r of the haptic stylus in the recorded screenshot images. Given the recorded HIP position $P_i = (P_{i_x}, P_{i_y})$, we can then map the position points between image and haptic coordinate spaces as following through the affine transformation:

$$P_{i_x} = aQ_{i_x} + bQ_{i_y} + c \quad (1)$$

$$P_{i_y} = bQ_{i_x} - aQ_{i_y} + d \quad (2)$$

All position points, Q_i and P_i, where $\|F_i\| = 0$, $i = 1 \ldots m$, and m is the total number of position points between AB and CD as shown in Figure 2, are used to solve a, b, c and d in the following equation:

$$\begin{pmatrix} P_{1_x} \\ P_{1_y} \\ \vdots \\ P_{i_x} \\ P_{i_y} \\ \vdots \\ P_{m_x} \\ P_{m_y} \end{pmatrix} = \begin{pmatrix} Q_{1_x} & Q_{1_y} & 1 & 0 \\ -Q_{1_y} & Q_{1_x} & 0 & 1 \\ \vdots & & \vdots & \\ Q_{i_x} & Q_{i_y} & 1 & 0 \\ -Q_{i_y} & Q_{i_x} & 0 & 1 \\ \vdots & & \vdots & \\ Q_{m_x} & Q_{m_y} & 1 & 0 \\ -Q_{m_y} & Q_{m_x} & 0 & 1 \end{pmatrix} \begin{pmatrix} a \\ b \\ c \\ d \end{pmatrix} \quad (3)$$

All detected haptic stylus positions Q_l between the correspondent HIP trajectory section BC are then transformed into the position points T_l in haptic coordinate space, where $\|F_l\| \neq 0$, $l = 1 \ldots k$, k is the total number of correspondent HIP position points between BC. By using the similar transformation method, the haptic stylus radius r can be transformed into r' in the haptic coordinate space.

A quadratic function $f(x) = A_1 x^2 + B_1 x + C_1$ is used to fit all the points T_l and determine the constants, A_1, B_1 and C_1. An adjustment should be made to get the real virtual object's contact surface. For each point T_l, the correspondent virtual object's surface contact point can be computed as: $T'_l = T_l + r' \nabla f(x)$, where $\nabla f(x)$ is the

gradient of the function $f(x)$. Appling the virtual object's surface contact points T'_l, a new quadratic function $f'(x) = A_2 x^2 + B_2 x + C_2$ can be finally determined to model the virtual object's contact surface.

Physical Properties Identification

Regarding the surface model $f'(x)$, we can conceive that the haptic rendering method takes the HIP positions and force feedback as the input and output respectively with the parameter settings of stiffness constant s and friction coefficient μ. In order to replay the haptic feeling of the user interaction in the original HVE, the parameters should be estimated based on the recorded HIP position and force data. We code the physical parameters in a chromosome $\phi = \{s, \mu\}$, which is to be evolved by the GA. Since the force feedback is the output of the haptic rendering method, we can use the root-mean-square (RMS) force error to define the fitness function:

$$Fitness(\phi) = \frac{1}{RMS(\phi)} \quad (4)$$

$$RMS(\phi) = \sqrt{\frac{1}{n}\sum_{i=1}^{n}\|F_{r_i} - F_{e_i}\|^2} \quad (5)$$

where n is the number of recorded haptic data samples, F_{r_i} and F_{e_i} are recorded and estimated force feedback at sample i respectively. And the GA's termination condition is defined as:

$$Fitness(\phi) \geq \frac{1}{\sqrt{\dfrac{k^2}{n}\sum_{i=1}^{n}\|F_{r_i}\|^2}} \quad (6)$$

where k is the deadband value [1], $k = 2.5\%$. The friction cone haptic rendering method [2] is used to analyze the recorded HIP position data and estimate the force F_{e_i} at each sampling step.

Results

The 2D HVE shown in Figure 1 is setup to allow users manipulate a quadratic shape

$F(x) = -1.12x^2 - 0.6x + 0.72$ configured with stiffness $s = 6.43$, friction coefficient $\mu = 0.58$ and the haptic stylus radius $r = 0.08$. The friction cone haptic rendering method [2] is used to render the surface frictional feeling. Total 339 visual-haptic data is recorded at the frequency of 40 frames per second from the 2D HVE. After the process of contact surface modeling, the final quadratic is determined as $f'(x) = -1.1219x^2 - 0.5997x + 0.7197$. The GA is set to run with the population size of 100, the crossover rate set as half of the population size and the mutation rate set as $\frac{1}{15}$. The parameters optimization results of the GA's three runs are shown in Table 1. We take the mean values of the estimated parameters as the final results, which are very close to the original settings. Regarding the friction cone haptic rendering method [2], the haptic rendering can then be reproduced with the estimated stiffness constant, friction coefficient and the contact surface model.

Parameters	Run 1	Run 2	Run 3	Mean	Orig. Value
s	6.5159	6.3491	6.5510	6.47	6.43
μ	0.5544	0.5703	0.5608	0.56	0.58
RMS err. (N)	0.0481	0.0493	0.0506	0.0493	-
Time spent (Sec.)	18	29	33	26.67	-

Table 1: Results of the GA runs.

Discussion

Regarding the experimental results, it is proved that the geometric and physical properties of the virtual object's contact surface can be estimated sequentially in different processes. Given the contact surface model, the GA's search space is narrowed and the GA has good optimization results for the physical properties based on the recorded haptic data.

In the contact surface modeling process, the haptic stylus motion is tracked from the recorded 2D screenshot images and the quadratic function is used to model the virtual object's contact surface. This solution is sufficient for 2D HVEs, where the haptic stylus motion is parallel to the image plane. For 3D cases, it is hard to track the haptic stylus motion which is perpendicular to the image plane. One solution we are investigating is to adopt the manual data sampling process, which allows users to probe and slip on the virtual object surface to generate surface contact points for modeling the contact surface.

References

[1] Hinterseer, P., and Steinbach, E. A psychophysically motivated compression approach for 3d haptic data. In *Haptic Interfaces for Virtual Environment and Teleoperator Systems, 2006 14th Symposium on*, IEEE (2006), 35–41.

[2] Salisbury, K., and Tarr, C. Haptic rendering of surfaces defined by implicit functions. In *ASME Dynamic Systems and Control Division*, vol. 61 (1997), 61–67.

[3] Yan, Y., Ruthenbeck, G. S., and Reynolds, K. J. A genetic algorithm approach to identify virtual object properties for sharing the feel from virtual environments. In *EuroHaptics 2014* (2014).

[4] Yan, Y., Ruthenbeck, G. S., and Reynolds, K. J. Hapteo: Sharing visual-haptic experiences from virtual environments. In *Haptics Symposium (HAPTICS), 2014 IEEE*, IEEE (2014), 257–262.

Toward Playmate Robots that can Play with Children Considering Personality

Kasumi Abe
The University of
Electro-Communications
1-5-1 Chofugaoka, Chofu-shi,
Tokyo 182-8585, Japan
k.ishii@apple.ee.uec.ac.jp

Chie Hieida
The University of
Electro-Communications
hchie@apple.ee.uec.ac.jp

Muhammad Attamimi
The University of
Electro-Communications
m.att@apple.ee.uec.ac.jp

Takayuki Nagai
The University of
Electro-Communications
tnagai@ee.uec.ac.jp

Takayuki Shimotomai
Tamagawa University
6-1-1 Tamagawa-gakuen,
Machida-shi, Tokyo 194-8610,
Japan
shimotomai@lab.tamagawa.ac.jp

Takashi Omori
Tamagawa University
omori@lab.tamagawa.ac.jp

Natsuki Oka
Kyoto Institute of Technology
Hashigami-cho, Matsugasaki,
Sakyo-ku, Kyoto 606-8585,
Japan
nat@kit.ac.jp

HAI '14, Oct 29-31 2014, Tsukuba, Japan
ACM 978-1-4503-3035-0/14/10.
http://dx.doi.org/10.1145/2658861.2658913

Abstract

It is difficult to design robotic playmates for introverted
children. Therefore, we examined how a robot should play
with such shy children. In this study, we hypothesized and
tested an effective play strategy for building a good
relationship with shy children. We conducted an
experiment with 5- to 6-year-old children and a humanoid
robot teleoperated by a preschool teacher. We developed
a valid play strategy for shy children.

Author Keywords

Robotic playmate, children, personality

ACM Classification Keywords

H.5.m [Information interfaces and presentation (e.g.,
HCI)]: Miscellaneous.

Introduction

Playing with introverted children is not easy because they
can be unassertive and uncommunicative. Many
researchers have proposed robots to interact with children
[1, 2]; however, none have considered the interaction with
introverted children. Current communication robots would
find playing with introverted children difficult. In this
study, we analyzed the interaction between introverted
(i.e., shy) children and a teleoperated robot. Because the
robot was operated by a preschool teacher during the

experiment, we expected the robot to be able to play with all children regardless of their personality. Our aim was to abstract effective strategies taken by the preschool teacher in order to play with shy children. This expertise can be useful to building robots for communicating with children.

Teleoperated robotic playmate system

Our future goal is for our robotic playmate to be able to play with a child at home in order to decrease the childcare burden on caregivers [1]. Therefore, this robot can play with a child on a one-on-one basis indoors. The robot is targeted toward 5- to 6-year-old children.

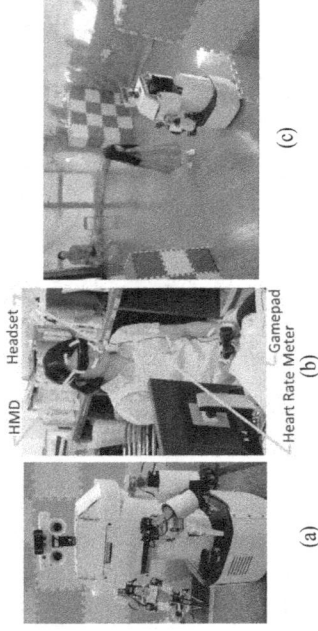

Figure 1: Experiment environment: (a)robot platform LiPRo, (b)operator (preschool teacher), and (c) play room.

Teleoperation system

In this work, we used our developed robot platform "LiPRO" (Fig. 1 a). LiPRO is approximately 105 cm in height. The base consists of four omnidirectional wheels. A webcam and Kinect, which consists of an RGB camera and depth sensor, is mounted on its head. Figure 1b shows a photograph of the operator putting on the teleoperation interface. The operator can control

- the movement of the robot's head with the head-mounted display (HMD);

- the utterances of the robot with the headset microphone;
- the movement of the robot with the joystick on a game pad; and
- the execution of play modules with the game pad.

Each play module is semiautomated and requires only simple operation. Table 1 lists details of the play modules that were prepared for the experiment.

Table 1: Details of play modules prepared for experiment.

Play	Contents
Rock-paper-scissors	The robot makes a rock, paper, or scissors shape selected by the operator with its hand and utterance to play rock-paper-scissors with the child
Quiz	The robot quizzes the child on preschool. The child raises a true-false stick held in each hand and replies. Then, the robot displays the correct answer with the true-false stick.
Playing dice	The robot and child each throw a die and compete on the numbers on the dice or add the numbers.
Sing a song	The robot sings the songs "The 100% of Braveness," "Under the Spreading Chestnut Tree," or a song from the child's preschool alone or with a child.
Hide and seek	One of the robot and child acts as the tagger and looks for the other player who is hiding. Two obstacles are located in the experiment room for hiding.

Experiment between the robot and a child

Thirty-nine 5- to 6-year-old children (25 boys and 14 girls with an average age of 5 years 9 months, $SD = 5.0$ months) participated in this experiment. Four female preschool teachers with 10 years' experience (average age: 36 years) worked as operators of the robot, and one parent of each child helped in completing questionnaires. The experiment was carried out for 12 days at the preschool that the children and teachers attended.

Each parent sat down on a chair near the door, and the child was free to move around in the playroom (Fig. 1c). The robot was operated by a teacher; it was initially in the "robot house" at the back of the room, and freely played with the child. This interaction took approximately 30 min. We logged the utterances of the robot and the duration of each executed play module during the experiment with the teleoperated system. After the interaction, the parent answered a questionnaire to evaluate the child's impressions of the robot on a five-point Likert scale.

Results

All 39 children were able to play with the robot for the entire 30-min interaction. Data of 31 children had valid responses with no missing information. Therefore, we analyzed the data of these 31 children.

The aim of this experiment was to verify the hypothesis that there is an effective play strategy for building a good relationship with a shy child. Thus, we confirmed whether or not play actions affected the relationship. In order to evaluate the relationship, we asked the parents the question "Did your child seem to have a sense of intimacy with the robot?" and used this friendliness score as a measure of the relationship. We also asked "Is your child relatively not shy?" and used this shyness score as a measure of shyness. The analytical procedure was as follows:

1. Confirm whether shyness affected the relationship between the child and robot. We counted the number of children based on the friendliness score and shyness score.
2. Search for play actions that positively impacted the relationship between a shy child and the robot. We calculated the correlation coefficients between the friendliness score and play actions, such as the time duration of the play action. The results revealed play actions that were carried out many times by the shy children who felt intimacy with the robot.

Effect of shyness on friendliness

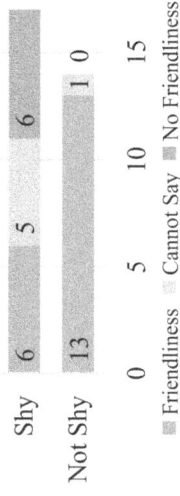

Shy	6	5	6
Not Shy	13	1	0

0　　　5　　　10　　　15

■ Friendliness　■ Cannot Say　■ No Friendliness

Figure 2: Breakdown of number of children by friendliness score and shyness score.

Based on the shyness scores, 17 children were shy (S group: score of 1–3), and 14 children were not (non-S group: score of 4–5) out of the 31 children in total. Figure 2 breaks down the number of children by the friendliness score and shyness score. All of the children who were not shy were friendly with the robot; conversely, the children who were not friendly with the robot were shy. The personality of the child clearly affected the relationship between the child and robot. Note that one-third of the shy children (six out of 17) were friendly with the robot.

Analysis of effective actions

In this analysis, we focused on the S group and analyzed the relationship between the friendliness score and the play actions taken by the preschool teachers. The time duration of each play action (five play modules), conversation, and movement of the robot) was measured in intervals of 0–10, 10–20, and 20–30 min. The numbers of times the robot made an utterance, called the child's name, and used the final particle "ne" (in Japanese) to express an attitude of intimacy were counted in the same intervals. We also counted the utterances in intervals of 0–15 min. Then, we calculated the product–moment correlations between the friendliness score and measured time durations and the counts.

Table 2: Correlation between play actions and friendliness score. (*: $p < 0.05$, †: $p < 0.1$, none: no significant difference.) Play actions include time of each play and number of robot's utterance: C = Conversation, M = Move, R = Rock-paper-scissors, Q = Quiz, D = Playing dice, S = Sing a song, H = Hide and seek, Name = Utterance of child's name, Ne = Utterance of final particle "ne."

time	play actions	S r	p		Non-S r	p	
0~10	C	0.118	0.653		0.597	0.024	*
	M	-0.030	0.908		-0.259	0.371	
	R	-0.115	0.660		0.034	0.909	
	Q	0.568	0.017	*	0.093	0.752	
	D	0.016	0.952		-0.237	0.414	
	S	-0.455	0.066	†	-0.162	0.579	
	H	-0.379	0.133		0.033	0.910	
10~20	C	-0.327	0.200		-0.130	0.657	
	M	-0.247	0.340		-0.107	0.715	
	R	0.353	0.165		0.214	0.463	
	Q	-0.413	0.099	†	0.575	0.032	*
	D	-0.098	0.709		-0.075	0.800	
	S	0.100	0.702		0.072	0.807	
	H	0.492	0.045	*	-0.255	0.379	
0~15	Name	0.419	0.087	†	-0.117	0.664	
	Ne	0.459	0.083	†	-0.505	0.070	†

Table 2 presents the results. Play actions omitted from the table had no correlation with the friendliness score. For comparison, the same correlations were calculated for the non-S group and are presented in Table 2.

Extracted strategies

Figure 3 summarizes the results, which represent strategies employed by the preschool teachers to enhance the friendliness between the robot and children.

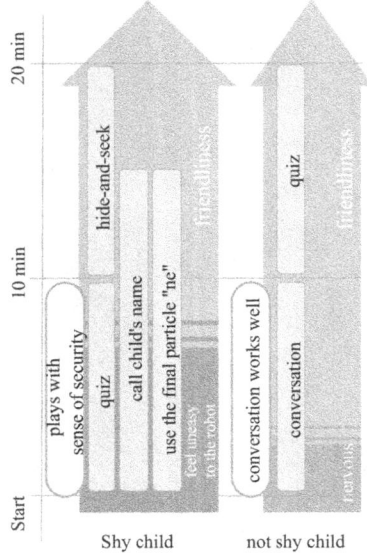

Figure 3: Play plans for building sense of friendliness.

Conclusion

We proved our hypothesis that there is an effective play strategy for building a good relationship with a shy child. To implement a robot that can play with shy children autonomously, we need to study how a robot can estimate a child's personality.

Acknowledgments

We thank the staff of Kakinomi Kindergarten for their devoted help and support. This work was supported by a Grant-in-Aid for Scientific Research (C) (20500179, 23500240) and Grant-in-Aid for Scientific Research on Innovative Areas.

References

[1] Abe, K., Iwasaki, A., Nakamura, T., Nagai, T. et al. Robots that play with a child: application of an action decision model based on mental state estimation. J. of the Robotics Society of Japan 31, 3 (2013), 263–274 (in Japanese).

[2] Belpaeme, T., Baxter, P. E., Read, R., et al. Multimodal child-robot interaction: Building social bonds. J. of Human-Robot Interaction 1, 2 (2013), 33–53.

Affective Agents for Enhancing Emotional Experience

Takahiro Matsumoto
NTT Service Evolution
Laboratories, NTT Corporation
1-1 Hikari-no-oka,
Yokosuka-Shi, Kanagawa,
239-0847 Japan
matsumoto.takahiro@lab.ntt.co.jp

Shunichi Seko
NTT Service Evolution
Laboratories
seko.shunichi@lab.ntt.co.jp

Ryosuke Aoki
NTT Service Evolution
Laboratories
aoki.ryosuke@lab.ntt.co.jp

Akihiro Miyata
NTT Service Evolution
Laboratories
miyata.akihiro@lab.ntt.co.jp

Tomoki Watanabe
NTT Service Evolution
Laboratories
watanabe.tomoki@lab.ntt.co.jp

Tomohiro Yamada
NTT Service Evolution
Laboratories
tomohiro.yamada@lab.ntt.co.jp

HAI 2014, October 29–31, 2014, Tsukuba, Japan.
ACM 978-1-4503-3035-0/14/10.
http://dx.doi.org/10.1145/2658861.2658914

Abstract

We propose shared emotional experience agents. They enhance the user's emotional experience by emotional contagion. Our experiment has 12 participants watch videos together with a robot that expresses an emotional state by body and voice. The results suggest that the affective robot will make user more excited and relaxed and make user less depressed and afraid than they view it alone.

Author Keywords

Affective computing; Emotional contagion; Social actors;

ACM Classification Keywords

H.1.2[Models and Principles]:User/Machine Systems human factors;

Introduction

Being able to evoke the user's emotions like excitement or relaxation is a key goal for media contents like movies, games, music, and books. To enhance the perceived value of contents, positive emotions like excitement should be strengthened while negative emotions like fear could be strengthened or weakened to suit the user.

Since it is impractical to change the contents to suit the user, we focus on his/her emotions can be altered by sharing. A social psychology study showed watching a humorous film with another strengthened positive feelings [1]. However, such sharing is all-too infrequent, and the impact of sharing is not clear for other contents.

Our solution is the sharing experience agent to enhance user's emotions. An experiment finds that this agent can alter the user's emotion.

RELATED WORK

When we share an experience with another, emotional contagion is a one reason of altering our elicited emotion. Emotional contagion is the tendency for people to mirror the emotions of the other. According to simulation theory, it is caused by mimicking to understand other's emotional expression. And it is supported by research on mirror neurons in neuroscience [7].

In the field of human-agent interaction (HAI), virtual agents and social robots are known as they can behave social actors. They behave as if they have their own emotions and can elicit social responses from people. There are many studies on the interactions between humans and agents behaving as social actors [5] [6]. And human-agent emotional contagion was partially ascertained by previous experiments [3] [4].

AGENTS FOR ENHANCING EMOTIONAL EXPERIENCE

We propose shared emotional experience agents. They watch, play, listen or read media contents with user and exhibit the same emotion as contents elicit. User's emotion is effected from emotional contagion with agents as well as contents. So we make a hypothesis that affective agents can enhance user's emotional experience.

In this study, we deal with **human-content-agent interaction**. Our aim is to show how human emotional experience is altered by affective agents in various emotion eliciting conditions.

EXPERIMENT

A video viewing experiment is conducted to reveal the impact of an affective robot on human emotions. In this experiment, we used 4 emotional types of videos that they were selected by following procedures.

We prepared 206 movie scenes clipped from 24 movies, each scene is 1 to 3 min in length and four testers checked the coherence of all movie scenes. Each scene was scored by 16 participants (8 males and 8 females) using Russell's 2D model of emotion. As the score, two questions and a 7 level Likert scale was used: Q1 asks "how pleasant" (1 = very unpleasant and 7 = very pleasant) and Q2 asks "how arousing" (1 = very sleepy and 7 = very aroused). We selected 3 movies that got most extreme score for each of 4 types of emotion (total 12 movies). 1): highest arousal - highest pleasance (AP), this type elicits excited feeling. 2): highest arousal – lowest pleasance (AU), this type elicits afraid. 3): lowest arousal – lowest pleasance (SU), elicits depressed feeling. 4): lowest arousal – highest pleasance (SP), elicits relaxed feeling.

Viewing Condition

For each video stimulus condition, we prepared 3 types of viewing condition to reveal affective robot's impact. 1): Participants view videos alone (Alone). 2): Participants view videos with robot expressing emotion to suit video (Appropriate). 3): Participants view videos with robot expressing random emotional behavior (Random).

We used Robo Danboard a programmable humanoid robot manufactured by Vstone Co.,Ltd. Figure 1 (left) shows the appearance of Robo Danboard, it has 11 degrees of freedom (Head has 3 DoF, Arm 2, and Leg 2).

The robot was given 4 emotional expressions. Each emotion expression set was composed of three actions: viewing, speaking, and pointing. In viewing, the robot turned its face to the display and expressed emotion by body movement. For speaking, the robot turned its face to the display and expressed emotion by body movement and voice. For pointing, the robot turned its face to the participant, pointed to the display by its right arm, and expressed emotion by body movement and voice. Body expressions were based on the Laban-Based approach [8]. For vocalization, the robot spoke its own language much like R2-D2 in Star Wars. Sound emotion was expressed by sound pitch average, pitch range, intensity, pitch change and sound change rate; parameters that were extracted from human emotional speech expressions [2].

We picked three characteristic points in each video. The robot spoke at the first two points and pointed at the last one. Other times, the robot performed viewing action repeatedly.

Experimental Procedure

Our experiment used 12 participants (5 males and 7 women, average age 27.8), and a within-subjects design was used. Figure 2 shows the experiment's flow.

Each participant watched the 12 movies under the three viewing conditions. To suppress order effects, viewing condition was counterbalanced. After watching each movie, participants scored their feelings of pleasance and arousal. This scoring method is the same with previously described. We set the robot to the right front of participants to allow them to simultaneously see both the movie and the robot.

Figure 1: Experimental Environment.

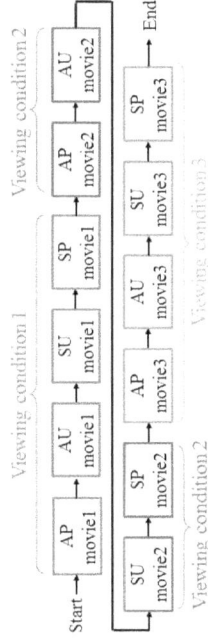

Figure 2: Experiment's Flow.

our proposal with more participants. A more comprehensive analysis based on participant's empathy scale value and video footage is also needed.

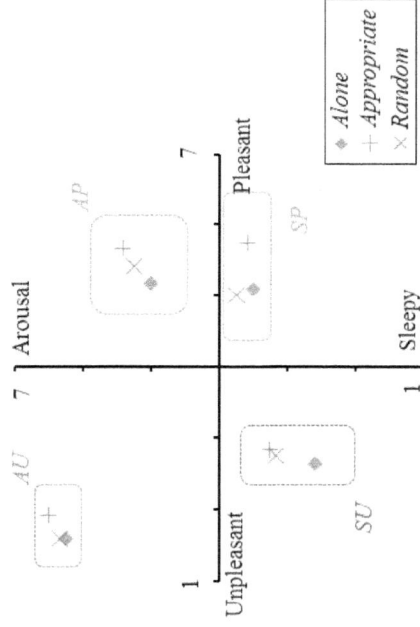

Figure 3: Experiment's Flow.

RESULTS & DISCUSSIONS

Figure 3 plots the average scores of arousal and pleasance for each video emotional condition and each viewing condition. In AP, AU and SU conditions, participants felt more arousal and pleasance when they watch under Appropriate condition than Alone. In SP condition, they feel more pleasance under Appropriate than Alone. It suggests that Appropriate condition make user more excited and relaxed and less depressed and afraid than Alone. Additionally in SP and AU conditions, Random condition has little effect, and in AP conditions, Random has smaller effect than Appropriate. It suggests that appropriate emotional expression enhanced excited and relaxed feeling, but it depressed afraid and depressed feeling.

CONCLUSION & FUTURE WORK

We have proposed that affective agents be used to change the user's emotional experience through emotional contagion. Future work includes confirming

REFERENCES

[1] E.Jakobs, A. S. R. Manstead and A. H. Fischer, Social Motives and Emotional Feelings as Determinants of Facial Displays: The Case of Smiling. Personality and Social Psychology Bulletin (1999), 25, 424-435.

[2] I. R. Murray and J. L. Arnott, Towards the simulation of emotion in synthetic speech: A review of the literature on human vocal emotion. Journal of the acoustic society of America (1992). 93, 1097-1108.

[3] J. Tsai, E. Bowring, S. Marsella, W. Wood and M. Tambe, A Study of Emotional Contagion with Virtual Characters. In Proc. IVA 2012, 81-88.

[4] J. Xu, J. Broekens, K. Hindriks and M. A. Neerincx, Robot mood is contagious: effects of robot body language in the imitation game, In Proc. AAMAS 2014, 973-980.

[5] H. Osawa and M. Imai, Enhancing Empathy toward an Agent by Immersive Learning, In Proc. HAI 2013.

[6] L. Moshkina, S. Trickett and J. G. Trafton, Social Engagement in Public Places: A Tale of One Robot, In Proc HRI 2014, 382-389.

[7] M. Dapretto, M. S. Davies, J. H. Pfeifer, A. A. Scott, M. Sigman, S. Y. Bookheimer and M. Iacoboni, Understanding emotions in others: mirror neuron dysfunction in children with autism spectrum disorders, Nature Neuroscience 2005, 28-30.

[8] M.Masuda, S. Kato and H. Itoh, A Laban-Based Approach to Emotional Motion Rendering for Human-Robot Interaction. In Proc. ICEC 2010, 372-380.

The hybrid Agent MARCO: A Multimodal Autonomous Robotic Chess Opponent

Christian Becker-Asano
Albert-Ludwigs-Universität
Freiburg
Georges-Köhler-Allee 052
79108 Freiburg, Germany
basano@cs.uni-freiburg.de

Eduardo Meneses
National Polytechnic Institute,
CIC Computing Research
Center
Av. Luis Enrique Erro S/N
Mexico City, Mexico
eduarmeneses@hotmail.com

Nicolas Riesterer
Albert-Ludwigs-Universität
Freiburg
Georges-Köhler-Allee 052
79108 Freiburg, Germany
riestern@cs.uni-freiburg.de

Julien Hué
Albert-Ludwigs-Universität
Freiburg
Georges-Köhler-Allee 052
79108 Freiburg, Germany
hue@cs.uni-freiburg.de

Christian Dornhege
Albert-Ludwigs-Universität
Freiburg
Georges-Köhler-Allee 052
79108 Freiburg, Germany
dornhege@cs.uni-freiburg.de

Bernhard Nebel
Albert-Ludwigs-Universität
Freiburg
Georges-Köhler-Allee 052
79108 Freiburg, Germany
nebel@cs.uni-freiburg.de

Abstract

This paper introduces MARCO, a hybrid, chess playing agent equipped with a custom-built robotic arm and an emotionally expressive, virtual face presented on a small, servo-controlled display. MARCO was built to investigate the hypothesis that hybrid systems capable of displaying emotions make playing chess more personal and enjoyable. In addition, it is our aim to realize emotional contagion between man and machine in that the agent has the power to influence the human player on an emotional level and vice versa. The hardware components consist of eight Dynamixel servos, an Arduino-based control board, a 5.6 inch display, and a DGT chessboard. The software components run concurrently as separate processes. The main components are the virtual agent framework MARC, the WASABI Affect Simulation architecture, and the TSCP chess engine.

ACM Classification Keywords

I.2.9 [Computing Methodologies]: Artificial Intelligence— *Robotics*

General Terms

Chess, Robotics, Human-agent interaction, Hybrid agent, Affective Computing

HAI 2014, October 29-31, 2014, Tsukuba, Japan.
ACM 978-1-4503-3035-0/14/10.
http://dx.doi.org/10.1145/2658861.2658915

Introduction & Motivation

With the advent of humanoid agents—both robotic and virtual or even hybrid as presented here—chess offers a good opportunity for system evaluation. Robotics researchers find an interesting challenge for both hardware and software design in grabbing and moving chess pieces. Researchers in the fields of human-computer interaction and affective computing use chess as a situational context, which does not need to be explained to most people letting them instantly dive into the interactive experience. Questions such as how different embodiments might change player satisfaction and how the integration of a virtual agent expressing emotions influences a human's stance towards a computer system have recently been investigated [8].

MARCO features a low-cost robotic arm to autonomously move chess pieces. A custom built, small sized, robotic display presents a highly anthropomorphic virtual agent's head to realize a hybrid embodiment. Its modular software architecture relies on an established emotion simulation architecture as one of its core modules.

We aim to address the following research questions: (1) Is it more enjoyable to play against MARCO (i.e. the robotic arm with the virtual agent) when the agent expresses emotions as compared to when it remains equally active but emotionally neutral? (2) How contagious is the agent on the emotional level and which behavioral factors are best suited to maximize emotional contagion?

Additionally, MARCO allows us to tackle systematically the general question of how and when "mindfulness" is ascribed to machines [9]: (3) Is the most human-like and emotional agent evaluated as more (socially) intelligent than its less complex/human-like versions?

The remainder of the paper is structured as follows. First, we explain how the employed chess engine evaluates board positions. Subsequently, MARCO's hardware components are detailed, before its software components are described. The paper is summarized by presenting our ideas for future research.

Hardware description

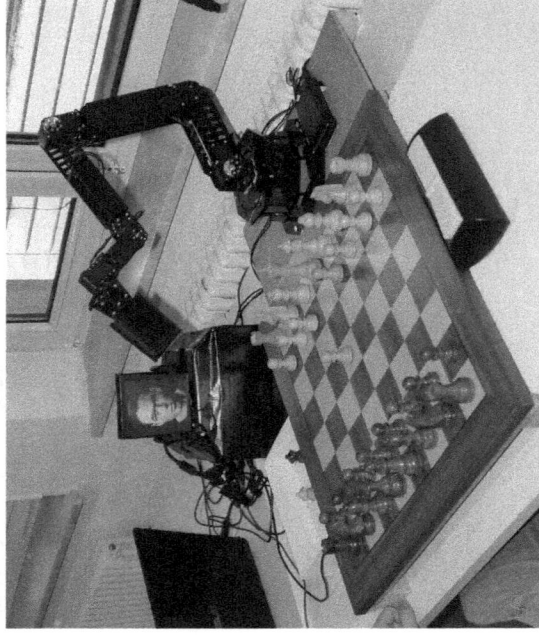

Figure 1: The pan-tilt-roll agent display, the robotic arm, and the digital chess board with the chess clock after MARCO performed its opening move. The laptop in the back is running MARCO's software modules and the small black box next to the robotic arm contains the Arduino components. A Kinect sensor for human player tracking is mounted on a tripod behind the robotic arm (not visible in this picture).

The complete setup is presented in Figure 1. It comprises a pan-tilt-roll display with the virtual agent's face, a robotic arm, and a digital chess board with a chess clock.

The design of the robot's arm is based on the "WidowX Robotic Arm Kit Mark II" [1] available from Trossen Robotics. The rotational base remained unchanged, but the arm itself needed to be extended and the gripper modified. The custom extensions for the arm were printed with a 3D printer. Five Dynamixel servos of four different families move the robot's arm. For the base and wrist two MX-28 servos are used. An MX-64 servo moves the robot's elbow and an MX-106 servo its shoulder. The gripper is opened and closed by an AX-12A servo. With a maximum reach of $550mm$ the robotic arm can reach all 64 squares of the $480mm \times 480mm$ DGT tournament chess board.

The pan-tilt-roll display component features a 5.6 inch upright TFT LCD display with a physical resolution of 640×480 pixels at 16bit color depth. It is positioned to the left of the robotic arm to give the impression that these two components belong together and it is mounted high enough that the virtual agent could potentially overlook the complete chess board. Three Dynamixel AX-12A servos are connected to the same Arduino-based control board as the robotic arm to change the display orientation during the game along all three axes.

The DGT chess board is a wooden board with standard Staunton pieces and $55mm \times 55mm$ squares. Each piece is equipped with a unique RFID chip that makes it recognizable. The board is connected to the computer with a USB cable, and it transmits the position in FEN format to the engine every time a change is performed.

Software description

Except for the external MARC framework, the complete system is implemented in C++ using the Qt SDK [2] to enable cross-platform functionality. Communication with

the hardware parts (i.e. the DGT chess board and the Arduino board) is realized by relaying their output to the Qt-specific event loop.

Figure 2: The virtual agent expressing *anger*, *neutral*, and *joy* (left to right)

The system consists of five main components which are linked together by the main module to form the chess playing agent: (1) the DGT board controller, (2) the TSCP chess engine, (3) the WASABI emotion simulation, (4) the robot arm controller, and (5) the MARC animation framework. The NovA toolkit for tracking the human player runs on a separate computer, because of its high demand of processing power.

The general design follows the one described in [4]. The main information flow originates, on the one hand, from the DGT chess board, which detects when pieces are lifted or put down. On the other hand, the chess engine reacts to a human player's moves by calculating MARCO's move in response. This is sent as movement commands to the robotic arm and, at the same time, the virtual agent receives a behavior description in the behavior markup language (BML) to respond non-verbally with eye-gaze and head movements. The latter are realized by physical movement of the display (instead of rotating the virtual representation alone).

The TSCP chess engine [7] evaluates the position using an alpha-beta algorithm based on a number of criteria like: pieces left on the board, activity of these pieces, security of the king, etc. The greater the depth the more precise is the evaluation. Apart from determining MARCO's next move, the changes in chess board evaluations over time are used to derive emotional impulses that drive MARCO's emotion dynamics inside the WASABI emotion module [5].

The virtual agent is animated by the MARC framework [6] and displayed on the 5.6 inch pan-tilt-roll display next to the robotic arm. Emotional facial expressions (see Fig. 2 for examples) are triggered by WASABI and are combined with text-to-speech synthesis provided by OpenMARY inside the MARC framework to create lip-sync animations of emotional verbal utterances.

For tracking and analysis of the human players' nonverbal behaviors during gameplay the "NovA - Nonverbal Behavior Analyzer" is integrated into our setup [3]. In combination with the Microsoft Kinect sensor this framework allows for the automatic detection, recording, and offline analysis of head orientation and body posture.

Summary

This paper introduced MARCO, a chess playing hybrid agent equipped with a robotic arm and a screen displaying a virtual agent capable of emotional facial expressions. The system can play chess autonomously against a human player, whose non-verbal behavior is recorded for later analysis.

This combination of hard- and software components allows us to empirically investigate next, which factors support emotional contagion between artificial agents and humans. We speculate that a human player's enjoyment will increase together with higher levels of emotional contagion.

References

[1] http://www.trossenrobotics.com/widowxrobotarm.

[2] Qt: Cross-platform application and UI framework. http://qt-project.org/, 2014.

[3] Baur, T., Damian, I., Lingenfelser, F., Wagner, J., and André, E. Nova: Automated analysis of nonverbal signals in social interactions. In *Human Behavior Understanding*, vol. 8212 of *LNCS* (2013), 160–171.

[4] Becker-Asano, C., Stahl, P., Ragni, M., Martin, J.-C., Courgeon, M., and Nebel, B. An affective virtual agent providing embodied feedback in the paired associate task: system design and evaluation. In *Intelligent Virtual Agents (IVA 2013)* (2013), 406–415.

[5] Becker-Asano, C., and Wachsmuth, I. Affective computing with primary and secondary emotions in a virtual human. *Autonomous Agents and Multi-Agent Systems 20*, 1 (2010), 32–49.

[6] Courgeon, M., Martin, J.-C., and Jacquemin, C. MARC: a Multimodal Affective and Reactive Character. In *Proc. 1st Workshop on AFFective Interaction in Natural Environments* (2008).

[7] Kerrigan, T. Tom kerrigan's simple chess program. http://www.tckerrigan.com/Chess/TSCP.

[8] Leite, I., Martinho, C., Pereira, A., and Paiva, A. icat: an affective game buddy based on anticipatory mechanisms. In *Autonomous agents and multiagent systems*, AAMAS '08 (2008), 1229–1232.

[9] Nass, C., and Moon, Y. Machines and mindlessness: Social responses to computers. *Journal of Social Issues 56*, 1 (2000), 81–103.

Artificial Endocrine System for Language Translation Robot

Wu Jhong Ren
National Taipei University
wujhongren@gmail.com

Hooman Samani
National Taipei University
hooman@mail.ntpu.edu.tw

HAI '14 , Oct 29-31 2014, Tsukuba, Japan
ACM 978-1-4503-3035-0/14/10.
http://dx.doi.org/10.1145/2658861.2658916

Abstract

A novel robot with the purpose of translation is presented in this paper. The proposed system consists of a mobile robot which carries a smart phone that language translation APP, including audio, text and audio, is running on it. It also equipped with extra touch and voice sensors for input, micro controller for process and speaker and wheels for output. The proposed system is equipped with state flow mechanism, which is managed by an artificial endocrine system that employs the PID controller in order to navigate between interacting people. This robot provides an embodied system which could function as a robotic translator that navigates between interacting people and facilitates the communication.

Author Keywords

Translator robot; Human – Agent Interaction; Translation; Smart System

Introduction

In the age of digital technology, smart phones became an essential tool for everyone. Moreover, several software and APPs have been developed for the purpose of language translation. The state of the art in using APPs for translation enables us to benefit from basic translation between languages. Even though the accuracy is not perfect yet, but the current technology can help us to understand the basic meaning of statements in a different language. Our motivation in this research was to equip the available APPs on smart phones with embodiment and navigation facility in order to develop a mobile translator robot. Despite various APPs, translation application has been very limited in robotic systems. The wearable translation robot is basically intelligent glasses, which can automatically translate multiple languages in real-time [1]. Such kind of technology could be promoted with applications such as Google's glass. Our aim was to change the wearable nature to a robot shape. Various humanoid robots are equipped with certain translation capabilities. However, that is still limited to expensive robots, which are currently in the research phase. Our goal was to make the robotic system low cost, functional and available for public use. Considering the limited functionality of available translation software, we tried to keep our design simple and believable where the user does not expect perfect translation but enjoys the help of the robot of conveying the message in different language. We hope with further improvement in language translation systems our robot could be also improved in functionality. We have considered various modes for the functionality of the translation robot. The main function is to have voice as the medium of communication. Furthermore, users can use text for data entry. Additionally, the robot can use the camera of the smart phone in order to scan, identify and translate any written text in the environment which is shown to the robot. In order to give an appropriate command, we have employed extra sensors such as touch sensor to incorporate with the translation APP. Such interaction is not limited to direct commands. We have developed Artificial Intelligent (AI) systems, which can process the user input for smooth

and correct functionality of the robot. Our ultimate goal is that the translation robot can function fully autonomous, and that is why AI modules such as artificial endocrine system and state flow are employed in our system.

SYSTEM ARCHITECTURE

Data from touch and sound sensors are transmitted to the processor unit which includes three modules. The State Flow module handles state transitions of the robot. Artificial Endocrine System (AES) is highest level of AI for smooth behavior generation . Finally, the Control unit includes a PID controller for navigation of two motors, which are connected to wheel.

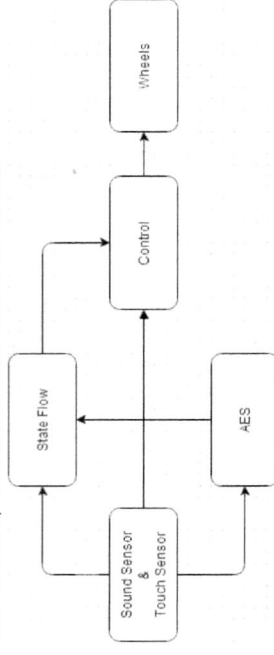

Figure 1. Overall structure of the software architecture

Artificial Intelligence

We have employed Artificial Endocrine System (AES) on top layer of our robot navigation system. Artificial endocrine system concept is inspired from the biological system which empowers the robot to behave smoothly like the way hormones help biological system to behave smoothly with collaboration with the emotional system.

AES is the calculation of the biological role of the endocrine system containing the basic model and the endocrine system by biological principles, models inspired by the wisdom of generic methods [2]. With such system, we will be able to make a response to external stimuli, and has control of the system using artificial hormones.

AES system has been used in various robotics applications such as Lovotics [3]. Physiological unit of the Lovotics artificial intelligence employs artificial endocrine system consisting of artificial emotional and biological hormones. Artificial emotional hormones include Dopamine, Serotonin, Endorphin, and Oxytocin. For biological hormones Melatonin, Norepinephrine, Epinephrine, Orexin, Ghrelin, and Leptin hormones are employed which modulate biological parameters such as blood glucose, body temperature and appetite [4].

By using the artificial endocrine system in the robot AI, the robot can operate smoothly in an unstable environment. Another advantage of AES system is to make it possible to express "slow" relation between causes and effects as it takes time for an artificial hormone to be effective. Such property generates smooth and realistic behaviors by the robot. One unit of our developed AES is presented in Figure 3.

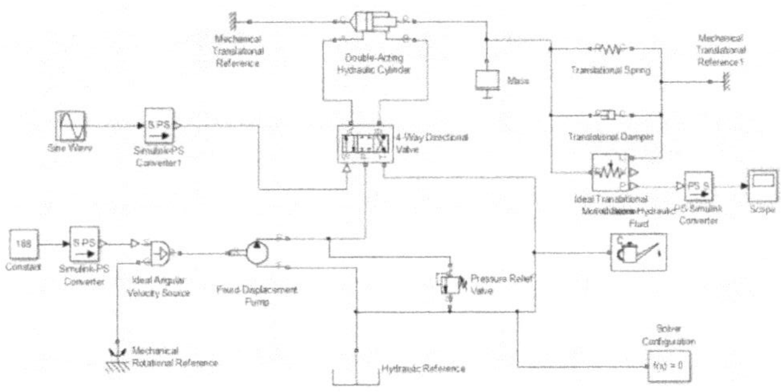

Figure 1. The structure of the one unit of AES system

When the system receives external signal information, which in our translator robot is touch and sound, the system behaves naturally to use that cause to define two artificial hormones. One relates to sound and one to touch. For example, if the input sound signal is active for long duration, it increases the level of artificial sound hormone which leads that robot navigates slower to hear all the conversation. We defined various commands for the touch sensors for changing mode. For example if touch sensor is activated multiple times, the level of relevant hormone increases, which makes the robot to change between modes frequently.

An example of changes in these two hormones is illustrated in Figure 4 when we tested it for sinusoid input signals.

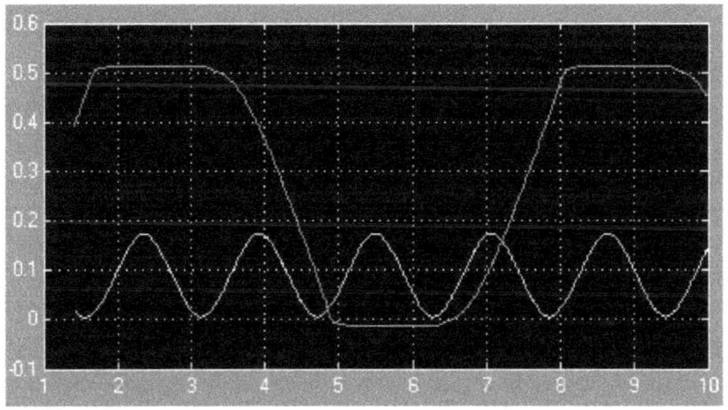

Figure 2. AES Hydraulic translate simulation with touch sensor and sound sensor

The output of AES is related to the State Flow module where several states are defined and managed in the robot. The detail of state flow is illustrated in Figure 5.

In the state flow module, we let the robot translate back and forth between two people. Based on our experiments, we adjusted the timing. The default value for changes of navigation between two people is 5 seconds. Users can commend the robot via voice or more directly via touch sensor. We explain the way of handling the robot for the user before experiment. In many cases, users also like to use the smartphone interface which can simply interrupt the robot movement using the touch sensor.

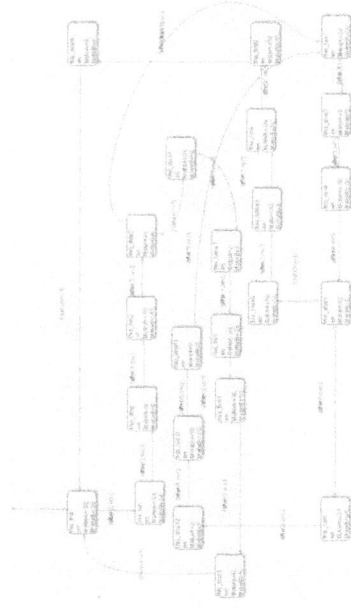

Figure 3. Translate Robot State Flow

Conclusion

In this paper, we have presented a robotic system which is used for the purpose of translation between different humans using various modes of interaction such as audio and text. The proposed system empowers available APPs with embodiment which enables the translation system to navigate in the environment and facilitate multilingual communication between users. We have tested this system in the country were English is not the main language and communication between foreigners is often troublesome because of the language barriers. Our robotic design also triggers positive interaction between users due to curiosity about the developed robot. This system can be used in various applications such as meetings, ordering foods in restaurants, shops, museums and tourist attractions. In future, we aim to further develop this robot with more extra performance and behavior such as adaptive movements. We also plan to perform formal user studies to improve the design and behavior of the robot.

Acknowledgements

Authors would like to thank the funding resource for this project and various people who participated in our user tests and experiments.

References

[1] Xi Shi, Yangsheng Xu, A Wearable Translation Robot,

[2] Scaramuzza. Introduction to autonomous mobile robots. .Neal, M., Timmis, Z. Timidity: A Useful Emotional Mechanism for Robot Control, Informatica, vol. 27(2), pp 197-204, 2003.

[3] H. Samani, A. D. Cheok. Probability of love between robots and humans. In Intelligent Robots and Systems (IROS), 2010 IEEE/RSJ International Conference on (pp. 5288-5293). IEEE. 2010.

[4] H. Samani. Lovotics. Loving Robots. Book. LAP LAMBERT Academic Publishing, ISBN: 3659155411, 2012.

Pointing Gesture Prediction using Minimum-jerk Model in Human-Robot Interaction

Ren Ohmura
Toyohashi University of
Technology
Aichi, Japan
ren@tut.jp

Yuki Kusano
ShinMaywa Soft Technologies,
Ltd.
Hyogo, Japan
kusano.y@shinmaywa.co.jp

Yuta Suzuki
Tokai Rika Co., Ltd.
Aichi, Japan
yuta@usl.cs.tut.ac.jp

HAI '14 , Oct 29-31 2014, Tsukuba, Japan
ACM 978-1-4503-3035-0/14/10.
http://dx.doi.org/10.1145/2658861.2658917

Abstract

A pointing gesture has an important role in human-human
interaction. From our observation, we predict a pointing
target before finishing the gesture in human-human
communication. This paper, thus, proposes a method for
a robot to predict human pointing gesture using the
minimum-jerk model. Analytically, the final position of a
wrist can be obtained by detecting the first acceleration
peak, which corresponds to first 21% of the entire gesture.
We implemented and evaluated the method with a
desktop size robot named Robovie-W. The result showed
that our method improves naturalness and smoothness.

Author Keywords

Human-robot Interaction; Gesture Prediction; Pointing
Gesture; The minimum-Jerk Model; Impression Evaluation

ACM Classification Keywords

H.5.2. [Information Interfaces and Presentation (e.g.
HCI)]: User Interfaces

Introduction

In human-agent interaction, a pointing gesture is
frequently used and an important method for joint
attention. Since we can observe that we turn his/her face
to the pointing object before finishing the gesture in

horizontal plane, as the following C_J get minim value.

$$C_J = \frac{1}{2}\int_0^{t_f}\left(\frac{d^3\boldsymbol{x}}{dt}^2\right) \qquad (1)$$

While the original model is defined in two dimensional space, we extend it into three dimensions.

Under the constraint of zero velocity and acceleration at the start and end, Equation 1 obtains a trajectory of

$$\boldsymbol{x}_\tau = \boldsymbol{x}_0 + (\boldsymbol{x}_f - \boldsymbol{x}_0)(6\tau^5 - 15\tau^4 + 10\tau^3) \qquad (2)$$

where $\tau = t/t_f$, $\boldsymbol{x}_0$ is the initial position of the hand, and $\boldsymbol{x}_f$ is the final position.

By setting the third derivative of Equation 2 to zero, we can get maximum acceleration. The first maximum value is when

$$\tau_1 = \frac{3-\sqrt{3}}{6} \approx 0.21 \qquad (3)$$

and the final position is estimated as follows.

$$\boldsymbol{x}_f = \frac{4\boldsymbol{x}_{\tau_1} - (2+\sqrt{3})\boldsymbol{x}_0}{2-\sqrt{3}} \qquad (4)$$

Thus, the first acceleration peak is at 21% of the entire motion, and the final hand position can be calculated. The algorithm is shown in Figure 2.

In the algorithm, the threshold to detect the start of a pointing gesture is decided by discriminant analysis and currently set $200mm/sec$. The first peak, τ_1, is detected as the time $t-1$ that gives first $a_t \leq a_{t-1}$ in current implementation.

---

human-human interaction, predicting the pointing gesture is expected to improve the human-agent interaction.

Importance of pointing gesture has been realised in several studies of mediated human-human and human-agent interaction[1, 3, 4]. Most of them, however, focused on how to recognise the pointing target, but not on when the target is recognised. As one of exceptions, Sugiyama et. al[5] focused on predicting a pointing gesture of a communication partner and showed its prediction improved a feeling of naturalness in communication. The method just follows the estimated finger position after 0.3 seconds, but we observe that we usually predict the target by the partner's initial motion as mentioned above.

Thus, we propose a method to predict the final hand's position of a human pointing gesture only with its initial motion. The method uses the minimum-jerk model[2], which is one of the mathematical models of a human hand motion. We implemented the method on a desktop size humanoid robot, named "Robovie-W"(Figure 1), and evaluated it comparing with a method used in Sugiyama et al[5] and no prediction.

Basics of Proposed Method

There are some other mathematical models for human hand motion, such as a minimum-torque change model[6]. However, the minimum-jerk model is simple and can be analytically solved under certain conditions with output of a unique trajectory. Moreover, the minimum-jerk model gives basic characteristics, bell-shape velocity, considered in most of other models. Thus, we use the minimum-jerk model to predict the human pointing gesture.

The minimum-jerk model is contrived for representing a trajectory of human hand motion between two points on a

---

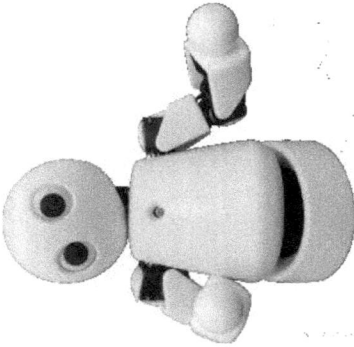

Figure 1: Robovie-W

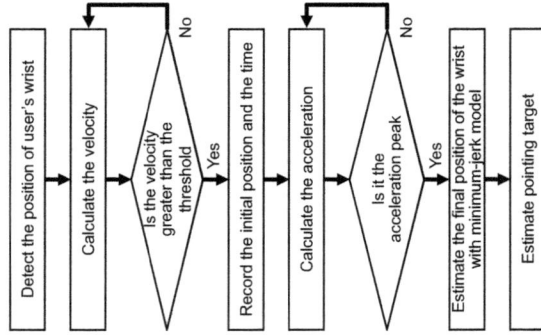

Figure 2: The flowchart of proposed method

Detect the position of user's wrist

Calculate the velocity

Is the velocity greater than the threshold — No / Yes

Record the initial position and the time

Calculate the acceleration

Is it the acceleration peak — No / Yes

Estimate the final position of the wrist with minimum-jerk model

Estimate pointing target

Evaluation

Experiment Environment

We implemented our method on a desktop size (30cm height) robot named "Robovie-W". For detecting hand motion, Microsoft Kinect placed at the side of the robot and OpenNI were used.

Figure 3 shows the experiment environment. A subject and the Robovie-W were positioned $3m$ in face-to-face condition. Three objects, whose size were $10cm(W) \times 10cm(D) \times 60cm(H)$, were placed on the line at the middle between a subject and the Robovie-W. Distances between objects were $40cm$ each.

The Robovie-W performed following three control method.

NoPre The Robovie-W just gazes and points the current position of the subject wrist. (No prediction)

PA0.3sec The system predicts the wrist position after 0.3 seconds by linearly extending current direction of hand velocity. The Robovie-W gazes and points to the predicted position. (A method used in [5])

PMJ The system predicts the final position using the minimum-jerk model. The Robovie-W immediately gazes and points the predicted position. (Proposed method)

Sixteen subjects were involved. Each subject randomly pointed to three objects several times, and this trial is repeated three times. Before the experiment, they were told that the robot would show different responses in each trial but not told detailed difference. Order of control methods was random for each subject. After each trial, the subject answered inquiries of a semantic differential (SD) method.

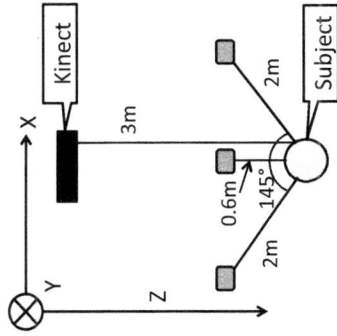

Figure 3: Experiment Environment for Impression Evaluation

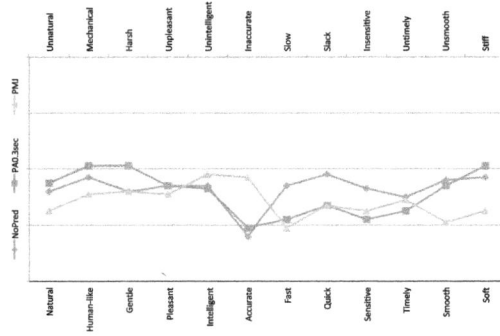

Figure 4: Result of inquiry of SD method

Results

In the questionnaire, the scale between an adjective pair was divided into five levels. Figure 4 shows the mean score, and Table 1 shows result of t-test in each adjective pair between two of three methods ("*" is $p < 0.10$ and "**" is $p < 0.05$). The order of these adjective pairs is changed from the sheet a subject marked. It was random to prevent the subject from being impressed with similar adjectives.

Adjective pair	NoPred vs PMJ	PA0.3sec vs PMJ	NoPred vs PA0.3sec
Natural vs Unnatural	**	**	−
Human-like vs Mechanical	−	**	−
Gentle vs Harsh	−	**	**
Pleasant vs Unpleasant	−	−	−
Intelligent vs Unintelligent	−	*	−
Accurate vs Inaccurate	**	**	−
Fast vs Slow	**	−	**
Quick vs Slack	**	−	**
Sensitive vs Insensitive	*	−	**
Timely vs Untimely	−	*	−
Smooth vs Unsmooth	**	**	−
Soft vs Stiff	**	**	−

Table 1: Result of inquiry of SD method ("**" represents $p < 0.05$, and "*" represents $p < 0.10$)

In "Natural", "Human-like", and "Gentle", PMJ marks best result, and PA0.3sec marks worst. This implies that although both are predicting human motion, PMJ gives natural impressions for a robot motion, and PA0.3sec conversely gives more unnatural and harsher impressions.

In "Pleasant", there are no significant difference between three.

In "Intelligent", NoPred and PA0.3 are almost same, and PMJ is lower with marginal significance. In "Accurate",

NoPred and PMJ are also same, but PMJ is lower with significant difference. These are because sometimes PMJ gives a wrong prediction, which never happens on PA0.3sec and NoPred.

In "Fast", "Quick", and "Sensitive", both predicting method, PMJ and PA0.3sec, are almost the same and mark higher than NoPred. These seem to be the main effects of prediction of human motion.

In "Timely", PA0.3sec is slightly higher than PMJ and NoPred. The reason may be that the response of PA0.3sec is quicker and clearer than others, because PMJ waits 21% of a pointing gesture for the start and NoPred points to the current position of human wrist.

In "Smooth" and "Soft", PMJ marks higher than PA0.3sec and NoPred with significant difference. These results are as same as the results of "Natural", "Human-like" and "Gentle".

Thus, result shows that both predicting methods improve the impression related to speed. Moreover, PMJ improves naturalness and smoothness of a robot motion instead of decreasing prediction accuracy. PA3.0sec doesn't decrease prediction accuracy, but it gives unnatural and harsh impressions.

An interesting thing here is that naturalness (and human-likeness) is increased in spite of lower accuracy. More detailed experiment is required, but it implies that a temporal factor is more important for giving natural or human-like impression in a robot motion.

Conclusion

For improving human-robot interaction, this paper proposed a method to predict the final wrist position of human pointing gesture with initial 21% motion using the minimum-jerk model. Evaluation with a desktop size robot shows that our method improves naturalness and smoothness despite decreasing prediction accuracy.

References

[1] Brooks, A. G., and Breazeal, C. Working with robots and objects: Revisiting deictic reference for achieving spatial common ground. In *Proceedings of the 1st ACM SIGCHI/SIGART Conference on Human-robot Interaction (HRI2006)* (2006), 297–304.

[2] Flash, T., and Hogans, N. The coordination of arm movements: An experimentally confirmed mathematical model. *Journal of Neuroscience 5* (1985), 1688–1703.

[3] Kuzuoka, H., Oyama, S., and Suzuki, K. Gestureman: A mobile robot that embodies a remote instructor's actions. In *Proceedings of the ACM 2000 Conference on Computer-supported cooperative work 2000 (CSCW2000)* (2000), 155–162.

[4] Nagai, Y. Learning to comprehend deictic gestures in robots and human infants. In *Proc. of the IEEE International Workshop on Robot and Human Interactive Communication 2005. (ROMAN 2005)* (2005), 217–222.

[5] Sugiyama, O., Kanda, T., Imai, M., Ishiguro, H., and Hagita, N. Natural deictic communication with humanoid robots. In *Proceedings of the 2007 IEEE/RSJ Internation Conference on Intelligent Robots and Systems (IROS2007)* (2007), 1441–1448.

[6] Uno, Y., Kawato, M., and Suzuki, R. Formation and control of optimal trajectory in human multijoint arm movement. *Biological Cybernetics 61*, 2 (1989), 89–101.

Digital Play Therapy for Children with Learning Disabilities

Yukako Watanabe
Shibaura Institute of
Technology.Toyosu 3-7-1.
al11126@shibaura-it.ac.jp

Yoshiko Okada
Shibaura Institute of
Technology.Fukasaku Miuma-ku
Sautama,337-8570
y-okada@shibaura-it.ac.jp

Hirotaka Osawa
University of Tsukuba
Tenno-dai 1-1-1, Tsukuba, Ibaraki,
Japan
osawa@iit.tsukuba.ac.jp

Midori Sugaya
Shibaura Institute of
Technology.Toyosu 3-7-1.
doly@shibaura-it.ac.jp

HAI '14 , Oct 29-31 2014, Tsukuba, Japan
ACM 978-1-4503-3035-0/14/10.
http://dx.doi.org/10.1145/2658861.2658918

Abstract

Children who are suffering on learning and
developmental disabilities require daily trainings for
social skills. However, such daily training is not
provided occasionally because it requires interactive
helps from therapists. In this paper, we propose a
digital dollhouse that enhanced traditional psychological
play therapy with digital sensors and computer graphics.
The digital dollhouse provides immersive space to
children which grows children's communication skill
through their imaging play. This device allows non-
professional like parents to make play therapy. In this
paper, we show details about prototype of digital
dollhouse. We also categorize requirements for digital
play therapy that are given by psychological viewpoints
based on the prototype. Interdisciplinary design
process collaborating with engineers and psychologists
shows the possibility that digital dollhouse is enough to
enhance empathy of children and such empathy will be
enhanced by creating immersive characters.

Author Keywords

Digital Therapy; Learning Disabilities; System Design;
Human Computer Interaction; Orange Roof House.

ACM Classification Keywords

Human Factors; Miscellaneous.

Introduction

Learning and developmental disabilities are intrinsic to the individual, presumed to be due to central nervous system dysfunction, and may occur across the life span [1]. These brain's disabilities will cause not only the learning difficulties, but also communication, and physical difficulties in various situations. To moderate the difficulties, it requires daily trainings of social skills that have interaction and communication with others.

To grow up the social skills, play therapy has been acknowledged as a major method by which to help children communicate and express their emotin with counseling [2]. Play therapy is a "here are now" approach to play therapy that is considered similar to a behavioral approach in which children practice new behaviors to prepare for real-life settings[3]. However, there are problems that these settings requires expensive, and need the trained therapiest for supporting their enrolling and immersing the settings interactively. Sometimes, it requires come to a special care-center, therefore it is difficult to train their skills with using this method with settings in daily-life. In the therapy method that could grow up the social skill, it is important to hear of others, and express their emotion about their imminent environment with their language. Since daily training is required, the device should not be large and hopefully not installed any specific place, and it is desirable to have a theme children want to get involved spontaneously. Based on above requirements, we present a digital dollhouse that enhanced traditional psychological play therapy with digital sensors and computer graphics. For the children, it is familiar with the house environment like their home, it is possible to immerse themselves into doll play space in their pretended roll play as a family member. We consider this environment is suitable to train the children to

grow up the required social skills. To accelerate the basic effect of the dollhouse and compensate to meet the requirements, various sensors are installed to sense their physical world, the result would be visualized in the screen of the computer to share the information more easily. We discussed with the psychologist who uses play method for learning disabilities' children that there are important social skills, which should be trained. As the first stage of the discussion, we discuss the idea with an expert, who has experience of the method of play therapy, and organize the requirements for the device, and have developed a prototype. In this paper, we describe the design and prototype implementation, and describe how to apply in the discussion, about the challenges of the future.

Digital Play Therapy: Design and Implementation of Prototype
1. Proposal

We propose a digital dollhouse that enhanced traditional psychological play therapy with digital sensors and computer graphics. The digital dollhouse provides immersive space to children to train their social skill. For the chi   ldren, it is familiar with the house environment; it is possible to immerse themselves in doll play space in their pretended rolls. We consider this environment is suitable to train the children to grow up the required social skills that we discussed in the previous section. We prepare a dollhouse device that is possible to treat in small space and their roof will be opened with their small hand, since it is important for these children, who are in the stage of pre-operational age, tends to think intuitively through the concreate device and to have a interest for the "touch" itself. Based on the idea, we installed the following futures of the device that have pupose to grow up the three social skills.

(1)Training for hearing and speaking: in the dollhouse, we installed temperature sensor, and a light sensor (photo detector), and this sense the changing of physical situation reflects to the virtual room is illustrated in the screen. The roof can be opened easily, and if it opened, the rooms in the virtual space also light up reflecting to the physical world change. Children can play with the roof open/close and see the rooms right up and darken by their play. Computer graphics (CG) interface can express the physical world change such as bright and dark, and warm and cool with sensors, and illustrate it with more easily understand pictures. We assume that children easily understand the changing of the environment with these pictures and express the situation with their word. This device will facilitate to choose an appropriate word for express their feeling with the objective viewpoint.

(2)Training for choosing appropriate word for explaining the changing situation: we installed the switch that could change the situation of the room. Since a change supposed to the result the operation that the children pushed the button. We assume that the reactive system could help children to express the changing situation by their operation.

(3) Training for choosing appropriate word for expressing feeling and empathy to share the situation with others. In the room that is illustrated in computer graphic, we prepare a window that shows the changing of seasonal views. We assume that hat encourage training into words subtle changes in season. Through the share the sense of the physical world in the dollhouse and the augmented reality in the computer with visual appeal, we assumed that children easily immerse the play and express their word by sharing the situations in visually and sensuously with the trainee.

2. System Design

In the Figure 1, we illustrate the abstract image of training in the therapy.

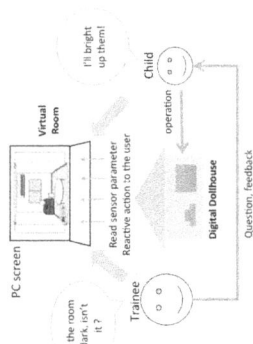

Figure 1. Sharing the visual and tactile through the screen of personal computer

Figure 2. Dollhose (Left: Front, Right: Back)

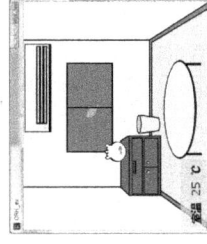

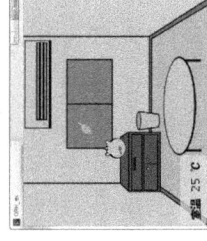

Figure 3. Inside the room on the screen, Right: Without Light/Roof, Left: Natural Light

Our prototype is controlled with the Arduino[4] that is a open-source electronics prototyping platform. On the board, we installed a temperature sensor, light sensor, and switches.

Discussion

We developed a prototype of our proposed system, and demonstrate it in front of the experienced expert. We discuss about the issues and detect the problems with digital play therapy that are given by psychological viewpoints. We categorize the four issues about the device as follows.

1. Using the method of play therapy
2. Providing functions to the development of skills
3. CG supports the immersive augmented reality
4. Augmented Reality and development empathy with an agent

The contribution of our work is to show why digital technology support children abilities in psychological viewpoint. We conducted interdisciplinary discussion between engineer and psychologist. The result of discussion shows with real prototype reveals that digital dollhouse will support children's abilities to shift viewpoint. It also suggests that our approach is also improved by applying human-agent interaction technologies. Our interdisciplinary works are just a start point. Further researches will be required to verify our hypothesis.

Conclusion

In this paper, we propose a digital dollhouse for the children who are suffering on learning and developmental disabilities who require daily trainings for social skills. It can enhanced traditional psychological play therapy with digital sensors and computer graphics. It provides immersive space to children which grows children's abilities to hearing and speaking through their imaging paly, and allows non-professional like parents to make Play therapy. In the discussion, we categorize the requirements, and get aware of a new requirement character that would promote the training effectively. In the future, we try to improve this house based on the discussion, and discuss about the evaluation method for the device.

REFERENCES

[1] National Joint Committee on Learning Disabilities: Learning disabilities: Issues on definition. Asha, 33,(Suppl. 5),1991,pp.18-20.

[2] Dale, M.A., & Lyddon, W. J. Sandplay: An investigation into a child's meaning system via the self-confrontation method for children. Journal of Constructivist Psychology, 16, pp. 17-36.

[3] Mary Frances Russo, Jody Vernam, Amanda Wolbert, Sandplay and storytelling: Social constructivism and cognitive development in child counseling. The Arts in Psychotherapy, 33, 2006, pp. 229-237.

[4] Arduino : http://www.arduino.cc/

Amae and Agency Appraisal as Japanese Emotional Behavior: Influences on Agent's Believability

Koushi Mitarai
Tokyo Institute of Technology
2-12-1-W9-67 O-okayama
Meguro-ku, Tokyo 152-8552
Japan
mitarai.k.aa@m.titech.ac.jp

Hiroyuki Umemuro
Tokyo Institute of Technology
2-12-1-W9-67 O-okayama
Meguro-ku, Tokyo 152-8552
Japan
umemuro.h.aa@m.titech.ac.jp

Abstract

Recently, autonomous agents with emotional behavior are developed to improve the human-agent interaction. Users' perceived "believability" of autonomous agents is considered to affect interactions with agents. While human-like emotional behavior is considered to increase believability, actual emotional behaviors differ across cultures. Therefore culture-specific emotional behaviors of agent might increase believability. In this paper, two kinds of emotional behaviors specific in Japanese culture, namely *amae* and Japanese way of agency appraisal, were implemented in agents. Influences of these behaviors on believability were investigated experimentally. Results showed that both Japanese behaviors increased believability. Especially *amae* increased personality factor, which is one of the factors of believability.

Author Keywords

Autonomous agent; believability; emotional behavior; Japan; *amae*; agency appraisal; MikuMikuDanceAgent

ACM Classification Keywords

I.2.11 [Artificial Intelligence]: Distributed Artificial Intelligence—Intelligent agents.; H.1.2 [Models and Principles]: User/Machine Systems—Software psychology

Permission to make digital or hard copies of part or all of this work for personal or classroom use is granted without fee provided that copies are not made or distributed for profit or commercial advantage and that copies bear this notice and the full citation on the first page. Copyrights for third-party components of this work must be honored. For all other uses, contact the Owner/Author. Copyright is held by the owner/author(s).
HAI 2014, Oct 29-31 2014, Tsukuba, Japan
ACM 978-1-4503-3035-0/14/10.
http://dx.doi.org/10.1145/2658861.2658919

Introduction

Believability of Autonomous Agent

In order for autonomous agents to spread more, higher believability is considered as an essential factor[5] . If the believability is perceived as low or not sufficient, users feel disbelief, anoetic or odd with the agent. While physical features of agent have already matured well, these days, emotional behaviors of agent are studied as increasing factor of believability[2] . As emotional behavior might contribute for agents to be perceived as more like human, people are likely to communicate more with agents with emotional behavior[1]. Therefore, implementation of realistic emotional behavior with agent is essential to promote interactions with autonomous agents.

Emotional Behavior and Culture for Autonomous Agent

Some studies have implemented culture-specific behaviors into agents to increase realism or preference[4] . They showed that participants prefer the agents when the agents act partcipants' cultural behavior. However, previous studies have not focused on emotional behavior of agent in the context of culture. As emotional behavior may vary across cultures, agent's emotional behaviors specific in cultures should increase believability.

Purpose of This Study

The purpose of this study is to investigate how emotional behaviors specific in a culture might influence on believability of agents. This study focused on Japanese culture for the feasibility of research. Firstly, two emotional behaviors specific in Japanese culture, namely *amae*, or indulgent dependency[9], and Japanese way of agency appraisal[6], are discussed. Then these behaviors were implemented with software agents. Finally, influences of these behaviors on believability were investigated through experiments using the agent.

Japanese Emotional Behaviors

Amae

Doi[3] defined *amae* as "to behave depending someone's generosity," and mentioned that *amae* is the key concept to understand Japanese specific interpersonal emotion. *Amae* always exists and remains through whole life of people in Japanese society[3].

Among various kinds of *amae* actions mentioned in previous researches, this study focused on the *amae* of wanting substitution that Kobayashi and Katou[8] suggested, because it is natural for agents to behave this kind of action, while other actions are not visible or not natural.

In implementation with the agents, *amae* action was expressed in situations where the agent had troubles in her task. They wanted the user to substitute her task. For example, when the agent was searching for some information and the browser did not work smoothly, the agent would say "It doesn't work. Please do this instead of me."

Japanese Agency Appraisal

Agency is attributions for success or failure, and appraisal is to interpret to what extent individuals contributed or are responsible for the situation. Imada and Ellsworth[6]showed that in a successful situation, Americans reported stronger self-agency emotions than did Japanese, whereas Japanese reported a stronger situation-agency emotion, and vice versa (Table 1).

Situation	Japanese	Americans
Success	Situation-agency	Self-agency
Failure	Self-agency	Situation-agency

Table 1: Japanese and American agency appraisal[6]

In implementation, agency appraisal was expressed in situations where the agent succeeded or failed in doing her task. The agent attributes her success or failure in the ways shown in Table 1. For example, if the agent with Japanese agency appraisal fails in doing her task, the agent blames herself and attributed failure to her own.

Implementation

Then both Japanese behaviors were implemented in agents with a computer software, MMDAgent[10]. It is a toolkit for building voice interaction systems.

Five tasks were prepared as scenarios in which users ask the agent to work. One is the example task. Others tasks are to ask the agent to help searching where to go out, to book a very popular concert ticket, and so on. Each task had variations in emotional behaviors, whether agency appraisal is Japanese or not, and whether do *amae* or not.

Experiment

Experiment Design and Participants

A 2 (do *amae* action or not) × 2 (Japanese agency appraisal or not) factorial design was employed for this study. Thirty-two Japanese university students (20 males and 12 females), aged between 18 and 23 years old ($M = 21.0$, $SD = 1.36$) participated in the experiment. Eight participants were randomly assigned to each of four between-participants conditions.

Procedure

The experimenter showed the first task as a demonstration. Then participant was asked to act as if he/she was in such situations of the four tasks and started the tasks with instructions printed on paper and guide sentence on the screen. Finally, the participant answered the questionnaire.

Measures

Two types of measurements were employed in this study: question about believability and the measure of Computer-Mediated Communication (CMC)[7] in order to measure general impression of agents.

Question for believability

Gomes et al.[5] proposed the dimensions and metrics of believability. Dimensions are: awareness, behavior understandability, personality, visual impact, predictability, behavior coherence, change with experience, social, and emotional expressiveness. The templates Gomes et al.[5] proposed, were employed for the questionnaire, e.g. "The agent perceives the world around her(awareness)." Participants evaluated to what extent each of the sentences above matched with the agent, using seven-point Likert scales (1: "Not at all", 7: "Definitely").

Results

A two (*amae* action or not) × two (participant's gender) analysis of variance was conducted for each of characteristic variables.

Believability

There was a significant main effects of *amae* on personality score ($F(1, 24) = 6.107$, $p < .05$). This result suggested that *amae* increases perceived personality.

There was a moderately significant interactions between gender and agency appraisal on social score ($F(1, 24) = 3.119$, $p < .10$). Female participants rated agents with Japanese agency appraisal higher than non-Japanese agency appraisal ($p < .10$). Finally, there was a significant interaction between gender and *amae* in social score ($F(1, 24) = 4.874$, $p < .05$). Male participants rated agents doing *amae* higher than those not doing *amae* ($p < .05$).

CMC

Agents with Japanese agency appraisal were perceived more earnest than those with non-Japanese agency appraisal ($p < .05$). Agents doing *amae* were perceived more casual talk ($p < .05$), short-tempered ($p < .05$), less objective ($p < .05$), and more volatile($p < .10$), than agents without *amae* action.

Conclusion

This study proposed two emotional behaviors of autonomous agents that are specific in Japanese culture, which are *amae* action and Japanese agency appraisal. Influences of the proposed emotional behaviors on user's perceived believability were investigated through experiment. Results showed that agents with Japanese emotional behaviors obtained higher believability than those without Japanese emotional behaviors. To summarize, Japanese emotional behavior can be useful to increase agent's believability for Japanese users.

Endrass et al.[4] implicated Japanese behavior might have bigger influence on believability for Japanese people than foreign people. Comparative studies with participants from broader cultures should be conducted in future.

References

[1] Bates, J. The role of emotion in believable agents. *Communications of the Association for Computing Machinery 37*, 7 (1994), 122–125.

[2] Demeure, V., Niewiadomski, R., and Pelachaud, C. How is believability of a virtual agent related to warmth, competence, personification, and embodiment? *Presence: Teleoperators and Virtual Environments 20*, 5 (2011), 431–448.

[3] Doi, T. *Zoku "Amae" no kōzo*. Kōbundo, Tokyo, Japan, 2001.

[4] Endrass, B., M., R., and E., A. Culture-specific communication management for virtual agents. In *Proc. the 8th International Conference on Autonomous Agents and Multiagent Systems 1*, International Foundation for Autonomous Agents and Multiagent Systems (2009), 281–287.

[5] Gomes, P., Paiva, A., Martinho, C., and Jhala, A. Metrics for character believability in interactive narrative. In *Interactive Storytelling*, Springer (2013), 223–228.

[6] Imada, T., and Ellsworth, P. C. Proud Americans and lucky Japanese: Cultural differences in appraisal and corresponding emotion. *Emotion 11*, 2 (2011), 329–345.

[7] Kim, K. An exploratory study of impression formation in computer-mediated communicaiton. *Japanese Journal of Social Psychology 14*, 3 (1999), 123–132.

[8] Kobayashi, M., and Katou, K. A development of "emotional and practical amae scale". *Kyushu University Psychological Research 10* (2009), 81–92.

[9] Smith, H. W., and Nomi, T. Is amae the key to understanding japanese culture? *Electronic Journal of Sociology 5*, 1 (2000).

[10] Tokuda, K., Lee, A., and Oura, K. MMDAgent (version 1.3.1). http://www.mmdagent.jp, 2012.

Weight-Aware Robot Motion Planning for Lift-to-Pass Action

Oskar Palinko
Istituto Italiano di Tecnologia
via Morego 30
16163 Genova, Italy
oskar.palinko@iit.it

Alessandra Sciutti
Istituto Italiano di Tecnologia
via Morego 30
16163 Genova, Italy
alessandra.sciutti@iit.it

Francesco Rea
Istituto Italiano di Tecnologia
via Morego 30
16163 Genova, Italy
francesco.rea@iit.it

Giulio Sandini
Istituto Italiano di Tecnologia
via Morego 30
16163 Genova, Italy
giulio.sandini@iit.it

HAI '14, Oct 29-31 2014, Tsukuba, Japan
ACM 978-1-4503-3035-0/14/10.
http://dx.doi.org/10.1145/2658861.2658920

Abstract

Passing an object between two humans is a very
natural and seamless operation, mainly thanks to non-
verbal cues which facilitate the process. Just from
action observation, humans can easily anticipate where
and when a passing movement will end and how heavy
the transported object is. But how could this natural
understanding be ported to non-human agents? We
introduce a simple robotic architecture to enable the
iCub humanoid robot to visually recognize the weight of
an object and select a lift-to-pass motion which
implicitly communicates such information to the action
partner. In this work we mainly focus on the building
and training of the procedural memory module needed
to store the association between the mass of an object
and its visual appearance, and we propose how such a
model can be used to successively select
communicative lifting motions.

Author Keywords

Human robot interaction; motion understanding; visual
classification; force sensing.

Introduction

Humans pass objects to each other with ease. Even in
complex environments or when our attention is focused
elsewhere, we handle objects gracefully. However, from
a robotics standpoint passing objects in a natural way is

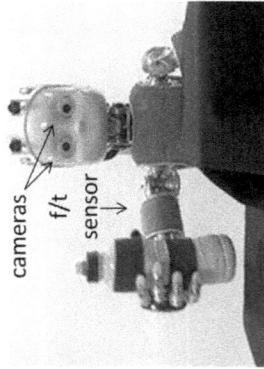

Figure 1. iCub lifting a bottle.

a very complex technical task. Studies have been devoted to determining the optimal location of the passage during a handover; to showing the intention of passing and to coordinating the dynamics of the process [1; 2; 10]. Here we focus on another important aspect of the process: the readability of the object's properties from the robot's passing motion. A good estimate of the weight is important for an agent to safely receive the object. Indeed, humans tend to plan their forces *before* manipulating an object, rather than reactively adjusting their grip force after sensing its weight [6]. This memory-based predictive planning yields to a quicker and more accurate manipulation, as it is not limited by delays in the tactile feedback. The resulting lift is fluid, without corrective motions and appropriately speeded as a function of the lifted weight. This latter information is implicitly read by observers, who can in turn anticipatorily plan the most efficient receiving action [8; 9]. It would be important to incorporate this capability on robots to learn the weight of the objects and to be able to implicitly communicate it to the action partner, as humans do in everyday life. This way, with no need of overt attention and even in noisy and cluttered environment the human partner could be prepared from the very beginning of the passing motion to receive efficiently and safely the passed object. In this work we propose an architecture for a humanoid robot which enables it to associate

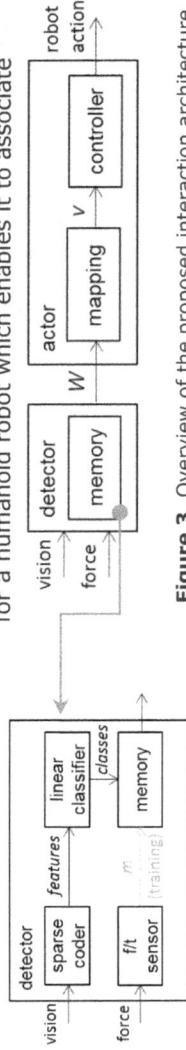

yielding to the construction of a sort of procedural memory for object weights [6]. Exploiting this memory, the robot can then tailor its own lifting and passing movements to maximize the transfer of implicit information (e.g. weight estimate) to the human participant.

Architecture

The architecture of the proposed interaction system consists of a *Detector* and an *Actor*, see Figure 3. The Detector determines the weight of an object (m) and passes the information to the Actor. This subsystem then selects the appropriate motion trajectories for lifting and passing (mapper) which are finally sent to the motor controllers for execution. The input to the Detector is the object weight and object image from the visual system of the robot. In this work we introduce the *Memory* element in the Detector module which enables the robot to associate expected weights with images of the observed objects, see Figure 2.

The interaction system has two basic states: *building the memory* and *object recognition with lifting*.

Building the memory
In this phase the robot learns to associate the weight with the appearance of objects. The process starts by presenting n objects to the robot seen from a number of angles. Each of these images is processed by the sparse coder, which extracts a feature vector. It is assumed the object is segmented from the camera image to be classified. From this cropped image, SIFT (scale-invariant feature transform) local descriptors are extracted and then fed to a spatial pyramid matching kernel based on sparse coding [5]. The output feature vector of this stage has been proven to be a very

Figure 3. Overview of the proposed interaction architecture

the visual appearance of an object to its weight,

Figure 2. Detector module in detail.

effective tool for real-time image classification [4]. This vector is then fed to the linear classifier, which learns to discriminate between feature vectors. For each object class a one-versus-all strategy is employed to train a binary linear SVM (support vector machine), yielding to n linear SVM classifiers, where n is the number of objects. (For a more detailed explanation of feature extraction and classification methods, see [4].)

After all the images are acquired the robot grasps and lifts the object to measure its weight and associates it with the learned class. To infer the weight, the force measured from the force/torque sensors located in the upper arms of the robot (Figure 1) is recalculated in the palms of the hands using the recursive Newton-Euler algorithm [3]. The object's weight is then calculated by subtracting the vertical resultant force while the hand is empty (baseline) from the vertical resultant force while holding the object. This way the association between object weight and its visual appearance is learned by the robot.

Object recognition and lifting

Once the training is complete, the robot is ready to perform object recognition, lifting and passing with appropriate motion. Again, we start with visual observation of the object, but this time only one image is taken. Feature vectors are extracted using the sparse coder and recognition is performed by the linear classifier which was trained in the previous step. The classifier gives results in the form of levels of confidence for each trained class. The highest scoring class is declared winner. In the third step the weight associated with the winning class is retrieved from the previously built memory. This is the expected mass of the object. Based on this mass, an appropriate lifting and passing action is selected that will convey

information about the weight of the object to the human participant. This is achieved by selecting a lifting speed inversely proportional to the mass (see inset). Hence, if the recognized mass is larger, the motion will be slower, thus implicitly communicating to the human the object's weight. This strategy has been already demonstrated as effective in communicating weight in a previous work with the same platform [9].

Experimental results

Visual learning and recognition

We ran a preliminary visual recognition study using 6 objects of different weights which could be grasped by the iCub (Fig. 4) [7]. We recorded 11 images for each of the 6 objects. The images of the objects were captured using one of the robot's cameras located in the right eye, while the robot was within grasping distance. The 11 images were taken with different orientations (around the vertical axis) of the objects on the table. They were manually cropped to include only the objects themselves before feeding them to the sparse coder for feature extraction. The linear classifier was trained by 10 images of each object, while leaving one testing image out (for each class). During the recognition phase, the class with the highest score was declared the winner. This procedure was repeated for each of the 66 images. Table 1 shows averaged accuracy of the classifier in percentages. Rows of the table represent actual objects, while columns denote the output of the classifier. Values on the diagonal of Table 1 represent correct classifications. It can be noticed that the recognition system performs fairly well even with a limited number of low resolution images and objects of similar shape.

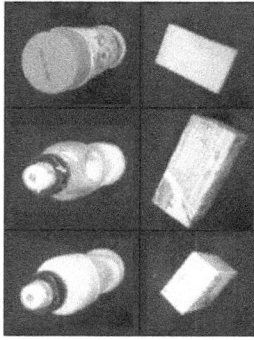

Figure 4. Objects for recognition: full bottle, empty bottle, a can of paint, a small box of cereal, tea box and sponge.

%	bottle	ebottle	paintcan	cereal	teabox	sponge
bottle	72,7	9,1	0,0	0,0	9,1	9,1
ebottle	9,1	81,8	9,1	0,0	0,0	0,0
paintcan	9,1	18,2	72,7	0,0	0,0	0,0
cereal	0,0	0,0	0,0	72,7	0,0	27,3
teabox	18,2	0,0	0,0	0,0	63,6	18,2
sponge	18,2	0,0	0,0	27,3	18,2	36,4

Table 1. Average object classification accuracy [%].

Velocity mapping

Motion velocities are going to be mapped to the weight estimate retrieved from the robot's memory. In particular the peak vertical velocity of the motion will be selected following a linear dependency from object mass, as:

$$v_v \left[\frac{cm}{s}\right] = 30 \left[\frac{cm}{s}\right] - 50 \left[\frac{cm}{s \cdot kg}\right] \cdot m[kg],$$

where v_v is the end effector vertical velocity and m is the expected mass of the object from the previous step. This approach has been found to be functional in communicating weights in the common range of 100-400g to human observers [9].

Acknowledgements

This work has been conducted in the framework of the European project CODEFROR (PIRSES-2013-612555). The authors thank Sean Ryan Fanello for his expertise on machine learning.

Memory building

Once the objects are classified and their weights are determined, a memory lookup table can be built. This table contains the object's class, its expected weight and optionally a confidence value which expresses how sure the robot is about the memorized expected weight. For example, if over time the robot lifts the same box but measures different weight each time (due to a change in the contents of the box), its confidence in the expected mass would be low. On the contrary, if the measured weight of the object of a given class is repeatedly measured with little variability, the confidence level would be deemed high. This measure could then be used by the robot in preparation to lift: if confidence in object weight is low, be prepared to adjust the lift during the motion; if it's high and the real weight is different, show surprise to the human partner.

Conclusion

Interaction between humans is efficient because of its perfect timing, which is often achieved by predicting rather than reacting to the action of the other agent. In this work we tried to extend such prediction also to humanoid lifting action. More precisely, memory based architecture was shown for learning and recalling object weights based on their visual appearance, to allow the robot to select the lifting action which could immediately communicate to the observer the lifted weight.

References

[1] Cakmak, M., Srinivasa, S. S., Lee, M. K., Kiesler, S. and Forlizzi, J. Using spatial and temporal contrast for fluent robot human hand-overs, *in Proceedings of the 6th International Conference on Human-Robot interaction*, 2011, pp. 489-496.

[2] Chan, W. P., Parker, C. A., Van der Loos, H. M., and Croft, E. A., A human-inspired object handover controller, *The International Journal of Robotics Research*, vol. 32, pp. 971-983, 2013.

[3] Del Prete, A., Natale, L., Nori, F., and Metta, G., Contact Force Estimations Using Tactile Sensors and Force / Torque Sensors, *Human Robot Interaction*, 2012.

[4] Fanello, S.R., Ciliberto, C., Natale, L. and Metta, G., Weakly supervised strategies for natural object recognition in robotics, *ICRA*, 2013.

[5] Fanello, S.R., Noceti, N., Metta, G. and Odone, F., Multi-class image classification: sparsity does it better, *VISAPP*, 2013.

[6] Gordon, A. M., Westling, G., Cole, K.J., and Johansson, R.S., Memory representations underlying motor commands used during manipulation of common and novel objects, J Neurophysiol. 69(6):1789-96. 1993.

[7] Metta, G., Natale, L., Nori, F., Sandini, G., Vernon, D., Fadiga, L., Hofsten, C., Rosander, K., Lopes, M., Santos-Victor, J., Bernardino, A., and Montesano, L., The iCub humanoid robot: an open-systems platform for research in cognitive development, *Neural Netw*, vol. 23, no. 8-9, pp. 1125-1134, 2010.

[8] Runeson, S. and Frykholm, G., Visual perception of lifted weight, *J. Exp Psychol Hum Percept Perform*, vol. 7, pp. 733-40, Aug 1981.

[9] Sciutti, A., Patanè, L., Nori, F. and Sandini, G., Understanding object weight from human and humanoid lifting actions, *IEEE Transactions on Autonomous Mental Development*, vol. 6, no. 2, pp. 80-92, 2014.

[10] Sisbot, E. A. and Alami, R., A Human-Aware Manipulation Planner, IEEE Transactions on Robotics, vol. 28, pp. 1045 -1057, 2012.

Emotion Recognition and Expression in Therapeutic Social Robot Design

Sun Jie
Keio-NUS CUTE Center,
National University of Singapore
idmsunj@nus.edu.sg

Daniel Peng Zhuo
Department of Mechanical
Engineering,
National University of Singapore
A0056600@nus.edu.sg

Li Qinpei
Department of Mechanical
Engineering,
National University of Singapore
Philip.li1990@gmail.com

Wong Chern Yuen, Anthony
Institute for Infocomm Research,
Agency for Science Technology
and Research, Singapore
cywong@i2r.a-star.edu.sg

Rui Yan
Institute for Infocomm Research,
Agency for Science Technology
and Research, Singapore
ryan@i2r.a-star.edu.sg

HAI '14, Oct 29-31 2014, Tsukuba, Japan
ACM 978-1-4503-3035-0/14/10.
http://dx.doi.org/10.1145/2658861.2658921

Abstract

To improve the healthcare and wellbeing of the elderly population, a therapeutic social robot was designed and its interaction with human was investigated in this research. The focus is to enable the designed robot to understand human's emotion and express emotion through gestures accordingly. To identify human emotion, tactile sensors were utilized and installed on the robot's head to detect users' touch signals, and classify them into four patterns (hit, pat, stroke and unknown). The classification task was performed based on three methods (Localist Attractor Network, Temporal Decision Tree and Naive Bayes Classifier). Exploration of the trade-off between high accuracy and low computing workload was also carried out for all three methods. Four gestures were designed to respond to the four emotion recognition patterns, which can express some basic human emotional statuses such as unhappiness, love, relaxation and confusion.

Author Keywords

Therapeutic robot; social robot; emotion recognition; tactile sensor; classification

ACM Classification Keywords

I.2.9 Artificial intelligence: Robotics.

Introduction

To improve healthcare of people with mental disabilities, researches working on social robotics start to focus on assistive technologies on treatment of mental disorders such as dementia, autism and so forth. These social robots aim to engage people through attentional and emotional behaviours, provide assistance physically and mentally, and collaborate with nursing stuff and family members to form a life support network [1]. Being aware of the promising future of social robot applications in healthcare, the objective of this work is to build a therapeutic social robot (The Panda) to improve human robot interaction by 1) making the robot understand human emotion through tactile information, 2) classifying different touches into four categories: hit, pat, stroke or unknown, and 3) generating gestures according to the output of pattern recognition algorithms, to express basic human emotions such as unhappiness, love, relaxation and confusion. The tactile pattern classification procedure is shown in Figure 1.

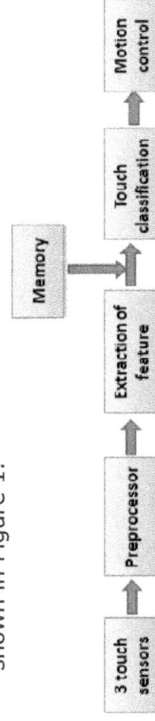

Figure 1. Tactile Pattern Classification Procedure

Robotic Structure And Motion Design

Design Criteria

The social therapeutic robot built in this project is named the Panda, which provides both elderly and young children with a form of companionship in hospitals and nursing. Glocker M.L. et al. [2] provided experimental evidence that cuteness motivates caretaking in adults. Therefore, the Panda should be designed as a cute companion that invites users of all ages to initiate interaction with it and take care of it.

In addition, the design should be human-centered, focusing upon understanding and satisfying the needs of users. To cater the needs of the elderly from all background, a simple, user-friendly operating system and user experience to raise people's acceptance level and motivation is a must. The robot should also be designed in a way to make the elderly feel capable, empowered or even independent. When introduced as common property like in a nursing house, the robot can also increase and enhance the communication among the users so that they can express and exchange their opinions on it.

Design Overview

Figure 2 shows a photo of the Panda, which allows freedom in behavior design due to less expectation of a specific behaviour. The Panda consists of arms, legs, head, shoulder/neck and trunk. The trunk contains embedded microprocessors, processing sensory circuit board, motion driving system and power. In this design, complicated gestures can be simplified into a combination of motions to achieve 9 degree of freedom (DOF): 3 DOF in the neck (raw, pitch, yaw); 2 DOF in each arm (forearm and upper arm); 1 DOF for eyes and 1DOF for mouth. Mini gear DC motors actuate all these motions. Rotary encoders are used as position sensors for these DC motors, where 1024 bytes are mapped to 360 degrees. To avoid collision, the position range of each motor was determined by manually tuning motors to the boundary positions and noting down the encoder output.

Figure 2. The overview of the Panda.

Robot Body Design

Our intention was to design the Panda to be convenient for users to hold, touch and hug, therefore, upright standing or sitting posture are preferred. A bear-like model was tentatively chosen since the bulky body of this model is sufficient to hold inner mechanical structure and electrical components and at the same time big round body and face are considered features that make something look cute according to cute factor study reported by Angier [3].

Emotion Recognition By Tactile Sensor

Tactile Sensors

Three force sensitive resistor tactile sensors (SEN-09375), were utilized to detect the pressure given by human as shown in Figure 3. Its resistance drops from more than 1MΩ (no pressure) to 1KΩ (under pressure). As shown in Figure 3(a), a layer of foam (skin) was attached to robot head and tactile sensors are mounted on the foam. Another layer of foam was applied to cover the sensors to imitate robot skin as Figure 3(b) in the final robot.

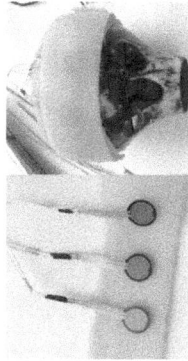

(a)   (b)

Figure 3. Tactile sensors arrangement (a) Tactile sensors; (b) Tactile sensor on the robot head

Touch Pattern Classification

The outputs from tactile sensors were used in touch patterns classification, and three touch patterns were defined in Table 1. If the touch data cannot be classified under any category, it will fall into the unknown status.

	Force	Contact Time	Repeat	Contact Area Change
Hit	High	Short	No	No
Pat	Low	Short	Yes	Yes
Stroke	Low	Long	Yes	Yes

Table 1. Definitions of the three touch patterns.

Comparison of Pattern Classification Methods

Three pattern recognition methods (Localist Attractor Network, Temporal Decision Tree and Naive Bayes Classifier) were compared in this study to explore the trade-off between high accuracy and low computing workload. All the pattern classification methods are based on features extracted from force signals of tactile sensors. The size of data set for this study is 150, and each pattern has 50 sets.

• *Localist Attractor Network*

In Localist Attractor Network (LAN), the touch pattern models are achieved using an off-line classification, and the first ten real part coefficients from fast Fourier transform are chosen to depict touch features. The first 10 sets of data for each pattern are taken as training data, and the attractor is obtained by taking the mean of them. Other parameters are determined by 5-fold cross-validation for the 50 data sets under each pattern.

• *Temporal Decision Tree*

In temporal decision tree, force magnitude, repetition and contact time are identified as features to differentiate the three patterns. In temporal decision tree, the classifier is trained off-line first to set up all necessary parameters and then tested on-line using contact time, force magnitude and repetition property in a sequent way.

• *Naïve Bayes Classifier*

In naïve Bayes classifier [4], the same training data set from LAN is used to develop this classification model, where mean and variance of force, contact time and repetition under each pattern were calculated.

199

In the experiment, all the three methods can achieve more than 90% classification accuracy. While, the computing workload for both LAN and Naïve Bayes classification is a bit high. The advantage of temporal decision tree classifier is the low computation cost and fast processing speed. The corresponding results from temporal decision tree are shown in Table 2.

Gesture Design and Generation

Typical gestures were designed to respond to different touch pattern from the users, and also a sequence of gestures were selected to respond to the same class to make the interaction less mechanical and more natural. Four gestures were designed in the first version of prototype to respond to the four pattern recognition outcomes, which respectively indicate the users' current emotions, unhappiness, love, relaxation and confusion.

Hits from users convey an emotion of unhappiness or anger, and the robot's reaction was naturally designed to show an emotion of sadness and being wronged to pursue affection and sympathy. Pats from users convey an emotion of affection and love, therefore, the robot's reaction gesture was designed to show a happy and cheerful emotion. Strokes from users convey a peaceful and relaxing emotion, meanwhile, strokes on human or pets usually bring a comfortable feeling for the acceptors. Therefore, the gestures were designed to reciprocate this feeling back to the users. Since no specific feelings are expressed in unknown state, the designed gesture shows a cute look and a little

confusion. A further improvement is needed on expressing the desired emotions to users.

Conclusion

For future research, to implement sensors on the skin is proposed so that robot can have the sense of touch in every part of the body, intelligent classification method to differentiate touch from humans and tactile contact from other objects, and diverse senses to induce more natural human robot interaction.

Acknowledgements

This research is supported by the National Research Foundation, Prime Minister's Office, Singapore under its International Research Centre @ Singapore Funding Initiative and administered by the Interactive & Digital Media Programme Office.

References

[1] Sasaki, J., Yamada, K., Tanaka, M. and Funyu, Y. An experiment of the life support network for elderly people living in a rural area. In *Proc. The 7th WSEAS International Conference on Applied Computer Science* 7 (2004), 316-321.

[2] Glocker, M. L., Langleben, D. D., Ruparel, K., Loughead, J. W., Gur, R. C., & Sachser, N. (2009). Baby schema in infant faces induces cuteness perception and motivation for caretaking in adults. *Ethology*, 115(3), 257-263.

[3] Angier, Natalie. The Cute Factor. The New York Times, 2006-01-03.

[4] Leung, K.M. Naïve Bayes Classifier. New York, NY, 2007. http://cis.poly.edu/~mleung/FRE7851/f07/naiveBayesianClassifier.pdf

Classifi-cation	Hit	Pat	Stroke
Hit	47	0	0
Pat	2	50	0
Stroke	0	0	50
Unknown	1	0	0
Accuracy	94%	100%	100%

Table 2. Classification results from the temporal decision tree.

Luminous Device for the Deaf and Hard of Hearing People

Akira MATSUDA
Shibaura Institute of
Technology Department of
Information Science and
Engineering
Toyosu 3-7-5, Koutouku,
Tokyo, 135-8548 JAPAN
al11103@shibaura-it.ac.jp

Midori SUGAYA
Shibaura Institute of
Technology Department of
Information Science and
Engineering
Toyosu 3-7-5, Koutouku,
Tokyo, 135-8548 JAPAN
doly@shibaura-it.ac.jp

Hiroyuki NAKAMURA
Shibaura Institute of
Technology School of Arts and
Sciences
Toyosu 3-7-5, Koutouku,
Tokyo, 135-8548 JAPAN
nkmr@shibaura-it.ac.jp

Abstract

People with hard of hearing and the deaf often face
difficulties to recognize things happening in their
surroundings. Imagine you cannot hear the sound,
because you are with hard of hearing or using iPod with
earphones, you would not able to recognize the car
coming behind of you. It may cause a fatal collision. The
purpose of this study is to develop the device mostly for
the deaf or hard of hearing people, for persons temporarily
with hard of hearing besides.

The device can be applied to multi modal accessibility,
which transforms the sound information to the visual
information. It also provides the direction to the sound
source using a light. The device is compact in an attempt
to be used in everyday life.

Author Keywords

Accessibility, Assistive Technology, Deaf, Hard Hearing,
Alert Device

ACM Classification Keywords

H.1.2 [User/Machine Systems]; H.5.1 [Multimedia
Information Systems]; H.5.5 [Sound and Music
Computing]; K.4.2 [Social Issues]

General Terms

Documentation, Standardization

Introduction

People with hard of hearing, or hearing impaired, and the deaf often face difficulties to recognize things happening in their circumstances. Fire alarm, for instance, sounding the imminent danger, is not accessible to those people.

American with Disabilities Act (ADA) and Section 508 of The Rehabilitation Act require alert systems visually accessible to those at hotels and motels, like other places of public accommodation[6, 7, 2].

The ratio of senior citizens, age 65 and over, is increasing in the global community. Japan in particular is the fastest country in terms of aging. Its ratio of this age group to the entire population is 25.1% (as of Oct. 1, 2013), which is the highest in the world. The fail of the hearing function by aging makes elderly people difficult to obtain various auditory information.

Disability is caused by not only nature but situation. Imagine you hold bags on your both hands. You are not able to use your hands for other purposes. This difficulty is similar to what a person with paralysis has.

When we focus on the deaf or hard of hearing, listening music in large volume and/or concentrating on a smartphone are/is same as disability. When you cannot hear the sound, you are no longer recognizing a car coming behind.

It has been proposed that the danger prediction method using sound localization[5, 4]. However, no device is yet actually suggested. An alert device and an accident prevention device have been demanded[1, 8]. While the device for visual disorder is already developed as Forehead Sensory Recognition System[3], no device for the deaf and hard of hearing people is found.

In this study, authors propose the alert device for the deaf and hard of hearing people. The device offers both sound localization and alert function.

In addition, considering the property of this device as both an attention awakening device and an everyday device, this device's portability and usability must be considered when determining its shape and size.

Device

The device architecture is elaborated in the following sections.

Device Architecture

The device consists of a sound localization unit using microphone array and an alert unit.(fig1). An alert unit is using not only light by LED but also another component such as vibrator, speaker or another 'human acceptable' component for this propose.

A sound localization unit and an alert unit are separated but these are connected by radio.

Usage

A user puts the alert device and the microphone array on his/her body or belongings. Once something happening with certain sound occurs around a user, the sound localization unit detects the direction which the sound comes from. The result of the detection is notified to the alert unit so that it presents the information using alerting component such as flash light.

Discussion

Separating the sound localization unit and the alert unit gives great advantages to this device.

These advantages make the device possible to be equipped for various use cases. The alert unit attached on glasses, for instance, makes this device as a wearable alert system.

Another way to use this device is to notice the situation in the remote place. For example, when an alert unit is attached to a baby, a person in the next room is able to find something happening around the baby.

Furthermore, the alert unit is attached to a person (User A) and the sound localization unit is attached to another person (User B). User B is able to call User A when User B gets lost.

Separating the localization unit and the alert unit lets us use several components corresponding to various user experience. LED is able to provide the direction using light, vibrators can provide it using haptics and so on.

Conclusion

Authors developed the device, which offers the sound localization and the alert function using light. Separating the sound localization unit and the alert unit creates various use cases and frees users from places. Further studies on this device are in progress. Details will be described, the device and some use cases will be demonstrated at iHAI 2014.

References

[1] NTT Docomo.
https://www.nttdocomo.co.jp/info/news
_release/2013/12/03_00.html, in Japanese, Last
accessed date 2014-02-17.

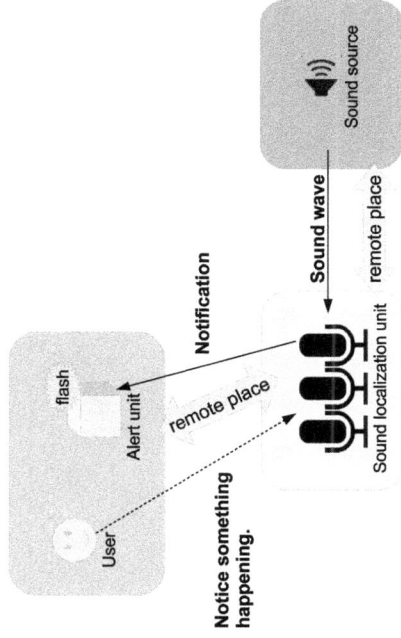

Figure 1: Schematic diagram of device usage.

Prototyping

Prototype device is in fig.2. An alert unit using light by LED and a sound localization unit are connected over smartphone by Bluetooth LE.

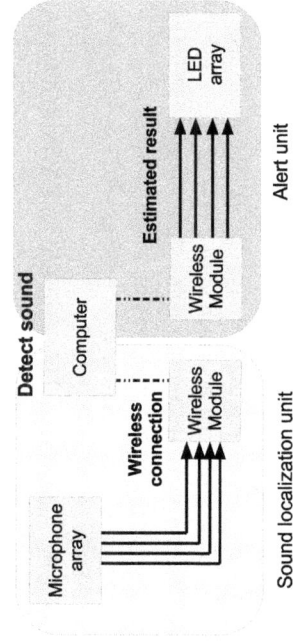

Figure 2: Schematic diagram of prototype device

[2] Accessibility Study Group. *Information Accessibility and Universal Design*. ASCII publishing, 2003, in Japanese.

[3] Eyeplus Co. inc. Information on auxdeco. http://www.eyeplus2.com/product-2/about-auxdeco, in Japanese, Last accessed date 2014/02/17.

[4] Yusuke Mochida and Ito Katunobu. Danger prediction by measuring the direction of sound with using binaural microphones. *Proceedings*, 2011(1):123–125, March in Japanese, 2011.

[5] SHIMADA Naoto, ITAI Akitoshi, and YASUKAWA Hiroshi. A study on an approaching vehicle detection using a linear microphone array-based acoustic sensing. *Smart Info-media System (SIS) of IEICE*, 109(447):125–128, February 2010.

[6] United States Department of Justice. 2010 ada standards for accessible design. http://www.ada.gov/2010ADAstandards.index.htm, Last accessed date 2014/02/17.

[7] National Association of the Deaf. Hotels and motels. http://www.nad.org/issues/transportation-and-travel/hotels-and-motels, Last accessed date 2014-02-17.

[8] Chiyoda City's webpage. http://www.city.chiyoda.lg.jp/koho/kuse/koho/pressrelease/h25/h2507/h250729.html, in Japanese, Last accessed date 2014-02-17.

Development of Werewolf Match System for Human Players Mediated with Lifelike Agents

Yu Kobayashi

Tokyo Polytechnic University
Graduate School of Engineering
1583 Iiyama Atsugi-city
Kanagawa, Japan
kbys.yu3ant10@gmail.com

Hirotaka Osawa

University of Tsukuba
1-1-1 Tennodai Tsukuba
Ibaraki, Japan
osawa@iit.tsukuba.ac.jp

Michimasa Inaba

Hiroshima City University
3-4-1 Ozuka-Higashi
Asa-Minami-Ku
Hiroshima, Japan
inaba@hiroshima-cu.ac.jp

Kosuke Shinoda

University of Electro-
Communications
1-5-1 Chofugaoka Chofu
Tokyo, Japan
kosuke.shinoda@is.uec.ac.jp

Fujio Toriumi

University of Tokyo
7-3-1 Hongo Bunkyo-ku
Tokyo, Japan
tori@sys.u-tokyo.ac.jp

Daisuke Katagami

Tokyo Polytechnic University
1583 Iiyama Atsugi-city
Kanagawa, Japan
katagami@cs.t-kougei.ac.jp

HAI '14 , Oct 29-31, 2014, Tsukuba, Japan
ACM 978-1-4503-3035-0/14/10.
http://dx.doi.org/10.1145/2658861.2658923

Abstract

"Are You a Werewolf?" is a conversation type game. We
construct a Werewolf match system for humans with
lifelike agents. We evaluate whether it is possible to
realize conversation space of "Are You a Werewolf?"
with the system.

Author Keywords

Werewolf AI; lifelike agents; Werewolf Match System

ACM Classification Keywords

H.5.m. Information interfaces and presentation (e.g.,
HCI)

Introduction

It is possible for computers to win human in perfect
information game. The fact has become evident from
the recently result of computer chess [1] or computer
shogi [2]. In the other hand, incomplete information
game is unexplored field.

"Are You a Werewolf?" or werewolf game in popular
name is one of incomplete information game. This
game is considered to be used as standard problem to
evaluate the performance of general artificial
intelligence [3]. And, by modeling werewolf game,
werewolf game is attempted to make a platform for
playing werewolf game in humans versus agents or

agents each other [4]. However, lifelike agent system, which can discuss with humans in "Werewolf" while exchanging non-verbal information such as gestures and verbal information such as utterances, have not been developed around the world.

In this paper, we aim to let subject acquire advanced skill in conversation by playing "Werewolf" mediated with lifelike agents. The space of discussion between humans mediated with lifelike agents is realized.

Werewolf Game

Werewolf game is conversation type party game. Werewolf game is the game that players discuss about who has the role of "Werewolf". A player determines the role of the other players from their content of utterances and gestures. However, he do not execute player having a valuable role. Therefore, the players need advanced skill in conversation.

The players are divided into two teams, "Villagers side" and "Werewolf side". In this time, no player knows who has which role. This game has two phases: "Day" and "Night". On "Day" phase, living players discuss to find out a player having the role of "Werewolf". After that, players decide one player to be excluded in the form of executing werewolf found out. On "Night" phase, players living and having special skill use their own skill. For example, as shown below, there are some skills.

Werewolf
Werewolf players exclude one Villagers side player from the game. This action is called "Attack".

Seer
Seer player can be sure whether one living player designated by Seer player is Werewolf player or not.

Medium
Medium player can be sure can be sure whether the player executed yesterday is a werewolf.

Bodyguard
Bodyguard can defend only one player designated by Bodyguard player from werewolf's attack.

This game repeats such "Day" and "Night". Finally, if all Werewolf players are executed, Villager side players win. Or, if it is same numbers between living Werewolf players and the other players, Werewolf side players win.

Match System for Werewolf Game

We develop lifelike agent control system for playing werewolf game with lifelike agent. We use MMD Agent [5] for lifelike agent. MMD Agent can communicate with other programs through plugins. We call the system to control MMD Agent and make us play smoothly "MMDAWOZ for Werewolf".

We show the system chart of MMDAWOZ for Werewolf in Figure 1. All players play werewolf game by controlling his lifelike agent with the system. Players discuss mediated with his lifelike agent. When player's lifelike agent speaks, the system enable players to control agent's motion. The system sends Request Message: Vote and Night Actions, to Game Server. Game Server returns to each player the appropriate information of game results. At Night phase, in order to avoid knowing the role of the players who don't control

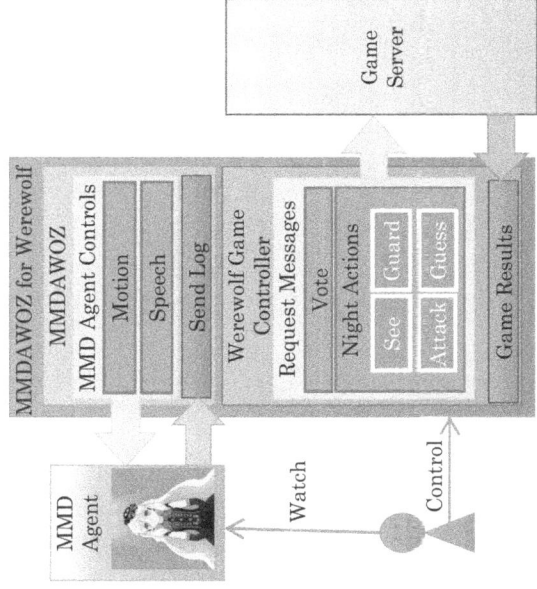

Figure 1. Schematic Drawing of MMDAWOZ for Werewolf

MMDAWOZ, players having no special ability guess who is werewolf. The system records all utterances and information sent to Game Server in text format.

We show system chart in Figure 2. All players allow watching and listening in lifelike agent conversation space.

Conclusion

In this paper, we aim to realize the space of discussion between humans mediated with lifelike agents. We constructed a Werewolf match system for humans with lifelike agents.

In the future, we aim to realize the conversation of Werewolf AI by using lifelike agents.

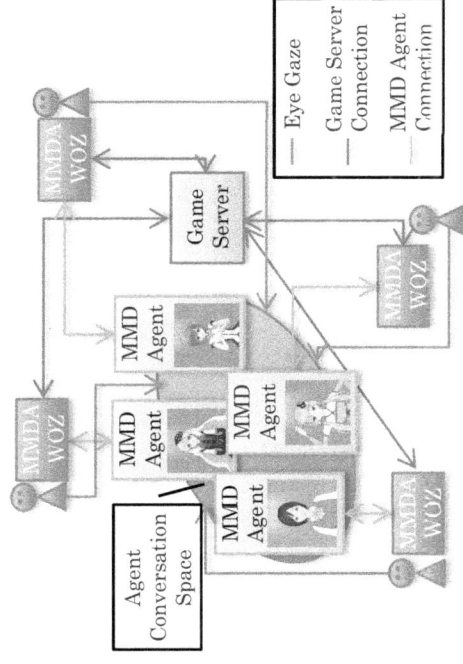

Figure 2. System Chart

Acknowledgements

This work was partially supported by JSPS KAKENHI Grant Number 25330243.

References

[1] Deep Blue http://www-03.ibm.com/ibm/history/ibm100/us/en/icons/deepblue/

[2] Denousen http://www.shogi.or.jp/kisen/denou/

[3] Shinoda, K. Toriumi, F. Katagami, D. Osawa, H. Inaba, M. "Are you a Werewolf?" becomes a Standard Problem for General Artificial Intelligence. In Proc. The 28th Annual Conference of the Japanese Society for Artificial Intelligence, 2014, (2014).

[4] Osawa, H. Communication Protocol for the "Werewolf" game. In Proc. HAI2013, (2013).(Japanese)

[5] Lee, A. Oura, K. Tokuda, K. Mmdagent—A fully open-source toolkit for voice interaction systems. In Proc. 2013 IEEE International Conference on Acoustics, Speech, and Signal Processing, (2013).

Development of Smart Infant-Parents Affective Telepresence System

Elham Saadatian
Keio-NUS CUTE Center
Interactive and Digital Media
Institute
National University of
Singapore
elham@nus.edu.sg

Reihaneh Hosseinzade Hariri
Faculty of Computer Science
UPM University
Malaysia
rhariri2003@gmail.com

Adrian David Cheok
City University
College Building, Room A304J
St John Street EC1V 4PB
London, UK
adriancheok@gmail.com

Ryohei Nakatsu
Keio-NUS CUTE Center
Interactive and Digital Media
Institute
National University of
Singapore
idmnr@nus.edu.sg

HAI 2014, October 29–31, 2014, Tsukuba, Japan.
ACM 978-1-4503-3035-0/14/10.
http://dx.doi.org/10.1145/2658861.2658924

Abstract

Crying is the language of babies. Inability of parents in understanding the needs of babies causes stress and anxiety. The aim of this study is to develop a rapid prototype of infant-parent communication system. The system was tested on real babies and parents, while they were apart. The Results pointed to the overall acceptance and effectiveness of the system in cry translation and reducing the parents anxiety with regards to baby cries.

Author Keywords

Smart sensing, Affective presence, virtual presence

Introduction

Cry is the language of the babies. They try to express their needs and status using the language of cry and nonverbal cues. Inability of parents to understand this language causes stress and anxiety. In this study we have developed a system to support affective communication between remotely located baby and parents

previous researchers have also attempted to interpret the baby needs and status based on their cry signals and other nonverbal cues. For instance, an automatic infant cry recognizer is developed by [6] to distinguish between normal and pathological cries. The Smart Jacket, provides reliable health monitoring for critically unhealthy newborn babies [1]. Another similar system uses a biosensor belt for monitoring the heart rate, breathing frequency, body movements and temperature of the new born baby with embedded sensors [5]. There has been a study on development of a mobile-based monitoring and advisory system that continuously monitors the baby and remotely updates the mother on child status [7]. There are several studies with the goal of emotion detection such as: A study that demonstrated an innovative method of emotion detect through facial recognitions [3] and another research which analyzed relationship between emotional responses with skin conductance[4].However, as can be seen there are very few studies that could address the issue of affective communication between baby and mother.

Developing Infant Cry Translator system

Since the language of babies is cry, the first step that we take in creating the system is developing baby cry translator. It is proven that baby cries contain many information about health and internal status of the baby [2]. We have developed a cry recognition system which can identify the cry signal, translates the meaning of the cry and communicate it to the remotely located parents through a Graphic User Interface (GUI). The following explanation describes our methodology in development of the described system.

Automatic infant cry recognition system distinguishes the cry meaning, of babies aging from one day up to one year old. The system is activated automatically when baby cries and captures the cry through microphone and translates and communicates the meaning to parents in real time. The classification is done through a pattern classification, where the crying waves are taken as the input patterns. The acoustic feature vectors are classified based on their corresponding type of cry, using Neural Network algorithm.

The implementation procedure is described below:

- Data Collection: A corpus of cry signals which are labeled for each type is needed. The corpus can be obtained in hospital or child care center. Signals should be recorded in a quiet room and labeled using the help of experts. In this study, we have used prerecorded cry signals. The database of infant cry is downloaded from the Baby Chillanto database as an initial dataset [1].

- Sound Recorder: A module is available in the system to be automatically activated when baby cries and captures the cry signals in real-time.

- Voice Activity Detection: This function role is to separate cry and non-cry (noises) signals. Therefore this function separates the sounds caused by the vibration of the vocal cords (cries) from the sounds of the inspiratory ,coughing, silences, and other noises.

- Segmentation: Cry signals are divided to small segments of one or few seconds, to enhance the accuracy of the output silent moments and noises should be removed. This part is done using available audio processing software called Praat [2].

---

[1]http://ingenieria.uatx.mx/orionfrg/cry/, The Baby Chillanto Data Base is a property of the Instituto Nacional de Astrofisica Optica Electronica - CONACYT, Mexico
[2]http://praat.en.softonic.com/

- Feature Extraction: Relevant acoustic features for each category of cries is extracted. We have used Mel-frequency cepstral coefficients (MFCC) feature extraction technique to retrieve the features.

- Data Compression: After feature extraction we need to compress the data, using audio signal compression techniques. No compression, PCA, and FRP, were tested and PCA resulted to the highest accuracy of 97.33 for compression.

- Classification: and Decision Display: Classifier is developed based on neural network algorithms.

- Communication: Communication module transfers the data to the parents via internet. the initial communication module is a simple GUI developed in visual studio that shows the baby video and translates bay cry meanings in real -time. The following figures show the print screen of the system GUI

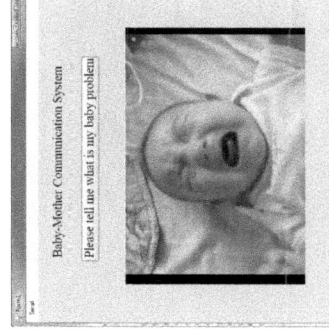

Figure 1: Cry translator GUI main window.

Results and Conclusion

The classifier was tested using unlabeled cry signals and we got accuracy rate of 97%. We have also tested the system in terms of user perception on system as a remote communication tool with the baby. For this purpose we have installed the system on the computers of five working mothers that were remote from their babies during the office hours and asked them to try it for a week, then we asked for their opinion about the system through informal interview. Overall from their feedback we realized that they liked the idea of being connected to their babies while they were away and felt less stressed, although they had concerns regarding the reliability of the system. One of them pointed that it would be better if they could know about the baby status and needs even when the baby is not crying.

Acknowledgments

This research is supported by the Singapore National Research Foundation under its International Research Center Keio-NUS CUTE Center @ Singapore Funding Initiative and administered by the IDM Program Office. We like to thank Dr. Carlos A. Reyes-Garcia, Dr. Emilio Arch-Tirado and his INR-Mexico group, and Dr. Edgar M. Garcia-Tamayo for their dedication of the collection of the Infant Cry data base.
We would also like to thank the participant of the user study for their cooperation and other members of CUTE center for their collaborations during brainstorming.

References

[1] Bouwstra, S., Feijs, L., Chen, W., and Oetomo, S. B. Smart jacket design for neonatal monitoring with wearable sensors. In *Wearable and*

Figure 2: communicating translated baby cry.

Implantable Body Sensor Networks, 2009. BSN 2009. Sixth International Workshop on, IEEE (2009), 162–167.

[2] LaGasse, L., Neal, A., and Lester, B. Assessment of infant cry: acoustic cry analysis and parental perception. *Mental retardation and developmental disabilities research reviews 11*, 1 (2005), 83–93.

[3] Lau, B. T. Portable real time emotion detection system for the disabled. *Expert Systems with Applications 37*, 9 (2010), 6561–6566.

[4] Moscovitch, D. A., Suvak, M. K., and Hofmann, S. G. Emotional response patterns during social threat in individuals with generalized social anxiety disorder and non-anxious controls. *Journal of anxiety disorders 24*, 7 (2010), 785–791.

[5] Piccini, L., Ciani, O., Grönvall, E., Marti, P., and Andreoni, G. New monitoring approach for

neonatal intensive care unit. In *5th International Workshop on Wearable Micro and Nanosystems for Personalized Health* (2008).

[6] Reyes-Galaviz, O. F., Cano-Ortiz, S. D., and Reyes-Garcia, C. A. Evolutionary-neural system to classify infant cry units for pathologies identification in recently born babies. In *Artificial Intelligence, 2008. MICAI'08. Seventh Mexican International Conference on*, IEEE (2008), 330–335.

[7] Saadatian, E., Iyer, S., Lihui, C., Fernando, O., Hideaki, N., Cheok, A., Madurapperuma, A., Ponnampalam, G., and Amin, Z. Low cost infant monitoring and communication system. In *Humanities, Science and Engineering (CHUSER), 2011 IEEE Colloquium on*, IEEE (2011), 503–508.

COLUMN: Persuasion as a Social Mediator to Establish the Interpersonal Coordination

Yasutaka Takeda*
takeda@icd.cs.tut.ac.jp

Shotaro Baba*
baba@icd.cs.tut.ac.jp

Michio Okada*
okada@tut.jp
Interactions and
Communication Design Lab*,
Toyohashi University of
Technology*, Toyohashi
441-8580, JAPAN

Kohei Yoshida*
yoshida@icd.cs.tut.ac.jp

P. Ravindra S De Silva*
ravi@tut.jp

Abstract

We developed soccer ball-shaped interactive artifacts (COLUMN) consisting of eight modules that are connected to twelve servomotors. In the interaction, COLUMN becomes a social mediator to prompt the connectivity of the users. We claim that the above process generates a variety of user's interpersonal coordinates and these can be mapped to the shape of COLUMN's. Therefore, the motivation of our study is to extract the patterns of user's interpersonal coordination. It is also interesting to explore how these patterns lead to imagine behavior for an artifact which has different degree of freedom of its body than the existing.

Author Keywords

Social mediator, Interpersonal coordination, visually-mediated connectedness, COLUMN

ACM Classification Keywords

H.1.2 [Models and Principles]: User/Machine Systems-Human Factors; H.5.2 [Information Interfaces and Presentation]: User Interfaces—
Evaluation/methodology, User-Centered Design

HAI 2014, October 29-31, 2014, Tsukuba, Japan.
ACM 978-1-4503-3035-0/14/10.
http://dx.doi.org/10.1145/2658861.2658925

Introduction

HRI community has been exploring how robot can become social mediators for children with special needs (autism) to enhance their social interaction by investigating a variety of collaborative (with caregiver or teacher, parent ect) play [3]. The play scenarios were designed by centralizing the robot-based interaction which comport as social mediator to the context while grounding the communicative connective among the children, teacher/caregiver, and parent. All of the above terminations indicate the usage of the robot as social mediator [2].

In contrast to the above approach, strategically we can utilize a robot as a social mediator to connect the users while establishing the co-action in order to extract patterns of dynamic connectives of the users. The finding is thoroughly beneficial to invent a variety of behaviors for this kind of unique artifact of COLUMN.

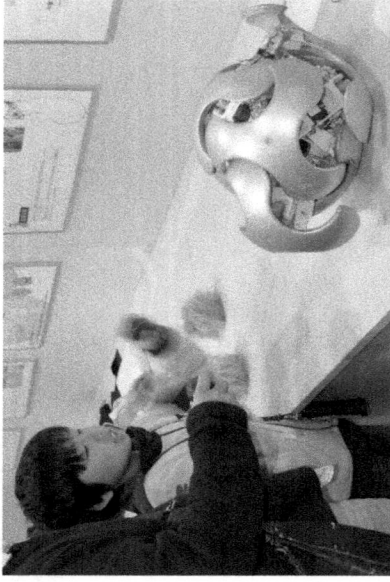

Figure 1: Appearance of the COLUMN

Architecture of the COLUMN

The COLUMN is a soccer ball-shaped interactive artifact consisting of eight modules that are connected to the twelve servomotors (Figure 1). We can transfer the COLUMN body shape by moving the actuators with modules, and these actuators can be controlled by a wireless communicator called a "COLUMN Gear." Each of the users (three participants) can control the 4 servo-motors of the COLUMN, and a user can swing the COLUMN gear to change its body shape (transfer its modules) [4].

The modules (eight) are situated at the corners of the cubic, and each module is designed for gibing with other modules. The cross-section of the module where other modules are fit is cut at a tilt for avoiding interfering with other modules. Because of absorbing the frame distortion by using the ball-shaped moving part of joint, the COLUMN is protected from damage. The modules are made of artificial wood (chemical wood) and are moderately hard but lightweight. We used AX-12+ for the servo-motors, which are small-scale but high-powered and used mainly for the self-produced robot. The electrical circuit of the COLUMN is specialized for controlling AX-12+. AX12+ servomotors connect to a ZigBee wireless communication module via a microcomputer. We can transfer the COLUMN body shape by moving the actuators with the modules, and these actuators can be controlled by a wireless communicator called a "Column Gear." The acceleration of swing (each of the users) map to change the degree of the servo motors; changing the body shape of the COLUMN is proportional to acceleration of the swing.

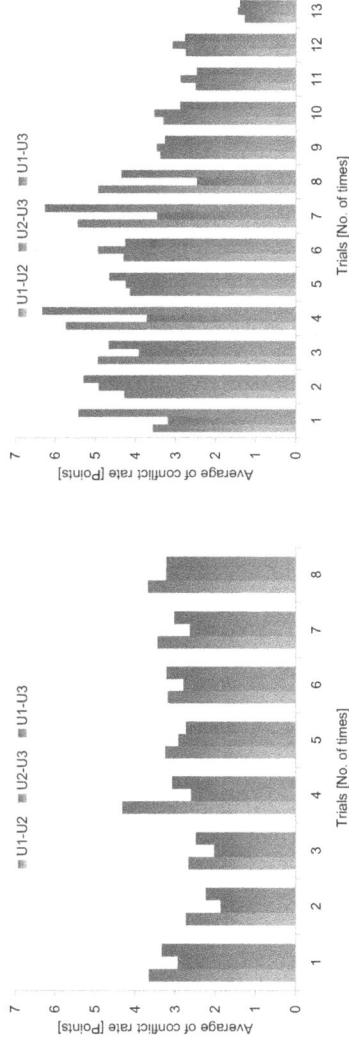

Figure 2: Figure shows the average conflict rates of each user combinations in each trial for groups $G1$ and $G5$. Here the x-axis represents the trials and the y-axis represents the average conflict rate.

Experiment

Three users have to proceed to the COLUMN from the starting point to goal point by using their swing interaction while coordinating with each other efforts. Within five minutes users have to reach the goal, otherwise, again they have to begin from the starting point. At least each of the groups has to participate in five trials, and the groups also have to undertake more trials if they cannot reach the goal at least once within five trials. The reason for the five-trial setup is that sometimes it is possible for a group to reach to goal with their random swings during the initial trials. Five groups (15 users, aged between 22-24 years old) participated in the experiment and were randomly assigned as members of a group. All of the users had no prior experience about controlling a robot. During the interactions, we gathered the user's swing acceleration, COLUMN degree of freedom, and videos (to obtain the states of rolling and behaviors).

Results

Conflict Rates and Interpersonal Coordination

If an interactive user increases the swing acceleration parallel to the partner's, then the conflict rate will be quite higher. Oppositely, if we have a lower conflict rate, then there is potential to have cooperation of the users. In our COLUMN mechanism, cooperation of interactions can be determined as interpersonal coordination of the users, because in order to obtain the rolling behaviors of the robot, each of the users has to coordinate their swings in the dynamic interactions.

Our next step is to explore conflict rate of the group by considering the pair of the users in each trial. To estimate the conflict rate of the users, we employed the swing acceleration to the following equation (Equation 1, where $i, j = 1, 2, 3$) by considering each of the pairs.

$$Conflict_t^{u_i, u_j} = Acceleration_t^{u_i} \times Acceleration_t^{u_j} \quad (1)$$

Figure 2 depicted the number of trials (y-axis) against the average conflict rate (x-axis) for group $G1$ and $G5$. In initial trials, every group has higher conflict rates than the later trials of the interactions. Also, the average conflict rate for every pair-combination of the users ($U1 - U2$, $U2 - U3$, and $U1 - U3$) became approximately equal in the later trials of the interactions. In addition, the conflict rates gradually converged to interval; e.g., in $G1$ it varied between 0-3, and between 0-2.5 for $G2$, etc., and the $G5$ group clearly showed a convergence in the conflict rate.

In the initial trials, most groups did not exhibit an interpersonal coordination among the each user's combinations; however, after having experience with a few trials, the results showed that some of the user's combinations gradually started to connect with each other. These kinds of interpersonal coordination disclose the variety of shape changes of the COLUMN to obtain the rolling behaviors.

Discussion

The lower conflict rate of the users had a direct connection to the interpersonal coordination between the users. The overall results showed that when a user experienced with several interactive trials, then the conflict rate of the user combination became lower than initially. As such, equal swing acceleration between users, and low conflict rates indicates that the users' connectivity was obtained to be the COLUMN rolling behaviors.

Conclusion & Future Works

The results showed that the defined interactive scenario was motivated by connecting the interactive users, which indicated the powerfulness of the COLUMN as a social mediator. Therefore, our future work is direct to extract the body configuration (patterns) with low-level features

by extracting the patterns of interpersonal coordination to attain self-automation behaviors for COLUMN. Also, utilization of social mediator might be thoroughly beneficial to invent variety of behaviors for this kind of unique artifact.

Acknowledgments

This research has been supported by Grant-in-Aid for scientific research of KIBAN-B (26280102) and JSPS fellowship (247630) from the Japan Society for the Promotion of science (JSPS).

References

[1] E. Ferari, B. Robins, and K. Dautenhahn. Robot as a social mediator - a play scenario implementation with children with autism. In *8th International Conference on Interaction Design and Children IDC2009*, 2009.

[2] M. Okada, S. Sakamoto, and N. Suzuki. Muu: Artificial creatures as an embodied interface. In *In ACM SIGGRAPH Conference Abstracts and Applications*, page 91, 2000.

[3] F. Papadopoulos, K. Dautenhahn, and W. C. Ho. Exploring the use of robots as social mediators in a remote human-human collaborative communication experiment. *Paladyn*, 3(1):1–10, 2012.

[4] Y. Takeda, Y. Yoshiike, R. S. D. Silva, and M. Okada. Column: dynamic of interpersonal coordination. In *HRI*, pages 389–390, 2011.

Towards Better Eye Tracking in Human Robot Interaction Using an Affordable Active Vision System

Oskar Palinko

Istituto Italiano di Tecnologia

via Morego 30

16163 Genova, Italy

oskar.palinko@iit.it

Alessandra Sciutti

Istituto Italiano di Tecnologia

via Morego 30

16163 Genova, Italy

alessandra.sciutti@iit.it

Francesco Rea

Istituto Italiano di Tecnologia

via Morego 30

16163 Genova, Italy

francesco.rea@iit.it

Giulio Sandini

Istituto Italiano di Tecnologia

via Morego 30

16163 Genova, Italy

giulio.sandini@iit.it

HAI '14, Oct 29-31 2014, Tsukuba, Japan

ACM 978-1-4503-3035-0/14/10.

http://dx.doi.org/10.1145/2658861.2658926

Abstract

Knowing where a person is looking is an important parameter of every human-human interaction. Detecting a person's gaze could significantly improve the interaction capabilities of today's robotic agents. But many robots' visual systems are limited by data bandwidth and optical hardware. We propose a low-cost high-def pan/tilt/zoom active vision system that could significantly improve the robot's eye tracking capabilities. We tested the proposed system for improving mutual gaze detection in a human-robot interaction scenario and found significant results compared to systems without zoom capability.

Author Keywords

Eye tracking; human robot interaction; active vision.

Introduction

Gaze plays an important role in human-human interaction. People exchange many glances while communicating with each other. However, our eyes do not only provide us with visual information but they also serve as tools for implicit interaction: in a busy administrative office, the attending clerk needs only to glance at the next client's eyes to initiate the transaction. We are also very much able to guess about someone's object of attention by just observing the eyes: a customer's glance reveals which item s/he is interested in and tells the seller which product's presentation to focus on. It is thus evident that robots could also benefit from knowing their human collaborator's gaze direction. But from the technological point of view robot camera system are not as sophisticated as the human eye: they do not have the necessary spatial resolution nor sensor distribution of the human eye. The robot needs a wide field of view (FOV) in order to locate potential human collaborators but then it needs a narrow field of view to zoom in on the face of the detected person to figure out their gaze. This is an approximation of how human peripheral and foveal vision works. Finally, today's robots have a very limited data bandwidth over their inner networks, which puts a limit on the spatial and temporal resolution of the imaging system.

We propose a low-cost active camera system that addresses the before mentioned issues: we use a high definition (1080p) stereo pair of webcams in a robot head setup (see Fig. 1) which in its currently limited repertoire performs only pan and tilt movements. Such a system could

a) provide a wide field of view (64°) low resolution (VGA) image feed for locating collaborators,

b) use its unused pixel density to digitally zoom in to the face (30° FOV) of the detected person to perform eye tracking

c) use pan and tilt for keeping focus on the face.

After discussing related work and a technical description of the system, we will report on a short experiment which validates the proposed camera system's ability to detect mutual gaze better than regular non-zoom camera solutions.

Related Work

Since their appearance, eye tracking systems have found many applications in human-machine interaction [2]. Remote eye trackers started becoming more used than head mounted ones, as they are more convenient and less intrusive. The benefit of remote systems has also been recognized in human-robot interaction studies [3]. Commercially available eye tracking systems, however, are in general very expensive and require ad hoc hardware, making the system less affordable and not customizable enough for the use in a robotic device. Our work proposes instead an active vision system developed by using affordable webcams. Drawing inspiration from the work of Atienza and Zelinsky [1], we present an active vision system with zoom capabilities, to cope with a wide interaction space and moving subjects. Our work expands on previous ideas by using affordable modern technology and by validating the benefits of a zoom system in a human subject pilot study. An important goal for eye tracking in HRI is the detection of mutual gaze [5], the exploration of which is also one of the goals of our research.

System Implementation

The robot head system consists of the visual and actuator system, see Figure 2.

Visual System

The visual system is a stereo mount of two Microsoft LifeCam Studio webcams. These cameras were selected for their high resolution (HD, 1080p, 1920x1080 actual pixels), compact size (for installing them in a humanoid robot), auto-exposure and auto-focus capabilities.

Because of the limited data bandwidth of the communication networks on modern robots we decided

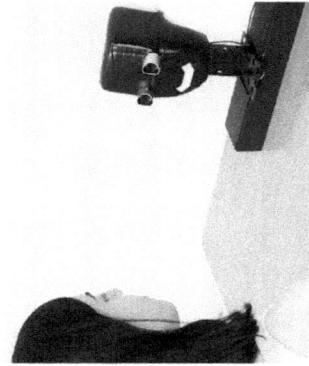

Figure 1. Human-agent interaction.

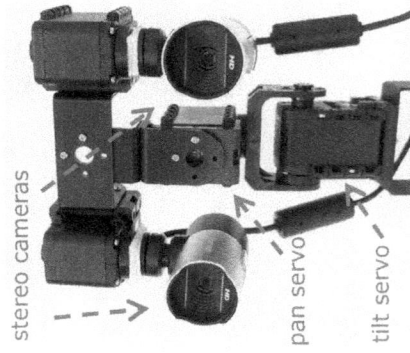

stereo cameras

pan servo

tilt servo

Figure 2. Camera and motor setup.

to constrain our system to VGA resolution of the cameras (640x480). Such a setup provides a relatively wide field of view (64°) that is adequate for recognizing people's faces in the robot's environment (using the Viola-Jones face detection algorithm in OpenCV [6]). Precise eye tracking is enabled by the cameras' digital zoom capability. This allows narrowing the field of view to 30°, while using the cameras actual sensor pixels instead of interpolation as in non-HD webcams. This dual purpose narrow-wide FOV operation mode addresses the necessity to perceive details of what is fixated rather than out-of-focus elements: we see much more precisely in a narrow cone of our eyes called the fovea, while we have lower resolution outside of it, i.e. our retina is a space-variant sensing surface [4].

Motor System

The pan and tilt movements are performed by two Dynamixel AX-12 digital servo motors. They are mounted in the neck of the robot. Additional servos will provide head roll, eye vergence, and eye tilt in future implementations. The motors are controlled in a closed loop to track the face of the human conversant and keep their face in the middle of the image.

Operation procedure

The robot head starts its operation by panning left and right. When a face is detected, the motors start to track it, keeping it in the middle of the camera images. At the same time the cameras zoom in on the face and change the zoom level continuously to keep its size in the image nearly constant even when the subject moves closer or further away. This way facial features occupy a large area of the camera images, thus providing enough pixels for eye tracking. Once a face is detected, the Viola-Jones algorithm is again used for roughly detecting the eyes. Within this area the corners

of the eyes are found using template matching and the iris is located by a circle fitting algorithm (Hough transformation), Figure 3. If the cameras lose the face for more than a second they automatically zoom out and start looking for a new face to detect, effectively restarting the process. It is worth mentioning that the proposed system uses visual light without Purkinje image tracking. It also does not need supervised face model learning for each subject.

Validation Experiment

We designed and ran a pilot study to verify some of the benefits of our system: namely, we were interested to see if mutual gaze could be more precisely detected and tracked using our pan/tilt/zoom mechanism compared to a non-zoom system. For this task only the right webcam was used. Three subject completed the test. They were asked to look either straight at the camera (mutual gaze) or 5 and 10 degrees to the left of it, as we made ten angle calculations for each offset. The distance of observation was either 40cm (near) or 80cm (far). The near condition didn't require any zooming, because the subjects' faces already occupied most of the camera image. The far condition had two options: using zoom and not using zoom. In the first one we let the previously described algorithm enlarge the face (Figure 3. below) while the latter condition did not use any zoom (Figure 3. above). Gaze direction was calculated as the angle between straight ahead position (baseline) and the detected position of the eyeball, by assuming an eyeball diameter of 24mm. Figure 4. shows the absolute error between real and detected gaze direction, averaged over all three subjects and all three angle positions. It can be noticed that the error is quite low for the "close" and "far zoom" conditions while it's much higher for the "far no-zoom" option. We

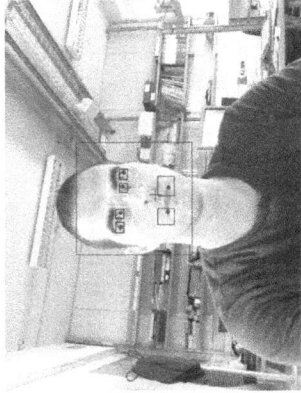

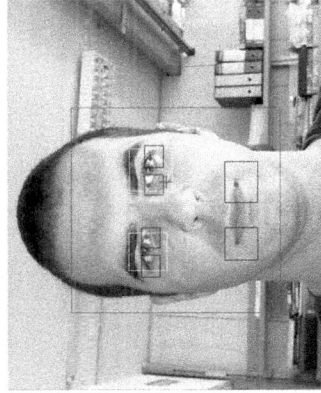

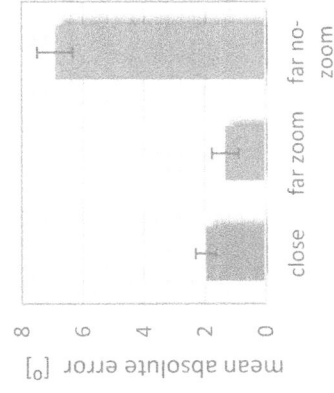

Figure 3. Zoomed out (above) and maximum zoomed in (below) images.

Figure 4. Mean absolute error.

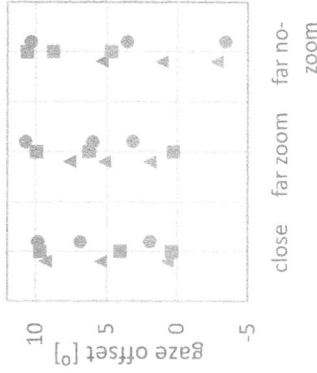

Figure 5. Average gaze points for each subject, each gaze offset and each condition. Triangular markers denote Subject01, squares Subject02 and circles Subject03. Gray markers denote straight ahead gazes, orange ones 5 degree offset, while blue stands for 10 degree offsets.

Future Work

We plan to further develop the eye tracking capabilities of our system in order to put the active vision hardware to full use. First steps will include ellipse matching of the iris and compensation for head movement/rotation. The long term goal is to make a robotic platform contingently react to the gaze of its human partner.

Acknowledgements

This work has been conducted in the framework of the European project CODEFROR (PIRSES-2013-612555).

performed a Friedman ANOVA test on the absolute errors for each subject and found that differences were highly significant ($p<0.001$). This confirmed our expectation that when the subject is far away from the robot and the face is not zoomed in, the results will have high rates of error. These levels of error effectively prohibit from detecting mutual gaze in systems with only a wide FOV. Indeed, if we assume a threshold of 4° for discriminating between mutual gaze or not, then the zoom enabled system was 90% accurate on average while the no-zoom system's performance was only 42%. Hence, mutual gaze can be detected more easily using a system like ours.

Figure 5. shows detailed results for each subject and each angle. It can be seen that for the "close" and "far zoom" options, the angle estimates for all subjects cluster around their nominal values (e.g. orange markers around 5 degrees). At the same time the "far no-zoom" option shows erratic results (markers of different colors are mixed around different nominal gaze offsets) which confirms that mutual gaze detection is very difficult when not zooming in on the face.

Conclusion and Discussion

In this paper we presented an active camera system that is designed to facilitate eye tracking for use in human-robot interaction. The pan/tilt mechanism allows the robot to a) scan its environment to find interaction partners while it's zoomed out and b) track a detected face while it is moving around in zoomed in mode. The digital zoom lets the robot perceive more details about a subject's face features, e.g. the eyes and the mouth. These details enable more precise eye tracking compared to a system without zoom. This advantage becomes evident in situations when the subject is more than 40cm away from the robot. Since

many interaction scenarios involve distances greater than 40cm, such a system would benefit most robots. A digital zoom system can be faster and much cheaper than an optical zoom lens.

The proposed active vision system is very affordable as it uses off the shelf web cameras and servo motors (less than 250EUR total), thus allowing wider and quicker dissemination. As web cameras' performance rapidly increases with every new generation, they could slowly replace much more expensive systems for robot applications, also thanks to OpenCV library, which makes it simple to calibrate these low-cost cameras for manufacturing imperfections.

References

[1] Atienza, R., and Zelinsky, A., Active Gaze Tracking for Human-Robot Interaction, Proceedings of Intl. Conf. on Multimodal Interfaces, 2002.

[2] Jacob, R. J. K. and Karn, K. S., Eye tracking in human-Computer interaction and usability research, in The Mind's Eye: Cognitive and Applied Aspects of Eye Movement Research, 2003.

[3] Matsumoto, Y., Sasao, N., Suenaga, T, and Ogasawara, T., 3D Model-based 6-DOF Head Tracking by a Single Camera for Human-Robot Interaction, Proceedings of ICRA 2009.

[4] Sandini, G., Questa, P., Scheffer, D., Diericks, B., & Mannucci, A., A retina-like CMOS sensor and its applications. Proc. of Sensor Array and Multichannel Signal Processing Workshop. 2000.

[5] Scassellati, B., Imitation and mechanisms of joint attention: A developmental structure for building social skills in a humanoid robot. In Comput. for Metaphors, Analogy and Agents (Nehaniv, C., ed.), Vol. 1562,1998.

[6] Viola, P., and Jones, M., Rapid object detection using a boosted cascade of simple features. Proceedings CVPR, 2001.

Evaluation of a Video Communication System with Speech-Driven Embodied Entrainment Audience Characters with Partner's Face

Yutaka Ishii

Faculty of Computer Science and Systems Engineering,
Okayama Prefectural University
111 Kuboki, Soja, Okayama, Japan
ishii@cse.oka-pu.ac.jp

Tomio Watanabe

Faculty of Computer Science and Systems Engineering,
Okayama Prefectural University
111 Kuboki, Soja, Okayama, Japan
watanabe@cse.oka-pu.ac.jp

Abstract

We previously proposed an embodied video communication system called E-VChat, in which a

HAI '14, Oct 29-31 2014, Tsukuba, Japan
ACM 978-1-4503-3035-0/14/10.
http://dx.doi.org/10.1145/2658861.2658927

computer-generated (CG) avatar is superimposed on the other talker's video image in a face-to-face scene, so that they can better comprehend their mutual interactions during remote communication. In this study, an advanced video communication system that includes audience characters showing a partner's face is proposed. This system provides a more interactive space that makes it easy to communicate by clearly distinguishing the simple audience characters from the functional substitutes of the partner. A communication experiment is performed to confirm the effectiveness of the system for 12 pairs of 24 talkers.

Author Keywords

Video communication; human interaction; embodied avatar; virtual face-to-face communication; decision making

ACM Classification Keywords

H.5.1 Multimedia Information Systems.

Introduction

Video chat systems provide a means to show nonverbal behavior such as a nod or facial expression of a person who is speaking. People communicate smoothly using nonverbal information such as a gesture and a nod in face-to-face communication; thus, various communication supports that focus on this nonverbal information were examined previously [1],[2].

We developed a video communication system called E-VChat [3] that provides support for the sharing of a physical rhythm with a partner. The system uses a speech-driven embodied entrainment computer-generated (CG) character called InterActor [4] which automatically generates communicative motions such as a nod on speech input in order to activate embodied interactions.

In this study, we describe a new video communication system with audience characters that have a partner's face. This system provides a more interactive space that makes it easy to communicate by clearly distinguishing between simple audience characters and functional substitutes of a partner. This system has audience characters, with the partner's face detected using face tracking by way of image processing.

E-VChat System

Overview

In the E-VChat system, talkers can smoothly realize mutual interaction awareness by generating a virtual face-to-face scene. A CG character that is substituted for the talker aids in the sharing of physical rhythms by performing the speaker and listener motions according to speech inputs such as a gesture and a nod. Moreover, the system prototype was developed to link the head motion of a speaker to a self-character. This system can reflect the speaker's intentions onto the self-character such as affirmation and negation. In addition, we confirm the effectiveness of this system by

performing a communication experiment in free conversation. Furthermore, we developed an advanced system that superimposes not only a self-character but also audience characters, which perform listener motions on a partner's video image (Figure 1).

Self-character configuration

The self-character to be used in the E-VChat is the InterActor. First, the moving-average (MA) model, which nods in correspondence with the talker's voice data, generates character motions for the listener character model [4]. The MA model of the speaker allows the avatar's head and body motions to be linked to the on-off pattern of speech. A motion-capture device that monitors the head is also used to facilitate communication and avoid misunderstanding. The avatar's motions are generated using measurements of the talker's motions that are recorded by a motion-capture device (Kinect for Windows L6M-00005). The avatar's motions are represented on the basis of the measured head motions.

Method of Character Superimposition

When a camera is mounted on the monitor, a camera will look down the talker, and the gap between the gaze line of the talker gazing at the screen and the gaze line for the camera is calculated. Then, the partner's image from the frontal viewpoint appears to face the self-character by arranging the self-character in the center of the lower part of the screen. Virtual face-to-face projection using the self-character and the partner's image reduces the incongruity caused by the gaze gap.

Figure 1. E-VChat System.

E-VChat System with the Characters with the Partner's Face

Concept

We propose a new video communication system with audience characters that have the partner's face around the partner's image. The talker can recognize interactive avatars of the partner instead of just audience characters by superimposing the partner's face image on the characters. These audience characters also perform the communicative listener motions on the basis of speech input. Even when the partner's reaction is subtle and cannot be expressed for various reasons, audience characters can perform skillful communicative reactions and give affirmative impressions to the talker.

Method of Superimposing a Partner's Face on a Character

A partner's face is detected using position information of the face that is obtained by using the face-tracking feature of Kinect. The circumference of the partner's face is saved as a picture by performing a keystroke, and the partner's face compounds as a texture to the face of audience characters. A face picture composition image is shown in Figure 2. The screenshot of usage is shown in Figure 3. A self-character is arranged in the destination of the gaze line of the partner, and audience characters are arranged around the partner.

Communication Experiment

Experimental Setup

We performed an experiment to evaluate E-VChat in two different

rooms, both having the same layout. In the experiment, we compared two operation modes. In both modes, the talker's head motions were reflected, and all characters were based on the talker's voice. In Mode A, the self-character and the audience characters were arranged. In Mode B, the self-character and the audience characters with the partner's face were arranged. First, the subjects (12 pairs of Japanese students) used the system, and we confirmed that they were familiar with its operation. They were then introduced to the two operation modes and the differences between them while using the system. In addition, they practiced so that they would become accustomed to the key operation, and they communicated with the system in freely conversation to experience the difference of both modes. This phase took approximately 10 minutes. Next, the subjects were instructed to perform a paired comparison of each mode as an overall evaluation. Finally, the subjects scored their rating using a seven-point bipolar scale from -3 (not at all) to 3 (extremely). A score of 0 denotes "moderately" for the eight items, which were "Enjoyment," "Ease of talking," "Sense of unity" (a subject can feel a sense of unity with a partner), "Relief" (a subject can feel secure with the partner), "Excitement," "Reaction of the partner," "Like," and "Preference." After performing their tasks in each mode, the subjects filled out a questionnaire.

After the experiment in freely conversation, we performed the experiment under the decision-making task that subjects selected an answer from opinions different each other. These claims based on the questionnaire of 40 items about daily life, such as "Is it a dog or a cat if you have a pet?" The decision-making experiment was also consisted of a paired comparison

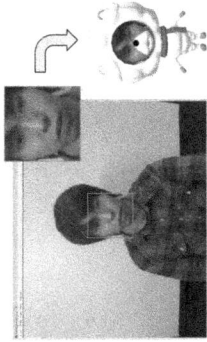

Figure 2. Image of compounding partner's face.

Figure 3. Screen shot.

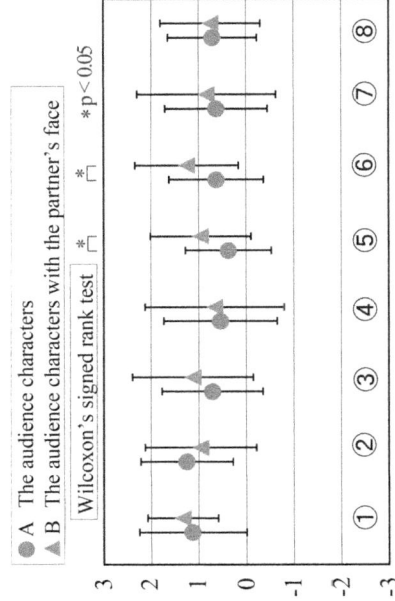

● A The audience characters
▲ B The audience characters with the partner's face

Wilcoxon's signed rank test   * $p < 0.05$

① Enjoyment, ② Ease of talking, ③ Sense of unity, ④ Relief
⑤ Excitement, ⑥ Reaction of the partner, ⑦ Like, ⑧ Preference

Figure 4. Seven points bipolar rating in the experiment under the freely conversation.

References

[1] Ishii, R., Ozawa, S., Mukouchi, T., and Matsuura, N.: MoPaCo: Pseudo 3D Video Communication System, Human Interface, Part II, HCII 2011, LNCS 6772, pp. 131–140 (2011).

[2] Kim, K., Bolton, J., Girouard, A., Cooperstock, J., and Vertegaal, R.: TeleHuman: Effects of 3D Perspective on Gaze and Pose Estimation with a Life-size Cylindrical Telepresence Pod, Proc. of CHI2012, pp. 2531–2540 (2012).

[3] Takada, T., Ishii, Y., and Watanabe, T., "Development of an Embodied Video Communication System with a Superimposed Entrainment Character Driven by Voice and Head Motion Inputs", Proc. of STSS2012, No.40, pp.1-4 (2012).

[4] Watanabe, T., Okubo, M., Nakashige, M., and Danbara, R.: InterActor: Speech-Driven Embodied Interactive Actor; International Journal of Human-Computer Interaction, Vol.17, No.1, pp.43–60 (2004).

and a seven-point bipolar scale of the same eight items. Subjects made a decision in 10 minutes. If they couldn't, the extra time was added just 1 minute.

Results

For the reader's convenience, the results of the means and the standard deviations for seven-point bipolar scales are shown in Figure 4 for the freely conversation and Figure 5 for the decision-making task, respectively. In Figure 4, a significance level of 5% was obtained for the "Excitement," and "Reaction of the partner" by administering the Wilcoxon rank sum test for multiple comparisons. In Figure 5, a significance level of 1% was obtained for the "Reaction of the partner." Mode B was positively evaluated from these results in both figures. The results of the paired comparison of the two modes are shown in Figure 6. In a freely conversation situation, 17 subjects selected the scene using the audience characters with the partner's face. A significance level of 5% was obtained by administering the Chi-square test. Result of the mode using for selected user in the decision-making task is shown in Figure 7. The opinions of subjects using the mode B were selected in the tests of 61%.

Conclusions

In this paper, we developed a video communication system with audience characters that have a partner's face and examined the effectiveness of this system by the sensory evaluation of a communication experiment.

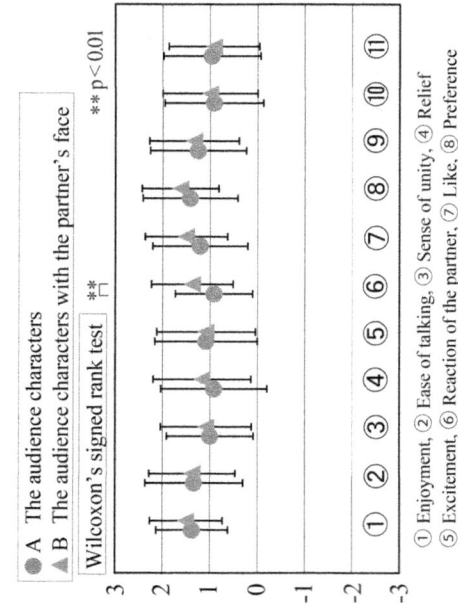

Figure 5. Seven points bipolar rating in the experiment under the decision-making task.

① Enjoyment, ② Ease of talking, ③ Sense of unity, ④ Relief
⑤ Excitement, ⑥ Reaction of the partner, ⑦ Like, ⑧ Preference

● A The audience characters
▲ B The audience characters with the partner's face

Wilcoxon's signed rank test ** ** p<0.01

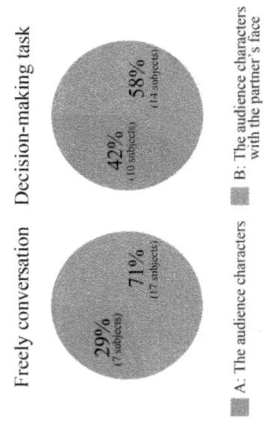

Figure 6. Result of the Mode using for selected user in the decision-making

Freely conversation   Decision-making task

A: The audience characters   B: The audience characters with the partner's face

29% (7 subjects)   71% (17 subjects)

42% (10 subjects)   58% (14 subjects)

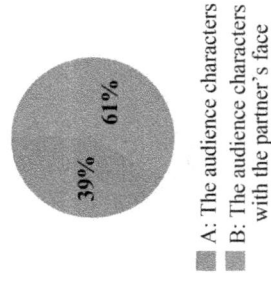

A: The audience characters
B: The audience characters with the partner's face

39%   61%

Figure 7. The results of the paired comparison in two experiments.

Dynamic Dialog System for Human Robot Collaboration - Playing a Game of Pairs

First Author

1st Andreas Kipp
Applied Informatics,
Bielefeld University
Universitätsstr. 1-3,
Bielefeld Germany
akipp@techfak.uni-bielefeld.de

Second Author

Franz Kummert
Applied Informatics,
Bielefeld University
Universitätsstr. 1-3,
Bielefeld Germany
franz@techfak.uni-bielefeld.de

HAI 2014, October 29-31, 2014, Tsukuba, Japan.
ACM 978-1-4503-3035-0/14/10.
http://dx.doi.org/10.1145/2658861.2658928

Abstract

This paper presents results of a first study for a human-robot-interaction in which the robot Flobi autonomously plays the game "pairs" against a human player. Integrated is a dialog system which can use different dynamic sentence structures for altering the verbal output during the interaction. The system is compared with a dialog system using static sentences with high information detail and a system using static short sentences. The results suggest that using a dynamic system results in a more satisfying gameplay.

Author Keywords

Humanrobot interaction; Interaction aware robot; Socially interactive robot; Entertaining robotic gameplay; Spoken dialog system

ACM Classification Keywords

I.2.1 [Applications and Expert Systems]: Games.

Introduction and Related Work

To establish a social interaction between humans and robots most scenarios are designed to fulfill a collaborative task. The human supports the robot by performing a specific task and vice versa. In many cases this is realized by verbal communication using a dialog system. Both parties explain their wishes and beliefs and comment on the partners actions.

In this paper a first study is discussed, where a human and a robot play the game "pairs". In our study we use the robot head Flobi (see figure 1), which lacks the ability to turn cards on its own. To cope with this disadvantage he needs to tell his opponent how to play with him by using verbal communication.

Castellano et al.[1] showed that a robot playing chess can be seen as a companion which must be able to display a social behavior. Emotional feedback based on context information was used to analyze the humans engagement towards the robot while playing the game.

To support this a dynamic verbal communication may be helpful. Qvarfordt et al.[4] showed that if a system provides information and answers every time the same way, users tend to classify the system to be tool-like. If a system is capable of giving different answers and vary the verbal output the system will be classified more human like.

The following sections give a coarse description of our system, the design of the first study and presents the results.

Game-play for Human-Robot Interaction

The robot platform used for the study is the anthropomorphic robot head Flobi[2] developed at the Bielefeld University.

Due to the lack of manipulators Flobi communicates its wishes and beliefs to the player via speech output. For this a dialog system [3] is integrated which allows Flobi to structure the verbal interaction and to react on feedback

given by the human player. While playing Flobi can give explanations about the rules, how cards should be turned and he notifies the player about results (e.g. pair or no pair, winner, etc.). A speech recognition component records the players answers with a wireless microphone and forwards the results to the dialog system. To control and structure the interaction a state-machine is implemented representing the game "pairs". This component is used to orchestrate robot control, vision and dialog system and allows a full autonomous interaction.

For every verbal action of the game different sentences were defined in the dialog system. Multiple sentences are given for one action to create more variance for the output. Sentences are given in hierachical order beginning with a high information value down to very short sentences containing only needed information for the action. When a sentence is used for output for the first time it consist of a higher information detail giving the user a good insight of what the robot wants the player to do. If the action occurs again, the dialog system selects the next shorter version from the alternatives. This procedure is repeated until the shortest version for a given action is reached. At this point the dialog selects only the shortest sentence for the rest of the game (example see table 1).

Study Design

To analyze the effect of using the different sentence structures in an human-robot interaction 30 participants (age 22-61, 18 female and 12 male) were recruited for the study. In this first study the facial expression and motion possibilities of Flobi are left out to focus on the dialog elements.

Our hypothesis is that a non static communication will enrich the interaction and result in a higher user

Figure 1: The robot head Flobi[2].

(1)	"From your point of view in the first row turn the third card."
(2)	"Please turn in the first row the third card."
(3)	"Turn the third card in row one."

Table 1: Dialogexamples for the dynamic structure.

satisfaction. Using dynamic sentence structures will also lead to a more fluent and faster game-play. If the dialog consist of repeated static sentences the user will get bored and will not play consecutive rounds. If only short and less informative sentences are used the user will get confused which results in misunderstanding and frustration.

For the study the participants were divided into three groups. Each group plays one condition. Flobis speech output for the group one (9 participants) consists only of the long sentences (L) designed for the dialog system. Group two (12 participants) gained the dynamic speech output (D). The third group (9 participants) directly received the shortest version of each sentence (S) from the beginning until the end of the game. The whole interaction was recorded by using an external camera, a microphone and Flobis cameras (see figure 2). A questionnaire was given to the participant before and after the interaction. The range for an answer to a question goes from one to six. When filling the first questionnaire the participant did not know that the game "pairs" will be played.

Results

All questionnaires are compared between the three conditions. For each item a Kruskal-Wallis-Test was performed on the three groups. From the results only the item "has the robot a mind or not" ($\chi^2(2,N=30)=8.031$, $p=.018$) shows significance. The items "artificial vs realistic" ($\chi^2(2,N=30)=5.895$, $p=.052$) and "lacy vs active" ($\chi^2(2,N=30)=5.588$, $p=.061$) show a tendency for significance. For our hypothesis we focus on the dynamic system and its advantages against the long static sentences and the short ones. For this we tested for significance by using the Mann-Whitney for condition D versus the condition S and L. Looking at the user's feeling

of the speed of the whole interaction, condition D ($M=2.5$, $SD=1.83$) does not significantly differ from condition L ($M=2.19$, $SD=0.82$), $U=58.0$, $p=.39$, and S ($M=3.63$, $SD=1.32$), $U=60.5$, $p=.16$). Checking item "Does the robot speak too much?" results show that the participants preferred condition D compared to L ($U=78.0$, $p=.04$). Considering an effect of missing information which results in confusion of the participant by using only S no significant effect could be found from the questionnaire. From all answers given to questions concerning the coordinate system or instructions given by Flobi no misunderstandings or the need for more information could be found. The question "Is the robot more machine or human like?" showed a significant difference for condition L to D ($U=80.0$, $p=.032$) and to S ($U=60.5$, $p=.038$) pointing out that L makes the human see the robot more tool-like. This is supported by the questions "Is the robot artificial or realistic?" for D compared to L ($U=86.0$, $p=.011$). For S this question showed no significant difference to L ($U=56.0$, $p=.08$). The question "Mind vs. no mind" is also significant comparing L to D ($U=91.0$, $p=.004$). For this question there was again no significant difference between L and S ($U=55.5$, $p=.09$). For analyzing the objective measures the videos recorded were annotated regarding the length of the robots speech synthesis and how long a participant played with flobi (by marking all rounds in one game). The length of a game and its rounds are used to check how fluent a game is and if condition D results in faster game-play. From the annotated results the mean time per round does not significantly differ between all three conditions. Condition D ($M=8.72$ min, $SD=2.73$ min) is in average 0.6 minutes faster then condition L ($M=9.39$ min, $SD=4.89$ min) with $U=96.0$, $p=.29$. Compared to condition S it is nearly 0.6 minutes slower with $U=96.0$, $p=.34$.

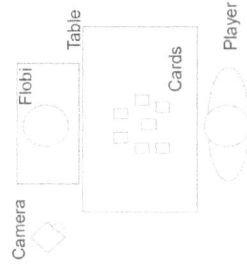

Figure 2: The setup for the experiment with the player and Flobi.

Discussion

By using a dynamic sentence structure for a human-robot interaction the humans perception of the system results in a less tool-like manner. A dynamic structure allows to remove unnecessary information in later situations which results in a more interesting and faster game-play. This can enhance the satisfaction of the user and increase his experience made by playing the game. The results of the study are used to extend the system for the main study. The data from the positive feedback on dynamic sentence structures suggests that users would prefer a robot which alters more elements in the communication instead of repeating static announcement on its beliefs. Breaking the communication down to simple and short sentences results in a tool-like perception of the system. This shows that starting with full information and then shorten the information up till the end of a game may be a good way to keep the human players satisfaction at a higher level. Results taken from the logging files support this showing that the dynamic system needs less utterances for the communication. As result from this insight additional sentences structures for the dynamic system have been added. Also a randomization process is integrated switching between sentences whenever a given action reaches the shortest versions of a sentence. Another addition is the integration of more feedback upon request by the user. Users argued that sometimes the system did not show its state on important elements like whose turn it is or who leads the current round. The underlying state system is extended to cope with this and to allow the dialog to give more feedback upon request.

Conclusion

The study focused on testing the implemented autonomous system for its capability to perform in a long term isolation study. We found that the dialog system with altering dynamic responses is preferred by the user and results in an interesting game-play and a good rate of user satisfaction. Compared to a static system with longer sentences results show that user rate such a system more like a tool. For the future several additions for the scenario are planned, like adding a memory component which allows the dialog to access information about past games with a specific user. Also the possibilities of adding more emotional feedback given by the robot is a topic which is under heavy development to enrich the interaction.

Acknowledgments

This work is supported by the DFG, EXC 277 CITEC and the German Aerospace Center (support code 50RA1023) with funds from the Federal Ministry of Economics and Technology due to resolution of the German Bundestag.

References

[1] Castellano, G., Leite, I., Pereira, A., Martinho, C., Paiva, A., and McOwan, P. W. It's all in the game: Towards an affect sensitive and context aware game companion. In *Affective Computing and Intelligent Interaction and Workshops, 2009. ACII 2009. 3rd International Conference on* (2009), 1–8.

[2] Lutkebohle, I., Hegel, F., Schulz, S., Hackel, M., Wrede, B., Wachsmuth, S., and Sagerer, G. The bielefeld anthropomorphic robot head flobi. In *Robotics and Automation (ICRA), 2010 IEEE International Conference on* (2010), 3384–3391.

[3] Peltason, J., and Wrede, B. Modeling human-robot interaction based on generic interaction patterns. In *AAAI Fall Symposium: Dialog with Robots*, AAAI (2010).

[4] Qvarfordt, P., Jnsson, A., and Dahlbck, N. The role of spoken feedback in experiencing multimodal interfaces as human-like. In *In Proceedings of ICMI03* (2003).

Unification of Demonstrative Pronouns in a Small Group Guided by a Robot

Takashi Ichijo

Graduate School of Information
Science and Technology,
Hokkaido University, Japan
ichijo@complex.ist.hokudai.ac.jp

Nagisa Munekata

Graduate School of Information
Science and Technology,
Hokkaido University, Japan
munekata@complex.ist.hokudai.ac.jp

Tetsuo Ono

Graduate School of Information
Science and Technology,
Hokkaido University, Japan
tono@ist.hokudai.ac.jp

HAI '14, Oct 29-31 2014, Tsukuba, Japan
ACM 978-1-4503-3035-0/14/10.
http://dx.doi.org/10.1145/2658861.2658929

Abstract

For realizing smooth communication, participants'
viewpoints and usages of demonstrative pronouns
assume an important role. Moreover, they both are
strongly associated and construct a dialogue structure
among participants. In this study, we investigate the
relation constructed by their viewpoints and usages of
demonstrative pronouns in a small group. Especially,
we conducted experiments to verify whether
demonstrative pronouns were unified in a small group
consisted of two participants and a robot guided by the
robot, and evaluate participants' psychological factors
on this occasion. As a result of experiments, the
unification of demonstrative pronouns in the small
group guided by the robot led participants to smooth
communication.

Author Keywords

Robot; Group interaction; Pronouns; Joint attention;

ACM Classification Keywords

I.2.9 [**Artificial Intelligence**]:Robotics

Introduction

Usage of demonstrative pronouns plays significant
roles for realizing smooth communication [1]. One of
the roles is to indicate an object for communication
more briefly. Moreover, the pronouns are used for a

number of descriptive purposes, e.g., indicating unknown and unspeakable objects, because the usages of those are simple. From another perspective, the usages of pronouns can promote communication due to simplify repeated objects in communication by using the pronouns.

Moreover, participants' viewpoints and the usages of demonstrative pronouns are strongly associated in communication [2]. To make the pronouns work adequately, participants need to understand the indicated object mutually [3]. In fact, it is difficult to identify the object only using other participant's utterances. Therefore, we can identify the object being guided by the participant's viewpoint in accordance with day-to-day manner.

In daily communication, the usages of misidentified pronouns happen routinely because they are subjective described in Table 1, and change dynamically in themselves along with conversation progresses. Accordingly, the disagreement of the pronouns may obstruct smooth communication because each participant has to transform the meaning of the pronouns. To put it the other way around, unification of demonstrative pronouns achieves smooth communication.

In this study, we investigate the relation constructed by their viewpoints and usages of demonstrative pronouns in a small group. Especially, we conduct experiments to verify whether demonstrative pronouns should be unified in a small group guided by the robot (see Fig. 1), and evaluate participants' psychological factors on this occasion.

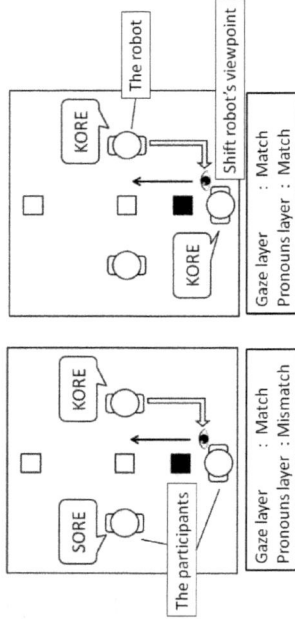

Fig. 1 Outline of this study.

Demonstrative Pronouns	Meaning by oneself and an object	Meaning including a partner
KORE (this)	The short distance from oneself	Near the oneself
SORE (that)	The middle distance from oneself	Near the partner
ARE (that over there)	Far side from oneself	Far side from them

Table. 1 The meaning of Japanese demonstrative pronouns.

Experiment Environment

Fig. 1 shows an outline of experiment environment. We placed a robot (Robovie-R) and one participant (Left) across the table. And the other participant (Center) was located in front of the display across the table. We set the distance between the robot and participants to 1.2 m [4]. Three differently numbered objects (1, 2, and 3) were displayed on the table. The object 2 was placed between the robot and one participant (Left). And the distance between the object 1 and 2 was 60 cm, meanwhile the distance between the object 2 and 3 was 150 cm. 10 participants took part in the experiment (male: 9, female: 1).

In this experiment, the robot shifted its viewpoint to the center participant's and used the pronouns which s/he was using. It meant the robot used the unified pronouns with him/her.

Moreover, we achieved conversation with the robot by the WOZ method [5] in the experiment.

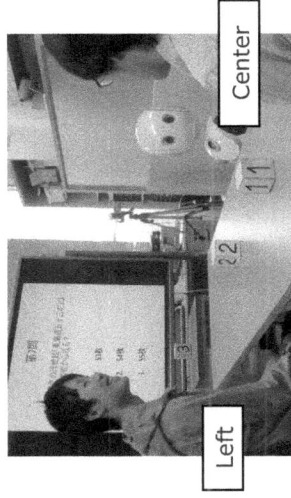

Fig. 2 Experiment environment.

Experiment Procedure

In the experiments, we gave three-choice questions to the participants. The content of questions was not only one based on knowledge but also open questions that provoke thought. The participants and the robot discussed and unified their answer by using their pronouns. After unifying the answer, participants gave it to the experimenter by using the pronouns. It repeated 10 times.

Then there were three experimental constraints in the experimental procedure. First, the participants were set the position limit. Second, they could not express the choices verbally nor the number of choices in the discussion. Third, they could not use pointing gestures. Therefore, participants suggested their choices by using pronouns and the line of sight to the numbered objects.

In the questionnaire, participants were asked to guess 1) how cooperative the robot was, 2) which participant constructed better relationship with the robot, 3) how much attention to the robot's viewpoint, and 4) whether the robot's pronouns was unnatural or not.

Experimental Results

Fig. 3 shows the results of the questionnaires on robot's cooperativeness. All participants felt good about robot's responses. It suggested that there was no difference between the robot's behaviors such as pros and cons by using WOZ method.

Fig. 4 shows which participant constructed better relationship with the robot. The center participants constructed better relationships significantly (p < .05). In all groups, there was no answer that the left participants constructed better relationship. Accordingly, in the condition of unification of the pronouns, the participants constructed better relation than in that of confusion of them.

The participants did not pay attention to the robot's viewpoint (Fig. 5). Moreover, eight participants did not feel anything wrong about the robot's pronouns (Fig. 6). It could be said that participants had much tolerance for changing pronouns. However, two participants noticed and felt that the usage of these pronouns was unnatural. We need to investigate about a method of the changing pronouns naturally depending on circumstances.

confusion of them. Moreover, they had much tolerance for changing pronouns.

We think the unification of the pronouns leads participants to smooth communication. Therefore, we will need to investigate about a method of changing pronouns naturally depending on circumstances. Moreover, if robots can shift their viewpoints and move toward unification naturally, human-robot communication will become more smoothly.

Reference

[1] H. Ishiguro, T. Ono, M. Imai, T. Maeda, T. Kanda, and R. Nakatsu: Robovie: A robot generates episode chains in our daily life, { Proceedings of the 32nd ISR(International Symposium on Robotics) }, pp.1356-1361 (2001)

[2] M. Imai, K. Hiraki, T. Miyasato, R. Nakatsu, and Y. Anzai: Interaction With Robots: Physical Constraints on the Interpretation of Demonstrative Pronouns, {International Journal of Human-Computer Interaction}, 16(2), pp.367-384 (2003)

[3] Y. Matsusaka, T. Tojo, S. Kubota, K. Furukawa, D. Tamiya, K. Hayata, Y. Nakano, and T. Kobayashi: Multi-person conversation via multi-modal interface-a robot who communicate with multi-user-, { EUROSPEECH }, Vol. 99, pp.1723-1726 (1999).

[4] J. Mumm, and B. Mutlu: Human-robot proxemics: physical and psychological distancing in human-robot interaction, {Proceedings of the 6th International Conference on Human-Robot Interaction}, pp.331-338 (2011).

[5] N. M. Fraser and G. N. Gilbert: Simulating Speech Systems, {Computer Speech and Language}, Vol.5, No.1, pp.81-99 (1991)

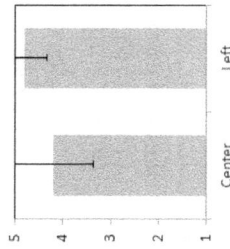

Fig.3 Cooperative attitude towards the robot.(5=high, 1=low)

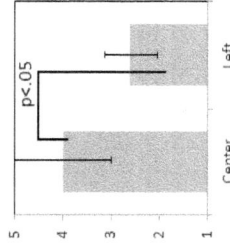

Fig.4 Which participant constructed better relationship with the robot? (5=you, 1=other participant)

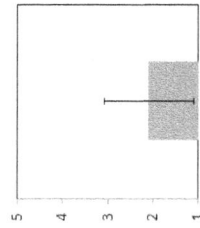

Fig. 5 Participants' attention to the robot's viewpoint.(5=high, 1=low)

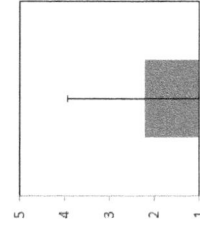

Fig.6 unnaturalness about robot's pronouns.(5=unnatural, 1=not unnatural)

Conclusion & Future Work

In this study, we investigated the relation constructed by participants' viewpoints and usages of demonstrative pronouns in a small group. We set two conditions: one was in the unification of pronouns, the other was in the confusion of them. As a result of the experiments, in the condition of the unification, the participants constructed better relation than in that of

Evaluating an Intuitive Teleoperation Platform Explored In a Long-distance Interview

Ritta Baddoura

Université Lyon 1 ; INSERM U846
18 avenue du Doyen Lépine,
69500 Bron, France
ritta.baddoura@inserm.fr

Gentiane Venture

Tokyo University of Agriculture and Technology
2-24-16 Nakacho Koganei-shi
184-8588 Tokyo, Japan
venture@cc.tuat.ac.jp

Guillaume Gibert

Université Lyon 1 ; INSERM U846
18 avenue du Doyen Lépine,
69500 Bron, France
guillaume.gibert@inserm.fr

HAI '14, Oct 29-31 2014, Tsukuba, Japan
ACM 978-1-4503-3035-0/14/10.
http://dx.doi.org/10.1145/2658861.2658930

Abstract

SWooZ is an intuitive teleoperation platform using a humanoid robot as a proxy between two humans: a remote user teleoperating the robot and a local user interacting directly with it. NAO (Aldebaran) is the proxy used in this study. The remote user controls its head motion with his own movements (live) while his real voice is transmitted to the local user with an unnoticeable lag time. This paper presents a user study of the platform in the context of a long-distance survey and investigates the possible effect of the remote user's previous experience with robots on the local users' evaluation of the proxy. Although found useful, likable and satisfying by all the local users, only the ones interviewed by the non-naive user find it averagely credible. Results fail to validate an effect of the remote users' previous experience with robots on the local users.

Author Keywords

Teleoperation; user study; humanoid proxy; social robotics; previous experience with robots; head motion.

ACM Classification Keywords

Design; experimentation; human factors; measurement.

Introduction

Various studies show the interest of using teleoperation and telepresence robots [2, 4] in different fields such as remote education health care environments or offices. We developed SWoOZ, a teleoperation setup that mirrors face, eye and head motion on a humanoid robot and consequently allows the generation of spontaneous movements in order to support a natural interaction [1]. In this setup, a humanoid robot is used as a proxy between two humans. One human, the remote user, is bound with the humanoid robot and controls its head motion in real-time and free of attached sensors. The remote user perceives the scene almost as if she or he was present in the same room with his human interlocutor, called the local user. The humanoid head motion for instance, as the local user sees it, is the direct translation of the remote user's motion. In order to evaluate this teleoperation platform, we started a study in the context of a realistic long-distance survey.

Methods

Experimental Setup & Equipment

The SWoOZ platform consists of A) a system able to estimate the remote user's head pose thanks to a consumer depth camera [1]. B) A software program to apply online manipulation to specific parameters. C) A humanoid robot: NAO (Aldebaran). Once the data are estimated, they are sent to the robot so that it mimics the estimated motion of the remote user's head. Further information about the SWoOZ platform can be found in [2]. The remote user's voice captured by a microphone is transmitted to the local user interacting with the robot through a small speaker positioned behind it. To bind the remote user to the robot and enable her or him to sense the scene almost as if she

or he was seated in its place, auditory and visual feedbacks are transmitted to her or him using a High Definition webcam positioned behind the robot and binaural microphones discreetly placed on its body.

Participants

Two male remote users (one naive and another non-naive) and 20 naive local users (previous exposure to robots was controlled prior to the experiment) volunteered to take part in the study. The 22 candidates are Japanese students from Tokyo University of Agriculture and Technology (TUAT). All of them range in age from 19 to 25 years old. The naive remote user (never used or interacted with robots before) interviewed 14 local users (9 males, 5 females). This group of local users will be referred as X in the rest of the text. The non-naive remote user (who has previously used NAO for HRI studies) interviewed 6 local users (5 males; 1 female). This group of local users will be referred as Y. Both were trained to perform the interview. More generally, the experimental design aims at defining a precise and repeatable conversational context.

Materials, Procedure & Data collection

The experiment took place on a Japanese university campus. The local and the remote users volunteered to participate in an anonymous survey lead by a Japanese researcher working in France. They were informed about the following: a) The interview is live mediated by a humanoid robot, b) The interview room is filmed using two cameras, c) The remote user's and the local user's voices are recorded and IMU sensors are used for head motion capture for future analysis. The remote user teleoperating the robot is in room A while the robot NAO and the local user are facing each other in room B, a real meeting room. When the local user is seated, the remote user addresses him or her, and provides a recapitulation of the survey context. The local user is reminded that there are no false and right answers: only personal opinions are expected. Then the interview starts. It consists of 15 questions revolving around the specificities of the Japanese and French cultures. The interview's overall duration is 10 min and when it is completed, the remote user asks the local user to fill the questionnaire placed on the table.

The questionnaire consists of 40 items divided into 5 sets assessing various aspects of the local users' evaluation of the proxy. At this first phase of the study, only two sets of the questionnaire (the first and the fourth) are used to investigate (1) the local users' evaluation of the robot proxy as teleoperated through the SWoOz platform, (2) the effects of the remote user's previous exposure to robots on the local users' evaluation. These two sets use a 5-point Likert scale (the points go from 0 to 4; 0 = not at all; 4 = to a high degree). The Cronbach's alpha of the questionnaire is 0.91 which shows a good internal reliability.

Hypotheses

We first hypothesize that the remote user's previous exposure to HRI will impact the local users' experience of the interaction as well as their ratings and that the evaluations made by X will be significantly different from the ones made by Y (H1). Regarding the local users' evaluation of the proxy, the focus is on their ratings of its usefulness, likability, credibility and on their satisfaction with it. Based on a preliminary study performed using the SWoOz setup [2] as well as on the proxy's capacity to mirror the remote user's head motion and transmit his real human voice in real-time, we expect the local users' ratings of usefulness, likability and satisfaction to be above the average

score, 2 being the average on this 5-point Likert scale (H2). From another perspective, the authors in [3] showed that the participants expect the robot's appearance to match its task during an interview context. Knowing that the appearance of this 58-cm tall humanoid does not seem the most appropriate to match the image of a researcher, we expect that the local users give poor ratings to its credibility (H3).

Results

We calculated the descriptive statistics (95% CI) based on the local users' ratings of the humanoid proxy's performance. X and Y generally gave it medium-to-low ratings and Y seemed to have given more generous scores than X. X considered that the robot failed in being credible (X: $M= 1.28$, $SD= 1.03$) (H3 validated for X). Nevertheless, they found the proxy rather satisfying (X: $M= 2.14$, $SD= 1.30$), likable (X: $M= 2.07$, $SD= 1.10$) and useful (X: $M= 2.5$, $SD= 1.11$) (H2 validated for X). Y found the proxy averagely satisfying (Y: $M= 2.00$, $SD= 0.81$), likable (Y: $M= 2.83$, $SD= 0.68$) and useful (Y: $M= 2.5$, $SD= 1.11$) (H2 validated for Y). Contrary to X, they found the NAO proxy rather credible (Y: $M= 2.33$, $SD= 1.10$) (H3 infirmed for Y).

We did a Mann-Whitney test to ascertain if the differences between X and Y scores are statistically significant, thus implying an effect of the remote users' previous experience with robots on their evaluations. The observed U-values ranged between 22 and 41.5 and failed to be significant as they were superior to the U critical value (17) at $p \leq 0.05$ (H1 infirmed). Some interesting associations regarding the useful aspect of the proxy were revealed for both X and Y when calculating the Spearman rank correlations. These positive dependencies showed that the more the local users found NAO useful, the more they appreciated its credibility (X: corr.= 0.61, p= 0.01; Y: corr. = 0.78, p= 0.06) and the more they found it satisfying (X: corr.= 0.57, p= 0.03; Y: corr.= 0.91, p= 0.01).

Discussion and Conclusion

The local users showed a moderate to low appraisal of the proxy's performance. The results failed to validate an effect of the remote users' previous experience with robots on their answers (H1 infirmed). The hypotheses 2 and 3 were validated for X but only hypothesis 2 was confirmed for Y who rated the proxy as averagely credible. The validated correlations also showed that the proxy's credibility is positively correlated with its usefulness which is also associated to the satisfaction of the local users with it. Based on that and knowing that the proxy's usefulness was averagely rated, it is possible to suggest that in order to improve the local users' evaluation of the proxy's usefulness, one interesting possibility would be to work on enhancing its credibility by investigating what might have limited it in this study: the lack of adequacy of the robot's appearance with the researcher's role or its limited communication and expressive features. Indeed, it is possible that NAO's appearance and its interactive abilities did not match its role as a mediator.

When considering the difference between X and Y when rating the proxy's credibility, the question of whether the remote users' previous experience impacted their evaluations or not, appears legitimate. But the statistical results did not validate this effect. The small size of the sample interviewed by the non-naive user could explain this lack of significance. Also, the intuitive mediation characteristics of the SWoOZ platform might have mitigated the remote users' effect. The proxy's mediation, as it interferes in the human dyad, is in favor of rendering a rather homogeneous behavior of the robot, especially that only the remote users' head motion is mirrored here. The failure to prove a significant effect of the remote users' previous experience with robots is interesting in regards to the platform's usability as it strongly suggests that any naive person could, with some preparation, successfully use SWoOZ as a remote user and be as equivalently effective as a more experienced person. Knowing that the SWoOZ setup is compatible with different humanoid robots, the replication of our experiment with another humanoid would probably clarify our findings.

Acknowledgements

This work was supported by the ANR SWoOZ project (11PDOC01901) and the « Techno-Innovation Park » grant from TUAT.

References

[1] Gibert, G., Lance, F., Petit, M., Pointeau, G. and Dominey, P.F. Damping robot's head movements affects human-robot interaction. In *Proc. of the 2014 ACM/IEEE HRI* (2014).

[2] Kristoffersson, A., Coradeschi, S. and Loutfi, A. A review of mobile robotic telepresence, *Advances in Human-Computer Interaction*, 3 (2013).

[3] Li, D., Rau, P.P. and Li, Y. A cross-cultural study: effect of robot appearance and task. *International Journal of Social Robotics 2* (2010), 175-186.

[4] Nishio, S., Ishiguro, H., Anderson, M. and Hagita, N. Representing Personal Presence with a Teleoperated Android: A Case Study with Family. In *AAAI Spring Symposium: Emotion, Personality and Social Behavior* (2008), 96-103.

Analysis of Personality Traits for Intervention Scene Detection in Multi-user Conversation

Shochi Otogi
Graduate School of
Information Science and
Engineering, Ritsumeikan
University, Japan

Hung-Hsuan Huang
Graduate School of
Information Science and
Engineering, Ritsumeikan
University, Japan
hhhuang@acm.org

Ryo Hotta
Graduate School of
Information Science and
Engineering, Ritsumeikan
University, Japan

Kyoji Kawagoe
Graduate School of
Information Science and
Engineering, Ritsumeikan
University, Japan

Abstract

As the advance of embodied conversational agent (ECA) technologies, there are more and more real-world deployed applications of ECA's like the guides in museums or exhibitions. However, in these applications, the agent systems are usually used by groups of visitors rather than individuals. In such multi-user situation, which is more complex sophisticated than single user one, specific features are required. There can be difference in how and when to intervene in the conversation of others due to the variety of personality. In order to realize a more implement the human-like and more helpful guide agent, this work tries to explore the relationship between personality and the willing to intervene in users' conversation as the role of a guide. In this paper, the analysis results of the intervention action and personality traits are reported.

Author Keywords

Multiple-conversation, human-agent

ACM Classification Keywords

H.5.m [Information interfaces and presentation (e.g., HCI)]: Miscellaneous.

Introduction

As the advance of embodied conversational agent (ECA) technologies, there are more and more real-world deployed

HAI 2014, October 29-31, 2014, Tsukuba, Japan.
ACM 978-1-4503-3035-0/14/10.
http://dx.doi.org/10.1145/2658861.2658931

applications of ECA's like the guides in museums or exhibitions. However, in those these situations applications, the agent systems are usually used by groups of visitors rather than individuals. In such multi-user situation, which is much more complex sophisticated than single user one, specific features are required. One of them these features is the ability for the agent to smoothly intervene user-user conversation. Intervention this feature is supposed to facilitate mixed-initiative human-agent conversation and to provide more proactive service for the users. However, there are can be difference in how and when to intervene in the conversation of others due to the variety of personality individual differences in the intervention to conversation by the character of human. In order to realize a more implement the human-like and more helpful guide agent, this work tries to explore the relationship between personality and the willing to intervene in users' conversation as the role of a guide, from the data of a Wizard-of-Oz (WOZ) experiment. with more coordination by analysis of interventions and the character of human. In order to realize this, at first, a Wizard-of-Oz (WOZ) experiment was conducted for collecting human interaction data. By analyzing the collected data corpus, four kinds of timings which allow the agent to do intervention potentially were found. Also, the relationship between intervention timings and personality is analyzed. Second, experiment to find out relation the intervention and character of human by Big Five inventory[1]. In this paper, report the result of the analysis.

Interaction corpus collecting WOZ experiment

To collect the video corpus for an analysis of the situations when the agent can potentially intervene the situations when users to provide information, a WOZ experiment on three collaborative decision making tasks was conducted. We expect that the subjects' reactions toward the agent may differ to how they talk with a human information provider. To observe the natural interaction with humans and agents, we chose the WOZ experiment setting instead of a human–human one. Pairs of experiment participants were instructed to interact with a life-size female character on a screen. They had to retrieve information from the character in order to make a decision regarding the given tasks until the agreement between them achieved. The conversation experiment was conducted with the following premises:

-The participants want to make a decision base on their agreement from multiple candidates with the help of the agent who is knowledgeable about that task domain.

-The participants have a rough image of what they want, but they do not have idea about particular candidates in advance.

-The conversation ends when the participants made the final decision.

A total of 12 pairs of college students were recruited as the participants in the experiment, all of whom were native Japanese speakers. Each pair was instructed to complete three decision-making task of Travel planning and Lecture registration, Part-time job hunting. These tasks were chosen because the student participants are supposed to be familiar with these issues. In order to stimulate more active discussion, the participants were instructed to make rankings on the three final choices.

Experiment of interven exploration

The appropriate timings when to intervene the inter-user conversation for a guide agent is a subjective issue and has no correct answers. In order to find the timings supposed to be reasonably appropriate, another experiment was conducted. The video clips of 12 sessions from the corpus collecting experiment were evaluated by

20 recruited evaluators. Each video clip was assigned to five evaluators. The evaluators were instructed to annotate the video when they want to provide additional and on-time information for the users, if they were a proactive guide agent. The evaluators watched the video and input four possible timings with a game pad. The A, B, C, D button of the game pad were assigned to the following four possible timings.

A: switch the topic and provide new information to the users

B: provide more detailed information in compensating the information provided previously

C: remind the user about the information provided by the agent if they forgot it

D: sort out and conclude the discussion up to now

In the case when the evaluator wanted to use intervene the inter-user conversation in another way, he / she can pause the video and freely type "other" types of timings. In order to investigate the individual difference in evaluating the video clips, NEO-FFI personality test was conducted for each evaluator.

Analysis of the intervention scene

Totally there were 440 timings labeled by the 20 evaluators upon the 12 video clips (five evaluators for one clip, averagely 36.7 timings for one clip). In order to analyze these timings, it divided by the speech segment of the following I,II,III,IV. It was excluded timing that occurred in the utterance of the agent does not become a object of the intervention agent.

I: immediately after the utterances of the agent

II: immediately after the utterances of the user

III: silent period (at least three seconds)

IV: during the user's utterances

Next, it was grouped in order to reduce the feature to target the 20 participants in order to explore the relationship of intervention to the conversation and personality traits based on personality diagnosis by BIGFIVE that was performed on the experimental participants. It classified the five elements of Extraversion・Neuroticism・Consxientiousness・Ageeablenss・Openess to experience. By using the Ward method[2], were divided into three groups of 4 participant table1. As a feature of the group of classification, Extroversion and Ageeablenss is high in group2. In addition, I can be seen that the value of Neuroticism and Openness is high in group3.

Table 1: The clustering result of the personality traits

	N	E	O	A	C
group1	21.75	25.25	22.25	28.00	23.75
group2	23.50	33.75	22.50	34.25	32.50
group3	35.50	26.25	35.50	27.50	31.50

First, analyzed the frequency of intervention in utterance scene is how high each group. It can be seen that chance utterance of the user of IV intervention most often looking at the figure1. This is a need assistance from the agent highest in utterance of the user. It is believed that it is the least respect silent section of III, but this is because it is smaller than the speech segment of the other. However, the frequency of intervention are arranged orderly in a section of each groups. Opportunities for intervention has become less group2 that Ageeablenss and Extroversion is high. On the other hand, intervention frequency, the higher the value of group3 Openness and Neuroticism is high.

believed to be able to vary the behavior of the agent depending on whether to focus characteristic which when considered separately the personality traits.

Conclusion and Future Works

At first, a Wizard-of-Oz (WOZ) experiment was conducted for collecting human interaction data. By analyzing the collected data corpus, four kinds of timings which allow the agent to do intervention potentially were found. Also, the relationship between intervention timings and personality is analyzed and reported. Second, experiment to find out relation the intervention and character of human by Big Five inventory. As a result, the frequency of need or what kind of support in which the speech segment is different in character each was obtained. However, it is expected to be carried out next additional experiments to capture the trend of the character each, because the number of data is not sufficient. Further, it is expected to be detected intervention scene to the conversation with the non-verbal information based on the results obtained. Finally, we would like to incorporate the intervention timing estimation feature into an ECA system and test it in a real-world application.

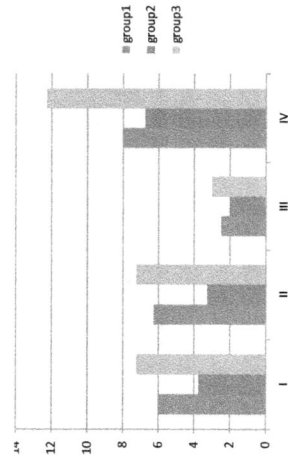

Figure 1: Number of timing of each group of per video in the speech segment

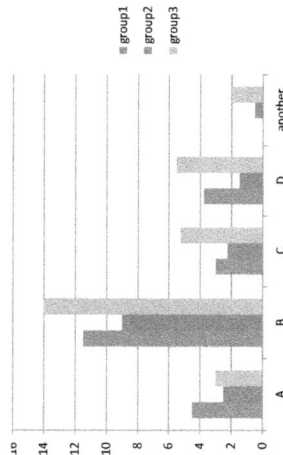

Figure 2: Number of types of timing of each group in one video per

In terms of figure2, B becomes significantly larger than the other in every group. In scene of the guide, it can be seen that the scene the user is in need of more information are many and some still. In addition, it is the result of the A frequency is greater than the other groups only group1 considering each type. There is no feature of the value of personality traits Group 1. Therefore, the other two groups are not trying to switch the topic actively. Some kind of intervention, by the timing difference by personality traits from this result. It is

References

[1] Warren T Norman. Toward an adequate taxonomy of personality attributes: Replicated factor structure in peer nomination personality ratings. *The Journal of Abnormal and Social Psychology*, Vol. 66, No. 6, p. 574, 1963.

[2] Laurence Claes, Walter Vandereycken, Patrick Luyten, Bart Soenens, Guido Pieters, and Hans Vertommen. Personality prototypes in eating disorders based on the big five model. *Journal of Personality Disorders*, Vol. 20, No. 4, pp. 401–416, 2006.

A Design Method Using Cooperative Principle for Conversational Agent

Masahide Yuasa

Shonan Institute of Technology
1-1-25 Tsujido-Nishikaigan
Fujisawa, Kanagawa, Japan
yuasa@sc.shonan-it.ac.jp

HAI '14, Oct 29-31, 2014, Tsukuba, Japan
ACM 978-1-4503-3035-0/14/10.
http://dx.doi.org/10.1145/2658861.2658932

Abstract

It is usually difficult to pre-determine the various verbal and nonverbal behaviors that an agent will exhibit in conversation. In order to develop an efficient conversational agent, a better design method is therefore required, preferably one that is relatively simple and easy to use. In this study, I propose a novel method for designing the verbal and nonverbal behaviors of conversational agents, employing the cooperative principle observed in human behavior. This paper presents examples of research related to the underlying hypothesis of the model, which asserts that humans tend to be cooperative by nature. The applicability of the proposed model for agent behavioral design is also discussed.

Author Keywords

Animated agent; conversational robot; conversation; cooperative principle; human-agent interaction.

ACM Classification Keywords

H.5.m. Information interfaces and presentation (e.g., HCI): Miscellaneous.

Introduction

Plenty of research on the appearance, gestures, personalities, and emotional expressions (via voices as well as facial expressions) of conversational agents/robots exist. Additionally, a great deal of practical design methods and techniques have been proposed [1]. Social behavior and interaction design methods for agents/robots have also been investigated [2], the findings of which will help develop an agent that can perform complex social behaviors and interactive actions involving humans, including engaging in collaborative work and multi-party conversations, or, even, generating better conversational moods.

However, unified and simplified principles for the design of conversational agents have yet to be identified, due to the fact that agents have largely been developed by individual designers/researchers, depending on their respective research aims and interests. Although each research finding is remarkable and practical, implementing all these findings in the design of a single agent is both complicated and impractical, and the agent will be unable to function sufficiently.

Simplicity is an important factor, and such unified and simplified principles are required for agents to function. Subsumption architecture [3], an approach which enables the development of complicated intelligent behaviors from a combination of simple modules, is a good example of such simple and clear design principles. It has been applied in artificial intelligence (AI) research, where robots capable of performing complex behaviors have been successfully designed. Richard Williams, a famed animator, has pointed out a general rule for effective animation design: "Keep it short and simple" [4]. The rule does not allow overly exaggerated facial, mouth, or body movements, and the use of too much action in the development of characters in animation. In order to design efficient

conversational agents with wide applicability across multiple situations, having a better design method based on unified and simplified principles is crucial.

Therefore, a novel method of designing conversational agents is proposed in this paper, using the cooperative principle, which has been widely explored in conversation research. Here, it will be applied to the design of both verbal and nonverbal behaviors of conversational robots and agents for HAI.

The Cooperative Principle in Human Activity

Humans tend to "cooperate" with one another by virtue of the innate cooperative tendencies. These tendencies have been described in many areas of research [5-7]. Our cooperative tendencies commonly surface, for instance, in group settings, where we exhibit cooperative attitudes and work collaboratively [5], because any individual who does not work with others in the group will be excluded from that group. The tendency to cooperate, stemming from the basic sense of equality that humans have, has also been explored widely in game theory and described in detail in the fields of mathematics and economics [6]. The prisoner's dilemma is the most representative example of such tendencies: humans tend to divide their money equally among themselves. Henrich et al. conducted ultimatum game experiments in many different parts of the world, and arrived at the same results every time on our tendency to cooperate as humans [7]. In fact, our cooperative tendencies in everyday verbal communication have also been discussed in the area of linguistics and conversation. Grice described the "cooperative principle" [8] as a way in which people interact with one another cooperatively and achieve effective communication. One of Grice's maxims is to "make your contribution as informative as is required," to enable sufficient understanding among one's receivers. Clerk [9], who agrees with Grice's views, and Sperber and Wilson, who studied relevance theory [10], have also noted that the tendency to cooperate with others is inherent in humans. In research on turn-taking conducted by Sugawara [11] and Kimura [12], cooperative patterns were also observed in the conversational behaviors of former foragers, even though they had different cultural and linguistic practices.

From the evidence presented thus far, the tendency to cooperate is applied to a wide expanse of human activity. Cooperative tendencies may be "guidelines" for human behavior and contribute toward sustaining long-term social relationships with others. Thus, they need to remain an integral part of human society [5]. Although cooperative tendencies are fundamental to human-to-human interactions, such tendencies are also evident in human interactions with agents. In an experiment conducted by Kisler et al. exploring the prisoner's dilemma, humans as well as animated agents were assigned as game partners to research participants [13, 14].

Proposal for Designing Conversational Agents Using the Cooperative Principle

Applying the cooperative principle to the development of conversational agents could be helpful in resolving design principle issues with regard to simplicity. Table 1 presents several examples of previous designs of agent verbal and nonverbal behaviors incorporating the cooperative principle. These designs often had a "social aim" in fostering the desire to cooperate with one another, and were built to participate in "social

relationships" that allowed collaborative archiving. It is important for researchers to focus on these social aims and relationships in their designs of each individual verbal and nonverbal behavior. We aim to conduct additional studies in the future to investigate the relationship between cooperative attitudes and sociality.

	Social Aim	Relationship	Design Object
Conversation [8] (Grice)	Mutual understanding	Participants in conversation	Verbal behavior
Retrieval system with agent [15]	Foster continuous system use	User requests retrieval, agent retrieves information	Nonverbal behaviors of agent during retrieval
Utterance attitude [16, 17]	Cooperate and share the floor equally	Participants in conversation	Facial expression, gesture, timing

Table 1. Examples of designs of verbal and nonverbal behaviors using the cooperative principle. Grice's cooperative principle [8] describes how people archive mutual understanding. Yuasa et al. showed that users tend to continue using a retrieval system when an agent expresses cooperative attitudes [15], and that utterance attitudes [17] expressing the desire to speak create better moods than do neutral ones [16].

Conclusion

This paper explained the tendency to cooperate with one another by describing examples in several different fields of human activity. Examples of how the cooperative principle may be applied were discussed. This method could facilitate designs of agents capable of mimicking human-human communication.

References

[1] Gulz, A. and M. Haake, Design of animated pedagogical agents—A look at their look. *International Journal of Human-Computer Studies 64.* 4 (2006), 322-339.

[2] Gulz, A., et al., Building a Social Conversational Pedagogical Agent: Design Challenges and Methodological approaches, in *Conversational Agents and Natural Language Interaction: Techniques and Effective Practices,* D. Perez-Marin and I. Pascual-Nieto, Editors, IGI Global, 2011.

[3] Brooks, R.A., A robust layered control system for a mobile robot. *IEEE Journal of Robotics and Automation 2.* 1 (1986).

[4] Williams, R., *The animator's survival kit.* Expanded ed., Faber and Faber, London, 2009.

[5] Tomasello, M. and A. Vaish, Origins of human cooperation and morality. *Annu Rev Psychol 64.* (2013), 231-55.

[6] Nowak, M.A., Evolving cooperation. *J Theor Biol 299.* (2012), 1-8.

[7] Henrich, J., et al., "Economic man" in cross-cultural perspective: behavioral experiments in 15 small-scale societies. *Behav Brain Sci 28.* 6 (2005), 795-815; discussion 815-55.

[8] Grice, H.P., *Studies in the way of words.* Harvard University Press, Cambridge, Mass., 1989.

[9] Clark, H.H., *Using language.* Cambridge University Press, Cambridge England, New York, 1996.

[10] Sperber, D. and D. Wilson, *Relevance : communication and cognition.* Language and thought series. Harvard University Press, Cambridge, Mass., 1986.

[11] Sugawara, K., Interactive significance of simultaneous discourse or overlap in everyday conversations among |Gui former foragers. *Journal of Pragmatics 44.* 5 (2012), 577-618.

[12] Kimura, D., Utterance Overlap and Long Silence among the Baka Pygmies:Comparison with Bantu Farmers and Japanese University Students. *African study monographs. Supplementary issue 26.* (2001), 103-121.

[13] Kiesler, S., L. Sproull, and K. Waters, A prisoner's dilemma experiment on cooperation with people and human-like computers. *Journal of Personality and Social Psychology 70.* 1 47-65.

[14] Parise, S., S. Kiesler, and L. Sproull. *My Partner is a Real Dog: Cooperation with Social Agents.* in *Proc. CSCW96,* ACM (1996), 399-408.

[15] Yuasa, M. and S. Aya, A Method to Foster Continuous System Use through a Cooperative Animated Agent - Agent Interface Design by Cooperative Principle - (in Japanese). *IEICE TRANSACTIONS on Fundamentals of Electronics, Communications and Computer Sciences 97-A.* 6 (2014), 396-405.

[16] Yuasa, M. Can Animated Agents Help Us Create Better Conversational Moods? An Experiment on the Nature of Optimal Conversations. in *Proc. HCI2014,* (2014), 634-640.

[17] Yuasa, M., et al. *An utterance attitude model in human-agent communication: from good turn-taking to better human-agent understanding.* in *Proc. Ext. Abstracts CHI 2010,* ACM (2010), 3919-3924.

Experimental Study of Empathy and Its Behavioral Indices in Human-Robot Interaction

Yuichiro Tsuji
Ami Tsukamoto
Takashi Uchida
Yusuke Hattori
Ryosuke Nishida
Chie Fukada
Motoyuki Ozeki
Kyoto Institute of Technology
Matsugasaki, Sakyo-ku
Kyoto 606-8585 Japan
tsuji@ii.is.kit.ac.jp

Takashi Omori
Tamagawa University
6-1-1 Tamagawagakuen, Machida
Tokyo 194-8610 Japan

Takayuki Nagai
The University of Electro-
Communications
1-5-1 Chofugaoka, Chofu
Tokyo 182-8585 Japan

Natsuki Oka
Kyoto Institute of Technology
Matsugasaki, Sakyo-ku
Kyoto 606-8585 Japan
nat@kit.ac.jp

HAI '14 , Oct 29-31 2014, Tsukuba, Japan
ACM 978-1-4503-3035-0/14/10.
http://dx.doi.org/10.1145/2658861.2658933

Abstract

Similar to relationships between humans, a person desiring to form a good relationship with a robot needs to be able to empathize with it. However, the specific kinds of human-robot interactions that would arouse and enhance empathy for the robot in the user's mind have not yet been clarified. In addition, the human behavioral traits that may be regarded as indices of empathy have not been investigated extensively. In an attempt to address these two issues, a preliminary experiment on empathy in human-robot interaction is conducted. The results suggest that the actions of naming or comforting a robot could contribute to enhancing its user's empathy and that eye fixation could be used as an index of empathy even when the use of a subjective index is inconclusive.

Author Keywords

empathy; behavioral indices; visual fixation time

ACM Classification Keywords

I.2.0 General: Cognitive simulation.

Introduction

Robots are increasingly being integrated into our everyday lives. One of the most significant topics in the field of human-agent interaction research is to understand the factors responsible for encouraging long-term interactions between human users and their robots. If the assumption that interactions of this nature can be established when users empathize with robots is true, it would be necessary to explore the kind of human-agent interactions capable of prompting the arousal and enhancement of empathy. It is known that eye contact, social touch, and imitation serve to enhance empathy in human–human interaction [1, 2, 3], that humans are capable of showing emotional reactions towards a robot [4], and that humans become emotionally attached to a facsimile by giving it a name [5]. However, the nature of the human-robot interactions that would invite empathy and the types of human behavior that could be regarded as indices for empathy, have not yet been clarified. In an attempt to address these two issues, this paper presents a preliminary experiment on empathy in human-robot interaction. Assuming that physical contact with the robot or the action of giving the robot a name would instill a feeling of affection, we investigate the effect of these two actions on participants' sense of empathy. The eye movements, facial expressions, and body movements of the participants are recorded throughout the experiment to establish whether they provide an indication of the degree of empathy.

Method

Participants

Four university students (two women and two men), all aged 21 years, participated in the experiment.

Apparatus

Figure 1 shows the experimental setting. Two humanoid robots, model Nao T14 (ALDEBARAN Robotics), and a display monitor were positioned in front of the participant. An eye mark recorder, EMR-9 (nac Image Technology), and a digital video camera, iVIS HF11 (CANON), were used for recording eye and body movements, respectively.

Procedure

The participants were seated face-to-face with the two robots with the instruction to observe them playing the game "rock paper scissors" (RPS). The robots' respective hand signs were displayed on the monitor placed between them, because they could not form the hand shape representing a pair of scissors. The two robots were programmed to behave differently during the game: one produced the sounds "Rock, paper, scissors!" and "Yeah!" (when it won the game), and performed the actions of clenching its fist (when it won) and lowering its head (when it lost) as well as the actions associated with the RPS game, whereas the other produced the same sounds without performing any actions. We named the former 'E-robot' and the latter 'U-robot.'

We separated the participants into two groups depending on the way they were expected to interact with E-robot. Group A was instructed to comfort the robot by patting it when it lost the game ('Patting condition'), while group B was instructed to name the robot before the game of RPS started ('Naming condition'). After a short demonstration of our RPS system, two experimental sessions (each consisting of four matches) were presented to each participant with a brief interval in between. The combined experimental sessions lasted about 30 min for each participant. Group A was asked to comfort E-robot in the first session, but to refrain from doing so in the second

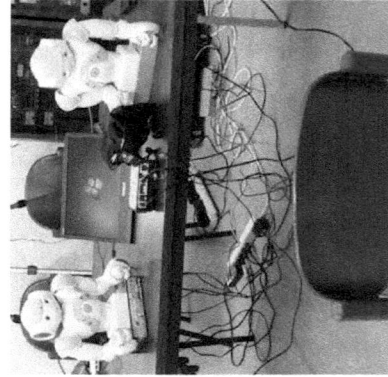

Figure 1. Experimental environment.

session. Participants in Group B received no instructions for the first session, but were asked to name the robot before the second session started. After each session, all participants were requested to answer the following questions:

Questionnaire (five-point scale, using a score of 1: U-robot; 2: Mostly U-robot; 3: neutral; 4: Mostly E-robot; 5: E-robot):

Q1: "Which robot do you want to talk with?"

Q2: "In which case did you feel happy, when E-robot won the game or when U-robot won the game?"

Q3: "In which case did you feel sad, when E-robot lost the game or when U-robot lost the game?"

Results

The video data shows that, contrary to our expectation, none of the participants imitated E-robot's actions such as clenching their fists in triumph, and lowering their heads in disappointment. None of them expressed their facial emotions in accordance with the outcome of the RPS game. This indicates that the participants did not strongly empathize with the robot. As seen in Table 1, however, the responses to the questionnaire, which were mostly scores of four or five, indicate participants' empathy with E-robot. Figure 2 shows the difference between the visual fixation patterns displayed by each participant during the first and the second sessions. The eye movement data represented in Figure 2 indicates that participants tended to look at E-robot when required to perform naming and patting, suggesting that these interactions could make participants pay attention to the robot.

Discussion

Participants' self-evaluations revealed that they mostly empathized with E-robot, and the recorded eye movement patterns showed that the participants looked at E-robot longer. However, the participants neither imitated the robot's actions nor displayed empathetic facial expressions. Based on the interviews with the participants, we ascribed the absence of imitational behavior and facial expression to the following possible reasons:

- The participants have felt as if they were prohibited to perform actions other than those they had been instructed to perform, namely patting or naming; hence, they suppressed their natural reactions intentionally.

- The head-lowering action of the robot may not have been clear or easy to understand. Considering that the speed of the gesture of triumph by the robot was considerably slower than when it results from human action, the slower gestures may not have evoked strong sympathy.

- The duration of the experiment may have been too short for the participants to develop a noticeable degree of empathy with the robot.

Group	Participant	Session	Q1	Q2	Q3
A	a	Patting	4	4	3
		w/o Patting	4	3	3
	b	Patting	4	4	3
		w/o Patting	4	4	3
B	c	w/o Naming	3	3	3
		Naming	4	4	4
	d	w/o Naming	5	4	4
		Naming	5	4	4

Table 1. Responses to the questionnaire: Participants' self-evaluation of the degree of empathy for E-robot.

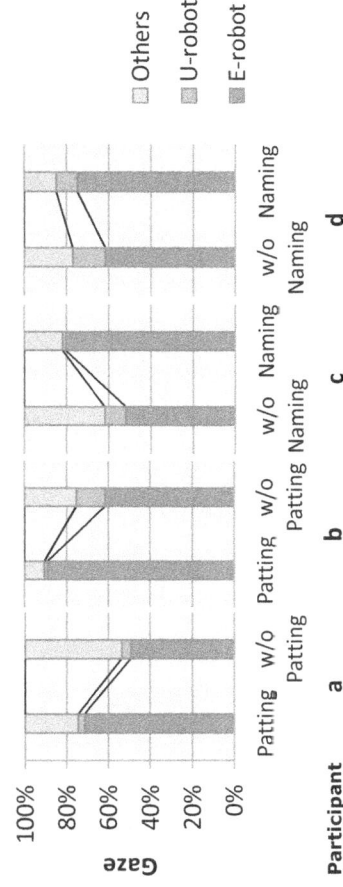

Figure 2. Shift in eye fixation pattern of each participant between two experimental sessions.

results suggested that a user could enhance his or her empathy for a robot by performing actions such as naming or comforting it and that eye fixation might be an index of empathy in situations in which the use of a subjective index does not provide clarity. However, the interpretation of the results should not be considered conclusive, because the factors that were evaluated were not completely separated in our preliminary experiment, and also because the number of participants in the study was very small.

Acknowledgements

This work was supported by JSPS KAKENHI 25330260.

References

[1] Iacoboni, M. Imitation, empathy, and mirror neurons. Annu. Rev. Psychol. 60 (2009), 653-70.

[2] Montague, E., Chen, P., Xu, J., Chewning, B., & Barrett, B. Nonverbal interpersonal interactions in clinical encounters and patient perceptions of empathy. Journal of Participatory Medicine 5 (2013).

[3] Chartrand, T.L., Maddux, W.W., & Lakin, J.L. Beyond the perception-behavior link: The ubiquitous utility and motivational moderators of nonconscious mimicry. In R.R. Hassin, J.S. Uleman & J.A. Bargh (Eds.), The new unconscious. New York: Oxford University Press (2005), 334-361.

[4] Rosenthal-von der Pütten, A.M., Schulte, F.P., Eimler, S.C., Sobieraj, S., Hoffmann, L., Maderwald, S., Brand, M., & Krämer, N.C. Investigations on empathy towards humans and robots using fMRI. Computers in Human Behavior 33 (2014), 201-212.

[5] Yamamoto, Y. Ethical relationships between humans and machines. The 29th Annual Meeting of the Japanese Cognitive Science Society (2012), P2-7 (in Japanese).

• The participants may have been too tense to show enough empathy, because of the unfamiliar experimental environment that required them to interact with an eye mark recorder, an unfamiliar device.

In the first session to which the naming condition was applied, the only difference between the two robots was a display of movement or the lack thereof. While the eye fixation data of the session revealed that both participants spent more time observing E-robot, the questionnaire revealed that one participant empathized with E-robot, but the other did not. Therefore, eye fixation could be an index of empathy even when this is not obvious when using a subjective index. The possible causal relations between a robot's motion, gaze, and the empathy are shown in Figure 3.

Participants who named E-robot were observed to gaze at the robot, and they reported that they felt empathy for the robot. However, Figure 3 suggests that naming may not be the exclusive cause of the gaze and the empathy, as the motion of E-robot and the continuation of the sessions may also have had an influence on the result.

Comforting the robot by patting it also seemed to affect gaze and empathy, but again the effect of the robot's motion on participants' gaze and empathy cannot be completely separated from that of the patting action. Figure 3 illustrates possible causal relations between the various factors in our experiment.

Conclusion

This paper described a preliminary experiment aimed at assessing empathy in human-robot interaction. The

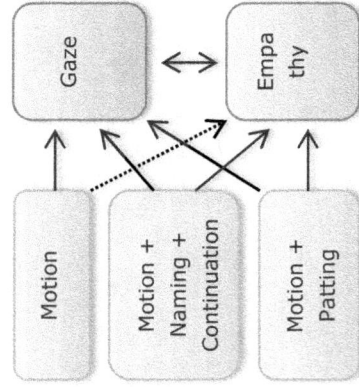

Figure 3. The possible causal relations among robot's motion, naming, continuation, patting, gaze, and empathy.

Huggable Communication Medium Encourages Listening to Others

Junya Nakanishi[1,2]
nakanishi.junya@irl.sys.es.osaka-u.ac.jp

Hidenobu Sumioka[1]
sumioka@atr.jp

Masahiro Shiomi[1]
m-shiomi@atr.jp

[1]ATR
2-2-2 Hikaridai, Keihanna Science City
Kyoto 619-0288, Japan.

Daisuke Nakamichi[1,2]
daisuke-nakamichi.daisuke@irl.sys.es.osaka-u.ac.jp

Kurima Sakai[1,2]
sakai.kurima@irl.sys.es.osaka-u.ac.jp

Hiroshi Ishiguro[1]
ishiguro@sys.es.osaka-u.ac.jp

[2]Osaka Univ.
1-3 Machikaneyama, Toyonaka
Osaka 560-8531, Japan

HAI 2014, October 29–31, 2014, Tsukuba, Japan.
ACM 978-1-4503-3035-0/14/10.
http://dx.doi.org/10.1145/2658861.2658934

Abstract

We propose a huggable communication device called Hugvie that encourages children to concentrate on listening by reducing their stress and strengthening the feeling that the storyteller is close. We observed a group of preschool children who listened to a story and conclude that Hugvie has the potential to facilitate attention on stories. This indicates its usefulness to relieve the educational problem where children show disobedient or restless behavior during class. We discuss Hugvie's effect on learning and memory and potential applications to special-needs children.

Author Keywords

Tactile interaction; social presence; education support

ACM Classification Keywords

H.5.m [Information interfaces and presentation (e.g., HCI)]: Miscellaneous.

Introduction

Being with a familiar person provides positive health benefits for us. Researchers in robotics have enhanced the feeling of a human presence to realize similar effects with a teleoperated android that closely resembles a living individual [2] and have designed robots as a minimalistic human [4]. Hugvie, a human-shaped cushion phone that enhances such feelings with voice and tactile stimulation, reduces stress during conversation when it is hugged [3].

We believe that Hugvie can be a useful tool to support education because its stress reduction and enhancement of the feelings of human presence allow younger students to concentrate on listening to their teacher. They have not learned yet that listening to others is a very active process and is critical for learning and memory [6].Despite listening's importance, many young students have a problem with it; they walk around the classroom, chat with friends, and exhibit other restless/disobedient behaviors during class. The inability to concentrate in class causes many problems for children, especially those in the lower grades of elementary school, because it lowers their academic performance in later life. Hugvie can relieve this problem by encouraging children to pay more attention in class.

We explore the potential of a huggable communication device to support listening ability by introducing Hugvie into a classroom situation. In this paper, we report a case study where we applied Hugvie in an environment where preschool children listened to a story and discuss how a huggable communication medium helps them listen to others.

Importance of attention on listening process

Listening is modeled as three internal processes: receiving, attending, and assigning meaning [5]. While listening to another person, listeners have to pay attention as they receive sensory information from their surroundings including the person. By attending to the speaker, they can interpret the speech's content, memorize useful information, and respond to the speaker. Students who cannot pay attention in class fail to pay attention to a speaker, even though attending is a fundamental process in listening.

Hugvie helps students pay attention to their speaker by two effects: stress reduction and enhancement of the feeling of a speaker's presence. Stress reduction by holding Hugvie enables people to relax and prepare for listening. The speaker's voice close to their ear heightens the feeling that the speaker is talking near them and focuses their on attention on the speech.

Equipment

Huggable communication medium: Hugvie

Hugvie is a human-shaped cushion phone (75 cm high and 600 g) that was designed as a communication device that focuses on the hugging experience. It is a soft cushion filled with polystyrene microbeads and is covered with spandex fiber. It enables us to import the hug experience into telecommunication by putting a hands-free mobile phone inside a pocket of its "head". Since the phone is in Hugvie's pocket, people can talk while hugging it, increasing the feeling they are actually hugging a distant conversation partner.

Storytelling system

Although Hugvie is generally used in one-to-one interactive communication (e.g. [3]), storytelling in elementary school is done in one-to-many and one-way communication, where a storyteller reads a picture book to a group of children. Therefore, we applied radio broadcasting to one-to-many storytelling by putting a radio receiver inside Hugvie instead of a mobile phone.

Figure 1 shows our system for storytelling. Storytellers tell the child-listeners a story through a microphone connected to an FM radio transmitter. All of the children listen to the storyteller's voice that is near their ears through radio receivers while they hug their Hugvies. Note that the children can also directly listen to the storyteller's voice since they are both in the same room. However, they will experience the storyteller's voice as a whisper since they simultaneously hear the storyteller directly and through the radio receivers.

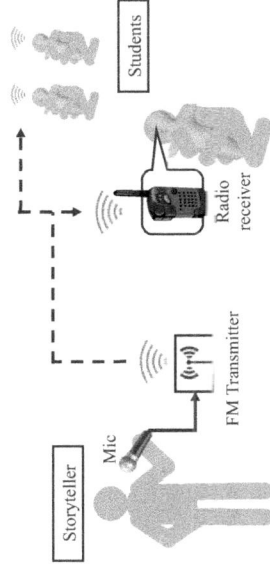

Figure 1: System overview

Case study: storytelling to preschool children

We report how Hugvie changed children's attitude toward listening in a storytelling environment to preschool children. Since this is a preliminary study, we cannot provide any quantitative results. But observing children's behavior offers an insight into the potential impact of huggable communication devices on their attitudes to listening.

We introduced Hugvie into a storytelling context to 33 preschool children who will soon start elementary school. They were given Hugvies and instructed how to use them. At the beginning, a volunteer did some tricks and sang action rhymes with the children. Then three other volunteers told them a story that was illustrated with picture cards for about seven minutes (storytelling 1). After a three-minute trick show, another story was told for about eleven minutes (storytelling 2). After that, the

Hugvies were collected from the children, and two other volunteers began a paper-cutout activity.

Surprisingly, no child walked around the room or chatted with friends during the talking stories of the volunteers. Figure 2(a) shows a typical scene during storytelling 2. Before it, we worried that some children might play with their Hugvies. But all of them calmly listened to the volunteers in both storytellings 1 and 2. About two-third listened to the volunteer voices from their Hugvies; the rest used them like cushions. Many children preferred to listen to the storytellers through Hugvies.

Interestingly, the children at the back of the room seemed to listen to the volunteers' voices from Hugvies without any complaints, even though they had difficulty seeing the picture cards. One girl in the back appeared to be having fun and mentioned this feeling to an experimenter during the storytelling. Hugvie seemed to help children continue to pay attention even from the back of the room.

On the other hand, the interest of the children in the back lagged in the paper-cutout activity and their attention shifted to other things while the children in the front continued to focus on the volunteers. Some children in the back walked around the room and others played with their friends (Fig.2(b)). This might be because the volunteers sometimes concentrated on cutting paper without addressing the children. However, since more of the children who showed restless behavior were observed in the back of the room than in the front, perhaps the children in the back had less feeling that the volunteers were talking to them due to the distance.

These observations suggest that stress reduction and the feeling of a speaker's presence through Hugvie helped the children maintain their attention on the story.

data around the children to investigate how they behaved during the storytelling from a quantitative perspective. Currently we are analyzing these data using our human tracking system [1].

Acknowledgements

We thank the staff at the Higashi-Hikari elementary school, its students, and their parents for their cooperation. We also appreciate K. Kuwamura helping with the experimental setup. This work has been supported by JST CREST research promotion program "Creation of Human-Harmonized Information Technology for Convivial Society" Research Area.

References

[1] Brscic, D., Kanda, T., Ikeda, T., and Miyashita, T. Person tracking in large public spaces using range sensors. *IEEE Transaction on Human-Machine Systems 48* (2013), 522–534.

[2] Nishio, S., Ishiguro, H., and Hagita, N. Geminoid: Teleoperated android of an existing person. *Humanoid Robots: New Developments* (2007), 343–352.

[3] Sumioka, H., Nakae, A., Kanai, R., and Ishiguro, H. Huggable communication medium decreases cortisol levels. *Scientific Reports* (2013), 3034.

[4] Sumioka, H., Nishio, S., Minato, T., Yamazaki, R., and Ishiguro, H. Minimal human design approach for sonzai-kan media: Investigation of a feeling of human presence. *Cognitive computation* (2014). DOI:10.1007/s12559-014-9270-3.

[5] Wolvin, A., and Coakley, C. *Listening, 5th ed.* McGraw Hill, 1996.

[6] Wolvin, A. D. *Listening and human communication in the 21st century.* Wiley Online Library, 2010.

Figure 2: (a) Storytelling with Hugvie and (b) paper-cutout activity without Hugvie

Conclusion and discussion

This paper investigated the potential of a huggable communication device called Hugvie to help children maintain their attention to listening to others by reducing their stress and strengthening the feeling that a storyteller is close. Our observation of storytelling to children supports such potential, suggesting that Hugvie is a useful tool to relieve the educational problem caused by children who show restless and disobedient behavior during class. We believe that concentration on listening can improve learning and memory performances, as suggested in a listening model [5]. Future work will evaluate the effect of Hugvie on learning and memory.

We also believe that Hugvie's effect is useful for children with such developmental disorders as attention deficit and hyperactivity disorder (ADHD) because they have difficulty maintaining attention in class. We have begun applying our system for storytelling to such special-needs children. We installed two depth sensors to gather depth

Tap Model to Improve Input Accuracy of Touch Panels

Takahisa Tani
The Graduate University for
Advanced Studies
2-1-2 Hitotsubashi, Chiyoda
Tokyo 101-8430, Japan
tani@nii.ac.jp

Seiji Yamada
National Institute of
Informatics
2-1-2 Hitotsubashi, Chiyoda
Tokyo 101-8430, Japan
seiji@nii.ac.jp

Abstract

In recent years, devices that use touch panels as
interfaces, such as smart phones and tablet PCs, have
spread. These devices have many advantages. For
example, operating the panel can be done more
intuitively in comparison with using conventional
physical buttons, and the devices are quite more
flexible than those that use a traditional fixed UI.
However, mistakes frequently occur when inputting
with a touch panel because the buttons have no
physical boundaries and users cannot get tactile
feedback with their fingers because the panels never
change physically. Thus, the input accuracy of
touch-panel devices is lower than that of devices with
physical buttons. There are studies on improving input
accuracy. Most of them use language models for typing
natural language or probabilistic models to describe
the errors made when users tap their fingers. However,
these models are not practical, and the experiments
are preliminary. Thus, in this paper, we propose a more
practical model for improving input accuracy, in which
the relative relationships between a target object and
neighbor objects that might influence error making
when touching the target are tested. We consider that
our model can describe important properties for
designing various UIs depending on practical
applications. We also conducted preliminary

Figure 1: Example of software keyboard on smartphone

HAI 2014, October 29–31, 2014, Tsukuba, Japan.
ACM 978-1-4503-3035-0/14/10.

http://dx.doi.org/10.1145/2658861.2658935

experiments in order to build our model in a calibrated way and discuss our evaluation of the model.

Author Keywords
user interface; touch panel; tap model; touch accuracy.

ACM Classification Keywords
H.5.2. [Information Interfaces and Presentation: Input devices and strategies (e.g. mouse, touchscreen)]

Introduction
In recent years, devices that use touch panels as interfaces, such as smart phones and tablet PCs, has spread. These have many advantages. For example, operating the panel can be done more intuitively in comparison with using conventional physical buttons, and the devices are quite more flexible than those that use a traditional fixed UI.

However, mistakes frequently occur when inputting with a touch panel because the buttons have no physical boundaries and users cannot get tactile feedback because the panels never physically change when being tapped. Thus, the input accuracy of touch-panel devices is significantly lower than those using physical buttons in a traditional way. In addition, users often make unintentional mistakes when using the panels for input. In particular, smartphones usually have a smaller screen and smaller UI in comparison with conventional large UIs on a computer display. Thus, the lack of high input accuracy is serious, and this problem with using small screens for input is called the *fat finger problem*[5]. This problem is a problem of accuracy in pointing manipulation. In the future, input devices will progress, and pointing accuracy beomes more important. Thus, improving accuracy improvement is important.

There are many studies such as on improving the accuracy of software keyboards (Figure 1). The software keyboard needs to place a lot of keys in a small area. Hence, this is a typical example of the fat finger problem because the keys are too small for a user to correctly tap them. The some of these uses the tap models[1, 2]. The model has information on the difference between the locations of buttons and the points where a user taps. The system revises points on the panel of the screen.

There are fundamental studies in which limited and concrete applications to practical UIs are not assumed[3, 6]. Although these studies might provide novel knowledge in a general aspect, it is very difficult to use this knowledge to design UIs practically. Thus, these models are not practical, and the experiments are preliminary. This means that the models may be influenced by more complex factors such as the layout or color of the interface.

Thus, in this study, we focus on a method that predicts a touch point from multiple sensors that was proposed by [6]. Also, we propose a more practical model that includes the influence of neighbor objects, e.g., buttons and links.

Method of Estimating Tap Points with Multiple Sensors.
The previous studies[6] proposed the following method. Let s be the input of the multiple sensors and (x, y) be the intended location of a user. Here, multiple sensors means the output of the touch panel (e.g., location,

time, size of area, pressure), accelerometer, and so on. Then, they calculate the function $(x,y) = f(s)$ by regression, and the system estimates the intended location from the sensor input by f.

Next, we extend this touch model to a more practical one by introducing the relationship between a target object and a neighbor object. Furthermore, we try to introduce incremental learning to improve the touch model through user execution of the UI.

Influence of Interface Layout on Tap Model

The tap location in practical use changes with various factors. In particular, it is known that the tap model significantly changes with the differences in how the device is held and how the fingers operate the device. We call this difference of tap point *kinematic error* (e_k). This influence may be solved by estimating these factors with sensors like acceleration sensors.

However, the tap model may change with the interface layout. In Figure 2, let the blue square be a target. The tap location has a distribution like the blue line (a), where a Gaussian distribution is assumed for the touch model. If there is another object (the green square) on the right hand side, the distribution will move to the left side because the user is aware of the green squire and tries to avoid miss-touching the green squire instead of the blue squire. We call this difference of tap point *cognitive error* (e_c). In addition, there might be an influence from the position, size, color, or shape of the object.

The previous studies do not consider this kind of influence because the sensor inputs s do not include this information. Therefore, we propose adding interface layout i as a variable of f. We consider this

information makes a touch model quite more practical. Since our touch model with interface layout is basically characterized with (x, y) coordination on the touch panel, it can be applicable to the various UIs independent of the properties of tappable objects like buttons and icons. Thus, this model has a wide coverage to be applied to the same as conventional touch models. Furthermore, this proposed touch model is very practical and precise because it effectively introduces the influence of neighbor objects in contrast with traditional touch models[3, 6].

Experiment

We conducted the experiment to obtain a large number of training data and to evaluate the accuracy of our touch model as follows.

Method

In order to evaluate the influence of the interface layout on the tap model, we developed the method of obtaining the training data implicitly. Participants perform a task in which they tap a marker on a touch panel. The marker disappear, and another ones appear in another position when the markers are tapped. A marker does not disappear until being tapped. The target marker which a participant should tap has a while circle in the center, and various neighbor makers appear around it. We instruct participants to tap as quickly as possible.

Result

Figure 3 shows the kinematic error(e_k) for horizontal and vertical axis. The curve is estimated by Gaussian Process Regression (GPR)[4]. Tap points (white circles) shift to the side of an operate hand($e_k > 0$) and gaps in points distant from an operate hand are larger

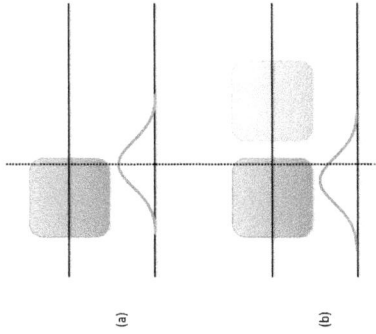

(a)

(b)

Figure 2: Tap target and tap location

than gaps in near points. These features are the same tendencies as previous works[3, 6].

Figure 4 shows the cognitive error(e_c) for each axis. Here, we use data which has only one neighbor marker, and the effect of e_k is eliminated. Tap points shift to upper right when a neighbor marker is at lower left side, shift to up when a neighbor marker is at lower right side and shift to lower left when additional marker is at right side. These results suggest that cognitive error exists.

Conclusion

In this study, we considered that our tap model can describe important properties for designing various UIs depending on practical applications. We conduct an experiment in order to build our model in a calibrated way and discuss the evaluation of our model. The results suggested that cognitive error existed, In the future study, we will additional experiment and evaluate our method.

References

[1] Findlater, L., and Wobbrock, J. Personalized input: improving ten-finger touchscreen typing through automatic adaptation. In *Proceedings of the SIGCHI Conference on Human Factors in Computing Systems, CHI '12*, ACM (2012), 815–824.

[2] Himberg, J., Häkkilä, J., Kangas, P., and Mäntyjärvi, J. On-line personalization of a touch screen based keyboard. In *Proceedings of the 8th international conference on Intelligent user interfaces, IUI '03*, ACM (2003), 77–84.

[3] Holz, C., and Baudisch, P. Understanding touch. In *Proceedings of the SIGCHI Conference on Human Factors in Computing Systems, CHI '11*, ACM (2011), 2501–2510.

[4] Rasmussen, C. E., and Williams, C. K. I. *Gaussian Processes for Machine Learning (Adaptive Computation and Machine Learning)*. The MIT Press, 2005.

[5] Siek, K. A., Rogers, Y., and Connelly, K. H. Fat finger worries: how older and younger users physically interact with pdas. In *Proceedings of the 2005 IFIP TC13 international conference on Human-Computer Interaction, INTERACT'05*, Springer-Verlag (2005), 267–280.

[6] Weir, D., Rogers, S., Murray-Smith, R., and Löchtefeld, M. A user-specific machine learning approach for improving touch accuracy on mobile devices. In *Proceedings of the 25th annual ACM symposium on User interface software and technology, UIST '12*, ACM (2012), 465–476.

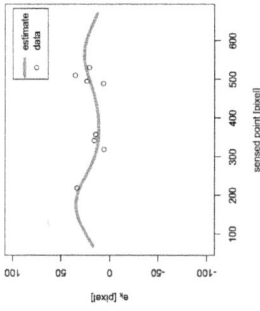

Figure 3: Tap points vs. kinematic errors for each axis

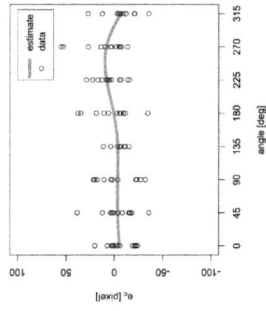

Figure 4: The angle of an additional marker vs. cognitive errors for each axis

Modeling of Cooperative Behavior Agent Based on Collision Avoidance Decision Process

Kensuke Miyamto
Keio University
Fujisawa City
Kanagawa Prefecture
Endo 5322
kmiya@sfc.keio.ac.jp

Hiroaki Yoshioka
Keio University
Fujisawa City
Kanagawa Prefecture
Endo 5322
yoshi09@sfc.keio.ac.jp

Norifumi Watanabe
Tokyo University of Technology
Hachioji Tokyo
Katakura-Cho 1404-1
watanabenr@stf.teu.ac.jp

Yoshiyasu Takefuji
Keio University
Fujisawa City
Kanagawa Prefecture
Endo 5322
takefuji@sfc.keio.ac.jp

HAI '14, Oct 28-31 2014, Tsukuba, Japan
ACM 978-1-4503-3035-0/14/10.
http://dx.doi.org/10.1145/2658861.2658936

Abstract

Recent years, robots are useful at home such as cleaning task or communication tools. So there are a lot of studies about cooperative behavior with robots. In order to realize cooperative tasks with robots, it is necessary that robots estimate human intention from human behavior and act in the context based on the intention.

In this research, we construct an agent model that enables coordinated behavior by estimating human intention. We focus on collision avoidance as an example of a simple cooperative behavior. We implemented that a agent has Meta-Strategy model in a virtual environment. We have a collision avoidance experiment between virtual agent and human subject and analyzed subject's behavior. It was confirmed that the agent's behavior can influence the human avoidance behavior from experimental results. By indicating the agent's intention, we consider it is possible to achieve cooperative collision avoidance.

Introduction

It is popular that many robots are used in the home, we must consider to cooperative task of human and robot. To realize human robot interactions, it is necessary for the robot to estimate human intention and take actions based on the estimation.

There are some robotics researches of various path finding [3][4][5][6]. But these studies have not focused on human intention.

Some studies evaluate a locus of human motion with real robot [7][8][9]. In these studies, robots work passively in environment.

In this study, we aim at constructing an agent which enables a cooperative action by estimating human intention. Specifically, we took up collision avoidance as an example of cooperative task and analyzed the human behavior. We tested on SIGVerse [1] simulator and an agent acts according to Meta-Strategy[2] theory. Furthermore, we consider cooperative behavior between human and robot with Meta-Strategy. Specifically, we compare a timing and distance between agent and human subject collision avoidance. We argue whether subjects recognized agent's strategy based on the results.

Meta-Strategy Model

We don't decide our behavior by looking other peoples all the time. We show an explicit action to others, for example, when others intention is not clear. Meta-Strategy model is one of internal model of human robots interaction process [2]. This Model formulated passive and active strategy of action decision as a computational model. We estimate other people intention first in passive strategy. We decide own action to adapt other's purpose. Passive strategy is classified by some levels. Yokoyama et.al discuss a level 1 strategy that we decide own action by estimation of other people intention. To estimate the intention, they define equation (1) (G: goal, s: state, a: action).

$$\bar{G}_o = \arg\max_G P(G|S_o, a_o) \qquad (1)$$

After that, we set our Goal, and decide our action by equation (2).

$$a_s = \arg\max_a P(a|S_s, G_s) \qquad (2)$$

The simplest strategy, decide our action with no estimation but by our state action value function, is defined level 0 strategy.

On the other hand, we make sure of own purpose in active strategy. To achieve the purpose, we should choose the action which is the easiest to understand own intention. There are differences in action value for the purpose in each action. The differences let us choose the best action (eq. 3).

$$a_s = \arg\max_a (P(G_s|S_s, a_s) - P(\tilde{G}_o|S_s, a_s)) \qquad (3)$$

We will not change own objective, so the strategy is defined level 0* because it's considered as improved strategy of level 0.

Between these strategies, there is difference in usage of the state action value function. By applying the function to the state of opponent, we estimates opponent intense. Meta-Strategy is an overarching strategy determining which strategy to use in a given situation.

Collision Avoidance Experiment based on Meta-Strategy Model

In this study, we analyze human behavior when they interact with an agent based on Meta-Strategy model. We examined 4 subjects who are 20s.

Subjects avoid an agent in SIGVerse simulator. Subject's action is reflected in the virtual space by motion sensor (Microsoft Kinect). We also measure subject's waist by using Kinect. To deal with measuring range of Kinect, position of subjects is reflected only horizontal direction in the virtual space. Subject's model moves vertical direction automatically, but the subjects stamp until starting avoidance in real world (Fig. 1). Virtual subject's sight is showed by head mount display (Video Eye-wear Wrap 1200).

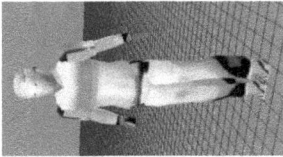

Figure 2. Agent model in

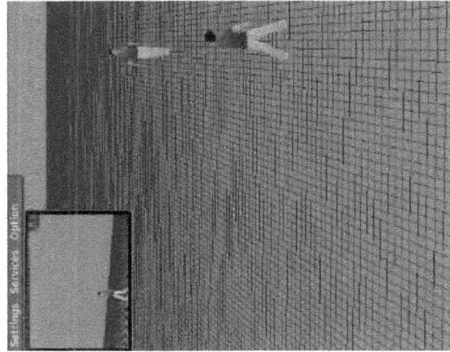

Figure 3. Collision Avoidance in SIGVerse (Left upper area is view of subjects)

Agent movement was selected by 3 strategies pattern level 0, level 1 and level 0* (Fig. 4). On level 0 strategy pattern, agent goes straight on regardless of the subject's action. In this strategy, subjects should avoid agent. In level 1 strategy pattern, agent changes direction after subject's movement for avoiding agent. The timing is instructed by experimenter. In level 0* strategy patterns, agent changes direction before subject's movement for avoiding agent. The timing of direction changing is almost 5 seconds from starting trial.

Angle of agent avoidance in level 1s and 0* strategy patterns is 30 and 60 degrees. We experimented five trials each patterns, but in the analysis, we ignore 30 degrees patterns because subjects didn't perceive agent's change of direction in the patterns.

Result

Figure 5 shows maximum value of avoidance distance in SIGVerse coordinate space. This graph is average of 5 trials. Subject 1, 2 and 4 move the longest distance in level 0 strategy pattern. When agent avoids before subjects movement (level 0*), subject 2, 3 and 4 avoid smaller than level 1 strategy pattern. On the other hand, subject 1 moves longer distance in level 0* strategy pattern.

Discussion

If subjects estimate that opponent doesn't avoid, they avoids more long distance in order to avoid opponent. Though an agent is an opponent in this experiment, subjects moves less distance in level 0* pattern than level 1 pattern.

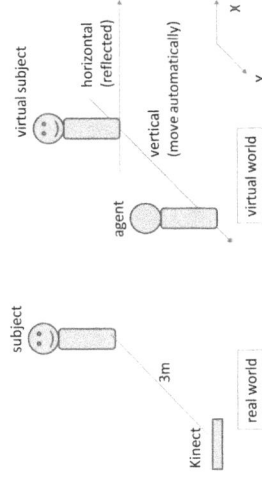

Figure 1. Experiment environment

Bipod humanoid model is used as agent (Fig. 2). Agent movements were read walking motion of experimenter prepared beforehand, and switch the direction in the timing of ground leg or top of free leg to avoid unnatural motion.

As the result, we affected the subject avoidance by agent movement. When we avoid a person, we estimate the intention of the person and change the action accordingly.

We experimented to confirm whether the action of the human changed by changing the movement of agent. It is concluded that subjects estimated the intention to avoid earlier of an agent. In particular, subject 2 had a big difference between level 1 and 0*. However, some subjects showed not clear reaction. We might not show that an agent has cooperative strategy pattern enough.

In next experiment, we are planning to present agent's strategy through collision avoidance between the agent and other pedestrians before subject's avoidance.

Conclusion

In collision avoidance, we reported that agent movement based on Meta-Strategy can affect subject's estimation of intention. Subjects recognized an agent as a partner of cooperation like a human and switched their movement by corresponding to active strategy agent. In future study, we make a robot that be clearly shown cooperative strategy pattern by considering agent behavior.

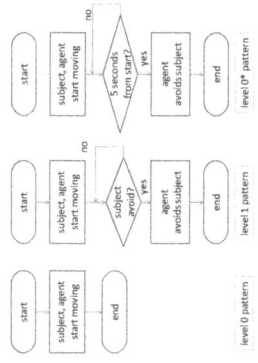

Figure 4. Flow of 3 strategies pattern

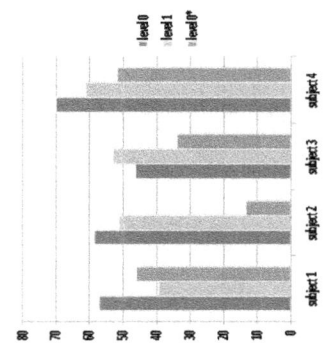

Figure 5. Result of avoidance distance

References

1. Special Interest Group for SocioIntelliGenesis, SIGVerse, http://sigveerse.org/sigverse/main/

2. Yokoyama, A., Omori, T., Model Based Analysis of Action Decision Process in Collaborative Task Based on Intention Estimation, The Journal of the Institute of Electronics, Information and Communication Engineers (2009), vol.192-A, no.11, pp.734-742 (in Japanese)

3. Jen-Hui C. et al, An analytically tractable potential field model of free space and its application in obstacle avoidance, IEEE TRANSACTIONS ON SYSTEMS, MAN, AND CYBERNETICS-PART B:CYBERNETICS, VOL.28, NO.5 (1998) p.729-736

4. Michael G.H., James L.R., Walter F.T., Christoper A.R., Two Formal Gas Models for Multi-agent Sweeping and Obstacle Avoidance, Formal Approaches to Agent-Based Systems (2005), pp.111-130

5. Silvia M., Dusan M.S., Christoper R.G., Koji A.I., Mark W.S., Formation Control and Collision Avoidance for Multi-agent Nou-holonomic Systems:Theory and Experiments, The International Journal of Robotics Research (2011), pp.1037-1071

6. Brost, R.C, Computing Metric and Topological Properties of Configuration-Space Obstacle Proc, IEEE Conf. Robotics and Automation (1989) pp.170-176

7. Yoda M., Shiota Y., A Study on the Mobile Robot which Passes a Man, Journal of the Robotics Society of Japan, vol.17, no.2, (1999) pp.202-209 (in Japanese)

8. Yoda M., Shiota Y., Mobile Robot's Passing Motion Algorithm Based on Subjective Evaluation, Transactions of the Japanese Society of Mechanical Engineers, vol.66, no.650, (2000) pp.156-163 (in Japanese)

9. Nakano H., Shimowaki Y., Katayama A., Watanabe M., Research of foot pursuit method for the autonomous mobile robot based on prediction by Kalman Filter, The Special Interest Group Technical Reports of IPSJ, CVIM, vol. 2004, no.113, (2004) pp.9-16 (in Japanese)

Representation of Gaze, Mood, and Emotion: Movie-watching with Telepresence Robots

Ken Yonezawa
Kyoto Sangyo University
Motoyama, Kamigamo, Kita-ku,
Kyoto, Japan
i1258159@cc.kyoto-su.ac.jp

Hirotada Ueda
Kyoto Sangyo University
Motoyama, Kamigamo, Kita-ku,
Kyoto, Japan
ueda@cc.kyoto-su.ac.jp

HAI 2014, October 29–31, 2014, Tsukuba, Japan.
ACM 978-1-4503-3035-0/14/10.
http://dx.doi.org/10.1145/2658861.2658937

Abstract

Two methods to enhance viewer's presence in movie-watching by telepresence robots in remote rooms are proposed. To keep coherance of eye-direction in all rooms, the system detects the object gazed by the viewer and controles the robot's face direction. To effectively express an affect change, which is tough to notice in non-face-to-face communication, the system interprets it into robot body action. These methods realize the suitable remote communication environment for movie-watching in remote places.

Author Keywords

Telepresence robot; Movie-watching; Non-verbal behavior; Gaze direction; Affect; Mood; Emotion.

ACM Classification Keywords

H.4.3. Information systems applications: Communications Applications—computer conferencing, teleconferencing, and videoconferencing.

Introduction

A discrepancy in eye-direction is a typical problem in remote communication support system. Otuka [1] synchronized head movements of participants and displays that represent participant's faces and solved this problem. Guizzo [2] has shown the great power of expression by behavior freedom of the robot. Hasegawa [3] developed a telepresence robot that represents user's unconscious behavior and solved speech collision. We aim at a support of entertaining remote communication and focused on atmosphere as if participants enjoy watching a movie in the same room with the remote friends. Therefore, the presence of the remote friends should be expressively represented. In our system, affect is the key to convey the presence of the remote users. Affect can be roughly divided into emotion and mood [4]. We developed a system that carefully convey not only gaze but emotion and mood. Furthermore, environments that each participant can feel comfortable should be provided. In the previous study, it is necessary to keep the same spatial relation of the people and robots in each rooms, but our system allows free placement of them in all rooms. An illustration of the proposed system is shown in Fig.1. The system control flow is shown in Fig.2.

Figure 1. Movie-watching with telepresence robots.

System Implementation

In order to represent the presence of remote viewer, non-verbal behavior should be properly represented. We divided non-verbal into three components. Eye-directions is "attention". Face expression is "emotion". Head gesture such as nod or shaking head is "intention". Robot's representation of "attention" guarantees the coherent eye-direction even in the free placement of people and robots, as mentioned above. Since almost communication in movie-watching is a conversation during watching a television screen, it is not easy to notice a change in facial expression each other. However, representation of "emotion" by the robot action solve this problem. To convey "intention", robot imitates the remote person's head movement by a method of the previous study [3], which a robot undisguisedly behaves head movements by remote person.

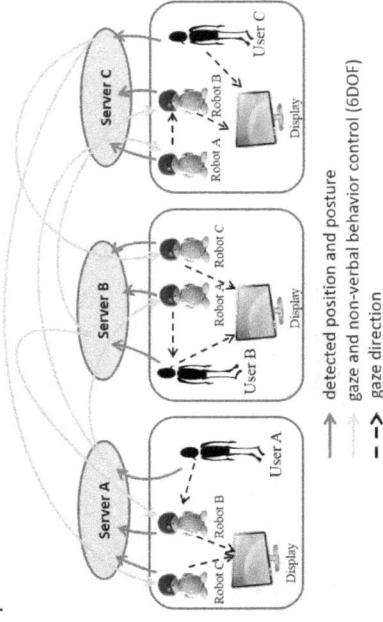

Figure 2. System control flow.

Conveyance of Attention

We propose a method that identifies a gazed object and controls robot's face direction to the object in the remote room. The system detects most important two types of gaze directions; (A) one to the robots that are avatars for remote people and (B) a television screen. This limitation of the gaze recognition provides the stable system operation and keeps coherent eye-direction even in different spatial relation well. In order to do that, it is necessary for two procedures: to estimate spatial relation of a user and the robots in the room and to detect user's gaze-direction to an object. To detect user's position and posture invisible markers that Nakazato proposed [5] is used. To detect the user's gaze-direction an acceleration and geomagnetism censer attached user's head is used. The head direction may not directly turn to a gazed object, and eye movement complements the rest of direction. Considering that, whether the object exists or not is judged from direction of one-and-a-half move degree of head.

Conveyance of Affect

To convey affect to remote place even in non-face-to-face communication, we propose a method that estimates affect of a user and makes remote robots express it. Since human beings have strong peripheral vision, we believed they can easily notice such an expressive robot's behavior even when they are watching movie screen. As mentioned above, affect is divided into emotions and moods. "Emotions" are strong and last only for a short time, but "Moods" are week and last for a long time. Affect can be more effectively conveyed by distinguishing "emotions" and "moods". Our system has two procedures; estimation

of an affect and interpretation of the affect into robot behavior.

For the emotion estimation, the image recognition library Okao Vision[6] is used. It can estimate six kinds of face expression such as anger, disgust, fear, happiness, sadness, and surprise. For the mood estimation, we assumed four moods shown by behavior or posture. For instance, behavior touching a part of the body shows anxiety. An unconscious behavior such as stretch or yawn shows boredom. Forward-bent posture shows interest. Folding hands back of head shows relax. To detect such behavior or posture and estimate the four moods, Kinect is used. To estimate the moods more precisely, we are considering not only a part of body but whole body comprehensively. If behavior or posture showing displeasure mood in upper and lower body are both detected, the system should express higher displeasure than when detecting a part of body.

For the interpretation of emotions and moods into robot action, we adapt an algorithm proposed by Maeda [7]. This algorithm is based on Russell's circumplex model of affect and Laban Movement Analysis and determines parameters of robot action: velocity, height, and area, from two factors of affect, which are pleasure and arousal. When the pleasure degree increases, Area is set bigger and height of the center of the gravity (CG) is set higher. When the arousal level increases, area is set smaller and velocity is set faster. Velocity is simply the speed of robot action and CG height is represented by the head and hands of the robot. When CG height is higher, the robot turns head up and raises both arms higher, when CG height is lower, the robot turns head down and lowers both arms. Regarding area, the color effect is used. The front body color of the robot is dark and the side body color is bright as shown in Fig.3. Therefore when the robot rotates the user feels that robot has become large. Hands-up action makes CG rise and body area large. Therefore, a correction for this effect is taken.

Figure 3. Conversational robot Phyno

According to Russell's cuicumplex model of affect, the emotions are in the high arousal position whereas the moods are in the low arousal position. To represent the arousal level, velocity of robot action is suitable. Thus, the emotions are represented by fast action, and the moods are represented by slow action. In addition, emotions end in short time, and moods last for a long time. Therefore, while a mood is estimated, the robot regularly repeats the action. On the other hands, while an emotion is estimated, the robot represents the emotion preferentially because of the high arousal degree. As a result, the robots enhance the presence effectively, and the user understand both the emotions and the moods of the remote viewers clearly.

Conclusion

We proposed two methods for the movie-watching system with telepresence robots and developed a prototype system. Coherency of eye-direction in different spatial relation is maintained by the user's gaze direction detection and robot's face direction control. The user's affect that is not easy to be noticed in the non-face-to-face communication situation like movie-watching is translated into the robot body action for the effective representation. We are going to conduct subject experiment to prove the effect that can enhance viewer's presence.

References

[1] K, Otsuka. MM-Space: Recreating Multiparty Conversation Space by Using Dynamic Displays. *NTT Technical Review 10*, 11(2012), 1-5.

[2] Guizzo, E. When My Avatar Went to Work. *IEEE Spectrum 47*(2010), 26-50.How to Classify Works Using ACM's Computing Classification System.

[3] K, Hasegawa et al. Preliminary Evaluation of a Telepresence Robot Conveying Pre-motions for Avoiding Speech Collisions, 1st International Conference on Human-Agent-Interaction, 2013.

[4] A, Judge et al. Emotions and Moods. *Organizational Behavior*, 13(2008), 258-297

[5] Y, Nakazato et al. Localization of wearable users using invisible retro-reflective markers and an IR camera, SPIE (2005), 1234-1242.

[6] Image Sensing Technology

[7] http://www.omron.com/ecb/products/mobile/

[8] Y, Maeda and N, Tanabe. Basic Study on Interactive Emotional Communication by Pet-type Robot (in Japanese). SICE 42, 4 (2006), 359-366

A Hierarchical Structure for Gesture Recognition using RGB-D sensor

Hyunsoek Choi
School of Electrical Engineering
and Computer Science,
Kyungpook National University.
Sangyuk-dong, Buk-gu, Daegu,
702-701, KOREA
choihs@ee.knu.ac.kr

Hyeyoung Park
School of Computer Science
and Engineering,
Kyungpook National University.
Sangyuk-dong, Buk-gu, Daegu,
702-701, KOREA
hypark@knu.ac.kr

HAI'14, Oct 29-31, 2014, Tsukuba, Japan
ACM 978-1-4503-3035-0/14/10.
http://dx.doi.org/10.1145/2658861.2658938

Abstract

Recently, gesture recognition using visual sensors has been
paid increased attention as an intelligent technology for
human-computer interaction. To achieve good recognition
performance in vision-based gesture recognition, it is
important to find an efficient representation of complex
visual signals and a robust classification method that can
deal with diverse variations of gesture data. To treat these
challenging topics, we propose a hierarchical structure for
feature extraction and measuring similarity between two
gestures obtained through RGB-D video sensors such as
Kinect. The efficiency of the proposed method is
confirmed through computational experiments on a public
benchmark database.

Author Keywords

Gesture recognition; Feature extraction; Similarity
measure; RGB-D sensor; Kinect

ACM Classification Keywords

H.5.1 [Information interfaces and presentation (e.g.,
HCI)]: Multimedia Information Systems.; I.5.0 [Computing
Methodologies]: Pattern Recognition.

Introduction

In order to analyze gesture data obtained from the visual
sensors, it is important to find an appropriate feature

extraction method and a robust data classification method[8, 9]. In the classic approaches, these two topics - feature extraction and classification - have been studied separately[3, 6, 7]. Recently, there have been a number of studies on finding efficient features and classification function in a single deep network structure through learning[1, 2, 4]. Though these deep learning approaches show remarkably successful results in various pattern recognition tasks, it still needs long learning time and large training data set in order to obtain good results. In addition, once a fixed number of gesture types are trained for classification, newly given gesture types cannot be easily added without additional training.

To solve the problem, we develop a hierarchical structure that can extract efficient features from two gesture video and calculates similarity between two gestures. Instead of determining class labels of a given gesture data, the proposed structure is designed to calculate similarity between two gestures in order that the similarity values can be used in the distance-based classifier such as K-nearest neighbor classifier for identifying the membership of a given gesture video. Using this approach, it is possible to change the number of gesture types (classes) adaptively. In addition, the proposed structure can be applied to RGB signal as well as depth signal. Also we can use both of the two signals together to get more robust recognition results.

Proposed Hierarchical Structure

Figure 1 shows the overall structure of proposed hierarchical system. When a sequence of (RGB or depth) images $\mathbf{X}$ with $N + 1$ frames is given as

$$\mathbf{X} = [\boldsymbol{x}_0, \boldsymbol{x}_1, \cdots, \boldsymbol{x}_N], \quad (1)$$

we first represent it by using a sequence of difference images $\boldsymbol{\Xi}$ with N frames, which is defined as

$$\boldsymbol{\Xi} = [\boldsymbol{\xi}_1, \boldsymbol{\xi}_2, \cdots, \boldsymbol{\xi}_N], \boldsymbol{\xi}_i = f(\boldsymbol{x}_i - \boldsymbol{x}_{i-1}), i \in [1:N], \quad (2)$$

Where f is a nonlinear filter for removing infinitesimal noise. When the vision sensor is fixed and does not move, the obtained difference image is expected to be robust against illumination and background. The difference images $\boldsymbol{\xi}$ are further transformed by using a matrix $\boldsymbol{W}$, to obtain a low-dimensional feature vector $\boldsymbol{z} = \boldsymbol{W}^T \boldsymbol{\xi}$. The transformation matrix $\boldsymbol{W}$ is defined as a multiplication of two matrices $\boldsymbol{W}_{PCA}$ and $\boldsymbol{W}_{LPP}$, each of which is obtained through linear subspace analysis, PCA(principal component analysis) and LPP(locality preserving projection), respectively. Consequently, a gesture data $\mathbf{X}$ with $N + 1$ image frames is represented by a feature matrix $[\boldsymbol{z}_1, \boldsymbol{z}_2, \cdots, \boldsymbol{z}_N]$, where each column vector $\boldsymbol{z}_n$ ($n \in [1:N]$) is calculated by

$$\boldsymbol{z}_i = \boldsymbol{W}^T \boldsymbol{\xi}_i = (\boldsymbol{W}_{PCA} \boldsymbol{W}_{LPP})^T \boldsymbol{\xi}_i. \quad (3)$$

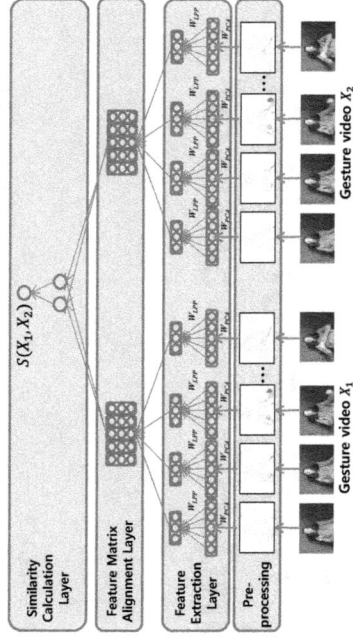

Figure 1: Proposed structure for feature extraction and calculating similarity of two gestures.

Once two gesture signals X_1 and X_2 are given as shown in Figure 1, the two signals are pre-processed and linearly transformed separately and two feature matrices are obtained. We should note here that the obtained two feature matrices may have different size of columns due to the variable lengths of image sequences, and they need to be aligned with each other. In this work, we used DTW (dynamic time warping) algorithm to make the best alignment, and finally obtain two matrices Z_1 and Z_2 with same size.

In order to calculate the similarity between two matrices Z_1 and Z_2, we use a correlation distance. Since the column and row vector of the feature matrix have different information (the spatial and temporal information), we extend the conventional vector correlation into a matrix version, which can be defined as

$$S(Z_1, Z_2) = \frac{tr\{(Z_1 - M_1)^T(Z_2 - M_2)\}}{\sqrt{tr\{(Z_1 - M_1)^T(Z_1 - M_1)\}}\sqrt{tr\{(Z_2 - M_2)^T(Z_2 - M_2)\}}}$$
$$+ \frac{tr\{(Z_2 - M_2)(Z_1 - M_1)^T\}}{\sqrt{tr\{(Z_1 - M_1)(Z_1 - M_1)^T\}}\sqrt{tr\{(Z_2 - M_2)(Z_2 - M_2)^T\}}}, \quad (4)$$

Where M_i is the mean of all elements of Z_i. In the classification stage, we apply K-nearest neighbor classifier with the proposed similarity measure.

So far, we described the case that a single (either RGB or depth) signal is given. When both of them are given, we can combine them by extracting features separately and concatenating them horizontally. Then we can simply use the same similarity measure for the concatenated matrices.

Experimental Results

In order to confirm the efficiency of the proposed method, we conducted computational experiments on a benchmark dataset, SKIG[5], which contains 2160 hand gesture sequences (1080 RGB sequences and 1080 depth sequences) collected from 6 subjects through a Kinect sensor. It consists of ten categories of hand gestures as shown in Figure 2. In the collection process, all the ten categories are performed with three hand postures: fist, index and flat. To increase the diversity, the gestures were recorded under three different backgrounds (wooden board, white plain paper and paper with characters) and 2 illumination conditions. Consequently, for each subject, 360 gesture sequences were recorded.

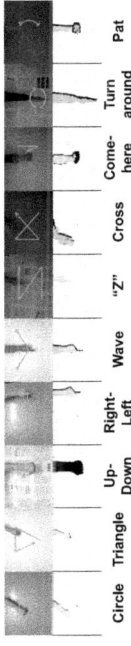

Figure 2: Examples of SKIG database.

We basically used the same experimental conditions as those used in [5]; each image was resized to 96×72 pixels and three-fold cross-validation was used for obtaining average results. One exceptional difference is about treating length of image sequences. Whereas the conventional method[5] normalized the length of all the sequences to 50 frames, we just shortened each sequence to one-fifth of its original length using subsampling. Since our structure has DTW component for size alignment, we do not have to normalize the length in a lump, which may cause some loss of information.

In Table 1, we compared the proposed method with the results given in [5]. From the table, we can see that the proposed method can give the best results with depth signal and RGB-D signal. In addition, we can also confirm that the combination of RGB and depth signal can improve the performance.

Table 1: Recognition rates (%) on SKIG database.

Method	RGB Signal	Depth Signal	RGB-D Signal
RGGP[5]	84.6	76.1	88.7
CNN[5]	81.7	72.6	83.8
DBN[5]	83.1	73.8	85.9
Proposed	82.0	91.3	91.9

Conclusions

The proposed hierarchical structure is basically designed for representing gesture video efficiently and measuring the similarity between two gestures. Though we used the data obtained from Kinect sensor, it is also possible to apply other types of visual sensors to the proposed system. In further works, it would be interesting to use various types of feature extractors such as HOG and combine all the features to obtain more robust recognition performance.

Acknowledgements

This research was supported by Basic Science Research Program through the National Research Foundation of Korea(NRF) funded by the Ministry of Education(2013R1A1A 2061831).

References

[1] Chen, B., Ting, J.-A., Marlin, B., and de Freitas, N. Deep learning of invariant spatio-temporal features from video. In *Proc. NIPS* (2010).

[2] Ji, S., Yang, M., and Yu, K. 3D convolutional neural networks for human action recognition. *IEEE transactions on pattern analysis and machine intelligence 35*, 1 (2013), 221–231.

[3] Kim, T.-K., Wong, S.-F., and Cipolla, R. Tensor Canonical Correlation Analysis for Action Classification. In *Proc. CVPR*, IEEE (2007), 1–8.

[4] Le, Q. V., Zou, W. Y., Yeung, S. Y., and Ng, A. Y. Learning hierarchical invariant spatio-temporal features for action recognition with independent subspace analysis. In *Proc. CVPR*, IEEE (2011), 3361–3368.

[5] Liu, L., and Shao, L. Learning Discriminative Representations from RGB-D Video Data. In *Proc. IJCAI*, AAAI Press (2013), 1493–1500.

[6] Lui, Y. M. A least squares regression framework on manifolds and its application to gesture recognition. In *Proc. CVPRW*, IEEE (2012), 13–18.

[7] Lui, Y. M., Beveridge, J. R., and Kirby, M. Action classification on product manifolds. In *Proc. CVPR*, IEEE (2010), 833–839.

[8] MarketsandMarkets. Gesture Recognition & Touchless Sensing Market (2013 - 2018). Tech. rep., April 2013.

[9] Weinland, D., Ronfard, R., and Boyer, E. A survey of vision-based methods for action representation, segmentation and recognition. *Computer Vision and Image Understanding 115*, 2 (2011), 224–241.

Communicating Emotions: A Model for Natural Emotions in HRI

Oliver Damm
Applied Informatics
Bielefeld University, Germany
odamm@techfak.uni-bielefeld.de

Britta Wrede
Applied Informatics
Bielefeld University, Germany
bwrede@techfak.uni-bielefeld.de

Abstract

Based on different psychological models of emotion, we argue that an intrapersonal account of emotion is not sufficient. Rather, we need interpersonal accounts of emotion that go beyond the assumption that a communicative agent simply displays her internal affective state and takes situational aspects into account. In this paper a computational model for the application of natural emotions in HRI is presented. Having a robot which is able to mimic emotional expressions and also use emotions in a strategic manner will enhance its emotional and social competence.

Author Keywords

Social Robotic; Emotions; Emotional Alignment; human-robot interaction; Strategic Emotions; Context Events

ACM Classification Keywords

H.5.m [Information interfaces and presentation (e.g., HCI)]: Miscellaneous.

Introduction

Several findings in research of social interaction indicate the importance of expressing and understanding emotions [4]. So every interaction between humans is emotionally colored [3]. A study conducted by Eyssel and Colleagues

HAI 2014, October 29–31, 2014, Tsukuba, Japan.
ACM 978-1-4503-3035-0/14/10.
http://dx.doi.org/10.1145/2658861.2658939

[2] exemplifies the relevance of emotions in human-robot interaction. They found that people sympathize more strongly with a robot if it communicates emotions. Another important point is the response given by the emotional display. So people form expectations about the behavior. They wait for reactions which they often express themselves in their real-life interactions [6]. In other words: There are many emotion expressions in human-human interaction (HHI), and therefore people presume the same for human-robot interaction (HRI).

Developing a computational model of emotional alignment requires building a system which is able to produce the similar phenomena and behavior that can be observed in human-human interaction. On a interpersonal level such phenomena might be emotional mimicking or empathy, on a intrapersonal level the system has to anticipate in which manner the currently computed emotion will influence the actual interaction.

Computational Model

In the following section the computational model of emotional alignment (fig. 2) will be described in more detail. This model was implemented and evaluated using the anthropomorphic robot head Flobi [5] (fig. 1).

Processing perception

As aforementioned in the proposed model the processing of the emotional feedback may occur on several layers of complexity. On the one hand the choice of the level depends on the level of understanding, i.e. in case of non-understanding only the level of automatically emotional alignment can be reached. On the one hand the necessity is a crucial factor in selecting the level of processing.

Figure 1: The anthropomorphic robot head Flobi.

On the lowest level (automatic) the processing is limited to perception of an emotional expression and the copy process. Depending on the modality of the stimulus, this process maps the received features into motor-commands or prosodic features of the emotional display.

The middle level (schematic), uses the features previously extracted by the underlying level to compute a hypothesis with respect to the observed expression. So a motor program produces an emotionally aligned output on all relevant channels.

The third level (conceptual), is the top-level process. On this level the situational context as well as the internal emotional state of the robot is taken into account. So the process of adaption is influenced by the current emotional state of the robot.

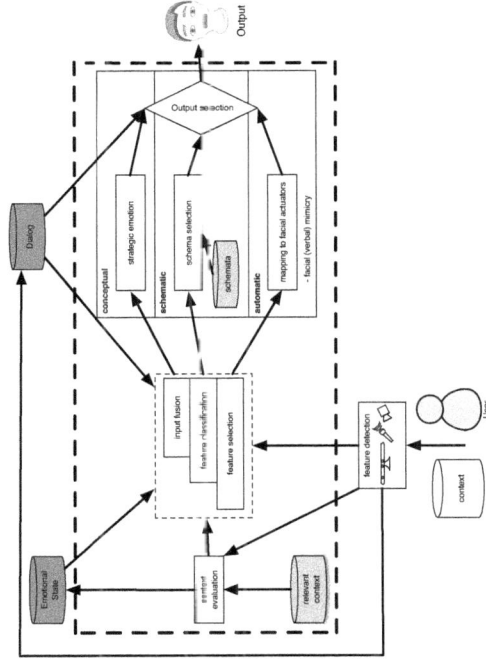

Figure 2: The proposed computational model for emotional alignment.

Emotional Response

The level of output generation has to handle the results from all three layers of processing. On this stage of processing it is important to determine which expression should be displayed and which has to be suppressed. For modeling this behavior it is necessary to integrate an emotional memory to store all stimuli acquired by the sensors.

According to the facial feedback hypothesis [1] the process for output generation is linked directly to the emotional state of the robot.

Imagine having the situation, the robot is facing a familiar user. The user is smiling at the robot, but he has the intension of lying to it. According to the proposed model, the robot would evaluate this situation as following. The perception process is detecting the emotional features and use these feature to mimic the expression. In contrast the conscious evaluation of the situation generates the hypothesis, given the familiarity, the user is lying to the robot. That will lead the robot to compute an angry emotion. According to the emotional memory the process of output generation has to decide which emotion is adequate for the situation.

In summary, this model is not limited to describe only one alignment process, e.g. empathy or mimicry. It regards emotional interaction processes from a more communicative perspective and integrates alignment processes, which can be allocated to the three layers (automatic, schematic, conceptual). In addition, the model is influenced on all three layers of processing by internal and external context factors. Communication with an (emotionally) aligning robot is supposed to be much easier than with less adaptive partners.

Evaluation

The above-described system was evaluated in a study at the Bielefeld University. In total 86 students participated in this study and played the "Who Am I?" game against the robot. During the interaction the three layers produced different emotional expressions.
The lowest level where used to produce a facial mimicry.
The schematic level enables the robot to react to context events. This contextual events were prearranged

interruptions by a confederate. On these interruptions the robot responded with an angry face and sent the confederate out of the room.
The conceptual level were used to influence the interaction. Every time the robot is losing the game he showed a sad face and asked the participant if he doesn't want to reconsider his last action. If he then asked a wrong question, the robot may perhaps ask another question and win the game.
Afterwards they were asked to rate the robot and the interaction. First results show that the robot was rated better when all layers of emotional alignment were enabled.

Conclusions

With this computational model of emotional alignment an approach is presented which includes communicative adaptation processes and can be observed in human-human interaction. It will also be able to form expectations in which manner the currently computed emotion will influence the actual interaction. The was to develop a system, which aligns in communication to the emotions expressed by the human partners. The robot equipped with it will not only be perceived as more natural and emotionally more competent but will also enhance successful communication. The robot reacts emotionally to its communication partner alternatively on the three described layers. He is able to react on contextual events and integrate them into the current interaction. The further analysis of the results will show that the integration of these system will enhance the human-robot interaction.

Acknowledgments

This research is partially supported by the German Research Foundation (DFG) in the Collaborative Research Center 673 "Alignment in Communication".

References

[1] Buck, R. Nonverbal behavior and the theory of emotion: The facial feedback hypothesis. *Journal of Personality and Social Psychology 38*, 5 (1980), 811–824.

[2] Eyssel, F., Hegel, F., Horstmann, G., and Wagner, C. Anthropomorphic inferences from emotional nonverbal cues: A case study. *RO-MAN, 2010 IEEE* (2010), 646–651.

[3] H Delhees, K. *Soziale Kommunikation: psychologische Grundlagen für das Miteinander in der ...* Opladen: Westdt. Verlag, 1994.

[4] Hielscher, M. Emotion und Sprachproduktion. *Gert Rickheit/Theo Herrmann/Werner Deutsch (Hg.), Psycholinguistics/Psycholinguistik. Ein internationales Handbuch, Berlin/New York* (2003), 468–490.

[5] Lütkebohle, I., Hegel, F., Schulz, S., Hackel, M., Wrede, B., Wachsmuth, S., and Sagerer, G. The bielefeld anthropomorphic robot head "Flobi". In *Robotics and Automation (ICRA), 2010 IEEE International Conference on* (2010), 3384–3391.

[6] Weiss, A., Mirnig, N., and Foerster, F. What users expect of a Proactive Navigation Robot. In *Proceedings of the workshop "Expectations in intuitive interaction" on the 6th HRI International conference on Human-Robot Interaction* (2011).

How does emphatic emotion emerge via human-robot rhythmic interaction?

Hideyuki Takahashi
Osaka University.
F1-401, 2-1, Yamadaoka, Suita
565-0871, Osaka, Japan
hideyuki@ams.eng.osaka-u.ac.jp

Takato Horii
Osaka University.
F1-401, 2-1, Yamadaoka, Suita
565-0871, Osaka, Japan
takato.horii@ams.eng.osaka-u.ac.jp

Nobutsuna Endo
Osaka University.
F1-401, 2-1, Yamadaoka, Suita
565-0871, Osaka, Japan
endo@ams.eng.osaka-u.ac.jp

Tomoyo Morita
Osaka University.
F1-401, 2-1, Yamadaoka, Suita
565-0871, Osaka, Japan
Morita@ams.eng.osaka-u.ac.jp

Hiroki Yokoyama
Osaka University.
F1-401, 2-1, Yamadaoka, Suita
565-0871, Osaka, Japan
yokoyama@ams.eng.osaka-u.ac.jp

Minoru Asada
Osaka University.
F1-401, 2-1, Yamadaoka, Suita
565-0871, Osaka, Japan
asada@ams.eng.osaka-u.ac.jp

HAI 2014, October 29-31, 2014, Tsukuba, Japan.
ACM 978-1-4503-3035-0/14/10.
http://dx.doi.org/10.1145/2658861.2658940

Abstract

Sharing a same rhythm among different agents matures close empathic relationship. However it is still unclear how rhythmic information is transferred to emphatic emotion in our brain. In this paper, we propose human-robot drumming interaction system to investigate how rhythmic physical interaction brings emphatic emotion. In this paper, we introduce the detail of our proposed system.

ACM Classification Keywords

J.4 Social and Behavioral Sciences: Psychology

Introduction

Empathy is a capacity for experiencing and inferring other's internal feeling and it is one of core components for animal social cognition [?]. Over the past few decades, a considerable number of studies have been made on psychological and neural mechanisms of empathy. One of interesting topics about empathy is how empathic relationship (e.g. bonding) occur via a physical non-emotional interpersonal interaction. For example, bidirectional mother-infant body imitation matures the mother-infant bonding [?]. Further even in adults, implicit mimicry brings empathic relationship between two individuals (chameleon effect) [?]. Although there are many psychological and neural experimental findings suggesting the strong link between physical interaction and empathy, it is still unclear what kinds of information in physical interaction are transformed to empathic emotion.

Figure 1: Our proposed human-robot drumming interaction system named "AOKICHI"

One of possible hypotheses is that the arousal of empathic emotion strongly links to rhythmic synchronization among different agents. If audiences are emotionally excited in a concert, their body movements tightly synchronize with the music rhythm. The link between rhythm and emotion is investigated in some previous literatures [?]. For example, a child tended to show helping behaviors for other person when the child and the person shared a common musical rhythm [?]. However it is still unclear how rhythmic information connects to empathic emotion in our brain, because there are few suitable experimental platforms connecting rhythm information to subject's empathic response. In an interpersonal interaction, it is quite difficult to control the degree of rhythmic synchronization between two individuals. Hence the experimental platform that can strictly control the degree of the synchronization is required. .

Figure 2: An example scene of the robot suffering

We have conducted several studies using robots as the method for social neuroscience research [?] [?]. Robots can be recognized as a social partner by us. Meanwhile robot's appearance and behavior are absolutely controllable and it is useful for constructing well-controlled experimental tasks for social interaction.

In this paper, we propose a human-robot drumming interaction system to elucidate how rhythmic physical interaction brings empathic emotion (Figure1). In this system, we can strictly control the degree of human-robot rhythmic synchronization in a joint drumming task by programing the robot's drumming behavior. This system enables to investigate how the degree of rhythmic synchronization with the robot modulates empathic response when subjects watch the movie of the robot suffering (Figure2).

The detail of our proposed system

In our system, a drumming robot named "AOKICHI" hits a taiko (Japanese drum). The robot consists of 1 degree-of-freedom (maxon DC motor RE 35, 90[W]). The position of the motor is controlled by an Arduino Uno board and a motor driver (TITECH PC-0120-2). The taiko is equipped with a piezo film sensor. The Arduino Uno board detects hitting times of subject and the robot and sends the data to PC. The overview and the system configuration of AOKICHI system are shown in Figure 3.

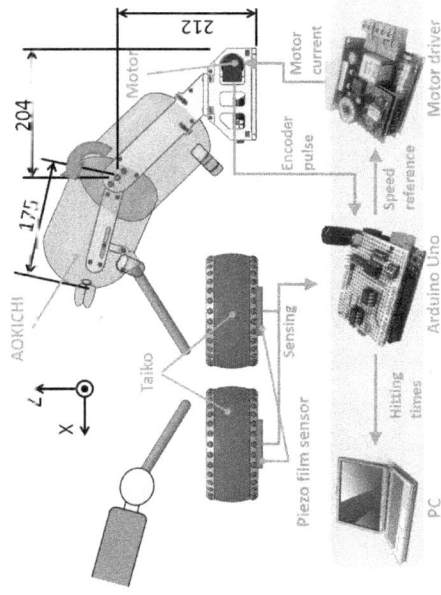

Figure 3: The overview of the system

On going project and discussion

We are now conducting several experiments in both adults and children with this system. As a preliminary finding in adults, we found that a subject who was aware of mutual rhythm coordination (not one-way coordination) with the robot tended to show empathic response to the robot

suffering by questionnaires rating (Figure 4). This result suggests that ambiguous initiative in rhythmic interaction might bring the empathic emotion. In a child experiment, we are now investigating how the visual appearance of the robot influence child drumming behavior. Our hypothesis is that the appearance leading empathic emotion (e.g. very pretty animal-like stuff) improves the rhythm synchronization between child and robot.

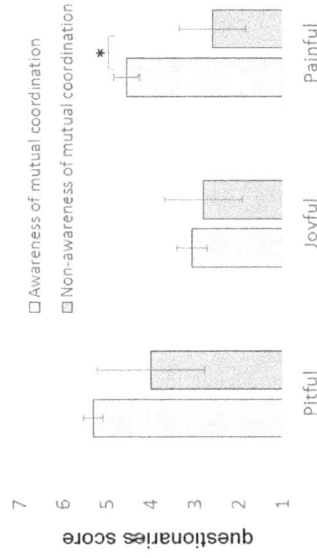

Figure 4: Preliminary questionnaire result

We believe that rhythmic information and empathic emotion tightly interact in our brain and our proposed system is very useful for elucidating the link between rhythm information and empathic emotion.

Acknowledgements

This study was supported by a Grant-in-Aid for Specially Promoted Research (No. 24000012), a Grant-in-Aid for Scientific Research on Innovative Areas "Founding a creative society via collaboration between humans and robots (No. 4101)" (No. 24118708), Grant-in-Aid for Young Scientists (B) (No. 23700321) and the MEXT project "Creating Hybrid Organs of the future" at Osaka University. I am deeply grateful to Shinsuke Shimojo,

Jimmy Baraglia, Paul Hendi, Ban Midori and Takako Shibata for their helpful comments and kindly supports.

References

[1] Davis, Mark H. *Empathy: A social psychological approach.* Westview Press, 1994.

[2] Stern, Daniel N. *The first relationship: Infant and mother.*. Harvard University Press, 2009.

[3] Chartrand, Tanya L., and John A. Bargh. *The chameleon effect: The perceptionbehavior link and social interaction.*. Journal of personality and social psychology 76.6 (1999): 893.

[4] Kawasaki, Masahiro, et al. *Inter-brain synchronization during coordination of speech rhythm in human-to-human social interaction.*. Scientific reports 3 (2013)

[5] Cirelli, Laura K., Kathleen M. Einarson, and Laurel J. Trainor. *Interpersonal synchrony increases prosocial behavior in infants.* Developmental Science (2014)

[6] Takahashi, Hideyuki, et al. *An investigation of social factors related to online mentalizing in a human-robot competitive game.* Japanese Psychological Research 55.2 (2013): 144-153.

[7] Takahashi, Hideyuki, et al. *Different impressions of other agents obtained through social interaction uniquely modulate dorsal and ventral pathway activities in the social human brain.*. Cortex (2014).

Determining Robot Gaze According to Participation Roles in Multiparty Conversations

Takashi Yoshino
Seikei University
Musashino-shi, Tokyo, Japan
dm146213@cc.seikei.ac.jp

Yuki Hayashi
Osaka Prefecture University
Sakai-shi, Osaka, Japan
hayashi@kis.osakafu-u.ac.jp

Yukiko I. Nakano
Seikei University
Musashino-shi, Tokyo, Japan
y.nakano@st.seikei.ac.jp

Abstract

Gaze is an important nonverbal feedback signal in multiparty face-to-face conversations. To build a robot that can convey the appropriate attentional behavior in human-robot multiparty conversations, this paper analyzes human attentional behaviors in multiparty conversations, and establishes gaze-transition models for speakers, addressees, and side participants. Further, the model was implemented in a humanoid robot that can control its gaze.

Author Keywords

Gaze; Participation role; Multiparty conversation

ACM Classification Keywords

H.5.2. Information interfaces and presentation: User Interfaces – Interaction styles; Theory and methods; Prototyping

Introduction

In face-to-face communication, gaze is an important nonverbal feedback signal for the speaker. Specifically in multiparty conversations, the gaze or attentional behavior of each participant is more complex [1]. Such behavior differs depending on the participation roles [2, 3]. A speaker looks at the addressee during most of the

Figure 1: Snapshot of interaction in the data collection experiment

speaking, occasionally paying attention to the side participants. The side participants, on the other hand, tend to look at either the speaker or the addressee.

Therefore, in order to introduce a communication robot as a participant in multiparty interactions with human users, it is indispensable to generate the appropriate gaze and attentional behavior that corresponds to the robot's role at any given time. Previous studies on communication robots demonstrated the importance and effectiveness of a robot's gaze in human-robot interaction [4, 5].

With the goal of building a robot that can convey the appropriate attentional behaviors in human-robot multiparty conversations, this paper establishes attentional behavior models by analyzing human multiparty conversations, and implements a robot that can control its gaze based on these models.

DATA COLLECTION AND ANNOTATION

First, we collected face-to-face multiparty conversations to analyze human attentional behaviors. To do so, a group of four people was asked to have a conversation about where to go on the weekend. The experiment included 11 male and 7 female university students. Participants were divided into six groups of three people. A fourth member, well acquainted with possible weekend destinations (hereafter referred to as the "guide"), joined each group. Any of the three participants could ask the guide questions about the various locations. Each group conversed in three sessions, and the 18 conversations from the 6 groups were collected for analysis.

The overall interactions were recorded on video. In addition, each participant's speech was recorded using headset microphones, and each participant's point of view was recorded using a web camera mounted on a cap worn by the participant. We also used augmented reality (AR) markers to identify each subject. A snapshot of the experiment is provided in Figure 1. As shown in the figure, a unique marker was placed in front of each subject.

The speech intervals were detected using Julius adintool speech-recognition software, and the gaze direction during each speech interval was registered using ELAN, a video-annotation tool. Furthermore, we used the AR-marker recognition results to report the gaze direction.

HEAD-GAZE ANALYSIS

We analyzed the time during which the human gaze was maintained before it transitioned to another.

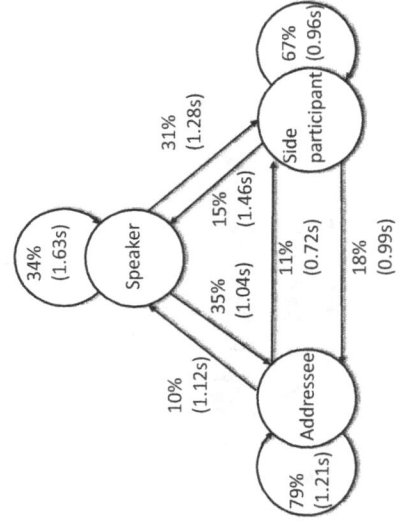

Figure 2: Analysis of gaze transition for the guide acting as a side participant

Because of the potential for the guide's attentional behavior to differ from the other participants, separate analyses were deemed necessary. Moreover, because the gaze direction may differ depending on the participation role, we analyzed the gaze of the speakers, addressees, and side participants.

Figure 2 illustrates the analysis of the gaze transition and duration for the guide acting as a side participant—that is, when the guide was neither a speaker nor an addressee. The labels in each arc indicate the average proportion for the transition. The number in parentheses represents the average time during which the gaze was maintained. For example, when the guide acted as a side participant and looked at the current speaker, the gaze was redirected towards the addressee 35% of the time and continued for an average of 1.04 s. The guide redirected the gaze toward another side participant 31% of the time, sustaining it for an average of 1.28 s. The gaze was maintained at the speaker 34% of the time for an average of 1.63 s. Moreover, the graph reveals the proportion and duration of the gaze when it was directed at the addressee and when it was directed at another side participant.

We also created models reflecting the attentional behavior of the guide acting as a speaker and an addressee, and similar models for the other participants who were not the guide. In total, we created six gaze-transition models.

Implementation

We used the results of the gaze-transition analysis described above to develop models that were implemented in a humanoid robot, named Robovie-R3

(Figure 3). The system architecture is provided in Figure 4.

Recognizing the participation roles

Speaker diarization: A microphone array in the Kinect sensor is used to detect speech sounds and to estimate the audio-source angle. When speech sounds are detected, the system assumes that the participant closest to the audio-source angle is the speaker.

Addressee identification: We assume that a speaker will look directly at the addressee upon speaking. Hence, the system identifies the addressee by recognizing the target for the speaker's gaze when the speaker begins talking. We used AR markers in front of each participant to recognize the target of the gaze. When the speaker's web camera recognizes the AR marker of a participant, the latter is understood to be the target of the speaker's gaze. When the robot acts as the speaker, the cameras installed in the robot's eyes are used to find the AR markers.

Side-participant identification: After determining the current speaker and the corresponding addressee, the person who is neither the speaker nor the addressee is identified as the side participant.

Control the robot's gaze

Once the participation roles are recognized, the robot's gaze is determined by referring the gaze-transition models obtained from our data analyses. The system measures the angle between the current head direction and the direction of the next target. First, the system recognizes the position of the person's head that will be the next target of the robot's gaze. For this purpose, we use the head position in the Kinect skeleton data.

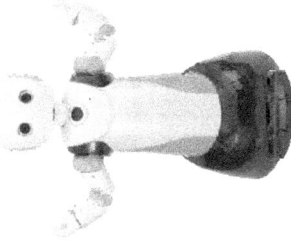

Figure 3: Humanoid robot, Robovie-R3

Moreover, the gaze-transition models will be improved by considering the context as well as the utterance content. In the current implementation, we used AR markers to recognize who is looking at whom, but we plan to use Kinect's face-tracking functions to recognize the gaze target for each participant.

Acknowledgements

This work was supported by JSPS KAKENHI Grant Number 25280076.

References

[1] Vertegaal, R., The GAZE Groupware System: Mediating Joint Attention in Multiparty Communication and Collaboration, *In CHI 1999*, 1999.

[2] Goffman, E., *Forms of Talk*, Philadelphia, PA: University of Pennsylvania Press, 1981.

[3] Clark, H.H., *Using Language*, Cambridge: Cambridge University Press, 1996.

[4] Moubayed, S. AI, Beskow, J., Skantze, G., and Björn, G. Furhat: A Back-projected Human-like Robot Head for Multiparty Human-Machine Interaction, *Cognitive Behavioural Systems*, Lecture Notes in Computer Science Volume 7403, pp 114-130, 2012.

[5] Mutlu, B., Shiwa, T., Kanda, T., Ishiguro, H., and Hagita, N. Footing In Human-Robot Conversations: How Robots Might Shape Participant Roles Using Gaze Cues, *HRI '09 Proceedings of the 4th ACM/IEEE International Conference on Human-Robot Interaction*, pp 61-68, 2009.

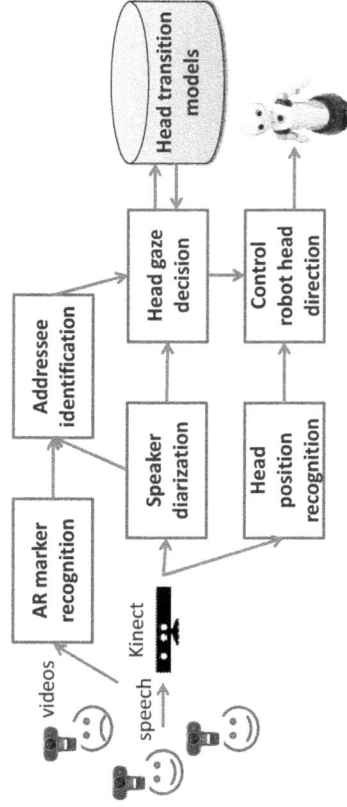

Figure 4: System architecture

Then, the system calculates the angle between the head position and the robot's current head direction, and uses this as the angle for rotating the robot's head. The head gaze is maintained for the time period provided by the model. If the speech continues past a certain time period, the robot has the opportunity to change its gaze and determines the direction for this change by referring once again to the transition model.

Conclusion

This paper analyzed attentional behaviors in multiparty conversations, and proposed gaze-transition models for speakers, addressees, and side participants. We also implemented these models in a humanoid robot, and built a prototype system for changing the gaze of the robot depending on its participation role.

We proposed separate models for the guide and the other participants. Because we could not recruit multiple guides, the current models are based on data obtained from only one guide. Therefore, additional data is needed from different subjects acting as guides.

Interactions on Eyeballs of Humanoid-Robots

Takayuki Todo

Institute of Advanced Media Arts
and Sciences.(IAMAS)

4-1-7 Kagano, Ogaki-shi, Gifu

503-0006 JAPAN

todzilla11@iamas.ac.jp

Takanari Miisho

Institute of Advanced Media Arts
and Sciences(IAMAS)

4-1-7 Kagano, Ogaki-shi, Gifu

503-0006 JAPAN

tmiisho2011@iamas.ac.jp

Author Keywords

Humanoid robots; Androids; Interaction; Animatronics;

ACM Classification Keywords

H.5.1 Multimedia Information Systems: *Artificial,
augmented, and virtual realities.*
H.5.2 User Interfaces: *Interaction styles.*
I.2.9 Robotics.

Prolution

There has previously been a plethora of research
studies conducted on humanoid robots (especially
"Androids" the robots designed with photorealistic
appearances to look and act like a real human).
However, these studies have still not found a solution
to creating robot facial expressions, and the sense of
discomfort created from interaction with a human and a
robot without facial expressions or abnormal facial
expressions. In this study, we focused on the gaze
expressions of humanoid robots' eyes. We hypothesized
that by constructing a more adequate interaction
between the [visual object - eyeballs - head], we can
make the movements of a humanoid robots' gaze more
natural and less discomforting, or give them more
impressive expressiveness. In order to explore this
hypothesis, we have created and tested "GAZEROID",
an original humanoid robot.

Problem and Solution

During target observation by humans (fixed gaze or tracking movements), both eyes maintain contact with their visual target, independent of head movement. However, in the case of humanoid robots, previous work has shown robot eyes that successfully track a target, but the head may move in various directions, sometimes even opposing the direction of eye movement. These awkward movements cause humans interacting with the robot to lack the feeling that the robot is looking or gazing at them (the impression that they are directing their attention on something), and this may cause humans to feel the interaction with the robot is strange or creepy.

If "gaze" is defined as the vector between the eyeballs and the visual object, we can evaluate it from the current relative locations and directions of the each eyeball, the head which the eyes embedded in, the visual object, and the sensor. By constructing the motion mechanism which reflects this relation, we made "GAZEROID" a humanoid robot prototype which is able to represent the "gaze" and perform more natural eye-contact.

System

The software system has the ability to calculate the vector between the current locations of right and left eyeballs and the visual object, from the accurate figures of relative positions between the centers of both eyeballs, the rotation of head, and the lens of the depth camera sensor. We use the Microsoft Kinect as the sensor that is able to capture the facing person as a 3 dimensional figure, and the system estimates the location of his or her eyes to create a target point.

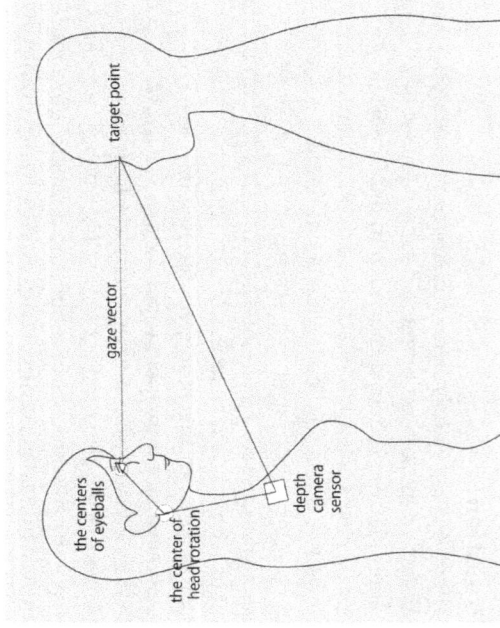

Figure 1. GAZEROID generates gaze vector from relative vectors between current locations of the centers of eyeballs, the rotation of head, depth camera sensor, and the target point.

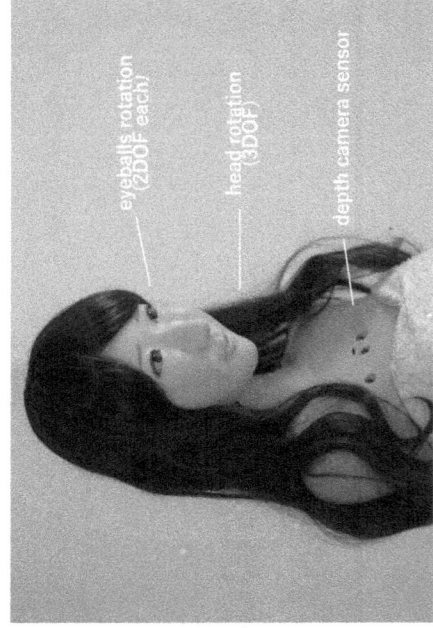

Figure 2. Hardware appearance of GAZEROID

The hardware system has servos to give each eyeball rotation in 2 dimension of freedom (DOF, as pitch and yaw), and the head has rotation in 3DOF (as pitch, yaw, roll). These systems are packaged in the housing, which is shaped in appearance like real human.

Experiment and the Result

We exhibited our robot "GAZEROID" at open events that are accessible by the general public, and surveyed over 5000 men and women. Results showed almost half the people gave positive evaluations, describing the robot with adjectives such as "pretty" and "approachable". On the other hand, the other half gave negative evaluations, in some cases describing the robot as "scary" or "creepy". However, 90% of those surveyed felt like the robot was staring at them. In the negative evaluations, there were many answers such as "It's scary because it's too realistic", "I felt like I was being glared at" and "It casts a cold eye".

Discussion

In both positive or negative evaluations, we can estimate that the eye-contact interaction achieved great effectiveness. We postulate lack of eyelids' connected motion to the eyeballs is thought as the reason why it caused negative impressions. In the case of real human, eyelids have movement related to eyeball motion. However, this robot did not have this feature, and it often makes unnatural faces with the eyes rolled askance too much.

Conclusion and Future perspectives

Both positive and negative feedback regarding the robot was received. However, both groups of respondents showed a majority felt the effectiveness of "gaze" impressions. Therefore, we think it is possible to improve the positive impressions on humanoid by construction of higher level of interactions with additional implements of eyelids' related to eyeball motion, gaze-to-gaze interaction by using gaze tracking sensor, and so on.

References

[1] Mori, M. (1970/2012). The uncanny valley (K. F. MacDorman & N. Kageki, Trans.). IEEE Robotics & Automation Magazine, 19(2), 98–100.

[2] Bartneck, C., Kanda, T., Ishiguro, H., & Hagita, N. (2007). Is the Uncanny Valley an Uncanny Cliff? Proceedings of the 16th IEEE, RO-MAN 2007, Jeju, Korea, pp. 368–373.

[3] T. Minato, M. Shimada, S. Itakura, K. Lee, and H. Ishiguro. (2006) Evaluating the human likeness of an android by comparing gaze behaviors elicited by the android and a person, Advanced Robotics, Vol.20, No.10, pp.1147-1163.

Video-Based Emotion Identification Using Face Alignment and Support Vector Machines

Gil-Jin Jang
School of Electronics
Engineering
Kyungpook National
University
80 Daehakro, Bukgu Daegu
702-701, South Korea
gjang@knu.ac.kr

Jeong-Sik Park
Department of Information and
Communication Engineering
Yeungnam University
280 Daehak-ro, Gyeongsan-si,
Gyeongsangbuk-do 712-749,
South Korea
parkjs@knu.ac.kr

Ahra Jo
School of Electrical and
Computer Engineering
Ulsan National Institute of
Science and Technology
(UNIST)
UNIST-gil 50, Ulsan 689-798,
South Korea
araya23@unist.ac.kr

HAI 2014, October 29-31, 2014, Tsukuba, Japan.
ACM 978-1-4503-3035-0/14/10.
http://dx.doi.org/10.1145/2658861.2658943

Abstract

This abstract introduces an efficient method for
identifying various facial expressions from image inputs.
To recognize the emotions of the facial expressions, a
number of facial feature points were extracted. The
extracted feature points are then transformed to
49-dimensional feature vectors which are robust to scale
and translational variations, and the facial emotions are
recognized by a support vector machine (SVM). Based on
the experimental results, SVM performance was obtained
by 50.8% for 6 emotion classification, and 78.0% for 3
emotions.

Author Keywords

Emotion Recognition, Active Shape Model, Support
Vector Machine.

ACM Classification Keywords

I.5.4 [Pattern Recognition]: Applications.

General Terms

Algorithms, Performance.

Introduction

This abstract introduces a human emotion recognition
system using facial images. To achieve the goal, the facial
components such as eyes, brows, nose, ears, and mouth

are aligned by active shape models (ASMs) [1, 3], and 49 feature values are then extracted from the aligned facial points so that they are invariant to scale and translation changes. Using the feature vectors, support vector machine (SVM) is used to recognize the facial expressions.

Method and Results

One of the most popular pattern classifiers these days is support vector machine (SVM) [4, 5]. When there are not enough training samples, most pattern recognizers such as neural networks and Bayesian pattern classifiers fail to perform well. The advantage of SVM is that it is very robust with few number of training samples because the classification boundary is built only from a small number of samples that lie on the decision boundary. In our work, we used radial-basis function kernels whose shape is very similar to Gaussian functions [2].

Table 1

No. Emotions	6	5	4	3
Anger	34.4%	25.0%	N.A.	N.A.
Disgust	59.3%	65.3%	80.7%	77.3%
Surprise	55.5%	63.9%	74.8%	76.5%
Fear	20.0%	N.A.	N.A.	N.A.
Happiness	74.7%	76.4%	79.2%	80.3%
Sadness	60.9%	60.9%	60.9%	N.A.
Average	50.8%	58.3%	73.9%	78.0%

The advantage of Gaussian kernel functions is that it can localize the model to a bounded region so that it can distinguish one class to the others, and multi-class classification can be implemented by one-versus-others method. We have carried out emotion recognition experiments on a set of 517 images u 153 different subjects. The experimental results are shown in Table 1.

Emotions are gradually excluded one by one, and the performances were measured for 6, 5, 4, and 3 emotions.

Acknowledgements

This research was supported by Kyungpook National University Research Fund, 2014.

References

[1] Ahn, B., Han, Y., and Kweon, I. S. Real-time facial landmarks tracking using active shape model and lk optical flow. In *Proc. International Conference on Ubiquitous Robots and Ambient Intelligence (URAI 2012)* (11 2012), 541–543.

[2] Chang, Y.-W., Hsieh, C.-J., Chang, K.-W., Ringgaard, M., and Lin, C.-J. Training and testing low-degree polynomial data mappings via linear svm. *Journal of Machine Learning Research 11* (2010), 1471–1490.

[3] Cootes, T., Taylor, C., Cooper, D., and Graham, J. Active shape models - their training and application. *Computer Vision and Image Understanding 61* (1995), 38–59.

[4] Cristianini, N., and Shawe-Taylor, J. *An Introduction to Support Vector Machines and other kernel-based learning methods.* Cambridge University Press, 2000.

[5] Vapnik, V. *The Nature of Statistical Learning Theory.* Springer-Verlag, 1995.

Social Networking Sites Photos and Robots: A Pilot Research on Facebook Photo Albums and Robotics Interfaces for Older Adults

Angie Lorena Marin
Self-Scholar
Tokyo, Japan.
angielorena@gmail.com

Author Keywords

Robotics Interfaces; Facebook; SNS; elderly; HRI; HCI; photo albums.

ACM Classification Keywords

J. Computer Applications. J.4 SOCIAL AND BEHAVIORAL SCIENCES. Subjects: Sociology; Psychology

HAI 2014, October 29–31, 2014, Tsukuba, Japan.
ACM 978-1-4503-3035-0/14/10.
http://dx.doi.org/10.1145/2658861.2658944

Abstract

Human Computer/Robot Interaction has concerned about developing agents and tools for an effective performance in a user interaction scenario. In particular, the study on the usage of social media tools by older adults has been of a core theme to investigate. In this study, the interaction with a social network site tool, Facebook photo albums, supported by an agent embedded in an assistant robot is analyzed. Therefore, we present a study that explores the relationship between the type of interaction with the social network tool, and the level of perceived usefulness, ease of use, ease of learning and satisfaction by the elderly as users. The study found that the type of interface interaction with the social media tool affect the perception of the older adults in usefulness, ease of use, ease of learning and satisfaction: the older adults perceived the Facebook photo albums tool more useful, easy to use, easy to learn and felt more satisfied during the interaction with the robotic interface supported by the agent. Based on the results of this work, we can approach toward the integration of social network sites technologies for older adults and robots, not only for interaction design considerations, but also to help the seniors to overcome technological and social isolation.

Introduction

In the modern digital connected society social networks have become one of the most popular fashions of making friends and communicating with them. It is widely known that people can keep in touch not only with their friends, but also with their relatives using Social Network Sites (SNS) such as Facebook.

Smart devices are surrounding us, and its inclusion in our individual needs is increasing day by day. However, although social networking behaviors are a common habit for adults and younger people, still some limitations persist when it refers to elder's technology use. How can a robot help in the process? Can older adults become in active users of social networks tools?

Literature review

Older generations do not use the internet for socializing and entertainment as much as they do it for searching information, emailing, and buying products [1]. Regarding demographic population, Internet users older than 50, have nearly doubled from 22% to 42% in 2010. Almost half of Internet users 50-64 and about 26% users age 65 and older now use social networking sites [2]. However, while online news and email are still more appealing to older users, the interest toward social sites is increasing, and older adults are becoming in frequent users. One aspect that can influence older users' interest in Social Network tools, is the possibility of reconnecting with people from their past. "The use of technology and its' providing information allows the elderly to face more easily the difficulties of modern life, trespassing the limits of their social and emotional isolation, thus achieving a more qualitative living" [3].

The Internet community is facing not only the boom of technological creations, but also challenges in terms of social interaction and social organization. The process of creation and inclusion of new technologies may result in new difficulties. However, these problems may light the responsibilities of facilitating and encouraging successful interaction. [4].

Regarding robotics systems, not many studies have been done for Social networks and robots. Facebot Project [5] explores how a mobile robot with vision, a dialogue system, a social database and a Facebook connection was created. The research claims to study the first robot that is embedded in a social website and a system that can purposefully exploit and create social information that is available online. Diverging from their approach, this study is focused into facilitate Social Network use on robotic interfaces for older

adults, investigating how is the relationship between the type of interface (robotic vs. conventional) for a Social Network tool (Facebook photo albums) and the perceived usefulness, ease of use, ease of learning and satisfaction of older users.

Method

Participants

Twenty four participants from the Jongno Senior Welfare Service Center in Seoul, South Korea were recruited to participate in the experimental design. N=24 (12 Males, 12 Females) with ages ranging from 63 to 80.

Stimulus Materials

KORUS Tech - Homemate Robot from Intelligent Systems Research Institute in Sungkyunkwan University, South Korea. Facebook desktop application and Android Application were configured for the study. (Figure 1)

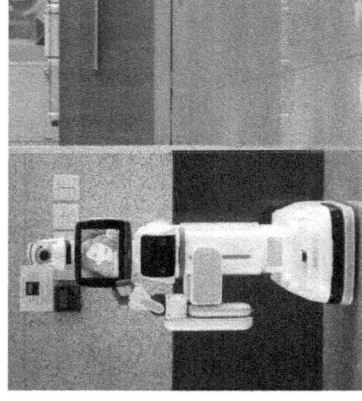

Figure 1. Homemate Robot.

Hypothesis

- H1: In the design of interaction scenarios for the elderly, assistantship of a robotic agent could affect the perceived usefulness of the Facebook Photo albums tool more than the conventional user interface. Therefore, older adult's perceived usefulness of the tool is affected by the type of interaction with the system.

- H2: Robotic Interface assistance could affect the sense of complexity to perform a task. Therefore, older adult's perceived Ease of use and Ease of learning will be affected by the type of interaction with the robot or the computer system.

- H3: Satisfaction level will be higher in conditions where the system (Robot agent vs computer) initiates the interaction for the Facebook Photo albums tool.

Manipulation. Independent Variables

Type of Interaction with a Social Network tool (Facebook Photo Album)

Condition 1. Elderly Computer Interaction (ECI):

- Conventional Facebook photo album interface.
- 2 clicks per Interaction
- High Visual Complexity

Condition 2. Elderly Computer Interaction (ERI):

- Robotic Interface for Facebook photo album tool.
- Robot agent announcing and assisting the interaction
- 3 taps per interaction

- Low Visual Complexity

Measurements/Dependent Variables

- Usefulness of the Facebook photo albums tool.
- Perceived Ease of Use of the Facebook photo albums Interface tool.
- Perceived Ease of learning of the Facebook photo albums Interface tool.
- User Satisfaction during the interaction.

The USE questionnaire was used in this study. [6].The items of the questionnaire were convenient to the study because it's evaluated items and declared face validity for both users and researchers.

Procedures

Users were asked to rate agreement with the statements in a five-point Likert scale, ranging from strongly disagree to strongly agree.

Condition 1. Elderly Computer Interaction (ECI):

1. The researcher asks the participant for his permission to take a picture of her/him and upload it to Facebook.

2. Then, the researcher uploads the picture using Facebook android application and asks the participant to use the computer interface to find the picture (The interface is two clicks far from watching the picture)

3. The researcher asks the participant to fill the USE a questionnaire in a paper.

Condition 2. Elderly Computer Interaction (ERI):

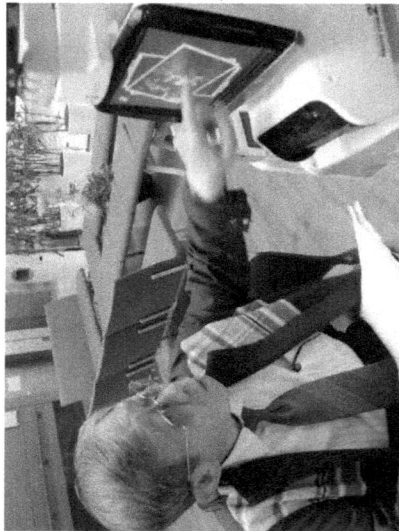

Figure 2: Participant in the ERI Condition.

1. The researcher asks the participant for his permission to take a picture of her/him and upload it to Facebook.

2. The researcher uploads the picture using Facebook Android application and asks the participant to listen the robot.

3. The robot says to the participant: 'The center has uploaded new photos. Do you want to see the pictures? Please touch the photos Icon". (see Figure 2)

4. The researcher asks the participant to fill the USE questionnaire in paper.

Results

Descriptive statistics and inferential statistics

Participants were 50% females and 50% males. The mean age of the respondents was approximately 72.38 years (SD=5.1) ranging between 62 and 91 years. A multivariate analysis was implemented for each one of the items evaluated.

In Table 1, the results for T-test by stimulus show that among constructs there is a statistical significant value for Usefulness, Ease of Use, Ease of learning and satisfaction.

Discussion

Practical Implications

A better interaction scenario using a robot and Facebook photo albums, can help ensure that needed connection that may otherwise get excluded from a technological gap or visual complexity on web applications.

CONSTRUCT	ECI MEAN	ERI MEAN
Usefulness	1.57	4.20
Ease of use	1.85	3.99
Ease of learning	1.73	4.04
Satisfaction	1.99	4.23

Table 1. Means by construct for the Elderly Computer Interaction Condition 1, and Elderly Robot Interaction Condition 2.

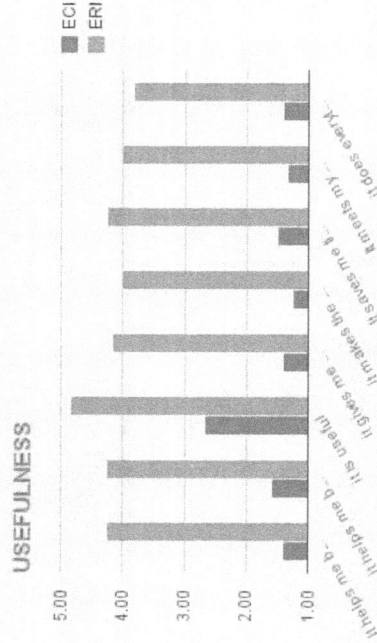

Figure 3: Detail for Usefulness Data Analysis Comparison from the t-test.

Although the mean and SD data for individual questions expressed several variations, the overall results have shown a clear difference among conditions.

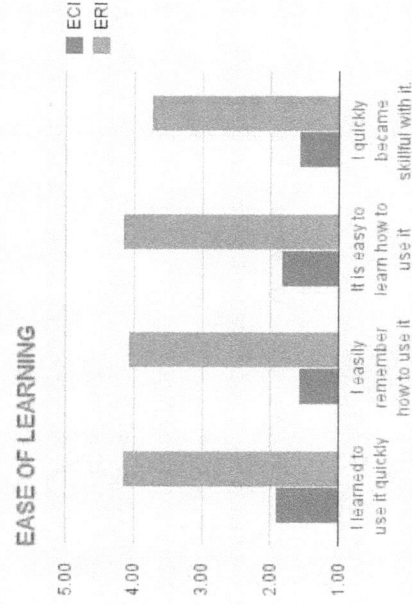

Figure 4: Detail for Ease of learning Data Analysis Comparison from the t-test.

This study can contribute into the interaction design for a cognitive consumer robot "Homemate" from the Korus Tech Project in the Intelligent Systems Research Institute In Sungkyunkwan University. Homemate robot plays a role as a recommendator agent with an Avatar+Interface in a screen instead of a head. This robot has a female voice and gives assistance to the elderly for different scenarios such as Errand service for water, beverages, etc. facilitates communication through video chatting, entertainment such as games and karaoke and health assistance.

Additionally, the application of USE questionnaires that are originally designed for usability tests In conventional systems, conduce us to analyze whether the same principles from HCI can be applied for Human Robot Interaction interfaces.

Limitations and future research

Few limitations of the study should be acknowledged in order to interpret its findings effectively. First, while there are several assistant robots and photo sharing tools, our focus in this pilot study was on Homemate Consumer Robot and Facebook photo albums using an API (Application programming interface) of our own design. Second, the subjects were only Korean older adults without including individuals with serious physical or psychological disabilities. Third, reconsidering the two conditions is needed in order to identify in more detail the effect of the robot and to exclude the novelty of the interface itself from the results. In addition, deeper data analysis is needed since our conclusions are based in a very initial comparison of means. Thus, the results in the study have a limited generalizability are just intended to be

used as information source for the correct design of the main experiment.

A long-term study with a home-setting robot agent, where each senior individual can experience the continuous communication with their relatives through agent assistantship and Facebook Photo Albums, is being considered. This could lead us to very interesting findings toward the real effect of social media tools on the social isolation of older adults.

Acknowledgements

This research was performed for the Intelligent Robotics Development Program, one of the 21st Century Frontier R&D Programs (F0005000-2010-32), and in part for the KORUS-Tech Program (KT-2008-SW-AP-FSO-0004) funded by the MKE, Korea. This work was also partially supported by the MEST, Korea, under the WCU Program supervised by the KOSEF (R31-2008-000-10062-0), and by MKE, Korea under ITRC NIPA-2010-(C1090-1021-0008)(NTIS-2010-(1415109527).

References

[1] Pew Internet & American Life Project. Generations Online (2009).

[2] Hewie. Hewie's Views & Reviews August 31 (2010).

[3] Roupa, Z., Nikas, M., Gerasimou, E., Zafeiri, V., Giasyrani, L., Kazitori, E., & Sotiropoulou, P. (2010) The Use of Technology by the elderly. Health Science Journal, 4(2), 118-126.

[4] Kollock, P. Design principles for online communities. (1998).

[5] Mavridis, N., Datta, C., Emami, S., Tanoto, A., BenAbdelkader, C., & Rabie, T. FaceBots: Steps Towards Enhanced Long-Term Human-Robot Interaction by Utilizing and Publishing Online Social Information. In Human-Robot Interaction (HRI), 2009 4th ACM/IEEE International Conference on (pp. 273-274). IEEE.

[6] Frøkjær, E., Hertzum, M., & Hornbæk, K. Measuring usability: are effectiveness, efficiency, and satisfaction really correlated?. In Proceedings of the SIGCHI conference on Human factors in computing systems (2000, April). (pp. 345-352). ACM.

[7] Travis, D. Measuring satisfaction: Beyond the usability questionnaire. Online at http://www. userfocus. co. uk/articles/satisfaction. html (2008).

Telepresence Robot that Exaggerates Non-verbal Cues for Taking Turns in Multi-party Teleconferences

Komei Hasegawa
University of Tsukuba
1-1-1 Tennodai, Tsukuba, Ibaraki,
Japan
komei@hri.iit.tsukuba.ac.jp

Yasushi Nakauchi
University of Tsukuba
1-1-1 Tennodai, Tsukuba, Ibaraki,
Japan
nakauchi@iit.tsukuba.ac.jp

HAI 2014 , Oct 29-31 2014, Tsukuba, Japan
ACM 978-1-4503-3035-0/14/10.
http://dx.doi.org/10.1145/2658861.2658945

Abstract

In this paper, we propose a telepresence robot that exaggerates non-verbal cues for taking turns in multi-party teleconferences. In multi-party teleconferences, it is more difficult that the remote participants to take their turns than face-to-face. Therefore, it is assumed that the remote participants' turns are tended to decrease. It is said that addressee tends to be next speaker. Therefore, becoming addressee is previous step to become speaker and take turns. In order to make remote participant become addressee, proposed system recognized remote participant's non-verbal cues such as attention directions, nod motions and back-channels. Then, the system exaggerates the cues and expresses them as the telepresence robot's motions.

Author Keywords

Telepresence robots; turn taking; multi-party conversations; teleconference; non-verbal communication

ACM Classification Keywords

H.5.3. Information interfaces and presentation (e.g., HCI): Group and Organization Interfaces.

294

Introduction

In recent years, video chat systems are widely used to communicate with remote persons. It is a general situation that most of all members can meet together but a few members cannot. Then, most members communicate in face-to-face and a few remote members attend the conversation via a video chat. In this situation, it is assumed that opportunities which remote participants give utterances are decreased. Then, it is more difficult that the remote participants to take their turns than face-to-face. Because it is difficult to exchange non-verbal cues in video chat since two-dimensional vision could convey poor presences. While it is said that embodied robots make people feel stronger presence than visions. Therefore we think robots could be used for conveying the presences to remote sites.

Humans can conduct smooth turn-taking in face-to-face situations. It is because humans are able to exchange non-verbal cues. Especially in turn-taking, non-verbal information is used as a cue, which enables participants to predict the next speaker [1]. Thus, it is important to express non-verbal cues in order to take turns via robots.

Goffman proposed the participation framework [2]. The participation framework defines conversational roles such as speaker, addressee (currently being spoken to), side participant (not currently being spoken to) and so on. In multi-party conversations, participants dynamically change these roles. Further, participants change their roles according to various verbal and non-verbal cues such as gaze direction, postures and gestures [3]. It is said that addressee tends to be next speaker than other side participants. Therefore,

becoming addressee is previous step to become speaker and take turns.

In this paper, we propose a telepresence robot for taking turns in multi-party teleconferences. In order to make remote participant become addressee, proposed system recognizes remote participant's non-verbal cues. Then, the system exaggerates the cues and expresses them as the telepresence robot's motions. We expect that these exaggerated motions expressed by the robot help us to become addressee and take turns.

Related Work

Some existing telepresence robots for remote communications were developed. MeBot having a movable neck and arms enabled communications using various kinds of head and hand gestures [4]. However, this research focused on only one-to-one communications. There was no consideration about multi-party conversations and turn-taking.

There were some researches that developed a robot attending multi-party conversations [5]. The conversational robot used non-verbal cues such as head direction, body direction and gestures for taking turns. However, this was an autonomous system not for telecommunications.

System Design

Participation status transition diagram
Based on the Goffman's participation framework, we prepared the participation status transition diagram shown in Figure 1. To become next speaker, we aim to become addressee at first step because it is said that addressee tends to become next speaker. Then, to become addressee, it is important to get the address

and continue it when the remote participant is a listener.

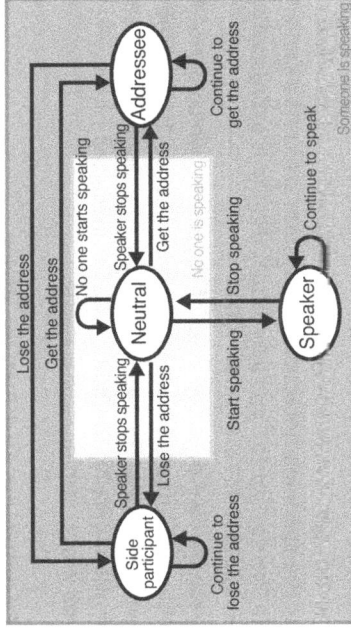

Figure 1. Participation status transition diagram

Cues of recipiency

We enumerated following non-verbal cues that was assumed to obtain the address.

- Gaze directions
- Body directions
- Nod motions
- Back-channels

By expressing these non-verbal cues, it is expected to get more addresses from the speaker. We called these cues as cues of recipiency. Cues of recipiency argue the speaker that the listener is receiving and has some interests.

Exaggerates cues

It is said that remote participants in front of the video chat tend to reduce the frequency of their gestures [6]. It is also seemed that their gestures' intensities become weaker. Accordingly, proposed system exaggerated

cues of recipiency. Cues of recipiency can be divided in two types, attention directions and response cues. Gaze directions and body directions belong to attention directions. While, nod motions and back-channels belongs to response cues. We exaggerated cues among same type of cues. For example, when the remote participant faced a participant, the telepresence robot turned to the participant not only the face also body as an exaggerated cue. Table 1 shows other examples of relationships between input cues and exaggerated cues.

Implementation
System configuration

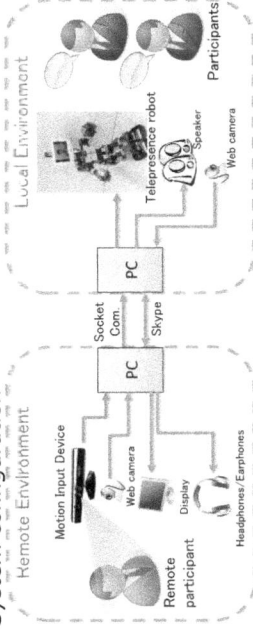

Figure 2. System configuration

Proposed system's configuration is seen in Figure 2. A remote participant attended the meeting via the telepresence robot (shown in Figure 3). Kinect sensed the remote participant's motions. Then, the motion data were sent to the computer at the local place via socket communications. The motion data were processed and expressed by the robot. In each environment, web cameras and microphones captured participants' appearances and voices. Then, those were exchanged through Skype. Especially, the remote participant's facial expression was displayed by a small display set up on the robot's head.

Input (Remote participant's cues of recipiency)	Output (Exaggerated cues that telepresence robot express)
Turn face to a participant	Turn face and body to a participant
Nod slightly	Nod more intensely
Nod intensely	Nod intensely with the whole body
Back-channel	Nod

Table 1. Examples of input cues and exaggerated cues

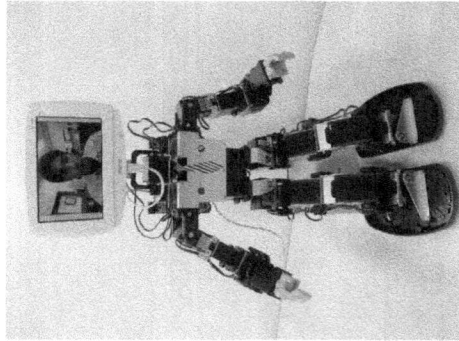

Figure 3. Telepresence robot. We employed KHR-3HV that is a desktop sized humanoid robot by Kondo Kagaku Company. The robot had two 4 DOF arms which enables various kinds of hand gestures. It also had a 2 DOF waist, which allows leaning forwarding motions and changing body directions. For expressing head motions and looking directions, it had a 3 DOF neck. As the robot 's face, a small size display was fixed on the neck. We used mimo um-430 (usb connectable 4.3 inch display) as the face display. The display showed the operator 's face video so that it conveyed the facial expressions.

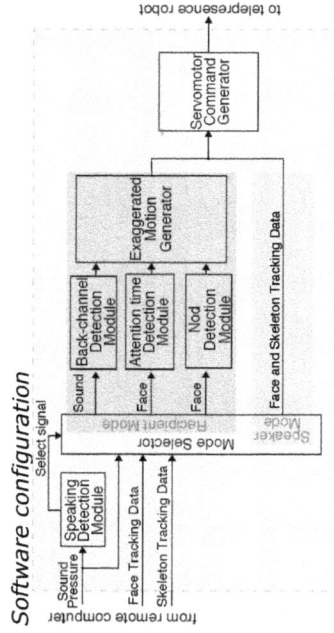

Software configuration

Figure 4. Software configuration

Figure 4 shows the system's software configuration. First, the system received the input data such as sound pressure, face tracking data and skeleton tracking data from the remote computer. Then, the speaking detection module estimated whether the remote participant was speaking or not. According to the result of the speaking detection, the system selected a mode. In the case of the speaker mode, the robot expressed motions without change. While, in the recipient mode, each module detected cues of recipiency, which back-channels, attention time and nod motions. Then, based on these cues, the system generated exaggerated motion. Finally, the motion was transmitted to the robot as a servomotor command.

Conclusion and Future Work

In this paper, we proposed a telepresence robot that exaggerates non-verbal cues for taking turns in multi-party teleconferences. In order to make remote participant become addressee, proposed system detected remote participant's non-verbal cues such as attention directions, nod motions and back-channels.

Then, the system exaggerates the cues and expresses them as the telepresence robot's motions.

In the next step, we will conduct an experiment that makes a subject to attend a multi-party conversation via proposed system. Then, we will confirm how exaggerated cues affect becoming the addressee and taking turns.

References

[1] Marjorie F. Vargas: Louder Than Words: An Introduction to Nonverbal Communication, Iowa State Press (1986)

[2] Goffman, E. Replies and Responses, Language in Society, 5 (1982), 257–313

[3] Clark, H. H. Using Language, Cambridge University Press (1996)

[4] S. O. Adalgeirsson, C. Breazeal: MeBot: A Robotic Platform for Socially Embodied Telepresence, HRI2010 (2010), 15–22

[5] T. Tojo, Y. Matsusaka, T. Ishii, and T. Kobayashi, "A con- versational robot utilizing facial and body expressions," in 2000 IEEE International Conference on Systems, Man, and Cybernetics, 2 (2000)

[6] Hidekazu Tamaki, Suguru Higashino, Minoru Kobayashi, Masayuki Ihara: Reducing Speech Contention in Web Conferences, 2011 IEEE/IPSJ International Symposium on Applications and the Internet, (2011), 75-81

Emotional Scene Understanding Based on Acoustic Signals Using Adaptive Neuro-Fuzzy Inference System

Taewoong Kim
School of Electronics Engineering
Kyungpook National University
1370 Sankyuck-Dong
Buk-Gu Daegu Korea
twkim@ee.knu.ac.kr

Minho Lee
School of Electronics Engineering
Kyungpook National University
1370 Sankyuck-Dong
Buk-Gu Daegu Korea
mholee@gmail.com

Abstract

We propose a novel approach to recognize positive or negative emotions from acoustic signals in movies by extracting musical components such as tempo, loudness and melody and then by applying ANFIS Model with fuzzy clustering. In order to extract emotional features in acoustic signals, we first transform the sound into a spectrogram. The spectrogram visually represents characteristic information of sound such as tempo, loudness and melody. Then, we apply the fuzzy model on spectrogram to get the effective emotion features of sound. The extracted tempo, loudness and melody information is used as inputs for an adaptive neuro-fuzzy inference system (ANFIS) with fuzzy c-means clustering (FCM). Finally, the ANFIS classifies the sound as positive or negative emotion, which is compared with a mean opinion score of human in test movies.

Author Keywords

Short Time Fourier Transform (STFT); fuzzy C-means clustering (FCM); Adaptive Neuro Fuzzy Inference System (ANFIS); emotive sound recognition

ACM Classification Keywords

H.1.2 [Models and principles] : User/Machine Systems

HAI 2014, October 29–31, 2014, Tsukuba, Japan.
ACM 978-1-4503-3035-0/14/10.
DOI: 10.1145/2658861.2660591

Introduction

Relation between sound and emotion is well known in multimodal communications such as cinema. It has been argued that images are for visual aesthetic and sound is for evoking emotions [1]. While this relation between sound and emotion is studied in various fields, it has got a considerable attention in artificial intelligence too. The attempt has been to, at least, make computers understand (if not feel) emotions like humans for quality human-computer interactions. In rest of the paper, we discuss our approach and explain our method which combines musical component with intelligent signal processing using FCM, and ANFIS model to classify sound data into positive or negative emotion. We also present the experimental result and show that our method can be a good candidate to classify human emotion based on non-linguistic sound signal.

Overview of Emotion Inference System

We propose a method to extract emotional valence of acoustic signals in movies using musical components, FCM and ANFIS model. It is done in three steps: In the first step, sound is converted into spectrogram using short-time Fourier transformation (STFT) as shown in Figure 1. By using this method, tempo, melody, loudness of sound can be represented as pattern such as envelop, intensity, interval etc. Those features in the spectrogram are particularly associated with emotions [2]. In the second step, those musical features are clustered using FCM clustering to generate emotional descriptors. Finally in the third step, emotional descriptors generated by the musical components are used as inputs for an ANFIS. At the end of three-step method, the system classifies the sound as having positive or negative emotion in valence domain.

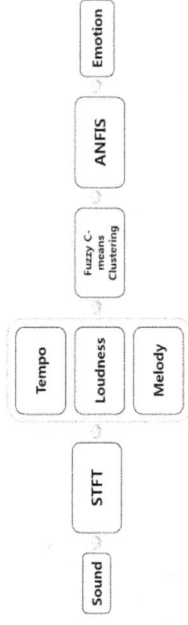

Figure 1. Process of emotion inference system

Spectrogram from STFT

The process of emotion inference system starts with STFT of the sound which contains the sound information such as "tempo", "loudness" and "melody". It represents various patterns according to the contents of acoustic signals. The two axes represent the spectrogram. One is time-domain and the other is frequency-domain. "Tempo" of sound is represented with the density of spectrogram in time-axis. "Melody" is represented with high-low pattern in frequency-axis, and "loudness" is represented with the color information of spectrogram. To summarize, in the first step, we convert acoustic signals extracted from the multimedia clips into musical component features, which can then be used as an input for fuzzy logic model.

Fuzzy C-means clustering model from musical components

FCM is a data clustering technique wherein each data point belongs to a cluster to some degree that is specified by a membership grade. We apply this method to separate musical components into two groups to put as input data of ANFIS.

ANFIS model and emotion complexity

After FCM processing, using the musical components, we classify the features into two values (positive or negative) on the emotive axis. To classify emotive features into two values, we use the ANFIS. The clustering of the emotional features using FCM forms the primitive knowledge about emotion. Based on this knowledge, the neuro-fuzzy system develops its understanding of emotion under the control of an ANFIS network. By interacting with human, the learning procedure searches for the optimal membership functions and optimal parameters of the consequent models [3]. Mean opinion scores (MOS) are used as teaching signals for the neuro-fuzzy system.

Fuzzy logic and developmental emotion recognition

The fuzzy system extracts emotional features by clustering musical components. This emotional feature is a higher-level feature with semantic meaning. The feature space is constructed by combining the membership grades from clustering each basic musical feature. And the subject's response is used to make teaching signals to supervise the learning process of the ANFIS. Using such a developmental process, the proposed system can develop a mental ability to understand more complex human emotions by mining the characteristics of emotional features and interacting with its environment. The developmental emotion recognition procedure for a particular subjects is shown in Figure 1. The subject specific developmental emotion recognition performance of the proposed system is evaluated by comparing the outputs of system with each subject's feedback. The results of the system performance are summarized in Table 1.

Experiment

In order to test our method which determines the emotional valence aspects from non-linguistic sound in movies, we conducted an experiment. We describe the procedure and results in this section.

Material

We collected the movies' sound data from internet. Four participants, whose data are used for training procedure, listened to these files and classified them into two groups: (1) positive and (2) negative. Negative test sounds were recordings from real life sound such as sliding car, horn of vehicle, siren of emergency vehicle and so on in movie. Positive test sounds included baby laughing sound, classical music pieces and so on. To classify the emotion as positive or negative, we used 30 samples of sound, with distribution expressed in Figure 2.

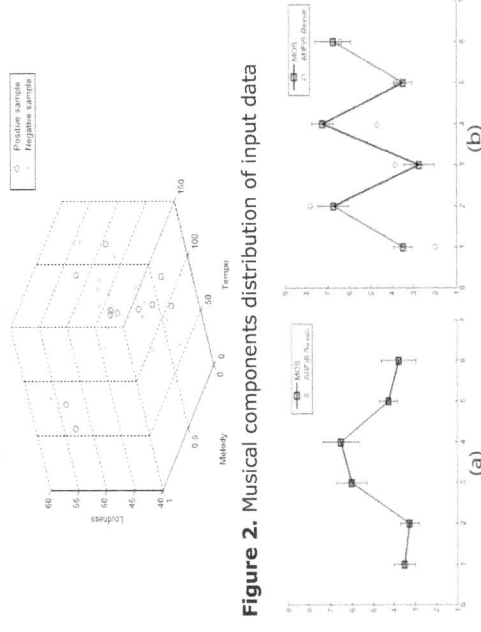

Figure 2. Musical components distribution of input data

Figure 3. (a) one example of MOS and ANFIS output set in training data (b) one example of MOS and ANFIS output set in Test data using k-fold verification

We used MOS mean of participants' feedback as a target value for training the system to classify sound into two groups such as positive and negative emotion.

MOS scores are acquired by 8 subjects after listening the signals, thus we have 8 subjects for test. The test data included a total of 6 sound files among positive and negative emotional movies. The test data were randomly selected. Then we applied the sound data as our model input. From overall data, 24 samples are used for training. To check our model efficiency, k-fold verification is applied. From the musical components extracting process, we can acquire the acoustic features, which are projected in the high dimension of region like human perception. That is to say, multi-dimension features are combined and abstracted using fuzzy clustering.

The MOS mean values with variances and ANFIS one example of output set in training data is expressed in Figure 3(a), where it can be seen the relative results of each value intuitively. Figure 3(b) shows the MOS mean values with variances and ANFIS values obtained from the test data group 1. Notice that values above MOS five are positive and the ones below are negative. This way, it is possible to classify the emotion in those two groups with 83.3% efficiency rate of positive or negative valence tendency prediction, even if the exact value of MOS is not inferred. Results of proposed system are summarized in Table 1. Notice that our test results indicate an average of 76.7% successful classification of acoustic signals in movies.

Objects	Test 1	Test 2	Test 3	Test 4	Test 5	Test 6	Total
Training Error	83.3%	100%	50%	100%	100%	100%	86.7%
Test Error	83.3%	83.3%	66.7%	83.3%	83.3%	83.3%	76.7%

Table 1. Inference system efficiency

Conclusion

In this study, we developed a novel scheme for understanding human emotion based on sound signals in movies. In this system, the emotional feature space is built based on the fuzzy logic and musical components. In order to develop an emotion recognition system from non-linguistic acoustic signals in movies signals, we proposed a method, which converts acoustic signals in movie data into spectrogram and cluster extracted musical features using FCM and classify them as emotionally negative or positive sounds by using ANFIS model. In short, based on the relationship between emotional factors and the characteristics of spectrogram of musical components are adapted to analyze the sound features by incorporating the fuzzy concept.

Acknowledgements

This research was supported by Basic Science Research Program through the National Research Foundation of Korea(NRF) funded by the Ministry of Education, Science and Technology (2014011672) (50%) and the Ministry of Science, ICT and future Planning (2013R1A2A2A01068687) (50%).

References

[1] COHEN, A. J. Music as a source of emotion in film. Music and emotion. *Theory and research* (2001), 249-272.

[2] GABRIELSSON, A., LINDSTRÖM, E. The influence of musical structure on emotional expression. Music and emotion. *Theory and research* (2001), 223-248.

[3] WEI-NING, W., YING-LIN, Y., SHENG-MING, J. Image retrieval by emotional semantics: A study of emotional space and feature extraction. *Systems, Man and Cybernetics*, 2006. SMC'06. IEEE International Conference on. IEEE, (2006). 3534-3539.

SB Simulator: A Method to Estimate How Relation Develops

Taichi Sono
Keio University
sono@ayu.ics.keio.ac.jp

Toshihiro Oosumi
Keio University
toshihiro@ayu.ics.keio.ac.jp

Michita Imai
Keio University
michita@ayu.ics.keio.ac.jp

ABSTRACT

People spend their everyday life while expecting social relations between them and the others. However, the expectation causes a trouble or a misunderstanding because they grasp the relations from their subjective viewpoint. It is useful that a computer software assists people to grasp the relations by showing the possible variations of the relation. This paper proposes a simulator named SB Simulator that accepts current relations which a user grasps and simulates the course of the development of relations between them based on Heider's balance theory and Socion theory. The aim of SB Simulator is to make the user know what changes in the relations happen if s/he takes an action. In particular, SB Simulator generates possible initial relations before starting the simulation, which compensate for the possibility that the user grabs the current relations incorrectly from her/his subjective viewpoint. The function of generating the initial relations has a role in raising a user's awareness of the other possibilities of relations. Moreover, since SB Simulator employs Socion Theory to express the relations, it can distinguish relations which people recognize subjectively from the ones existing objectively, and simulate possible relations based on dynamics between the subjective and objective relations. The paper evaluates SB Simulator in terms of whether the results of the simulation are acceptable in contrast to the typical course of relation development. The result indicated that SB Simulator simulated the relations properly based on the initial relations.

Author Keywords

human relation; Socion theory; Balance theory; agent simulation;

ACM Classificatio Keywords

H.5.m. Information Interfaces and Presentation (e.g. HCI): Miscellaneous

INTRODUCTION

Keeping a good relationship is sometimes difficul because of misunderstandings in a daily communication. Since the relationship is based on social balance between people, the relationship varies significantl depending on who interacts with whom and how s/he behaves at the time. People select their behaviors to interact with the others while considering what effects their utterance and behaviors give to the relationships with the others. However, the relationships that people grasp may not be the same as the correct ones because they recognize and simulate the relationship from their subjective viewpoint. The paper consider the way to estimate possible relationships between people even though they have only the subjective comprehension of the relationships.

The problem of estimating the possible relationships is to fin a way for a computer to deal with human relations. In particular, the computer needs the method to express human relations and to simulate the transition of the relations in the courses of a development.

The simulation of human relations has been studied in the area of multi-agent researches. For example, Ohsumi et al. found that the relations which each agent grasp subjectively became similar to the one gasped by an agent who communicates with the others most frequently than the other agents [6]. They employed Socion theory [2] to express and simulate the relation between the agents. Honda et al. indicated that the propagation of information among a group has the structure of small world network [4]. Dias et al. [1] simulated relations between a user and agents on a game scenario by using Balance Theory [3]. Kadowaki et al. investigated that a system persuades a user to buy goods which an agent recommends by using the effect of Balance Theory [5].

Although multi-agent simulation for human relations is designed for simulating interaction on a specifi scenario, it is also important to develop a general simulation method as a basis for simulating the human relations on each scenario. The researches [1] and [5] are not proposals for considering the general simulation method. Moreover, the models which the researches employ cannot express the difference between the relations which an agent grasps subjectively and the ones existing in actual. In addition, a multi-agent simulator is not designed for consulted about the social problem that a person has against the others because it is a research tool for investigating the mechanism of social dynamics such that what social relation appears under a condition and rules. It does not need to consider the correctness of relations given by a user because the initially given relation is a seed for a simulation. On the other hand, a simulator to give a user advice has to consider the possibilities that the initial relation given by the user includes wrong information. It is important for the simulator to take account of the incorrectness of an initial relation given by the user. The paper [6] does not also deal with the incorrectness of the initial relations even though it distinguishes the subjective relations from the objective ones. The paper focuses on achieving three features in designing a simulator as follows.

- The generality of a simulation algorithm

- Distinguishing relations recognized subjectively from the ones existing in actual

- Dealing with relations including incorrect relations

The paper proposes a simulator named Socion-Balance Simulator (SB Simulator) which expresses human relations based on Socion Theory [2] and simulates changes in the relations based on Balance Theory [3]. SB simulator deals with the relations between three people which include a user who want to consult SB simulator about relations with two others. The user can input three types of information into SB Simulator: The relations which s/he grasps subjectively, the relations for which s/he hopes, and her/his action for achieving the hope. SB Simulator simulates how the initial relations vary when the user takes the input action, and confir whether the desired relations emerges in the course of the simulation. SB Simulator employs Balance Theory because the theory provides a general rule to simulate the changes in the relations and it does not depends on any specifi scenario. SB Simulator also employs Socion theory to introduce the distinctive expressions of subjective relations and objective relations. Moreover, SB Simulator generates several varieties of initial relations based on the user input to compensate for the user's ability to recognizing human relations.

The rest of the paper is organized as follows. Next section explains Socion theory and Balance theory. In addition, it discusses the features of a human relationship which SB Simulator has to handle. Third section proposes SB Simulator and explains how SB Simulator simulates the changes in the human relations and reveals the resultant relations coming from the simulated interaction between three people. Then, the paper evaluates the performance of SB Simulator. At last, the paper concludes by discussing the result of the evaluation and the current problems of SB Simulator.

BACKGROUND

Socion Theory
Socion Theory [2] is the theory which can express subjective and objective relationships on a single diagram. The basic unit of the diagram is an expression of a person. The expression consists of three types of selves as follows.

- A self which is considered by one's inner self: a relation between a person and its own self.

- A self which is considered by the other: a relation from the other to a person.

- A self which is exposed toward the others: a relation from a person to the other.

Figure 1 indicates the relation between three people each of which appears as a big circle in the figure The small circles in each big circle correspond to that three selves. The small circle which has an arrow toward the big circle to which the small one belongs expresses a self considered by her/his own self (the firs self). The small circle which has an arrow toward the other bigs circle expresses a self exposed toward

the other (the third self). The self exposed toward the other can be interpreted as a self considered by the others from the viewpoint of the other big circle (the second self). Also, the small circle can express a positive or negative relation. The white and black circle represent the positive and the negative respectively.

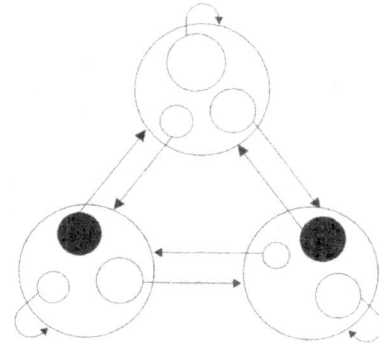

Figure 1. Socio-gram

Figure 1 shows a diagram named Socio-gram that can express both of the relations which each people recognize subjectively and the ones which exist in actual between them. The objective relation is called C-net and the subjective one is called P-net. The big circles in Socio-gram also expresses three persons. The big circle has middle and small circles to construct P-net. The relations which a person grasps subjectively is expressed by the arrows from small circles to the middle circles inside a big circle. For instance, the small circles are used to express a subjective understanding of how the other considers the other self (the arrow from a small circle to the middle circle to which it belongs) and how the other considers her/himself (the arrow from a small circle to the middle circle which does not have a small circle). The small circles also express a subjective understanding of how the others consider each other (the arrows from a small circle to the other middle circle which has small circles). Those relations in P-net may include misunderstandings because it is impossible to know how the other consider the others and the only way to know the relation is to observe the others' behaviors. On the other hand, C-net does not include misunderstanding because it consists of how self consider its own self and the others (the arrows started directly from the middle circle). The paper employs the word P-net for indicating the subjective relations and C-net for the actual relations.

We introduce symbols to express relations on Socion Theory.

W indicates the state of the relations and has a positive (1) or negative (-1) value to express a positive or negative relation. a indicates a person and we use i to identify a person a_i. W_{ij} indicates the relation from a_i to a_j. W_{ij} corresponds the relation on C-net (also see W_{01} on Figure 2). Since a relation on P-net is based on someone's subjective recognition, the relation on P-net has one's ID on it such as W_{ij}^k which means that a person a_k considers that a person a_i has a relation W_{ij}^k toward a person a_j. Here, a relation W_{ij}^i on P-net is the same as W_{ij} on C-net because what relation toward a person a_j a

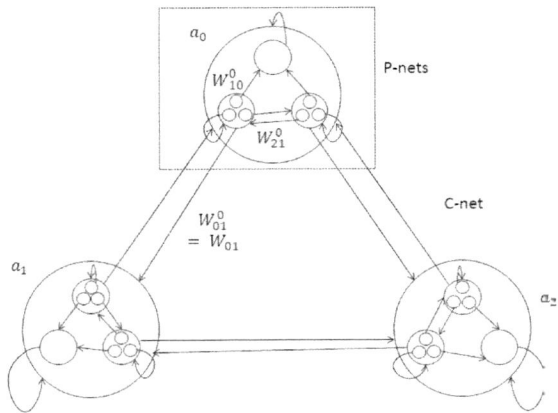

Figure 2. P-net and C-net

person a_i considers that s/he has is the same as what a person a_i has in actual. The relation between a_i and its own self a_i is expressed as W_{ii}. Also, the relation which a_k considers a_i has toward its own self is expressed as W_{ii}^k.

Figure 2 indicates an example of relations. For example, W_{21}^0 denotes that a_0 considers that there is a relation W_{21}^0 from a_2 to a_1. W_{10}^0 indicates that a_0 considers that there is a relation W_{10}^0 from a_1 to her/himself a_0. In addition, Figure 2 shows that W_{01}^0 is the same as W_{01}.

Balance Theory

Balance Theory is an interpersonal theory and also known as POX model. P is oneself, O is another person, and X is a target person or object of P and O. Balance Theory define a balanced and an unbalanced state on the relations between P, O, and X. Also the theory suggests that the unbalanced state changes into the balanced one by altering one of the relations between P, O, and X. Figure 3 shows the patterns of relations on POX model. The positive relation is expressed as +, and the negative one is - on Figure 3. The balanced state is define as the result of multiplication of the sign on the relations. If the result is plus, the state is balanced. If it is minus, the state is unbalanced. The unbalanced relation becomes the balanced one by changing one of the sign on the relation between P, O, and X

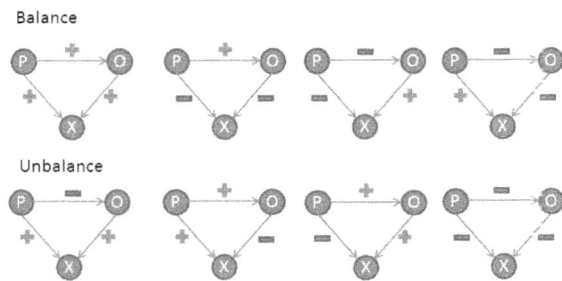

Figure 3. POX model from Balance Theory

Two People's Balance Theory

Original Balance Theory does not cover the relation between a person and her/his own self which corresponds to the firs

self of Socion Theory. However, Balance Theory can also deal with the relations by considering Balance Theory between two persons. Balance Theory for two persons considers that P is a person and X is also the same person observed by P. As Figure 4 shows, Balance Theory can considers the relations between two persons based on the modification P→X

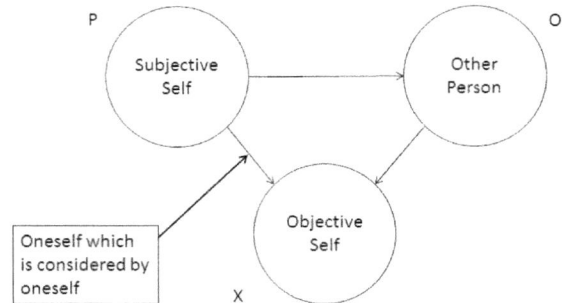

Figure 4. POX model in two person

in the figur is a relation to oneself. This paper employs Balance Theory for two persons for simulating a relation between a person and her/himself.

Incorrectness of user input

We must distinguish the relation which people recognize from the relation which exists in actual because the relations are sometimes inconsistent. The inconsistent causes a difficult for a system to be consulted about the problem of the relations which a user has because the user cannot prepare correct relations as a seed for a simulation. We have to take account of the difficult when designing a method for a simulator to deal with the relations provided by a user.

SB SIMULATOR

Overview

SB Simulator simulates human relations between three people which includes a user who want to consult it about a problem related to human relations. The simulation is based on the relations and the action which the user provides as an initial seed for the simulation. The result of the simulation is the probability that the user can achieve her/his desired relations. SB Simulator not only uses the given initial relations but also generates other varieties of the initial relations by modifying some parts of the given relations. The method compensates for the subjective relations which includes wrong information. Figure 5 shows the overview of SB Simulator.

Input of GUI accepts the human relations which a user grasps, an action whose effect the user want to confirm and a desired relations which the user want to achieve. Initializer generates the initial state of relations by modifying the relations given by the user, and feeds it into Simulator. Since the input relations are based on only user's subjective viewpoint, SB Simulator needs to generate the initial relations to examine the other possible relations. Simulator simulates the transition of human relations using the algorithm based on Balance Theory. The simulation starts from the generated initial state. In addition, Simulator counts the number of achieving

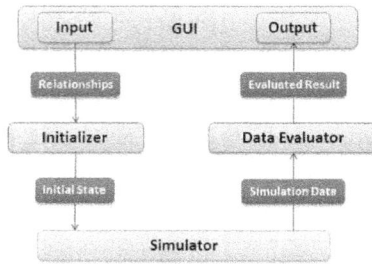

Figure 5. Overview of SB Simulator

the desired relations and the average time steps to achieve the relations. Data Evaluator evaluates how well the initial relation and the action of the user inputs achieve the desired state based on the result of Simulator. Although Initializer generates all possible relations as the initial states of the simulation, the number of the results is too many for the user to see. Data Evaluator calculates the rank of the results to eliminate the number of data to give the user more important results. GUI Output shows the user the top of the ranked results.

UI Input

Figure 6 shows the input part of GUI. The aim of SB Simula-

Figure 6. UI Input

tor is to suggest how well a user action has an effect on establishing a desired relations. The simulation of SB Simulator requires four types of inputs: Initial relations for simulating changes in the relations, the degree of certainty that the initial relations are correct, the action which the user takes, and the relations which the user desires.

Since SB Simulator takes account of the possibility that the initial relations which the user grasps subjectively are different from actual ones, it calls the initial relations input by the user "your assumption" (see also Figure 6). The user can input relations between her/him and two other people at Your

assumption. Certainty degree in GUI allows the user to input how certainly s/he believes that the inputs at Your assumption are true. The degree is used at Data Evaluator to evaluate the result of the simulation. Your action in GUI requires what action the user will take to change the relations. Purpose in GUI accepts a desired relation which the user wants to achieve. We explain each input in detail as follows.

- Your assumptions
  SB Simulator asks the user nine relations. Since the relations is recognized by the user subjectively, they corresponds to P-net of user's Socion.

- Certainty degree
  Although SB Simulator generates the other varieties of initial relations based on Your assumption, it needs to estimate which initial relations are reliable to show the user the result of simulation. Since the importance of the simulation result depends on not only how well desired relations are established but also how reliable the initial relations of the simulation are, SB Simulator uses the certainty degree to evaluate the importance of a simulation result. The paper employs s_{in} to denote the certainty degree.

- Your action
  SB Simulator supposes that the user takes an action to change relations. SB Simulator deals with Your action as a relation between the user and the target person for which the user takes the action because all interaction between people is considered based on only relations in Socion theory. SB Simulator fi es the relation between the user and the target person when the user sets an action to her/him; a positive action is set as a positive relation and a negative one is set as a negative relation. For example, when a user a_0 takes a good action to a person a_2, the value of relation W_{02} between them is fi ed to 1.

- Purpose
  SB Simulator asks the user his desired relation which s/he wants to achieve by changing the initial relation. For example, the user a_0 wants to have a good relation from a person a_1, the desired relation is expressed as $W_{10} = 1$.

Initializer

Initializer generates initial relations for the simulation to complement the relations which the user recognized subjectively. Initializer sets all P-nets on Socio-gram after generating possible initial relations.

At first P-nets of the other two persons are set by the same value as user's P-net by copying user's P-net to P-nets of the others. Here, each value of user's P-net is each value of Your assumption. The copying is define as $W_{nl}^0 = W_{nl}^1 = W_{nl}^2$ where there are three persons: A user a_0 and two persons a_1 and a_2. n and l are in the range of $0 \leq n \leq 2$ and $0 \leq l \leq 2$.

Initializer generates the other possible initial relations by changing some values of Your assumption. For example, Initializer prepares a new relation of W_{12}^1 by $W_{12}^1 \leftarrow -W_{12}^0$. The change in the value means that a user a_0 misunderstood what relation between a person a_1 and a person a_2 a person a_1 grasps. Initializer applies the change in the values into all parts of Your assumption to generate all possible patterns of different relations.

After generating the possible patterns of the relations, Initializer apply Your action to them. For example, when the user sets that the user a_0 takes a negative action toward the person a_2, Initializer sets $W_{02} = -1$, no matter what value is in W_{02}. SB Simulator does not change the relations set by Your action in the course of the simulation because it confirm the effect of the action on the relations between tree persons.

Degree of Difference

SB Simulator covers all of possible relations generated from Your assumption. However, there are cases that the result of the simulation is not meaningful if the generated possible initial relations does not exist in actual. SB Simulator calculates an existing probability for each generated initial relations based on Certainty degree. For the calculation, we define the degree of the difference, d, to estimate the difference between Your assumption and each generated initial relation. The small value of d indicates that the generated initial relations are similar to Your assumption.

Simulation Algorithm

Select a relation to update

Simulator changes the relations by findin unbalanced relations on Socio-gram based on POX model. The change employs not only three people POX model but also two people POX model. If Simulator find the unbalanced relations, it selects a relation from the unbalanced relations and reverses the plus or minus sign. If the selected relation is the target of Your action, Simulator skips the changing.

Relation Update

There are three relations on the target of Balance theory. Simulator selects one relation from the three in random and reverses its sign as follows.

- If the selected relation is the target of Your action, the other relation is selected from the remaining two.

- If the relation also belongs to C-net, the sign of the relation is reversed directly. The direct change means that a person can decide the relation belonging to C-net freely because the relation belonging to C-net also belongs to a person's own relation toward the others.

- If the relation belongs to P-net, Simulator checks a corresponding relation on C-net. If the sign of those relations are different, the sign of the selected relation is reversed. If those are the same, Simulator select the other relation again. The reason of the process is that the relation belonging to only P-net is the result of a subjective observation which the target person does. The person cannot change the relation freely without the observation. We introduce an observation failure to emulate someone's misunderstanding. The misunderstanding happens in random. If it happens, Simulator updates the sign of the target relation by using the reversed sign of the corresponding relation on C-net.

Simulator executes one updating in each simulation step. The updating continues until all relations are balanced.

Data extraction

Simulator confirm whether the desired relation is achieved in C-net at the end of the simulation. Simulator extracts the number of the times m that the desired relation is achieved, and the sum of the simulation steps R to achieve the desired relation. The data is used in Data Evaluator to show the user important simulation results. Simulator also stores the samples of the simulation steps to show the user the examples of the relation transition.

Data Evaluator

Purpose of Evaluation

The purpose of Data Evaluator is to reduce the number of simulation results and show the user only important results. Data Evaluator selects the results by evaluating the data extracted by Simulator and ranking the initial relations used for the simulation. SB Simulator show the user top ranked results based on the result of Data Evaluator. The ranking is based on the evaluation value calculated from an achievement probability and an existence probability. Some of ranking is based on the the degree of the difference d.

Achievement probability

The achievement probability, named P_1, is calculated by Equation (1).

$$P_1 = \frac{m}{M} \cdot A^{\frac{R}{m}} (0 < A < 1) \tag{1}$$

M is the whole number of simulation trials. A is the value of noise coming from the randomness of the relation transition.

Existence probability

The existence probability, named P_2, is calculated by Equation (2). transition.

$$P_2 = -A((18 - s_{in}) - d)^2 + B \tag{2}$$

A and B are coefficients for normalization.

Evaluation value

The evaluation value E is the product of P_1 and P_2. If m is 0, Data Evaluator considers that the initial relations does not have the value of E.

UI Output

Figure 7 shows a captured image of the output on GUI. We call it UI Output. UI Output selects five simulated results. First one is the result started from the initial relations that user's and the others' P-net are completely based on Your assumption. Second one is the result started from the initial relations that only user's P-net is based on Your assumption, and user's and the other's P-net are completely different. Remaining three are the results which has high E value except for the firs and the second one. Since the number of whole data is 262144, it is impossible for the user to grasp the simulation results without the selection.

The selected results are shown as a sentence on UI Output. The view buttons located at the end of the sentences on UI Output are the functions to show the user the log of changing relations stored at Simulator.

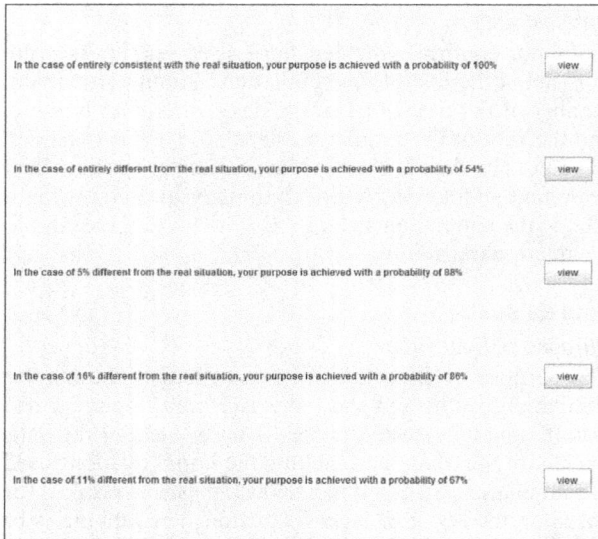

Figure 7. UI Output

Table 1. Valuation Result

Purpose		Is The Purpose achieved in the input?	output
W_{10}	1	yes	86
		no	81
	-1	yes	67
		no	90
W_{20}	1	yes	86
		no	82
	-1	yes	78
		no	90
W_{11}	1	yes	86
		no	76
	-1	yes	nonsuc
		no	nonsuc
W_{22}	1	yes	86
		no	76
	-1	yes	nonsuc
		no	nonsuc

EVALUATION

We confirme a performance of SB Simulator.

Purpose

The Purpose of the valuation was to verify that Simulator produces the results which match our intuitive knowledge about human relations.

Process

We entered 16 patterns of inputs to SB Simulator and compared the results. We selected the patterns based on following Criterion.

Criterion

If user's desired relation is already achieved in user's input, the evaluation value E should be higher than the not achieved case. To verify it, we set eight desired relations and two kinds of relations; one is that the desired relation is already achieved and the other is that the desired relation is not achieved. And we compared the simulated results.

Result

Table 1 is the result of the evaluation. The Purpose shows the relations corresponding to desired relations prepared in the input pattern. The output shows maximum E in simulating the corresponding input pattern. The nonsuc shows that the simulation did not achieve the desired relation.

Discussion

This subsection discusses the result of the evaluation.

The result indicates that the case that the desired positive relation has already been achieved at the initial relations has higher value of E than the case that it has not. However, the case that the desired negative relation has already been achieved at the initial relations has lower E than it has not. This is because Balance theory tends to judge the relations

including more positive ones to be stable. Therefore, if initial relations include more negative relations, Simulator needs more simulation steps to stable the relations. These results matches our intuitive knowledge about human relations.

On the other hand, the simulation could not reach a stable state in the case that a person does not like her/himself such as $W_{11} = -1$ and $W_{22} = -1$. The result comes from the stable structure of Balance theory. It is impossible for the self-hated state to be stable on the network managed by Balance theory. We needs to consider the simulation algorithm of dealing with the self-hated state to improve the ability of SB Simulator.

The evaluation verifie the effect of the difference between the desired relation and the initial ones. However, we needs to evaluate SB Simulator from the other aspect and improve the algorithm. In particular, a user study is important to develop a simulator which gives her/him an advice. We will take both approaches of developing algorithm and conducting a user study.

CONCLUSION

We have developed SB Simulator which simulates the course of the development of relations between a user and two persons based on Heider's balance theory and Socion theory. SB Simulator prepares a general algorithm to simulate relations between three people. The aim of SB Simulator is to be consulted about the problem of human relations which a user has. Since the relations which the user grasps subjectively are sometimes different from the ones in actual, SB Simulator employs Socion theory to express the difference. Moreover, SB Simulator generates possible initial relations from the input initial ones in order to confir other possible course of interaction which the user does not recognize. The function improves the ability of SB Simulator to estimate the development of human relations.

REFERENCES

1. Dias, J., and Paiva, A. I want to be your friend: establishing relations with emotionally intelligent agents.

In *Proceedings of the 2013 international conference on Autonomous agents and multi-agent systems*, International Foundation for Autonomous Agents and Multiagent Systems (2013), 777–784.

2. Fujiwara, H. *an introduction to Socion Theory (in Japanese)*. Kitaooji Shobo Publishing, 2006.

3. Heider, F. The psychology of interpresonal relations *In Lawrence Erlbaum Associates* (1958).

4. Honda, H., and Matsuka, T. How is knowledge transmitted in a small world network through communicative interaction? In *the Proceedings of the 33rd Annual Conference of the Cognitive Science Society* (2011), 1841–1846.

5. Kadowaki, K., Kobayashi, K., and Kitamura, Y. Influenc of social relationships on multiagent persuasion. In *Proceedings of the 7th international joint conference on Autonomous agents and multiagent systems-Volume 3*, International Foundation for Autonomous Agents and Multiagent Systems (2008), 1221–1224.

6. Osumi, T., Osawa, H., and Imai, M. Proposal for an agent model which has imagined human relationship. *The 1st International Conference on Human-Agent Interaction* (2013).

Modeling Perception-Action Loops: Comparing Sequential Models with Frame-Based Classifiers

Alaeddine Mihoub
GIPSA-Lab & LIRIS
Grenoble, France
alaeddine.mihoub@gipsa-lab.fr

Gérard Bailly
GIPSA-Lab
Grenoble, France
gerard.bailly@gipsa-lab.fr

Christian Wolf
Université de Lyon, CNRS
INSA-Lyon, LIRIS, UMR5205
F-69621, France
christian.wolf@liris.cnrs.fr

Abstract

Modeling multimodal perception-action loops in face-to-face interactions is a crucial step in the process of building sensory-motor behaviors for social robots or users-aware Embodied Conversational Agents (ECA). In this paper, we compare trainable behavioral models based on sequential models (HMMs) and classifiers (SVMs and Decision Trees) inherently inappropriate to model sequential aspects. These models aim at giving pertinent perception/action skills for robots in order to generate optimal actions given the perceived actions of others and joint goals. We applied these models to parallel speech and gaze data collected from interacting dyads. The challenge was to predict the gaze of one subject given the gaze of the interlocutor and the voice activity of both. We show that Incremental Discrete HMM (IDHMM) generally outperforms classifiers and that injecting input context in the modeling process significantly improves the performances of all algorithms.

Keywords

Social behavior model, HMMs, SVMs, cognitive state recognition, gaze generation

INTRODUCTION

The design of social robots/agents able to engage efficient and believable face-to-face conversations with human partners is still an open issue. Although this kind of communication is considered as one of the most basic and classic forms of communication in our daily life [23], it is a complex and sophisticated bi-directional multimodal phenomenon in which partners continually convey, perceive, interpret and react to the other person's verbal and co-verbal displays and signals [26]. Studies on human behavior has confirmed for instance that co-verbal features – such as body posture, arm/hand gestures , head movement, facial expressions, eye gaze– strongly participate in the

encoding and decoding of linguistic, paralinguistic and non-linguistic information. Several researchers have notably claimed that these features are largely involved in maintaining mutual attention and social glue [18].

Human interactions are paced by multi-level perception-action loops [2]. Thus, social robots/agents aiming at monitoring a multimodal and natural communication should mimic the very aspects of this complex close-loop system. In concrete terms, the robot has to couple two principal tasks: (1) scene analysis and (2) behavior generation. A multimodal behavioral model is responsible for computing behavior generation given the scene analysis and the intended goals of the conversation.

Our goal is to train statistical multimodal behavioral model that learns by observation of human-human interactions i.e. that maps perception to action. In this context, we present and compare three different candidate models: the first one is based on Hidden Markov Models (HMMs) and models the evolution of joint perception/action features over time. The two others are standard classifiers (Support Vector Machines and Decision Trees) that perform direct mapping without any explicit sequential modeling.

The paper is organized as follows: The next section reviews the state-of-the art of trainable multimodal generation systems. The three models are introduced in section 3. Section 4 illustrates the application of our models on data collected in a previous experiment [1]. We analyze the impact of contextual data in section 5. Finally, we conclude in section 6.

RELATED WORK

The analysis of multi-party interaction is an interdisciplinary domain spanning research not only in signal and image processing but also in social and human science involving sociology, psychology and anthropology [24]. In recent years, it is becoming an attractive research area and there is an increasing awareness about its technological and scientific challenges. Actually, automatic conversation scene analysis copes with several issues, including turn taking, addressing, activity recognition, roles detection, degree of engagement or interest, state of mind, personal traits and dominance. Several computational models have been proposed to predict or generate observed multimodal human behavior.

For instance, Otsuka et al. [22] proposed a Dynamic Bayesian Network (DBN) to estimate addressing and turn taking ("who responds to whom and when?"). The DBN framework is composed of three layers. The first one perceives speech and head gestures; the second layer generates gaze patterns while the third one estimates conversations regimes. While the first layer is observable, the others are latent and should be estimated. In order to recognize individual and group actions, Zhang et al. [30] suggested a two layered HMM. The first layer estimates personal actions taking as input raw audio-visual data. The second one infers group actions taking into account the estimations of the first layer. A Decision Tree is used in [3] for automatic role detection in multiparty conversations. Based mostly on acoustic features, the classifier assigns roles to each participant including effective participator, presenter, current information provider, and information consumer. In [13], Support Vectors Machines have been used to rate each person's dominance in multiparty interactions. The results showed that, while audio modality remains the most relevant, visual cues contribute in improving the discriminative power of the classifier. More complete reviews on models and issues related to nonverbal analysis of social interaction can be found in [10] [9][29].

For multimodal behavior generation, several platforms have been proposed for virtual agents and humanoid robots. Cassel et al. [6] notably developed the BEAT system ("Behavior Expression Animation Toolkit") which processes textual input and generates convenient and synchronized behaviors with speech such as intonation, eye gaze and iconic gestures. The synthesized nonverbal behavior is assigned on the basis of a contextual and linguistic analysis that relies on a set of rules inspired from research on conversational social human behavior. Later, Krenn [17] introduced the NECA project ("Net Environment for Embodied Emotional Conversational Agents") which aims to develop a platform for the implementation and the animation of conversational emotional agents for Web-based applications. This system hosts a complete scene generator and has the advantage of providing an ECA with communicative attitudes (e.g. head nods, eye brow raising) as well as non communicative attitudes (e.g. moving/walking in the scene, physiological breathing). Another major contribution of the NECA platform is Gesticon [16]. It consists of repository of predefined co-verbal animations and gestures that can drive both virtual and physical agents. "MAX", the "Multimodal Assembly eXpert" developed by Kopp and colleagues [14], interacts with humans in a virtual reality environment and collaborates with them in order to achieve some tasks. MAX is able to ensure reactive and deliberative actions via synthetic speech, facial expressions, gaze, and gestures. Most mentioned platforms have many similarities: multimodal actions are selected, scheduled and integrated according to rules-based configurations. The SAIBA framework [15] has been developed to establish a unique platform, unify norms and accelerate advancements in the

field. It is organized into three main components: "Intent planning", "Behavior planning" and "Behavior realization". It's worth noticing that SAIBA offers only a general framework for building multimodal behavioral models. In fact, the modeling within each component and its internal processing is treated as a "black box" and it is to researchers to fill the boxes by specifying their own models. One missing aspect of SAIBA is the perception dimension. In [26] a specific representation of perceptual cues was introduced to fill this gap. Many systems have adopted the SAIBA framework, particularly the GRETA platform [19] and the SmartBody system [28].

In the next section we will present our proposed models that, unlike pre-mentioned rule-based models (BEAT, SAIBA, etc), rely on machine learning and statistical modeling to intrinsically associate actions and percepts and to organize sequences of percepts and actions into so-called joint sensory-motor behaviors.

SOCIAL BEHAVIOR MODELING

This section presents statistical/probabilistic approaches for modeling jointly multimodal sensory-motor behaviors. Thus, these models should enable an artificial agent (1) estimate its cognitive state from perceptual observations (e.g. speech activity/gaze fixations of the partner), this state should reflect the joint behaviors of the conversation partners at that moment; (2) generate suitable actions (e.g. its own gaze fixations) that should reflect its current cognitive state and its current awareness of the evolution of the shared plan.

Each situated conversation is controlled by a specific syntax that defines a particular sequencing of joint cognitive states by a sort of behavioral grammar. As matter of fact, we chose HMMs because they have intrinsic sequential and temporal modeling capabilities. We compare here their performance with those of two well-known powerful classifiers (SVMs and Decision Trees).

HMMs

For each dyad, we model each cognitive state with a single Discrete Hidden Markov Model (DHMM) and the whole interaction with a global HMM, that chains all single models with a task-specific grammar. The hidden states of these HMMs model the perception-action loop by capturing joined behaviors. In fact, the observations vectors are composed by two streams: the first stream contains the perceptual observations and the second stream observes actions. The "hidden" states are then sensory-motor. In the training stage, all data are available while in testing only perceptual observations are available. After training, two sub-models are thus extracted: a recognition model that will be responsible of estimating sensory-motor states from perceptual observations and a generation model that will generate actions from these estimated states. In our model, these two phases of decoding and generation are performed incrementally using a modified version of the Short-Time Viterbi algorithm [5]. Since observations here have discrete values, we called this model IDHMM (for Incremental

Discrete HMM). For more details about the IDHMM model see [21].

SVMs and Decision Trees

SVMs and Decision Trees are among the most used and powerful classifiers. In our context, we will train two distinct classifiers: the first one will estimate the most likely cognitive state from perceptual observations while the second one will directly determine the most likely actions from perceptual observations.

APPLICATION TO A FACE-TO-FACE INTERACTION

Experimental setting

The dataset used has been collected by Bailly et al. [1]. The setting is shown in Figure 1. It consists of speech and gaze data from dyads playing a speech game via a computer-mediated communication system that enabled eye contact and dual eye tracking. The gaze fixations of each one are estimated by positioning dispersion ellipsis on fixation points gathered for each experiment after compensating for head movements. The speech game involved an instructor who reads and utters a sentence that the other subject (respondent) should repeat immediately in a single attempt. Dyads exchange Semantically Unpredictable Sentences (SUS) that force the respondent to be highly attentive to the audiovisual signals. The experiment was designed to study adaptation: one female main speaker LN interacted with eight subjects (females) both as an instructor for ten sentences and as a respondent for another set of ten sentences.

Data and models

For each dyad, we have two observations streams: voice activity ($v1/v2$ with 2 modalities: on/off) and gaze fixations ($g1/g2$ with 5 regions of interest ROI: face/mouth/left eye/right eye/else) of both speakers. Seven cognitive states (CS) [4] have been labeled semi-automatically ('Read', 'Prephon', 'Speak', 'Wait', 'Listen', 'Think' and 'Else'). For SVMs and Decisions Trees, a first classifier is used to estimate the CS of the principal subject LN from ($v1$, $v2$, $g2$). Then a second classifier is used to estimate her gaze ($g1$) from the same data. Similarly for the IDHMM, the recognition model is used to estimate the CS from ($v1,v2,g2$) and the eye fixations ($g1$) are synthesized using the generation model.

Gaze data have been monitored by two Tobii® eyetrackers operating at 25Hz. Voice activity detection has been sampled at the same rate.

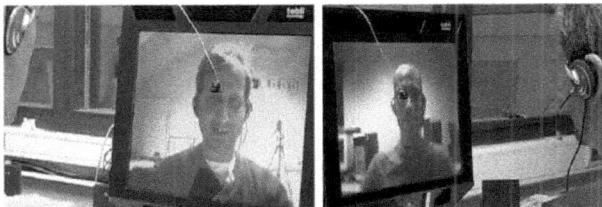

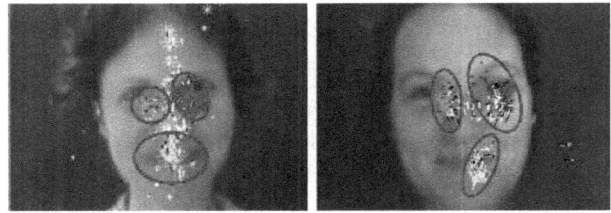

Figure 1: Experimental setting (only female subjects are included in our dataset)

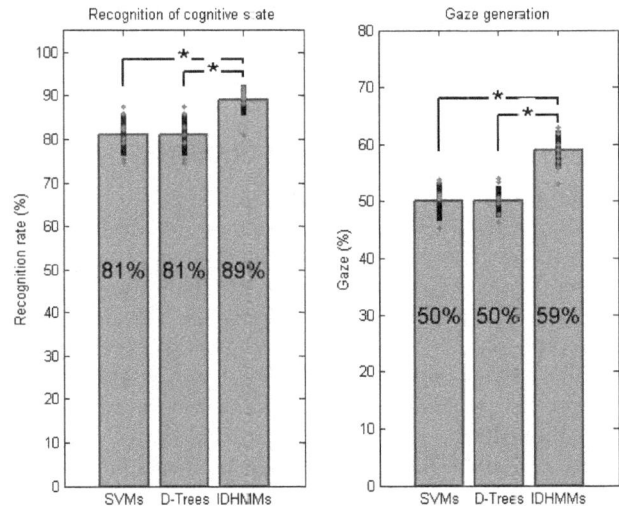

Figure 2: Results of the three models: SVMs, Decision Trees and IDHMMs

Results and comparison

DHMMs are trained with HTK [12], the IDHMM model was implemented in Matlab using PMTK3 toolkit [8]. For SVMs/Decision Trees, the Weka java package [11] has been used for both training and testing. For all models, 8-fold cross validation was applied: 7 subjects have been used for training while the eighth for testing.

Accuracy rates are used to evaluate cognitive state recognition, where the Levenshtein distance [20] is adopted for the evaluation of gaze generation because it allows more adequate comparison between generated and original signals. In fact, The Levenshtein distance is a metric for measuring the difference between two sequences; it computes the minimum number of elementary operations (insertions, deletions and substitutions) required to change one sequence into the other. From this optimal alignment, recall, precision and their harmonic mean (the F-measure) can be directly computed. In this paper all generation rates represent F-measures.

Figure 2 clearly shows that there is no significant variation between the two classifiers. However, the IDHMM model outperforms the two classifiers and the improvement provided by this model is quite significant ($p<0.05$). The IDHMM model has a rate of 89% for cognitive state detection and 59% for eye gaze generation. Moreover Figure 5 shows that the IDHMM model is more efficient in detecting the structure of the interaction. We can see that the estimated path of cognitive states reflects correctly the predefined syntax of the task. In comparison, the SVMs have more difficulty in capturing the organization of the real path (see Figure 5) and discard short transition states: we can see that the estimated states are principally « Speak », « Wait » and « Listen ». This is in not in contradiction with the 81% recognition rate because these three cognitive states alone represent 85% of the ground truth. This performance gap is mainly due to the sequential constraints afforded by HMMs. This lack of sequential organization impairs the performance of SVMs and Decision Trees that should exclusively exploit bottom-up information provided by the observations.

MODELS WITH CONTEXTUAL ATTRIBUTES

New models

In order to build a generation model of demonstrative pronouns in dialogues of a collaborative situated task, Spanger et al. [27] proposed an SVM classifier that uses actual and historical information about the interaction. This idea is also used by [7] in order to generate beat gestures from the acoustic signal. In fact, classifier performance can be improved by adding memory (historical values) to each observation. In the previous section, at a time t, the initial models use only the data of that moment. In the new configuration, we added the same three attributes (v1,v2,g2) but from a previous instant t-T, T being the size of the memory. Moreover we have varied this sole instant T from 1 frame to 80 frames to find the optimal delay.

Results and comparison

Our tests revealed that there is no significance difference between SVMs and Decision Trees, thus, in the rest we will focus on comparative performance of SVMs vs. IDHMMs. Figure 3 shows that the optimal delay for this task is T= ~55 frames (~ 2 seconds). We got the same value for Decision Trees. This optimal delay corresponds exactly to [25] in which authors demonstrate that, if a speaker looks at an object, 2 seconds after the listener will most likely be looking at the same object. From Figure 4, we can see that the addition of past observations results in better performance ($p<0.05$) for both SVM recognition (91%) and generation (59%). This memory injection leads also to a better modeling of the interaction structure. In fact, in Figure 5 we can obviously notice the improvement of the recognition of cognitive states.

Likewise, we added this past observation to the sensory stream of the IDHMM. As a result, we also observe a significant improvement in the gaze generation (59% to 63%) while the recognition rate remains the same at a 95% confidence level.

In the initial configuration, we concluded that IDHMM model was the most efficient due to the sequential property of Markov Models. In the second configuration, the results are generally improved; while the IDHMM is still better in gaze generation (63% vs. 59%), the SVM model leads to a higher rate (91% vs. 87%) for a 95% confidence level. Hence, supplying the SVM model with memory has relatively addressed the missing temporal aspect.

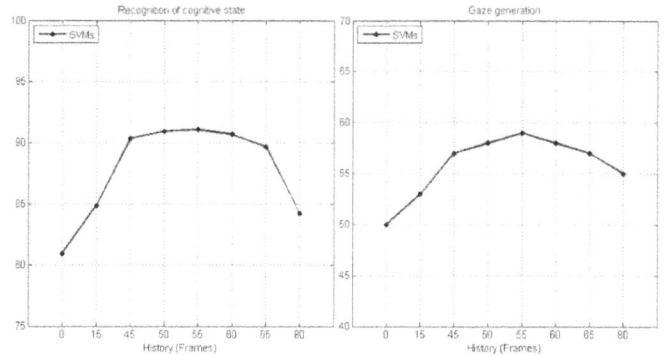

Figure 3: Optimal memory instant for the SVM

CONCLUSIONS

In this paper, we presented a comparative study of three behavioral models designed for social robots/agents (SVMs, Decision Trees and IDHMMs). These models have been tested in two different configurations: with & without history features. Comparison results showed that, in both settings, the IDHMM, thanks to its sequential modeling properties, remains a robust model for cognitive state recognition and eye gaze generation, and that classic classifier like SVMs could result in high performance if a certain memory (~2 seconds in our case) was included in the input observations.

Currently, we are studying a new scenario of a face-to face interaction that allows generating not only gaze but also deictic gestures. For the IDHMMs, we are also studying the influence of the number of hidden sensory-motor-states on the performance of each cognitive state and thus the impact on the generation figures.

ACKNOWLEDGMENTS
This research is financed by the Rhône-Alpes ARC6 research council.

(a)   (b)

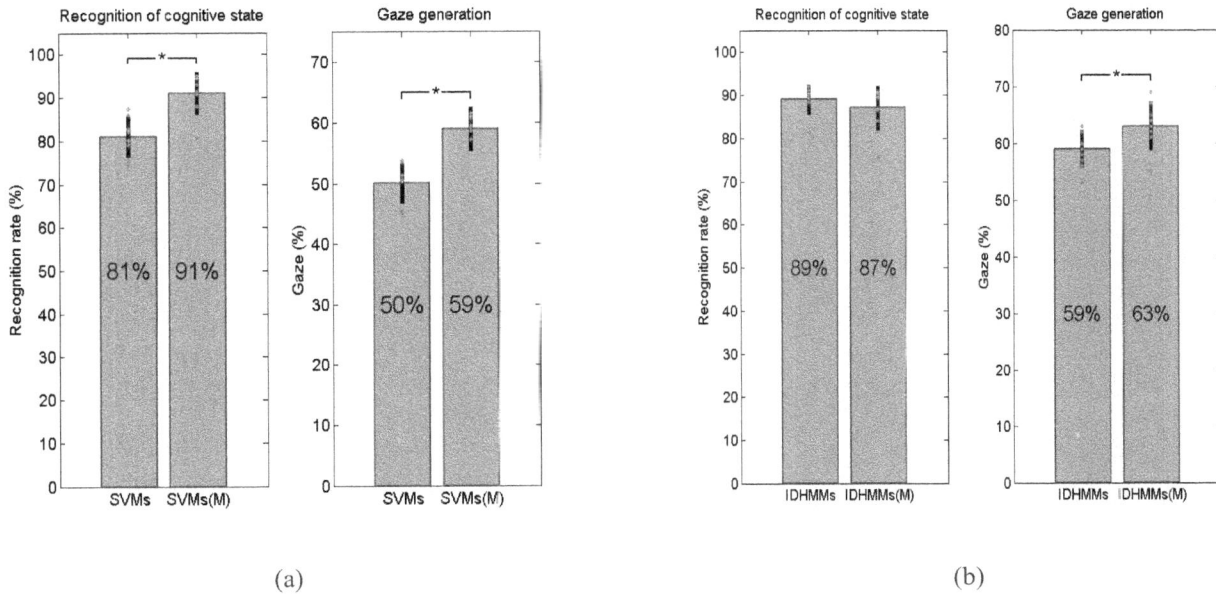

Figure 4: No memory / Memory (M=55) (a) for SVMs (b) for IDHMMs

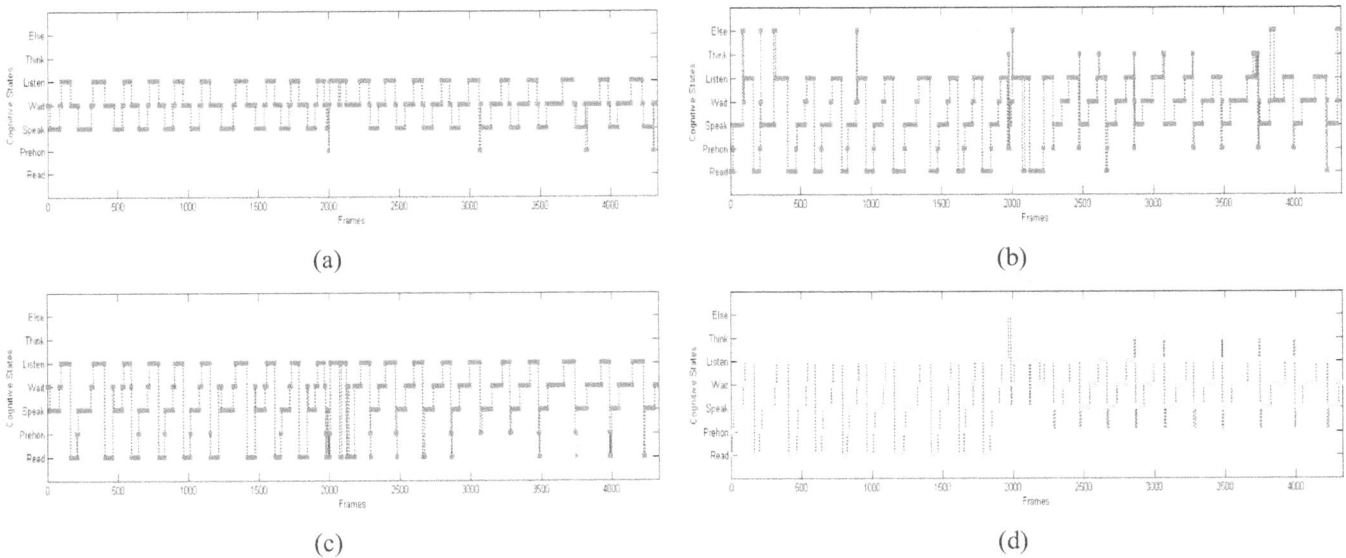

(a)   (b)

(c)   (d)

Figure 5: Estimation of the cognitive state (CS) for a specific subject (a) using SVMs (b) using IDHMM (c) using SVMs and memory attributes (d) the real CS path

REFERENCES

1. Bailly, G., Raidt, S., and Elisei, F. Gaze, conversational agents and face-to-face communication. *Speech Communication 52*, 6 (2010), 598–612.

2. Bailly, G. Boucles de perception-action et interaction face-à-face. *Revue fran\ccaise de linguistique appliquée 13*, 2 (2009), 121–131.

3. Banerjee, S. and Rudnicky, A.I. Using simple speech-based features to detect the state of a meeting and the roles of the meeting participants. (2004).

4. Baron-Cohen, S. *Mind Reading: The Interactive Guide to Emotions*. Jessica Kingsley Publishers, London u.a., 2004.

5. Bloit, J. and Rodet, X. Short-time Viterbi for online HMM decoding: Evaluation on a real-time phone recognition task. *IEEE International Conference on Acoustics, Speech and Signal Processing, 2008. ICASSP 2008*, (2008), 2121–2124.

6. Cassell, J., Vilhjalmsson, H., and Bickmore, T. *BEAT: the Behavior Expression Animation Toolkit*. 2001.

7. Chiu, C.-C. and Marsella, S. Gesture Generation with Low-dimensional Embeddings. *Proceedings of the 2014 International Conference on Autonomous Agents and Multi-agent Systems*, International Foundation for Autonomous Agents and Multiagent Systems (2014), 781–788.

8. Dunham, M. and Murphy, K. *PMTK3: Probabilistic modeling toolkit for Matlab/Octave, http://code.google.com/p/pmtk3/.* .

9. Gatica-Perez, D. Analyzing group interactions in conversations: a review. *Multisensor Fusion and Integration for Intelligent Systems, 2006 IEEE International Conference on*, (2006), 41–46.

10. Gatica-Perez, D. Automatic nonverbal analysis of social interaction in small groups: A review. *Image and Vision Computing 27*, 12 (2009), 1775–1787.

11. Hall, M., Frank, E., Holmes, G., Pfahringer, B., Reutemann, P., and Witten, I.H. The WEKA data mining software: an update. *SIGKDD Explor. Newsl. 11*, 1 (2009), 10–18.

12. HTK, The Hidden Markov Model Toolkit. *http://htk.eng.cam.ac.uk/.* .

13. Jayagopi, D.B., Hung, H., Yeo, C., and Gatica-Perez, D. Modeling dominance in group conversations using nonverbal activity cues. *Audio, Speech, and Language Processing, IEEE Transactions on 17*, 3 (2009), 501–513.

14. Kopp, S., Jung, B., Lessmann, N., and Wachsmuth, I. Max - A Multimodal Assistant in Virtual Reality Construction. *KI 17*, 4 (2003), 11.

15. Kopp, S., Krenn, B., Marsella, S., et al. Towards a Common Framework for Multimodal Generation: The Behavior Markup Language. *INTERNATIONAL CONFERENCE ON INTELLIGENT VIRTUAL AGENTS*, (2006), 21–23.

16. Krenn, B. and Pirker, H. Defining the gesticon: Language and gesture coordination for interacting embodied agents. *Proc. of the AISB-2004 Symposium on Language, Speech and Gesture for Expressive Characters*, (2004), 107–115.

17. Krenn, B. The NECA project: Net environments for embodied emotional conversational agents. *Proc. of Workshop on emotionally rich virtual worlds with emotion synthesis at the 8th International Conference on 3D Web Technology (Web3D), St. Malo, France*, (2003).

18. Lakin, J.L., Jefferis, V.E., Cheng, C.M., and Chartrand, T.L. The Chameleon Effect as Social Glue: Evidence for the Evolutionary Significance of Nonconscious Mimicry. *Journal of Nonverbal Behavior 27*, 3 (2003), 145–162.

19. Le, Q.A. and Pelachaud, C. Generating Co-speech Gestures for the Humanoid Robot NAO through BML. In E. Efthimiou, G. Kouroupetroglou and S.-E. Fotinea, eds., *Gesture and Sign Language in Human-Computer Interaction and Embodied Communication*. Springer Berlin Heidelberg, 2012, 228–237.

20. Levenshtein, V. Binary Codes Capable of Correcting Deletions, Insertions and Reversals. *Soviet Physics Doklady 10*, 8 (1966), 707–710.

21. Mihoub, A., Bailly, G., and Wolf, C. Social Behavior Modeling Based on Incremental Discrete Hidden Markov Models. In *Human Behavior Understanding*. Springer International Publishing, 2013, 172–183.

22. Otsuka, K., Sawada, H., and Yamato, J. Automatic inference of cross-modal nonverbal interactions in multiparty conversations: "who responds to whom, when, and how?" from gaze, head gestures, and utterances. *Proceedings of the 9th international conference on Multimodal interfaces*, ACM (2007), 255–262.

23. Otsuka, K. Multimodal Conversation Scene Analysis for Understanding People's Communicative Behaviors in Face-to-Face Meetings. (2011), 171–179.

24. Otsuka, K. Conversation Scene Analysis [Social Sciences]. *IEEE Signal Processing Magazine 28*, 4 (2011), 127–131.

25. Richardson, D.C., Dale, R., and Shockley, K. Synchrony and swing in conversation: coordination, temporal dynamics, and communication. In I. Wachsmuth, M. Lenzen and G. Knoblich, eds., *Embodied Communication in Humans and Machines*. Oxford University Press, 2008, 75–94.

26. Scherer, S., Marsella, S., Stratou, G., et al. Perception markup language: towards a standardized representation of perceived nonverbal behaviors. *Intelligent Virtual Agents*, (2012), 455–463.

27. Spanger, P., Yasuhara, M., Iida, R., and Tokunaga, T. Using extra linguistic information for generating demonstrative pronouns in a situated collaboration task. *Proceedings of PreCogSci 2009: Production of Referring Expressions: Bridging the gap between computational and empirical approaches to reference*, (2009).

28. Thiebaux, M., Marsella, S., Marshall, A.N., and Kallmann, M. Smartbody: Behavior realization for embodied conversational agents. *Proceedings of the 7th international joint conference on Autonomous agents and multiagent systems-Volume 1*, (2008), 151–158.

29. Vinciarelli, A., Pantic, M., Heylen, D., et al. Bridging the Gap between Social Animal and Unsocial Machine: A Survey of Social Signal Processing. *IEEE Transactions on Affective Computing 3*, 1 (2012), 69–87.

30. Zhang, D., Gatica-Perez, D., Bengio, S., and McCowan, I. Modeling individual and group actions in meetings with layered HMMs. *Multimedia, IEEE Transactions on 8*, 3 (2006), 509–520.

PaintBoard – Prototyping Interactive Character Behaviors by Digitally Painting Storyboards

Daniel J. Rea
University of Manitoba
daniel.rea@cs.umanitoba.ca

Takeo Igarashi
The University of Tokyo
takeo@acm.org

James E. Young
University of Manitoba
young@cs.umanitoba.ca

ABSTRACT

The creation of interactive computer-controlled characters in interactive media is a challenging and multi-faceted task requiring the skills and effort of professionals from many fields. This work addresses authoring the interactive aspect of these characters' behaviors – how characters act automatically in response to a dynamic user-controlled character. We present PaintBoard, a system that enables users to prototype and test discrete, real-time, interactive movements in a 2D grid environment simply by digitally painting a storyboard. We designed and developed a novel authoring technique for creating behaviors (painting storyboards) and a novel algorithm based on machine-learning, that analyzes a storyboard to create a behavior that works beyond situations provided in the input storyboard. We conducted two exploratory studies that grounded the prototype design, and present the results of a proof-of-concept workshop with game developers. Finally, we performed a comparison of machine learning algorithms' performance on our storyboard data.

Author Keywords

End-user programming; interactive systems; sketch interface; prototyping; interface design; machine learning

ACM Classification Keywords

H.5.2. User interfaces: Prototyping, User-centered design

General Terms

Design; Human Factors

INTRODUCTION

Computer controlled characters are an integral component of modern video games and other interactive media. The creation of these characters is a difficult task that, at the professional level, can demand a broad range of specialized and highly-skilled collaborating individuals, including artists for creating 3D models and animations, writers and voice actors for dialogue, and a range of programmers to implement artificial intelligence and system logic. This is particularly challenging when the computer-controlled characters are highly

HAI '14, October 29 - 31 2014, Tsukuba, Japan
Copyright is held by the owner/author(s). Publication rights licensed to ACM.
ACM 978-1-4503-3035-0/14/10…$15.00.
http://dx.doi.org/10.1145/2658861.2658886

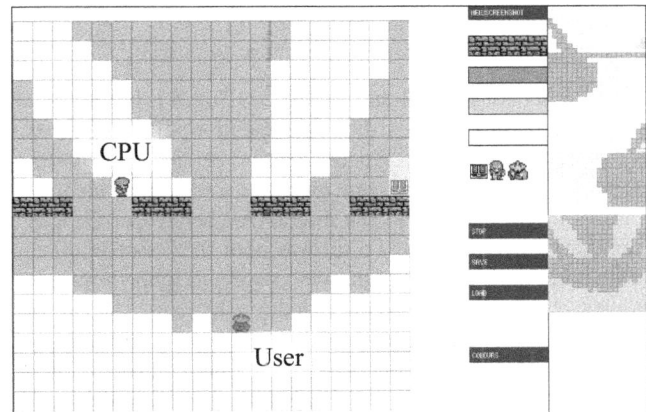

Figure 1: A participant sketches a storyboard to show that a computer-controlled interactive character (CPU) should approach yellow squares (the treasure) while staying out of the red squares (user controlled character's sight). PaintBoard extrapolates and generates the interactive behavior of sneaking to the treasure when the user's character is not looking.

interactive—when the characters must, in real-time, assess and interact appropriately to dynamic input from users and their environment. These highly-dynamic *interactive behaviors* can demand programming expertise and significant amounts of time. For example, in a role playing game, a designer may want a computer-controlled thief character to "sneak": avoid the user-controlled character when they are nearby while simultaneously approaching a treasure box, all without being seen. Such behaviors usually require the logical definition of multiple conditions based on user activity, and all details of the behavior that occur in each condition.

Researchers have proposed various methods to reduce the amount of expertise and time required for creating content for interactive systems. This includes enabling people to create 3D models simply by sketching in 2D [12], to author advanced animations through simple mouse gestures [13], or to create complex interactive stories through point-and-click visual logic programming [15]. Simplifying the creative process further provides experts and non-experts alike with prototyping tools for quickly testing, visualizing, and sharing their ideas [18]. We extend this body of work with PaintBoard: a simple and visual prototyping method that aims to reduce the effort and skill required for the creation of interactive behaviors for computer controlled characters.

Paper sketching and other related low-fidelity techniques (such as storyboarding) are low-cost, fast, easy-to-use tools that support creativity and exploration [4,14] by assisting and enabling rapid iteration of ideas, and by providing immediate visual feedback of those ideas [4,14,18]. They also enable and inherently support communication with others, as well as storytelling [11]. Because of this, low-fidelity techniques are part of standard toolkits across a broad range of fields including human-computer interaction [14], film [10], and animation [13]. PaintBoard leverages the benefits of these exploration techniques by enabling people to create behaviors by digitally painting rough ideas on virtual storyboards, similar to sketching, and by generating results that people can interact with, test, refine, and show to others.

In this paper we present an initial PaintBoard prototype that provides a novel storyboarding interface for painting interactive behaviors. We developed a feature set for representing the behaviors, and employed machine-learning using these features to generate real-time interactive behaviors from the user-drawn storyboards. To inform both the PaintBoard interface and algorithm design, we conducted interviews with industry professionals and analyzed results from a behavior-programming workshop with experienced programmers. We present the results of a proof-of-concept, hands-on Paint-Board workshop and an evaluation of our algorithm by comparing its performance in alternative configurations.

RELATED WORK

Existing research that simplifies the creation of interactive characters and systems has aimed to reduce the programming requirements typical to such tasks. One example uses accessible drag-and-drop textual representations of game objects combined with programming-like elements [15] to create story-based interactive worlds (their focus was not on interactive behavior movement). Another powerful work allows authors to explore complex interactive story narratives by specifying details about the characters and the world they act in [16]. Others enable users to build up an interactive behavior with gesture grammars and state machine logic [17]. PaintBoard focuses on prototyping, and because linear, detail-oriented thinking can hinder prototyping and exploration [20], our work aims to avoid requiring users to explain their behavior logically and enable them to describe it in a visual, story-like, less detail-oriented way.

Programming by demonstration, where a designer can author a behavior by simply providing a performance demonstration, is a common technique for authoring interactive behaviors. Although this is well established in animation [6,13] and robotics [19], most of this work has been for the creation of *static* behaviors without an interactive element. Interactive work has focused on, for example, learning reactive body language from motion-capture data with user-controlled parameters [7], or well-defined sequences of actions that fit into a state-machine model [9,17]. PaintBoard extends this work by targeting movement in response to unpredictable users in continuous real-time interaction throughout a 2D environment. Further, programming by demonstration can often require large numbers of repetitive demonstrations (e.g. [8]), real world data of many types of movement (e.g. [8]), or still

uses programming in the process (e.g. [21]). To enable its use as a low cost rapid-prototyping tool, PaintBoard can work with as little as one example.

Perhaps closest to our work is the Puppet Master programming-by-demonstration project [22], which enables authors to rapidly prototype interactive animation or robotic motion behaviors similar to the ones targeted by PaintBoard. While Puppet Master emphasizes interactive movement "style" of two interacting characters, PaintBoard builds upon their results to cover multi-part behaviors (e.g., hide when seen, get some treasure when guards are not looking), and enable characters to interact with the environment (e.g., walls, important objects such as treasure chests). Further, Puppet Master's evaluations indicated that users had difficulty envisioning the result from their performance demonstration due to the mental load from Puppet Master requiring the user to successfully author the whole behavior in real-time in one attempt; To avoid such issues, we extend Puppet Master's approach by enabling more complex interactive behavior authoring in a visual way with frame-by-frame storyboards.

Low-fidelity prototyping techniques such as sketching have been used to successfully simplify other forms of digital content design, for example, by using 2D sketches to create 3D character models [12], or to design and implement user interfaces [14]. These tools are accessible as design and prototyping tools to both professional and amateur designers. We follow this approach by applying rough painting to simplify the creation of interactive motion behaviors

EXPLORATORY INVESTIGATION

To inform our interface and algorithm design, we conducted two exploratory studies. First, we performed semi-structured interviews with video game designers and developers to uncover common problems faced and workflows used during the creation process. To inform the design of our behavior generation algorithm, we conducted a second investigation (programmer study) with 26 undergraduate programmers, where we explored the range of interactive behaviors people may author, and analyzed implementations (computer code) to extract strategies and techniques used to implement them.

Interviews with Industry

We conducted four, one-hour semi-structured interviews with professional game designers and developers. Questions we asked include "How are certain interactive behaviors difficult to create, specifically because of interactions with the player?" and "How do you create these interactive behaviors?" We recorded the interviews and qualitatively analyzed transcripts through open coding to identify key themes.

Participants reported spending significant time planning behavior implementations due to the even higher time cost of actually implementing them with programming. In addition, participants heavily relied on experimentation and iterative prototyping (writing programs and observing results). This grounds our initial rapid prototyping motivation in the needs of real users. Further, participants reported having difficulty communicating and understanding how an interactive behavior should look. We saw this reported by both technical developers as well as artistic designers. As visual tools improve communication [4,11], one aim of PaintBoard was leveraging painting's visual nature as the main interaction metaphor.

Programmer Study: Analysis of Implementations

To investigate programming strategies that may be useful for generating behaviors, we conducted a programming workshop to explore methods used by developers to implement interactive behaviors. We asked 26 fourth-year undergraduate Computer Science students in a Human-Computer Interaction class to program a set of behaviors; such participants have the skills to work in the video game industry. We used a medieval-theme (common within the role-playing video game genre) as a representative scenario. Participants were provided a simple graphical game board (that looked similar to PaintBoard, e.g., Figure 1) and Java API, and were tasked with creating three behaviors each. They were encouraged to develop their own behaviors, and were described "follow," "protect treasure," and "escape" as examples.

We received 78 unique behavior implementations that we categorized into 19 distinct types. The three most common of these were our suggested "follow the user" (24 participants), "protect treasure" (18), and "escape from the user" (13) behaviors. The remaining behaviors had less overlap (16 types over 23 implementations). Common behavior types, however had significant variation, for example, some "follow the user" implementations would stay close behind the user, others would walk side by side, and yet others would follow from a distance. Thus behaviors are envisioned differently by different authors; PaintBoard will need to accommodate not only a variety of behaviors, but allow for variations of those behaviors.

Our post-workshop analysis of the developers' behavior implementations illuminated strategies that participants used to define their behaviors. Across behaviors, we found that participants consistently leveraged a small set of commonly calculated quantities, such as the characters' visibility and relative positions, to decide on how the computer character should interact with the user; we distilled these into a set of features that our algorithm used to analyze painted storyboard input (detailed in Section 4.3). Additionally, programmers commonly specified points of interest, for example, a treasure chest to "guard," a "hideout" to run to, or even staying in "close proximity to the user." Thus PaintBoard enables users to define such goal areas with the interface.

PAINTBOARD PROTOTYPE

Our PaintBoard prototype provides a sandbox setting that enables people to author a behavior by digitally painting on a screen. Users paint a storyboard consisting of static *snapshot* panels that each convey the behavior in a specific situation. The storyboard represents a full behavior, and is used as input to the PaintBoard algorithm to generate the interactive

result. The interface and logic was programmed in Java using Processing[1] and the ControlP5 library[2] was used for the GUI.

User Interface

The sandbox area of the interface is a 20x20 2D character movement grid where the user constructs snapshots from an overhead view (Figure 2a). Users can drag objects (from Figure 2d), including both the computer and player characters (maximum one of each), points of interest (treasure chest, maximum one), and environment (walls, from Figure 2c), onto the grid, and position them as desired.

Users can select a color from the palette (Figure 2c) and then paint on the grid by clicking and dragging the mouse; cells can only have one color at a time. Red paint denotes areas where the computer character should *not* go, for example, when painting a "sneak" behavior all grid cells that the user character can see should be red because a sneaking character does not want to be seen. Gold paint indicates *goal* areas: where the computer character wants to go (Figure 3). This differs from points of interest in that it is based on the user and computer characters' current configuration (e.g., "behind the user") and as such are more dynamic than stationary points of interest. Unpainted (white) squares are neutral and the character neither avoids nor tends toward them. In other words, the computer character should try to go toward gold areas, while passing through uncolored areas and avoiding red ones. Thus the PaintBoard interface addresses the features uncovered during our programmer study: visibility can be defined simply by painting where a character can see (Figure 3), relative position is defined by how the user and computer characters are placed, and the gold paint and points of interest enable the author to designate goals.

PaintBoard Interaction Flow

To facilitate rapid and iterative prototyping, PaintBoard enables users to quickly create behaviors, and easily test and modify them. While painting, users can test their behavior by pressing a single button ("play"), and the system instantly

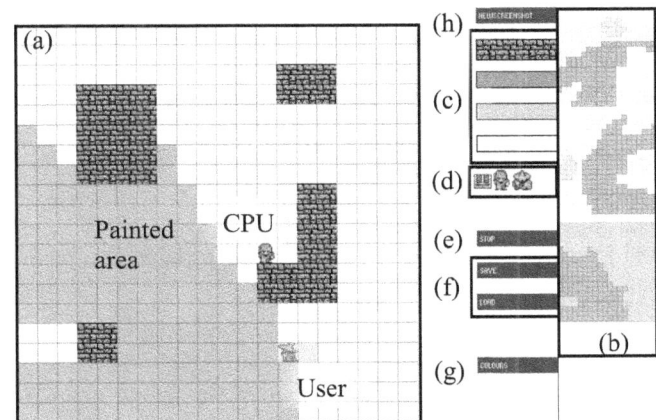

Figure 2: The PaintBoard interface: (a) sandbox area, (b) storyboard snapshots, (c) paint palette, (d) point of interest (chest) and characters, (e) play and pause, (f) save and load behavior, (g) debug mode, (h) new snapshot.

[1] http://www.processing.org/

[2] http://www.sojamo.de/libraries/controlP5/

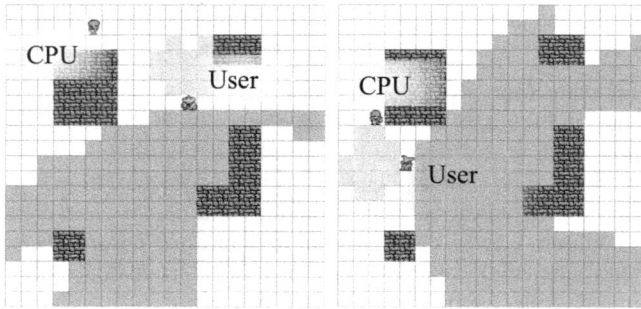

Figure 3: A sample two-part behavior storyboard of a character that sneaks up on the user. In this case, the computer character should not enter the sight of the user character, (red squares) and should stay close to and behind the user (gold).

compiles the behavior and generates a result that the users can interact with using the keyboard controls (arrow keys). At any time, the author can press "stop," edit any of the snapshots in the storyboard, or create a new snapshot to modify the behavior. While testing, if the computer character moves in an unintended way, the user can capture the real-time scenario as a new snapshot, and paint it.

PaintBoard has a debug mode that is identical to testing ("play" mode) except that it provides real-time visual feedback regarding what the character is trying to do. Based on the storyboard input, PaintBoard will display red and gold squares to indicate where – in the given situation – it believes the character should and should not go. For example, given the snapshots in Figure 3 as the storyboard input, Figure 2 is the debug-mode output, a visual representation of what PaintBoard has learned.

Enabling rapid and iterative prototyping of ideas was a major interface priority, as it has been shown to aid creativity and exploration [14,18,20]; PaintBoard enables users to quickly create, modify, and delete snapshots, as well as test the interactive results without requiring any programming or logic definition. With PaintBoard, authors create behaviors *in-situ* (e.g., [12,17]): they create in the same environment where the behavior will be used. This enables authors to bypass conceptual translations required when moving from an authoring to a testing medium (such as moving from visual programming to a game), helping visualize the final result [2].

Algorithm
The PaintBoard algorithm must analyze a painted storyboard and generate an interactive character that matches the qualities given in the storyboard.

Given an input storyboard and a new, live situation, PaintBoard first generates a new *synthetic snapshot* to have similar characteristics to the input examples (e.g. red paint in user's line-of-sight). For example, given the two snapshots as input from Figure 3, PaintBoard generated the painting in Figure 2a to have similar characteristics. Then, PaintBoard uses this synthetic snapshot to determine the interactive character's next move. After moving, the process is repeated, generating a new synthetic snapshot for each new situation.

Generating Synthetic Snapshots
We employ a Support Vector Machine (SVM) [5] classifier to iterate over all cells of the unpainted snapshot and label them as red, gold, or unpainted, creating the synthetic snapshot. We selected an SVM as a standard, fast classifier and used the LibSVM library [5] with its default settings.

To train the SVM, we calculate a feature vector for every cell in every snapshot, and label it with the color painted by the author (red, gold, unpainted). Thus, the SVM would ideally label cells of the synthetic snapshot to match characteristics (the features) of the training data (as show in Figure 2).

A challenge of using machine learning is to select representative features that capture the appropriate characteristics of the scene. This is non-trivial, and we developed our own domain-specific features given the lack of prior work; this problem and challenge is common in machine learning (e.g., [7,22]). PaintBoard uses the features identified in our programmer study, with the final set selected informally through experimentation. We call these *state features*, detailed below (Figure 4):

Cell Position Relative to the User in the Screen's Coordinate System. For example, in Figure 4 the bold cell is two to the left and three above the user. This captures absolute relation to the user (e.g., stay to the left side of the environment).

Cell Position Relative to the User's Orientation. For example, in Figure 4 the bold cell is two cells in front of and 3 cells to the right of the user character. This captures position from the user's point of view (e.g., stay behind them).

Cell Position in a Coordinate System Rooted at the User and Oriented to the Point of Interest. For example, in Figure 4 the bold cell is 2.6 cells behind and 2.5 to the left of the user and chest. This captures the context of the point of interest (e.g., do not go between the user and the chest). This is not used when there is no point of interest.

Visibility: we cast rays from the user to the cell and its neighbors to calculate visibility, with those blocked by walls not counted. For example, the bold square in Figure 4 has visibility 0.6 (6/9). This captures line of sight information (e.g.,

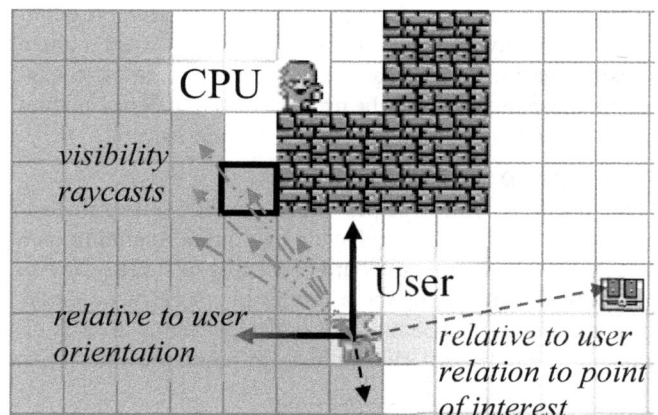

Figure 4: How state features are calculated for the bolded cell.

how visible cells are to the user), and the non-binary classification enables the computer character to capture the difference between being partially and fully seen.

Euclidean Distances from the Cell to the User and Point of Interest. For example, in Figure 4 the bold square is 3.6 and 7.3 from the user and point of interest respectively. This helps emphasize proximity (e.g., how close to be to the user).

These features form a multi-dimensional vector for each cell which is labeled with the color painted by the author. We use all vectors from all snapshots in a storyboard to train the SVM. During interaction, the features are calculated for each cell in real time and the SVM is used to classify (paint) them to generate the synthetic snapshot.

Using a Synthetic Snapshot to Generate the Behavior
After generating the synthetic snapshot, the computer character moves toward the closest goal space (gold paint), while not walking through walls, and avoiding red spaces if possible. The algorithm does a breadth-first search spiraling out from the computer character (we saw this in our programmer study), where walls are considered impassable. Red cells may not be completely avoidable, for example if all other paths are blocked. We address this by giving them a penalty distance of four. For the case when the character is stuck with large red areas between it and the goal, we added a path-length threshold of 20 so the character simply would wait in safety rather than traversing large red areas. Both of these quantities were selected through experimentation.

PAINTBOARD WORKSHOP
We conducted a proof-of-concept workshop to explore reactions to our PaintBoard approach and interaction design by potential end-users. Formal, targeted evaluations (e.g., investigating how PaintBoard can integrate into a designer's workflow) remain important future work.

We recruited five professional and hobbyist game developers for the 1.5 hour workshop, where they received a 15 minute tutorial on how to use PaintBoard to prototype interactive behaviors. Afterwards, they were given one hour to freely create any behaviors they wished (using the same medieval theme as above), and were given a 15 minute questionnaire at the end. Although each person worked independently, the atmosphere was friendly and collaborative, and people were having spontaneous discussions about their experiences. Researchers took notes throughout the workshop

Participants were asked to save their storyboards (through the PaintBoard functionality) for later inspection. In addition, we performed broad qualitative analysis on the notes and questionnaire answers in order to identify themes and insights of our participants' experiences on topics such as viability of painting as a behavior authoring technique, or ways that PaintBoard could be leveraged in real-world situations.

Results
Overall, participants were able to use PaintBoard to quickly and successfully prototype a range of interactive behaviors

such as "follow the user," "hide," "obstruct the user," "guard an area," and "sneak to treasure." This was achieved in spite of minimal training, lending support to our painting and storyboarding approach and implementation.

Participants reported feeling that PaintBoard would be useful for planning and prototyping ideas:

> *In its current state, could be handy for prototyping and visualizing scenarios. - P3*

> *I would use this as a prototyping tool to make quick behaviors that I would then implement with code - P2*

and for communicating with others:

> *Easy to visually show others simple behavior that can be expanded to more complex situations. - P5*

Some noted that it may be useful for team members with less technical expertise:

> *I'm not sure if it'll be useful in my workflow (yet), but I think it'll be great for designers - P1*

Although this is far from rigorous proof, the previous two quotes highlight our motivation of making a tool that facilitates communication between designers and developers: the visual and interactive nature is important as the resulting behavior prototypes can be shared and discussed with coworkers. As PaintBoard requires no coding knowledge, it enables two-way communication as both designers and developers can modify behavior prototypes to enhance discussions.

Participants praised the benefits of PaintBoard's iterative nature, noting that it matches their existing workflows:

> *I like the iterative design process. Games tend to follow on iterative design, so this fits nicely. - P1*

Even though our participants were experienced programmers, they were very receptive to the use of painting in the behavior design process:

> *The abstraction of the concepts is very easy to understand ... as well as the ability to alter states during play, and ability to watch the goal and avoid state change - P4*

All participants also felt the performance of the test mode was reasonable. However, some did show concern over PaintBoard's ability to scale up to more complex behaviors:

> *It's a bit hard to convey a behavior sometimes, but maybe that doesn't need to be a goal. It seems to work with simpler behaviors and I think it can be used as such usefully - P1*

There were several examples where the painted storyboard was very clear and descriptive from a person's perspective, but the resulting behaviors were not generated successfully. While this is a difficulty with the current learning algorithm, we believe that this is a success for the painting interface: it illustrates the ability to represent and communicate a desired result through our storyboards. See Figure 5, a storyboard produced by a participant in our workshop: it has easy-to-understand snapshots of specific behavior aspects and the overall storyboard clearly describes a complete behavior, but the generated behavior usually predicted only unpainted cells.

In addition to reflecting on the potential benefits of Paint-Board, participants described specific functionality that they believed could improve PaintBoard. For example, participants requested the addition of story branches, where a condition indicated in a snapshot may lead to a new set of snapshots. This could fit within the storyboard interaction, but would require new algorithmic solutions. Participants also suggested adding the ability to weigh painted cells, where some are more important than others (e.g. prefer not being seen over reaching the treasure), or the ability to make hard rules about the environment, for example, to mark specific squares in the environment which should always be avoided. While these would give more creative power and control to a PaintBoard user, such features should be added with careful consideration of the speed and simplicity of PaintBoard's interaction flow, else they may slow down PaintBoard's rapid and iterative nature.

COMPARISON OF CLASSIFIERS AND FEATURE SETS ON STORYBOARD DATA

To understand how our choice of learning algorithm and training features were linked to some of our users' behavior generation problems observed in our workshop, we analyzed the performance of different variations of our algorithm. We modified our algorithm on two dimensions: classifier, and

feature set used to train the classifier. This analysis has three components: we developed a dataset and accuracy metric that could be used to test a given configuration, we tested the accuracy of each classification algorithm, and using the best performing classifier we greedily selected state features to form a possible variant feature set for training.

To build a dataset for training and testing classifiers, we recruited developers and had them use PaintBoard to paint behaviors. Participants were 4th year and graduate computer science students. They were given an explanation of how PaintBoard worked, including a demonstration of painting a "follow" behavior. Each participant was asked to paint three behaviors: escape from the user character, sneak up to the user character, and protect a treasure from the user character. For each behavior, the participant was instructed to create 10 different storyboard examples with each example fully defining a behavior and containing one or more snapshots. Thus, there were 30 example storyboards per user.

Comparison of Classifiers

We compared the performance of five different machine-learning classifiers for our behavior generation algorithm: SVM with a radial basis kernel (which we used in our initial PaintBoard implementation), SVM with a polynomial kernel,

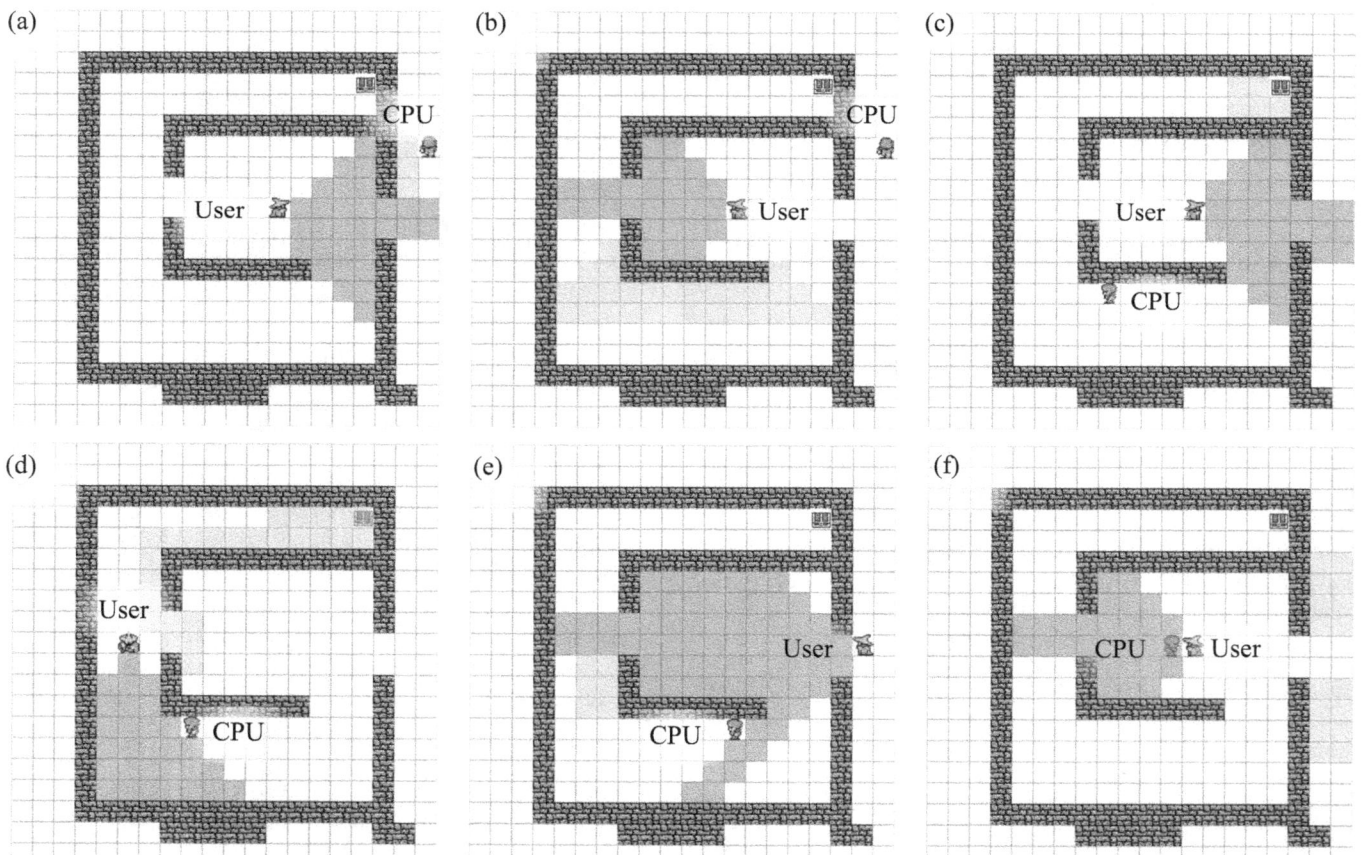

Figure 5: A storyboard authored by a participant during our workshop, showing how a computer character should sneak around a user to get treasure. (a) hide by the only entrance to the room (b) when the user is not looking, sneak into the room and stay out of sight (c) when the user is not looking at the inner hallway, run to the treasure (d) if the user is in the hallway, sneak around the other way (e) get as close to the treasure as possible without being seen, and (f) if spotted by the user, run out of the room.

K-Nearest Neighbors, Random Forest, and Naïve Bayes classifier. We used the implementations of these algorithms provided by the Java Machine Learning Library [1]. The two SVMs used the LibSVM default parameters; k was chosen as 5 for K-Nearest Neighbors as it had similar performance to higher values (e.g. k=10) with faster run-time; the tree count for the random forest was set to 100, based on the evidence suggesting random forests do not often overfit [3].

For each algorithm, we performed cross-validation to better understand its predictive accuracy with PaintBoard. For one participant's behavior, we trained PaintBoard with only one of the provided 10 storyboard examples: our target use case is rapid prototyping and, ideally, a user will paint minimal data and test in many situations. For each of the remaining examples, we generate a synthetic snapshot for the same situation and calculate accuracy as the percent of true positives (direct cell matches) between the two. This is done for each example, training a new classifier each storyboard and averaging the accuracies together. The accuracy of an algorithm is the mean accuracy over all participants and behaviors.

Results

We present accuracy of each algorithm in Figure 6. There was a main effect of the algorithm on the accuracy of the synthetic snapshot ($F(4, 120) = 11.9$, $p < .001$, $\eta^2 = .284$). Post-hoc tests (with Bonferroni correction) revealed that the radial basis function SVM performed better than Naïve Bayes ($p<.001$), and polynomial SVM ($p<.05$). All other comparisons were not significant.

The behavior type impacted the accuracy of the synthetic snapshot ($F(2, 120) = 8.0$, $p=.001$, $\eta^2 = .117$). Post-hoc tests (with Bonferroni correction) revealed that "sneak" was more accurate than "escape" or "protect" (10% more) $p<.005$. There was no interaction effect between algorithm and behavior type on accuracy.

One problem with interpreting the above accuracy results is that, in our data, a cell is much more likely to be unpainted (clear) than painted (red or gold); this biases classifiers to give us high accuracy for unpainted cells while possibly lowering the accuracy for the other colors. To provide insight we present a confusion matrix for the radial basis SVM (Figure 7), showing the average accuracy across all participants and

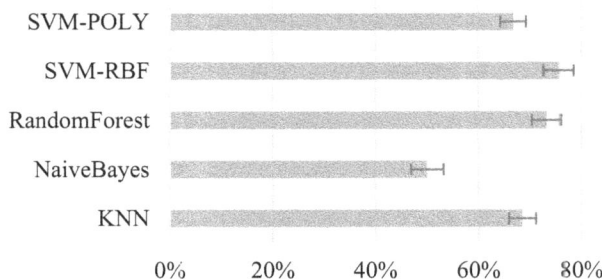

Figure 6: Accuracy of each algorithm for our dataset. Error bars are standard error. SVM polynomial kernel, SVM radial basis function kernel, Random Forest, Naïve Bayes, and K-Nearest Neighbors.

behaviors as a percentage. Each entry can be read as "[entry value] percent of all author-painted [column] cells in the test data were predicted to be [row] by PaintBoard." For example, we can see that, across all participants and behaviors, 76% of gold painted cells were predicted to be unpainted in the synthetic snapshots. In our case, a possible solution is to carefully balance the data fed into the SVM by clustering the disproportionately large number of uncolored squares to a representative subset is similar in size to the other colors. Despite this limitation we highlight that labelling a square as unpainted is as equally important as painting it, and the results were robust enough for our workshop.

SVM-RBF	red	unpainted	gold
red	0.25	0.09	0.09
unpainted	0.70	0.85	0.76
gold	0.05	0.06	0.15

Figure 7: The confusion matrix for the radial basis function SVM. Columns are input labels, and rows are output labels.

Although our current implementation is sufficiently fast for interactive results, we analyzed execution time as a significantly faster algorithm could be important for future work. There was a main effect of the algorithm execution time per participant per behavior ($F(4, 42) = 19.4$, $p<.001$, $\eta^2 =.649$). Post-hoc tests (with Bonferroni correction) revealed that all algorithms ran at least 650% faster than polynomial SVM, $p<.001$. No other effects were found.

Evaluation of State Features

We explored variations of our feature set in order to explore if any of our features were poorly chosen. Using a naïve greedy selection approach using the radial basis kernel SVM, we first measured the accuracy (as above) with each state feature on its own, picked the single feature with the highest accuracy, and iteratively added features in the same fashion. We found no significant improvement of accuracy over our existing feature set as described earlier.

LIMITATIONS & FUTURE WORK

To expand the behavior vocabulary, PaintBoard should be extended to incorporate other state features such as the movement speed of the character. In addition, we should explore if PaintBoard should consider the order of the snapshots in the storyboard, as storyboards are inherently chronological. Along similar lines, it may be useful to explore how PaintBoard could use layers (e.g., as used in Adobe Photoshop). This may enable users to separate varying aspects of what they are authoring, and may be useful for representing speed, or other features such as character orientation, without cluttering the snapshots.

Our current studies served as a proof-of-concept of painting storyboards as a behavior generation tool, but targeted follow up studies with more rigorous evaluations need to be conducted. For example, we will conduct a follow-up study where developers and non-technical designers work together to create a behavior, and use PaintBoard as the prototyping and communication medium. For future algorithmic work, investigating new state features may greatly improve accuracy. For evaluating behaviors, we relied on user self-reporting and naïve accuracy metrics; improving the behavior validation method is important future work.

CONCLUSION

This paper detailed PaintBoard: a novel interaction and algorithmic technique for prototyping interactive character behaviors by painting and storyboarding. We presented results from exploratory interviews and a programmer study, which informed our interface design and algorithm development. PaintBoard's algorithm was based on machine learning, and can generate real-time interactive behaviors based solely on a few painted examples. We presented a feature set (state features) that can represent important characteristics of paired interactive behaviors. Our proof-of-concept workshop highlighted the usability of PaintBoard's storyboard painting approach, showing how developers, with minimal training, can successfully and quickly prototype behaviors. Finally, we gave insight into the PaintBoard's algorithm with a comparative study. Overall, we believe that PaintBoard is a clear proof-of-concept for the approach of authoring interactive behaviors through visual painting and storyboarding.

ACKNOWLEDGMENTS

We would like to thank NSERC and JSPS for providing funding for this research.

REFERENCES

1. Abeel, T., de Peer, Y. V., and Saeys, Y. Java-ML: A Machine Learning Library. *Journal of Machine Learning Research 10*, (2009), 931–934.

2. Beyer, H. and Holtzblatt, K. *Contextual design: defining customer-centered systems*. Elsevier, 1997.

3. Breiman, L. Random Forests. *Machine learning 45*, 1 (2001), 5–32.

4. Buxton, B. *Sketching User Experiences: Getting the Design Right and the Right Design*. Morgan Kaufmann Publishers Inc. 2007.

5. Chang, C.-C. and Lin, C.-J. LIBSVM. *ACM Transactions on Intelligent Systems and Technology 2*, 3 (2011), 1–27.

6. Dontcheva, M., Yngve, G., and Popović, Z. Layered acting for character animation. *ACM SIGGRAPH 2003 Papers on - SIGGRAPH '03*, (2003), 409.

7. Förger, K., Takala, T., and Pugliese, R. Authoring Rules for Bodily Interaction: From Example Clips to Continuous Motions. *Intelligent Virtual Agents*, (2012), 341–354.

8. Forte, D., Gams, A., Morimoto, J., and Ude, A. On-line motion synthesis and adaptation using a trajectory database. *Robotics and Autonomous Systems 60*, 10 (2012), 1327–1339.

9. Gebhard, P., Kipp, M., Klesen, M., and Rist, T. Authoring scenes for adaptive, interactive performances. *Autonomous agents and multiagent systems*, (2003), 725.

10. Goldman, D.B., Curless, B., Salesin, D., and Seitz, S.M. Schematic storyboarding for video visualization and editing. *ACM Transactions on Graphics 25*, 3 (2006), 862.

11. Greenberg, S., Carpendale, S., Marquardt, N., and Buxton, B. The narrative storyboard: telling a story about use and context over time. *interactions 19*, 1 (2012), 64–69.

12. Igarashi, T., Matsuoka, S., and Tanaka, H. Teddy: a sketching interface for 3D freeform design. *SIGGRAPH*, ACM Press (1999), 409–416.

13. Igarashi, T., Moscovich, T., and Hughes, J.F. Spatial keyframing for performance-driven animation. *ACM SIGGRAPH/SCA '05*, ACM Press (2005), 107.

14. Landay, J.A. and Myers, B.A. Interactive sketching for the early stages of user interface design. *SIGCHI*, ACM Press (1995), 43–50.

15. McNaughton, M; Cutumisu, M; Szafron, D; Schaeffer, J; Redford, J; Parker, D. ScriptEase : Generative Design Patterns for Computer Role-Playing Games. *Automated software engineering*, (2004), 386–387.

16. Pizzi, D. and Cavazza, M. From Debugging to Authoring : Adapting Productivity Tools to Narrative Content Description. *Lecture Notes in Computer Science 5334*, (2008), 285–296.

17. Shen, E.Y. and Chen, B. Toward gesture-based behavior authoring. *International 2005 Computer Graphics*, (2005), 59–65.

18. Shneiderman, B. Creativity support tools: accelerating discovery and innovation. *Communications of the ACM 50*, 12 (2007), 20–32.

19. Suay, H.B., Toris, R., and Chernova, S. A Practical Comparison of Three Robot Learning from Demonstration Algorithm. *International Journal of Social Robotics 4*, 4 (2012), 319–330.

20. Terry, M. and Mynatt, E.D. Recognizing creative needs in user interface design. *Creativity & cognition - C&C '02*, (2002), 38–44.

21. Wolber, D. Pavlov: Programming by stimulus-response demonstration. *SIGCHI*, (1996), 252–259.

22. Young, J.E., Sharlin, E., and Igarashi, T. Teaching Robots Style: Designing and Evaluating Style-by-Demonstration for Interactive Robotic Locomotion. *Human–Computer Interaction 28*, 5 (2013), 379–416.

Voice Interaction System with 3D-CG Virtual Agent for Stand-alone Smartphones

Daisuke Yamamoto
Nagoya Institute of Technology
CREST, JST
Gokiso, Showa, Nagoya, Japan.
daisuke@nitech.ac.jp

Keiichiro Oura
Nagoya Institute of Technology
CREST, JST
Gokiso, Showa, Nagoya, Japan.
uratec@nitech.ac.jp

Ryota Nishimura
Nagoya Institute of Technology
CREST, JST
Gokiso, Showa, Nagoya, Japan.
nishimura.ryota@nitech.ac.jp

Takahiro Uchiya
Nagoya Institute of Technology
CREST, JST
Gokiso, Showa, Nagoya, Japan.
t-uchiya@nitech.ac.jp

Akinobu Lee
Nagoya Institute of Technology
CREST, JST
Gokiso, Showa, Nagoya, Japan.
ri@nitech.ac.jp

Ichi Takumi
Nagoya Institute of Technology
CREST, JST
Gokiso, Showa, Nagoya, Japan.
takumi@nitech.ac.jp

Keiichi Tokuda
Nagoya Institute of Technology
CREST, JST
Gokiso, Showa, Nagoya, Japan.
tokuda@nitech.ac.jp

ABSTRACT

In this paper, we propose a voice interaction system using 3D-CG virtual agents for stand-alone smartphones. Because the proposed system can handle speech recognition and speech synthesis on a stand-alone smartphone differently from the existing mobile voice interaction systems, this system enables us to talk naturally without encountering delays caused by network communications. Moreover, proposed system can be fully customized by dialogue scripts, Java-based plugins, and Android APIs. Therefore, developers can make original voice interaction systems for smartphones easily based on proposed system. We have made a subset of the proposed system available as open-source software. We expect that this system will contribute to studies of human-agent interaction using smartphones.

Author Keywords: Voice interaction system; Mobile application; Open-source software

ACM Classification Keywords
H.5.2. Information interfaces and presentation (e.g., HCI): User Interfaces

HAI 2014, October 29–31, 2014, Tsukuba, Japan.
ACM 978-1-4503-3035-0/14/10.
http://dx.doi.org/10.1145/2658861.2658874

INTRODUCTION

Recently, voice interaction systems for mobiles, such as Apple's Siri [1], have become widely popular. These systems enable users to obtain information—from map navigation to weather forecasting—by talking with virtual agents. These systems adopt a server-side speech recognition method to achieve a high speech recognition accuracy.

On the other hand, these systems have the following problems. One is that these system don't display 3D-CG virtual agents. We believe that 3D-CG virtual agent is effective for voice interaction systems to archive more user-friendly interface. The other is that the delay in voice interaction is considerably long because of both network communication and server-side processing costs. In general, the delay is an important factor for facilitating a natural voice interaction. Importantly, the more natural the voice interaction system is (such as in a voice interaction system with virtual agents that adopts real-time 3D-CG rendering), the more serious the delay problem becomes.

The purpose of this study is to develop a voice interaction system that can function on stand-alone smartphones with a virtual agent. They enable users to talk with 3D-CG virtual agents more naturally and smoothly. Moreover, the proposed system can be fully customized by dialogue scripts and Java-based plugins using the smartphone's functions effectively. Therefore, users can develop original voice interaction systems for smartphones freely and easily based on proposed system. Concretely, we ported the existing toolkit for building voice interaction systems MMDAgent [2] to the Android OS and extended it for smartphones. MMDAgent archives not only advanced speech technologies but also various and detailed managements of virtual agents.

In order to meet the goals of this study, we need to solve the following problems.

Problem 1. The response time for the voice interaction system must be minimized. Response time is an important factor in natural voice interaction systems [3]. This hypothesis must be confirmed with subjective experiments.

Problem 2. The proposed system must be able to be extended easily by not only dialogue scripts but also plugin mechanisms to utilize smartphone-specific functions, such as email, calendar, and networking.

Problem 3. The power consumption for the proposed system must be minimized because it is a crucial issue for smartphone users.

In the PROBLEMS section, we describe in detail the problems outlined above. Next, in the PROPOSED SYSTEM section, we explain our method. The PROTOTYPE SYSTEM section discusses the prototype for the proposed system. In the EXPERIMENTS section, we evaluate the prototype in terms of its response time, power consumption, and subjective experiments. The RELATED WORK section describes comparable systems. Finally, the CONCLUSION section summarizes our research with concluding remarks.

Furthermore, we unlocked a subset of the proposed system to present it as open-source software[1]. We expect that the proposed system can contribute to studies of human-agent interaction systems for smartphones.

PROBLEMS

Comparison of voice interaction methods for mobiles

First, in order to address **Problem 1**, we compared the various methods adopted by mobile voice interaction systems.

Many existing voice interaction systems for smartphones adopt server-side speech recognition (we call it the "cloud method"). The cloud method requires transfer time to record a voice into the smartphone and then upload it to the server before processing it in the recognition server. The cloud-method thus has the disadvantage of a response time for voice interaction that may be longer than one might expect in, say, a natural human dialogue.

In general, response time is an important factor for making natural interaction systems [4],[5]. Shiwa [6] suggests that

---

[1] http://www.mmdagent.jp/

the response time should be within 2 s. Although the response time of existing cloud-method systems may take several seconds, the delay might not be noticeable because these systems adopt a question-and-answer type interface instead of a natural voice interaction interface. However, we believe that the delay will become significant as more natural voice interaction interfaces are developed, such as in using 3D-CG virtual agents.

Therefore, we compared and studied the following three methods to examine the delay.

Cloud method: this method records a voice in the smartphone and then uploads it to the server before recognizing it.

Streaming method: this method recognizes a voice in the server in real-time because the smartphone transfers the voice to the server in a streaming manner.

Stand-alone method: this method recognizes a voice in the smartphone in real-time without using any servers or networks.

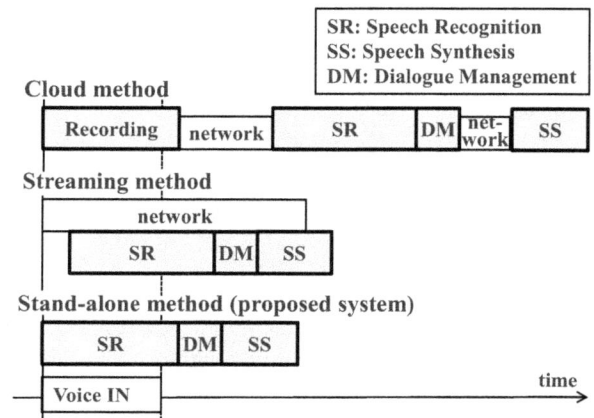

Figure 1. Response time for voice interaction of each method. "Network" refers to the delay in network communication.

	Cloud	Streaming	Stand-alone
Cost for client	good	good	poor
Cost to network	fair	poor	good
Cost to server	poor	poor	excellent
Delay in interaction	poor	good	excellent

Table 1. Costs and delay in various voice interaction methods for smartphones.

Figure 1 and Table 1 show the features for each method. The cloud method has certain advantages. For instance, the computational cost for the smartphone itself is low because voice recognition is not performed by the smartphone. However, the cost to the server is high and the response time is long. Apple's Siri adopts this method.

The streaming method has the advantage that the computational cost to the smartphone is low while the response time is shorter than with the cloud method. However, that comes at a cost to both the server and network. This method requires constant communication with the server while talking with agents. Mobile Mei-chan [7] adopts this method.

The stand-alone method has the advantage that both the cost to the server and the delay in communicating is nil. Although the calculating cost to the smartphone is high, the processing speed of current smartphones is sufficiently high for recognizing a voice in real-time.

A toolkit for building voice interaction systems

We have developed MMDAgent in our past research. MMDAgent is the toolkit that includes advanced speech and graphics technology such as speech recognition, speech synthesis, 3D-CG rendering, dialogue management, and a physics engine. MMDAgent adopts Julius [8] as a speech-recognition engine, Open JTalk [9] for speech synthesis, OpenGL for 3D-CG rendering, MikuMikuDance [10] format for 3D modeling, and Bullet Physics [11] for the physics engine.

MMDAgent can manage voice interaction scenarios based on FST script. FST script, which is based on the FST (Finite State Transducer) format as shown in Figure 2, can handle dialogue scenarios by triggering various events including speech keywords, sensor values, timers, and so on. MMDAgent performs real-time voice recognition with a slight delay.

a) FST script

```
 1 10 RECOG_EVENT_STOP|Hello   <eps>
 1 10 RECOG_EVENT_STOP|Hi      <eps>
10 11 <eps>     MOTION_ADD|mei|greet|greet.vmd
11 12 <eps>     SYNTH_START|mei|normal|Hello
12  1 SYNTH_EVENT_STOP|mei     <eps>
```

b) FST diagram

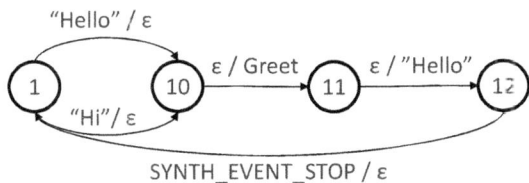

Figure 2. a) A sample FST script for MMDAgent and b) its diagram. In this FST, if the agent recognizes voice "Hello," the agent greets and speaks "Hello."

Although the existing MMDAgent was compatible with PC platforms including Windows, Linux, and Mac OS X, it did not support smartphone platforms such as Android OS. Therefore, we needed to port MMDAgent for PCs to Android OS in order to render it compatible with smartphones.

PROPOSED SYSTEM

Porting MMDAgent to Android OS

There were many challenges in porting the existing MMDAgent for PCs to Android OS. First, Android applications are expected to be written in Java whereas the existing MMDAgent was written in C++. Fortunately however, Android OS can support the C++ language by using Android NDK (Native Developer Kit) [12]. Therefore, we adopted Android NDK for porting MMDAgent. We used the OpenSL ES [13] library for Audio I/O.

Second, we changed Julius, the acoustic model, because the existing acoustic model was too demanding for smartphones. We adopted IPA's PTM model, which is smaller in size than the existing acoustic model. However, we did not change the language model, which can handle about 60,000 words [14]. This language model is the same as that in the existing MMDAgent. The text-to-speech engine, Open JTalk, is also the same as that in the existing MMDAgent. Since a microphone of a smartphone is close to its speaker in general, moreover, we developed the echo suppressor to cut off microphone when playing voices.

Although we changed some of the specifications for MMDAgent, both MMDAgent for PCs and MMDAgent for smartphones are based on the same scripts and materials. Therefore users can develop a common dialogue content for both PCs and smartphones.

Plugin extension based on Android OS APIs

Android NDK doesn't support some Android OS APIs such as mail management, calendar, live wallpaper, and application launcher. To address **Problem 2**, we developed a bridge module to connect existing C++ modules with Android's Java modules, as shown in Figure 3.

To explain in more detail: with MMDAgent, all internal messages between modules are communicated via the Global Message Queue. The bridge module transfers the internal messages in the Global Message Queue to PluginListener, written in Java. The bridge module adopts JNI (Java Native Interface), which can communicate between C++ and Java. Similarly, internal messages based on the Java language can be transferred to the Global Message Queue. This mechanism provides an easy way to communicate easily between modules written in C++ and those written in Java.

Therefore, developers can extend the proposed system by implementing PluginListener class of Java. A sample implementation of PluginListener is shown in Figure 4. In this sample, if the plugin receives the internal message 'Hello' command, the plugin returns the internal message 'Hello' event. Moreover, the proposed system can support plugins based on Android's standard GUI by using PluginListener. Figure 5 shows a sample of the GUI. In that sample, users can add text, select items, and push buttons.

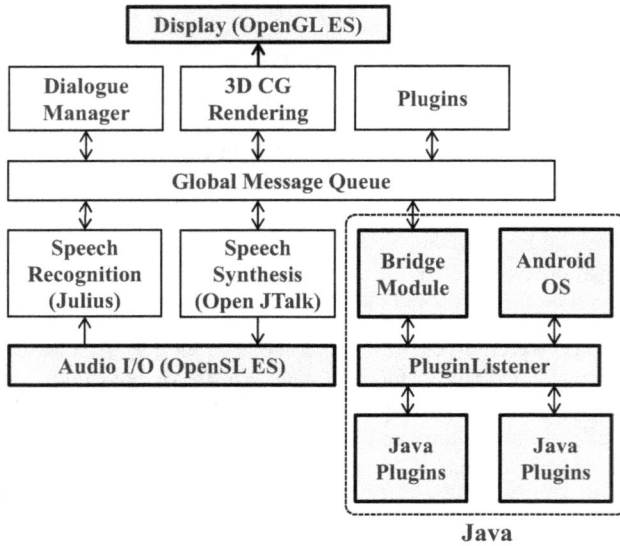

Figure 3. System configuration of MMDAgent for Android. To use Android OS functions, we implemented the Java module and Audio I/O module using OpenGL ES.

```
public class Sample implements PluginListener{
  public void onCommandMessage(String message){
    if(message.equals("Hello"))
      MMDAgentJNI.sendMessage("Hello");
  }
  public void onEventMessage(String message){
    ...
  }
}
```

Figure 4. Sample implementation for PluginListener. Here, if the plugin receives the internal message 'Hello,' the plugin returns the internal message 'Hello.'

Figure 5. Sample plugin based on the standard Android GUI. In this sample, users can input using standard GUIs.

MMDAgent in live-wallpaper mode

The proposed system enables the live-wallpaper mode, as shown in Figure 6. Live-wallpaper is resident software operating in the background of Android smartphones. In live-wallpaper mode, users can use the voice interaction system without launching any applications because the system is already working as resident software. We expect that in the live-wallpaper mode, our proposed system will work more quickly and easily.

There may be a concern with power consumption because the proposed system in live-wallpaper mode requires running the speech-recognition process at all times. In order to reduce power consumption, the proposed system can halt the speech recognition process while other applications are being used. This simple technique will be extremely effective for reducing power consumption because wallpaper is not visible at all times.

Figure 6. The proposed system in the live-wallpaper mode.

PROTOTYPE SYSTEM

We developed two prototypes. One is the application mode for smartphones shown in Figure 5. The second is the live-wallpaper mode shown in Figure 6. Live wallpaper is resident software working in the background of Android smartphones.

This section describes the prototype system and its interfaces in detail.

Virtual agent

For this proposed system, we created a disproportionately shaped woman as the virtual agent we call "SD Mei-chan." Because SD Mei-chan's head is so big, users can more easily understand her facial expressions even if the display is relatively small. Icons near the virtual agent show the active functions for voice interaction. For example, the weather forecast icon permits users to talk about the weather with the agent. All objects including the virtual agent, icons, and images are rendered as 3D computer graphics.

Table 2 presents a list of the motions, expressions, and speaking styles for SD Mei-chan. SD Mei-chan expresses herself vividly by combining these motions, expressions, and speaking styles. Since these resources can be created by using free software, her motions and voices can be customized freely if necessary.

Type	Resources
Motion	breath, good-bye, greeting, guide, idle, imagine, laugh, look panel, point, self-introduction, surprise, wait
Expression	anger, bashfulness, happiness, listening, sadness, normal
Speaking style	angry, bashful, happy, normal, sad

Table 2. List of resources for motion, expression, and speaking style.

Basic voice interaction

The voice interaction function can be used in the proposed system exactly as it is in the existing MMDAgent for PCs. Dialogue scenarios can be written with FST script as well as with the existing MMDAgent.

Figure 7 provides examples of the voice interaction function showing SD Mei-chan in normal status, sleeping status, and interacting with a forecast panel.

Figure 7. Example of voice interaction with the proposed system. In order: normal status; sleep status; and interacting with a forecast panel.

Voice interaction based on Android OS API

Android OS provides some APIs such as calendar, email management, and networking. Our proposed system can use these APIs by implementing PluginListener for Java.

For example, users can run the calendar service by using the calendar API. Were the user to say "please tell me my schedule for today," the agent will answer "you have two appointments: a conference at 10 a.m., and a planning meeting at 1 p.m." by referring to schedule data in the Android OS.

Voice interaction based on network services

The proposed system can retrieve weather information by connecting with forecasting web services. Users can find weather information using their voice and an image, as shown in Figure 7 (right). For example, when the user asks "how is the weather today?," the virtual agent replies "today's weather is sunny." Similarly, users can ask their horoscopes and get directions.

Idle function

Because the speech-recognition process is running continuously, unintended voices and agent-performed actions from falsely recognized noises might pose a problem.

Therefore, the proposed system includes an idle as well as an active mode for preventing false recognition. In active mode, the virtual agent answers all recognized user voices. In idle mode, the virtual agent does not answer any user voices not prefaced with "hello." In idle mode, when a user says "hello," the state changes to active mode replacing the point of view, as shown by "normal status" in Figure 7 (left and center).

EXPERIMENTS

We evaluated the delay in voice interaction, power consumption, and usability of the proposed system by comparing the cloud and streaming methods with our proposed method. Apple's Siri served as the representative cloud model, and Mobile Mei-chan stood as the streaming model. In Siri and Mobile Mei-chan, we used iPhone 4S. In proposed system, we used Galaxy S3. We used b-mobile[2]'s 3G network for network communications. Table 3 shows the applications and smartphones used in the experiment. Both of the iPhone 4S and Galaxy S3 were flagship smartphones in the summer 2012.

	Application	Smartphone
Cloud method	Apple's Siri	iPhone 4S
Streaming method	Mobile Mei-chan	iPhone 4S
Stand-alone method	Proposed system	Galaxy S3

Table 3. Applications and smartphones for comparative analysis

Evaluation of the delay of voice interaction

First, we evaluated the delay in the voice interaction of our proposed system by measuring the response time in order to verify **Problem 1** (described in the INTRODUCTION above). In our experiment, "response time" means the

---

[2] http://www.bmobile.ne.jp/english/

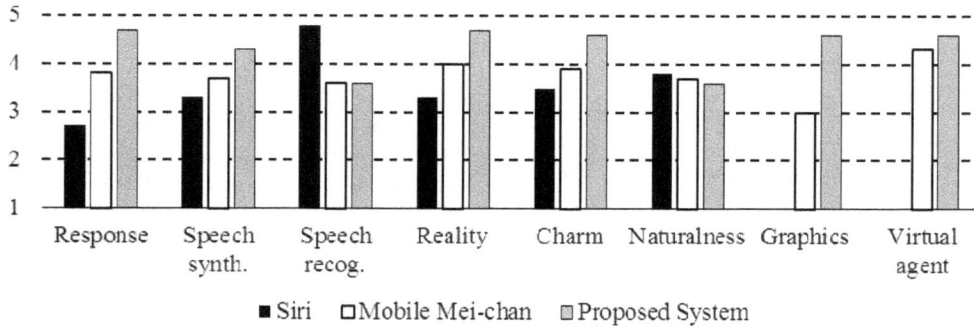

Figure 8. Results of the usability questionnaire for each system

elapsed time from the terminus of the user's speech to the time when we first hear the synthesized voice—as shown in Figure 1. The experimental conditions were as follows: the speech text was "What is the weather like today?" The target language was Japanese. We recorded the voice with a microphone and measured the response time by measuring the elapsed silence. We measured the response time five times for each system.

Table 4 shows the results, listing response times for each method. The response time for the proposed method (0.82 s) is faster than both the streaming method (1.1 s) and cloud method (4.1 s). The reason for why the proposed method is faster than the streaming method is that our method is not susceptible to network delays. These results suggest that the proposed method is the best approach for mobile voice interaction systems where delay is concerned.

There is some concern that, with the proposed system, the response time will be longer when the size of the language model is larger. Server-side recognition methods need not share this concern. However, we believe that this problem is easily overcome given that the processing speed of smartphones has been increasing at a rapid pace in recent years.

	Response time
Cloud method	4.1 s
Streaming method	1.1 s
Stand-alone method	0.82 s

Table 4. Response time for each voice interaction method.

Evaluation of power consumption

Next, we tested the power consumption rate for the proposed system in order to address **Problem 3** (described in the INTRODUCTION). In general, power consumption is an important factor for smartphone applications. Because a voice interaction system needs to monitor audio input continuously in order to process speech recognition, we needed to verify that the power required for our proposed system is not excessive.

The experimental conditions were as follows: The target smartphone was a Sony Xperia TX with its brightness display at 50%. We disabled the wireless function—both Wi-Fi and 3G networks. We measured the remaining battery power after keeping the terminal running at 1 h from full battery. We compared our prototype system with the system that displays only a static image.

Table 5 shows the experimental results. The remaining battery power for the proposed system (58%) is less than the system displaying only static image (93%). These results suggest that the proposed system can work continuously for 143 min. Whereas one might be concerned that the power required for the proposed system is considerably high for an average smartphone, we think that the power consumption is sufficient to operate in a usual manner because users will not be running the proposed system at all times. Because other applications, such as a web browser or an email application is active more often, the overall power consumption for the proposed system is relatively nominal. Nevertheless, we will study the power consumption issue in future work.

	Remaining battery level (60 min.)	Estimated time
Proposed System	58%	143 min.
Wallpaper	93%	857 min.

Table 5. Evaluation of power consumption. Wallpaper means a static image of background of Android OS.

Evaluation of the usability

Finally, we evaluated the usability of the proposed system. Experimental conditions were as follows: 16 university students participated in the experiment as target users. They were asked to communicate with the voice agents using Siri, Mobile Mei-chan, and the proposed system. We conducted a five-stage questionnaire to obtain our results, asking the students to judge the following:

1. **Response** time of voice interaction

2. The quality of **speech synthesis**

3. The quality of **speech recognition**

4. Did the virtual agent seem **real**?

5. Is the virtual agent **charm**ing?

6. Do you feel the system is **natural**?

7. How is the **graphic** quality of the virtual agent?

8. Do you feel the **virtual-agent** displayed is desirable?

Figure 8 shows the results of the questionnaire. In **response**, the proposed system (4.7 point) scored better than not only Siri (2.7 point) but also mobile Mei-chan (3.8 point). Although the difference in response time between mobile Mei-chan and proposed system is relatively small—as shown in Table 3—the proposed system is better than we expected. The **reality** (4.7 point) and **charm** (4.6 point) of the proposed system is also better than other systems tested. The **speech recognition** (3.6 point) of the proposed system is worse than that of Siri (4.8 point). We found that the high scores for both **response** and **graphic** quality affected the **reality** and **charm** in spite of the poor **speech recognition** scores. Moreover, the results for **virtual-agent** suggest that the 3D-CG virtual agent is receptive for voice interaction systems. On the other hand, in terms of whether the system is **natural**, our results show the difference between methods is relatively minor. Although the **speech recognition** of the proposed system is worse than that of Siri, we will improve it by adopting higher accuracy models for speech recognition when the processing speeds of smartphones are improved in the future.

We also obtained supplementary comments for our proposed system. Typical positive comments included: virtual agent is cute and natural; CG rendering is beautiful; synthesized voice is clear and pleasant. Typical negative comments suggested: there are fewer responses available than with Siri; it is shameful to always have women agents on smartphones.

RELATED WORK

We have developed other MMDAgent-based voice interaction systems, such as a voice interactive digital signage for campus guide [15] and mobile Mei-chan.

The voice interactive digital signage for campus guide is implemented in a digital signage placed at the main gates of Nagoya Institute of Technology. This system enables users to talk with a female CG virtual agent. Both students and staff can post their event information with synthesized voices by using a web browser, and the virtual agents can then advertise the posted events with voice, gesture, and images.

Mobile Mei-chan is a voice interaction system for mobiles based on video communication systems such as Skype or Google Hangout. With this system, MMDAgent is connected with Skype using Skype API. Users can converse with CG virtual agents using Skype-installed terminals, such as smartphones and PCs. Although both this system and proposed system can be worked in smartphones, we confirm that proposed system is better than Mobile Mei-chan in EXPERIMETNAL RESULT section.

Talkman [16] is an early voice interaction system based on a 3D-CG virtual agent. The purpose of Talkman is to develop a virtual agent with natural human facial features and expressions based on speech synthesis and speech recognition technology.

There are other agent-based voice interaction systems such as *Takemaru-kun* and *Kita-chan* [17]. These system can be worked as an agent robot. Furthermore, there are voice interaction systems for public transit such as Let's Go bus system [18]. Using these systems, users can query bus information by speech using their phones.

Galatea toolkit [19] is a voice interaction toolkit along with MMDAgent used in this research. Galatea toolkit can develop a spoken dialogue system with a life-like animated agent. Galatea toolkit cannot be worked in smartphones differently from proposed system.

CONCLUSION

This paper proposed a voice interaction system with a 3D-CG virtual agent for stand-alone smartphones. The proposed system enables users to talk with a 3D-CG virtual agent more naturally than with existing systems because the delay in voice interaction is relatively short. Moreover, the proposed system can be fully customized by not only dialogue scripts but also Java-based plugins using the smartphone's APIs such as email management, calendar, and networking. Since the system also can run in live-wallpaper mode for Android smartphones, users can use this system easily without running any applications explicitly.

The response time, power consumption, and usability of proposed system is better than that of existing voice interaction systems such as Siri and mobile Mei-chan. We found that the response time and graphics quality affect the reality and charm of the virtual agents.

Because we have made a subset of the proposed system available as open-source software, it can be easily downloaded from the Web. A demonstration video of the proposed system is also released here[3]. In the future, we will develop several applications based on this proposed system. Since proposed system can be easily customized based on scripts and plugins, we expect that this system will contribute to studies of human-agent interaction using smartphones.

---

[3] https://www.youtube.com/watch?v=eR7aUh9RBio

ACKNOWLEDGEMENTS
This research was partly funded by Core Research for Evolutionary Science and Technology (CREST) from Japan Science and Technology Agency (JST).

REFERENCES

1. Apple Inc. Siri, http://www.apple.com/ios/siri/

2. Lee, A., Oura, K., and Tokuda, K. MMDAgent - A fully open-source toolkit for voice interaction systems. *In Proc. ICASSP 2013* (2013), 8382-8385.

3. Ward, N., Rivera, A., Ward, K., and Novick, D. Root causes of lost time and user stress in a simple dialog system. *In Proc. INTERSPEECH 2005*, (2005), 10.

4. Miller, R.B. Response time in man-computer conversational transactions. *In Proc. Spring Joint Computer Conference*, AFIPS Press (1968), 267-266.

5. Starner, T. The Challenges of Wearable computing: Part 2, *IEEE Micro*, Vol.21, issue 4, (2001), 54-67.

6. Shiwa, T., Kanda, T., Imai, M., Ishiguro, H., Hagita, N., and Anzai, Y. How quickly should communication robots respond? *Journal of RSJ*, Vol.27, No.1, (2009), 87-95.

7. Uchiya, T., Yamamoto, D., Shibakawa, M., Yoshida, M., Nishimura, R., and Takumi, I. Development of spoken dialogue service based on video call named 'Mobile Mei-chan' (in Japanese). *In Proc. JAWS2012*, (2012), Interaction 1-3.

8. Lee, A., and Kawahara, T. Recent Development of Open-Source Speech Recognition Engine Julius. *In Proc. APSIPA*, (2009), 131–137.

9. Open JTalk, http://open-jtalk.sourceforge.net/.

10. MikuMikuDance, http://www.geocities.jp/higuchuu4/index_e.htm.

11. Bullet Physics, http://bulletphysics.org.

12. Android NDK, http://developer.android.com/tools/sdk/ndk/index.html.

13. OpenSL ES, http://www.khronos.org/opensles/.

14. Lee, A., Kawahara, T., Takeda, K., Mimura, M., Yamada, A., Ito, A., Ito, K., and Shikano, K. Continuous Speech Recognition Consortium — an Open Repository for CSR Tools and Models —. *In Proc. LREC*, (2002), 1438–1441.

15. Oura, K., Yamamoto, D., Takumi, I., Lee, A., Tokuda, K. On-Campus, User-Participatable, and Voice-Interactive Digital Signage (in Japanese), *Journal of Japanese Society for Artificial Intelligence*, Vol.28, No.1, (2013), 60-67.

16. Nagao, K., Takeuchi, A. Speech dialogue with facial displays: Multimodal human-computer conversation, *In Proc. ACL-94*, (1994), 102-109.

17. Shikano, K., Tobias, C., Kawanami, H., Nisimura, R., Lee, A. Development and Evaluation of Takemaru-kun Spoken Guidance System and Portability to Kita-chan and Kita-robo Systems (In Japanese). *In Proc. IPSJ SIG Notes*, Vol.2006 (107), (2006), 33-38.

18. Raux, A., Bohus, D., Langner, B., Black, A.W. and Eskenazi, M. Doing Research on a Deployed Spoken Dialogue System: One Year of Let's Go! Experience. *In Proc. INTERSPEECH 2006*, (2006), 65-68.

19. Kawamoto, S., Shimodaira, H., Nitta, T., Nishimoto, T., Nakamura, S., Itou, K., Morishima, S., Yotsukura, T., Kai, A., Lee, A., Yamashita, Y., Kobayashi, T., Tokuda, K., Hirose, K., Minematsu, N., Yamada, A., Den, Y., Utsuro, T., Sagayama, S. Open-source software for developing anthropomorphic spoken dialog agent. *In Proc. PRICAI-02, International Workshop on Lifelike Animated Agents*, (2002), 64-69.

Assigning a Personality to a Spoken Dialogue Agent through Self-disclosure of Behavior

Yoshito Ogawa
Graduate School of Human
Sciences, Waseda University
2-579-15, Mikajima,
Tokorozawa-shi, Saitama-ken
359-1192, Japan
stream@toki.waseda.jp

Kouki Miyazawa
RIKEN Brain Science Institute
2-1, Hirosawa, Wako-shi,
Saitama-ken 351-0198, Japan
kouki.miyazawa@riken.jp

Hideaki Kikuchi
Faculty of Human Sciences,
Waseda University
2-579-15, Mikajima,
Tokorozawa-shi, Saitama-ken
359-1192, Japan
kikuchi@waseda.jp

ABSTRACT

In this study, we propose a method to assign a personality to a spoken dialogue agent and evaluate effectiveness of the method. Recently, some research studies on human-agent interaction (HAI) showed that it is possible to assign a personality by controlling non-verbal information of an agent. However, we consider that verbal information sent from an agent would result in the agent developing a personality. In this paper, we focus on self-disclosures about behavior as an important factor of assigning a personality, and analyze the effects of self-disclosures on assigning a personality to the agent by evaluation of impressions. We discovered that self-disclosures performed by the agent are as effective for personality recognition as those performed by humans. Further, self-disclosures allow a user to recognize an agent's personality, and humanlike self-disclosure does not impede personality recognition even if utterer of these self-disclosures is an agent. Based on these facts, we verified effectiveness of our proposal method to assigning a personality by self-disclosures about behavior.

Author Keywords

Humanlike virtual agents; personality assigning; personality model; self-disclosure;

ACM Classification Keywords

H.1.2. MODELS AND PRINCIPLES: User/Machine Systems

INTRODUCTION

Currently, facilitated by advances in key technologies such as speech recognition and natural language processing, advanced systems for verbal communication with users are being implemented. Some of them aim at interaction with users and giving pleasure to users via interaction [4].

Some studies have shown that users often recognize personalities in such systems [11]. In the human-agent interaction (HAI) field, the effect of agent personality is being studied. Nass et al. showed that commonality in "dominant-submissive" of personalities between a human and an agent leads to more satisfaction regarding the result of a task with the agent [11]. In contrast, Isbister et al. showed that complementarity in "introvert-diplomatic" personalities between a human and an agent leads to higher evaluation for the agent [3]. Vugt et al. indicated that the reality of an agent's personality causes a human to want to continue the dialogue [17]. Moreover, Takeuchi and Murakami et al. proposed methods for inducing a human to follow an agent's instructions by assigning the agent with an authoritative personality [16, 8]. Nakagawa et al. showed that a "dominant-submissive" personality in a health care robot affects human acceptance of proposals from the robot [9]. These studies suggest the possibility of improving the impression of an agent and inducing human behavior according to agent personality by assigning an apposite personality to the agent.

However, these studies dealt with broad classifications of personality such as "dominant-submissive". If some personalities are in same broad classification, they probably are in different classes from each other based on narrower classification, and their effects probably are different. Establishing a method for assigning various personalities to agents and clarification of their effects results in improved user satisfaction, a desire to continue dialogue, higher rating of task achievement, and so on by assigning an apposite personality to the agent [7, 19]. For assigning various personalities, it is necessary to construct an implementable model of the process when a human recognizes an agent personality and design agent behavior according to the model. According to Media Equation theory [12], it is expected that the process is basically similar to the process when he recognizes another human personality. For this reason, we construct a model of the personality recognition process of another human personality and confirm through an experiment that the model can be adapted to the process of an agent personality.

In brief, in this paper, we aim to establish a method for assigning various personalities to an agent. For this purpose, we construct an implementable model of the process when a human recognizes another personality, and we propose a method for designing agent behavior according to the model. To evaluate our proposed method, we conducted an impression evaluation experiment and reported its results.

METHOD

Behavior-oriented Personality Model

Before we construct a model of the process by which a human recognizes another personality, we need to define personality. Some previous studies on HAI or personality psychology have defined personality as something that determines and provides consistency to the behavior, thought, and feelings of a human [5, 10, 6]. and we adopt this definition in the present study. When we consider the guidelines for a person's behavior (thoughts, and feelings) in a particular environment or situation, it can be said that some behaviors determined by the same guidelines are consistent. Therefore, we can think that the set of all such guidelines comprises that person's personality. In this study, we name the "behavior guideline trait", and we construct a personality model as a set of behavior guideline traits.

The thought processes to comprehend personality as a set of human traits has been addressed in personality psychology for a long time. [1] Mischel et al. explained trait handling in personality psychology, for example, in the studies of Allport and Cattell [6]. Allport and Cattell classified traits based on their influence on behavior and as being "apparent or latent". They also studied what trait is the most basic and what types of structure traits comprise human personality. Our study is similar to these previous studies of a personality model as a set of traits, but different from them the properties of traits for plain implementation. First, a behavior guideline trait is a more restrictive concept to describe behavior information than the traits studied by Allport and Cattell. A behavior guideline trait only means that certain behavior arises when a person possessing the trait is in a certain environment or situation. Therefore, a human possesses many behavior guideline traits in our model. This is because we think that we can address narrowly and clearly defined traits more accurately than broadly and vaguely defined ones when developing an artificial personality. Allport then showed that different people did not possess same traits; however, we allow different people to possess the same behavior guideline trait in our personality model. This is because behavior guideline traits describe restricted information; therefore, it is possible for different people to possess the same behavior guideline trait. However, the number of behavior guideline traits that a person can possess in our personality model is large, and consequently different people do not possess the same personality as a set of behavior guideline traits.

Also, our model is different from other influential personality models like Big 5 Scales[2] or Egogram[1]. Those models portray a personality as a several dimension vector using several dozens of questionnaire items. The number of dimensions and items are determined in advance. This means that

those models determined the number of traits composing personality. Therefore those model are suited to consider a personality to be static. In contrast, our model doesn't determine the number of behavior guideline traits. This is because our model portray a personality that someone recognizes to another person in a certain moment. Therefore our model is suited to consider a personality to be dynamic. A personality recognized to another person gradually changes according to experience of interaction with the person. For that reason, our model allow a personality to change the number of behavior guideline traits it contains.

Personality Recognition Process Model

We constructed a personality recognition process model based on the above-mentioned personality model. As personality recognition processes, observing the behavior of others directly and recognizing a personality in them are probably the most basic. However, assigning a personality by direct observing behavior is not realistic owing to development cost. Therefore, we propose a method to assign a personality by conveying agent behavior in dialogue. Self-disclosure is a means to inform others about oneself, and self-presentation is a means to introduce information and make one look good in dialogue between humans. Existence of these behaviors suggests the possibility of a controlling personality that others recognize by utterance behavior.

A personality recognition process model based on self-disclosure of behavior is shown in Figure 1. The flow of this model is as follows:

precondition1 Person A determines his behaviors with according to his behavior guideline traits ((1) in Figure 1).

precondition2 Person B knows nothing about person A's behaviors and personality at first.

1 Person B is conveyed person A's behaviors by his self-disclosure ((2) in Figure 1).

2 Simultaneous, person B observes person A's self-disclosure as a behavior of person A ((3) in Figure 1).

3 If person B discovers some consistencies in person A's behaviors, he evaluates the behavior guideline traits of person A ((4), (5) in Figure 1).

4 Person B recognizes the set of only behavior guideline traits that he evaluates as person A's personality.

5 As the number of conveyed behaviors increases, the recognized personality gets closer to the person A's correct personality.

If person B doesn't discover any consistency, he still knows nothing about person A's personality. Person B recognizes person A's personality after he is conveyed enough behaviors to discover some consistencies. In the case that there are no consistencies among the behavior guideline traits person A possesses, plural behaviors determined by a specific behavior guideline trait possess a consistency that induces to evaluate that behavior guideline trait. Person B evaluates each behavior guideline trait after he is conveyed enough behaviors

---

[1] In personality psychology, a trait is explained as a consistent difference from others that determines a personal reaction to stimulation. It is a broader concept than "behavior guideline trait".

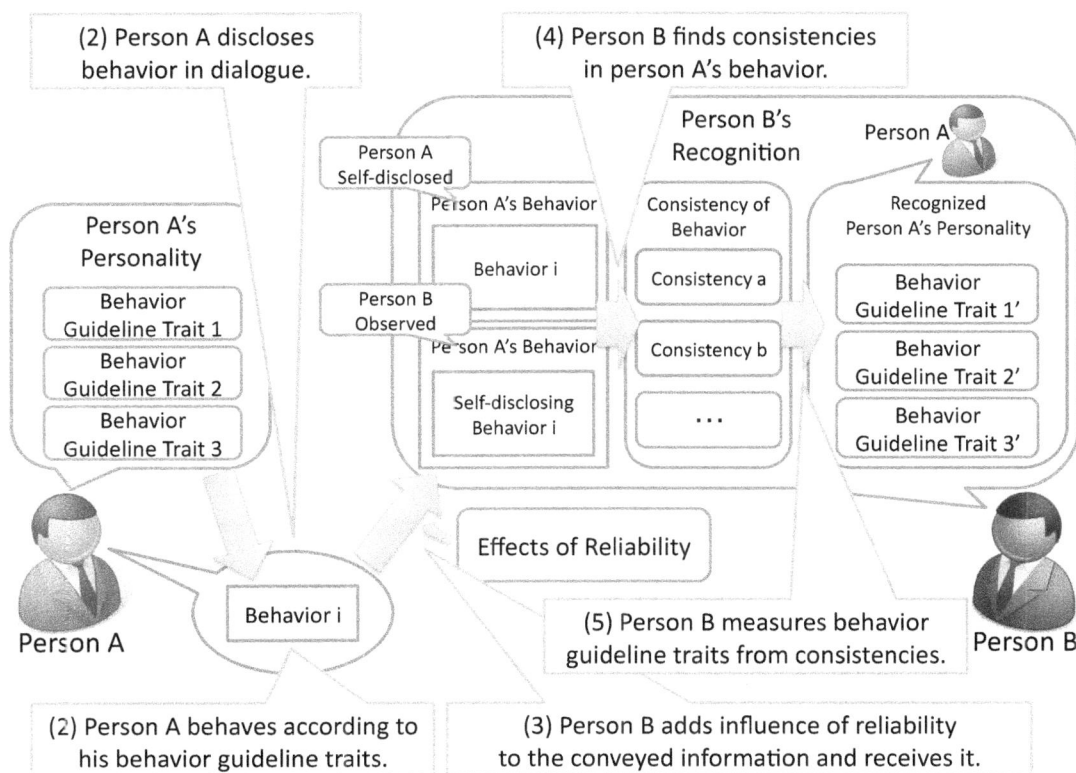

Figure 1. Model of personality recognition by self-disclosure process.

determined by that behavior guideline trait, and recognizes person A's personality consisting of only behavior guideline traits that he evaluates.

Method for assigning a Personality

Our proposal method to assign a personality to an agent using self-disclosure of behavior is shown in Figure 2. In this method, the frequently exhibited behaviors of the person possessing the personality being assigned (stereotype about behavior) is collected and stored in a database beforehand. The agent selects a behavior to portray from behavior database of the personality whenever the agent performs an interaction with an user. The agent then discloses this behavior by utterance of sentences to the user. As the number of interactions and quantity of disclosed behavior increase, the user who received the self-disclosure finds consistency in the disclosed behaviors and evaluates the behavior guideline traits of the agent. Because all disclosed behaviors are tied to the personality in the behavior database, these behaviors cause the user to perceive consistency and behavior guideline traits that cause him to recognize the personality being assigned. As a result, the user recognizes the personality assigned to the agent. This is the flow of the method for personality assignment.

In this study, we propose a method to assign a personality by disclosed agent behavior. However, it is thought that per-

sonality can be assigned by other cues, for instance, by presentation of agent profile information. Actually, Wilks et al. and Sugiyama et al. proposed a method to assign a personality by responding to questions about personality [18, 15]. As having mentioned it above, it is thought that personality recognition is affected by how a human obtains information from an agent. It is expected that the most effective means of information transmission varies with the environment and situation. In the present study, at first we show the possibility of assigning personality by self-disclosure and treat the characteristics of the means of information transmission as a future work.

Evaluation

For verification of our proposed method, we performed an impression evaluation experiment. In this experiment, we made the same agent perform different self-disclosures, which were designed using a behavior database, and compared the personalities that subjects recognized in these agents. In addition, we examined whether humanlike self-disclosure performed by an agent obstructed personality recognition.

Behavior Collection

In accordance with our proposal method, we needed to collect frequently exhibited behaviors from the person possessing the personality to be assigned. We adopted the Tokyo

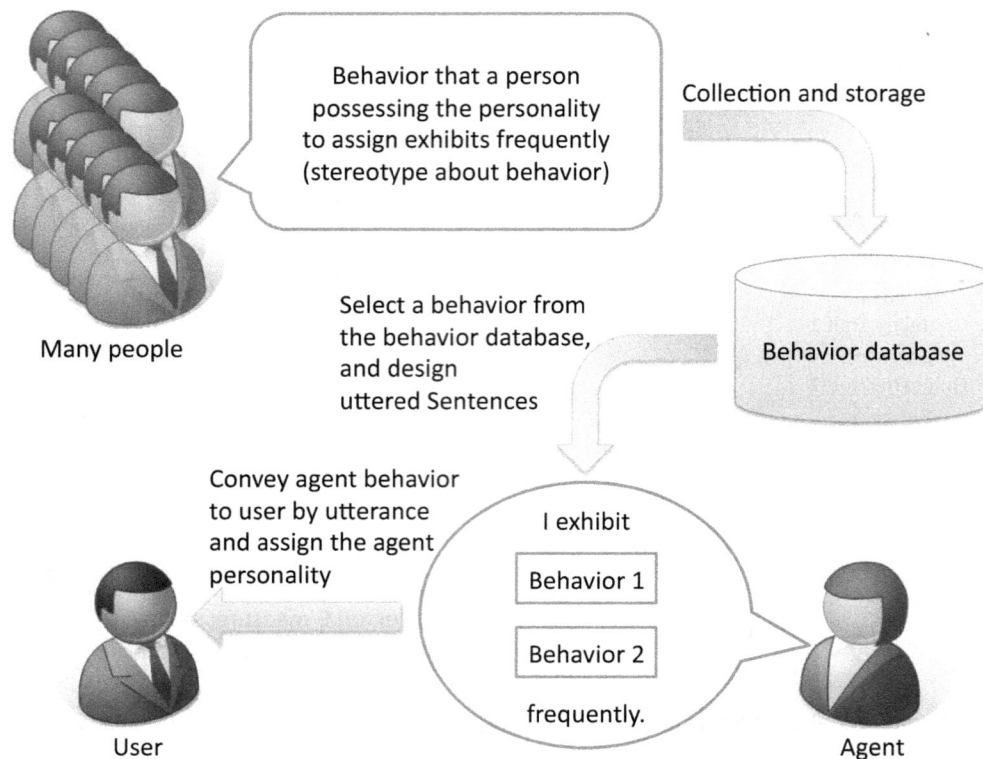

Figure 2. Proposed method for assigning various personalities to an agent.

University Egogram (TEGII) [14] for classification of personality. TEGII classifies personality in 29 categories according to the intensity of five ego-states: Critical Parent (CP), Nurturing Parent (NP), Adult (A), Free Child (FC), and Adapted Child (AC). Each ego-state is expressed in 20 points of perfect scores. Magnitude correlation of ego-states has influence to TEGII classification and concrete scores of each ego-states are not important. However, for convenience, we defined the three categories:

- high intensity : > 15 points

- medium intensity : "$>= 6$ points" and "$<= 15$ points"

- low intensity : > 6 points

We adopted five categories with each having one ego-state with high intensity and four ego-states with medium or low intensity as personalities to assign. In the following, we refer to the five personality categories by their respective intense ego-states, for instance, "personality category CP".

We had created the behavior database which was constructed with the following method. Subjects had accessed to the experiment website. They had been presented 29 personality categories and characteristics of each category defined in TEGII. Then, they had been asked to list the behaviors considered that a person possessing each personality exhibit it frequently for each personality category. Subjects had been

16 Japanese people aged between 20 to 50 years. As a result, 659 behaviors had been collected in total. We diverted behaviors contained by the behavior database to this experiment. We extracted 143 behaviors related to five personality categories that we adopted from this database.

Stimuli

In this experiment, we did not focus on conversational exchange but on one-time agent utterances to simplify the experiment. We used single-utterance animations of agents upon their first meeting with a subject as experiment stimuli. For each personality category, five behaviors were selected from the behavior database and edited in the form of self-introduction. Therefore, 25 stimuli were used in this experiment. We show a partial stimulus (corresponding to personality category CP) in Table 1. Agent animations were made from uttered sentences using MMDAgent [13]. We show the face image of the agent in Figure 3.

Impression Evaluation Items

Because we adopted five personality categories prescribed in TEGII as personalities to assign, we also adopted the method of personality evaluation prescribed in TEGII. Subject replied to a questionnaire consisting of 50 items, for instance, "Is the person easily to be influenced by what another person says?" Possible answer were "yes", "no", or "neither", and 50 items were associated to each a ego-state. The intensity of each

Personality Category	Self-introduction (translated to English)
Personality Category CP	I make a manual before acting and I keep it in mind to obey the manual.
	My creed is never to change my opinion.
	It is often said that I do not hear opinions of other people.
	I like to please people by introducing them to something that I think is good for them.
	I am good at leading a group.

Table 1. Part of an Uttered Sentence.

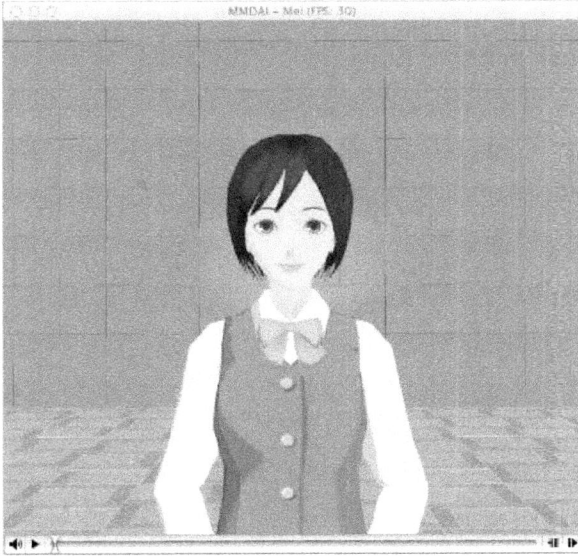

Figure 3. Face image of the agent.

Personality category	p-value
CP	6.87e-10***
NP	1.94e-10***
A	2.20e-16***
FC	5.66e-10***
AC	2.20e-16***

Table 2. Result of the Wilcoxon rank sum test of each personality category.

Ego-state	p-value
CP	1.36e-8***
NP	2.58e-12***
A	2.22e-16***
FC	3.89e-9***
AC	2.20e-16***

Table 3. Result of Wilcoxon rank sum test of each ego-state.

ego-state was calculated as the sum of the scores for each item with each "yes" answer receiving two points and each "neither" answer receiving one point.

Procedure

This experiment was performed on a website. On the page for the questionnaire, agent animations were shown one by one in random order, and subjects replied each question after the seeing and hearing each animation. Subjects were 14 colorredJapanese people aged between 20 to 50 years. Half of the subjects is university and graduate school student. Japanese was used exclusively in this experiment.

RESULT

In this section, the evaluation results of five stimuli corresponding to a personality category x were described $R(x)$. $R(x)$ was a set of five-dimensional vectors consisting of dimensions corresponding to CP, NP, A, FC, and AC and one dimension corresponding to a ego-state y in $R(x)$ were described $R(x, y)$. Because there were five stimuli for each personality category and 14 subjects, $R(x, y)$ contained 70 scalars.

The distributions of the evaluation results of five stimuli for each personality category and averaged every subject are shown in Figure 4. These figures show that magnitude relations among the five recognized ego-states are greatly dif-

ferent among the personality categories. In addition, the ego-state corresponding to each personality category was recognized emphatically.

To confirm the above statistically, we performed statistical testing on the averages of the two groups. We adopted five categories with each having one ego-state with high intensity and four ego-states with medium or low intensity as personalities to assign. Therefore, if the intensity of the ego-state corresponding to personality category is larger than the other ego-states, it is said that agent personality corresponding to the personality category was recognized. Accordingly, we compared $R(x, y)$ when x is equivalent to y ($n = 70$) to $R(x, y)$ when x is not equivalent to y ($n = 280$) for each personality category x. First, we performed a Kolmogorov-Smirnov test. As a result, normality of distribution was controverted in all personality categories. Next, we performed a Wilcoxon rank sum test. We show the p-values of each personality category in Table 2. The result shows that there is a significant difference between $R(x, y)$ when x is equivalent to y compared to when x is not equivalent to y in all personality categories x. Therefore, it is confirmed that the ego-state corresponding to each personality category was recognized emphatically, and the personalities corresponding to personality categories were recognized.

Next, we performed statistical testing to confirm that distinct personalities were recognized among the personality categories. In this experiment, each personality category corresponding to an ego-state possesses that ego-state with high intensity, and the four other personality categories possess it with low intensity. Accordingly, we can confirm the above by comparing $R(x, y)$ when x is equivalent to y ($n = 70$) with $R(x, y)$ when x is not equivalent to y ($n = 280$) for each ego-state y. Similarly to the preceding paragraph, we performed a Kolmogorov-Smirnov test first. As a result, normality of distribution was controverted in all ego-states. Then, we performed a Wilcoxon rank sum test. We show the p-values of each ego-state in Table 3. The result shows that there is a significant difference between $R(x, y)$ when x is equivalent to y compared to when x is not equivalent to y in all ego-states y. Therefore, it is conformed that distinct personalities were recognized among personality categories.

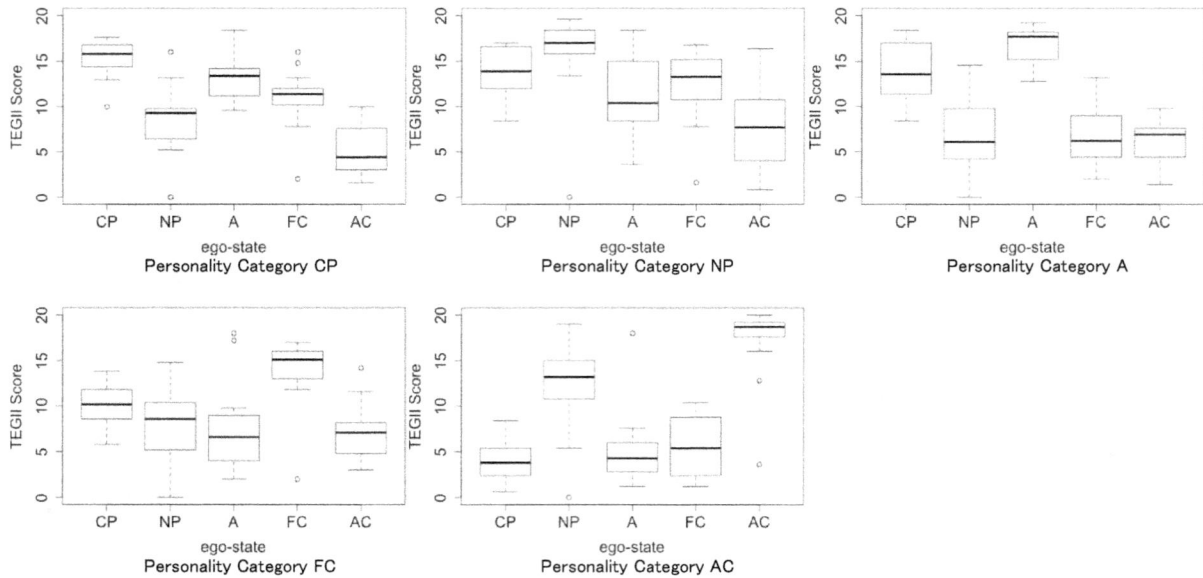

Figure 4. Evaluation result of each personality category.

DISCUSSION

From the results of the evaluation experiment, it can be said that our proposed method can assign personalities corresponding to self-disclosure. We used only five personality categories in the experiment. However, this method is logically applicable to any personality if we can collect behavior information corresponding to the personality. Our method will contribute to studies on the effects of agent personalities.

The result suggests that it is possible to assign personalities to agents via self-disclosure of behavior using a stereotype about behaviors. By reason of influence that a stereotype receives from society and culture, utterances we used in the evaluation experiment are not able to apply to subjects of another language and cultural sphere. However, by collecting behavior information from people sharing stereotypes and designing utterances based on the behavior information, the proposed method of assigning personality to agents seems to be effective in another language and cultural sphere. Verification in another language and cultural sphere is a part of future work.

In the experiment, there exist some ego-states noncorresponding to personality categories with comparatively high intensity, for instance, $R(CP, A)$, $R(A, CP)$, and $R(AC, NP)$. It is believed that this problem occurs because some behaviors that cause subjects to recognize ego-states that do not correspond to the personality categories are present in the behavior database. In addition, it is thought that improving the accuracy of the behavior database, for example, by impression evaluation for each behavior would be effective to address this problem.

Finally, we used a personality recognition process model for recognizing other human personalities and human behaviors as self-disclosure. Our results indicated that the model can be adapted to agent personality and agent personality can be

assigned by human behavior. However, the degree for how humanlike behavior can assign an agent personality was not clarified and remains a part of future work.

REFERENCES

1. Dusay, J. *EGOGRAMS: How I See You and You See Me.* Harper & Row Publishers, 1977.

2. Gough, H., and Heilbrun, A. *The adjective check list mannual*, 1983 ed. Consulting Psychologist Press, Palo Alto, C.A., 1983.

3. Isbister, K., and Nass, C. Consistency of personality in interactive characters: verbal cues, non-verbal cues, and user characteristics. *International journal of human-computer studies 53*, 2 (2000), 251–267.

4. Ishiguro, H., and Hiura, R. Business of communication support robots. *Journal of the Robotics Society of Japan 20*, 7 (2002), 672–675.

5. Loyall, A. B., and Bates, J. *Believable Agents: Building Interactive Personalities.* PhD thesis, Dept. Comp. Sci., Carnegie Mellon Univ., 1997.

6. Mischel, W., Shouda, Y., and Ayduk, O. *INTRODUCTION TO PERSONALITY Toward an Integrative Science of the Person*, 8th ed. John Wiley & Sons, 2007.

7. Miyake, T., Omoto, Y., and Nishida, T. Investigation of influence of agent's personality parameters on negotiation. In *Proc. 72th National Convention of IPSJ*, IPS Japan (2010), "2–335"–"2–336".

8. Murakami, N., Katagami, D., and Yamada, S. Human-robot interaction by applying authority. In *IPSJ SIG Technical Reports ICS*, no. 105, IPS Japan (2002), 105–110.

9. Nakagawa, K., Shinozawa, K., Matsumura, R., Ishiguro, H., and Hagita, N. Persuasive effects of robots' presonality. In *Proc. Forum on Information Technology 2010*, Committee of Forum on Information Technology (2010), 89–92.

10. Nakajima, H., Morishima, Y., Yamada, R., Brave, S., Maldonado, H., Nass, C., and Kwaji, S. Social intelligence in a human-machine collaboration system - social responses of agents with mind model and personality. *Transactions of the Japanese Society for Artificial Intelligence : AI 19* (2004), 184–196.

11. Nass, C., Moon, Y., and Fogg, B. Can Computer Personalities Be Human Personalities? *International Journal of Human-Computer Studies 43* (1995), 223–239.

12. Reeves, B., and Nass, C. *The Media Equation*. Cambridge University Press, 1996.

13. Ri, A., Oura, K., and Tokuda, K. An open-source toolkit realizing attractive voice interaction systems : Mmdagent. In *IEICE Technical Report. SP*, vol. 111 (2012), 159–164.

14. Suematsu, H., Nomura, S., and Wada, M. *Tokyo University Egogram New Ver. II*. KANEKOSHOBO, 1993.

15. Sugiyama, H., Meguro, T., Higashinaka, R., and Minami, Y. Response generation for questions about dialogue system's personality. In *JSAI Technical Report SIG-SLUD* (2014), 33–38.

16. Takeuchi, Y. Ethopoeia in social human-computer interaction. *Journal of the Japanese Society for Artificial Intelligence 16*, 6 (2001), 826–833.

17. van Vugt, H., Konijn, E., Hoorn, J., Keur, I., and Eliëns, a. Realism is not all! User engagement with task-related interface characters. *Interacting with Computers 19*, 2 (2007), 267–280.

18. Wilks, Y., and Catizone, R. Human-conputer conversation. *arXiv:cs*, 9906027v1 (2000), 1–14.

19. Yasuda, A., Yamamoto, K., Kuramoto, I., Minakuchi, M., and Tsujino, Y. The influence of conversational agents' personality in decision making support system by discussion with them. In *Proc. Human-Agent Interaction Symposium* (2011).

Potential of Imprecision: Exploring Vague Language in Agent Instructors

Leigh Clark*, Khaled Bachour*, Abdulmalik Ofemile†, Svenja Adolphs†, Tom Rodden*

*Mixed Reality Lab   †School of English

University of Nottingham, UK

{psxlc, khaled.bachour, aexacof, svenja.adolphs, tom.rodden}@nottingham.ac.uk

ABSTRACT

As we find greater potential for agent instructors, we must be aware of how their language use can affect the user and interaction as a whole. This study investigates the use of intentionally imprecise or *vague* language as a communicative strategy to mitigate the impact of instructions. We look at the effects it has on improving the perception of agents and user performance. A series of assembly tasks were ran in which users constructed Lego models with the spoken instructions of vague and non-vague agents. Results show that though the non-vague agent was seen as more direct and authoritative, responses to other attributes and performance were much more varied. Findings suggest there is potential for vague language human-agent interaction, though there are several obstacles in agent design to overcome first.

Author Keywords

Human-agent interaction; instructions; vague language; communication strategies

ACM Classification Keywords

H.5.2 [Information Interfaces and Presentation]: User Interfaces – Interaction Styles

INTRODUCTION

The prevalence of agents in our lives continues to rise and our interactions with them are becoming more complex on both a communicative and social level. Conversational and relational agents in particular aim to achieve a sense of rapport with their users [3, 4]. These represent a move into the emerging science of human-agent collectives (HACS) and with them present new challenges as to how agents best convey information and an awareness of how their use of language can affect the interaction as a whole. In HACs humans and agents can take on a range of varying roles, and successful communication becomes crucial to the effective operation of the collective.

HAI '14, October 29 - 31 2014, Tsukuba, Japan.
Copyright 2014 ACM 978-1-4503-3035-0/14/10...$15.00.
http://dx.doi.org/10.1145/2658861.2658895

This study takes a similar but new approach with one particular arrangement of roles: it focuses on agents giving direct and vague verbal instructions to human participants. It also hopes to assess the effect of these on participants when agents employ politeness strategies and some issues that arise from the use of natural language to achieve this communication.

BACKGROUND

Agents as Instructors

When talking about Human-Agent Collectives, successful communication requires that humans be open to being directed [22], and able to engage with agents at a peer level [17]. Agents are capable of dealing with some types of information in quantities and complexities that would overwhelm humans [2], and it is in these situations that they are ideally suited for a role as instructor, making quick decisions with vast amounts of data. A lot of work has been done on the role agents can play in the management of complex and information rich situations such as emergencies [21] and damage control [6]. Agents have also been shown to be able to hold more advisory roles such as a personal tutor [14] or by assisting patients and medical staff in diagnoses [8, 11].

Vague Language

While machine communication is by design direct and unambiguous, everyday human communication often contains varying degrees of uncertainty know as vague language (henceforth VL) [9, 10]. This can arise from genuine uncertainty but when used deliberately is a communicative strategy used to achieve functional and relational goals simultaneously. For example, a student answering a mathematics questions in classroom may respond with, "but it's around 50 basically?" [20]. Here the speaker conducts the functional goal of answering a question given by a teacher, while also fulfilling the relational goal of protecting oneself from full commitment to the answer and potential error by being imprecise. VL is seen a wide array of other contexts such as medical examinations [1], academic conferences [25] and the workplace [15].

The example above shows the speaker using VL as a politeness strategy [5]. Politeness strategies allow speakers to convey information such as instructions and requests without encroaching upon the listener's independence and freedom of action without impediment known as *face* [12, 13]. Instructions in particular create an imbalance of power that can potentially create a social gulf between two speakers, so polite communication can be used to convey instructions through the medium of imprecise language.

There has been some work on incorporating politeness strategies into HAI. When used in the classroom polite agents were seen to improve learning outcomes [26]. Similarly, when used in advice giving robots for a baking task it was shown to make them appear more likeable, considerate and less controlling [24]. This explored the successful use of hedges and discourse markers as polite communication. Hedges such as *kind of* and *sort of* allow a speaker to express uncertainty and avoid being assertive [16, 19]. Discourse markers such as *basically* and *like* are able to soften commands and distance the speaker from the information they are delivering to the listener. Though not described as such, these both represent features of VL through their deliberate imprecision with a purpose of both interactional and relational success. For the purposes of this paper we adopt a similar approach in the creation of a linguistic framework. As both hedges and discourse markers were used for the same purpose with similar success we combine the two under the banner of VL. This also allows us to include words that may usually be assigned to other categories such as fillers in our framework, so long as it is used in accordance with VL definitions.

While the use of VL was able to make a difference perceived attributes of robots in advice giving, it is unknown whether the same can be achieved with instruction giving agents. Instructions represent a more rigid information structure in which there is a closed set of outcomes, particularly those in assembly where each step is dependent on the ones preceding it.

In investigating VL use with agent instructors we devised four hypotheses based on previous literature. Firstly, we envisage human users will rate a vague agent as more likeable, friendly, trustworthy and sociable than a non-vague agent (H1). Similarly, we believe the non-vague agent will be rated as more controlling, authoritative, clear and direct (H2). It is thought the protection of the user's face and attempts to create a socially level discourse [7] will create a notable difference in how the different agents are perceived. We also predict that user performance will increase when following the vague agent instructions by creating an equal relationship [18] in a similar vein to what they expect from human instructors (H3). Finally, we predict that the introduction of an external stress factor will see a reduction in the differences seen in H1-H3 (H4).

METHOD

To test the hypotheses we ran a series of simulated agent-instructed assembly tasks in which participants were verbally instructed to construct two different Lego models.

These were conducted though a mixed design approach. The first twenty-four participants were tested for the two agent conditions within-subjects (vague and non-vague) and the task condition between-subjects (stress and no-stress). This was partially balanced with the subsequent six participants being given the reverse: the agent conditions were between-subjects and the stress conditions within-subjects.

Each session was filmed from two angles. The native camera on a MacBook Pro 10.2, which provided the interfaces for each task, was set to record the entire session to capture the front facing angle of each task. This allowed for the recording of participant facial gestures. This was also the same machine that provided the interfaces for the assembly tasks. A Panasonic HDC-SD80 camera was also set up to record each session from the side to allow for a more detailed view of the model assembly (see Figure 1).

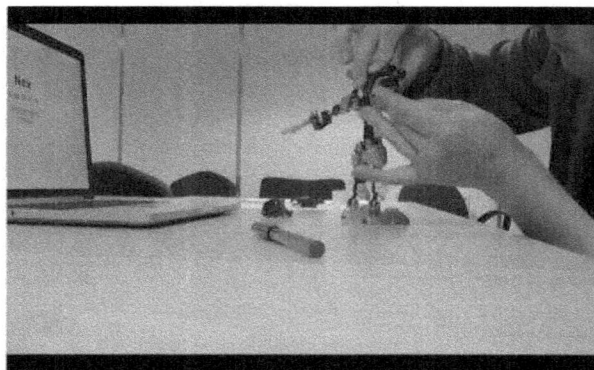

Figure 1. A participant constructs the model *Nex* in front of the agent interface.

Rather than develop an actual agent as such we created simulated agent interfaces that would provide a similar experience for the users. To create these agents each model was first split into 48 steps to produce the non-vague instructions. These were then altered to include VL items outlined in the framework to create the vague agent (Table 1).

	Non-Vague Agent	**Vague Agent**
Step 17 *Nex*	Twist this piece so the fin is pointing towards the desk	**Just** give this piece a **little bit** of a twist so the fin is **more or less** pointing towards the desk

Table 1. A comparison of non-vague and vague agent instructions from Step 17 of the model *Nex*.

Each set of instructions was inputted into the Text2SpeechPro software (http://www.hewbo.com) using the synthesised voice Cepstral Lawrence (http://www.cepstral.com) and exported as individual .mp3 files. Four separate HTML files were then created for the two versions of each model. These files functioned as the simulated agent interfaces and gave participants the options to request the next instruction and simulated agent interface and gave participants the options to request the next instruction and repeat the current one (Figure 2). As well as the interface they also functioned as tools for logging the number of repetitions requested in each task and the time taken to complete them.

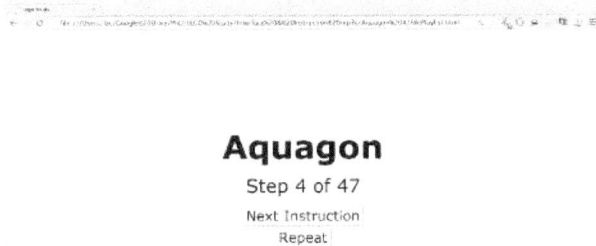

Aquagon

Step 4 of 47

Next Instruction
Repeat

Figure 2. The user interface for the model *Aquagon*.

For designing the two task conditions in the first 12 participants were given the no-stress condition and were timed in all three of their tasks, including the practice model. The mean average of these times was then calculated and each one increased by two minutes and thirty seconds. This total was used as the time limits for participants in the stress condition though they were not informed of the specific time, only that a limit was in place. As the research questions were primarily concerned with exposing subjects to vague language this time increase allowed for greater confidence in the majority of them finishing the task and being exposed to every instruction equally.

Participants

Thirty native English speakers studying at the University of Nottingham were recruited for this study and reimbursed with a £10 voucher for their participation. Nineteen students were male (63.3%) and eleven were female (36.7%). Of these, five were postgraduates and twenty-five were undergraduates. The ages of the participants ranged from 18-30 years old.

Procedure

Following a briefing participants were first tasked with constructing a practice Lego model using the manufacturer's instructions. Those undergoing the no-stress condition were told they had as much time as necessary for all tasks while those in the stress condition were made aware of the time limit known only to the researcher. The practice was followed by two further models using the agent instructions, with each of these proceeded by a questionnaire and interview.

Measures

Both quantitative and qualitative measures were used to assess the interactions with the agents.

Agent Perception

A five point Likert scale was used in post-task surveys to assess how participants rated the agent across eight attributes modified from an existing voice attribute scale [23] – likeable, friendly, trustworthy, sociable, controlling, authoritative, clear and direct – based on the hypotheses described earlier.

Open-ended questions in both the survey and semi-structured interviews were used to gain a greater understanding of their experience and attain a richer detail to as to their perception of the agent, thoughts on the language it used and if and how they would consider interacting with it again. An iterative content analysis approach was used to develop themes from this data.

Task Performance

Performance consisted of two measurements – the time taken to complete the task and the number of steps repeated.

RESULTS

Survey Measures

The results show that H2 was only partially correct. A mixed-design ANOVA revealed the non-vague agent was rated as more direct than the vague, but this was not affected by stress (Figure 3), F $(1, 26) = 14.62$, p $< .001$, $\eta_p^2 = .38$. Similarly, the non-vague agent was rated as more authoritative than the vague agent, which again was not affected by stress, F $(1, 26) = 15.79$, p $< .001$, $\eta_p^2 = .36$. The other hypotheses were not observed; no other attributes had a significant difference nor did any occur when comparing across the stress and no-stress conditions.

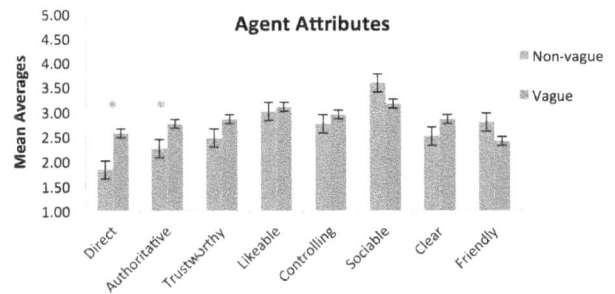

Figure 3. Comparison of vague and non-vague agent attributes measured in the survey showing the mean averages (*1= strongly agree, 5= strongly disagree*). Significant results are denoted with asterisks

User Performance

There was no marked difference in user performance across the two agent conditions (H3), however a one-way ANOVA revealed participants were seen to request less repeats in the stress condition than those in the no-stress F $(1, 59) = 5.97$, p $< .05$. There was no significant difference in time taken to complete the task.

Emerging Themes

These themes arose from the combination of the qualitative data discussed in the previous section. We observed no difference between the stress and no-stress conditions and as such this section focuses on the differences and similarities we observed between the agents.

Lexis

Almost all participants who interacted with both agents were able to identify lexical differences between them. The most commonly identified vague items were *basically*, *like* and *just*. These were followed by *kind of*, *sort of* and *more or less*, though participants mentioned *should*, *so* or *now*. For the direct tasks there was no explicit mention of any language.

Responses to particular words were mixed. The use of *basically* in particular appeared to cause an unfavourable perception of the agent, with it described as "inappropriate and somewhat demeaning" as well as being "annoying and too vague [and creating] a condescending tone". Similar responses were seen with *just*: "If I had this in my sat nav I would probably crash my car". Unlike *basically*, however, it also received positive feedback on its suitability with instructions that matched the procedure: "It was more consistent with the step "like it *was* just a little twist" and in creating a better impression of the agent: "I thought it was friendlier: "it sounded like a natural thing for him to be saying".

Similar mixed responses occurred when referring the to language as a whole, again creating a negative impression of the vague agent: "It felt like it was insincere"; "It seemed fake: "it was trying too hard", indicating a certain lack of success in creating a social leveling effect.

When participants were able to compare both agents there was a strong preference for the direct alternative due to its lack of vague language: "I liked the lack of fluffy words". Its simplicity in language was also praised: "It just said what was needed"; "It was much more straightforward so you just do what it tells you", indicating participants sometimes found the VL superfluous to the instructions as a whole.

VL Frequency

Although there was a mixed response to the vague agent, there were indications that reducing the frequency of VL in its instructions could change user perception of the agents: "I wouldn't mind it if they didn't say *like* so much"; "It's okay but think it says *just* too much"; "It's used too heavily", also pointing to a lack of variety in the language.

Voice Quality

There was a notable difference in how participants responded to the voice of the agent when the language changed. The non-vague tasks received better appraisals: "It was fine. I wouldn't really change anything"; "It's kind of what you expect from a computerised voice". Pairing the same voice with VL however produced difficulty in accepting the agent: "It's just the combination of the voice and script didn't work"; "It sounded too forced".

There was a general consensus that improving the voice would directly impact how the VL was received: "It would sound better with a more natural voice"; "The voice is holding it back". Specific recommendations included the addition of more sophisticated prosodic features: "Change the speed since it's quicker in human speech"; "It emphasized phrases like *more or less* strangely". This indicates a degree of technical limitation being on obstacle in the interactional success of the vague agent.

Context

The instructive nature of the task did not always combine well with the use of VL. It appeared to interfere with task performance and in turn agent perception: "I just wanted to get the job done"; "The extra information was meant to help but it ended up being confusing". Conversely, the non-vague agent received praise on the appropriateness of its instructions: "I think direct is just the way it has to be when getting instructions".

Using a vague agent in other contexts outside instructions received positive feedback, given it attends to the needs of the task at hand: "It's fine so long as it doesn't impact on what needs to be done"; "If it was for something that wasn't so precise [as instructions] then it'd work".

Multi-Modality

Having speech as almost the entire agent interaction had its drawbacks. The practice model using visual instructions resulted in the spoken instructions being less well received in some aspects of the task: "They're [visual] easier to relate to"; "Visual is easier for locating the right piece". Despite this, some elements were made easier with the spoken agents: "Verbal was easier for the actual assembly"; "It was easier to navigate around the 3D space with the spoken". This led to calls in combining the two to reap the positive aspects of each medium: "A visual supplement would make things easier"; "A mixture of both would be nice".

DISCUSSION

The aim of this study was to investigate the suitability of an agent instructing humans using vague language and its predicted effects on agent perception and task performance, using previous literature to create the language framework.

Responses from participants regarding the attributes of both agents were less definitive than in research studying advice-giving interactions, with only the key differences found only in the *direct* and *authoritative* characteristics. These two were expected as the lack of VL in the non-vague agent naturally creates a direct tone. This in turn produces an air of authority and a gap in social power between speaker and receiver. User performance did not vary significantly across the two agent conditions, though less repeats were used in the stress condition. This is likely a result of the unknown time limit creating a sense of urgency, leaving less time to check instructions again and perhaps forcing participants to employ greater focus during those tasks.

Though the results did not come out as expected, the interview data yielded a rich insight into why this may have occurred, as well as generating a greater understanding of the interaction as a whole. Some VL items, for example, were better received than others, either due to their appropriateness or frequency, but this was not overly consistent. VL was less well received in instructions than has been shown in advice giving, perhaps due to the inflexible nature of the outcomes that may warrant a more direct approach. The findings suggest, however, that there is also significant amount of individual preference at play. Some participants praised the use of VL, with several responses mimicking those seen in human interactions. Language is not a static entity that always warrants a general approach and perhaps more variety in the degrees of precision and imprecision are required. We must also strongly consider the individual user and their own preferences in agent design.

Other obstacles need to be overcome if VL is to be used successfully. The technical capabilities of the agent's voice were a strong barrier in acceptance as opposed to just the language. While VL is commonly used feature in everyday language, there is very little exposure to its use by an agent. As the agent lacked the vocal characteristics such as intonation and stress that accompany language, combining the two to create something more familiar could have greater success than either of them individually.

Limitations and Future Work

This study only used a simulated agent to create an interaction. It is unknown whether one agency could the change the outcomes seen here. Similarly, there could be significant differences with introduction of features such as embodiment and alternative exposure times (particularly in relational agents that may see interaction over a period of weeks). Investigating the multiple permutations available in these interactions would provide us with greater insight into how we may benefit from a greater awareness of agent language use.

Despite the mixed responses in this context, the data reveals there is potential in HAI for a greater human like approach to language. This study points towards the development of adaptive agents in the future – those that change their language depending on context and the individual user. For now though, further research in both instructive and non-instructive contexts is required so we may fully begin to understand the potential of alternative communicative strategies.

CONCLUSION

This study compared user reactions to vague and non-vague agent instructors. We ran a series of simulated agent-instructed assembly tasks to discover how agent perception is affected and how the interaction is experienced differently. Findings suggest that there is no one size fits all approach to language in agent design and there must be awareness of the context of the interaction, technical capabilities of the agent and the preferences of the individual user. Given the mixed responses there is potential for vague language in human-agent interaction, but these obstacles must first be researched in greater detail to achieve success.

ACKNOWLEDGEMENTS
This work was supported by EPSRC Grant No. EP/I011587/1.

REFERENCES
1. Adolphs, S., Atkins, S. and Harvey, K. Caught between professional requirements and interpersonal needs: Vague language in healthcare contexts, *Vague Language Explored* (2007), pp. 62-78.
2. Ball, M. and Callaghan, V. Introducing Intelligent Environments, Agents and Autonomy to Users. *IEEE* (2011), pp. 382-385.
3. Bickmore, T. and Cassell, J. Relational Agents: A Modl and Implementation of Building User Trust. Proc. *Human Factors in Computing Systems*, ACM Press, New York, NY (2001), pp. 396-403.
4. Bickmore, T. and Cassell, J. *Social Dialogue with Embodied Conversational Agents, Advances in natural multimodal dialogue systems*. Springer (2005), pp.23-54.
5. Brown, P. and Levinson, S.C. *Politeness: Some universals on language usage*. Cambridge University Press (1987).
6. Bulitko, V.V. and Wilkins, D.C. Automated instructor assistant for ship damage control. *AAAI/IAAI* (1999), pp.778-785.
7. Carter, R. Orders of reality: CANCODE, communication and culture. *ELT Journal,* 52 (1998), pp. 43-56.
8. Chan, V., Ray, P. and Parameswaran, N. Mobile e-Health monitoring: an agent-based approach, *IET communications*, 2 (2008), pp.223-230.
9. Channel, J. *Vague Language*. Oxford University Press (1994).
10. Cutting, J. *Vague Language Explored*. Palgrave Macmillan (2007).
11. Doswell, J. and Harmeyer, K. Extending the serious game boundary: Virtual instructors in mobile mixed reality learning games. *Digital Games Research Association International Conference*, Citeseer (2007)
12. Goffman, E. *The presentation of self in everyday* life. Garden City, NY (2002).
13. Goffman, E. *Interaction Ritual: Essays on Face-to-Face Behaviour*. Anchor Books (1967).
14. Heylen, D., Nijholt. R., Den Akker, O.P. and Vissers, M. Socially intelligent tutor agents. *Intelligent Virtual Agents*, Springer (2003), pp.341-347.
15. Koester, A. 'About twelve thousand or so': Vagueness in North American and UK offices, *Vague Language Explored* (2007), pp. 40-61.

16. Lakoff, G. *Hedges: A Study in meaning criteria and the logic of fuzzy* concepts. Springer (1975)

17. Maes, P. Agents that reduce work and information overload, *Communications of the* ACM, 37 (1994), pp.30-40.

18. McCarthy, M. and Carter, R. *As visible patterns of interaction*, Explorations in Corpus Linguistics (2006).

19. Prince, E.F., Frader. J. and Bosk, C. On hedging in physician-physician discourse. *Linguistics and the* Professions (1982), pp.83-97.

20. Rowland, T. 'Well maybe not exactly, but it's around fifty basically?' Vague language in mathematics classrooms. *Vague Language Explored* (2007), pp.79-96.

21. Schaafstal, A. M., Johnston, J. H. and Oser, R. L. Training teams for emergency management, *Computers in Human* Behaviour, 17 (2001), pp.615-626.

22. Sukthankar, G., Shumaker, R. and Lewis, M. Intelligent agents as teammates, *Theories of Team Cognition: Cross-Disciplinary Perspectives* (2012), pp.313-343.

23. Tamagawa, R., Watson, C.I., Kuo, I.H., Macdonald, B.A. and Broadbent, E. The Effects of Synthesized Voice Accents on User Perceptions of Robots, *International Journal of Social* Robotics, 3 (2011), pp. 253-262.

24. Torrey, C., Fussell, S. and Kiesler, S. How a robot should give advice, *Proceedings of the 8th ACM/IEEE international conference on Human-robot* interaction, IEEE Press, Tokyo, Japan (2013), pp. 275-282.

25. Trappes-Lomax, H. Vague language as a means of self-protective avoidance: Tension management in conference talks. *Vague Language Explored* (2007), pp.117-137.

26. Wang, Wang, N., Johnson, W.L., Mayer, R.E., Rizzo, P. Shaw, E. and Collins, H. The politeness effect: Pedagogical agents and learning outcomes, *International Journal of Human-Computer Studies,* 66 (2008), pp. 98-112.

Sharedo: To-Do List Interface for Human-Agent Task Sharing

Jun Kato[†]   **Daisuke Sakamoto**[‡]   **Takeo Igarashi**[‡]   **Masataka Goto**[†]

National Institute of Advanced Industrial Science and Technology[†], The University of Tokyo[‡]

{jun.kato, m.goto}@aist.go.jp[†], {d.sakamoto, takeo}@acm.org[‡]

ABSTRACT

In this paper, we propose a to-do list interface for sharing tasks between human and multiple agents including robots and software personal assistants. While much work on software architectures aims to achieve efficient (semi-)autonomous task coordination among human and agents, little work on user interfaces can be found for user-oriented flexible task coordination. Instead, most of the existing human-agent interfaces are designed to command a single agent to handle specific kinds of tasks. Meanwhile, our interface is designed to be a platform to share any kinds of tasks between users and multiple agents. When agents can handle the task, they ask for details and permission to execute it. Otherwise, they try supporting users or just keep silent. New tasks can be registered not only by humans but also by agents when errors occur that can only be fixed by human users. We present the interaction design and implementation of the interface, Sharedo, with three example agents, followed by brief user feedback collected from a preliminary user study.

Author Keywords

Human-robot interaction; social media platforms; to-do list.

ACM Classification Keywords

H.5.2. User Interfaces [Interaction styles]; I.2.9. Robotics [Commercial robots and applications].

INTRODUCTION

There is an increasing number of agents available in our daily lives, including software personal assistants on smartphones, e.g., Siri for iPhone and Cortana for Windows Phone, and robots at home, e.g. iRobot Roomba. While existing agents can handle various tasks through usable interfaces, e.g. speech and button-based interfaces, they are usually designed to instantly respond to the user. Therefore, to interact with such agents, the user needs to be prepared to clarify details. However, our daily lives are filled with ambiguity. We do not know what we want to eat tonight, who will cook it, whether to order books online or to buy them at a nearby bookstore, when we have time for watching videos

recommended by friends, etc. Such ambiguity in tasks does not need to be resolved instantly, and we sometimes want to keep them ambiguous till the time comes.

In addition, which agent should handle a task is sometimes ambiguous since multiple agents can handle it in different ways. For instance, to watch a movie, a shopping robot can buy a Blu-ray disc at a movie store and a web-based agent can show it online. Therefore, it is important to think of interaction techniques for task coordination as well as task specification.

For organizing ambiguous tasks whose details (who, when, how to handle them) are yet to be decided, a to-do list has been a good tool for human users [1]. Kreifelts investigated its use for human-human task sharing [8]. There are also many web services that allow sharing to-do lists with others such as Remember The Milk [10]. With these existing uses of to-do list interfaces for task sharing in mind, we propose Sharedo (Figure 1), a web-based to-do list interface that supports the ambiguous state in human-agent task sharing. It extends the use of the to-do list interface not only for humans but also for agents and allows them to share, discuss, and complete tasks together.

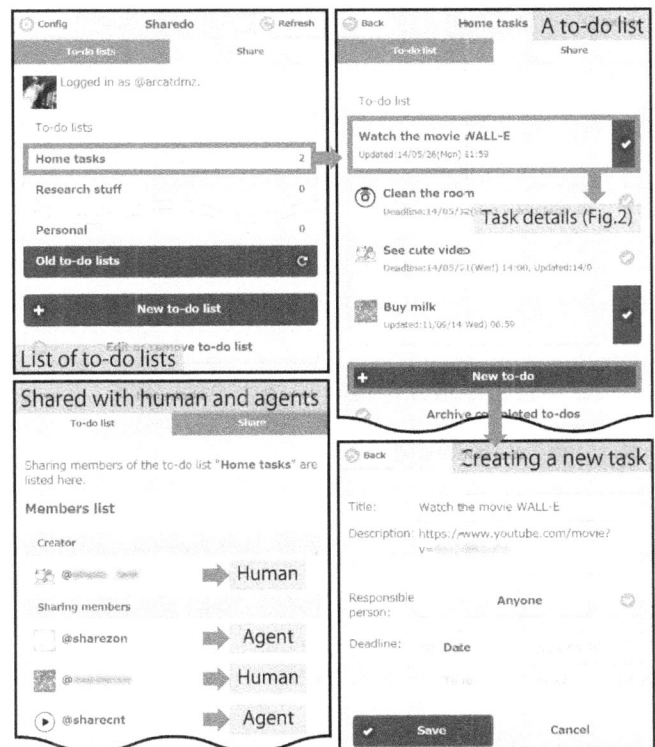

Figure 1. To-do list interface for human-agent task sharing

HAI 2014, October 29–31, 2014, Tsukuba, Japan.
Copyright is held by the owner/author(s). Publication rights licensed to ACM.
ACM 978-1-4503-3035-0/14/10...$15.00.
http://dx.doi.org/10.1145/2658861.2658894

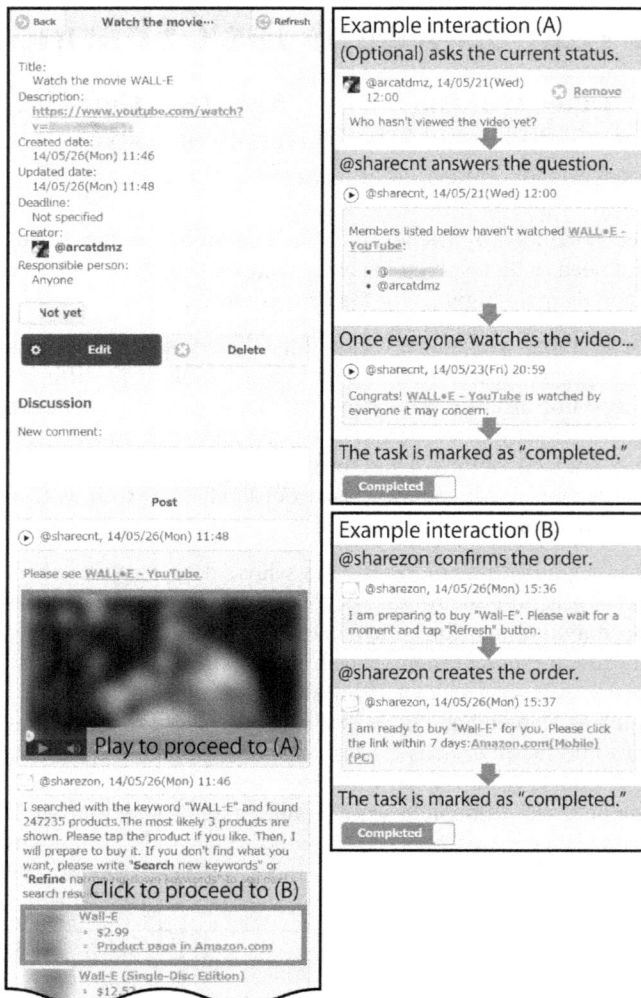

Figure 2. Discussion board for removing task ambiguity

All users and agents of the Sharedo interface have virtual embodiments associated with their social media accounts. Once they have logged-in to the platform by using the accounts, a to-do list can be created to share tasks with other users and agents. Both a user and agent can register new tasks to the list (the user through the web page and the agent through a web API). A task has its own page that shows its detailed information and a discussion board for discussing the details of a task, as shown in Figure 2. All users and agents are notified, whenever they edit the task information and create posts on the discussion board (the users through a message on the social media account and the agents through a web API hook). Discussion on the task gradually removes its ambiguity and leads to its completion. Finally, the task can be marked as completed either by a user or agent.

To provide concrete examples of human-agent interaction on the platform, three agents with different characteristics are implemented: a house cleaning agent that schedules the appropriate time for cleaning a room and executes it by controlling an iRobot Roomba robot, a shopping agent that

suggests, purchases, and delivers products to the home with the help of the Amazon API, and a media content agent that helps in consuming media content such as reading online articles and watching online videos. In the following sections, related work, interaction design, implementation details, and user experience collected from a preliminary study are reported.

RELATED WORK

Software Architectures for Task Coordination

Much work has been done proposing software architectures and algorithms for autonomous task coordination of multi-agent systems [2], aiming at efficient task completion. A notable example is Electric Elves [3], in which human users and agents are equally represented as proxies to achieve human-agent collaboration. The agents in the system support human organization by tracking schedules and the locations of human users with palmtop computers, deciding presenters for meetings, and arranging food for the meetings by faxing orders to restaurants. While these agents consider user input, e.g., accepting/declining meeting schedules, and achieve adjustable autonomy, the task coordination is an autonomous process without user input. In more recent work [11], a prototype infrastructure was proposed that allows the user to help in task coordination, which resulted in more efficient robot-agent-person collaboration for disaster rescue.

These papers do provide some information on their graphical user interfaces, but their focus is consistently on software architectures and algorithms for efficient (semi-)autonomous task coordination. In contrast, our work focuses on a user interface design that creates an intuitive mapping between actions on shared to-do lists and events of task coordination. It aims to allow human users to coordinate casual tasks on the basis of their occasional preferences.

Human-Robot Interfaces for Commanding Tasks

Various user interfaces have been proposed for operating robots interactively, such as use of a handheld device for the remote control of a mobile robot [6] and a multi-touch display for simultaneous control of multiple robots [7]. These interfaces allow real-time control and are suitable for tele-existence, military, and gaming applications in which the user needs to continuously monitor what the robot is doing.

Home robots are designed to complete household tasks by themselves and free the user from spending time on them. Therefore, it is desired that user interfaces for such robots can specify the details of repetitive and/or time-consuming tasks in intuitive ways. For instance, Cooky [12] allows the user to command multiple robots to cooperatively cook meals. Magic Cards [13] allows the user to put cards in a room where the user wants to particular tasks done such as "clean here" and "move objects from here" and "to there." Then, the system drives a card collector robot and delegates each task to an appropriate robot, e.g., cleaning task to a cleaner robot and delivering task to a carrier robot. When there is an error during the task execution, a printer robot prints error messages. This system and our work share the concept of commanding multiple kinds of agents and getting responses from them. The difference is that their system assumes the task details are clear when the user puts cards in the environment, while ours is capable of handling ambiguous tasks.

Instead of creating new interfaces for commanding robots, making use of social media platforms is proposed [9]. The system uses existing tools originally designed for human-human communication, including text messaging on cell phones, video chatting on personal computers, and an online shared calendar. Text messaging and video chatting both involve text-based dialogues and allow interactive task specifications, similar to the discussion board in our work. Though, there are two major differences. First, the prior work focuses on comparing social media to find the characteristics of each medium as a commanding interface. Our work, however, focuses on proposing a novel use of one social medium, a to-do list. The novelty is in its bi-directional commanding; it allows not only commanding *to* a robot but also *from* a robot. Second, in the prior work, each medium supports one-to-one communication between the user and a robot, but our work supports communication involving multiple users and multiple agents.

To-do List Interface for Task Management

A to-do list is one of the standard tools for task management. There are many web-based to-do list services, which often have an option to share the list with others for computer-supported cooperative work (CSCW). Within the research context, the effectiveness of sharing the lists in a distributed environment was discussed [8]. To-do lists have also often been discussed as part of personal information management (PIM) systems [1]. Intelligent assistance for to-do lists was proposed [5] that divides existing tasks into sub tasks, prioritizes tasks, merges similar tasks, and assigns tasks to automated programs on the basis of "common knowledge" collected in advance from volunteers and online corpora. In these cases, details on each task are shared and discussed with others via other conversation media, typically e-mail. In contrast, our interface has a discussion board that enables seamless integration of information sharing and discussion between human and agents.

Towel [4] is one of the closest examples in that it combines a to-do list interface with a text-based chat window for discussion between the user and a software personal assistant. While Towel provides a chat window for one-to-one human-agent communication to delegate digital tasks to a specific agent, our interface is designed to be a platform for collaborative completion of both physical and digital tasks. For instance, while Towel's chat log is only visible to the user and agent, our discussion board is accessible by all members of the to-do list, including human and agents. This allows support for more complex use cases, e.g., multiple agents propose handling the same task in parallel.

INTERACTION DESIGN

The main interface of the Sharedo platform looks like a standard web-based to-do list service, as shown in Figure 1 and Figure 2. The user can have more than one to-do list and switch between them in accordance with their purpose and context. For instance, one to-do list is for private use shared with the media content agent, while another is for sharing with family users and the cleaning agent, etc. Within each to-do list, multiple tasks can be registered. For each task, its own page shows the task details and a discussion board where human and agents can discuss the task. To identify each user and agent, we use the authorization API of an existing social medium, Twitter. Twitter is also used to send notifications to human users through its private messaging feature called "direct message."

Despite these standard features, the novelty of this interface comes from the platform being capable of hosting not only human-human but also human-agent interaction. In the following subsections, the human-agent interaction enabled on the platform is explained with concrete example scenarios with three agents: the house cleaning agent (@sharerom), the shopping agent (@sharezon), and the media content agent (@sharecnt). These agents are carefully designed to have different characteristics as shown in Table 1 to reveal the use cases of the platform.

Share Tasks

The user can add a task to a to-do list by specifying the title, e.g. "Buy milk," detailed description (optional), assignment, and deadline (optional). Options for the assignment are the user him/herself, a specific member among humans and agents sharing the to-do list, and anyone sharing the list. When a task is added to a list, it is immediately notified to all users and agents sharing the list. Each agent checks if it has anything to do with the task. For instance, the shopping agent is capable of buying milk, but the house cleaning and media content agents are not. In this case, the shopping agent proceeds to the next step of discussion, and the others keep silent.

An agent can also add a task to the list if it needs the help of human users or has some recommendations (Figure 3). For instance, the house cleaning agent might fail to complete cleaning because of errors such as low battery and being trapped in tangled cables on the floor. When the errors can

Agents and their features	Home Cleaning	Shopping	Media Content
Share – add user tasks	✓	-	✓
Discuss – clarify details	✓	✓	-
Discuss – notify progress	✓	-	✓
Complete tasks by itself	✓	✓	-
Tasks are…	Physical	Both	Digital

Table 1. Variety of agents with different characteristics

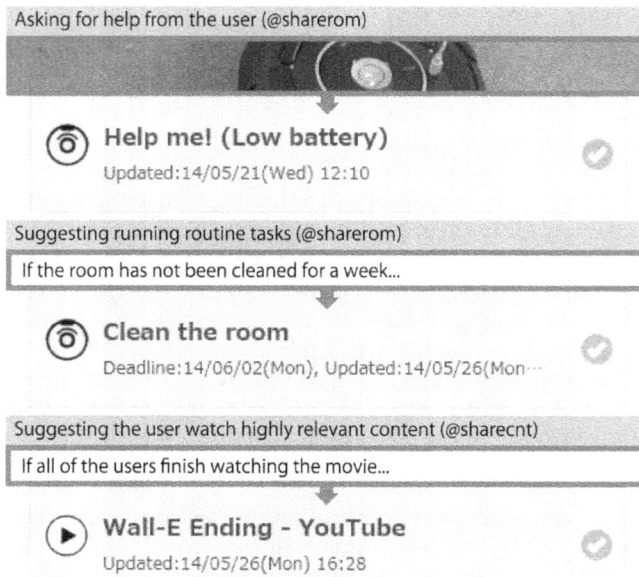

Figure 3. Examples of tasks created by agents

only be fixed by a human, the agent adds the to-do "Help me!" to the list and asks for help. The media content agent might also add a task for human users to watch a video that is considered highly relevant to recently watched videos. Please note that the tasks added to the list can be freely edited or removed if human users think they are not desirable. Once they are removed, the agents stop handling them. Every change the user makes on the Sharedo platform tells something to the agents, which in turn achieves a sort of non-verbal communication.

Discuss Tasks

After a task is shared in a to-do list, the discussion phase starts and continues till it is completed or removed from the list (Figure 2). The discussion takes place on a discussion board provided separately for each task in the list. This allows focused and effective discussion towards task completion.

One major role of the discussion board is to remove any ambiguity in the task and to create a complete task definition required to complete the task. The task definition in general consists of *who* should complete the task and *when* and *how* it should be completed. While *who* refers to one of the humans and agents sharing the list and *when* refers to a specific time and date, what kind of information *how* consists of is different from one task to another. On the Sharedo platform, each agent relevant to the task tries removing ambiguity in its own way in parallel. In other words, each agent has its own task definition and asks the user to fill in blank fields by concurrently posting comments. Such concurrent posts make the discussion board look similar to existing social media such as Twitter.

For instance, adding the task "Buy a broomstick and clean the room" makes both the shopping and house cleaning

agents post comments to the discussion board. The shopping agent searches for broomsticks on shopping sites, lists relevant products, and asks the user for a response. The house cleaning agent does not know if the user is going to use the broomstick to clean the room by him or herself, so it searches for time slots when the user is out of the house and offers those slots in which the Roomba robot will clean the room. The user can read these posts and assign the task to one of the two agents to mute further posts from the other agent. The user can even ignore these posts and go to the next step of completing the task by him or herself, making both agents stop posting to the discussion board.

Another example of ambiguous tasks is "Watch the Disney movie 'WALL-E'" accompanied with a YouTube URL (Figure 2). The shopping agent can buy and deliver the Blu-ray disc, shown as example interaction (B), but the media content agent can also show it online, shown as example interaction (A). The media content agent posts an inline YouTube video player to the discussion board.

The other role of the discussion board is to remind the user of the task. Since posting comments on the board triggers the sending of notifications to all users sharing the to-do list, agents sometimes make use of the board to make sure that human users complete the task. This is critical when a deadline is set to a task.

For example, suppose one user adds the task "See video before next meeting" to a to-do list shared with colleagues. The task is accompanied with a YouTube URL in its description and with a specific deadline. The user thinks that watching the video is mandatory to prepare for the meeting but is not sure if all of the colleagues will watch it. When the to-do list is shared with the media content agent, the agent addresses this concern. It posts a comment with an inline YouTube player allowing the colleagues to easily watch the video. Furthermore, it tracks the activity of the colleagues on the comment. When one starts playing the video with the inline player or clicks the link to watch it on the full YouTube site, the agent internally marks the user as "done." The creator of the task can post a new comment such as "Who hasn't watched the video yet?" to make the agent respond with a comment listing the colleagues whose activity has not been observed yet. Since the agent provides clear information on the progress, the creator of the task can be relieved from communicating with each colleague just to make sure whether they have watched the video.

Complete Tasks

Once any ambiguity in a task is removed, the last step is to complete it, mark the task as "done" on the system, and notify all users and agents of the task completion.

The user is allowed to complete tasks at any time, even if the discussion is in progress or if the user has already assigned the agent to handle it. For instance, the user might notice he can "buy milk" on his way back home. There are cases where agents cannot understand subtle nuance in the task definitions. For example, the user could find time to "clean the room" and actually want to do it by himself rather than asking the house cleaning agent, which does not consider the specific space he is temporarily using for an intricate jigsaw puzzle. Once the user completes a task and marks it as completed on the system, the agents do their best to cancel further actions. For instance, when the cleaning task is marked as done, the house cleaning robot cancels its scheduled cleaning.

Each agent has its own implementation for completing tasks. The task completion procedure can be self-contained as with the case of the house cleaning agent and the shopping agent. These agents can potentially complete the tasks without help from human users. Meanwhile, the procedure can depend on the human users' actions as with the case of the media content agent. It essentially observes the action of each user and marks the task as done when all conditions are met. During this procedure, new tasks are potentially made by agents. For such examples, see the second paragraph in the subsection "Share Tasks."

IMPLEMENTATION

Sharedo Platform

The Sharedo platform is implemented as a set of Java Servlets on the Google App Engine (GAE) server (Figure 4). Both the user client and agents call the Sharedo Web API to

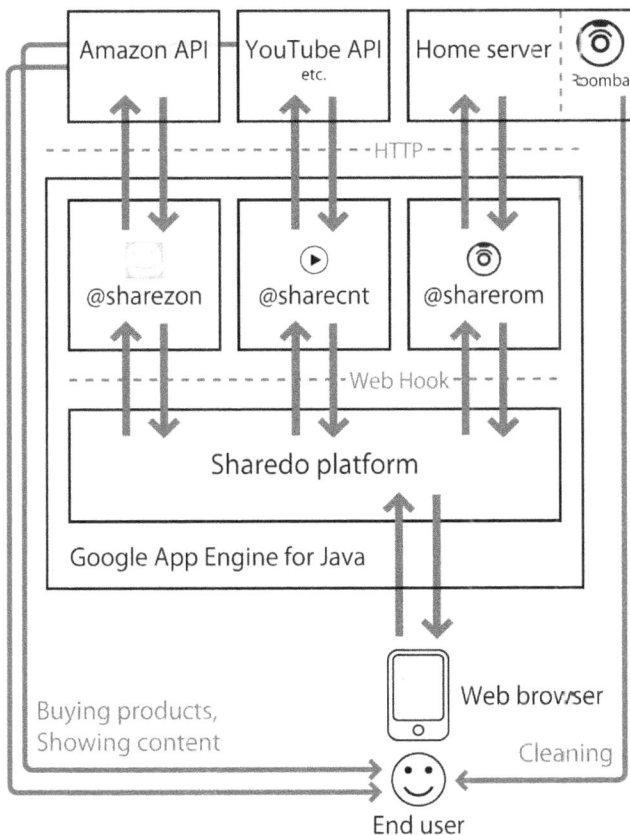

Figure 4. Sharedo platform with multiple agents

communicate with the platform. The agents also have a web hook mechanism, a Web API called by the platform for event notification. The implementation of the user client and agents is separated so that the user has control over the privacy policy (which agent to share what information) and to ensure capability for implementing more agents on the platform. Currently, the house cleaning agent, the shopping agent, and the media content agent are implemented on top of the platform.

User interface – The user interface is implemented with HTML5, CSS3, and JavaScript. All communication between the user interface and the platform is done via Asynchronous JavaScript + XML (Ajax), except for the authentication process that uses the OAuth API provided by Twitter and the initial load of the top page. Ajax allows smooth transitions between pages and provides a better browsing experience.

Event notification – The Sharedo platform notifies users of an event that has occurred in the to-do lists through a direct messaging API provided by Twitter. The notification is sent to their mobile phones or mailboxes, depending on their preferences. The platform also notifies the agents of the event through WebHook, which is a technique for sending HTTP requests to the Web APIs of agents. The current implementation notifies users and agents of events including the start and end of sharing, that is, the insertion, edit, and removal of a to-do, and the posting of a comment.

House Cleaning Agent

The house cleaning agent consists of two major components – the server-side implementation responsible for virtual embodiment of the agent and the client-side implementation responsible for physical embodiment of the agent.

The server-side implementation is installed on the GAE server. The implementation receives an event and responds to it on the Sharedo platform. It has various functions, e.g., to read the details of a task in the to-do list, to respond to comments, and to send instructions to the client-side implementation. When a new task is created, it finds a keyword related to cleaning in the text-based title and a description of the task by matching regular expressions. Then, with permission to access the user's online calendar (Google Calendar) granted beforehand, it looks for a time slot when the user is out of the house and offers a time in which the robot will work. Next, the agent waits for the user's response. If the user approves the offer by posting comments that contain "yes" or other similar words, the client-side implementation is commanded to handle the task at the selected time. If the user rejects the offer, the agent finds another appropriate time candidate. If the user does not respond, the agent will not work when the selected time comes. It will offer a new time for cleaning after the planned time has passed. The time can also be explicitly specified by commenting on it. The number of times for a thorough cleaning job can also be specified; for instance, commenting "twice" makes the robot repeat the cleaning twice. If the users have not added a cleaning task to the to-do list for more than a predefined period (a week by default), the agent adds the task "Clean the room" in the user's to-do list as a reminder.

The client-side implementation is installed on a personal computer in the user's house. It receives a HTTP request from the server-side implementation to control an iRobot Roomba doing an actual cleaning task in the real world. The Roomba robot is controlled wirelessly with the Roomba Open Interface protocol via a Bluetooth connection. When the task is finished, it notifies the server-side implementation to mark the cleaning task as completed. Otherwise, when a fatal error is reported by the robot that prevents task completion, it notifies the server-side implementation to add a new task that asks a human user for help.

Shopping Agent

While the shopping agent is implemented without any physical embodiment, it certainly affects the real world upon task completion (the product is delivered to the user's house). It is installed on the GAE server that orders products from an online shopping service (Amazon.com). In the future, it might be possible that we substitute the shopping service with a mechanical robot capable of buying and delivering the products to the mailbox.

The implementation finds a keyword in the title and description of the newly posted/edited task in a similar way to the house cleaning agent. It matches regular expressions to extract the keyword from a task, such as "buy something," and then searches for products by using the Product Advertising API by Amazon.com to show the most likely products (up to three) in the discussion board. The user can refine the result by posting a comment with the format "refine keywords" or instruct the agent to search again with "search new keywords." In addition, if the user wants to buy groceries, the user can narrow the results by including the category keyword "#Grocery." The search is repeated until the user is satisfied with the results. When the user approves an offer by clicking the product image on the discussion board, the shopping agent posts a comment with a link to make an order. Finally, when the order has been made, the task is marked as "completed." After the payment process, the ordered item will be delivered to the user.

Media Content Agent

The media content agent is installed on the GAE server and collects information about the URL mentioned in the task description. It posts a message that helps the human users to understand the media content pointed by the URL before they access it. In addition, by substituting the original URL with a redirection URL, the agent tracks which user has accessed the URL.

While the message depends on the content of the URL, a common procedure for the agent is to access the URL and try parsing the contents as a HTML document and retrieve the title. The message always starts with a hyperlink to the redirection URL such as "Please see <title of the web page>."

If the original URL is a YouTube video, the agent posts an inline player. The title text is shown as a hypertext link that navigates to a redirection URL, allowing the agent to track user activity with link clicking. Thanks to the YouTube Iframe API, the agent can also track user activity with the inline video player. When the user clicks the link or plays the video, the agent silently marks the user as "done." When all human users who are supposed to watch the video are marked as "done," the agent posts a congratulation to reward the users and to notify the task creator of it. In addition, the agent searches for highly relevant videos and posts them as a new task to the to-do list. Tasks posted by the agent can be easily distinguished on the list since all tasks made by other users and agents are shown with their social media icons.

Otherwise, when the original URL is not a YouTube video, the agent posts a thumbnail image showing the overview of the website instead of the inline player. While the video-specific interaction is omitted, all the rest remains the same; for instance, when all the users access the redirection URL, the agent congratulates them by posting a message.

PRELIMINARY USER STUDY

Method

We conducted a preliminary user study for two months by recruiting four participants in two families (one family with a 25-year-old male and 27-year-old female and the other with a 36-year-old male and 26-year-old female.) The study aimed to compare use of the Sharedo interface against the direct commanding of agents and to observe how the interface is used in a real setting. Besides the Sharedo interface, the participants were allowed to command an iRobot Roomba robot, access the Amazon website, or see other websites without the help of agents at any time during the user study.

Results

After two months, the participants made 179 to-dos with 111 comments including 61 from agents in 15 to-do lists. The Sharedo interface was used well to perform collaborative work between the participants and the agents.

For several times, the participants pushed the physical button of the Roomba robot to get the room cleaned immediately. Otherwise, they used our interface effectively to postpone their decision and later handled the cleaning on their own, asked their partner to do it, or made the robot do it at the correct timing. While the cleaning tasks done by the robot usually succeeded, one participant reported, *"I worried about the robot even when I didn't get messages while I was out."* and *"I came to feel more like cleaning the room by myself when possible. Otherwise, I often had to arrange the room to get it ready for robot cleaning."* Another participant said, *"When I made the robot clean the room, I wanted to specify the area to be cleaned. I did not want my Roomba to run over my belongings on the floor, though there was no other option than moving them by myself. Furthermore, I think such an option should not be told to other users and agents through text-based communication."*

Discussions about the shopping agent were interesting. Two of the participants were a married couple who reported, *"We felt like the shopping agent was a friend. The fact that it has its Twitter account as we do and it communicates with us through the account makes it more familiar. The Amazon.com website also has recommendations for us, but the feeling was very different,"* and, *"The recommendations made by the agents were sometimes beyond our expectations, expanding our choice."*

DISCUSSION AND FUTURE WORK

According to the preliminary user study, the platform itself was proved to work stably and is thought to be extendible enough to see a greater variety of agents being implemented in the future. The process of defining task details through the discussion board interface got favorable feedback from the users. While the board could not be used to get an immediate response from the Roomba robot, it has the potential to help create long-term good relationship between the user and the robot.

The server-side implementation of agents could be more convenient for the user if they can utilize the history of completed tasks. Agents could learn the timing patterns for cleaning a room and remember favorite products for shopping with the help of programming-by-example techniques. Some users complained that the text-based communication on the discussion board for specifying the details of cleaning tasks is not thorough enough. To address this issue, our future work will improve the agent implementation to integrate more interactive user interfaces within the discussion board.

Regarding the users' preference on the relationship with their agents through Twitter accounts, our future work might include more integration of our interface with Twitter. While the current implementation only uses a direct messaging API so that communication between the user and the agent cannot be seen from other followers of the user on Twitter, it might be interesting to see what happens when we allow public communication between them, which is shown in the Twitter timeline and visible to anyone on the Internet.

Collected comments from the study suggest that the platform can enhance communication between people. Deploying the interface as a communication medium for the user and professional housekeepers instead of the cleaning agent would also produce interesting results.

CONCLUSION

We presented a user interface design with which a user can share, discuss, and complete to-dos together with people and agents. Its implementation, named "Sharedo," can be accessed at http://www.sharedo.info/ and comes with three agents: house cleaning, shopping, and media content agents. A preliminary study showed that the platform could help remove ambiguity in task definition through the standard workflow of task management, showing a promising way to coordinate tasks for human-agent cooperation.

ACKNOWLEDGMENTS
This work was supported in part by JST, CREST.

REFERENCES
1. Bellotti, V., Dalal, B., Good, N., Flynn, P., Bobrow, D. G., and Ducheneaut, N. What a to-do: studies of task management towards the design of a personal task list manager. In *Proc. of CHI '04*, 735-742.

2. Campbell, A., and Wu, A. Multi-agent Role Allocation: Issues, Approaches, and Multiple Perspectives. *Autonomous Agents and Multi-Agent Systems 22(2)*, Springer (2011), 317-355.

3. Chalupsky, H., Gil, Y., Knoblock, C., Lerman, K., Oh, J., Pynadath, D., Russ, and T., Tambe, M. Electric Elves: Applying Agent Technology to Support Human Organizations. In *Proc. of AAAI IAAI '01*, 51-58.

4. Conley, K. and Carpenter, J. Towel: Towards and Intelligent To-Do List, In *Proc. of AAAI Spring Assistants*.

5. Gil, Y., Ratnakar, V., Chklovski, T., Groth, P., and Vrandecic, D. Capturing Common Knowledge about Tasks: Intelligent Assistance for To-Do Lists, *ACM Transactions on Interactive Intelligent Systems 2(3)*, Article 15.

6. Fong, T., Thorpe, C., and Glass, B. PdaDriver: A Handheld System for Remote Driving. In *Proc. of ICAR '03*.

7. Kato, J., Sakamoto, D., Inami, M., Igarashi, T. Multi-touch interface for Controlling Multiple Mobile Robots. In *CHI '09 Extended Abstracts on Human Factors in Computing Systems (CHI EA '09)*, 3443-3448.

8. Kreifelts, T., Hinrichs, E., and Woetzel, G. Sharing to-do lists with a distributed task manager. In *Proc. of ECSCW '93*, Kluwer Academic Publishers (1993), 31-46.

9. Ma, X., Yang, X., Zhao, S., Fu, C., Lan, Z., and Pu, Y. Robots in my Contact List: Using Social Media Platforms for Human-Robot Interaction in Domestic Environment. In *Proc. of APCHI '12*, 133-140.

10. RememberTheMilk. http://www.rememberthemilk.com/

11. Scerri, P., Pynadath, D., Johnson, L., Rosenbloom, P., Si, M., Schurr, N., and Tambe, M. A Prototype Infrastructure for Distributed Robot-Agent-Person Teams. In *Proc. of AAMAS '03*, 433-440.

12. Sugiura, Y., Sakamoto, D., Withana, A.I., Inami, M., and Igarashi, T. Cooking with Robots: Designing a Household System Working in Open Environments. In *Proc. of CHI '10*, 2427-2430.

13. Zhao, S., Nakamura, K., Ishii, K., and Igarashi, T. Magic Cards: A Paper Tag Interface for Implicit Robot Control. In *Proc. of CHI '09*, 173-182.

A Design Model of Emotional Body Expressions in Non-humanoid Robots

Jekaterina Novikova
University of Bath
Bath, UK
j.novikova@bath.ac.uk

Leon Watts
University of Bath
Bath, UK
l.watts@bath.ac.uk

ABSTRACT

Robotic emotional expressions could benefit social communication between humans and robots, if the cues such expressions contain were to be intelligible to human observers. In this paper, we present a design framework for modelling emotionally expressive robotic movements. The results demonstrate that such expressions can encode basic emotional information, in that the parameters of the proposed design model can convey the meaning of emotional dimensions of valence, arousal and dominance. The framework thus creates a basis for implementing a set of emotional expressions that are appropriately adapted to contexts of human-robot joint activity.

Author Keywords

Robot emotions; emotional body language; human-robot interaction; non-humanoid robots

INTRODUCTION

Robots are going to work together with people in human-robot teams in the future. In order to work successfully as a team, the members of that team should have a certain level of mutual understanding. Each team member should be able to understand the current status of the other team members: is (s)he successful in what (s)he is doing, does (s)he need help, what his/her intentions are. In human teams, this knowledge often comes from social communication and specific non-verbal behavioural cues, such as emotional expressions. However, in human-robot teams there is a lack of such a communication that often results in failures in jointly performed human-robot activities.

This paper presents a general design framework for expressing artificial emotional states in non-humanoid robots. It focuses on creating a system for designing a specific robotic body language that could help humans to better understand robot states and intentions in different situations that could occur in a simple working environment.

Previous studies have shown that people can understand emotional states expressed by robots using facial expressions [17, 26]. Less research has been conducted on the possibility

of expressing robotic emotions with sounds [24] and body language [3, 15] in humanoid robots. However, very little prior work has addressed the opportunities and challenges of creating an emotionally expressive body language for non-humanoid robots [28, 23].

There exists scepticism among researchers about the ability to reliably identify emotions from the body that has its roots in very early empirical results [13]. So why use bodies and not faces for expressing emotions? Reasons could be numerous [12] based both on a human psychology research and on the specifics of a robotics area.

1. First of all, in spite of the scepticism of recent decades, a number of behavioural experiments showed that recognition performance for bodily expressions is very similar for face and body stimuli [9].

2. Second, a major difference between facial and bodily expressions is that the latter can be recognized from a much bigger distance [31]. This potentially influences the communicative role of facial and bodily expressions, as for example facial expressions could give more information on an internal state of a person while bodily expressions direct attention to a person's actions.

3. Some emotions are more powerfully expressed and easier conveyed using a body than using a face [1]. Some previous studies showed that e.g. when viewing aggressive body pictures, observers spend the most of time looking at hands not faces [18].

4. Finally, it is not clear that robots could or even should have expressive human-like faces. Low and semi-expressive non-humanoid robots can be used more often for home-working tasks (e.g. a robotic vacuum cleaner Roomba), search-and-rescue [4], domestic assistance [33] and other tasks. The design of such robots is intended to match their purpose, e.g. designed to move across disaster zones to find and reach victims, or to be steady and move safely in order to help elderly or disabled people get out of bed and move around. Thus it's not always useful or possible for such robots to have human-like faces. However, it's still useful for them to be able to show expressive cues, as it is a fundamental social signal.

In our study we focus on emotional body language for non-humanoid robots. We propose a design framework for modelling emotionally expressive robotic movements. We hypothesize that expressions designed according to the framework help people to recognize five basic emotions implemented in a non-humanoid robot with a better-than-chance

HAI 2014, October 29–31, 2014, Tsukuba, Japan.
Copyright © 2014 ACM 978-1-4503-3035-0/14/10 ...$15.00.
http://dx.doi.org/10.1145/2658861.2658892

Parameter	Goal	Description of movement	Associated body part	Associated emotion
Approaching	Become closer to the object	Transfer weight forward	Upper body - forward	anger (12)
			Torso - forward	anger (12)
		Move limbs forward	Upper limbs - forward	interest (11)
			Step forward	anger (12)
		Move towards the object	Whole body - forward	anger (12)
	Become bigger for the object	Extend / expand yourself	Limbs - away from body	happiness (9), anger (8,11), surprise (12), fear (11)
			Head - up	happiness (3,12), pride (3,11)
Avoidance	Become further from the object	Transfer weight backward	Upper body - backward	fear, surprise (12)
			Torso - backward	fear, surprise (12)
		Move limbs backward	Upper limbs - backward	fear, surprise (12)
			Step backward	fear, surprise (12)
		Move away from the object	Whole body - backward	fear, surprise (12)
	Become smaller for the object	Reduce yourself	Limbs - close to body	sadness (8)
			Head - down	anger (3), sadness (12), shame, disgust (11)
			Upper body - down	sadness (11,12), boredom (11), shame, disgust (11)

(Modelling System → Shape)

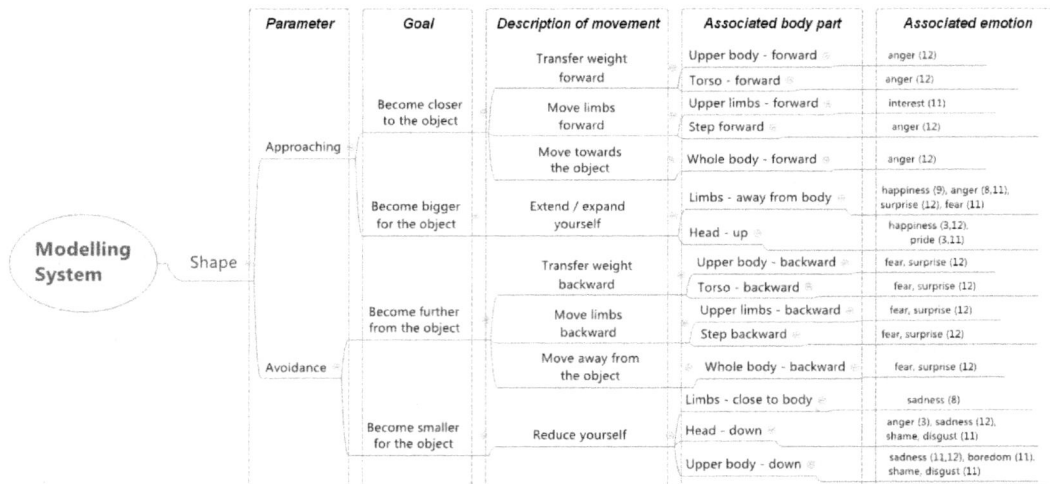

Figure 1. Shape as a category of the emotional modelling system.

recognition level. Previous psychological studies have suggested that the discrete model of basic emotions is not always enough to explain all the complicated nature of an emotional experience [8]. The dimensional approach has been argued to encompass a greater degree of subtlety that supports interpretation of emotional states [8]. In HRI research, a dimensional approach is often used as well for mapping emotional robot's expressions to a specific internal state [25]. In our study we also assume that basic emotions could not explain the whole image of how people see and understand robots. Thus we decided to analyse whether our proposed framework showed any relation between its parameters implemented in a robot and perceived emotional dimensions of valence, arousal and dominance.

The framework presented in our study is an important step in HRI research as it is expected to give other researchers a general design system for fast and easy creation of recognizable emotional expressions in different types of non-humanoid robots.

APPROACH

The expressive behaviours that have been programmed into the robot have been computationally modelled as a simplification of what is known about behaviours that are associated with human and animal emotions. The critical aspect of a robotic emotional signalling system is that the behaviours it generates must be well matched to what is familiar to people. This approach is intended to make a robot's behaviour accessible to the intuitions of a person who observes it. Thus our study focused on perhaps the most fundamental behavioural form of approach-avoidance, which is considered to be a set of universal movements of all animals [2]. Numerous studies have linked approach-avoidance motivations to emotional characteristics [16].

In our study, both approach and avoidance behaviours were analysed from the perspective of a robot's observer. In addition, we employed Laban's body expression theory [19].

Labanian theory, also used in HRI studies [27], classifies elements of expression contained in a body movement into two categories named Shape and Effort, where Shape is a feature that concerns overall posture and movement, while Effort is defined as a quality of the movement.

In order to define the Shape of emotional robot movements, we linked the emotional expression to a more general 'goal' of the expressive robot of either becoming closer to an observer by moving closer or becoming bigger without moving closer, as presented in the Figure 1. These two groups of movements although very different by their nature could both fulfil the purpose of a perspective approach from the observer's point of view and thus communicate a certain emotional cue. In order to generalize the framework of emotional expressions to different types of robots, we linked each possible movement to a specific part of a body in accordance with anatomical body planes that could be applied to both humanoid and non-humanoid bodies. Different features of Shape are organized hierarchically in Figure 1, with the highest level of abstraction on the left and the lowest - on the right. The lowest level of abstraction is a specific emotion associated with higher levels. The emotions are linked to higher level parameters based on previous research in human body language [3, 11, 18, 9, 32].

The Quality was used to capture dynamics of an expressive movement. Quality is divided into three subcategories: energy (strength of the movement), intensity (suddenness), and a flow/regularity category, which is itself subdivided into the duration of the movement, changes in tempo, frequency and trajectory of the movement. Figure 2 presents these subcategories as a part of the whole modelling system. Different features representing Quality of the movement are organized in the same hierarchical nature in the Figure 2, as the Shape's categories. The emotions on the lowest level are linked to higher level parameters based on previous research in human body language [15, 11, 18].

Modelling System → Quality

Parameter	Description	Description of movement	Associated emotion
Energy	Strength of the movement	strong	anger, joy (8)
		light	sadness (8,9)
Time / intensity	Tempo	fast	anger (1,8), fear (2)
		slow	sadness (1,8,9)
	Suddennes of the movement	sudden	anger, joy (8)
		not sudden	sadness (8)
	Duration of the movement	short	fear(2)
		long	sadness (9)
Flow / regularity	Changes in tempo	high	anger (9)
		low	
	Frequency of the movement	high	happiness (1,9)
		low	sadness (1)
	Trajectory of the movement	direct	
		indirect	happiness (9)

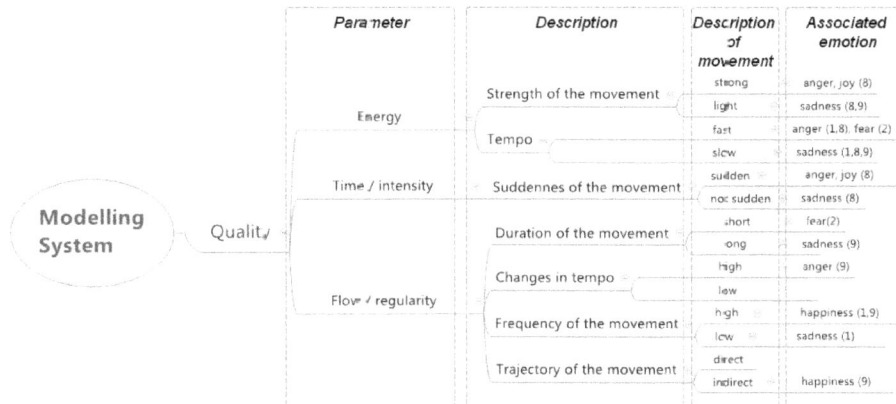

Figure 2. Quality as a category of the emotional modelling system.

METHOD

The robot we have been experimenting with is shown in Figure 3. It was implemented using Lego Mindstorms NXT and was based on a Phobot robot's design [10]. The robot had two motors that allowed it 1) to move forward and/or backwards on the surface, 2) to move its upper body part. The upper body part was constructed in such a way that the robot's hands were connected and moved together with robot's neck and eyebrows. Neck could move forward / backwards, hands could move up and down, and eyebrows could also rise up and down.

Figure 3. Lego robot used in the studies.

For programming robot's behaviours the RWTH – Mindstorms NXT Toolbox for MATLAB [1] was used. This software is a free open source product and is subject to the GPL. The RWTH toolbox was developed to control Lego Mindstorms NXT robots with Matlab via a wireless Bluetooth connection or via USB.

Use of Framework for Expressing Basic Emotions

Our first research question was formulated as follows: Do expressions designed according to the framework help people to understand five basic emotions implemented in a non-humanoid robot with a better than chance recognition level?

The independent variable here is the emotional expression presented by the robot. In our study we used five emotional expressions: afraid, angry, happy, sad and surprised. We also implemented a control expression with no emotion when a

[1] http://www.mindstorms.rwth-aachen.de/

robot doesn't react affectively to a change of the environment. The dependent variable was an emotional term, selected by participants and based on their recognition of the expressed emotion. We offered participants seven terms to select from: afraid, angry, happy, sad, surprised, not emotional, other. The measure used to obtain results for this research question was the recognition ratio $r(p_i, e_j)$ for each expression, which was calculated as defined by Eq. 1.

$$r(p_i, e_j) = \frac{N_{ij}}{N} \tag{1}$$

where p_i = expression number i , e_j = selected emotional code number j; N_{ij} = number of responses (p_i, e_j); N = total number of respondents.

Model's Parameters and Emotional Dimensions

We used an experimental study to investigate the causal relations between the parameters affective robotic expressions and a perceived emotional dimension. Due to the limitations of a robotic platform, not all the parameters of the model were implemented in our experiment. We implemented the following parameters in five affective expressions and one neutral:

1. Approach/avoidance parameter. This parameter was defined as +1 for approaching movements, -1 for avoidance and 0 for none.

2. Energy/speed parameter, defined as an average power of robot's motors per expression, where 100 (%) is a maximum.

3. Time/intensity parameter, defined as +1 when robot's expressive movements were programmed as sudden (Motors.SmoothStart = false) , and as 0 when the movements were programmed as smooth (Motors.SmoothStart = true).

4. Flow/regularity parameter, consisted of two sub-parameters:

   (a) Duration of the expression

   (b) Frequency of movement, defined as Number of hands' movements / Duration

EmotionID	Approaching / Avoidance	Energy	Intensity	Duration, sec	Frequency
1 (afraid)	-1	100	1	0.63	1.59
2 (angry)	1	75	1	2.58	0.78
3 (happy)	1	67	1	3.33	0.60
4 (sad)	mixed, not used in analysis	27	0	12.0	0.17
5 (surprised)	-1	75	1	1.0	1.00
6 (not emotional)	0	0	0	0.0	0.00

Table 1. Defining the main parameters of the framework.

EmotionID	Description	Valence / Pleasure	Arousal	Dominance
1	afraid	-1	+1	-2
2	angry	-1	+1	+2
3	happy	+2	+1	+1
4	sad	-2	-2	-1
5	surprised	0	+2	0
6	not emotional	0	0	0

Table 2. Mapping between discrete emotions and three emotional dimensions.

Context	Recorded emotional expression
Valence positive / negative	Happy, angry, neutral
Arousal positive / negative	Sad, surprised, neutral
Dominance positive / negative	Angry, afraid, neutral
Neutral	Afraid, angry, happy, sad, surprised

Table 4. A list of emotional expressions, presented to participants.

For each of the expressions the values of parameters presented in Table 1 were used as independent variables.

The values of recognized valence, arousal and dominance were used as dependent variables in our study. We used a Mehrabian model of emotions [20] to present five basic discrete emotions used in our study to a three-dimensional pleasure-arousal-dominance (PAD) space. We decided to use the PAD model firstly because it is often used to measure the affective value of facial expressions, and second because there was a validated questionnaire available.

The mapping between discrete emotions and the three dimensions was conducted based on previous studies in behavioural and experimental psychology [6, 14] and is presented in the Table 2. We scaled the values of all three dimensions to a 5-point scale [-2, 2] in order to proportion it to a 5-step Self-Assessment Manikin tool [5] we used for measuring participants' perception.

Creating Context
We used the same three-dimensional approach for creating a context for robot emotional expressions, as described in Table 3 .

As a result, we recorded a set of videos where each context was combined with a specific emotional expression of the same and the opposite level of the appropriate dimension. As a consequence, we got a list of twenty three emotional expressions of the robot in different contexts, as described in Table 4, each of the duration of about 5 sec.

A within-subject design was used to assign participants to a specific task condition, i.e. each participant was exposed to all the experimental conditions. In order to overcome limitations of a within-subject design and decrease the impact of a learning effect, the videos presented to each participant were randomized. We used a site `http://www.random.org` to randomize the conditions and ensured the two expressions of the same emotion were never presented one after another.

Participants were initially given a questionnaire containing demographic questions about age and gender, and the Toronto Empathy Questionnaire [30]. The participants were asked to sit on a chair at the table in a quiet room, watch the recorded videos and after each of them answer the questions from the prepared paper-based questionnaire. The questionnaire contained a Self-Assessment Manikin tool [5] and a forced-choice question regarding the perceived emotion of the robot. In order to produce reliable results we tried to eliminate and control biases that could appear during the experiment. In order to control biases, we prepared a written document with detailed instructions for participants and ran a pilot study before actual data collection to identify potential biases. In order to control biases caused by participants, we created task procedure that caused the least stress to the users and reassured the participants that we were testing the robot's behaviour, not them. The experimenter stayed neutral while supervising experiments thus reducing the chance to intentionally or unintentionally influence the experiment results. We controlled environment-introduced biases by making the experimental room without notable distractions. The participant was seated alone at the table and the experimenter was seating in another corner of the room in case the participant would need any help. The duration of the experiment didn't exceed thirty minutes.

One-way repeated measures ANOVA was used as a statistical test for evaluating the relation between each parameter and a perceived emotional dimension. The G*Power tool [2] was used to compute statistical power analyses for this test and an a priori calculation of a required sample size showed the need of 33 participants for our within-subject study in order to have an Effect size f= 0.3 (where err prob=0.05, Power (1- err prob)=0.95, Number of groups = 3).

RESULTS
34 people (9 females, 24 males and 1 preferred not to say) agreed to participate in a study, ranging in age from 18 to 46 (M=23.21, SD=7.42).

---

[2] `http://www.gpower.hhu.de/en.html`

Dimension of a context	Positive	Negative	Neutral
Valence	Something positive happens, e.g. robot finishes its task successfully.	Something negative happens due to e.g. robot's fault.	Nothing happens.
Arousal	Something sudden happens in the environment.	Nothing happens in the environment, robot's help isn't needed.	Nothing happens.
Dominance	Robot has no power to handle a situation as something dangerous prevents it from completing a task, e.g. a big obstacle.	Robot has a power to handle a situation as something harmless prevents it from completing a task, e.g. a small obstacle.	Nothing happens.

Table 3. Dimensional approach for creating a context for robot emotional expressions.

Expressed emotion	Recognition within appropriate context	Recognition within inappropriate context	Recognition without context
afraid	59%	35%	44%
angry	59%	48%	38%
happy	100%	34%	50%
surprised	88%	47%	47%
sad	12%	12%	9%

Table 5. Recognition ratios for presented expressions.

Recognition ratio

The values of recognition ratio for each presented expression are given in the Table 5. The recognition ratio for such emotions as surprise and happiness were the highest within an appropriate context (88% and 100% respectively). The lowest recognition ratio was for the emotion of sadness, as shown in the Table 5. An appropriate context added to an emotional expression increased the recognition rate for all the emotions, with the difference between an appropriate context and a context-neutral expression to range between 3 and 50%.

Modelling Parameters: Approach and Avoidance

We used a repeated measures ANOVA test for investigating a relation between different parameters of emotional robot expressions and a value of perceived valence, arousal and dominance. This test with a Greenhouse-Geisser correction didn't reveal any significant difference between the perception of arousal, although both approach and avoidance significantly (p<.0005) increased the perceived level of arousal comparing to a neutral robot expression. Mean scores of valence differed significantly between a neutral expression, approach and avoidance (F(1.74,57.49) = 32.399, p<.0005). The mean score of valence for the expression of avoidance was negative and was significantly lower (p<.0005) comparing it to a positive mean of valence for approach or to a neutral expression. Mean scores of dominance also differed significantly between a neutral expression, approach and avoidance (F(1.75,57.68) = 3.76, p=.035). Approach expressions determined a significantly higher positive value of a perception of dominance, avoidance a significantly lower negative value (p=.011).

We analysed an influence of different contexts on the perception of valence, arousal or dominance of an expression. The results of a repeated measures ANOVA with a Greenhouse-Geisser correction showed that positive valence of a context significantly increased (p<.05) a perceived level of valence of robot's expression, comparing to other contexts. At the same

time, positive valence of a context significantly (p<.0005) increased a perceived dominance of expressions. Negative arousal of a context significantly decreased (p<.05) a perception of arousal of an expression, although positive arousal didn't have any significant influence.

Modelling Parameters: Energy

A repeated measures ANOVA with a Greenhouse-Geisser correction revealed that the mean scores of valence for different energy levels differed statistically significantly (F(2.73,90.16) = 16.02, p<.0005), the same as the mean scores of dominance (F(2.19,72.58) = 9.94, p<.0005) and arousal (F(2.31,76.25) = 80.45, p<.0005). Expressions implemented with a high energy statistically significantly reduced the valence and dominance perception comparing to both a medium energy (p<.0005), low energy (p=.002 for valence and p=.038 for dominance) and a neutral expression (p<.0005 for valence and p=.022 for dominance). Therefore, we can conclude that a high energy of expression elicits a statistically significant reduction in the perception of valence and dominance. At the same time, higher speed representing higher energy of expressions significantly increased perceived arousal when changing from low to medium (p<.0005) and from medium to high level (p=.014).

Modelling Parameters: Intensity

A repeated measures ANOVA test with a Greenhouse-Geisser correction didn't find any statistically significant difference of perceived valence (F(1.00,33.00)=.28, p=.60) or dominance (F(1.00,33.00)=2.07, p=.16) between different intensity levels. However, higher intensity determined a significant increase in arousal perception of expression (F(1.00,33.00)=154.94, p<.0005).

Modelling Parameters: Duration

Regarding a duration of robot expressions, a repeated measures ANOVA with a Greenhouse-Geisser correction revealed a statistically significant difference in perception of both valence (F(2.72,89.74)=6.4, p<.005), arousal (F(2.54,83.87)=72.893, p<.0005) and dominance (F(2.23,73.51)=11.0,p<.0005). Valence perceived for the expression with a short duration (up to 1 sec) was significantly lower (p=.003) than valence of the expressions of a longer duration (2 to 3.3 sec). Low and medium duration of expressions (positive up to 3.3 sec) was perceived with a significantly (p<.0005) higher arousal level than a long duration of an expression (12 sec). However, any positive duration significantly (p<.0005) increased a perceived arousal score comparing to a neutral expression, which caused a negative arousal perception. Medium duration of expression caused a significantly (p<.05) higher perceived dominance level than low or high levels of expression's duration.

Modelling Parameters: Frequency

A repeated measures ANOVA with a Greenhouse-Geisser correction revealed a statistically significant difference in perception of both valence ($F(2.73, 90.16) = 16.02$, $p < .005$), arousal ($F(2.31, 76.25) = 80.45$, $p < .0005$) and dominance ($F(2.20, 72.58) = 9.94$, $p < .0005$) for different frequency levels. Valence perceived for the expression with a high frequency (1.6 movement/sec) is significantly lower ($p < .005$) than any other level of frequency (0-1 movement/sec). Any increase in frequency rate significantly increases ($p < .05$) a perception of expression's arousal. Both low and high frequency of emotional expressions corresponds to a negative dominance, which is significantly different ($p < .05$) from a positive perceived dominance of an expression of a medium frequency.

DISCUSSION

We proposed a framework for expressing and interpreting emotional movements in non-humanoid robots that is based on a behavioural form of approach-avoidance analyzed from an observer's point of view and the Labanian theory of movement analysis. We implemented the expressions of five basic emotions into a non-humanoid Lego robot. Let us examine how the study answered our research questions.

1. Do expressions designed according to the framework help people to understand five basic emotions implemented in a non-humanoid robot with a better than chance recognition level?

The results of the performed study showed that the values of recognition ratio exceeded the chance level for four recognized emotions: fear, anger, happiness and surprise. The recognition ratio for the emotion of sadness was lower than a chance level, so we can conclude that this specific emotional expression was not recognized correctly by the subjects. The reasons could be explained by comparing the current results with the results of several previous studies.

Table 6 compares the results of a recognition ratio within an appropriate context with the results of the similar previous experiments, where 1) the same robot expressed emotions in a dynamic way without a context [22], 2) the same robot expressed emotions in a static way without a context [21], 3) 70-cm tall Lego robot Feelix expressed emotions using facial features [7], 4) 23 DoF robot EDDIE expressed emotions using facial features and some animal-inspired attributes [29].

The recognition ratio for anger, happiness and surprise in our study were higher comparing to all previous experiments, as presented in the Table 6. The recognition ratio of fear in our study was higher than that of the studies with Feelix, Eddie and static pictures of the same robot, although lower than our previous study with dynamic robot expressions. The only difference in the current expression of fear with the previous study is the existence of a context. Thus we could suggest

Expressed emotion	Current study, appropriate context	Same robot, dynamic expressions, no context	Same robot, static images	Feelix	Eddie
afraid	59%	68%	42%	16%	42%
angry	59%	36%	15%	40%	54%
happy	100%	32%	36%	60%	58%
surprised	88%	57%	52%	37%	75%
sad	12%	14%	41%	70%	58%

Table 6. Comparison of our results with the results of the similar previous experiments.

that either a context for this expression was not chosen correctly, or the expression of fear is better recognized without any specific context. More experiments should be performed with this robotic expression in different contexts and without it in order to prove any of these hypotheses.

The recognition ratio of sadness was extremely low in our current study and hasn't even reached the chance level. However, a comparison with previous experiments suggests that the emotion of sadness is much better recognized from facial cues, as with Eddie and Feelix robots. On the other hand, a static picture of the expression of sadness is recognized with a significantly higher ratio than a dynamic expression. Earlier in this paper we have mentioned that some emotions are easier conveyed using a body than using a face [1]. Our results suggest that the emotion of sadness is the one which is expressed more powerfully using static facial feature and not the dynamic body language. If we focus on the specific features of the expression of sadness, we can notice that it is often described as slow, long movements of a low frequency, when limbs and head are kept close to the body, not moving. All this shows the intention to be as non-dynamic as possible during the expression of sadness. That's why, probably, the static picture represents sadness much better than any dynamic expression. However, more experiments need to be performed in order to prove this hypothesis.

In general, the results show that for such an emotional state as sadness a static facial expression fits more than dynamic bodily emotional expressions. Other emotions, especially surprise and happiness, can be expressed using a body language at least as successfully as facial features, and often even more successfully.

2. What is the relation between our framework's parameters and the recognized dimensions of valence, arousal and dominance?

The results of the study support our basic claim: the parameters of the design framework can be used as a model for implementation in a non-humanoid robot so that they can be related to perceived levels of valence, arousal and dominance. The design framework is conceptual tool that combines three dimensions of approach-avoidance, Shape and Effort. The model defines an architectural relationship between these ideas, bridging the framework and the implementation.

Arousal, according to the result of the study, was increased by both approach and avoidance behaviours, high intensity or an increase of speed of an expression, as well as an increase of frequency of limbs' movements. Decreased arousal, on the other hand, was related to a short or medium duration of an expression, low intensity and a context of a negative arousal.

The results show that it is easier to decrease a perceived valence of an expression by making it of a short duration or high speed, by increasing the frequency of limb movements to a high level, or by expressing avoidance. All the parameters mentioned make valence negative. In order to increase a perceived valence, an expression needs to be tied to a context of positive valence. An expression of approach increases a perceived valence and makes it positive.

Changing a perception of dominance by controlling parameters of our design model is similar to changing the perception of valence. As with valence, high speed of expression, high frequency of limb movements and avoidance all decrease the level of perceived dominance and make it negative (i.e. subjugated). Also as with valence, a context of positive valence tied to an expression increases the level of perceived dominance. However, the situation is different with a parameter of a duration of an expression: a medium duration of an expression increases the level of dominance and makes it positive, contrasting with duration's influence on valence.

In general, these results conform to a certain degree to what was shown by previous research that linked e.g. strong, jerk and intensive approaching movements to anger [11, 18, 9, 32], or linked a short and fast movements together with an avoidance behaviour to fear [15, 9]. Such a correspondence is suggested by making one more step and associating e.g. anger with a negative valence, high arousal and high dominance, while fear can be associated with a negative valence, high arousal and low dominance. However, such a link is not straightforward and is sometimes arguable. Our results however expand previous work by showing a direct link between the parameters of our suggested design framework and all the three emotional dimensions. Such a broader and more detailed model can help the researchers in implementing a broad range of emotions into non-humanoid robots.

CONCLUSION

This paper has presented research concerning the capacity for creating behavioural expressions of artificial emotions in human-robot interaction. As in human-human non-verbal social communication, expressive movements of the body play an important role in HRI. The goal of this research was to present and validate a general design framework for expressing artificial emotional states in non-humanoid robots. We proposed a design framework for modelling emotionally expressive robotic movements.

We posed two main research questions: Do expressions designed according to the proposed framework help people to understand five basic emotions implemented in a non-humanoid robot? What is the relation between our framework's parameters and the emotional dimensions recognized by human observers? We investigated these questions using

an exploratory study, where participants observed different expressions implemented in a non-humanoid robot according to the proposed design framework.

The results from this study demonstrate that the emotions of fear, anger, happiness and surprise are recognized on a better-than-chance level when implemented according to our proposed framework and expressed by a non-humanoid robot within an appropriate context. The results suggest that the emotion of sadness is more powerfully expressed using static facial features, not by dynamic body language. In addition, our results show that the parameters of our suggested model are related to the perceived level of valence, arousal and dominance. Thus, our model can be used by HRI researchers as a basis for implementing of a set of emotions in non-humanoid robots. It's important to consider the context of joint human-robot activity when deciding how to map from the VAD dimensional space into the behavioural space. The activity context will condition a person's ability to infer the meaning of a robot's behaviour: it cannot be understood in isolation from the task it is performing, or the human-robot joint activity in which it is engaged.

Future work will test the proposed design framework with other types of non-humanoid robots, as well as with humanoid robots. We also plan to analyse an effect of expressing artificial emotion on the efficiency of a joint human-robot activity.

ACKNOWLEDGMENTS
We thank all the volunteers and all publications support and staff, who wrote and provided helpful comments on previous versions of this document. Our thanks to Nova Novikova for her help with recording robot expressions for the study. The work was supported by a PhD studentship from the the University of Bath, UK.

REFERENCES
1. Aviezer, H., Trope, Y., and Todorov, A. Body cues, not facial expressions, discriminate between intense positive and negative emotions. *Science 338*, 6111 (2012), 1225–1229.

2. Baron-Cohen, S. Theory of mind and face-processing: How do they interact in development and psychopathology?

3. Beck, A., Stevens, B., Bard, K. A., and Cañamero, L. Emotional body language displayed by artificial agents. *ACM Transactions on Interactive Intelligent Systems (TiiS) 2*, 1 (2012), 2.

4. Bethel, C. L., and Adviser-Murphy, R. R. Robots without faces: non-verbal social human-robot interaction.

5. Bradley, M. M., and Lang, P. J. Measuring emotion: the self-assessment manikin and the semantic differential. *Journal of behavior therapy and experimental psychiatry 25*, 1 (1994), 49–59.

6. Broekens, J., and Brinkman, W.-P. Affectbutton: a method for reliable and valid affective self-report.

International Journal of Human-Computer Studies 71, 6 (2013), 641–667.

7. Canamero, L. D., and Fredslund, J. How does it feel? emotional interaction with a humanoid lego robot. In *Proc. of American Association for Artificial Intelligence Fall Symposium, FS-00-04* (2000).

8. Coppin, G., and Sander, D. Contemporary theories and concepts in the psychology of emotions. *Emotion-Oriented Systems*, 1–31.

9. Coulson, M. Attributing emotion to static body postures: Recognition accuracy, confusions, and viewpoint dependence. *Journal of nonverbal behavior 28*, 2 (2004), 117–139.

10. Cramer, H., Kemper, N., Zwijnenburg, A., and de Rooij, O. Phobot: Hri'08 student design competition winner.

11. Crane, E. A., and Gross, M. M. Effort-shape characteristics of emotion-related body movement. *Journal of Nonverbal Behavior 37*, 2 (2013), 91–105.

12. De Gelder, B. Why bodies? twelve reasons for including bodily expressions in affective neuroscience. *Philosophical Transactions of the Royal Society B: Biological Sciences 364*, 1535 (2009), 3475–3484.

13. Ekman, P. Differential communication of affect by head and body cues. *Journal of personality and social psychology 2*, 5 (1965), 726.

14. Hamann, S. Mapping discrete and dimensional emotions onto the brain: controversies and consensus. *Trends in cognitive sciences 16*, 9 (2012), 458–466.

15. Haring, M., Bee, N., and Andre, E. Creation and evaluation of emotion expression with body movement, sound and eye color for humanoid robots. In *RO-MAN, 2011 IEEE*, IEEE (2011), 204–209.

16. Harmon-Jones, E. Anger and the behavioral approach system. *Personality and Individual Differences 35*, 5 (2003), 995–1005.

17. Hashimoto, T., Hitramatsu, S., Tsuji, T., and Kobayashi, H. Development of the face robot saya for rich facial expressions. In *SICE-ICASE, 2006. International Joint Conference*, IEEE (2006), 5423–5428.

18. Karg, M., Hoey, J., Samadani, A.-A., Gorbet, R., Kulic, D., et al. Body movements for affective expression: A survey of automatic recognition and generation. *IEEE Transactions on Affective Computing* (2013), 1.

19. Laban, R., and Ullmann, L. The mastery of movement. boston: Plays. *Inc. LabanThe Mastery of Movement* (1971).

20. Mehrabian, A. *Basic dimensions for a general psychological theory: Implications for personality, social, environmental, and developmental studies.* Oelgeschlager, Gunn & Hain Cambridge, MA, 1980.

21. Novikova, J., and Watts, L. Artificial emotions to assist social coordination in hri. In *Workshop on Embodied Communication of Goals and Intentions at the International Conference on Social Robotics (ICSR) 2013* (2013).

22. Novikova, J., and Watts, L. Towards artificial emotions to assist social coordination in hri. *International Journal of Social Robotics* (submitted).

23. Novikova, J., Watts, L., and Bryson, J. J. The role of emotions in inter-action selection. *Interaction Studies 15*, 2 (2014), 216–223.

24. Read, R., and Belpaeme, T. People interpret robotic non-linguistic utterances categorically. In *Proceedings of the 8th ACM/IEEE international conference on Human-robot interaction*, IEEE Press (2013), 209–210.

25. Saerbeck, M., and Bartneck, C. Perception of affect elicited by robot motion. In *Proceedings of the 5th ACM/IEEE international conference on Human-robot interaction*, IEEE Press (2010), 53–60.

26. Saldien, J., Goris, K., Vanderborght, B., Vanderfaeillie, J., and Lefeber, D. Expressing emotions with the social robot probo. *International Journal of Social Robotics 2*, 4 (2010), 377–389.

27. Sharma, M., Hildebrandt, D., Newman, G., Young, J. E., and Eskicioglu, R. Communicating affect via flight path exploring use of the laban effort system for designing affective locomotion paths. In *Human-Robot Interaction (HRI), 2013 8th ACM/IEEE International Conference on*, IEEE (2013), 293–300.

28. Singh, A., and Young, J. E. Animal-inspired human-robot interaction: a robotic tail for communicating state. In *HRI* (2012), 237–238.

29. Sosnowski, S., Bittermann, A., Kuhnlenz, K., and Buss, M. Design and evaluation of emotion-display eddie. In *Intelligent Robots and Systems, 2006 IEEE/RSJ International Conference on*, IEEE (2006), 3113–3118.

30. Spreng, R. N., McKinnon, M. C., Mar, R. A., and Levine, B. The toronto empathy questionnaire: Scale development and initial validation of a factor-analytic solution to multiple empathy measures. *Journal of personality assessment 91*, 1 (2009), 62–71.

31. Walk, R., and Walters, K. Perception of the smile and other emotions of the body and face at different distances. In *Bulletin of the Psychonomic Society*, vol. 26, PSYCHONOMIC SOC INC 1710 FORTVIEW RD, AUSTIN, TX 78704 (1988), 510–510.

32. Wallbott, H. G. Bodily expression of emotion. *European journal of social psychology 28*, 6 (1998), 879–896.

33. Yamazaki, K., Ueda, R., Nozawa, S., Kojima, M., Okada, K., Matsumoto, K., Ishikawa, M., Shimoyama, I., and Inaba, M. Home-assistant robot for an aging society. *Proceedings of the IEEE 100*, 8 (2012), 2429–2441.

Signaling Trouble In Robot-To-Group Interaction. Emerging Visitor Dynamics With A Museum Guide Robot.

Raphaela Gehle
Interactional Linguistics and
Human Robot Interaction
Bielefeld University
raphaela.gehle@uni-
bielefeld.de

Karola Pitsch
Interactional Linguistics and
Human Robot Interaction
Bielefeld University
karola.pitsch@uni-bielefeld.de

Sebastian Wrede
Cognitive Systems
Engineering
Bielefeld University
swrede@cor-lab.uni-
bielefeld.de

ABSTRACT

Once a museum guide robot is deployed in the real world, it is faced with the difficulty to deal with user utterances within a noisy environment. We present explorative analysis of the ways in which visitors signal trouble on a multimodal level when they have difficulties in understanding the robot. Such moments of trouble are investigated in the context of robot-to-group situations. Analysis will give insights into the visitors conduct at moments of trouble in robot-to-single-user and robot-to-group interactions. In a limited data set, we found that members of a group show internal gaze coordination between each other when trouble occurs due to the robot's inadequate behavior. Implications will be drawn for further developing the interactional capabilities of an autonomous robot system to be attentive and responsive to the users' needs.

Author Keywords

multi-party; repair; user behavior; qualitative analysis

ACM Classification Keywords

H.5.m. Information Interfaces and Presentation (e.g. HCI): Miscellaneous

INTRODUCTION

Once robot systems are deployed in the real world they are faced with a range of insecurities. They not only have to orient themselves in a meaningful world [14] and to engage with multiple unknown, moving interaction partners [1], but they also have to deal with the users' verbal utterances which might be hard to understand in a noisy environment. In this vein, when a robotic museum guide presents some information to visitors it is faced with a range of verbal comments the visitors make both to the robot and to each other. To be attentive to the users' conduct, the robot would need to interpret whether visitors give positive feedback or might have a question about the explanation. On the level of utterances, it would be beneficial to know - for multiple user situations -

Figure 1. Nao as museum guide in multi-party interaction

whether they talk to each other because they would disengage from the interaction or rather attempt to clarify some aspect. Set aside improvements in speech recognition capabilities, it would be beneficial if the system could - without necessarily understanding the users' utterances - have hypotheses about the nature or interactional function of users' utterances.

In this paper, we explore - on the basis of a video corpus of human-robot-interaction in a real-world museum site - instances of the users' verbal utterances during a robotic guide's presentation. Starting from a general quantitative overview of user utterances, we focus on two particular questions using sequential qualitative micro-analysis:

(1) How do visitors *signal trouble* in understanding on a multimodal level and at which moment do they do it? (2) How do the visitors *deal with trouble* occuring due to a robot's non-understanding of their utterances in a robot-to-group situation? - Analysis will give first insights into visitor conduct at moments of trouble in robot-to-single-user and robot-to-group interactions. Implications will be drawn for further developing the interactional capabilities of an autonomous robot system to be attentive and responsive to the users' needs as part of a larger interest in our research ([9][13]).

BACKGROUND

The scenario of a robotic museum guide offers several degrees of scalable complexity for exploring human-robot-interaction. A robotic museum guide not only presents information to visitors, but also has to coordinate talk and gesture ([15]), attempt to open the interaction ([8]), recognize multiple visitors and judge about their engagement ([3]), shape their ways of participating ([7]), orient them in the environment ([6] [9]) and attempt itself to navigate in space ([1]). Focusing the field of verbal conduct, Yamazaki et al. [16] used involvement questions to increase visitors' engagement and actively direct their focus of attention in a museum setting. They arrange a question strategy - inspired by analysis of a human museum tour guide - where a first utterance prepares the visitors by directing their attention towards an essential detail and directing a follow-up question [16]. Kobayashi et al. [4] aim to prevent from choosing an answerer who would feel uncomfortable to be selected. Thus, after asking a question they monitor the consequent gaze behavior of the users to detect who is likely to answer. They also consider to preconfigure who is to answer with the help of looking at a particular user [4]. Nevertheless, if providing for user utterances, a robotic system has to classify and deal with the users' verbal reactions.

Insecurity of speech recognition reveals a central issue for developing a robotic system in the real-world. To increase robustness Hüwel and Wrede [2] attempt to integrate multimodal information, such as gestures. Krahmer et al. [5] aim to detect whether trouble is marked verbally without understanding the exact semantic information. They disambiguate users verbal "go back"-signals from "go on"-signals towards a spoken dialog system. They measured the length of utterances and found that humans tend to use the longer form when they mark that something goes wrong [5].

Inspite improvements in the perceptual capabilities in robotics, further-reaching strategies for recognizing and dealing with (potentially occuring) trouble are required. Süssenbach et al. ([13]) developed repair mechanisms for a robotic fitness companion, where an attentive system monitors several parameters of user behavior during an indoor-cycling session and provide support tailored to the user's action. On their way towards a responsive system Pitsch and Wrede ([9] developed suggestions for repair behavior to be attentive to the users' focus of attention and the context of establishing co-orientation in a museum guide setting. Although recent work has been unertaken in the field of HRI/HAI that focuses on repair in a range of settings, characteristics and challenges of repair in multi-party situations and emerging group dynamics have to be considered.

As a first step analysis of human interaction could serve as inspiration for structures robotic systems could use to deal with user utterances. In general, trouble in interaction between humans leads to a clarifiction requests (= initiation of repair, e.g. [11]), which occur even during ongoing speech of one participant. It is helpful to consider a speaker's talk as consecutive units, seperated by slots of silence where other participants have the chance to remark the need of clarification ("other-initiated repair"). Each repair initiation delivers information for helping to localize the trouble source. The realization of repair in human-human interactions gets proceeded subsequently [11].

DESIGN OF ROBOT CONDUCT: PROVIDING FOR USER UTTERANCES

A humanoid NAO robot was deployed as guide in an arts museum (see also [7] and [9]). We conducted two studies in which the robot was set up to (1) get in contact with visitors, (2) provide information about paintings and artists, and (3) finally close the encounter. At specific moments, it was set up to monitor the visitor's position in space and/or to check their verbal utterances for "yes/no"-answers to exhibit some basic reactive conduct. Despite the limits of the robot's interactional capabilities, the setup enables us to gain empirical insights into the ways in which users interpret the robot's conduct, how they behave towards the system and to pinpoint issues that need addressing for further developing the system towards an autonomous system attentive to the users conduct and engagement ([7][10]).

With regard to the users' verbal utterances during the three phases, we systematically provided for moments at which the robot's conduct would make user utterances relevant and thus structurally expectable, (e.g. after greetings, questions, etc). Additionally, there are moments at which user utterances *could* relevantly occur, but are not particularly provided for, such as backchannels, clarification requests etc. To investigate user conduct in such situations, the design of the robot conduct was specified in two subsequent studies.

Occasions for backchannels & "yes"/"no"-answers

In a **first study** ([7][9][10]), during which the robot provided information for about 2-3 minutes, the robot's conduct contained a set of 16 utterances providing information about the exhibits. Each utterance was followed by a short period of silence (for details about the robot's referential practices within these utterances, see [9]), during which visitors could provide backchannels if they wanted to engage with the robot. During the interaction, the robot additionally addressed several **closed questions** to engage visitors, which made a "yes"/"no"-answer relevant (1. *"Should I tell you something about this painting?"*, 2. *"Do you know Dokoupil?"*, 3. *"Have you seen the hole in the picture by Walter Dahn over there?"*, Fig. 2).

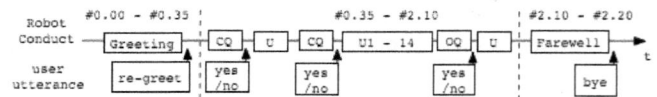

Figure 2. Study 1: Robot's utterance design

While the robot was able to monitor the visitors' position in space and orient its head to the nearest one, it did not dispose of auditory perception. Initially, the duration of silence periods were pre-designed and their duration ranges between 1.9 and 10.7 seconds depending on the system's processing power.

Increased complexity of robot questions

In a subsequent **second study**, the global structure of (1) opening, (2) explanation, and (3) closing was maintained. The interaction was extended to about five minutes during which the robot gave information about three paintings and walked across a table to assume different positions. This time, the questions which the robot would address to the visitors were more structurally differentiated. In addition to the closed questions asking for a "yes"/"no"-answer (study 1), also open questions were included (Fig. 3). We wanted to explore, if visitors that might not reply in the first instance, could be encouraged if the robot reformulated the question. This resulted in a structure of a first question followed by a short pause (1.7 sec.) and a second question (reformulating the first one). The overall structure contains the following question types:

(I) *Single closed questions (cf. study 1):* "Should I tell you something about these pictures?", "Would you like me to explain a third painting to you?"

(II) *Combined questions:* **(a) Type A: closed - closed:** "Do you see the yellow-white work of art ight at the top?" (pause) "What do you think, is that a painting at all?". - Visitors were expected to answer (if they choose to answer) "yes/no" for both questions. **(b) Type B: closed - open:** "Do you see the painting here behind me at the top left?" (pause) "What do you recognize?". - Visitors were expected to answer "yes/no" for the first question, and provide a free answer for the second one. This structure is comparable to Yamazaki's [17] concept of involvement questions as described in chapter 2. The first part orients users to the essential detail and prepares them for answering the second question. **(c) Type C: open - open:** *"How does the picture look like?"* (pause) *"What do you think does it represent?"*

We combined two open questions, where the content of the

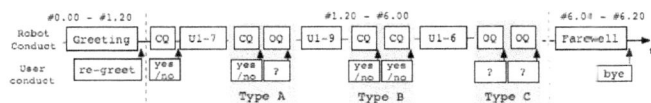

Figure 3. Study 2: Robot's utterance design

answers was highly expectable but the structure could be variable. The first question enables free utterance structures, whereas the second one could lead to a repetition or reformulation (e.g. simplification). Additionally, visitors who did not answer the first question, could be motivated to answer the second one. Both questions inquire the same answer (*"How does the picture look like?"* - *"What do you think does it represent?"*). Finally, the robot gives the answer by itself (*"Many consider it as a fried egg."*), regardless if a visitor did so anyway.

ROBOT SYSTEM

As the robotic platform should provide intuitive access for lay-users and be robust enough to be deployed in the real world, a humanoid NAO robot (Aldebaran, version 3+) was used. In both studies, the robot was set up to look at the visitors once they entered the room, to greet them and to ask whether they would be interested in some information about the paintings. Then it would deliver information about several paintings in the room using pre-defined talk and gestures. This explanation lasted for about 2-3 minutes (study 1) or about 5 minutes (study 2), and required visitors - if they were following the robots explanation - at moments to orient to different locations in the room as well as, at other moments, to look at the robot. The robot's verbal behavior provides for users' speech in expactable ways (re-greet, goodbye, "yes"/"no"), at other moments (esp. silence

between two robot utterances) the users get the chance to backchannel which is tentative.

In **study 1**, the robot was positioned on a small table in the corner of a room sized 5 x 6 meters (cf. [7][9][10]). During the explanation the robot was rather static, only moving the head and the right arm. The robot's perception was enhanced with a VICON motion capture system, which enabled the robot to show a certain degree of interactivity Therefore, participants had to wear specifically marked hats to track their position. The system was set to look at approaching visitors during the opening and afterwards look at the nearest visitor at pre-defined moments.

In **study 2**, the robot was placed on a table (1,20 x 2 meters, 0,7 meters high) at one side of a room sized 14 x 6 meters. For the explanation of several paintings, the robot assumed three different positions on the table between which it walked autonomously using tracking-markers in the four corners of the table. For visual perception we used the robot's internal cameras to track visitors during the opening phase as well as after the robot moved its head towards paintings (to orient visitors) or the installed tracking markers in the table corners (to navigate). During this study, the robot was provided with basic speech recognition capabilities allowing to detect "yes/no" answers after closed questions, the content of utterances after open questions could not be detected. We enhanced the users' utterances by close-talk microphones. To provide for multi-party interactions, we used three microphones at the same time.

STUDIES AND DATA

We conducted two explorative studies subsequently (study 1: 2010, study 2: 2011 - with more complex conduct, see section "Design of Robot Conduct"), where a basic system was deployed in the real world. In both studies the humanoid robot NAO was set up as tour guide in the local arts museum (Kunsthalle Bielefeld).

Studies

For **study 1**, the robot was deployed on seven days, for about six consecutive hours each day (cf. [7][9][10]). Ordinary visitors were asked if they were willing to participate and, if so, to wear hats equipped with markers. For **study 2**, the robot was deployed on four days during a science festival, where adults and children participated as uninformed users of the robot. They were largely attracted to the museum due to the robot appearance.

In both studies, visitors were informed that they would be video-recorded, but they did not get any information about the nature of the study nor the function of the equipment (markers/microphones) or how to handle the robot. Also, they could disengage and walk away at any time, and there was always the possibility of other visitors entering or leaving the room. The HRI trial was recorded with several HD video cameras, which were placed in the corners of the room. This way, we obtained recordings of the users talk, behavior in space, gestures, head orientation, gaze and facial expressions. At both studies, each participant was asked to fill in a short questionnaire after the trial (study 2 included a section with - partially misleading - questions about the content of the robot's explanations to test if the visitors catched the information provided by the robot).

Data

For quantitative analysis we used all cases, where the system runs without major technical issues and where at least one user starts to interact with the robot. Data from comparing conditions (where the robot was present but not interacting) was excluded. From **study 1** we thereby gain a subcorpus of 75 cases, for **study 2** a subcorpus of 37 cases. For qualitative analysis we consider two exemplary cases - one of each study.

ANALYTICAL METHOD

To explore the users' verbal conduct towards the robot system, quantitative and qualitative analysis is combined. This way, we are able to provide both - a general understanding of the frequency of user utterances and to gain new explorative insights into user conduct as a basis to further develop the system. *Quantification* leads to an overview of the users reactions on the designed structural moments of relevance (see section "Design of robot conduct"). Two independend coders did videobased annotations of the robot's and the users' behavior (Elan). These events were listed in Excel, related to the structural moments where the robot utterances of type A - C happen. Each case is included, regardless whether an answer occurs or not. In multi-party situations we do not differentiate whether one participant or more used speech as long the designed structural robot utterance leads to some verbal reaction of the user(s).

To gain new insights into the dynamics and emerging sequential structures of a setting in which a robot addresses multiple participants, explorative *qualitative analysis* is carried out. Using methods from Conversation Analysis (CA) [12] enables us to investigate - on a small data set - the interrelationship between robots and the visitors' multimodal actions and how they respond to each other on a structural level. We investigate the users perception and understanding of the robots actions and to which extent they constitute - for the participant - a meaningful, relevant action occurring at an appropriate moment ('member's perspective').

QUANTIFICATION: ROBOT MANAGES TO PROVIDE FOR USER UTTERANCES

With the help of quantification we found, on the one hand, that user utterances occur during the slots where the robot's conduct made user answers relevant (if they choose to interact with the robot this way) (see table 1). On the other hand we find user utterances which were not specifically provided for by the design of the robot's conduct. **For study 1**, we considered our subcorpus of 75 cases. With the help of simple descriptive statistics we find that users tend to verbally react after the designed structural moments for providing user utterances. Table 1 shows that 64% of the users utter a re-greet and 56% react on the farewell. Even more verbal reactions occur after the robot asks a closed question (84% an 32%). Additionally, the users also produced speech after the robot's utterances that were not constructed for providing user utterances. Considering the

cases, where users address clarification requests towards the robot, we find verbal requesting in 18 cases, that differ in their function: 1) acoustic non-understanding of robot utterances 2) content-related requests 3) requests in terms of orientation 4) others (e.g. *"can you fight"*, see table 2).

Table 1: User utterances at pre-designed moments
Total of subject groups (study 1): 75

Greeting	48 (64%)
Farewell	42 (56%)

Closed Questions	
Question	Answers
"may i tell you something about this picture"	65 (87%)
"do you know dokoupil"	65 (87%)
"have you seen the hole in the picture by walter dahn over there"	24 (32%)

Particularly interesting are those five cases (see table 2: acoustic clarification request towards NAO), in which a user addresses a clarification request towards the robot due to acoustic non-understanding. Four of which are addressed after the same robot's utterance (*"the speciality of this group is their dilettantism"*) and provide the same function (see table 2). To understand the emerging structures of these requests, we focus on one of these cases in qualitative micro-analysis (see chapter "Qualitative case analysis I").

Table 2: User questions (study 1)
Total of cases including requests: 18

Type of Request	towards NAO	towards others
Clarification Request (acoustic)	5 (28%)	3 (17%)
Clarification Request (content-related)	0 (0%)	1 (6%)
Clarification Request (Orientation)	6 (33%)	2 (12%)
Other Questions (others)	2 (12%)	n/a

For study 2, we also use the approach of considering the designed structural moments of the interaction, where user utterances are provided by the robot's more complex behavior consisting of several steps (as described in section "Design of Robot Conduct"). Our observations in the data of study 1 gets supported: table 3 shows that 84% of the users in our second study reacted verbally on closed questions of the robot. Type A question structures (closed - closed) entail 76% of user answers, 62% of type B questions (closed - open) and 65% of type C questions (open - open) are answered verbally by at least one user. Particularly interesting are the reactions on the Type C question structure, because variable reactions are possible. Table 3 shows, that the majority of answers occur after the first open question (58%).

Table 3: User utterances after combined questions

Total of subject groups (study 2): 37

Greeting	16 (43%)
Farewell	27 (73%)

Closed Questions - single	
"may i tell you something about these pictures"	31 (84%)
"do you want me to explain a third painting to you"	31 (84%)

Type A: closed - closed questions Cases with answers: 28 (76%) "do you see the yellow-white work of art right at the top" "what do you think is that a painting at all"	
no answer / answer	6 (16%)
answer / no answer	5 (14%)
answer / answer	16 (43%)

Type B: closed - open questions Cases with answers: 23 (62%) "do you see the here behind me at the top left" - "what do you recognize"	
no answer / answer	10 (27%)
answer / no answer	4 (17%)
answer / answer	7 (19%)

Type C: open - open questions "how does it look like" - "what does it represent" Cases with answers: 24 (65%)	
no answer / answer	14 (58%)
answer / no answer	4 (17%)
answer / answer	6 (25%)

We even find six cases in which users answer the second question (see table 3: type C - answer / answer), regardless of the fact, that they (most likely) already gave the required answer. To get an insight view how this repetition appears (if the user does not change his mind), we do a qualitative case analysis and describe the interactional structures emerging during this phase to deal with the type C structure (see section "Qualitative case analysis II").

QUALITATIVE ANALYSIS I: SIGNALING TROUBLE IN UNDERSTANDING

The quantitative overview of the users' utterances in **study 1** revealed four cases (table 2), in which users signalled non-understanding and adressed a clarification request to the robot. To gain a better understanding about how and when users signal trouble in understanding on a multimodal level, we firstly present a sequential micro-analysis of *one* case and then proceed to systematically consider our (small) collection of cases. In particular, we will show the moment at which users appear to address their clarification requests and the extent to which they are organized in a multimodal manner. The robot's lack of responding to the clarification requests has impact on the engagement of users and leads to visually perceivable effects on the interactional dynamics.

Case Analysis

Consider the following case (VP132), in which two visitors (V1: male, V2: female) are listening to the robot's

explanation since about one minute. They appear to be engaged in the activity, orienting to the robot (V1) and/or following its orientational hints to the painting (V2) (Fig. 4a).

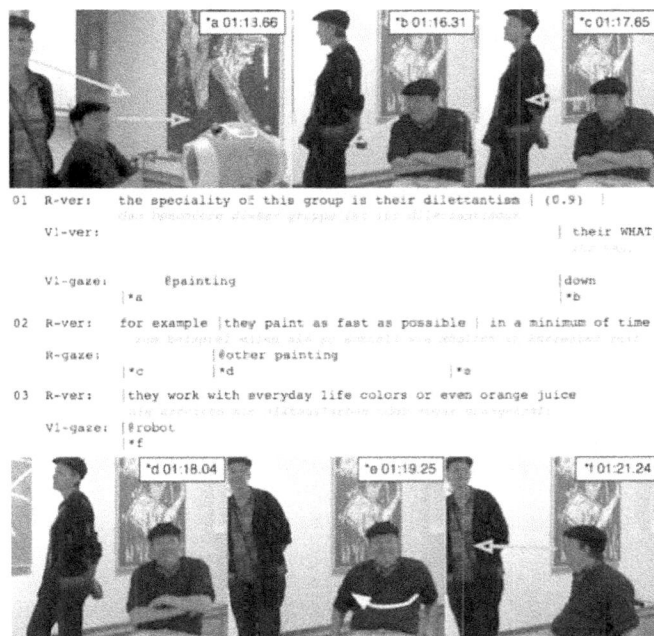

Figure 4. Case Analysis I: Dealing with trouble - step1: Marking trouble at a special structural moment of the interaction, step 2: Strategy for marking, step 3: Consequences on engagement level

a. Signaling trouble *immediately after* **the robot's utterance.** When the robot - being oriented with its head to V1 - produces the utterance *"the speciality of this group is their dilettantism"*, V1 signals trouble in understanding. After 0.9 seconds of silence he asks with rising intonation *"their WHAT,"* and thereby initates a repair on the last word of the robot's utterance (*"dilettantism"*) (see Fig. 4, line 01). In repeating the article *"their"* and attaching a "wh"-question he specifies his repair (cf. [11]). He indicates that he understood some parts of the previous utterances and that there is a lack of understanding related to the last word of the utterance.

b. Signaling trouble as a multimodal activity (speech, gaze, posture). In parallel to his verbal question, V1 bends forward to the robot and directs his head (gaze) to the floor (see Fig. 4b). He thus not only signals trouble in understanding verbally, but also organizes his request for clarification (therefore: an initiation of repair) as a multimodal event consisting of specific changes in gaze, body posture, speech and prosody.

c. Robot's lack of repair & user's temporary disengagement. With this request for repair V1 opens a side-sequence for repair. It is distinctive for this kind of interactional meaningful activity, that one participant initiates a repair, where the other is in charge of realising it. From that moment on, the robot is responsible for fulfilling the next action: repairing (e.g. repeating) the indicated trouble in the previous utterance. V1 maintains his body position and gaze direction for the robot's next actions. Against expectations, the robot continues with the explanations.

V1 remains oriented to the robot until it begins its next utterance (Fig. 4c), i.e. the moment where the repair action would be expectable. However, after the robot has produced "for example" (Fig. 4, line 02), V1 reacts by gazing away - potentially to another picture - smiles and changes his position (Fig. 4d and 4e) and thereby marks the robot's unconvenient behavior. For V1, it seems like the robot ignores his request for repair. To deal with this situation he distances himself from the interaction with the robot for several seconds.

d. Delayed return to the robot's explanation. The robot does not complete the side-sequence and V1 is not able to complete it either (see Fig. 4). This unpriviledged situation challenges V1 to deal with it. His reaction of temporary disengagement delays the moment of returning to the explanations. After this temporary state of disengagement he re-establishes his interactional connection to the robot in his role as listener (Fig. 4f). During the delay, V1 is at risk to miss parts of the robot's ongoing explanations. Temporary disengagement could possibly result in further trouble and thereby have impacts on the ongoing interaction.

Parallel cases and systematization

Considering further examples in our corpus (study 1), in four other cases visitors experience *and* verbally signal problems. We found 12 cases of signaling trouble, four of which occur with the same robot utterance (Fig. 5). This number of parallel cases might appear small from a quantitative point of view, yet the particular design of the study and robot system might have discouraged visitors from attempting to rely on sophisticated verbal cues as they were asked to wear specifically marked hats but no microphones, and as they have already experienced the system for about a minute. Given that signaling trouble and ways of dealing with it is a genuine building block of social interaction, this subset of cases provides a relevant basis for *explorative* analysis. In what follows, we focus on

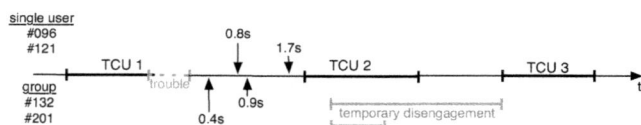

Figure 5. Timing of repair initiation, subcorpus study 1

instances of trouble with the same robot utterance as in the case analysis presented above. In these four trials (Fig. 5), we find that visitors verbally signal trouble in similar ways ("*sorry what*", "*the what*", "*their what*", "*the who*"). Also their timing is consistent, i.e. in the silence which occurs directly after the robot's utterance (Fig. 5). However, with regard to their bodily conduct, a difference between robot-to-single-user and robot-to-group interaction appears. Both individual visitors appear to not show any visible confusion after the robot's failure to engage in a repair sequence, while in another case of signaling trouble in robot-to-group-interaction the same phenomenon appears as in case analysis I (table 2). While we don't suggest for this difference to be significant, it opens up an interesting perspective for subsequent research

focusing on group conduct in situations of dealing with trouble. In particular, the users' disengagement after trouble in a group situation suggests that a disengaged visitor might miss relevant information from the explanation (Fig. 5, 'TCU 2'), which could lead to further trouble, which then would require more effort to deal with.

Implications of qualtitative case analysis (study 1)
From this exploratory analysis we get insights about dealing with trouble in HRI. We find first suggestion for potential difference between robot-to-single and robot-to-group situations. In group situations, participants show effects of trouble on a multimodal level: they use both verbal means and changes in head orientation and body posture to signal trouble. If we were able to robustly identify the users' multimodal actions in further data we could (1) establish a guideline for *detecting trouble* based on the participants signaling of trouble (with gaze, posture and speech) and related to visitor engagement. (2) *Detect the consequences* of unappropriate robot behavior in terms of disengagement and use them to trigger a suitable emergency strategy.

QUALITATIVE ANALYSIS II: USER'S ANSWER AND EMERGING GROUP DYNAMICS
The general quantitative overview of the users' utterances in study 2 reveals that there are six cases, in which the users answer both questions in the type C (open-open) question design (in which pause length were not interactionally established, but pre-defined). These instances are particularly interesting because both questions address the same topic. Hence the question arises, under what circumstances a participant would give the same answer twice or reformulate it. First, we conduct a case analysis based on video recordings to reveal the detailed ways in which a member of a visitor group deals with the robot's non-understanding of the answers he gave. We then evaluate the emerging group effects and in a second step we consider the collection of comparable cases from the corpus.

Case Analysis
We consider a case (VP03), in which a group of four visitors (V1: boy, V2: girl, V3: female adult, V4: male adult) are about to listen to the robot since about 3.30 minutes. They appear to be engaged in the activity, listening to the robot's explanations and its suggestions of orientation. We enter the scene at a moment where all members of the group orient to the robot, whereas the robot's head is directed to V2 (Fig. 6a). **a. Answering the robot's questions.** During the explanations about a second artwork the robot asks "*how does the picture look like*" (# 03:39.10, see Fig. 6, line 01). During this open question, V1 looks at the painting and afterwards to the robot. The robot finishes the question, steadily looking at V2 (Fig. 6a). After 1.14 seconds of silence, V1 answers "*like a fried egg*" (Fig. 6, line 02), although there is no mutual gaze situation between the robot and V1 (see Fig. 6a). **b. Gaze to other group members. Signaling overlap-trouble.** Before the end of V1s utterance the robot interrupts with "*what do you think does it represent*" (see Fig. 6, line 02). From an interactional perspective, the robot (a) behaves unpolitely and

(b) ignores that the conditional relevance already has been served. V1 reacts on the unpreferred robot behavior by explicitly looking to V3 during the robot's interruption. Nevertheless, V1 reacts on the additional conditional relevance that emerges with the robot's utterance. He repeats his previous answer in a short form *"a fried egg"* (Fig. 6, line 03) addressed to the robot (Fig. 6c).

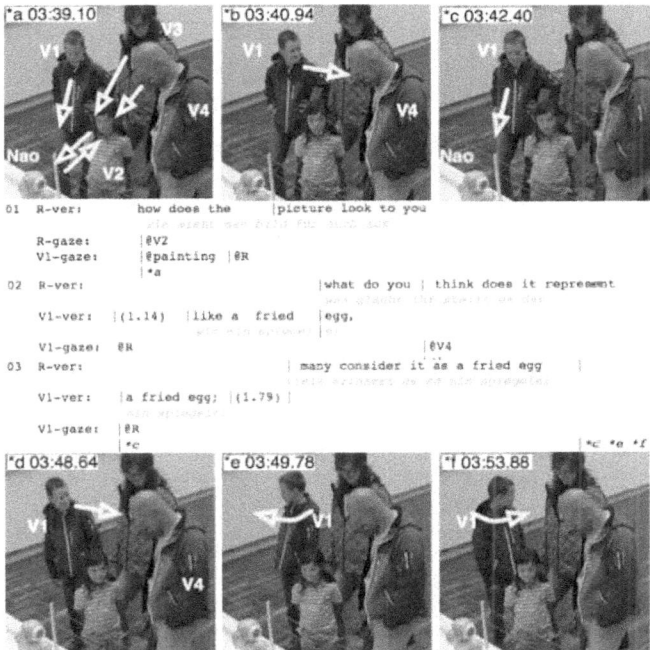

Figure 6. Case Analysis: Dealing with trouble due to pre-defined structures of robot's talk.

c. Temporary disengagement. After 1.79 seconds, the robot says *"many consider it as a fried egg"* (Fig. 6, line 3). The robot does not clearly ratify or refer to V1s answer and the pause appears quite long (cf. V1 himself reacted in a time-frame of about 0.9 to 1.14 seconds). The robot does not show, that V1s interactional work had any influence on the robot's actions. This leads to salient gaze behavior of V1. During the ongoing interaction, where the other group members stay oriented to the robot, V1 retires from the interaction. He rotates his upper body and looks at two study cams in the (far away) corners of the room Fig. 6e, f). V1 distances himself from the interaction with the robot (cf. case analysis I).

Parallel cases and systematization

At the moments of type C questions (study 2), we found that there were seven cases in which participants give the right answer but overlap trouble occurs (see Fig. 7). In three out of which the answering member of the group react on overlap trouble with temporary disengagement as also discussed in our first case analysis (see section "Qualitative Analysis I").

Implications of qualitative case analysis (study 2)

We find our suggestion supported, that robot-to-group situations provide for special emerging dynamics. A robot might have the chance to find these dynamics partially manifested

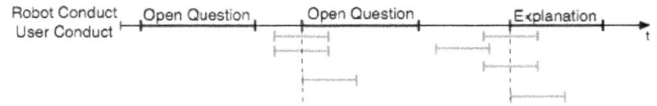

Figure 7. Overlaps between robot' and user's speech in severall cases

in a divergent gaze related to dealing with trouble as a group member. Beyond that, it would be beneficial, if the duration of silence could be adapted to the users' behavior. We find structural parallels to our first case study, concerning the dynamics that emerge in robot-to-group situations after trouble.

IMPLICATIONS & OUTLOOK

Using the example of the museum guide robot which presents information to visitors we were interested in gaining better understanding of the nature and timing of user utterances and the ways in which trouble is signalled and dealt with by the visitors. Based on videotaped data of two HRI studies in a real world museum site we addressed the following two questions: (1) How do visitors *signal trouble* in understanding, on a multimodal level and at which moment do they do it? (2) How do visitors in a robot-to-group situation *deal with trouble* that occurs due to a robot's non-understanding of their utterances? Our design of robot conduct included structural relevant moments that provide for user utterances as well as moments at which they could occur but are not necessary.

Analysis: In a first step we provided a general quantitative overview of where robot questions to engage the visitors provided for user utterances. We designed closed questions for engaging visitors and found that they indeed react verbally in 76 % (study 1) and 84 % (study 2) of the cases. In a second study we used more complex questions (double structure: question - pause - question) with the aim to involve visitors who might be shy to answer *open* questions. Combining questions in various ways (type A, B, C) manages to encourage visitors in 76% (type A), 62% (type B) and 76% (type C). In 25% of the cases, visitors' even answered both questions. The quantification also show, that there are 18 requests (study 1) on moments at which visitors' utterances were not demanded.

In a second step, we used qualitative analysis of two exemplary cases to investigate when and how visitors could signal trouble and found that in these cases clarification requests are addressed on a multimodal level right after the trouble-including robot utterances and without interrupting the robot. We also found effects of temporary disengagment when a visitor (as member of a group) realizes that the robot did not understand the utterance. The qualitative analysis of a case of study 2 - where the more complex double questions (open) were used - reveals that trouble of a second type occurs due to overlaps between the users' and the robot's talk. We investigated how the visitors deal with this type of trouble and found that - in several cases - members of a group orient their gaze to other group members and thereby also tend to temporary disengage from the interaction.

These results lead to the conclusion, that despite different types of trouble (in different studies with different robot conduct) lead to a similar way of dealing with trouble. In robot-to-group situations we found dynamics emerging between the group members. If the system does not deal with trouble immediately, in group situations participants tend to disengage and might miss (aspects of) the next utterance, which is shown by explorative analysis despite the small number of cases. For the future, this invites to consider repair on a multimodal level (cf. [9][13]) with regard to the special structures of multi-party interactions.

These observations lead to the following implications for further developing the museum guide robot (and presumably also in other scenarios) towards being attentive to user conduct and provide for an interactional dimension of human-robot-interaction:

- Moments after the robot's utterances should be considered as slots at which clarification requests of users are expectable. A short period of silence (here 0.4 - 1.7) appears to be necessary for the user to get the chance to formulate a clarification request. For future systems, the duration of silence should be adapted to the users' behavior.

- Our first insights into the multimodal nature of signaling trouble might reveal a strategy to deal with the limited capabilities of speech recognition to get hypotheses about the nature and function of user utterances. As next step, this should be explored systematically on a larger number of data.

- If the system does not deal with trouble immediately, in group situations visitors tend to disengage. Therefore, possibilities for dealing with trouble on the level of local and global sequential procedures have to be developed.

- In group situations, trouble seems to be manifested by gaze to another participant and / or (upper) body rotation while the robot continues to speak. Resulting from that, when a robot system is attentive and closely monitores user engagement ([7]) signaling trouble would be one aspect to take into account. If a system do not detect a trouble event, then the multi-party context provides a second possibility to recognize users actions and emerging group dynamics and thereby to detect and react on trouble (responsiveness).

Our future work will consist in further systematic study and implement it on the robot system, to explore the robustness of the described phenomenon.

ACKNOWLEDGMENTS

The authors acknowlegde the financial support from CITEC (project: "Interactional Coordination and Incremenality in HRI"), the Volkswagen Foundation (Dilthey Fellowship "Interaction & Space", K. Pitsch) and CoR-Lab.

REFERENCES

1. Bennewitz, M., Faber, F., Joho, D., Schreiber, M., and Behnke, S. Towards a humanoid museum guide robot that interacts with multiple persons. In *IEEE-RAS* (2005).

2. Hüwel, S., and Wrede, B. Spontaneous speech understanding for robust multi-modal human-robot communication. In *COLING/ACL* (2006), 391–398.

3. Klotz, D., Wienke, J., Peltason, J., Wrede, B., Wrede, S., Khalidov, V., and Odobez, J.-M. Engagement-based multi-party dialog with a humanoid robot. In *SIGDIAL* (2011), 341–343.

4. Kobayashi, Y., Shibata, T., Hoshi, Y., Kuno, Y., Okada, M., and Yamazaki, K. "i will ask you" choosing answerers by observing gaze responses using integrated sensors for museum guide robots. In *RO-MAN, 2010 IEEE* (2010), 652–657.

5. Krahmer, E., Swerts, M., Theune, M., and Weegels, M. Error detection in spoken human-machine interaction. In *International Journal of Speech Technology* (2001).

6. Kuzuoka, H., Pitsch, K., Suzuki, Y., Kawaguchi, I., Yamazaki, K., Yamazaki, A., Kuno, Y., Luff, P., and Heath, C. Effect of restarts and pauses on achieving a state of mutual orientation between a human and a robot. In *CSCW* (2008), 201–204.

7. Pitsch, K., Gehle, R., and Wrede, S. Addressing multiple participants: A museum guide robot's gaze shapes visitor participation. In *ICSR* (2013), 587–588.

8. Pitsch, K., Kuzuoka, H., Suzuki, Y., Süssenbach, L., Luff, P., and Heath, C. "the first five seconds": Contingent stepwise entry into an interaction as a means to secure sustained engagement. In *IEEE* (2009), 985–991.

9. Pitsch, K., and Wrede, S. When a robot orients visitors to an exhibit. referential practices and interactional dynamics in the real world. In press. RO-MAN, 2014.

10. Pitsch, K., Wrede, S., Seele, J.-C., and Süssenbach, L. Attitude of german museum visitors towards an interactive art guide robot. In *HRI '11*, ACM (2011).

11. Schegloff, E. When 'others' initiate repair. In *Applied Linguistics* (2000), 205–243.

12. Sidnell, J., and Stivers, T. *The Handbook of Conversation Analysis*. Blackwell Handbooks in Linguistics. Wiley, 2012.

13. Süssenbach, L., Riether, N., Schneider, S., Berger, I., Kummert, F., Lütkebohle, I., and Pitsch, K. A robot as fitness companion: towards an interactive action-based motivation model. In press. RO-MAN, 2014.

14. Weiss, A., Igelsböck, J., Tscheligi, M., Bauer, A., Kühnlenz, K., Wollherr, D., and Buss, M. Robots asking for directions – the willingness of passers-by to support robots. In *HRI '10* (2010).

15. Yamazaki, A., Yamazaki, K., Kuno, Y., Burdelski, M., Kawashima, M., and Kuzuoka, H. Precision timing in human-robot interaction: coordination of head movement and utterance. In *SIGCHI '08*, ACM (2008), 131–140.

16. Yamazaki, A., Yamazaki, K., Ohyama, T., Kobayashi, Y., and Yoshinori, K. A techno-sociological solution for designing a museum guide robot: Regarding choosing an appropriate visitor. In *HRI '12* (2012).

17. Yamazaki, K., Yamazaki, A., Okada, M., Kuno, Y., Kobayashi, Y., Hoshi, Y., Pitsch, K., Luff, P., vom Lehn, D., and Heath, C. Revealing gauguin: engaging visitors in robot guide's explanation in an art museum. In *SIGCHI '09*, ACM (2009).

Design Everything by Yourself

Takeo Igarashi
Professor, Department of Computer Science
Graduate School of Information Science and Technology
The University of Tokyo
takeo@acm.org

ABSTRACT

We live in a mass-production society today and everyone buy and use same things all over the world. This is cheap, but not necessarily ideal for individual persons. We envision that computer tools that help people to design things by themselves can enrich their lives. To that end, we have developed innovative interaction techniques for end users to (1) create rich graphics such as three-dimensional models and animations by simple sketching (2) design their own real-world, everyday objects such as clothing and furniture with realtime physical simulation integrated in a simple geometry editor, and (3) design the behavior of their personal robots and give instructions to them to satisfy their particular needs. I will introduce these result with live demonstrations.

Author Keywords

Computer Graphics; Fabrication; Human-Robot Interaction.

ACM Classification Keywords

I.3.5 [Computer Graphics]: Computational Geometry and Object Modeling—Physically based modeling.

BIO

Takeo Igarashi is a Professor of Computer Science Department at The University of Tokyo. He received a Ph.D from the Department of Information Engineering at The University of Tokyo in 2000. He then worked as a post doctoral research associate at Brown University (2000 - 2002). He joined the University of Tokyo as an Assistant Professor in 2002, and became a Professor in 2011. He also served as a director for JST ERATO Igarashi Design Interface project (2007 – 2013). His research interest is in user interfaces and interactive computer graphics. He is known for the development of a sketch-based modeling system (Teddy) and a performance-driven animation authoring system (MovingSketch). He has received several awards including the IBM Science Prize, the JSPS Prize, the ACM SIGGRAPH 2006 Significant New Researcher Award, and the Katayanagi Prize in Computer Science. He served as a program co-chair for ACM UIST 2013 and a program committee member for various international conferences such as ACM CHI, UIST, and SIGGRAPH.

HAI'14, October 29–31, 2014, Tsukuba, Japan.
ACM 978-1-4503-3035-0/14/10.
http://dx.doi.org/10.1145/2658861.2658946

Methodology for Study of Human-Robot Social Interaction in Dangerous Situations

David J. Atkinson
Institute for Human and Machine Cognition
15 SE Osceola Ave., Ocala, FL 34471 USA
datkinson@ihmc.us

Micah H. Clark
Institute for Human and Machine Cognition
15 SE Osceola Ave., Ocala, FL 34471 USA
mclark@ihmc.us

ABSTRACT

Applications of robotics in dangerous domains such as search and rescue require new methodology for study of human-robot interaction. Perceived danger evokes unique human psycho-physiological factors that influence perception, cognition and behavior. Human first responders are trained for victim psychology. Apart from real-life instances of disasters, studies of robots in this environment are difficult to perform safely and systematically with sufficient controls, fidelity, and in a manner that permits exact replication. Consequently, the trend to deploy rescue robots, for example, is proceeding largely without benefit of knowing whether human victims will readily cooperate with robot rescuers. The capability to deal with unique victim psychology has not been a testable requirement. We report on the methodology of an on-going study that uses virtual reality to provide a feature-rich immersive environment that is sufficient to evoke fear-related psychological response, provides simulation capability for robots, and enables systematic study trials with automated data collection via an embedded scripting language. The methodology presented provides an effective way to study human interaction with intelligent agents embodied as robots in application domains that would otherwise be impossible in the real world.

Author Keywords

Affective Computing; Artificial Intelligence; Autonomous Agents; Behavioral Science; Cognition; Disaster; Experimental Methods; Human-Robot Interaction; Intelligent Robots; Methodology; Second Life; Social Robots; Trust; Rescue Robotics; Virtual Environments

ACM Classification Keywords

H.1.2, H.5.1, H.5.2, I.2.9, I.2.11, I.6.3

INTRODUCTION

There is a demand for applications of intelligent robotics in domains and situations that may be dangerous for humans,

i.e., where there exist manifestly real or perceived threats to life or limb. Such threats may be due to environmental factors one might find in broad-area natural disasters (e.g., earthquakes) or local crises (e.g., urban structure fires). Threats may also be a result of adversarial factors due to crime or armed conflict. A prominent application for intelligent robots in dangerous situations is search and rescue, as evidenced by government programs (e.g., DARPA Robotics Challenge) and observed market growth for rescue robots.

Many of these danger-related applications demand interaction between humans and robots, including active cooperation. Real or perceived danger presents a multiplicity of stimuli that evoke human physiological and psychological factors that influence human perception, cognition and interaction. Yet very little can be said with scientific certainty about the impact of these unique psychological factors of danger on human-robot interaction owing to the difficulty of performing systematic, controlled studies in realistically high-risk situations. Apart from physical threat, researchers are compelled to minimize the psychological risk of causing trauma, or evoking a memory of trauma in participants. About 60% of men and 50% of women experience at least one trauma event in their lifetimes such as disaster, war, life-threatening assault or accident. Approximately 3.6% of Americans will experience a Post Traumatic Stress Disorder (PTSD) episode in any given year [13].

The challenge for researchers is to find methods for investigating human-robot interaction in dangerous situations safely, with sufficient controls, with situational and psychological fidelity, and with technical means that afford the opportunity for precise measurement. Experimental trials ideally are conducted in a manner that permits exact replication.

Immersive, virtual environments offer such capabilities by simulating physical robot features and behavior of interest, interfacing with external intelligent robot cognitive systems, and, most importantly, by simulating a dynamic, feature-rich environment in ways that safely increase a study participant's perception of risk and thus evoke the unique psychology present in dangerous situations.

Our research project is exploring how different factors are considered in a decision to trust and rely upon an intelligent, autonomous agent. We follow up on results reported by

Robinette [22], who investigated the role of appearance and certain robot behaviors for gaining trust of people in an evacuation scenario. However, that study used a fairly primitive virtual environment that could not evoke the unique victim psychology in dangerous situations.

Our study, in participant trials now, examines how perceived autonomous agent characteristics impact the attribution of benevolence on the part of the human toward the agent in a disaster scenario. Specifically, we are investigating how the human participants' perception of intelligent, autonomous system agency (i.e., ability to choose among many alternative actions) and autonomous system situational competence (specifically, role-based capability) affects their choice to rely (or not) upon an autonomous agent in a high-risk disaster scenario. Will they cooperate and comply with directions intended to help them? There is insufficient information to give a sure answer, and this is what we hope to contribute.

METHODOLOGY CHALLENGE

Intelligent robot capability has been studied in the context of actual dangerous crises as well as in isolated laboratory settings including simulations. These can provide useful context for analysis of human operator trust in autonomous robots [24]; however, they are insufficient for systematic study of interaction between robots and humans who perceive extreme personal danger.

Real-life instances of dangerous situations afford an excellent opportunity to evaluate engineered robot capability and the possibility to provide needed aid to rescuers and victims. Murphy provided a thorough review of activities of rescue robots at the World Trade Center during the 11 September 2001 crisis [15]. However, such instances are thankfully rare. They are also uncontrolled, thus rendering studies performed in real-life disaster conditions nearly impossible to replicate and therefore of limited utility.

One may reasonably ask whether some elements of human-robot interaction for dangerous situations may be studied in isolation – one at a time or in certain combinations. For many of the mechanisms of interest, such as methods of communication and others, the answer is yes. Specialized test-beds and competitions have been developed for this purpose [16, 17]. Certain danger stimuli may be included. However, heretofore system level testing in fully evocative environments has remained elusive due to unique factors of the psycho-physiology of victims.

Unique Psychological Factors of Danger

Actual dangerous situations present unique stimuli that evoke reflexive physiological and psychological reactions in humans such as fear-potentiated startle [10], anxiety, and stress [18] that are not ordinarily present in day-to-day life. As a result, human social interaction is affected by the perception of danger, depending on both situational and individual personality factors [12]. Human first responders who provide aid to victims must contend with the abnormal

psychology that such high-risk situations evoke; indeed, they receive special training for exactly this purpose [9].

How will survivors respond to a rescue robot? Our recent exploratory survey of individual choice to rely on an autonomous, intelligent agent in hypothetical dangerous scenarios revealed a strong correlation of the decision to become reliance with risk-related personality and situational factors [1, 2]. That study also indicated that the perceived qualities of competence, predictability, openness, and safety that are important in human interpersonal trust are likely carry over to trust of autonomous agents.

In high-risk situations, the symbolic meaning of situational cues interacts with social cues in ways that influence the interpretation of a physical and social situation, and thus behavioral response. These situations evoke an affective mental state with specific attributes and predictable psychological and behavioral results. These include fear, anxiety, panic, reduced compliance with social norms, hyper-vigilance and sensitivity to environmental cues, as well as avoidance behavior (references [10, 12, 18]). This is what we mean by the term victim psychology.

Given human propensity for anthropomorphic social treatment of robots, it seems likely that human-robot interaction in dangerous situations will be similarly influenced in ways that make it fundamentally different from interaction in other, non-threatening situations. To the extent that this influence is found to be significant, effective application of robots in dangerous situations where human interaction is a requirement (e.g., victim rescue, small team coordination) must account for the differences and adjust appropriately.

In a conventional laboratory setting, individual facets of threats can be studied in isolation (e.g., reaction to images) because potentially confounding cues can be controlled. However, the fear present in actual dangerous situations results from the perception of high risk [26]. To evoke the dynamics of human behavior and psychological factors that result in perception of high risk requires creating a laboratory environment with a large number of realistic danger cues. This is both difficult and likely to be judged unacceptable for human studies.

Use of Immersive, Virtual Reality

As an alternative to emulation of dangerous conditions in a physical test-bed, our proposition is that immersive, virtual reality affords us the opportunity to study human-robot interaction in situations that are perceived as high risk, thus evoking unique psychology and behavior present in the kinds of dangerous situations we have in mind for robot applications, such as urban search and rescue.

The study of HRI in virtual environments is a relatively recent activity. There are a number of commercial and open-source virtual reality tools available to researchers, each with their own strengths and weaknesses. Our primary selection criteria were a) affordance and ease of creating customized, feature-rich environments; b) embedded programming language for robot cognitive emulation; c) ability to interface with external software and servers for data collection, and; d) ready availability "in-world" of potential study participants who would require minimal training.

In addition, the efficacy of our methodological approach entails several important requirements with respect to behavioral realism, psycho-physiological effects, robotics fidelity, and experimental control. We discuss each of these in the following sections.

Behavioral Realism in Virtual Environments

Our methodology requires that human social behavior carries over and is consistent with behavior in virtual environments. It is essential that human behavior in our immersive, virtual reality be sufficiently similar to behavior in the physical world. This requires sufficient fidelity in the simulated environment to enable the mental state of "immersion" by participants.

Behavioral realism requires social presence, that is, the immersive feeling of embodiment and identification of an individual with their in-world avatar. Schultze [23] reviewed a number of studies and identified specific attributes that promote the sense of presence.

Our study has created a feature-rich virtual environment: a warehouse that is designed to enhance the participants' sense of immersion. Seen from overhead (see Figure 1), the warehouse layout is that of a typical psychological maze, with walls and stacks of boxes on pallets forming the structure of the maze. There is also the typical equipment found in warehouses, such as mechanical loaders, a crane, hand trucks, and other items that contribute to authenticity. Ambient sounds of machinery enhance the sense of immersion.

Figure 1. Warehouse Overhead View.
Fig.1@David. J. Atkinson. Courtesy D.J. Atkinson

As an aid to creating immersion, our study provides a period for acclimation to the task environment. This period limits the amount of distraction to participants that may occur when initially entering into the scenario. As discussed later, it also provides an opportunity for certain fear-potentiating cues to be noticed.

Our confidence that human social behavior carries over to virtual environments is buoyed by a number of relevant studies. Blascovich [4] provided a survey of social psychological studies and their methods that support the mirroring of virtual and real human social behavior, even using technology that by today's standards would appear fairly primitive.

Yee [29] established the persistence of social norms of gender, interpersonal distance, and eye gaze in virtual environments. This study investigated online immersive games as a platform to study physical social interaction at the micro and macro level.

With respect to social behavior, Harris [11] tracked a small population of interacting individuals over time in SecondLife™, providing additional evidence for social influence on individual and group behavior.

Prattichizzo [16] investigated social interaction in heterogeneous communities of robots and humans in SecondLife™. Burden [7] deployed a mix of chatbots and avatar-robots ("robotars") in SecondLife™ to study verbal interaction between humans and embodied virtual robots versus un-embodied chatbots.

Non-verbal communication was studied by Bailenson et al., [3] who found that people exhibited similar personal spatial behavior towards virtual humans (agents controlled by a computer) as they would towards real humans.

Evoking Disaster-Related Victim Psychology

To study human-robot interaction in the context of a disaster, we must assure that virtual environments evoke human perception of heightened risk in the absence of actual physical danger, and do so in a manner sufficient to create the unique psychological state in which we are interested. Previous influential clinical psychology studies give us a basis for this aspect of our methodology.

For example, it is well established in clinical psychology that immersive environments such as ours have the ability to evoke reflexive physiological and psychological reactions of the type in which we are interested. Wiederhold [27] provides a comprehensive review of clinical studies that demonstrate the effectiveness of virtual reality for treatment of phobias such as acrophobia and arachnophobia and anxiety disorders.

Immersion and visual features alone are enough to induce physiological arousal and strong negative affect [14]. The addition of other sensory modalities, such as audition, improves the sense of immersion and is a strong cue for eliciting fear and anxiety [25].

These studies have shown that specific situational cues elicit perception of high risk and fear-potentiated startle reflex. Based on those results, we have designed the warehouse task space to include many such cues on multiple sensory modalities.

As mentioned earlier, our study provides for an acclimation period to aid immersion. During the acclimation phase, prior to the onset of a simulated disaster, we potentiate the perception of high risk through a number of environmental cues, or "risk stimuli". The acclimation phase allows time for these stimuli to be processed, thereby paving the way for our disaster cues to elicit the desired psychological effect.

Risk stimuli include a worn-out appearance to the warehouse, messy and untidy rows of boxes, and signs of incivility such as trash on the floor, graffiti, and broken windows. In addition, some of the containers contain warning symbols for hazardous chemical materials. Finally, there are prominent warning signs and fire alarms.

In addition, the lighting in the warehouse is carefully controlled to create dark, shadowed areas. Atmospheric diffusion limits clarity of vision at longer distances. Visibility lines are also obstructed in many cases. These features combine to potentiate a fear of attack, evoking our evolutionary experience that predators may lurk in such places [6].

Figure 2. Warehouse Fire, Participants' View
Fig.2@David. J. Atkinson. Courtesy D.J. Atkinson

Following the acclimation phase, we begin our most significant manipulation of participants with the purpose of swiftly ramping up their affective sense of risk. There is a sudden very loud sound of a nearby explosion followed immediately by visible fire near the roof and smoke overhead (see Figure 2). Over time, the smoke lowers and increases in density, further obscuring vision. A loud warning siren commences along with an announcement to evacuate the building. Concomitant with the increasing smoke, fire appears among the stacked pallets and debris falls from the ceiling, blocking the entrance to the door used previously by the participant to enter the warehouse. Sparks erupt from electrical equipment nearby.

What was a moment ago a spacious warehouse is now a confined space. Our pilot tests during development indicate that at this point, a participant will feel a sense of entrapment, eliciting the goal of escape. In addition to evoking physical fear, we add additional cues such to raise the perception of

other types of risk and overall stress. It becomes incumbent on the participant to locate an exit to escape the disaster.

Each element of the simulated warehouse and disaster is designed to cue fear and heightened perception of risk without presenting any actual physical threat. We mitigate potential psychological risk to participants in the study with the use of screening protocols that eliminate individuals from the participant pool who may have, or be at-risk for, Post Traumatic Stress Disorder (PTSD). For this purpose, we use the U.S. Government Veterans Administration PC-PTSD screen, modified in consultation with a PTSD expert to include questions from the SCID-PTSD module [19].

The sudden appearance of a bystander or presence of a companion is another cue that elicits perception of high risk. In our study, a robot seen earlier in the warehouse, suddenly rushes over to the participant.

Emulation of Robots in Virtual Environments

As a practical matter, immersive, virtual reality must provide appropriate affordances to implement emulated robots of sufficient behavioral complexity. Both cognitive abilities and kinematic behavior (including plausible physics) are important.

Our study takes advantage of the "bystander effect" (mentioned earlier) when participants encounter a robot shortly after the onset of the simulated disaster (i.e., a fire-fighting robot "FireBot" or a janitorial robot, "JanitorBot", see Figure 3). The specific appearance, simulated physical behaviors, and interactive social behaviors of the robot in the study vary according to the specifications of the particular control or experimental trial.

Figure 3. "FireBot" and "JanitorBot"
Fig.3@David. J. Atkinson. Courtesy D.J. Atkinson

Programming the simulated robot requires software architecture choices between interfacing with the external "real world" for robot cognition or implementing these capabilities in a limited form within the virtual environment. Both approaches have met with success.

Our approach implements the robot's cognitive and control capability within the SecondLife™ script-oriented language LSL [8] to avoid latency introduced by external communications. We use an augmented subsumption architecture [5] with sensing, perception and individual behaviors implemented as individual scripts that do not directly depend upon or interact with each other. Rather, they interact via executive control scripts that implement activation and suppression consistent with the subsumption framework. Social interaction is implemented via behaviors that "overlay" robot kinematic behavior insofar as they are compatible [6]. Additional details on specific attributes of the robots in our study and their implementation of social interaction are left for later discussion.

Implementing robot cognition via external interface to the virtual world is also a viable option. Veksler [28] demonstrated that an external cognitive architecture, ACT-R, could be easily interfaced with SecondLife™ for studies of the differences in cognitive models with respect to performance, learning and decision-making in the presence of complex and dynamic environments full of distractive cues. Additionally, Ranathunga [21], who studied multi-agent interaction in virtual worlds using SecondLife™ as a platform, reported a key engineering result in the ease of interfacing external cognitive agent platforms such as Belief-Desire-Intention (BDI) programming frameworks with the virtual world.

With respect to robot kinematics and dynamics, Ranathunga also concluded that, unlike simpler simulation environments, SecondLife™ provided a dynamic world of sufficient high fidelity, complexity, constraints and physical laws consistent with object behavior and proportionally suitable sensory-motor capability. Similarly, Prattichizzo [20] concluded that the emulation (i.e., matching external behavior) of robotic control, sensing and perception mechanisms enabled reasonable reproduction of the kinematics of robot behavior.

Controlled Virtual Experiments and Data Collection

Our methodology also requires that we have the ability to capture useful data under controlled and repeatable experimental conditions.

Blascovich (cited earlier, see [4]) reviewed multiple studies that demonstrated how virtual environments enable social psychology studies to increase the level of "mundane realism" while maintaining experimental control.

We have fully automated execution of individual trials for this study, including participant consent, pre- and post-task questionnaires, provision task instructions to participants, all environmental dynamics during the participant's task, debriefing delivery, and data collection throughout. This will help ensure systematic, controlled execution of each trial and assist in future replication.

This automation is also implemented using scripts programmed in LSL (see reference [8]). These scripts include time-based events as well as events triggered by specific participant behaviors and human-robot interactions.

Data from each study trial is delivered automatically online from SecondLife™ in suitable format for storage in a MySQL database. In addition to the questionnaire data, we collect a variety of data during the participants' task. These include physical data of the robot and participant at specific intervals. We also collect a transcript of textual communication by the participant (if any, and only with permission). Our physical data collection is primarily oriented towards proxemics, including the relative geometry of participant and the robot, their absolute position, orientation, and movement vectors, and the continuous gaze direction and focal point of the study participant and robot.

CONCLUSION

To enable our investigation of human trust and human-robot interaction in the context of a disaster, we have created a virtual environment whose features evoke the affective state of high risk in study participants. Simulated robots and automation of study trial execution and data collection provide us with the methodological tools to conduct controlled and replicable studies in this important area. The key points of this paper follow below.

It is desirable to apply intelligent robotics in danger-related applications, many of which (e.g., urban search and rescue, dismounted infantry, humanitarian operations) require human-robot interaction and cooperation.

There are unique psychological factors evoked by dangerous situations that influence human perception, cognition and social interaction such that we anticipate similar impact on human-robot interaction.

Appropriate stimuli in feature-rich virtual environments can evoke physiological and psychological responses that manifest as a sense of high risk, fear, anxiety and stress similar to those seen in dangerous real-world situations.

Interactive human social behavior and the norms governing it carry over into immersive virtual environments. This provides the necessary psychological fidelity for human-robot interaction studies.

The methodological challenge of studying human-robot interaction in truly dangerous situations can be addressed using immersive virtual reality.

ACKNOWLEDGEMENT

This work was supported in part by the U.S. Air Force Office of Scientific Research under Grant FA9550-12-0097.

REFERENCES

1. Atkinson, D.J. and Clark, M.H. Autonomous Agents and Human Interpersonal Trust: Can We Engineer a Human-Machine Social Interface for Trust? In *Trust and Autonomous Systems: Papers from the 2013 AAAI Spring Symposium.* Technical Report No. SS-13-07, Menlo Park: AAAI Press (2013).

2. Atkinson, D.J. and Clark, M.H. Attitudes and Personality in Trust of Intelligent, Autonomous Agents. Manuscript in review (2014).

3. Bailenson, J.N., Blascovich, J., Beall, A.C. and Loomis, J.M. Interpersonal distance in immersive virtual environments, *Personality and Social Psychology Bulletin 29* (2003), 819–833.

4. Blascovich, J. et.al. Immersive Virtual Environment Technology as a Methodological Tool for Social Psychology." *PSYCHOL INQ 13*, 2 (2002), 103-124.

5. Brooks, R. A robust layered control system for a mobile robot". *IEEE J ROBOT AUTOM, [legacy, pre-1988] 2,* 1 (1988), 14–23.

6. Brooks, A.G., and Arkin, R.C. Behavioral overlays for non-verbal communication expression on a humanoid robot. *AUTON ROBOT 22* 1 (2007), 55-74.

7. Burden, D.J. Deploying embodied AI into virtual worlds. *KNOWL-BASED SYST 22* 7 (2009), 540-544.

8. Cox, R. and Crowther, P.S. A Review of Linden Scripting Language and Its Role in Second Life. In *Computer-Mediated Social Networking*, Volume 5322. M. Purvis and B. T. R. Savarimutha (Eds.). Berlin, DE: Springer-Verlag, (2009), 35-47.

9. Dorfman,W.I. and Walker, L.E. *First Responder's Guide to Abnormal Psychology.* New York: Springer-Verlag (2007).

10. Grillon, C. and Davis, M. Fear-potentiated startle conditioning in humans: Explicit and contextual cue conditioning following paired versus unpaired training. *PSYCHOPHYSIOLOGY 34* (1997), 451–458.

11. Harris, H., Bailenson, J.N., Nielsen, A. and Yee, N. The Evolution of Social Behavior over Time in Second Life. *PRESENCE 18* 6 (2009), 434-448.

12. Jorgensen, L.J. The Effect of Environmental Cues and Social Cues on Fear of Crime in a Community Park Setting. *University of Utah.* Ph.D Thesis. Dissertation Number 3304766 (2008).

13. Kessler, R.C., McGonagle, K.A., Zhao, S., Nelson, C.B., Hughes, M., et al. Lifetime and 12-month prevalence of DSM-III-R Psychiatric Disorders in the United States. *ARCH GEN PSYCHIAT 51* (1994), 8-19.

14. Macedonio, M.F., Parsons, T.D., Digiuseppe, R.A., Weiderhold, B.K., Rizzo. A. Immersiveness and Physiological Arousal within Panoramic Video-Based Virtual Reality. *CYBERPSYCHOL BEHAV 10* 4 (2007), 508-515.

15. Murphy, R.R. Trial by Fire: Activities of the Rescue Robots at the World Trade Center from 11-21 September 2001. *IEEE ROBOT AUTOM MAG* (2004).

16. Murphy, R.R., Casper, J., Micire, M. and Hyams, J. Assessment of the NIST standard test bed for urban search and rescue,. Presented at *NIST Workshop on Performance Metrics for Intelligent Systems* (2000).

17. Osuka, M., Murphy, R.R. and Schultz, A. USAR competitions for physically situated robots. *IEEE ROBOT AUTOM MAG 9* (2002), 26–33.

18. Pole, N., Neylan, T.C., Best, S.R., Orr, S.P. and Marmar, C.R. Fear-Potentiated Startle and Post-traumatic Stress Symptoms in Urban Police Officers. *J TRAUMA STRESS. 16* 5 (2003), 471–479.

19. PTSD Screening and Referral for Health Care Providers, [online] Retrieved 08 January 2014. http://www.ptsd.va.gov/professional/provider-type/doctors/screening-and-referral.asp

20. Prattichizzo, D. Robotics in Second Life. *IEEE ROBOT AUTOM MAG* (2009), 99-102.

21. Ranathunga, S., Cranefield, S. and Purvis, M., Extracting Data from Second Life. In *Proc. of 10th Int. Conf. on Autonomous Agents and Multiagent Systems (AAMAS 2011)*. Taipei, Taiwan (2011), 1181-1189.

22. Robinette, P., Wagner, A.R. and Howard, A.M. Building and Maintaining Trust Between Humans and Guidance Robots in an Emergency. In *Trust and Autonomous Systems: Papers from the 2013 AAAI Spring Symposium.* Technical Report No. SS-13-07, Menlo Park: AAAI Press. (2013), 78-83.

23. Schultze, U. Embodiment and presence in virtual worlds: a review. *J INF TECHNOL 25* (2010), 434-449.

24. Stormont, D.P. Analyzing Human Trust of Autonomous Systems in Hazardous Environments. In *Proc. of Twenty-Third AAAI Conference on Artificial Intelligence*. Chicago, Illinois (2008), 27-32.

25. Suied, C., Drettakis, G., Warusfel, O. and Via-Delmon, I. Auditory-visual virtual reality as a diagnostic and therapeutic tool for cynoophobia. *Journal of Cybertherapy and Rehabilitation 16* 2 (2013) 145-152.

26. Warr, M. Dangerous situations: Social context and fear of victimization. *SOC FORCES 68* (1990), 891–907.

27. Wiederhold, B.K. and Bouchard, S. *Advances in Virtual Reality and Anxiety Disorders.* Springer. Series in Anxiety and Related Disorders (2014).

28. Veksler, V.D. Second-Life as a simulation environment: Rich, high-fidelity world, minus the hassles. In *Proc. of the 9th International Conference of Cognitive Modeling.* Manchester, UK (2009) Paper 231.

29. Yee, N. et al. The Unbearable Likeness of Being Digital: The Persistence of Nonverbal Social Norms in Online Virtual Environments, *CYBERPSYCHOL BEHAV 10* 1 (2007).

More Human than Human? A Visual Processing Approach to Exploring Believability of Android Faces

Masayuki Nakane

University of Manitoba
umnakane@myumanitoba.ca

James E. Young

University of Manitoba
young@cs.umanitoba.ca

Neil D. B. Bruce

University of Manitoba
bruce@cs.umanitoba.ca

ABSTRACT

The issue of believability is core to android science, the challenge of creating a robot that can pass as a near human. While researchers are making great strides in improving the quality of androids and their likeness to people, it is simultaneously important to develop theoretical foundations behind believability, and experimental methods for exploring believability. In this paper, we explore a visual processing approach to investigating the believability of android faces, and present results from a study comparing current-generation android faces to humans. We show how android faces are still not quite as believable as humans, and provide some mechanisms that may be used to investigate and compare believability in future projects.

Author Keywords

Android Science; Human-Robot Interaction; Visual Processing; Uncanny Valley

ACM Classification Keywords

H.1.2 Models and Principles: User/Machine Systems. Software Psychology

INTRODUCTION

Androids are a class of robots that have the ultimate goal of being able to approximately pass for human [15]. To accomplish this, androids will eventually have to look, move, and interact the same as everyday people. When these goals are not met, not only are androids easily identifiable as non-human, but interaction can suffer in other ways, such as the android appearing eerie or making people uncomfortable (often referred to the Uncanny Valley problem [15]). Moving forward, android developers will need a solid understanding of which features and characteristics impact believability of their androids, understanding of the underlying perception mechanisms that impact believability, and tools and methods to help diagnose and determine their own android's believability.

In this paper, we take an initial step toward this goal by exploring visual perception and processing of android faces. We purposely select a heavy simplification of the broader problem, focusing on the visual perception of static images of android faces. This serves as an initial base case where believability is arguably more easily achievable than with real robots, motion, and interaction.

We present a visual processing discussion and initial foundations explaining how people may process android faces, and conducted a study based on this theory comparing human faces to faces of current-generation androids. While androids are becoming impressively believable, our results show that – as predicted by our theory – people are still faster at identifying human faces, find android faces more eerie, and make more mistakes with android faces.

This work provides an initial step toward building a theoretical foundation for the believability of android faces. At the very least, we have shown how simple studies examining face-identification times and error rates can be used to test android faces and infer potential believability.

RELATED WORK

The general study of how robotic design impacts interaction is well established in the field, e.g., comparing zoomorphic and anthropomorphic designs in terms of perceived animacy [1], or building frameworks for appropriate and believable social robot behaviors (e.g., [17]). We propose to extend this direction by specifically addressing the believability of android faces.

Most work on the believability of robots surrounds the eeriness problem (often called the uncanny valley problem). Since first postulated [22], this issue has been contentious [13], and many researchers have looked to unpack the issue in terms of robot dimensions, e.g., morphology [2, 8, 15], or realism and iconicity [5, 6]. While eeriness is inevitably a part of believability of android faces, we take a more holistic approach where eeriness is but one part of the issue.

There has been limited work in robotics and animation that looks at how people visually process artificial faces. One work looked at how people process a real face, an animated face, and various points "morphed" in between [8], and found that people took longer to classify ambiguous faces than clearly human or animated, with classification time decreasing as the ambiguity decreased. In our work we aim to continue this direction and explicitly target androids.

Some researchers have looked at the impact of faces, for example how modifying facial features can impact response such as perceived attractiveness of an agent [9], and similar work looked at how people can apply gender stereotypes to a robot based solely on the haircut [12]. We extend this direction by addressing believability.

VISUAL PROCESSING

Humans are hard wired to see and find faces, even where none exist: this can be illustrated by a common face-finding exercise in doodles [19], and has been linked to a human need for social interaction [10] – people can recognize a face in about 350ms [24]. As such, one would expect the creation of believable android faces to be fairly simple. Unfortunately, although people can easily understand even a crude android design as having a face, believability is a separate problem.

When a person sees a human face – or a face they believe may be human, such as an android – they conduct face-recognition processing, to determine if they know the face. Unlike the simple task of finding faces, this requires a great deal more sophistication given the range of differences and subtleties between people's faces. There is a body of work examining this processing, much of it dealing with how people scan and fixate on a potential face (e.g., [3, 24]).

When a person detects a face which at first-glance appears to be human, but deeper face-recognition processing detects a problem, we have an "expectancy violation" [21]. Such violations in processing draws a person's attention (even at the subconscious level) to the violation as a means of investigating why the violations happened; as such, we can expect that faces which are not quite normal will take more time for a person to process, given this violation. Further, expectancy violations have also been shown to impact anthropomorphism and believability in other contexts [21], and so we can anticipate similar results here. Arguably, if this violation is jarring and the drop in anthropomorphism is large, this may contribute to the eeriness problem.

There are standard ways that people scan faces, for example, many people initially look below the eyes [24], and usually look at the nose, mouth, and cheeks in some order [3], commonly forming a distinct "T" pattern (eyes and then down) [23]. There is also evidence that problems with eyes are more salient than other features [14]. Individual differences (e.g., based on culture [18] or gender [4]) do exist, which is important to consider for studying believability of androids; for example, some studies show women as having superior face processing [4] so they may be more difficult to deceive with androids. People also have varying tendencies to anthropomorphize (dispositional anthropomorphism) – to give non-human things such as images and potential faces human qualities [11]. Despite these differences, it may still be feasible to study general

eye-gaze patterns to help diagnose why an android face is not seen as human. For example by detecting uncharacteristically long fixations or fixation order across many people. In addition, it may be useful to measure a person's disposition to anthropomorphize as an important source of error in data analysis, where people with lower disposition may perhaps be better at detecting issues with an android face.

Some research has purposely distorted human faces to study results and infer about visual processing. For example, by inverting faces (upside-down) or components (inverting the mouth or ryes only), to separate whole-face from component processing [7]. Such techniques, including as hiding the eyes or mouth respectively and doing recognition tests (e.g., as in [7, 14, 25]), can be useful to diagnose components of an android face.

EXPLORATORY PILOT STUDY

We conducted an initial study looking at people's processing of android and human faces. As a pilot, we focused simply on people's classification of static images of faces as either android or human, following the experiment design of [8], and conducted a series of exploratory analyses.

As a primary base case, we wanted to investigate if current-generation android faces are sufficiently believable as human. Also, based on our visual processing background given above we hypothesized that people would take longer to process and classify android faces, would make more mistakes (higher error rate), and, due to the increased ambiguity, would find the android faces more eerie. We anticipated that a person's disposition toward anthropomorphism (general tendency to anthropomorphize) would negatively correlate with response time, as we postulated that they would more readily accept the android face as human, and would have higher error rates with android faces given their potential tendency to mistake them for human. Further, we expected that female participants would have lower error rates and quicker response times due to potential face recognition advantages.

Methodology and Procedure

We recruited fourteen participants from our general university population aged 18-58 (Mdn=20.5), with an equal male / female split, and paid them $10 for their participation. Participant nationalities were primarily Canadian, and also included Nigerian, Chinese, Brazilian, and Pakistani participants.

Experiments were conducted with one participant at a time. Participants were briefed about the study and we obtained informed consent. They then sat at a desk at a fixed distance (15cm) from a 24" wide-screen 16:10 monitor and fixed location (centered); we used a chin-rest (sanitized between participants) to ensure this, and participants wore a light-weight eye-tracking device (PT mini) – this was for technical pilot reasons only and the eye-tracking data was not used in our study. Participants completed the tasks where they classified faces as either human or android, and finished with a post-test questionnaire. The entire study took roughly 30 minutes.

Tasks

Our experiment consisted of two tasks: 1) classification accuracy priority, and 2) classification speed priority. In task 1, participants were shown a face for three full seconds, after which they were asked to classify it and were verbally asked post-stimulus questions before being shown the next face. The order of faces was counterbalanced using an incomplete Latin square. This design enabled the person to concentrate on the face and not to feel rushed in their decision making. In task 2, participants were shown the same faces (with a different counterbalanced order), but were asked to classify them as quickly as possible while the face was shown, with the response time being digitally recorded. The rest of the presentation style was the same except there were no post-stimulus questions here.

In both cases, faces were shown at random locations on the screen, and a blank screen with a fixation cross in the center was placed between faces (during questions) to minimize cross-over effect. Further, in both cases the participant held a mouse in their hand with thumbs on the two buttons, and use these to classify the faces by pressing one of them (left for human, right for android).

Instruments

We compiled a database of faces, consisting of ten android and ten human faces, with half of each category being female. Faces were selected as much as possible to have a neutral expression and to be fully front-facing. Figure 1 shows faces used and provides source attributions. All images were scaled to 324x386 for consistency across faces, which was 3.4" x 4.5" on our screen. For the post stimulus verbal questions, for task 1, we asked the participant to rate how "eerie" the image was on a scale of 1-7.

The post-test questionnaire collected basic demographics, and included the Individual Difference in Anthropomorphism Questionnaire [24] to measure the participant's disposition toward anthropomorphism.

Results

Based on task 1 results, overall androids were more likely to pass for human (57%) than android (43%), and humans were uncommonly mistaken for androids (10%), $\chi^2(1)=38.87$, $p<.001$, and $\chi^2(1)=2.86$, $p<.1$ for android faces only (Table 1). Despite this result, however, there were marked differences in how the faces were processed.

We used one-tailed, paired t-tests to further compare the results on android and human faces. On average, participants classified human faces faster ($M=1.66$s, $SE=.14$) than android faces ($M=2.00$s, $SE=.14$), ($t_{13}=-4.16$, $p<.01$, $d=.7$), reported that human faces were less eerie ($M=2.21$, $SE=.33$) than android faces ($M=2.57$, $SE=.36$, $t_{13}=1.87$, $p<0.05$, $d=.28$), and participants were found to have a lower error rate for classifying humans ($M=.12$, $SE=.06$) than androids ($M=.51$, $SE=.07$), ($t_{13}=3.77$, $p<.01$, $d=1.65$).

We performed correlation tests between the IDAQ (disposition toward anthropomorphism) questionnaire answers and other results, but all results were non-significant ($p>.50$). In addition, no effect of participant gender or face gender was found on any measure (F<1).

Discussion

Our results show that people classified android faces as human faces at the confidence level of 90% (or α=.1). At

Table 1 – cross tabulation of how human and android faces were classified, $\chi^2(1)=38.87$, p<.001.

Count

		classified as		Total
		human	android	
face	human	126	14	140
	android	80	60	140
Total		206	74	280

Figure 1 – Face images used in our study, human faces on the left and android faces on the right. The human faces are extracted from the FEI face database (http://fei.edu.br/~cet/facedatabase.html). We compiled the android faces through sources available online. From left to right, top row first: Hanson Robotics' Philip K. Dick, Bina 48, Jules (http://www.hansonrobotics.com/), ATR Geminoid and Geminoid F. Second row, FaceTeam FACE robot [18], JST ERATO Asada and Kokoro CB², Neurobiotics Alissa, KITECH Ever-2, National Taiwan University Robot (unnamed).

least for the simplified problem space of static images, we believe this demonstrates that android faces are doing quite well in terms of believability. Further, as expected, participants classified human faces faster than android faces, had a lower error rate, and found them less eerie. This shows that, even when android faces may pass for human, there are elements of visual processing and response that can highlight the differences between human and android faces. This initial pilot result lends support to our visual processing approach, and highlights how it can be applied to gain insight into believability of faces. For example, that through "expectancy violation" faces that have issues will take longer to process, and will be more ambiguous.

As the android faces were seen as being more eerie than the human faces, post-hoc we performed correlation tests between eeriness and the error rate and response time, to see if eeriness may predict the other factors. Unfortunately these tests were not significant. We believe that it will be important to continue to investigate how eeriness relates to visual processing and believability of faces.

The lack of results relating to disposition to anthropomorphize was surprising. Given the very poor results ($t<1$ in most cases, illustrated in Figure 2), we do not feel that this would become significant with more participants with our current setup. However, it is difficult to determine if the effect did not exist, if our sample size was too small, if other factors were larger than tendency to anthropomorphize, or if our IDAQ questionnaire did not measure it well, and so we encourage further inquiry in this area. Similarly, we suggest further inquiry into the effect of gender (both the person's [4] and the android's) on face believability.

LIMITATIONS
A key limitation of this study was the small sample size. Further work in the area must address this to find results that are more generalizable.

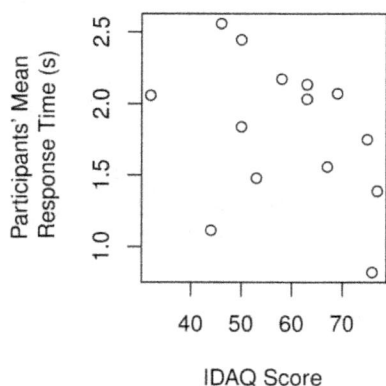

Figure 2 – Participant mean response time (s) against tendency to anthropomorphize (IDAQ score). As shown, there was little relationship found.

The primary purpose of this paper is to explore the visual processing approach to considering the believability of android faces, and so our primary limitation is the small scope of the work. We hope that this direction continues to be developed, and stronger android-centric visual processing theories can be developed to better inform design. From this, we hope that further studies will continue to be conducted to unpack the complexity of android face believability. For example, one element of our theory which we did not address yet is the gaze element of facial processing – how people fixate and process a face.

One facet which must be addressed for continuing work in this area is the development of a standardized face database. Our results are deducted from only ten faces of android faces. While we attempted to maintain uniform lighting, angle, and size across them, taking more care to develop such a database with more faces would provide an excellent benchmark for researchers to compare against. Such a database could include meta-data such as the race, supposed age, and gender of the face.

CONCLUSION
Understanding why a particular android's face is believable, and what can be done about it, is an important challenge for android science. While this is a large challenge, in this work we provided a new angle on the problem, explicitly looking to visual processing knowledge to understand how people are viewing faces. Using this, we have discovered how recognition time and error rate, as well as perhaps perception of eeriness, can all be indicators of believability of an android face as human. In addition, through our exploration we have highlighted various other future directions for explorations in this area.

REFERENCES
[1]   Bartneck, C. et al. 2009. Does the Design of a Robot Influence Its Animacy and Perceived Intelligence? *International Journal of Social Robotics*. 1, 2 (Feb. 2009), 195–204.

[2]   Bartneck, C. et al. 2007. Is the uncanny valley an uncanny cliff? *Proceedings - IEEE International Workshop on Robot and Human Interactive Communication* (2007), 368–373.

[3]   Barton, J.J.S. et al. 2006. Information processing during face recognition: the effects of familiarity, inversion, and morphing on scanning fixations. *Perception*. 35, (2006), 1089–1105.

[4]   Bate, S. et al. 2010. Socio-emotional functioning and face recognition ability in the normal population. *Personality and Individual Differences*. 48, 2 (2010), 239–242.

[5] Blow, M., Dautenhahn, K., Appleby, A., Nehaniv, C. L., & Lee, D. (2006, March). The art of designing robot faces: Dimensions for human-robot interaction. In Proceedings of the 1st ACM SIGCHI/SIGART conference on Human-robot interaction (pp. 331-332). ACM.

[6] Blow, M., Dautenhahn, K., Appleby, A., Nehaniv, C. L., & Lee, D. C. (2006, September). Perception of robot smiles and dimensions for human-robot interaction design. In Robot and Human Interactive Communication, 2006. ROMAN 2006. The 15th IEEE International Symposium on (pp. 469-474). IEEE

[7] Bombari, D. et al. 2009. Featural, configural, and holistic face-processing strategies evoke different scan patterns. *Perception*. 38, (2009), 1508–1521.

[8] Cheetham, M. et al. 2013. Category Processing and the human likeness dimension of the Uncanny Valley Hypothesis: Eye-Tracking Data. *Frontiers in psychology*. 4, March (2013), 108.

[9] Chen, H. et al. 2010. Crossing the "uncanny valley": adaptation to cartoon faces can influence perception of human faces. *Perception*. 39, 3 (2010), 378–386.

[10] Epley, N. et al. 2007. On seeing human: a three-factor theory of anthropomorphism. *Psychological review*. 114, (2007), 864–886.

[11] Epley, N. et al. 2007. On seeing human: a three-factor theory of anthropomorphism. *Psychological review*. 114, (2007), 864–886.

[12] Eyssel, F. and Hegel, F. 2012. (S)he's Got the Look: Gender Stereotyping of Robots1. *Journal of Applied Social Psychology*. 42, 9 (Sep. 2012), 2213–2230.

[13] Hanson, D. et al. 2005. Upending the Uncanny Valley. *Proceedings of the national conference on artificial intelligence*. 20, 4 (2005), 24–31.

[14] Hills, P.J. et al. 2013. First fixations in face processing: The more diagnostic they are the smaller the face-inversion effect. *Acta Psychologica*. 142, (2013), 211–219.

[15] Ho, C. et al. 2008. Human emotion and the uncanny valley: a GLM, MDS, and Isomap analysis of robot video ratings. *... conference on Human robot ...* (2008), 169–176.

[16] Ishiguro, H. 2007. Android Science - Toward a new cross-interdisciplinary framework -. *Robotics Research: Results of the 12th International Symposium ISRR. Springer, 2007* (2007), 118–127.

[17] Kitade, T. et al. 2013. Understanding suitable locations for waiting. *ACM/IEEE International Conference on Human-Robot Interaction* (2013), 57–64.

[18] Mazzei, D. et al. 2012. HEFES: An Hybrid Engine for Facial Expressions Synthesis to control human-like androids and avatars. *Proceedings of the IEEE RAS and EMBS International Conference on Biomedical Robotics and Biomechatronics* (2012), 195–200.

[19] McCloud, S. 1994. *Understanding Comics*.

[20] Miellet, S. et al. 2010. Investigating cultural diversity for extrafoveal information use in visual scenes. *Journal of vision*. 10, (2010), 21.

[21] Morewedge, C.K. 2009. Negativity bias in attribution of external agency. *Journal of experimental psychology. General*. 138, (2009), 535–545.

[22] Mori, M. et al. 2012. The uncanny valley. *IEEE Robotics and Automation Magazine*. 19, 2 (2012), 98–100.

[23] Peterson, M.F. and Eckstein, M.P. 2013. Individual differences in eye movements during face identification reflect observer-specific optimal points of fixation. *Psychological science*. 24, (2013), 1216–25.

[24] Peterson, M.F. and Eckstein, M.P. 2012. Looking just below the eyes is optimal across face recognition tasks. *Proceedings of the National Academy of Sciences of the United States of America*. 109, (2012), E3314–23.

[25] Schwaninger, A. et al. 2006. Chapter 18 Processing of facial identity and expression: a psychophysical, physiological, and computational perspective. *Progress in Brain Research*.

[26] Waytz, A. et al. 2010. Who Sees Human? *Perspectives on Psychological Science*. 5, (2010), 219–232.

Differences of Expectation of Rapport with Robots Dependent on Situations

Tatsuya Nomura
Department of Media Informatics,
Ryukoku University
Otsu, Shiga 520-2194, Japan
nomura@rins.ryukoku.ac.jp

Takayuki Kanda
ATR Intelligent Robotics and
Communication Laboratories
Keihanna, Kyoto 619-0288, Japan
kanda@atr.jp

ABSTRACT

An online survey for 1,200 Japanese participants from 20's to 50's was conducted to clarify what type of robot and under what situation humans expect rapport with, and explore human factors influential into these expectations. The survey was based on hypothetical situation method consisting of three situations: a vacuum robot, a pet-type robot, and a robot instructor. The results suggested that; 1) expectations of rapport with robots were dependent on types of robots and application contexts, and were directly not affected by experiences of robots; 2) these expectations were influenced by negative attitudes toward social influences of and emotional interaction with robots, and emotional sensitivity for others; 3) expectations of rapport with robots were influenced by different psychological factors dependent on robot types and application contexts.

Author Keywords

Expectation of rapport with robots; psychological scale; hypothetical situation method

ACM Classification Keywords

H.1.2 [User/Machine Systems]: Human factors

INTRODUCTION

Rapport or intimate relationships between humans and social robots are one of the most important themes human-robot interaction (HRI) studies have challenged. Tanaka, et al., [9] reported that children established peer-like relationships during long-term interaction with a robot. Lee, et al., [2] applied a personalization strategy to establish rapport with a robot in an office environment. Kidd [1] developed a robot designed to sustain long-term relationships with users to assist them lose weight. Leite, et al., [3] designed a robot for long-term interaction with a capability for empathetic interaction. These studies expect users to form rapport with social robots.

However, it has sufficiently not been investigated what factors increase or decrease rapport between humans and robots. In this stage, it is necessary to clarify what type of robot and under what situation humans expect rapport with. In addition to these robot and situational factors, human factors should also be investigated as influential ones.

As a preliminary study for the above aim, an online social survey was conducted based on a hypothetical situation method on robot types and contexts of robotics applications. Among many human factors, this survey focused on the following ones. The first one is negative attitudes toward robots. It was found that this factor can affect humans' communication behaviors toward robots [6]. The second one is experiences of robots. It was suggested that this factor can influence attitudes toward and expectation for robots [5, 7]. The third one is humans' empathy for others. It can be hypothesized that persons more empathic for others are more empathic for social robots, and as a result expect rapport with the robots.

The paper reports results of the survey, and then discusses about their implications on establishing long-term human-robot rapport.

METHOD

Data Collection

The survey was conducted in January, 2014. Respondents were recruited by a survey company at which about one million and thirty thousand Japanese persons have registered, via the Internet. Among people randomly selected based on gender and age, a total of 1,200 persons ranging from 20's to 50's participated in the survey. The respondents at each of the generations (20's, 30's, 40's, and 50's) consisted of 150 males and 150 females. A questionnaire was conducted online, via a WEB page.

Survey Design

After the face sheet and psychological scales of attitudes toward robots and empathy for others were commonly conducted for all the respondents, the survey consisted of three hypothesized situations where different types of robots behaved. Based on a between-participant design, each respondent was assigned to one of these hypothesized situations. Among 150 male and 150 female participants at each of the generations (20's, 30's, 40's, and 50'), 50 male and 50 female participants were assigned to each of the

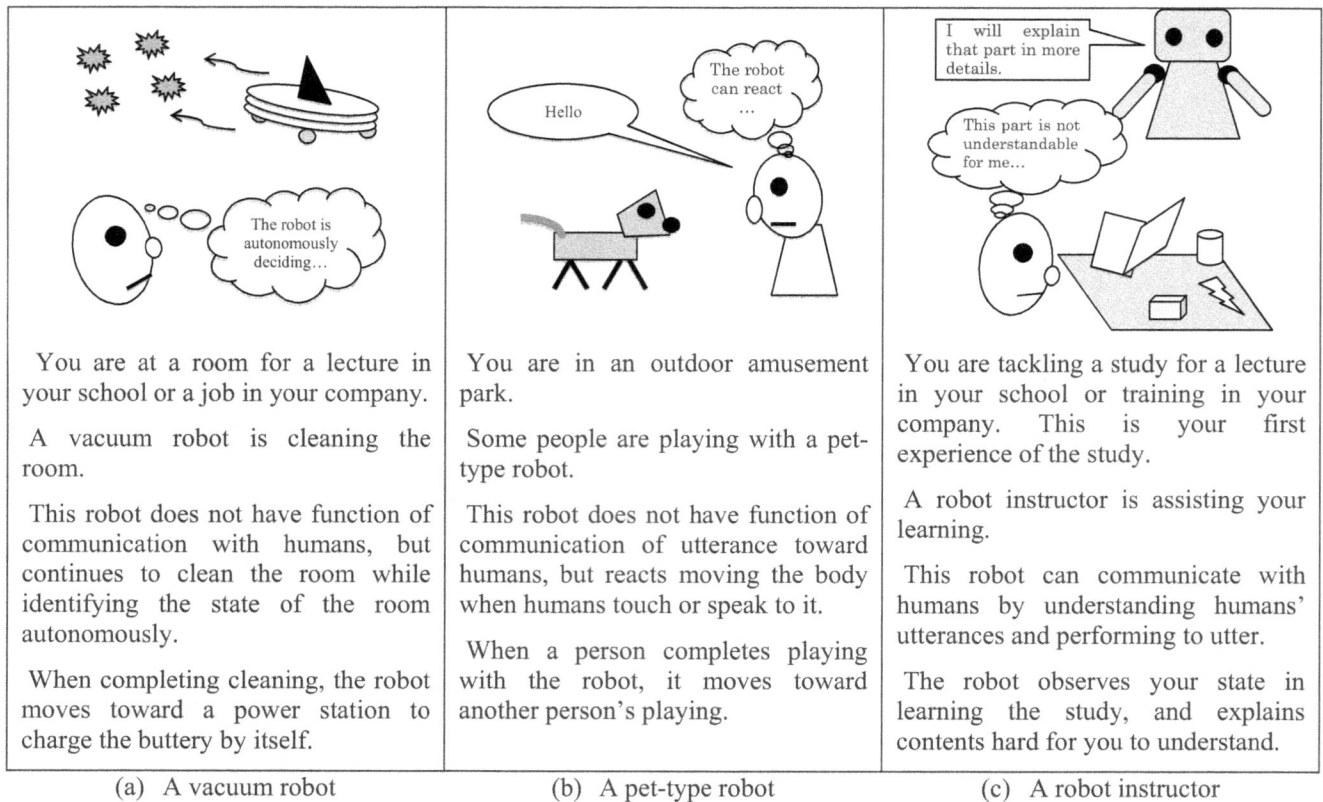

| (a) A vacuum robot | (b) A pet-type robot | (c) A robot instructor |

You are at a room for a lecture in your school or a job in your company.

A vacuum robot is cleaning the room.

This robot does not have function of communication with humans, but continues to clean the room while identifying the state of the room autonomously.

When completing cleaning, the robot moves toward a power station to charge the buttery by itself.

You are in an outdoor amusement park.

Some people are playing with a pet-type robot.

This robot does not have function of communication of utterance toward humans, but reacts moving the body when humans touch or speak to it.

When a person completes playing with the robot, it moves toward another person's playing.

You are tackling a study for a lecture in your school or training in your company. This is your first experience of the study.

A robot instructor is assisting your learning.

This robot can communicate with humans by understanding humans' utterances and performing to utter.

The robot observes your state in learning the study, and explains contents hard for you to understand.

Figure 1: Pictures and Texts in the Instruction of the Hypothetical Situations

three hypothetical situations. She/he was instructed to envision the assigned hypothesized situation, and then answer a psychological scale on her/his expectation of rapport with the robot that appeared in the situation.

The hypothesized situations in the survey were: 1) a vacuum robot having autonomy and no communication function, 2) a pet-type robot in an amusement park, and 3) a robot instructor in learning novel contents. The instruction of the situations was conducted with pictures and texts. Figure 1 shows these pictures and texts.

Measures

Experience of Robot
On the face sheet, respondents' experiences of robots were asked with a three-choice answer (1. I have seen real robots, 2. I have never seen real robots, but have seen those via media such as TV and newspapers, 3. I have never seen robots).

Negative Attitudes toward Robots
The Negative Attitudes toward Robots Scale (NARS [6]) was used to measure respondents' attitudes toward robots. This scale consists of 14 items classified into three subscales: (a) negative attitude toward interaction with robots (six items); negative attitude toward the social influence of robots (five items); and negative attitude

toward emotional interaction with robots (three items). Each item is scored on a five-point scale: 1) strongly disagree; 2) disagree; 3) undecided; 4) agree; 5) strongly agree, and an individual's score on each subscale was calculated by adding the scores of all items included in the subscale, with some items reverse coded.

Empathy for Others
The Multidimensional Empathy Scale (MES [8]) was used to measure respondents' empathy for others. This scale consists of 24 items classified into five subscales: (a) other-oriented emotional reactivity (five items); (b) self-oriented emotional reactivity (four items); (c) emotional susceptibility (five items); (d) perspective taking (five items); and (e) fantasy (five items). Each item is scored on a five-point scale: 1) It does not apply to me at all; 2) It does not apply to me; 3) Not decidable; 4) It applies to me; 5) It strongly applies to me. An individual's score on each subscale was calculated by adding the scores of all items included in the subscale, with some items reverse coded.

Expectation of Rapport with Robots
The Rapport-Expectation with a Robot Scale (RERS [4]) was used to measure respondents' expectation of rapport with three robots appearing in the hypothesized situations. This scale consists of 18 items classified into two subscales: (a) expectation as a conversation partner (eleven items) and

Scale	Subscale (# of items)	Example of Item Sentences
NARS	Negative attitude toward interaction with robots (6 items)	"I would feel very nervous just standing in front of a robot."
	Negative attitude toward social influences of robots (5 items)	"I feel that if I depend on robots too much, something bad might happen."
	Negative attitude toward emotional interaction with robots (3 items)	"If robots had emotions, I would be able to make friends with them."*
MES	Other-oriented emotional reactivity (5 items)	"When I see a person feeling sad, I would like to cheer up her/him.
	Self-oriented emotional reactivity (4 items)	"Sometimes, I cannot be pleased with others' successes."
	Emotional susceptibility (5 items)	"My feeling is easy to be influenced by others."
	Perspective taking (5 items)	"Even if I am opposed to another person, I will try to understand her/his perspective.
	Fantasy (5 items)	"I tend to dream or imagine repeatedly about things that may happen to me."
RERS	Expectation as a conversation partner (11 items)	"I wish to talk with the robot about hobbies and arts."
	Expectation for togetherness (7 items)	"I would accept this robot to attend my family dinner."

(*: reverse item)

Table 1: Examples of Item Sentences in Subscales Used in the Survey

(b) expectation for togetherness (seven items). Each item is scored on a seven-point scale (1: absolutely disagree – 4: undecided – 7: absolutely agree), and an individual's score on each subscale was calculated by adding the scores of all items included in the subscale, with some items reverse coded.

Table 1 shows examples of item sentences in these psychological scales.

RESULTS

Internal Consistency of Measures

Chronbach's α-coefficients of the RERS subscales were .915 and .867 in expectation as a conversation partner and expectation for togetherness, respectively. α-coefficients of the NARS subscales were .872 in negative attitude toward interaction with robots, .799 in negative attitude toward social influences of robots, and .753 in negative attitude toward emotional interaction with robots. It was found that these scales had sufficient internal consistencies.

On the MES, α-coefficients of the subscales were: .726 in other-oriented emotional reactivity, .668 in self-oriented emotional reactivity, .712 in emotional susceptibility, .688 in perspective taking, and .681 in fantasy. Although some subscales did not show sufficient internal consistencies, these scores were used in the regression analyses to explore influential factors into participants' expectation of rapport with robots.

Influences of Experiences of Robots

Table 2 shows the sample numbers on participants' gender, age groups, experiences of robots, and assigned hypothetical situations. There was no statistically significant relationship between age groups and experiences of robots ($\chi^2(6) = 10.618$, n.s.), although gender bias on experiences of robots was at a statistically significant level ($(\chi^2(2) = 13.867, p < .001)$.

For the scores of the RERS subscales, three-way ANOVAs with gender X experiences of robots X the hypothetical situations were conducted. Table 3 shows these results. On both expectations as a conversation partner and for togetherness, only the main effects of the hypothetical situations were at statistically significant levels, having moderate levels of effect sizes. There was no main effect of experiences of robots or gender, or interaction effect. Although the interaction effect between gender and situations on expectation for togetherness was at a statistically significant trend level, the effect size was small.

Post-hoc analyses with Bonferroni's method revealed that rapport-expectation with the robot instructor was higher than those with the vacuum robot and pet-type robot, and rapport-expectation with the pet-type robot was higher than that with the vacuum robot. Figure 2 shows the means and standard deviations of the RERS subscale scores based on the hypothetical situations.

On the other hand, two-way ANOVAs for the NARS subscale scores with gender X experiences of robots found

Hypothetical situations	Age group	Male				Female			
		Experiences of robots			Total	Experiences of robots			Total
		I	II	III		I	II	III	
Vacuum robot	20's	13	28	9	50	10	28	12	50
	30's	19	22	9	50	16	26	8	50
	40's	13	33	4	50	14	29	7	50
	50's	13	31	6	50	10	30	10	50
	Total	58	114	28	200	50	113	37	200
Pet-type robot	20's	18	25	7	50	10	31	9	50
	30's	13	25	12	50	6	34	10	50
	40's	19	22	9	50	10	31	9	50
	50's	19	28	3	50	9	32	9	50
	Total	69	100	31	200	35	128	37	200
Robot instructor	20's	7	27	16	50	9	24	17	50
	30's	9	34	7	50	13	28	9	50
	40's	10	37	3	50	12	26	12	50
	50's	22	23	5	50	6	33	11	50
	Total	48	121	31	200	40	111	49	200
Total	20's	38	80	32	150	29	83	38	150
	30's	41	81	28	150	35	88	27	150
	40's	42	92	16	150	36	86	28	150
	50's	54	82	14	150	25	95	30	150
	Total	175	335	90	600	125	352	123	600

I. Participants who had seen real robots,
II. Participants who had never seen real robots, but had seen those via media such as TV and newspapers,
III. Participants who had never seen robots

Table 2: Numbers of Samples based on Gender, Age Groups, Experiences of Robots, and Hypothetical Situations

the following statistically significant effects: experiences of robots ($F = 38.834$, $p < .001$, $\eta^2 = .061$) and interaction ($F = 4.203$, $p = .015$, $\eta^2 = .007$) on attitude toward interaction with robots, gender ($F = 11.259$, $p < .001$, $\eta^2 = .009$) and experiences of robots ($F = 9.012$, $p < .001$, $\eta^2 = .015$) on negative attitudes toward social influences of robots.

Post-hoc tests found that: toward interaction with robots, participants who had seen real robots had lower negative attitude than did the other participants in both male and female groups, female participants having seen robots via media had lower negative attitude than did female participants who had never seen robots, and males had lower negative attitude than did females in the group of participants who had seen robots via media. Moreover, it was found that participants who had seen real robots had lower negative attitude toward social influences of robots than did the other participants, and male participants had lower negative attitude toward social influences of robots than did female participants. However, the effect sizes of these factors were small except for experiences of robots on negative attitude toward interaction with robots. Moreover,

negative attitude toward emotional interaction with robots was not influenced by experiences or gender.

Relationships between Rapport-Expectation, Negative Attitudes toward Robots, and Empathy for Others

Linear regression analyses were conducted to explore influences of negative attitudes toward robots and empathy for others into expectation of rapport with robots. The RERS subscale scores were used as dependent variables, and the scores of the NARS and MES subscales and age were adopted as independent variables. The analyses were based on backward elimination method. Moreover, they were conducted for samples in each of the hypothesized situations to explore differences of influential factors between robot types and application contexts.

Table 4 shows the extracted models in the analyses. Both expectations as a conversation partner and for togetherness were negatively affected by negative attitudes toward social influences of and emotional interaction with robots in all the three hypothetical situations. Negative attitude toward interaction with robots positively influenced these

		Main			First Order Interaction			Second Order Interaction
		Hypothetical situations	Gender	Experiences of robots	Situations X Gender	Situations X Experiences	Gender X Experiences	
Expectation as a conversation partner	F	52.189	.124	.015	1.239	1.330	.422	.842
	p	< .001	.725	.985	.290	.257	.656	.498
	η^2	.076	.000	.000	.002	.004	.001	.003
Expectation for togetherness	F	31.219	.047	.940	2.874	1.468	.737	.657
	p	< .001	.829	.391	.057	.210	.479	.622
	η^2	.048	.000	.001	.004	.005	.001	.002

Table 3: Numbers of Samples based on Gender, Age Groups, Experiences of Robots, and Hypothetical

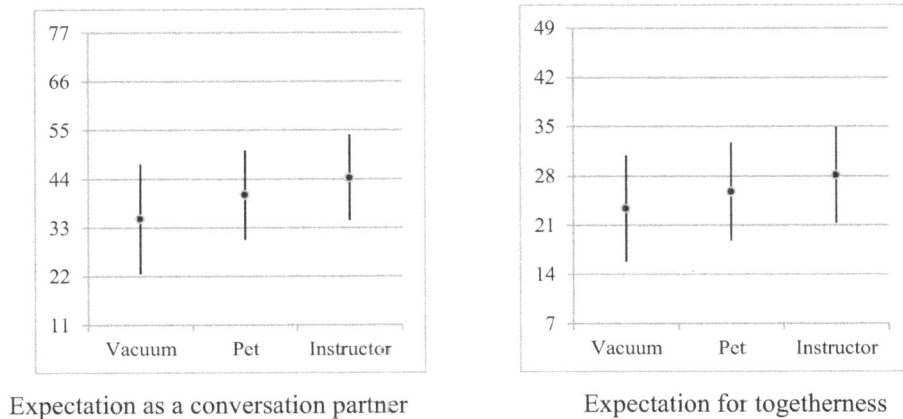

Expectation as a conversation partner   Expectation for togetherness

Figure 2: Means and Standard Deviations of RERS Subscale Scores based on Hypothetical Situations

expectations only in the situations of the vacuum robot and pet-type robot.

Moreover, both expectations as a conversation partner and for togetherness were positively affected by emotional susceptibility in all the three hypothetical situations. Fantasy positively influenced these expectations only in the situations of the vacuum robot and pet-type robot. Other-oriented emotional reactivity positively affected only expectation for togetherness in the situation of the pet-type robot. Self-oriented emotional reactivity positively affected only expectation for togetherness in the situation of the robot instructor. Participants' age positively affected both expectations only in the situation of the pet-type robot.

DISCUSSION

Findings
The results of the survey based on hypothetical situation method revealed that expectations of rapport with robots were dependent on types of robots and application contexts, and were directly not affected by experiences of robots. These expectations were influenced by negative attitudes toward social influences of and emotional interaction with

robots, and emotional sensitivity for others. Although negative attitude toward social influences of robots was affected by experiences of robots, this affection was weak. Thus, it was suggested that expectations of rapport with robots were mainly influenced by general attitudes toward robots and empathic characteristics, not related to experiences of robots.

The results of the survey also revealed that negative attitude toward interaction with robots, which was affected by experiences of robots, positively influenced rapport-expectation with the robots that had no function of utterances in the hypothetical situations. Moreover, the trend to imagine fantasy positively affected rapport-expectations with the robots that had communication functions in the hypothetical situations. They suggested that expectations of rapport with robots were influenced by different psychological factors dependent on robot types and application contexts.

Implications
The results of the survey imply that persons negative in influences of robots in the society and emotional bond with

Dependent variable	Independent variable	Vacuum robot			Pet-type robot			Robot instructor		
		β	t	p	β	t	p	β	t	p
Expectation as a conversation partner	NARS1	.343	6.451	.000	.131	2.305	.022			
	NARS2	-.201	-3.697	.000	-.159	-2.829	.005	-.207	-4.595	.000
	NARS3	-.337	-7.544	.000	-.332	-7.314	.000	-.347	-7.755	.000
	MES1									
	MES2									
	MES3	.143	3.211	.001	.179	3.783	.000	.111	2.495	.013
	MES4									
	MES5				.182	3.978	.000	.194	4.356	.000
	Age				.094	2.056	.040			
		$F(4,395) = 35.037, p < .001,$ $R^2 = .254$			$F(6,393) = 20.466, p < .001,$ $R^2 = .226$			$F(4,395) = 31.442, p < .001,$ $R^2 = .234$		

Dependent variable	Independent variable	Vacuum robot			Pet-type robot			Robot instructor		
		β	t	p	β	t	p	β	t	p
Expectation for togetherness	NARS1	.271	4.954	.000	.137	2.365	.018			
	NARS2	-.141	-2.532	.012	-.203	-3.584	.000	-.274	-6.052	.000
	NARS3	-.339	-7.384	.000	-.345	-7.583	.000	-.320	-7.166	.000
	MES1				.088	1.870	.062			
	MES2							.091	1.864	.063
	MES3	.132	2.887	.004	.124	2.611	.009	.087	1.895	.059
	MES4									
	MES5				.104	2.190	.029	.142	3.003	.003
	Age				.138	2.986	.003			
		$F(4,395) = 28.006, p < .001,$ $R^2 = .213$			$F(7,392) = 17.404, p < .001,$ $R^2 = .223$			$F(5,394) = 25.771, p < .001,$ $R^2 = .237$		

NARS1: Negative attitude toward interaction with robots, NARS2: Negative attitude toward social influences of robots, NARS3: Negative attitude toward emotional interaction with robots
MES1: Other-oriented emotional reactivity, MES2: Self-oriented emotional reactivity, MES3: Emotional susceptibility, MES4: Perspective taking, MES5: Fantasy

Table 4: Extracted Models in Linear Regression Analyses

robots tend not to expect rapport with robots. This tendency is hard to be improved only by advertisement of robotics applications in daily life. In order to have these persons accept robotics applications, it is necessary to explain benefits and risks of the applications more politely.

The results of the survey also imply that persons not sensitive for others and not liking to image fantasy tend not to expect rapport with robots having communication functions. If these persons can accept robotics applications, it is estimated that robots as just tools are preferred.

Limitations

Sampling in the survey was limited to the Japanese. Thus, cultural factors were not taken into account. The future survey should be extended to several countries including the USA, Korea, and the Europe.

Moreover, the results of the survey did not clarify differences between expectation as a communication partner and expectation for togetherness. It may be caused by a limit of hypothetical situation method. From the design perspective of robotics applications, it is important to investigate what type of rapport-expectation is evoked by a specific type of robot and application context. Thus, the future survey should adopt other types of stimuli such as videos.

ACKNOWLEDGMENTS
The research was supported in part by the Japan Society for the Promotion of Science, Grant–in–Aid for Scientific Research No. 25280095 and 25240042.

REFERENCES

1. Kidd, C. D. Designing for Long-Term Human-Robot Interaction and Application to Weight Loss. Massachusetts Institute of Technology, 2008.

2. Lee, M. K., Forlizzi, J., Kiesler, S., Rybski, P., Antanitis, J., and Savetsila, S. Personalization in HRI: A longitudinal field experiment. In Proc. 7th ACM/IEEE International Conference on Human-Robot Interaction (2012), 319-326.

3. Leite, I., Castellano, G., Pereira, A., Martinho, C., and Paiva, A. Long-Term Interactions with Empathic Robots: Evaluating Perceived Support in Children In Proc. International Conference on Social Robotics (2012), 298-307.

4. Nomura, T., and Kanda, T. Measurement of Rapport-Expectation with a Robot. In Proc. 8th ACM/IEEE International Conference on Human-Robot Interaction (2013), 201-202.

5. Nomura, T., Sugimoto, K., Syrdal, D. S., and Dautenhahn, K. Social Acceptance of Humanoid Robots in Japan: A Survey for Development of the Frankenstein Syndrome Questionnaire. In Proc. IEEE-RAS International Conference on Humanoid Robots (2012), 242-247.

6. Nomura, T., Suzuki, T., Kanda, T., and Kato, K. Measurement of Negative Attitudes toward Robots. Interaction Studies, 7, 3 (2006), 437-454.

7. Nomura, T., Suzuki, T., Kanda, T., Yamada, S., and Kato, K. Attitudes toward Robots and Factors Influencing Them. In New Frontiers in Human-Robot Interaction (K. Dautenhahn and J. Saunders (Eds)), John Benjamins Publishing (2011), 73-88.

8. Suzuki, Y., and Kino, K. Development of the Multidimensional Empathy Scale (MES): Focusing on the Distinction between Self- and Other-Orientation. The Japanese Journal of Educational Psychology, 56, 4 (2008), 487-497.

9. Tanaka, F., Cicourel, A., and Movellan, J. R. Socialization between Toddlers and Robots at an Early Childhood Education Center. Proceedings of the National Academy of Sciences of the USA (2007), 17954-17958.

Stage of Subconscious Interaction in Embodied Interaction

Takafumi Sakamoto
Graduate School of Science and Technology,
Shizuoka University
3-5-1 Johoku, Naka-ku, Hamamatsu, Shizuoka
4328011, Japan
dgs14010@s.inf.shizuoka.ac.jp

Yugo Takeuchi
Graduate School of Science and Technology,
Shizuoka University
3-5-1 Johoku, Naka-ku, Hamamatsu, Shizuoka
4328011, Japan
takeuchi@inf.shizuoka.ac.jp

ABSTRACT

Humans can interact with strangers because they can communicate with each other. On the other hand, developing a relationship with an unknown artifact is difficult. In order to address this problem, existing studies have explored various approaches to the artifact's behavioral design. However, little research has been done on interaction where there is no information about the interaction partner and where there has been no experimental task. Clarification of how people regard unknown objects as interaction partners is required. We believe that a stage of subconscious interaction plays a role in this process. We created an experimental environment to observe the interaction between a human and a robot whose behavior was actually mapped by another human. We observed this interaction under two different conditions; where the participants knew and where the participants did not know that the robot could interact. Both sets of participants approached or avoided the robot, but differences in the interaction property for each condition was confirmed. The results of our experiment suggest that a stage of subconscious interaction does exist for recognition of artifacts as interaction partners.

Author Keywords

Interaction; agency; communication relationship;

ACM Classificatio Keywords

H.5.m. Information Interfaces and Presentation (e.g. HCI): Miscellaneous

INTRODUCTION

It is expected that artifacts, such as robots, will increasingly be developed to cooperate with us and assume social roles in human society. While we can communicate with strangers because we know that other people possess the intellectual ability to form a relationship with us, it is difficult to communicate with an unknown artifact because whether it can communicate with us and how it will behave are unknown. As humans, we recognize an agency depending on actual interaction. For example, we do not regard others that we pass in

a crowd as communication partners, yet we often treat computers as agents [7].

It is necessary to clarify how people attribute agency status to an object through interaction. In order to encourage human interaction and communication with an artifact, several earlier studies focused on the design of the artifact's physical appearance. However, when human action is induced from previous knowledge, it is possible that this adaptation gap [6] may negatively influence continued interaction. Therefore, we focus on the artifact's behavior rather than its physical appearance. Humans can perceive the properties of an object or agent, such as its animacy and intention, by observing a moving geometric figure [3, 8]. It has been previously shown that humans can recognize animacy and intention through interaction with an abstract shape robot [2]. These researches indicate that only actual behavior during the interaction can encourage the development of communication relationships between humans and artifacts. However, the experiments for almost all of these previous studies involved interaction between participants and objects beforehand through the experimental task. Little research has been done on interaction when the participants have no prior knowledge of the subject object.

We focus on the primary stage in interaction between the human and the "other." We define "the stage of subconscious interaction" as the process through which humans realize that the object is behaving toward them and that it can interact with them. This process is considered to be the primary stage in which objects are attributed agency status through interaction. Assuming that this process exists, we conducted an experiment in which participants interact with an unknown entity. By modeling the process, artifacts that are able to form relationships with humans will be designed, thus contributing to the promotion of communication and interaction between humans and robots.

STAGE OF SUBCONSCIOUS INTERACTION

In human communication, we can immediately recognize a partner as human. The human brain possesses an area that is specifically designed to detect the human body [1]. In addition, as can be seen from the phenomenon called "biological motion," [4] we have a specific perception for recognizing human body movement. On the basis of these abilities, other people are regarded as agents with which we can communicate.

On the other hand, artifacts must have a physical appearance that can be recognized as an agency or, through interaction, encourage humans to perceive them as such. We focus on interaction, rather than physical appearance, because it can be used to design the form of an artifact. In previous research on interaction with artifacts, participant behavior based on the premise that the participants and artifacts can interact has been observed. However, in real situations, people must first realize that the artifacts are capable of interacting with them and react to their actions in the early stage of the interaction (Figure 1). We hypothesize that this process is carried out subconsciously and that, after this process, the interaction shifts to the stage of conscious interaction in order to create a relationship. We define this subconscious process as the "stage of subconscious interaction" and attempt to clarify it.

Until recently, many studies on interaction have used upper limb motion. Entire body movements, such as gait, differ from upper limb action [5]. While walking, humans unconsciously adjust direction and automatically avoid obstacles underfoot. Therefore, unconscious motions occur at a higher frequency than interaction using only the upper limbs. By using an abstract shape robot whose function is only moving a flower, we can observe lower-limb-driven interaction.

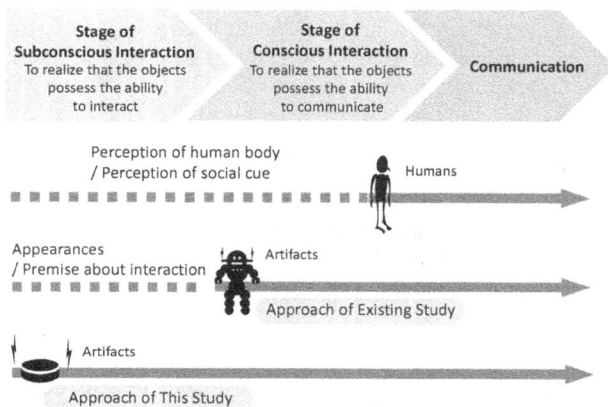

Figure 1. Stage of subconscious interaction

EXPERIMENT

Purpose

In this section, we provide the details of our experiment for detecting the process by which people perceive an object as an interaction partner capable of an interpersonal relationship. We observed interaction between humans because it is difficult to design agent behavior that can build relationships with people. However, the participants were unaware that the robot's behavior was capable of such interaction. In this way, we observed the interaction between a human and a robot that was not previously perceived as an agency but behaves as agent. We compared the behavior of participants who knew that the robot could interact with them with those of participants who did not know about the robot's motion. Through this interaction, participants who did not previously know about the robot's behavior may realize that the robot can interact with them. When this occurred, the behavior of

these participants changed and became similar to that of the participants who knew that the robot could interact with them beforehand. We analyzed the stage of subconscious interaction and tried to model the interaction by comparing these interactions (Figure. 2).

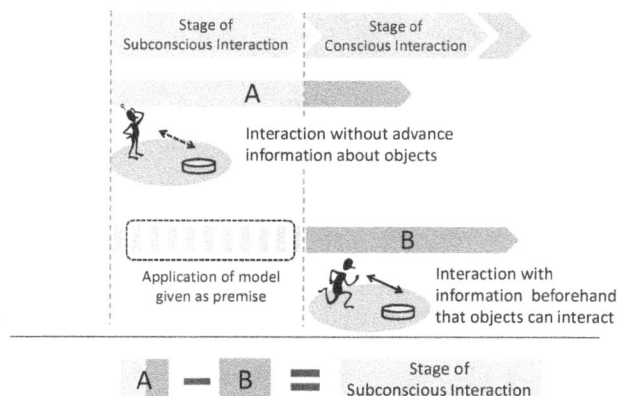

Figure 2. Method of selecting subconscious interaction

Method

Apparatus

As shown in Figure 3, we used two rooms as the experimental environment. Both rooms were constructed with similar appliances. The participants' movement was restricted within a three-meter square field. The positions of the participants were mirrored by the robots. That is, the position of the robot located in one room mirrored the position of the participant in the other room (Figure 4). In this way, each participant was able to interact with the other participant without recognition of each other (Figure 5). We used a Roomba controlled via Bluetooth. An encoder of the tires measured the robot's position. In addition, the robot's position was revised using a video camera. The participant's position was measured with a laser rangefinder.

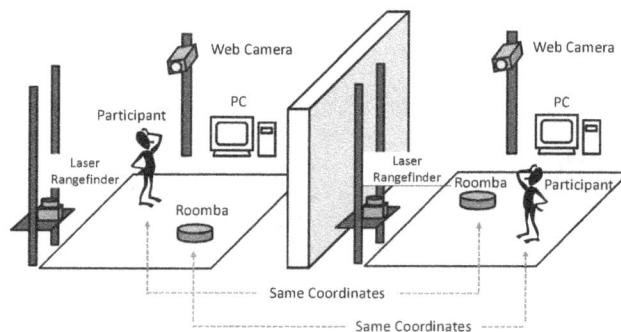

Figure 3. Experimental setup

Participants and Task

We assigned 10 pairs (20 university students) to the unknown condition and the known condition. The participant pairs were guided into the rooms separately without knowledge of their partners. All participants were instructed to move freely within the interaction field. The participants were provided

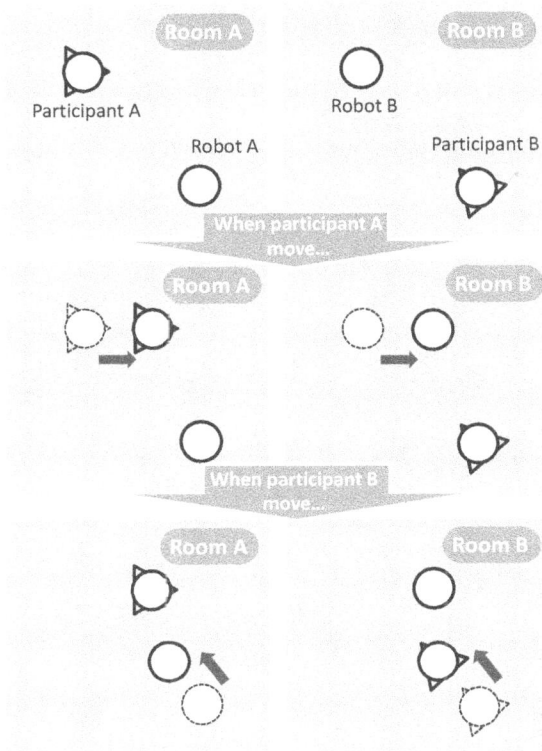

Figure 4. Behavior of robots

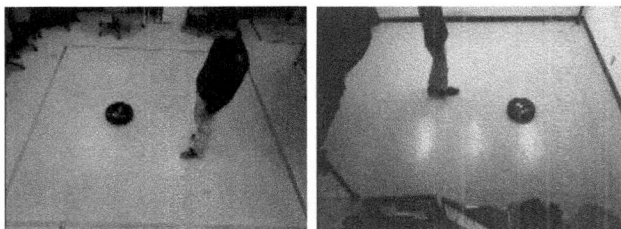

Figure 5. An interaction scene

information about the robot according to specific rules. In the unknown condition, the participants were not told about the robot's behavior. The pair participant who was assigned to the known condition group was instructed, "The robot moves as an entity that you want to relate to." Their partner was told, "The robot moves as an entity that you want not to relate to." Every participant was left alone in the room, and the interaction between the participants and the robot was observed for five minutes. The participants then responded to questionnaires.

Observed Data

We observed and analyzed the following data:

- Behavioral data
  - Log data of participant position (every 125 ms)
  - Log data of robot position (every 125 ms)
  - Interaction video

- Questionnaires
  - Free descriptions about behavior of participant and robot

Results

It is difficult to recognize a difference in overall tendency caused by varying conditions because the participants were able to move freely inside the experimental space. Therefore, we classified participant pairs with characteristics of the interaction that occurred. We calculated proximity, as shown in Figure 6, because the participants' main actions were to approach the robot or to stand away from it. On the basis of the variation in proximity between the pairs, we classified the pairs into the following four types:

(1) Pairs in which the role of each participant, as either chaser or escaper, was maintained stably

(2) Pairs in which the role of each participant was interchanged frequently

(3) Pairs in which one of the pair rarely moved and the other moved

(4) Pairs in which both participants rarely moved

In (1) and (2), it can be said that a relationship between the participants was established. In (3) and (4), an interpersonal relation was not formed. Below, we selectively compare the behavior of participants who are classified as type (1) and (2).

The upper portions of Figures 7 and 8 show the results of the change in distance between the participants who continued to approach or to avoid the robot without changing pattern. The lower portions of these figures show the change in proximity that was carried out by the participants. In both conditions, relations, that is, where one participant approaches the robot and the other participant moves away from the robot, were formed. The distance under the known condition changed more frequently than the distance under the unknown condition. Fast Fourier transformation results for the distance data are shown in Figure 9. The peak frequency under the

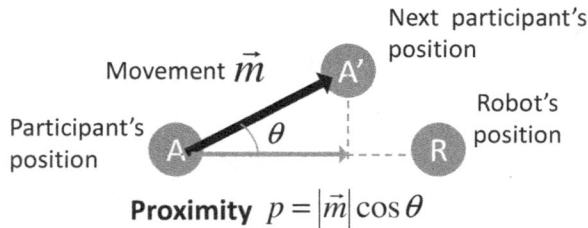

Figure 6. Proximity calculation method

$$\text{Proximity} \quad p = |\vec{m}| \cos \theta$$

known condition was larger than the peak frequency under the unknown condition, which supports the conclusion that the participants under the known condition approach or avoid the robot more frequently.

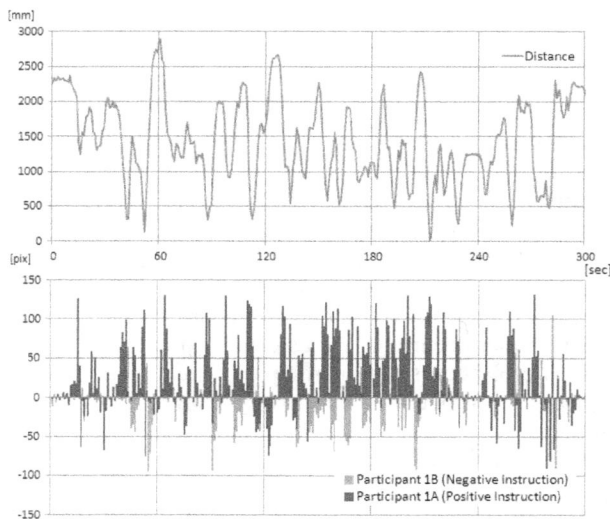

Figure 7. Distance and proximity data in resolute role interaction under the known condition

Figures 10 and 11 show the change in distance and proximity for the participants who interchanged roles. As shown in Figure 12, the time that the distance between participants under the known condition was maintained from 0 mm to 1000 mm was shorter than the time that participants under the unknown condition maintained the distance. Known Condition participants developed a sense of distance without getting too close to the robot. On the other hand, the Unknown Condition participants did not move immediately, even when the robot was too close.

Considerations

As shown by the results, the interaction pattern with an interaction partner that is a known entity differs from the interaction pattern with an unknown entity. The known condition results demonstrate that participants form relations with the robot by associating the robot's behavior with their actions. When participants P_A approach robot R_A, the opposite participants P_B immediately recognize robot R_B's behavior as an action for them. Then, by P_B moving away from R_B,

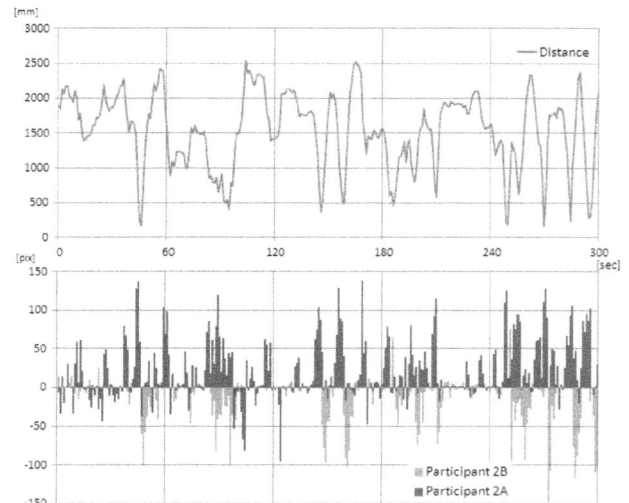

Figure 8. Distance and proximity data in resolute role interaction under the unknown condition

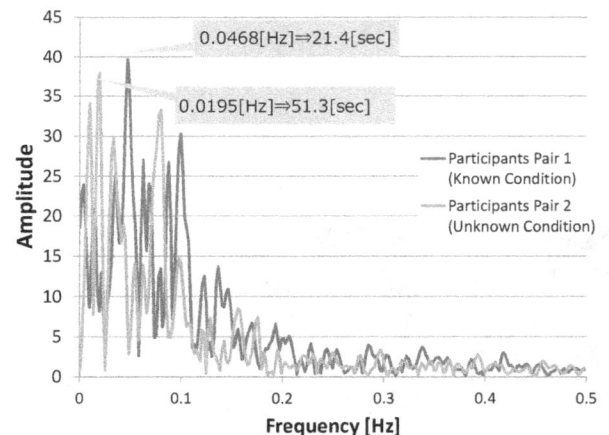

Figure 9. FFT processing result of distance data

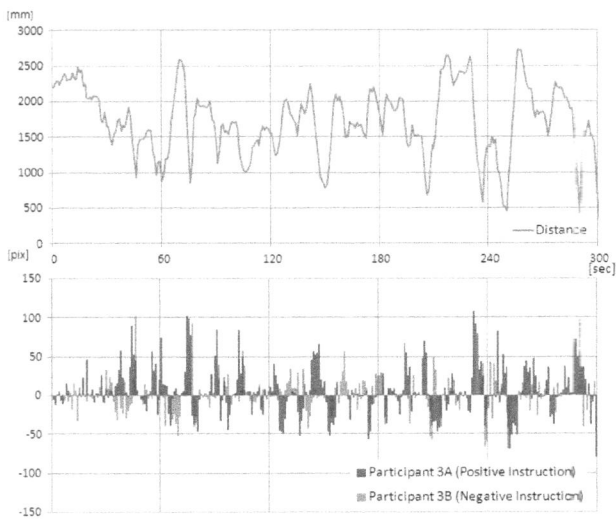

Figure 10. Distance and proximity data for flexibl role interaction under the known condition

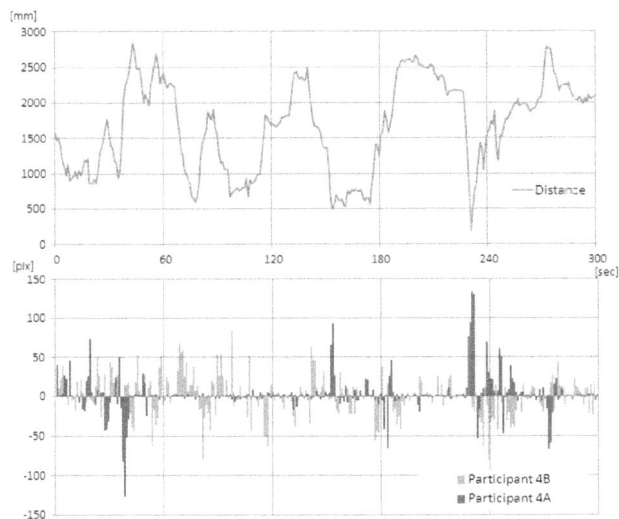

Figure 11. Distance and proximity data in flexibl role interaction under the unknown condition

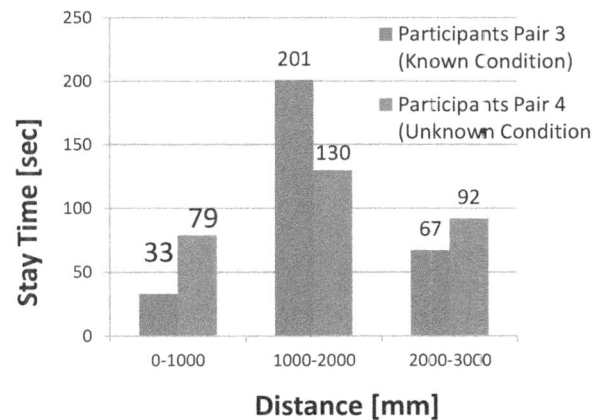

Figure 12. Maintained time according to distance

P_A recognizes R_A's avoidance as a reaction to P_A's action. It can be said that the participants anticipate robot behavior while interacting.

On the other hand, interaction under the unknown condition is established without participants' understanding the robot's behavior. When the Unknown Condition participants P_C approach robot R_C at the beginning of the interaction, the opposite participants P_D do not realize that robot R_D's behavior is approaching them. P_D avoid R_D if P_D assume that P_D and R_D will collide. P_C is likely to realize that R_C moves away from P_C in this situation. However, continuous interaction like the known interaction may not be carried out until P_D recognize that R_D's behavior is an action for P_D. In the questionnaire concerning the robot's behavior, a participant who had been assigned the unknown condition and stood away from the robot answered that the behavior of the robot had been random.

In addition, the Unknown Condition participants did not mind when the robot was close in comparison with those under the known condition. Unless the robot reached the closest limits, the participants did not react to the robot. Interchanging the role, as chaser or escaper, was one way to continue an interaction. It can be said that it is easy for an interaction with unknown entities to become deadlocked. This points to the importance of the primary stage of the interaction between humans and artifacts.

This experiment confirms the existence of the subconscious interaction phase. However, the process of recognizing the object's behavior as action has not become apparent. A further experiment will be necessary to model the process. It is difficult in this experiment to identify the point when the Unknown Condition participants realize that the robot can interact with them. We need to find that point, and will attempt to detect it using a think-aloud method and observe the interaction when one of the participant pair knows the robot and the other does not. In addition, we will examine the use of machine learning as a method to classify the unknown interaction and the known interaction.

CONCLUSION

In this study, we believe that a stage of subconscious interaction is the process in which participants regard objects as interaction partners. Through this process, humans appear to progress in establishing relationships with artifacts. In order to extract the subconscious interaction, we observed interactions with known and unknown robots whose positions were mapped by other participants. Under both conditions, some participants approached or avoided the robot throughout the entire experiment and the others changed roles frequently between chaser and escaper. The participants under the unknown condition interacted more infrequently, while participants under the known condition maintained their distance more than the unknown condition group. These results suggest that the stage of subconscious interaction for regarding objects as interaction partners exists. However, modeling this interaction process must await further investigation.

REFERENCES

1. Downing, P., Jiang, Y., Shuman, M., and Kanwisher, N. A cortical area selective for visual processing of the human body. *Science 293* (2001), 2470–2473.

2. Fukuda, H., and Ueda, K. Interaction with a moving object affects one's perception of its animacy. *International Journal of Social Robotics 2* (2010), 187–193.

3. Heider, F., and Simmel, M. An Experimental Study of Apparent Behavior. *American Journal of Psychology 57* (1944), 67–70.

4. Johansson, G. Visual perception of biological motion and a model for its analysis. *Perception & Psychophysics 14* (1973), 201–211.

5. Kannape, O., and Blanke, O. Agency, gait and self-consciousness. *International Journal of Psychophysiology 83* (2012), 191–199.

6. Komatsu, T., and Yamada, S. Adaptation Gap Hypothesis: How Differences Between Users' Expected and Perceived Agent Functions Affect Their Subjective Impression. *Journal of Systemics, Cybernetics and Informatics 9*, 1 (2011), 67–74.

7. Reeves, B., and Nass, C. *The Media Equation.* Cambridge University Press, 1996.

8. Tremoulet, P., and Feldman, J. Perception of animacy from the motion of a single object. *Perception 29* (2000), 943–951.

Author Index

Abe, Kasumi 165
Adolphs, Svenja 339
Alvarez, Celestino 113
Aoki, Ryousuke 169
Arimoto, Tsunehiro 97
Arras, Kai O. 91
Asada, Minoru 273
Atkinson, David J. 371
Attamimi, Muhammad 165
Baba, Shotaro 213
Bachour, Khaled 339
Baddoura, Ritta 233
Baek, Chaehyun 149
Bailly, Gérard 309
Becker-Asano, Christian 91, 173
Bruce, Neil D. B. 377
Cartwright, Stephen 39
Cheok, Adrian David 209
Chern, Yuen Wong Anthony 197
Choi, Hyunsoek 265
Choi, Jung Ju 137, 149
Clark, Leigh Michael Harry 339
Clark, Micah H. 371
Costa Sousa, Mario 39
Damm, Oliver 269
De Silva, P. Ravindra S. 213
Do, Ellen Yi-Luen 7
Dornhege, Christian 173
Endo, Nobutsuna 273
Fernández Cossío, Lucía 113
Fukada, Chie 245
Fukutome, Nami 117
Gaussier, Philippe 121
Gehle, Raphaela 361
Giannopulu, Irini 9
Gibert, Guillaume 233
Goto, Masataka 345
Grand, Caroline 121
Hagita, Norihiro ... 17, 83, 153, 157
Harris, John 59
Hasegawa, Komei 293
Hasnain, Syed Khursheed 121
Hattori, Yusuke 245
Hayamizu, Akira 67
Hayashi, Yuki 277
Hieida, Chie 165
Horii, Takato 273
Hosseinzade Hariri, Reihaneh .. 209
Hotta, Ryo 237

Hsu, Jane Yung-jen 103
Huang, Hung-Hsuan 237
Hué, Julien 173
Ichijo, Takashi 229
Igarashi, Takeo 315, 345, 369
Iio, Takamasa 17, 153
Imai, Michita 1, 3, 67, 301
Imamura, Yuto 105
Inaba, Michimasa 205
Ishiguro, Hiroshi 83, 97, 249
Ishii, Yutaka 221
Ishikawa, Shogo 141
Ito, Akira 105, 109
Jang, Gil-Jin 285
Jhong Ren, Wu 177
Jo, Ahra 285
Kamei, Koji 17, 153
Kanda, Takayuki 83, 383
Kanemoto, Yuka 117
Katagami, Daisuke 5, 205
Kato, Hiroshi 23
Kato, Jun 345
Kawagoe, Kyoji 237
Kikuchi, Hideaki 331
Kim, Taewoong 297
Kipp, Andreas 225
Kiriyama, Shinya 141
Kitamura, Yoshifumi 59
Kobayashi, Kazuki 5
Kobayashi, Yu 205
Komatsubara, Tsuyoshi 83
Kubota, Yoshihiko 23
Kumahara, Yuri 145
Kummert, Franz 225
Kuramoto, Itaru 133
Kusano, Yuki 181
Kuzuoka, Hideaki 23
Kwak, Sonya S. 137, 149
Law, Stephanie 59
Lee, Akinobu 323
Lee, Hyewon 137
Lee, Minho 297
Li, Nico 39
Lim, Qinpei 197
Lim, Yu De 75
Marin, Angie Lorena 287
Matsuda, Akira 201
Matsumoto, Takahiro 169
Meneses, Eduardo 173

Mihoub, Alaeddine 309
Miisho, Takanari 281
Minowa, Hirotsugu 125
Mitarai, Koushi 189
Miyamoto, Kensuke 257
Miyata, Akihiro 169
Miyawaki, Kenzaburo 117
Miyazawa, Kouki 331
Mizuki, Takakazu 109
Montreynaud, Valérie 9
Mori, Yoshikazu 145
Morita, Tomoyo 273
Mostafaoui, Ghiles 121
Munekata, Nagisa 29, 229
Nagai, Takayuki 165, 245
Nakadai, Kazuhiro 67
Nakamichi, Daisuke 249
Nakamura, Hiroyuki 201
Nakamura, Keisuke 67
Nakane, Masayuki 377
Nakanishi, Junya 249
Nakano, Yukiko I. 277
Nakatsu, Ryohei 75, 209
Nakauchi, Yasushi 293
Nebel, Bernhard 91, 173
Nishida, Ryosuke 245
Nishimura, Ryota 129, 323
Nishioto, Kazushi 1
Noda, Syogo 117
Nomura, Tatsuya 383
Novikova, Jekaterina 353
Nukushina, Harunobu 141
Ofemile, Abdulmalik 339
Ogawa, Kei 141
Ogawa, Yoshito 331
Ohmura, Ren 181
Oka, Natsuki 165, 245
Okada, Michio 213
Okada, Yoshiko 185
Omori, Takashi 165, 245
Ono, Tetsuo 1, 29, 229
Oosumi, Toshihiro 301
Osawa, Hirotaka 51, 185, 205
Otogi, Shochi 237
Oura, Keiichiro 323
Ozeki, Motoyuki 245
Palinko, Oskar 193, 217
Park, Hyeyoung 265
Park, Jeong-Sik 285

Peng, Zhuo Daniel 197
Pitsch, Karola 361
Rea, Daniel J. 315
Rea, Francesco 193, 217
Reynolds, Karen J. 161
Riesterer, Nicolas 173
Rodden, Tom 339
Rui, Yan 197
Ruthenbeck, Greg S. 161
Saadatian, Elham 75, 209
Saga, Tamami 29
Sakai, Kurima 249
Sakamoto, Daisuke 345
Sakamoto, Takafumi 391
Salafi, Thoriq 75
Samani, Hooman 75, 177
Sandini, Giulio 193, 217
Sano, Mutsuo Sano 117
Sciutti, Alessandra 193, 217
Seko, Shunichi 169
Sharlin, Ehud 39, 59
Sharma, Chandraprakash ... 17, 153
Shibata, Kenichi 141
Shimotomai, Takayuki 165
Shinoda, Kosuke 205
Shiomi, Masahiro 17, 83
                              153, 157, 249

Sono, Taichi 301
Sugaya, Midori 185, 201
Sumioka, Hidenobu 249
Sun, Jie 197
Suzuki, Hideyuki 23
Suzuki, Yuta 181
Takahashi, Hideyuki 105, 273
Takashima, Kazuki 59
Takebayashi, Yoichi 141
Takeda, Yasutaka 213
Takefuji, Yoshiyasu 257
Takeuchi, Yugo 391, 391
Takumi, Ichi 129, 323
Tanaka, Takahiro 5
Tani, Takahisa 253
Terada, Kazunori 105, 109
Todo, Takayuki 281
Tokuda, Keiichi 323
Toriumi, Fujio 205
Tsuji, Yuichiro 245
Tsujino, Yoshihiro 133
Tsukamoto, Ami 245
Uchida, Takashi 245
Uchiya, Takahiro 129, 323
Ueda, Hirotada 261
Uemura, Marie 133
Umemuro, Hiroyuki 189

Venture, Gentiane 233
Watanabe, Norifumi 257
Watanabe, Tomio 9, 221
Watanabe, Tomoki 169
Watanabe, Yukako 185
Watts, Leon 353
Wolf, Christian 309
Wrede, Britta 269
Wrede, Sebastian 361
Yamada, Seiji 253
Yamada, Tomohiro 169
Yamamoto, Daisuke 129, 323
Yamamoto, Keiko 133
Yamashita, Naomi 23
Yamazoe, Hirotake 35
Yan, Yongyao 161
Yano, Miyuki 45
Yokoyama, Hiroki 273
Yonezawa, Ken 261
Yonezawa, Tomoko 35, 45
Yoshida, Kohei 213
Yoshida, Naoto 45
Yoshikawa, Yuichiro 97
Yoshino, Takashi 277
Yoshioka, Hiroaki 257
Young, James E. 315, 377
Yuasa, Masahide 5, 241